QUEEN VICTORIA

CHRISTOPHER HIBBERT

QUEEN VICTORIA

✖✖✖✖✖✖✖✖✖✖✖✖

A Personal History

BASIC
BOOKS

A Member of thePerseus Books Group

Published by Basic Books,
A Member of the Perseus Books Group

First published in the United Kingdom by HarperCollins*Publishers*

Cataloging-in-Publication information is available upon request from
the Library of Congress.

ISBN 0-465-06761-1

00   01   02   03   /   10   9   8   7   6   5   3   2   1

For Amy, Lily and Rose with love

CONTENTS

List of Illustrations   xi
Author's Note and Acknowledgements   xv
Genealogy   xvi
Queen Victoria's Prime Ministers   xviii

PART ONE   1819–1861

1   The Family   3
2   The Parents   9
3   The Child   17
4   Conroy   25
5   Progresses   30
6   Uncles   41
7   The Young Queen   53
8   Melbourne   60
9   Coronation   70
10 The Hastings Affair   76
11 'A Pleasant Life'   85
12 'A Headstrong Girl'   90
13 German Cousins   98
14 Prince Albert   107
15 The Bridegroom   111
16 Honeymoon   120
17 Robert Peel   130
18 The Prince and the Household   137

19	Royal Quarrels	148
20	Osborne	157
21	Travelling	165
22	Balmoral	175
23	The Prince of Wales	183
24	Palmerston	193
25	Chartists	199
26	'Pam is Out'	204
27	The Great Exhibition	210
28	'Scenes'	216
29	Crimean War	221
30	Napoleon III	230
31	The Princess Royal	238
32	Indian Mutiny	248
33	The German Grandson	256
34	Death of the Duchess	264
35	The Disappointing Heir	268
36	Death of the Prince	276

PART TWO   1861–1901

37	The Grieving Widow	285
38	Séances and Services	293
39	Princess Alexandra	298
40	The Recluse	307
41	Disraeli	314
42	John Brown	321
43	'The Royalty Question'	331
44	'The Princely Pauper'	338
45	Typhoid Fever	342
46	Maids-of-Honour	349
47	Secretaries and Ministers	353
48	*Regina et Imperatrix*	360
49	'The Half-mad Firebrand'	367
50	Golden Jubilee	379
51	*Die Engländerin*	384

CONTENTS

52	The Daughters	391
53	The Sons	396
54	The Grandchildren	414
55	Would-be Assassins	420
56	Holidays Abroad	428
57	Death of Brown	440
58	The Munshi	446
59	Diamond Jubilee	455
60	Life at Court	461
61	Dinner Parties	468
62	Books	477
63	Bookmen	481
64	Failing Health	484
65	Death	492
66	Funeral and Burial	495
	References	503
	Sources	523
	Index	534

ILLUSTRATIONS

Princess Victoria aged two with her mother, by Sir William Beechey. © *Mary Evans Picture Library.*

Princess Victoria aged four, by Stephen Poyntz Denning. *By permission of the Trustees of Dulwich Picture Gallery.*

Princess Victoria with her spaniel, 'Dash', after Sir George Hayter. *The Royal Collection 2000. © HM Queen Elizabeth II.*

Sir John Conroy, painted by Alfred Tidey in 1836. *By courtesy of the National Portrait Gallery.*

Queen Victoria aged twenty, by Sir Edwin Landseer. *The Royal Collection 2000. © HM Queen Elizabeth II.*

Watercolour of Prince Albert by Queen Victoria. *The Royal Collection 2000. © HM Queen Elizabeth II.*

Prince Albert. A portrait by the miniature painter Sir William Charles Ross. *The Royal Collection 2000. © HM Queen Elizabeth II.*

Queen Victoria in her wedding veil, by Franz Xaver Winterhalter. *The Royal Collection 2000. © HM Queen Elizabeth II.*

Windsor Castle in Modern Times: Queen Victoria, Prince Albert and Victoria, Princess Royal, by Sir Edwin Landseer. *The Royal Collection 2000. © HM Queen Elizabeth II.*

Queen Victoria, painted in 1843 by Franz Xaver Winterhalter. *The Royal Collection 2000. © HM Queen Elizabeth II.*

La Filatrice Addormentata, by Julius Froschel. *The Royal Archives 2000. © HM Queen Elizabeth II/A Disderi.*

Florinda, by Franz Xaver Winterhalter. *The Royal Collection 2000. © HM Queen Elizabeth II.*

Queen Victoria with the Prince of Wales in 1846. A portrait of Franz Xaver Winterhalter. *The Royal Collection 2000. © HM Queen Elizabeth II.*

The Swiss Cottage at Osborne. A watercolour by William Leighton Leitch. *The Royal Collection 2000. © HM Queen Elizabeth II.*

The Prince of Wales just before his ninth birthday. A sketch by Queen Victoria. *The Royal Collection 2000. © HM Queen Elizabeth II.*

Princess Beatrice in a purple dress. A watercolour by Queen Victoria. *The Royal Collection 2000. © HM Queen Elizabeth II.*

Painting of Queen Victoria holding Prince Arthur, with the Duke of Wellington and Prince Albert. A painting by Franz Xaver Winterhalter. *The Royal Collection 2000. © HM Queen Elizabeth II.*

Queen Victoria opening the Great Exhibition. An illustration by André & Sleigh, after a painting by H. C. Selous. © *Mary Evans/Edwin Wallace.*

Fir trees decorated with lighted tapers at Windsor at Christmas. *The Royal Collection 2000. © HM Queen Elizabeth II.*

Princess Alice in 1861. A portrait by Franz Xaver Winterhalter. *The Royal Collection 2000. © HM Queen Elizabeth II.*

Sorrow by Sir Edwin Landseer. *The Royal Collection 2000. © HM Queen Elizabeth II.*

The Queen's dressing room at Balmoral, by James Roberts. *The Royal Collection 2000. © HM Queen Elizabeth II.*

The Queen's bedroom at Balmoral, by James Roberts. *The Royal Collection 2000. © HM Queen Elizabeth II.*

Victoria, Duchess of Kent, by Franz Xaver Winterhalter. *The Royal Collection 2000. © HM Queen Elizabeth II.*

Leopold I of Belgium. © *Mansell/Time Inc/Katz.*

Luigi Lablache. A sketch by Queen Victoria. *The Royal Collection 2000. © HM Queen Elizabeth II.*

Baroness Louise Lehzen. A sketch by Queen Victoria in 1833. *The Royal Collection 2000. © HM Queen Elizabeth II.*

Queen Victoria riding with Lord Melbourne, after a painting by Sir Francis Grant. © *The British Museum.*

Lord Melbourne. A portrait by Queen Victoria. *The Royal Collection 2000. © HM Queen Elizabeth II.*

Baron Stockmar. A painting by John Partridge. © *Mansell/Time Inc/Katz.*

Queen Victoria holding a portrait of Prince Albert. A photograph by B. E. Duppa. *The Royal Archives 2000. © HM Queen Elizabeth II/ B E Dupper.*

Prince Albert in 1854. A photograph by B. E. Duppa. *The Royal Archives 2000. © HM Queen Elizabeth II.*

The Great Exhibition of 1851. © *The Illustrated London News Picture Library.*

Prince Alfred, Frederick Waymouth Gibbs and the Prince of Wales. A photograph by Roger Fenton. *The Royal Archives 2000. © HM Queen Elizabeth II/Roger Fenton.*

The Princess Royal (with butterfly net), the Prince of Wales, Princess Alice and Prince Alfred at Osborne in 1853. *The Royal Archives 2000. © HM Queen Elizabeth II/Dr Ernst Becker.*

Prince and Princess Frederick William of Prussia at Windsor in 1858. *The Royal Archives 2000. © HM Queen Elizabeth II/Bambridge.*

Napoleon III, a sketch by Queen Victoria. *The Royal Collection 2000. © HM Queen Elizabeth II.*

The Royal Family at Osborne in 1857. *The Royal Archives 2000. © HM Queen Elizabeth II/Caldesi.*

Queen Victoria and Princess Alice with a bust of Prince Albert. *The Royal Archives 2000. © HM Queen Elizabeth II/Prince Alfred.*

The Blue Room at Windsor Castle, with a bust of the Prince Consort by William Theed. *The Royal Archives 2000. © HM Queen Elizabeth II/Hills & Saunders.*

The Prince and Princess of Wales with Prince Albert Victor in 1864. *The Royal Archives 2000. © HM Queen Elizabeth II/Prince Alfred.*

Queen Victoria on the throne in 1876. *The Royal Archives 2000. © HM Queen Elizabeth II/W & D Downey.*

Queen Victoria bestowing an earldom on Disraeli. *© Punch.*

Prince Leopold with Sir William Jenner and the Hon. Alec Yorke. *© Hulton Getty.*

Princess Louise in 1865. *The Royal Archives 2000. © HM Queen Elizabeth II/ Bingham.*

Princesss Beatrice in 1885. *© Hulton Getty.*

Attempt to shoot the Queen at Windsor in 1882. *© The Illustrated London News Picture Library.*

Queen Victoria smiling. A photograph by Charles Knight in c. 1887. *By courtesy of the National Portrait Gallery, London.*

Sir James Reid. *The Royal Archives 2000. © HM Queen Elizabeth II.*

Queen Victoria and the Empress Frederick in 1889. *The Royal Archives 2000. © HM Queen Elizabeth II.*

Queen Victoria in the garden at Osborne in 1889, surrounded by members of her family. *The Royal Archives 2000. © HM Queen Elizabeth II/Mullins.*

Queen Victoria in a carriage at Grasse in 1891. *The Royal Archives 2000. © HM Queen Elizabeth II/F Busin.*

Queen Victoria and the Munshi, Abdul Karim, at Balmoral in 1894. *The Royal Archives 2000. © HM Queen Elizabeth II.*

Queen Victoria with Prince and Princess Henry of Battenberg at breakfast in the Oak Room at Windsor in 1895. *The Royal Archives 2000. © HM Queen Elizabeth II.*

Queen Victoria wearing spectacles and reading a letter. *The Royal Archives 2000. © HM Queen Elizabeth II.*

Queen Victoria's funeral procession. *© Hulton Getty.*

The Royal Mausoleum at Frogmore with marble effigies of Queen Victoria and Prince Albert. *The Royal Archives 2000. © HM Queen Elizabeth II.*

AUTHOR'S NOTE
AND ACKNOWLEDGEMENTS

In an essay read to fellows and members of the Royal Society of Literature in 1972, Giles St Aubyn said that on average Queen Victoria wrote about 2,500 words every day of her adult life, achieving a total of some sixty million in the course of her long reign. If she had been a novelist her complete works would have run to seven hundred volumes, published at the rate of one a month. To her eldest daughter alone she wrote at least twice a week, and sometimes twice a day, for over forty years. Much of this material has been published in the various books mentioned in the preliminary note to the References on page 503. There remain at Windsor, however, many letters both to and from Queen Victoria which have never before been printed; and in 1983 the late John Murray and I were kindly allowed to consult these papers and to reproduce parts of them in a selection published under the title *Queen Victoria in Her Letters and Journals.* I have to acknowledge the gracious permission of Her Majesty the Queen for their publication as I do for the publication of all the other material of which she holds the copyright. I have been deeply indebted for their help to Sir Robin Mackworth-Young and Miss Jane Langton, Her Majesty's former Librarian and her Registrar of the Royal Archives, and to Mr Oliver Everett, the Queen's present Librarian at Windsor.

For their help in a variety of other ways I also want to thank Marian Reid, who edited the book, Juliet Davis, who helped me choose the pictures, Richard Johnson of HarperCollins, Bruce Hunter of David Higham Associates, John Kemmeer and Don Fehr of the Perseus Books Group, Dr Francis Sheppard, Captain Gordon Fergusson, John Paton, Margaret Lewendon, Richard Way, Diana Cook and the staffs of the British Library, the Bodleian Library, the London Library and the Ravenscroft Library, Henley-on-Thames. Hamish Francis and Ursula Hibbert have been good enough to read the proofs, and my wife has made the comprehensive index.

Finally I must say how grateful I am to Professor Paul Smith for having read the book in typescript and for having given me much useful advice for its improvement.

CHRISTOPHER HIBBERT

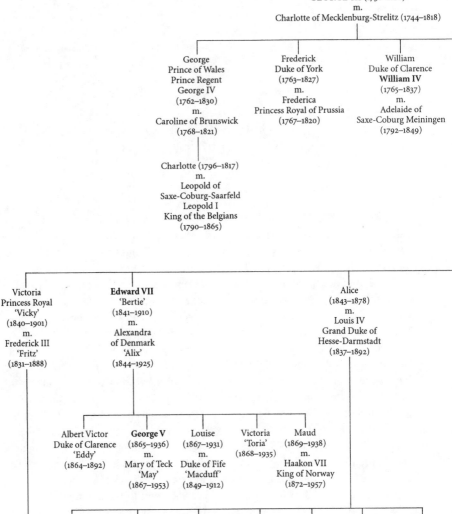

GEORGE III (1738–1820)
m.
Charlotte of Mecklenburg-Strelitz (1744–1818)

George
Prince of Wales
Prince Regent
George IV
(1762–1830)
m.
Caroline of Brunswick
(1768–1821)

Frederick
Duke of York
(1763–1827)
m.
Frederica
Princess Royal of Prussia
(1767–1820)

William
Duke of Clarence
William IV
(1765–1837)
m.
Adelaide of
Saxe-Coburg Meiningen
(1792–1849)

Charlotte (1796–1817)
m.
Leopold of
Saxe-Coburg-Saarfeld
Leopold I
King of the Belgians
(1790–1865)

Victoria
Princess Royal
'Vicky'
(1840–1901)
m.
Frederick III
'Fritz'
(1831–1888)

Edward VII
'Bertie'
(1841–1910)
m.
Alexandra
of Denmark
'Alix'
(1844–1925)

Alice
(1843–1878)
m.
Louis IV
Grand Duke of
Hesse-Darmstadt
(1837–1892)

Albert Victor
Duke of Clarence
'Eddy'
(1864–1892)

George V
(1865–1936)
m.
Mary of Teck
'May'
(1867–1953)

Louise
(1867–1931)
m.
Duke of Fife
'Macduff'
(1849–1912)

Victoria
'Toria'
(1868–1935)

Maud
(1869–1938)
m.
Haakon VII
King of Norway
(1872–1957)

Victoria
(1863–1950)
m.
Louis of Battenberg
(1854–1921)

Elizabeth
'Ella'
(1864–1918)
m.
Grand Duke
Serge of Russia
(1857–1905)

Irène
(1866–1953)
m.
Henry of Prussia
(1862–1929)
|
3 children

Ernest
Grand Duke
of Hesse
'Ernie'
(1868–1937)
m.
Victoria Melita
of Edinburgh
'Ducky'
(1876–1936)

Frederick
'Frittie'
(1870–1873)

Alix
'Alicky'
(1872–1918)
m.
Tsar Nicholas II
(1868–1918)
|
5 children

Mary Victoria
'May'
(1874–1878)

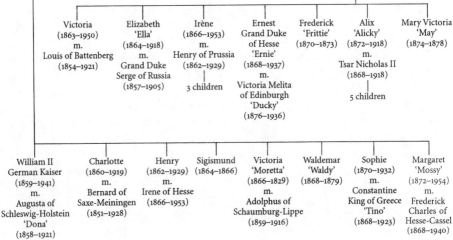

William II
German Kaiser
(1859–1941)
m.
Augusta of
Schleswig-Holstein
'Dona'
(1858–1921)

Charlotte
(1860–1919)
m.
Bernard of
Saxe-Meiningen
(1851–1928)

Henry
(1862–1929)
m.
Irene of Hesse
(1866–1953)

Sigismund
(1864–1866)

Victoria
'Moretta'
(1866–1829)
m.
Adolphus of
Schaumburg-Lippe
(1859–1916)

Waldemar
'Waldy'
(1868–1879)

Sophie
(1870–1932)
m.
Constantine
King of Greece
'Tino'
(1868–1923)

Margaret
'Mossy'
(1872–1954)
m.
Frederick
Charles of
Hesse-Cassel
(1868–1940)

VICTORIA'S FAMILY TREE

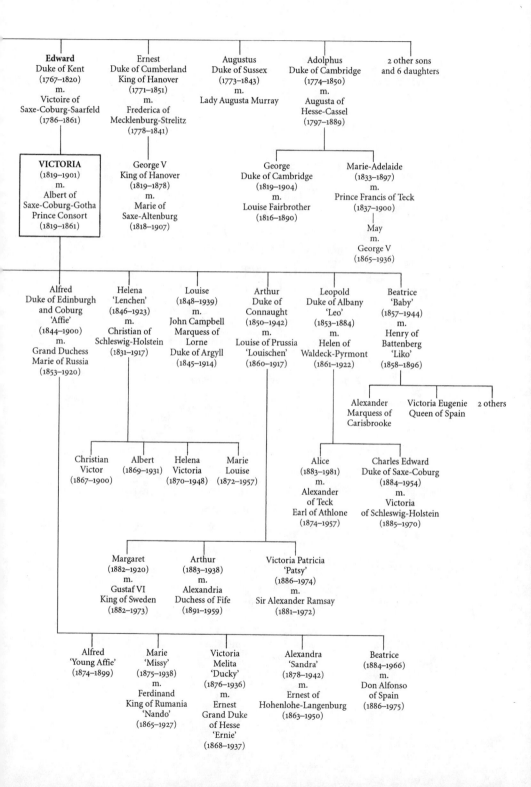

Edward
Duke of Kent
(1767–1820)
m.
Victoire of
Saxe-Coburg-Saarfeld
(1786–1861)

Ernest
Duke of Cumberland
King of Hanover
(1771–1851)
m.
Frederica of
Mecklenburg-Strelitz
(1778–1841)

Augustus
Duke of Sussex
(1773–1843)
m.
Lady Augusta Murray

Adolphus
Duke of Cambridge
(1774–1850)
m.
Augusta of
Hesse-Cassel
(1797–1889)

2 other sons
and 6 daughters

VICTORIA
(1819–1901)
m.
Albert of
Saxe-Coburg-Gotha
Prince Consort
(1819–1861)

George V
King of Hanover
(1819–1878)
m.
Marie of
Saxe-Altenburg
(1818–1907)

George
Duke of Cambridge
(1819–1904)
m.
Louise Fairbrother
(1816–1890)

Marie-Adelaide
(1833–1897)
m.
Prince Francis of Teck
(1837–1900)
|
May
m.
George V
(1865–1936)

Alfred
Duke of Edinburgh
and Coburg
'Affie'
(1844–1900)
m.
Grand Duchess
Marie of Russia
(1853–1920)

Helena
'Lenchen'
(1846–1923)
m.
Christian of
Schleswig-Holstein
(1831–1917)

Louise
(1848–1939)
m.
John Campbell
Marquess of
Lorne
Duke of Argyll
(1845–1914)

Arthur
Duke of
Connaught
(1850–1942)
m.
Louise of Prussia
'Louischen'
(1860–1917)

Leopold
Duke of Albany
'Leo'
(1853–1884)
m.
Helen of
Waldeck-Pyrmont
(1861–1922)

Beatrice
'Baby'
(1857–1944)
m.
Henry of
Battenberg
'Liko'
(1858–1896)

Alexander
Marquess of
Carisbrooke

Victoria Eugenie
Queen of Spain

2 others

Christian
Victor
(1867–1900)

Albert
(1869–1931)

Helena
Victoria
(1870–1948)

Marie
Louise
(1872–1957)

Alice
(1883–1981)
m.
Alexander
of Teck
Earl of Athlone
(1874–1957)

Charles Edward
Duke of Saxe-Coburg
(1884–1954)
m.
Victoria
of Schleswig-Holstein
(1885–1970)

Margaret
(1882–1920)
m.
Gustaf VI
King of Sweden
(1882–1973)

Arthur
(1883–1938)
m.
Alexandria
Duchess of Fife
(1891–1959)

Victoria Patricia
'Patsy'
(1886–1974)
m.
Sir Alexander Ramsay
(1881–1972)

Alfred
'Young Affie'
(1874–1899)

Marie
'Missy'
(1875–1938)
m.
Ferdinand
King of Rumania
'Nando'
(1865–1927)

Victoria
Melita
'Ducky'
(1876–1936)
m.
Ernest
Grand Duke
of Hesse
'Ernie'
(1868–1937)

Alexandra
'Sandra'
(1878–1942)
m.
Ernest of
Hohenlohe-Langenburg
(1863–1950)

Beatrice
(1884–1966)
m.
Don Alfonso
of Spain
(1886–1975)

QUEEN VICTORIA'S PRIME MINISTERS

1835	Viscount Melbourne (Whig)
1841	Sir Robert Peel (Tory)
1846	Lord John Russell (Liberal)
February 1852	Earl of Derby (Tory)
December 1852	Earl of Aberdeen (Tory)
1855	Viscount Palmerston (Liberal)
1858	Earl of Derby (Tory)
1859	Viscount Palmerston (Liberal)
1865	Earl Russell (Liberal)
1866	Earl of Derby (Tory)
February 1868	Benjamin Disraeli (Tory)
December 1868	W. E. Gladstone (Liberal)
1874	Benjamin Disraeli (Tory)
1880	W. E. Gladstone (Liberal)
1885	Marquess of Salisbury (Tory)
February 1886	W. E. Gladstone (Liberal)
August 1886	Marquess of Salisbury (Tory)
1892	W. E. Gladstone (Liberal)
1894	Earl of Rosebery (Liberal)
1895	Marquess of Salisbury (Tory)

A note on money:

According to figures recently compiled by the Bank of England, £41.03 would have been required in March 1999 for a person to have the same purchasing power as £1 in the middle of Queen Victoria's reign. That is to say, for instance, today's equivalent of the £45 10s a year paid to a maidservant at Windsor Castle in 1867 would be about £2,000 a year. The Lord Chamberlain received the equivalent of nearly £90,000 a year; and the President of Russia would now require over £1,000,000 to match the cost of the presents and gratuities given to the staff of the Royal Household by Tsar Nicholas I on his departure from the castle in 1844.

PART ONE

✳✳✳✳✳✳✳✳✳✳✳✳✳

1819–1861

I

✳✳✳✳✳✳✳✳✳✳✳

THE FAMILY

'God damme! D'ye know what his sisters call him?
By God! They call him Joseph Surface!'

SITTING AT HIS BREAKFAST TABLE in his rented house in Brussels
in December 1817, Edward, Duke of Kent, fourth son of King George III,
carelessly threw across the *Morning Chronicle* to his attractive mistress,
Julie de St Laurent, and began to open his letters. 'I had not done so but
a very short time,' he told Thomas Creevey, the witty, gossipy politician
who was then also living in Brussels for reasons of economy, 'when my
attention was called to an extraordinary noise and a strong convulsive
movement in Madame St Laurent's throat. For a short time I entertained
serious apprehensions for her safety; and when, upon her recovery, I
enquired into the occasion of this attack, she pointed to [an] article in
the *Morning Chronicle*.'[1]

This article – adverting to the death in childbirth of Princess Charlotte,
the only legitimate child of his eldest brother, the Prince Regent – called
upon the Duke of Kent and the other bachelor royal dukes to marry for
the sake of the family succession. For, although it was later calculated
that King George III had no fewer than fifty-six grandchildren, at this
time not one of these grandchildren was legitimate.

The Prince Regent, who was to become King George IV on his father's
death in 1820, was now fifty-five years old, separated from a detested wife
and living languorously in sumptuous grandeur at Carlton House in
London and the exotic Marine Pavilion at Brighton. The King's second
son, the Duke of York, was also married and also separated from a wife
who, childless, lived an eccentric life at Oatlands House in Surrey where,

surrounded by numerous pet dogs, monkeys and parrots, she was to die in 1820. The Regent's next brother, the Duke of Clarence, who, following the Duke of York's death, was to succeed to the throne as William IV in 1830, had lived contentedly for several years with the actress Dora Jordan, who had given birth to ten little FitzClarences, before dying the year before the death of Princess Charlotte. To be sure, the Duke of Clarence might marry now; and, indeed, after unsuccessfully pursuing various heiresses, both foreign and domestic, in the hope of paying off debts amounting to £56,000, he at last did find a bride in Princess Adelaide, the home-loving, good-natured but far from prepossessing eldest daughter of the Duke of Saxe-Coburg Meiningen. But she was not to prove so successful a mother as Mrs Jordan had been: her two daughters both died as babies.

Of the Duke of Kent's three younger brothers only one as yet had children. This was the asthmatic Duke of Sussex, a man whom Thomas Creevey described as 'civil and obliging' but about whom 'there was a *nothingness* that was to the last degree fatiguing'. He had been married in Rome in 1793 to a rather bossy lady some years older than himself, Lady Augusta Murray, daughter of the Earl of Dunmore, by whom he had had two children; but since the marriage had been contracted in breach of the Royal Marriages Act of 1772, which made it illegal for any member of the Royal Family to marry without the previous consent of the Crown, the King had declared the marriage void and the Sussex children were accordingly illegitimate. The Duke of Sussex's elder brother, the sardonic, much feared, widely disliked, reactionary and fiercely Protestant Duke of Cumberland, whose face had been given an alarmingly ugly cast by a head wound suffered while he was serving with the Hanoverian cavalry in the Low Countries, had managed to obtain permission to marry Princess Frederica of Mecklenburg-Strelitz, the niece of his mother, Queen Charlotte. But the marriage had not been easy to arrange since Queen Charlotte was bitterly opposed to it, having heard scandalous reports of the past behaviour of the Princess who had been married twice before and was widely rumoured to have murdered one of, if not both, her former husbands. She and the Duke had had a child but she was stillborn.

The youngest duke, the Duke of Cambridge, a man more respectable and financially responsible than his brothers, was not yet married; and when he did marry Princess Augusta of Hesse-Cassel in August 1818 the children of this marriage were so far down the line of succession that they could be dismissed by the Duke of Kent in his determined efforts to become the father of the future King or Queen of England.

The Duke of Kent was a disappointed man. Trained for a military career in Germany, he had not achieved the distinction or recognition which he believed he deserved. He had served in Gibraltar, in Canada and in the West Indies, and in all these places he had gained a reputation both for wild extravagance and the most strict and severe attention to military discipline: he would insist that the men under his command be roused at dawn and appear on the parade ground in impeccable condition and would punish infringements of his draconian rules by occasional executions and regular floggings of hundreds of lashes, as many as 400 being given for 'trifling faults in dress' and 999, the maximum permitted, for desertion. He left Canada accused of 'bestial severity'; and, upon his recall from Gibraltar in disgrace, he was accused by his elder brother the Duke of York – who had been appointed Commander-in-Chief of the Army – of provoking a mutiny by his conduct which 'from first to last was marked by cruelty and oppression'. He was given to understand that there would be no more military commands for him.[2]

Charles Greville, the diarist and Clerk to the Privy Council, contended that the Duke of Kent was 'the greatest rascal that ever went unhung',[3] while the Duke of Wellington, to whom Thomas Creevey related the story of the contretemps at Kent's breakfast table, regarded him as a figure of fun. At a ball in Brussels, where Wellington was serving as commander of the allied forces on the Continent after the defeat of Napoleon at Waterloo, Creevey was approached by the great Duke who said to him, 'Well Creevey, what has passed between you and *the Corporal* since you have met this time?' Creevey then told Wellington of a conversation he had recently had with the Duke of Kent 'Upon which,' so Creevey recorded, 'the Duke of Wellington laid hold of my button and said: "God damme! D'ye know what his sisters call him? By God! They call him Joseph Surface [the shameless hypocrite in Sheridan's *School for Scandal*]!" and then sent out one of his hearty laughs, that made every one turn about to the right and left to see what was the matter.'[4]

Yet the Duke of Kent had his good points as well as his bad, as Wellington conceded: he was a good and intelligent, if rather garrulous, conversationalist with a gift for mimicry, and an even better after-dinner speaker; he was also a conscientious correspondent, keeping three or four secretaries busy at their desks. He was fond of music and, when in funds, employed the services of a large band.

However, like all his brothers except the Duke of Cambridge, he was more or less constantly entangled in debt. The several charities to which he lent his name were supported by money which, as often as not, had been borrowed from men who were not always repaid. It was a perennial grievance with him that he was not provided with an allowance adequate to his high position as a prince of the blood.

Yet for all his faults, the Duke was capable of affection and this affection had been returned not only by Mme de St Laurent but also by Princess Charlotte, whose favourite uncle he had been, and by Mrs Maria Fitzherbert, the Roman Catholic widow whom the Prince Regent had illegally married and with whom the Duke conducted a correspondence of easy and intimate friendship. For nearly thirty years the Duke had lived contentedly with Mme de St Laurent, and he did what he could to soften the blow when he declared that duty to his family forced him to send her away to live in Paris with her sister. 'You may well imagine, Mr Creevey, the pang it will occasion me to part with her,' he said to the Whig politician. 'I protest I don't know what is to become of her . . . But before anything is proceeded with in this matter, I shall hope and expect to see justice done to her by the Nation and the Ministers . . . Her disinterestedness has been equal to her fidelity.'[5] He saw to it that she was provided with a generous allowance – which before long was much reduced – and he asked friends to go and see her to ensure that she was comfortable in Paris where she lived as the Comtesse de Montgenet, a courtesy title granted to her by King Louis XVIII. 'Our unexpected separation arose from the imperative duty I owed to obey the call of my family and Country to marry,' the Duke explained, 'and *not* from the least diminution in an attachment which had stood the test of 28 years and which, but for *that* circumstance' would have been kept up until one or other of them died.[6] He later thanked Creevey and his wife for their kind attentions to the 'dear Countess' and earnestly asked him to give him his 'opinion of her health, her looks and her spirits *very particularly*'.

*   *   *

The Duke at this time was forty-nine years old. He was tall and fat and stately in a ponderous way, with luxuriant whiskers dyed dark brown and a head without much hair. His breath smelled of garlic and his clothes of tobacco. He was attentive to women and very polite. He had the fleshy lips and rather protuberant eyes of the Hanoverians but he was handsome enough and carried himself like the soldier he was proud to have been.

He was of most regular habits, getting up at five o'clock, even earlier than his father, and eating and drinking sparingly. He had good reason to suppose that, if he found a suitable wife, he would soon be the father of children as healthy as he was himself. Already, before Princess Charlotte's death, he had begun the search for a wife, in the hope that Parliament would grant him a decent allowance to support one in the same way that his brother, the Regent, had been helped financially upon his disastrous marriage to Princess Caroline of Brunswick. Edward considered that the £25,000 a year settled upon the Duke of York after his marriage ought 'to be considered the precedent'.[7] Having borrowed £1,000 from the Tsar for the cost of his journey, he had travelled to Germany to inspect the Tsarina's sister, Princess Katherine Amelia of Baden, but he had not liked the look of the 'old maiden' of forty-one whom he had found at Darmstadt; and his thoughts had later turned to Princess Victoire – sister of Prince Leopold of Saxe-Coburg, who had married the Regent's daughter, Princess Charlotte.

The Regent had been against the marriage of his daughter to Prince Leopold at first. He had conceded that Leopold was a good-looking, gifted fellow, charming in a rather solemn kind of way, and that he would probably treat Charlotte well. But there was something in the ingratiating suavity of his manner which was decidedly distasteful, and the ponderousness of his cautious approach to life was rather irritating. Adept at choosing nicknames, the Regent called him 'le Marquis peu à peu'.[8] The less inventive Lord Frederick FitzClarence dismissed him as a 'damned humbug';[9] and Princess Lieven, the Russian Ambassador's wife, found him 'wearing and . . . with his slow speech and bad reasoning, a jesuit and a bore'.[10] He had his supporters and admirers, however. Lady Ilchester, for example, told a friend that he was 'enchanting as far as appearance and manner' were concerned. He was 'like an Englishman in all but the ease, elegance and deference of his manners'.[11] Having discouraged the match, the Regent had learned with annoyance that his brother, the Duke of Kent, was promoting it and allowing correspondence between the young couple to pass through his hands.

Princess Charlotte herself had not at first been much taken with her suitor, 'Prince Humbug'. If she were to marry him, she had said, it would be 'with the most calm and perfect indifference'.[12] But, as she had grown to know him better, she had fallen in love with him. He was, she decided, 'the only being in the world who would have suited me and who could have made me happy and a good woman'.[13] He, in turn, had been devoted to her; their short marriage spent mostly at Claremont Park, the handsome house built in 1771 for the first Lord Clive and bought for them on the outskirts of Esher, had been a very happy one, and Leopold had been distraught by her death, kneeling by her bed and kissing her lifeless hands for over an hour. He had not, however, been too upset to write to his sister at Amorbach, urging her to give an encouraging answer to the proposal of marriage which she had received from the Duke of Kent.

This proposal, conveyed precipitately in an extremely long letter soon after the Duke's arrival at Amorbach, had not at first been favourably received. Although she was only thirty-one, Princess Victoire had been married before to the grumpy, gouty Prince of Leiningen and had two children by him, Prince Charles, who was eleven years old, and Princess Feodora, aged ten; she was concerned about these children's future, about her son's succession, as well as by warnings about the Duke from certain members of her late husband's court. Besides, she had no wish to give up her independence, having been married at seventeen and not having enjoyed the experience much. But gradually the Dowager Princess was induced to change her mind. She spoke no English and was slow to learn it: later in England she was to have her speeches written out for her phonetically – 'Ei hoeve tu regrétt, biing aes yiett so littl cônversent in thie Inglisch, lenguetsch, uitsch obleitshes miy tu seh, in averi fiu words, theat ei em möhst grêtful for yor congratuleschen'[14] – but she was assured she would be well received in England where her brother, Prince Leopold, had made himself well liked since his wife's death.

2

✳✳✳✳✳✳✳✳✳✳✳✳

THE PARENTS

'Look at her well, for she will
be Queen of England.'

THE DUKE AND THE DOWAGER PRINCESS were married in the
Schloss Ehrenburg, Coburg on the evening of 29 May 1818. The Princess's
mother, the Dowager Duchess of Coburg, led them to their bedroom
where she saw them the next morning 'sitting together in friendly intimacy'.[1] Soon afterwards they left for their honeymoon at Claremont Park,
which had been lent to them by Prince Leopold who continued to hold
the house as tenant for life in addition to his enjoyment of the use of
Marlborough House in London and the remarkably generous allowance
of £50,000 which the Government provided for him.

The marriage of the Duke and Duchess of Kent continued, as it had
begun, in harmony. The Duchess was rather stout and no great beauty,
but she was warm-hearted and affectionate and, in need of guidance and
self-assurance, was ready to depend upon her much older husband in a
manner that appealed to him. To the letter which the Princess had written
to the Duke accepting his proposal, he had replied that he was 'nothing
more than a soldier, 50 years old and after 32 years service not very fitted
to captivate the heart of a young and charming Princess who is years
younger'; but that he would care for her with tenderness and affection
so that she might forget the difference in their ages. And so he did. 'She
is really happy and contented,' the Dowager Duchess of Coburg wrote
of her daughter in March the following year, 'and Kent makes an excellent
husband.' 'She quite adored him,' his sister, Princess Augusta, confirmed,
'and they were truly blessed in each other.'

The Duchess of Kent was by then pregnant and expecting her baby in May. Her husband was determined that the child should be born in England, so that there could be no possible grounds for denying its right to succeed to the throne; a fate which, so it was alleged, a gypsy in Gibraltar had predicted for it and of which the Duke himself protested to have no doubt, dismissing the possibility that, although the Duchess of Clarence's two babies had died, there was no reason to suppose she might not yet give birth to a child who would be nearer to the succession than his own. 'My brothers are not so strong as I am,' the Duke declared. 'I have led a regular life. I shall outlive them all. The crown will come to me and my children.'[2]

Yet for the moment he lacked the means to return with his wife to England for the birth. One of his friends, Joseph Hume, the radical politician, deepened his fear that the time might come when the child's legitimacy might be 'challenged, and challenged with effect, from the circumstance of the birth taking place on foreign soil.'[3]

In his dilemma the Duke turned to his brother, the Regent, for help. He had already been much disappointed when an ill-disposed House of Commons proved unwilling to increase the allowance paid to the royal dukes on their marriages in the manner they had hoped; a rebuff which the Duke of Wellington considered only too understandable. 'By God,' Wellington said, 'there is a great deal to be said about that. They are the damnedest millstone about the necks of any Government. They have insulted – personally insulted – two thirds of the gentlemen of England, and how can it be wondered at that they take their revenge upon them when they get them in the House of Commons? It is their only opportunity and, I think, by God! they are quite right to use it.'[4]

The Duke of Kent, who was hoping for a grant of £25,000 a year and a capital sum of £12,000, dismissed his debts with the observation that 'on the contrary the nation [was] greatly [his] debtor'; and he added in his characteristically long-winded approach to his brother that he would also need a yacht to cross the Channel, the loan of restored and redecorated apartments in Kensington Palace, the provision of meals for the Duchess and himself and their attendants on their arrival in England and, should their physician recommend sea bathing for the Duchess, the use of a house at Brighton or Weymouth.

These demands exasperated the Regent, who had never much cared for his brother and was much annoyed by his improbable friendships with such radicals as Joseph Hume and Robert Owen, the social reformer, and by his attendance at Noncomformist services. He instructed his Private Secretary, after a long delay, to turn down all the Duke's requests, with the suggestion that it would be much more sensible for the child to be born on the Continent, thus both saving money and relieving Her Royal Highness, the Duchess, from 'the dangers and fatigues of a long journey at [this] moment'. If the Duke was still bent upon returning, and succeeded in raising the money to do so, he could '*not expect to meet with a cordial reception*'.[5]

Momentarily downcast, the Duke soon recovered his spirits and set about raising the money elsewhere. By the end of March, with the help of the Duke of Cambridge and of various friends, including Lord Dundas, Earl Fitzwilliam, Lord Darnley and Alderman Matthew Wood (a chemist and hop merchant in a thriving way of business who was an extreme radical Member for the City of London), he had managed to collect over £15,000; and so, on the twenty-eighth of the month, the Duke's party set off from Amorbach for Calais, with several pet dogs and songbirds, in a strange, unwieldy caravan of carriages. The Duke and Duchess led the way in a phaeton, the Duke himself driving to save the cost of a coachman. They were followed by the Duke's barouche, containing the Duchess's lady-in-waiting, Baroness Späth, and Frau Siebold, a skilled obstetrician who had qualified as a surgeon at the University of Göttingen. Then, trundling after them, came a spare, unoccupied post-chaise, followed by a second post-chaise containing the Duchess's daughter, Princess Feodora, her governess and the English maidservants. Following these were a cabriolet with two cooks, a caravan with an English manservant looking after the royal plate, a second phaeton, two gigs (one containing the Duke's valet, Mathieu, and the Duchess's footman; the other, two clerks), and lastly a curricle with the Duke's personal physician, Dr Wilson.

The weather was fine, the pace slow but steady, and the inns at which the cavalcade stopped were not intolerably uncomfortable. The travellers passed through Cologne on 5 April and a fortnight later they reached Calais where, the Regent having relented, a yacht was waiting for them to take them across the Channel. After a few days' delay at Calais caused by unfavourable winds, they sailed on the 24th for Dover and were soon installed at Kensington Palace where, after a labour lasting just over six hours, at a quarter past four in the cold morning of 24 May 1819, a baby girl was born. She was 'as plump as a partridge',[6] and 'a model of strength and beauty combined', so her grandmother, the Dowager Duchess of Coburg, was informed by the Duke, who had remained with his wife throughout her labour. 'The dear mother and child are doing marvellously well ... It is absolutely impossible for me to do justice to the patience and sweetness with which [the mother] behaved.'[7]

'My God, how glad I am to hear of you,' the Dowager Duchess responded in a letter to her daughter. 'I cannot find words to express my delight that everything went so smoothly ... I cannot write much ... dear mouse ... for I am much too happy.' She hoped the mother was not disappointed that the baby was a girl: 'The English,' she said, 'like Queens.'[8] As for the child's father, he was to show her proudly to his friends, telling them to 'look at her well, for she will be Queen of England'.[9]

The Duke's excitement at the arrival of his little 'pocket Hercules' at Kensington was not shared by the rest of the family. According to Prince Leopold, the Prince Regent did not trouble to disguise his hope that his brother would soon clear off to Germany again, taking his wife and child with him. Certainly the Regent's behaviour at the baby's christening was far from fraternal. He announced that the ceremony must be a strictly private occasion and that it should take place on 24 June at three o'clock in the afternoon. The godparents were to be himself, Tsar Alexander, the child's grandmother, the Dowager Duchess of Coburg, and the baby's aunt Charlotte, her father's sister, widow of the King of Württemberg. None of these, apart from the Regent, was to be present and so they were represented by the Duke of York, and two others of the baby's aunts, the unmarried Princess Augusta and Mary, Duchess of Gloucester. The only other persons to attend, apart from the parents, were the Duke of Kent's cousin, the Duke of Gloucester, the Duchess of York and Prince Leopold.

As a matter of form, the parents sent a list of names proposed for the child to the Prince Regent – Victoire (her mother's name), Georgiana (in deference to the Regent), Alexandrina (in deference to the Tsar), and Charlotte and Augusta (the names of her aunts). Nothing was heard from the Regent until the day before the christening when he wrote to say that he could not allow the name of Georgiana to be used as he did not choose to place his name before the Tsar's, 'and he could not allow it to follow'.[10] He would indicate the other names at the ceremony, disapproving of Charlotte, the name of his dead daughter, and of Augusta as being too majestic.

The ceremony took place in the Cupola Room at Kensington Palace, the walls of which had been draped with crimson velvet for the occasion. In the room stood a splendid silver gilt font which had been ordered by Charles II and first used in 1688 for the christening of his nephew – Prince James Francis Edward Stuart, the 'Old Pretender'. Waiting beside it stood the Archbishop of Canterbury, Charles Manners-Sutton, a grandson of the Duke of Rutland, and the Bishop of London, William Howley, a scholarly but otherwise (in Charles Greville's opinion) 'very ordinary man' who was to succeed Manners-Sutton as Archbishop in 1828. Neither of them had any idea what the names were to be when the ceremony began and the Archbishop had the child in his arms. He looked towards the parents, then towards the Regent, for enlightenment. The Regent announced 'Alexandrina'. There was a pause. The father proposed Elizabeth. The Regent dissented, then, looking at the Duchess of Kent who had been reduced to tears, he said sharply, 'Give her the mother's name also then, but it cannot precede that of the Emperor.'[11] So the child was christened Alexandrina Victoria, and in her early years was generally known by the diminutive of the first name, Drina.

The Regent had not spoken to the Duke of Kent during the ceremony; nor had he seen fit to suggest that his other brother, the Duke of Sussex (with whom he was, as usual, quarrelling), should be asked to attend the ceremony, though he was then living in Kensington Palace in an apartment furnished with 50,000 books and numerous clocks. Nor did the Regent attend the dinner party which was given afterwards; nor yet did he deign to notice the Duke of Kent's presence a few weeks later at a reception given at the Spanish Embassy where he was seen actually to turn his back on him. That same month at a military review, to which the Duke and Duchess had ill-advisedly taken their baby daughter, the Regent was heard to expostulate, 'What business has that infant here?'[12]

There could be no question of the Regent coming to the help of the Duke who was once more deeply in debt, having spent with characteristic extravagance far more than he could afford on furniture and improvements for his apartments in St James's Palace, including several thousand pounds' worth of looking-glasses. He had a country house, Castle Hill at Ealing, on which equally lavish sums had been spent and which, with its furniture and land, was estimated to be worth about £70,000; but when he applied for parliamentary consent to sell the property by means of a lottery, the Leader of the House of Commons declined to consider the proposal. He then considered selling the place in lots but was advised by auctioneers to wait until the spring. So the Duke decided to move to the West Country where he and his family and household could live more modestly in a rented house and where the mother of his child might benefit from 'luke warm sea baths' and the healthy air of the Devonshire coast.

Accompanied by his equerry, John Conroy, the Duke set off for Devonshire by way of Salisbury where he caught a bad cold. He had been looking round the freezing cathedral and had called on the Bishop, John Fisher, who had been his childhood preceptor and was the uncle of Conroy's wife, Elizabeth, daughter of Major-General Benjamin Fisher. From Salisbury he sent a letter to his 'beloved and very dear wife' to whom he wrote affectionately every day.

In Devonshire the Duke and Conroy looked at various houses along the coast, none of which was satisfactory, until at Sidmouth they chanced upon a pretty house with a partly castellated roof and Gothic windows, Woolbrook Cottage, Woolbrook Glen.

The Duke decided to take it; and on Christmas Day he and his family moved in as snow covered the ground outside. For days it was dreadfully cold and wet. The Duchess and her daughter, Feodora, ventured out to take walks along the coast; but the Duke stayed indoors for most of the day, writing letters. His stomach had been upset when they first arrived and, so he complained, 'the water had already begun to play the very deuce with [his] bowels'. Then, at the beginning of January 1820 he caught another cold which became so feverish that the Duchess called in his physician, Dr Wilson, who was much concerned by his case. On the evening of the twelfth his patient complained of pains in his chest and was overcome by nausea. Soon he was delirious. The Duchess, distracted, rarely left his side. She sent an urgent request to London for Sir David Dundas, the eminent physician, to come to Sidmouth; but Dundas was in attendance on the dying King George III at Windsor. Dr William

Maton, who had been Queen Charlotte's physician, came instead. His arrival was no comfort to the Duchess: he spoke little French and scarcely any German, and the Duchess's English, despite her efforts to learn the language, was not yet good enough for her to communicate with him or adequately to protest against the tormenting treatment which he, like Dr Wilson, prescribed their helpless patient.

The Duke was bled and cupped day after day; blisters were applied to his chest; then he was cupped and bled again until, as the Duchess wrote to a friend, there was 'hardly a spot on his dear body which [had] not been touched by cupping, blisters or bleeding . . . I cannot think it can be good for the patient to lose so much blood when he is already so weak . . . He was terribly exhausted yesterday after all that had been done to him by those cruel doctors.'[13] Although 'half delirious' he was induced to sign a will, appending his signature to the document with the most pathetic determination before sinking back on to his pillow. He died the next morning. The Duchess, who had, she said, 'adored him', knelt beside his bed, holding his hand.[14]

She was now almost destitute and it was left to her brother, Prince Leopold, to come to her aid. Without his help, he later assured her daughter, Victoria, the Duchess could not possibly have remained in the country. The Regent's 'great wish was to get you and your mama out of the country,' he told her emphatically. 'And I must say without my assistance you could not have remained . . . I know not what would have come of you and your mama, if I had not then existed.'[15]

But Prince Leopold not only existed but still had so large an income that he could well afford to take his sister and his little niece into his care. He asked the Regent's sister, Princess Mary, Duchess of Gloucester, to seek permission from her brother – who was as fond of her as she was of him – to allow the stricken widow and her daughter to return to her late husband's apartments at Kensington Palace. 'Her situation is most melancholy,' Princess Mary wrote, 'for Edward had nothing in the world but debts & now there are all his old servants without a penny piece to provide for them. She knows what your goodness of heart is & she is sure you *will* do what you can for them.'[16] The Regent immediately gave his consent; and so the Duchess of Kent, assured of an annual allowance from Prince Leopold of £2,000, later increased to £3,000 a year, returned to Kensington Palace where they learned that the poor, blind, demented King had died at last on 29 January 1820 and the Prince Regent was now King George IV.

3

THE CHILD

'I never had a room to myself. I never had a sofa, nor an easy chair, and there was not a single carpet that was not threadbare.'

THE KING'S LITTLE NIECE, VICTORIA, was now eight months old. She had not been well at Sidmouth, suffering from a heavy cold for most of the time; and she had been 'very upset by the frightful jolting' of the carriage that brought her back to Kensington. But she was a strong child, as her father had been pleased to note of his 'little joy'; and at six months she had, in his opinion, been 'as advanced as children generally are at eight'. She had been vaccinated without ill effects and having been weaned – her mother having caused some disapproval by indelicately insisting on giving what her husband described as 'maternal nutriment' – 'she did not appear to thrive the less for the change'. The Duchess was delighted with her little 'Vickelchen', as she called her, although she had to admit that she was already showing 'symptoms of wanting to get her own little way'.

This stubbornness and independence of spirit became more pronounced as she grew older. So did her impatience, her wilfulness, outbursts of temper and defiant truthfulness. Frustrated, she would stamp her feet and would burst into tears when told to sit still or to pay closer attention during her reading lessons; and once, in a tantrum, she hurled a pair of scissors at her governess. Before her lessons began one day, her mother was asked if she had been a good girl that morning. 'Yes,' the Duchess replied, 'she has been good this morning but yesterday there was a little storm.' 'Two storms,' corrected the little girl, pertly interrupting her mother's account, intent as always on speaking and hearing the truth, 'one at dressing and one at washing.' She was similarly pert when her mother said to her, after one of her outbursts of temper, that she made them both very unhappy by such behaviour. 'No, Mama, not me, not myself, but *you*.'[1]

The Duchess's nervous temperament was not well adapted to dealing with such a child. 'To my shame,' she admitted, 'I must confess that I am over anxious in a childish way with the little one, as if she were my first child . . . She drives me at times into real desperation . . . Today the little mouse . . . was so unmanageable that I nearly cried.'

Wilful as she was, however, the little girl, intelligent and lively and with an astonishingly retentive memory, progressed satisfactorily with her lessons when these began to a regular timetable supervised by her Principal Master, the Revd George Davys, a Fellow of Christ's College, Cambridge, later Bishop of Peterborough. Davys came to live in Kensington Palace before the Princess was four years old. He helped to teach her to read by writing short words on cards and, as he put it, 'making her bring them to me from a distant part of the room as I named them'.[2] Admittedly, she was not very good at Latin, and piano lessons were often a trial: once, when told that there was 'no royal road to success in music' and that she must practise like everyone else, she banged shut the lid of the instrument with the defiant words, 'There! You see there is no *must* about it.' But she was patient and attentive in her history and geography lessons; she learned to speak French and German – the latter in particular with a 'correct pronunciation' – and a little Italian.* She soon became adept at arithmetic; her written English was exemplary and her soprano singing voice, trained by John Sale, the organist at St Margaret's Westminster, was delightful. She danced with easy grace, she listened dutifully to Mr Davys's religious instruction, she read poetry 'extremely well', he said, and understood what she read 'as well, as at her age, could reasonably be expected'. She displayed a precocious skill in drawing at which she was given lessons by Richard Westall, the prolific historical painter and book illustrator, and later, by Edwin Landseer, Edward Lear and William Leighton Leitch, the distinguished watercolourist.[3]

---

* Her first Prime Minister, Lord Melbourne, was later to comment, 'She is far too open and candid in her nature to pretend to one atom more knowledge than she really possesses . . . and yet, as the world goes, she would, as any girl, have been considered accomplished, for she speaks German well and writes it; understands Italian, speaks French fluently, and writes it with great elegance' (Benson and Esher, *The Letters of Queen Victoria*, 1st Series, i, 256: memorandum of George Anson, 15 January 1841).

In March 1830, when the Princess was ten years old, the Duchess decided that her daughter should be examined to ensure that her education was proceeding along the correct lines. The two invigilators chosen were Charles Blomfield, Bishop of London, described by Richard Porson, Regius Professor of Greek at Cambridge, as a 'very pretty scholar', and John Kaye, Bishop of Lincoln, who had been elected Master of Christ's College, Cambridge at the age of thirty and Regius Professor of Divinity two years later.

Having examined the Princess, these two eminent scholars expressed themselves as being 'completely satisfied' with her answers.

> In answering a great variety of questions [they reported] the Princess displayed an accurate knowledge of the most important features of Scripture, History and of the leading truths and precepts of the Christian Religion as taught by the Church of England; as well as an acquaintance with the Chronology and principal facts of English History, remarkable in so young a person. To questions of Geography, the use of Globes, Arithmetic and Latin Grammar, the answers which the Princess returned were equally satisfactory; and Her pronunciation both of English and Latin is singularly correct and pleasing. Due attention appears to have been paid to the acquisition of modern languages; and although it was less within the scope of our enquiry, we cannot help observing that the pencil drawings of the Princess are executed with the freedom and correctness of an older child.[4]

In later years she spoke of her childhood as being lonely and 'rather melancholy' and Kensington Palace as being bleak in the extreme. 'I never had a room to myself,' she complained. 'I never had a sofa, nor an easy chair, and there was not a single carpet that was not threadbare.' The food was boring and unappetizing: she promised herself that when she was grown up and could eat as she liked, she would never have mutton for dinner again. Yet the events of her early life as she recorded them were far from being all unhappy ones. Certainly there were recollections of bogeymen: she had 'a great horror of *Bishops*' with their strange wigs and incongruous aprons and of the Duke of Sussex, 'Uncle Sussex', who, she was told, would appear from his nearby rooms in the Palace and punish her when she cried and was naughty. She remembered screaming when she saw him.[5] But she was fond of her father's old preceptor, the kindly John Fisher, Bishop of Salisbury, who used to kneel down beside her and let her play with the badge he wore as Chancellor of the Order of the Garter; and she was fond, too, of her uncle, the childless Duke of York, who was very fat and very bald and held himself in such a way that it always seemed as though he would tumble over backwards. He was 'very kind' to her and gave her 'beautiful presents' including a donkey, and once he presided over a memorable party for her at the house of a friend where there was a Punch and Judy show.[6] As for her uncle, King George IV, he paid little attention to her when she was taken by her mother to see him at Carlton House; but one day while she was staying near Windsor with her aunt, the Duchess of Gloucester, at Cumberland Lodge, she was driven over to see the King at the Royal Lodge and found him in one of his happier moods. 'Give me your little paw,' he said, affectionately taking the hand of the seven-year-old child in his, and then pulled her on to his stout knee so that she could kiss him. It was 'too disgusting', she recalled more than half a century later, 'because his face was covered with grease-paint'. But at the time she had responded to his 'wonderful dignity and charm of manner': he never lost his way of pleasing young children. 'He wore the wig which was so much worn in those days,' she remembered clearly. 'Then he said he would give me something to wear, and that was his picture set in diamonds, which was worn by the Princesses as an order to a blue ribbon on the left shoulder. I was very proud of this – and Lady Conyngham [the King's plump and stately intimate friend, supposedly his mistress] pinned it on my shoulder.'[7]

Next day, while she was out walking with her mother, the King, who was driving along in his phaeton with the Duchess of Gloucester, overtook her. As his horses were brought to a halt, the King called out cheerfully, 'Pop her in!' So she was lifted up and placed between him and her aunt Mary, who held her round the waist as the horses trotted off. She was 'greatly pleased', though her mother appeared 'much frightened', fearful that her daughter would either fall out on the road or be kidnapped.

The King drove her 'round the nicest part of Virginia Water' and stopped at the Fishing Temple. Here 'there was a large barge and everyone went on board and fished, while a band played in another!' Afterwards he had his little niece conducted around his menagerie at Sandpit Gate where she inspected his wapitis, his chamois and his gazelles.

In the evenings, while staying at Cumberland Lodge, Princess Victoria was invited to watch the Tyrolese dancers creating a 'gay uproar' or listen to 'Uncle King's' band playing in the conservatory at the Royal Lodge by the light of coloured lamps. He asked her what tune she would like the band to play next. With precocious tact she immediately asked for 'God save the King!' 'Tell me,' he asked her later, 'what you enjoyed most of your visit?' 'The drive with you,' she said. He was clearly very much taken with her.[8]

As the Duke of Wellington's friend, Lady Shelley, said, she paid her court extremely well. When giving the King a bunch of flowers, she said, 'As I shall not see my dear uncle on his birthday I wish to give him this nosegay now'; and when wishing him goodbye she said with appealing if rather affected gravity, 'I am coming to bid you adieu, sire, but as I know you do not like fine speeches I shall certainly not trouble you by attempting one.'[9] Upon her return home she was most anxious that her mother should send 'her best love and duty to her "dear Uncle King"'.[10]

Although she remembered with pleasure her days at Windsor, the Princess enjoyed her visits to her uncle Leopold's house, Claremont, even more. So much did she enjoy these visits, indeed, that she cried when it was time to go back to Kensington. She remembered being allowed to listen to the music in the hall at Claremont when there were dinner parties there and being petted by Mrs Louis, Princess Charlotte's devoted former dresser. She was petted, too, by her own nurse, Mrs Brock, 'dear Boppy', and by her mother's lady-in-waiting, Baroness Späth, who had accompanied the Duchess from Germany. Indeed, Baroness Späth, so Princess Feodora said, idolized the child and would actually go on her knees before her.[11]

Very different was the behaviour of the Princess's governess, Louise Lehzen, a handsome woman, despite her pointed nose and chin, clever, emotional, humourless and suffering intermittently from a variety of complaints, mostly psychosomatic, including cramp, headaches and migraine. She claimed that she did not know what it was like to feel hungry: all 'she fancied were potatoes';[12] but she was forever chewing caraway seeds for indigestion, a habit which some maliciously attributed to a need to hide the alcohol on her breath.

In her mid-thirties at the time of her appointment, she was the youngest child of a Lutheran pastor from a village in Hanover. She was 'very strict', her former charge said of her in later years, 'and the Princess had great respect and even awe of her, but with that the greatest affection ... She knew how to amuse and play with the Princess so as to gain her warmest affections. The Princess was her only object and her only thought ... She never for the 13 years she was governess to Princess Victoria, *once left her*.'[13]

At night she stayed in the bedroom which the Princess shared with her mother until the Duchess retired; and in the morning, when the child was being dressed by Mrs Brock, she read to her so that the little girl would not get into the habit of talking indiscreetly to servants.

Yet Louise Lehzen's influence over Princess Victoria was not entirely beneficial, for the governess had her prejudices and these she implanted in her charge's mind. She encouraged the child to distrust her mother and her mother's friends and to tell people when they were wrong and 'to set them down'.[14]

If Princess Victoria's early childhood was not quite as melancholy as she afterwards decided when looking back upon it, it was – and was encouraged by Lehzen to be – certainly a lonely one. She was brought up in an adult world, rarely seeing children of her own age. 'Except for occasional visits of other children,' she said herself in later life, she 'lived always *alone*, without companions'. She was devoted to her half-sister, Princess Feodora, but Feodora, a pretty, attractive girl, was twelve years older than herself and longing to escape from Kensington where, so she claimed, her 'only happy time was driving out' with Princess Victoria and Louise Lehzen when she could speak and look as she liked. In February 1828, when Princess Victoria was nine, Princess Feodora did escape, her only regret being her separation from her 'dearest sister' of whom she so often thought and longed to see again.*[15]

Having married the impoverished, 32-year-old Prince Ernest Christian Charles of Hohenlohe-Langenburg, Princess Feodora went away with him to the enormous, uncomfortable Schloss Langenburg, leaving Princess Victoria to comfort herself with her dolls (one hundred and thirty-two of them – little wooden, painted mannequins made by herself and Lehzen and dressed as historical personages and characters from the theatre and opera, all of them listed in a copybook).[16]

*   *   *

* She did see Princess Victoria again when she visited England in 1834. The parting after that visit was a most painful one: 'the separation was indeed *dreadful*,' Victoria wrote. 'I *clasped* her in my *arms* and *kissed* her and *cried* as if my *heart* would break, so did the *dearest* Sister ... I sobbed and cried most violently the whole morning ... I love no one better than her' (RA Princess Victoria's Journal, 25, 26 July 1834).

Her mother had been lonely too. Having overcome the first shock of her husband's death, she had struck the few people with whom she came into close contact as being, in Lady Granville's words, 'very pleasing indeed', friendly and approachable.

But she herself, as she said, felt 'friendless and alone' in a country that was not her own, endeavouring to speak a language which she had not yet mastered, being, as she said with not altogether sincere self-denigration, 'just an old goose'.[17]

She was well aware that, as a German, she was not well liked in the country at large and, as the widow of the Duke of Kent and mother of Princess Victoria, much resented by the Duke of Clarence, heir to the throne after the death of his elder brother, the Duke of York, in 1827. Nor did King George IV care for her.

When the Prime Minister had suggested to the King that some provision ought to be made for his sister-in-law's child, the fatherless Princess Victoria, the King declared that he would not consider it: her uncle Leopold was quite rich enough to take care of her as well as her mother. The Duchess accordingly had to borrow £6,000 from Thomas Coutts, the banker.[18] Later, however, the Government came to her aid by proposing an allowance of £4,000 a year; but, since a grant of £6,000 was at the same time proposed for Princess Victoria's cousin, Prince George of Cumberland, son of the deeply distrusted and malignant Duke of Cumberland, she refused to consider the proposal. The offer to the Duchess was then raised to £6,000 and she accepted it.

At the same time, Prince Leopold assured her that he would be happy to continue the allowance he made her of £3,000 a year. She was at first reluctant to accept this; but being still heavily in debt she eventually agreed to it, even though she was finding her brother increasingly and tiresomely irritating and, as she put it, 'rather slow in the uptake and in making decisions' as well as annoyingly preoccupied.

Prince Leopold had, indeed, other matters on his mind, not to mention sexual desires to gratify. After pursuing a succession of other women, he had fallen in love with a German actress who, looking 'wondrously like' his departed Charlotte, was brought over to England and ensconced alternately in a house in Regent's Park and a 'lonely desolate and mournful' little house in the grounds of Claremont Park where he spent his time either gazing at her longingly while she read aloud to him or picking the silver from military epaulettes to make into a soup tureen.[19]

He had also become involved in negotiations for his elevation to a European throne. He had been offered the throne of Greece in 1830 after that country had secured its freedom from Turkish rule and, having declined to become King of Greece, he agreed two years later, after typical hesitation, to be crowned King of the Belgians once Belgium had secured its independence from the King of Holland. The next year he married Princess Louise, the daughter of Louis-Philippe, King of the French.

Before leaving for Brussels he volunteered to give up the grant of £50,000 a year he had received upon his marriage to Princess Charlotte but this gesture, gratefully accepted, was less well regarded when he announced that some £20,000 would have to be retained for various expenses, including the upkeep of Claremont.

Princess Victoria was very sad to have to say goodbye to her uncle. He had done his best to take the place of the father she had never known. Ponderous and, on occasions, exasperating as he could be, she loved him and admired him greatly. 'To hear dear Uncle Leopold speak on any subject,' she said, 'is like reading a highly instructive book.'[20] He was the first of those several older men upon whom, throughout her life, she was to rely for help and reassurance. But her mother bore her brother's departure for the Continent far more equably than she would have done at the time of her arrival in England. For the need she had always felt for support, protection and comforting advice had been met by her late husband's beguiling equerry, John Conroy.

4

CONROY

'I may call you Jane but you must not call me Victoria.'

PRINCE LEOPOLD described John Conroy as a 'Mephistopheles'; but the Prince's sister, the Duchess of Kent, did not know what she would do without him. He had been a 'dear devoted friend' of the Duke, she said, and he had not deserted the widow, doing all he could to help her by dealing with her affairs, financial and otherwise. Whereas Leopold was cautious and deliberate, inclined to see difficulties before advantages, Conroy exuded a confidence which the Duchess, comforted by positive men, found reassuring.

Although of Irish descent, with forbears who were proud to trace their lineage back to a royal chieftain of the early fifth century, Conroy had been born in Wales in 1786. He had obtained a commission in the Royal Artillery when he was seventeen and had been transferred to the Horse Artillery two years later. But thereafter he had not progressed as well in the Army as he considered his talents deserved, despite his marriage to a General's daughter, the rather nondescript, indolent niece of the Duke of Kent's friend, Bishop Fisher, by whom he was to have six children. He had not served in either the Peninsular War or the Waterloo campaign; and the Duke of Kent's attempts to find him a suitable staff appointment had not been successful. He had entered the Duke's household as equerry in 1817; and the death of the Duke three years later had given him the opportunity to worm his way into a position far more rewarding and influential than he could have hoped for in the Army.

The same age as the Duchess, he was a good-looking man of insinuating charm, tall, imposing, vain, clever, unscrupulous, plausible and of limitless ambition. Overbearing with those whom he sought to dominate, he was both short-tempered and devious. Charles Greville, the diarist and Clerk of the Privy Council, dismissed him as 'a ridiculous fellow'.[1] Conroy immediately recognized that by exerting a compelling influence over the susceptible and self-doubting Duchess of Kent, by isolating her household at Kensington from outside contacts and interference, he might be able to exercise unbounded control over her bright, spirited, affectionate and popular but obstinate and 'naturally passionate' child.

At the same time, Conroy made up his mind to win the confidence of King George IV's sister, Princess Sophia, who had apartments at Kensington Palace. She was nine years older than himself. Cloistered at Windsor in her father's lifetime, in what she and her sisters referred to as 'the nunnery', she had fallen in love with one of her father's equerries, General Garth, and had secretly borne him a child. Conroy had little difficulty in charming the impressionable and mentally rather unstable woman whose considerable finances he controlled, and with the help of whose liberality he was able to acquire a house in Kensington for £4,000 as well as a country house near Reading, Aborfield Hall, and an estate in Wales for £18,000.[2] Princess Sophia – whose generosity was said to be at least partly owing to Conroy's skill in dealing with the 'bullying importunities' of her illegitimate son, Captain Garth[3] – having appointed Conroy her unofficial Comptroller, was induced to apply to her brother, the King, for suitable ranks to be bestowed upon the Duchess of Kent's household. The King, who was fond of his adoring sisters, responded promptly: Louise Lehzen was created a Hanoverian baroness by His Majesty in his right as King of Hanover, while Conroy was created a Knight Commander of the Hanoverian Order.

Sir John Conroy, while so successfully beguiling both the Duchess of Kent and Princess Sophia, failed lamentably in his efforts to win the confidence of Princess Victoria whom he treated with that kind of bullying jocularity which children find so offensive. He told her she reminded him of the Duke of Gloucester, one of the least well-favoured members of her family; he said her economical habits, including the saving of her pocket money, must have been inherited from her parsimonious grandmother, Queen Charlotte; he teased her in the naive belief that she would be amused by his facetiousness rather than offended by what she described as 'personal affronts'. She grew to hate him. The Duke of Wellington believed that this hatred sprang from her having witnessed 'some familiarities' between her mother and Conroy; and when Charles Creevey remarked to the Duke that he 'concluded he was her lover', the Duke replied that he also 'supposed so'.[4] In later life Victoria strongly denied that her mother and Conroy could have been lovers, and she was no doubt right to disbelieve that they were; but her detestation of Conroy was nonetheless virulent and the Duchess's fond feelings for her Comptroller soured the feelings between mother and daughter. So too did they sour the friendly feelings which the Princess had earlier felt for Conroy's daughter, Victoire, a rather dull girl, and one of the few children of her own age with whom Victoria was allowed to associate.

Having established his position at Kensington, Sir John Conroy – who did not now trouble to conceal his occasional irritation with the Duchess who, so he said, lived 'in a mist' – set about what became known as 'the Kensington System', a process by which, in Conroy's words, Princess Victoria would become the 'Nation's Hope', the 'People's Queen'.[5] This entailed ensuring that the child became completely dependent upon her mother who – should the girl's uncle, the Duke of Clarence, die before she came of age at eighteen – would become Regent. In the meantime, there must be no risk of anyone beyond the Kensington household gaining any influence over the Princess. She must continue to sleep in her mother's room; she must never be left alone in any other room; when going downstairs she must be accompanied by an adult to hold her hand; she must never have the opportunity of talking to a visitor unless a third person were present. She must be strictly shielded from anyone who might endeavour to gain her confidence; furthermore, she must be separated from other members of the Royal Family, in particular from her uncle, the wicked Duke of Cumberland, who, so Conroy liked it to be supposed, as an additional reason for keeping her isolated, was quite capable of having her poisoned or otherwise disposed of so that he could succeed to his brother's throne.

Well aware of the system being adopted at Kensington, the Duchess of Clarence wrote to her sister-in-law to advise her against a policy which was attributed – 'rightly or wrongly', she could not judge – to Sir John Conroy, 'a man of merit' but one whose family was 'not of so high a rank that they *alone* should be the entourage and companions of the future Queen of England'. She must not allow Conroy to exercise '*too much* influence over her but keep him in his place'. The Duchess of Kent, a willing accomplice in the 'system', paid no attention.[6]

As well as being separated from the Royal Family, the Princess must also be shielded from any English lady who might have undesirable connections and friends; and Baroness Lehzen, being German, and 'entirely dependent' upon the Duchess, happily had none of these. The Princess must also, like her mother, 'acquire popularity and a wide following', clearly distinguishing her from all her dissolute relations.

Fortunately, though little was known about her, the glimpses which the public were permitted to see had already created a favourable impression of Princess Victoria. She had been seen riding her white donkey in Kensington Gardens with 'an old soldier, a former retainer of her father's, leading her bridle rein', 'riding in a pony chaise over the gravel walks, led by a page', and walking along the paths there followed by a very tall footman looking like 'a gigantic fairy'.[7] Lord Albemarle, a member of the Duke of Sussex's household, had watched from a window of the Palace 'a bright, pretty little girl' in a large white hat 'impartially' dividing the contents of a watering can 'between the flowers and her own little feet'.[8] Charles Knight, the publisher, also caught a glimpse of her one day having breakfast with her mother on the lawn outside Kensington Palace and running off to pick a flower in the adjoining meadow. 'I passed on,' Knight wrote, 'and blessed her.'[9]

Charles Greville saw her at a children's ball, given by the King and attended by the ten-year-old Queen of Portugal, and he thought that 'our little Princess' was a 'short, vulgar-looking child, and not near so good-looking as the Portuguese'.[10] But this was not a characteristic verdict. Most of those few people who came across her were more likely to share the opinion of Lady Wharncliffe, who was invited to dinner at Kensington where the Princess was occasionally allowed down from her bedroom to sit at the table, eating her 'bread and milk out of a small silver basin'. Lady Wharncliffe was delighted with 'our little future Queen'.

> She is very much grown, though short for her age [she wrote], has a nice countenance and distingué figure, tho' not very good; and her manner the most perfect mixture of childishness and civility I ever saw. She is born a Princess without the *least* appearance of

art or affectation ... When she went to bed we all stood up and after kissing *Aunt* Sophia, she curtsied, first to one side, and then the other, to all the Ladies, and then walked off with her governess. She is really very accomplished by *taste*, being very fond both of music and drawing, but fondest of all of her *dolls*. In short I look to her to save us from Democracy, for it is impossible she should not be popular when she is older and more seen.[11]

The Duke of Wellington's friend, Harriet Arbuthnot, was equally taken with the little girl, 'the most charming child' she ever saw. 'She is a fine, beautifully made, handsome creature,' Mrs Arbuthnot continued, 'quite playful & childish [she was nearly nine], playing with her dolls and in high spirits, but civil & well bred & Princess-like to the greatest degree.'[12] She was graceful in her movements and walked with a regal air, an accomplishment attributed to her having had to submit on occasions to a bunch of prickly holly pinned to the front of her dress to keep her head up.

It was not until she was nearly eleven years old that the Princess learned how near she was to the throne. Of course, she knew that she was an honoured little personage. Servants behaved to her with noticeable deference; when she was out walking, gentlemen touched or raised their hats to her. She herself once told a child who put a hand out to play with her toys, 'You must not touch those, they are mine. And I may call you Jane but you must not call me Victoria.' According to Baroness Lehzen, a few days after her charge had been cross-examined by the Bishops of London and Lincoln, and having discussed the matter with the Duchess of Kent, the Baroness placed a genealogical table into one of the Princess's history books. 'I never saw that before,' Victoria said; and, after examining the table, she commented, 'I see I am nearer to the throne than I thought.'[13] She then burst into tears. Lehzen reminded her that Aunt Adelaide was still young and might yet have children and, of course, if she did, it was they who would ascend the throne after their father died.

A few weeks later, on 26 June 1830, King George IV died at Windsor Castle and the short reign of King William IV began.

5

✳✳✳✳✳✳✳✳✳

PROGRESSES

'When one arrives at any nobleman's seat,
one must instantly dress for dinner and
consequently I could never rest properly.'

WHEN SHE WAS TWO YEARS OLD, Princess Victoria had received a letter from her 'truly affectionate Aunt', the Duchess of Clarence, in which the Duchess referred to her as 'my dear little Heart'; and, when she lost her second baby daughter, she wrote to the Duchess of Kent to say 'My children are dead, but yours lives and She is mine too.'[1]

A good-natured, unselfish and religious woman, almost thirty years younger than her husband, she was quite sincere in expressing these sentiments, and upon his accession to the throne she was as kind to her little niece as ever, doing all she could to persuade her guardians at Kensington to allow her to appear at Court. Her husband also strongly expressed his wish to see her there.

On becoming King, William, as good-natured as his wife, 'began immediately to do good-natured things'. He clearly loved being a king; and, excited by his rank, he strode about the London streets, nodding cheerfully to right and left, relishing his popularity. Expressing a general opinion, Charles Greville said that he was 'a kind-hearted, well-meaning . . . bustling old fellow [sixty-five years of age] and, if he doesn't go mad, may make a very decent King.' Contrasting his gregarious familiarity with the seclusion in which his predecessor had chosen to spend the last years of his life, the Duke of Wellington, the Prime Minister, told Dorothea Lieven that this was not so much a new reign; it was 'a new dynasty'.

At Kensington Palace, however, the new reign had no effect whatsoever upon the 'system' practised there. Sir John Conroy remained as the Duchess of Kent's Comptroller, organizing the household and all the particularities of its life, telling the Duchess to report to him upon '*everything*' that happened to the Princess down to the 'smallest and insignificant detail'. As soon as he heard of King George IV's death, Conroy wrote a letter which, signed by the Duchess, was sent to the Duke of Wellington for onward transmission to King William IV. This letter, referring to Princess Victoria as now being 'more than Heiress Presumptive' to the throne, required the appointment of the Duchess as Regent 'without any interference whatsoever'. It also required the appointment of an English lady of rank to be appointed governess to the Princess, superseding Baroness Lehzen, and requested the recognition of the Duchess as Dowager Princess of Wales with an increased allowance for her in her new position in the kingdom.

Dismayed by both the tone and the contents of this importunate letter, Wellington replied that he earnestly entreated her Royal Highness to allow him to consider it as 'a Private and Confidential Communication; or rather as never having been written'.[2] Angered by this rebuff, the Duchess, advised by Conroy, immediately returned a sharp reply, contending that she would find it irksome to be Regent but that she owed it to her conscience for her daughter's sake to undertake the duty. Wellington answered her letter in a mollifying tone but thought it as well to offer a guarded warning by urging her Royal Highness 'not to allow any Person' to persuade her to entertain the idea that there was any 'Party or Individual of influence in the Country' who wished to injure the interests of the Duchess and her daughter. Deeply offended by this reference to her Comptroller, the Duchess declined to see the Duke when he proposed to bring her a draft of a Regency Bill, telling him to communicate with Sir John Conroy, and refusing to talk to him for 'a long time after'.[3] The Regency Bill, introduced by the Lord Chancellor in Lord Grey's government which succeeded Wellington's in November 1830, did, however, provide for her appointment as sole Regent in the event of King William dying before her daughter reached the age of eighteen, the House of Commons recoiling in horror from the thought that the dreadful Duke of Cumberland might otherwise lay claim to share the appointment with her. When she was told of Parliament's decision, the Duchess, reduced to tears, said that it gave her more pleasure than anything else had done since the death of her husband.[4]

Yet the settlement of the Regency question, and the appointment of the Duchess of Northumberland as the Princess's English Governess, did nothing to improve relations between the Duchess of Kent and the Court which were also soured not only by the Duchess's attitude towards the King's illegitimate children but also by political differences; the King and Queen Adelaide both being strong Tories and known to be opposed to the Reform Bill which Lord Grey was endeavouring to push through Parliament; the Duchess of Kent, following her late husband's example, being as committed a Whig, and welcoming Whigs and reformers to Kensington Palace.

The family quarrel was exacerbated when the King proposed that the Princess's name of Victoria should be changed for an English one. Since Victoria had been named after herself, the Duchess naturally was upset by this request; but since the two names, Alexandrina and Victoria, her daughter bore had not been chosen by her but had been forced upon her by the late King, and since she was ready to concede that both, being foreign, were 'not suited to our national feeling', she agreed that they might be 'laid aside'. Soon afterwards, however, she changed her mind and much annoyed the King, who, persisting in his objection to Victoria as a name 'never known heretofore as a Christian name in this country', proposed Elizabeth instead. The Duchess declined to consider it.[5]

Then there was trouble over Princess Victoria's appearances at Court, which the King and Queen wished were more frequent and which the Duchess and Conroy wanted to be 'as few as possible'.*

One reason which the Duchess persistently gave for keeping her daughter away from Court as much as possible was the presence of the King's bastard children, the FitzClarences, who moved into Windsor Castle, one after the other, until it was 'quite full with *toute la bâtardise*'.[6] Queen Adelaide raised no objection at all to this, but not so the Duchess of Kent. She insisted that nothing would induce her to allow her daughter

---

* Years later, recalling these quarrels between her mother and the old royal family, Queen Victoria wrote, 'Oh, it was dreadful ... always on pins and needles, with the whole family hardly on speaking terms. I (a mere child) between two fires – trying to be civil then scolded at home' (Roger Fulford, *Dearest Child: Letters between Queen Victoria and the Princess Royal*; 8 March 1858, 72–3).

to mix freely with the offspring of such a shameful relationship. 'I never did, neither will I ever, associate Victoria in any way with the illegitimate members of the Royal Family,' she told the Duchess of Northumberland. 'Did I not keep this line, how would it be possible to teach Victoria the difference between vice and virtue?'[7]

Quarrels over Princess Victoria's attendances at Court were followed by a dispute over the Princess's style as Royal Highness, the word Royal having been omitted in a message to Parliament from the King concerning a proposed increased allowance of £6,000 for the Duchess. Then there was trouble over the Princess's precedence at the coronation, the King declaring that she must follow his brothers in the procession through Westminster Abbey, the Duchess insisting that she follow immediately after the King. When the King stood firm, the Duchess declared that, in that case, the Princess would not attend the coronation at all – maintaining that she could not afford the expense and that, in any case, the child's health made her attendance out of the question. The Princess, who had not been consulted, cried bitterly. 'Nothing could console me,' she said, 'not even my dolls.'[8] She would have loved to go, she said: it would have been a special treat like her rare visits to Windsor, even though, being well aware of how much her mother disapproved of them, she was sometimes so nervous in the King's presence on these visits that he once complained of her stony stares. 'I was very much pleased there,' she wrote of one such visit, 'as both my Uncle and Aunt are *so very kind* to me.' She felt nothing but 'affectionate gratitude' to the King whose wish it was that 'she should be duly prepared for the duties' which she was destined to perform.[9]

Kept apart from the King and Queen for months on end, with her uncle Leopold preoccupied with affairs in Belgium and with her half-sister, Feodora, now living in Germany, the Princess was more and more isolated at Kensington where she felt increasingly defenceless against the rule of Conroy so unquestioningly supported by her mother. Baroness Spāth, who had presumed to question the 'Kensington System' and was believed to indulge the Princess unduly, had been dismissed after having been in the Duchess's service for a quarter of a century. It was decided that the time would also soon come to get rid of the Duchess of Northumberland who was not sufficiently subservient to Conroy's rule. At the same time an extra lady-in-waiting was appointed to the Duchess of

Kent's household in the person of Lady Flora Hastings, daughter of the first Marquess of Hastings.

In the meantime steps were being taken to bring about the removal, or at least to lessen the influence, of Baroness Lehzen who was treated so rudely that it was hoped she would resign. This merely resulted in Princess Victoria becoming more attached than ever to Lehzen. 'I can never sufficiently repay her for all she has *borne* and done for me,' she wrote. 'She is the most affectionate, devoted, attached and disinterested friend that I have.' She was, the Princess added later, 'my ANGELIC dearest mother *Lehzen*, who I do so love'. It could not but give grim satisfaction to the Princess, as well as embarrass her, when the King, who warmly supported Lehzen, dismissed Conroy from the Chapel Royal – where his niece, looking so demure in a white lace dress and rose-trimmed bonnet, was about to be confirmed – on the grounds that the Duchess's retinue was too large. Upon her return to the Palace, upset as much by the Archbishop of Canterbury's admonitory sermon as by the stuffiness of the Chapel on that hot July day and by her mother's anger at the King's behaviour, she burst into tears.

On this day, 30 July 1835, Princess Victoria received a firm letter from her mother telling her that her relationship with Lehzen must now change: the Baroness was to be treated with more formality, less intimate affection. Dignity and friendly manners were 'quite compatible'. 'Until you are at the age of 18 or 21 years,' the Duchess added, 'you are still confided to the guidance of your affectionate mother and friend.'[10]

Nothing about the Duchess of Kent's behaviour exasperated King William more than what he termed the 'Royal Progresses' upon which she and Conroy took Princess Victoria so as to make her better known to the people over whom she was destined to rule and to introduce her to the leading families in the counties through which she passed.

The first of these journeys was undertaken in the summer and autumn of 1830 when the Duchess and Sir John Conroy and, as an unwanted companion for the Princess, Conroy's daughter Victoire, drove to Hollymount in the Malvern hills, calling on the way at Stratford-on-Avon, Kenilworth and Warwick, and paying a visit to the Duke and Duchess of Marlborough at Blenheim Palace. They also went to Earl Beauchamp's house, Madresfield Court, Malvern and to the Duke of Beaufort's Badminton House. They visited Hereford, Gloucester and Stonehenge; at Bath on 23 October the Princess opened the Royal Victoria Park; at Worcester she was taken round the porcelain works.

There was another tour two years later when, in the summer of 1832, the Princess and her incompatible entourage set off for north Wales by way of the Midland counties. With the utmost annoyance, the King read of these 'disgusting parades', of the vociferous welcome accorded to his niece, of the bands and choirs, of the loyal addresses delivered and graciously accepted, the decorated triumphal arches, the salutes of cannon from the walls of castles, the flags and flowers, the cheering crowds, the escorts of regiments of yeomanry, the presentation of medals. Drawn by grey horses, caparisoned with ribbons and artificial flowers, the post-boys wearing conspicuous pink silk jackets and black hats, the royal party – 'the Conroyal party' as the disapproving called it – passed through Welshpool to Powis Castle and Caernarvon, then on to Plâs Newydd on the island of Anglesey, home of the first Marquess of Anglesey, the one-legged cavalry commander, who had offered them the use of it. They returned by way of Eaton Hall in Cheshire, home of Lord Grosvenor, calling at Chester, where the Princess opened the Victoria Bridge spanning the river Dee, on their way to the Devonshires at Chatsworth where the Princess played her first game of charades and enjoyed her first tableaux vivants.

From Chatsworth they drove to the Earl of Shrewsbury at Alton Towers and then to Pitchford in Lancashire, seat of the Earl of Liverpool, half-brother of the former Prime Minister, whose daughter, Lady Catherine Jenkinson, a young woman of whom the Princess was fond, had been appointed lady-in-waiting to the Duchess of Kent two years before.

In November the royal party reached Oxford where, in the Sheldonian Theatre, to which they were escorted by a troop of yeomanry commanded by Lord Churchill, the Princess was obliged to watch the honorary degree of Doctor of Civil Law being awarded to Sir John Conroy and to listen to the speech of the Regius Professor of Civil Law who, having referred to the 'singular prudence' and 'much industry' with which Sir John had carried out his duties for the Duke of Kent, declared, 'Can you wonder that he who had gained the esteem of the Husband, should also have pleased His surviving Consort.'[11]

Despite the presence of Sir John and his daughter, the Princess had enjoyed the tour, the drives in the carriage, the rides at '*dear* Plâs Newydd' where her horse, Rosa, had taken her across the fields at an 'enormous rate. She literally flew.'[12]

The Princess had kept a journal of their travels as her mother had told her to do. The earlier entries were most precisely dated and, since both the Duchess and Lehzen read them, rather stilted in style and matter of fact in content, not to say boring:

> Wednesday, August 1st 1832. We left Kensington Palace at 6 minutes past 7 and went through the lower-field gate to the right. We went on and turned to the left by the new road to Regent's Park. The road and scenery is beautiful. 20 minutes to 9. We have just changed horses at Barnet, a very pretty little town. 5 minutes past half past nine. We have just changed horses at St Albans . . .'[13]

It was not until she was free to do so that she wrote from the heart and made full use of her powers of acute observation and a Boswellian ability to recall a conversation, the details of a man's appearance, a woman's dress. Even now, however, her writing was graphic when her imagination was aroused as it was, for instance, in her description of the mining districts of the Midlands, her first experience of such sights, such pitiable poverty which, in later years, she was rarely to witness again:

> The men, women, children, country and houses are all black [she wrote] . . . The country is very desolate Every Where . . . The grass is quite blasted and black. Just now I saw an extraordinary building flaming with fire. The country continues black, engines flaming, coals, in abundance, everywhere smoking and burning coal heaps, intermingled with wretched huts and carts and little ragged children.[14]

What a contrast these dark scenes were with country towns, with her reception elsewhere, in other places where, as at Oxford, her party 'were most WARMLY and ENTHUSIASTICALLY received!'[15]

The King read the reports of his niece's enthusiastic welcome with mounting annoyance and serious concern: the Princess was being presented, not so much as his rightful successor, as his rival, a friend of the people who, as the daughter of committed Whigs, was presumed to be in favour of the Reform Bill to which the Tory King and Queen were opposed.

So, when in 1833 the Princess was taken on another tour, this time to the south and west of England, the King decided to curb so far as he could the 'disgusting' excesses of these 'Royal Progresses' by putting an end to what he called the 'pop pop' of naval salutes whenever the Duchess, her daughter and their entourage sailed by one of His Majesty's vessels.

The Duchess was informed that since she was sailing for her own pleasure she must no longer expect to be saluted by any of the King's ships. Sir John Conroy replied that 'as H.R.H.'s *confidential adviser*' he could not recommend her to give way on this point.[16] So the King called a meeting of the Privy Council and issued an order requiring salutes to be given only for ships in which the King or Queen happened to be sailing.

Yet while the King was able to silence the naval 'pop pops', he could do little to prevent the unseemly excitement of the welcome accorded to his sister-in-law and niece on land; and reports of the 'progress' of 1833 were quite as irritating as those of previous years. On this occasion the royal party went to stay at Norris Castle on the Isle of Wight and at the beginning of August were sailing in the *Emerald*, tender of the royal yacht, the *Royal George*, when the ship ran foul of a hulk and broke her mast. The Princess was full of praise for the sailor in command of the *Emerald* who picked up her precious King Charles Spaniel, 'dear sweet, little Dash', and kept him 'under his arm the whole time, but never let him drop in all the danger'.[17]

That summer the Princess went to Portsmouth where she inspected Nelson's flagship, the *Victory*, and tasted some 'excellent' beef, potatoes and grog as a sample of the sailors' rations.[18] The *Emerald* anchored off Plymouth so that she could present new colours to the 89th Regiment; she was taken over the Eddystone lighthouse; she visited Torquay and Weymouth and Exeter; and she was driven in an open carriage, escorted by the Dorsetshire Yeomanry, to stay at Melbury House, Lord Ilchester's house near Dorchester.

No sooner had the disagreement about naval salutes been settled than there was further trouble over the provision of a country house for the Duchess of Kent and her daughter. The Duchess wrote to the Prime Minister asking for one. The King offered her Kew Palace for that summer. The Duchess did not want a house just for that summer but a permanent country residence; besides she had made arrangements to go to Tunbridge Wells in the summer. Well then, she might have Kew Palace on a more permanent basis. The Duchess went to see it. She did not like it: it was 'very inadequate in accommodation and almost destitute of furniture'.[19] The King replied that Kew had been considered perfectly satisfactory by his 'royal father and mother'. He had nothing else to offer.[20]

Disgruntled though she was by her brother-in-law's response, the Duchess seems to have enjoyed her autumn holiday at Tunbridge Wells in 1834. The Princess certainly did so, all the more so because she had been confined by illness to her room for over three weeks earlier that year, dutifully writing of her '*dear* Mama's' anxiety throughout her indisposition and 'dear Lehzen's unceasing' care. She described her rides in the lovely countryside around the town and the public dinners which were held for them, at one of which Sir John Conroy surprised his fellow-guests by singing a song called 'The Wolf'. The Princess left 'dear' Tunbridge Wells for St Leonard's-on-Sea and Hastings on 4 November with 'GREAT REGRET'.[21] At St Leonards, where she was given 'a most splendid reception', she showed her resourcefulness when the carriage in which she, her mother, Lehzen and Lady Flora Hastings were riding overturned, bringing the horses down with it. She called for her dog, Dash, to be rescued, then 'ran on with him in my arms calling Mama to follow', and then, when one of the horses broke loose and started chasing them down the road, she told them to take cover behind a wall.*[22]

Meanwhile another tour of England, this time in the northern and eastern counties, was being planned to start at the beginning of August 1835. There were to be excursions to some of the principal towns in Yorkshire, to Stamford and Grantham in Lincolnshire, to Newark in Nottinghamshire, to Belvoir Castle, home of the Duke of Rutland, and to the Marquess of Exeter's Burghley House, near Stamford.

The King made it known that he was firmly opposed to yet another 'progress'; and he wrote to say that he strongly disapproved of his niece being taken 'flying about the kingdom as she had been for the past three years'.[23] But the Duchess demanded to know from Lord Melbourne, who had succeeded Lord Grey as Prime Minister in 1834, 'on what grounds' she could be prevented from making these visits; and when Princess Victoria protested that she did not want to be taken on another one since

---

* An enterprising man who sat on one of the horses' heads while the traces were being cut, Mr Peckham Mickelthwaite, was created a baronet when the Princess became Queen.

the King did not approve of them, her mother wrote to remonstrate with her: the King was merely jealous of the reception accorded her; of course she must go; it was her duty to go: 'Will you not see that it is the greatest consequence that you should be seen, that you should know your country, and be acquainted with, and be known by all classes ... I must tell you dearest Love, if your conversation with me could be known, that you had not the energy to undertake the journey or that your views were not enlarged enough to grasp the benefits arising from it, then you would fall in the estimation of the people of this country. Can you be dead to the calls your position demands? Impossible ... Turn your thoughts and views to your future station, its duties, and the claims that exist on you.'[24]

They left the next morning. They attended the York Musical Festival and a performance in the Minster of *Messiah* which she acknowledged was considered 'very fine', but personally she thought the music 'heavy and tiresome', not sharing her grandfather George III's passion for Handel. She liked 'the present Italian school ... *much better*'. They were entertained by her grandfather's friend, the elderly, benevolent Archbishop Harcourt;* they went to Doncaster Races; they passed through Leeds and Wakefield and Barnsley; they inspected the Duke of Rutland's family mausoleum at Belvoir. Passing into East Anglia, they visited the Earl and Countess of Leicester at Holkham Hall where the Princess was so tired she nearly fell asleep at dinner; and they went to the Duke of Grafton's house, a rather decrepit Euston Hall. At Burghley House, after opening a ball with her host, the Marquess of Exeter, she had such a 'dreadful headache' that she went to bed after that one dance.[25]

'It is an end to our journey, I am happy to say,' the Princess wrote in her diary when it was all over. 'Though I liked some of the places very well, I was much tired by the long journey & the great crowds we had to encounter. We cannot travel like other people, quietly and pleasantly.'[26]

For most of the time on this tour she had been feeling unwell and had quite lost her appetite. There was no need now for those warnings occasionally despatched to her by her uncle Leopold who, in one of his arch letters, had written to say that he had heard that 'a certain little princess ... eats a little too much, and almost always a little *too fast*'.[27]

---

* Harcourt died at the age of ninety, after having fallen off a bridge into a pond. 'Well, Dixon,' he resignedly observed to his chaplain, 'I think we have frightened the frogs.'

Her 'dearest Sister' Feodora had also warned her that she ate too fast, and that in addition she helped herself to far too much salt with her meat.

Now the very thought of food sometimes made her feel sick. She was also suffering from intermittent headaches, back ache, sore throats, insomnia, and dreadful lassitude. 'When one arrives at any nobleman's seat,' she wrote, 'one must instantly dress for dinner and consequently I could never rest properly.'[28]

6

�֎✖✖✖✖✖✖✖✖✖✖

UNCLES

'There would be no advantage in having
a totally inexperienced girl of eighteen,
just out of strict guardianship to govern an Empire.'

THE PROSPECT OF an autumn holiday at Ramsgate did little to raise
the Princess's spirits, even though her uncle Leopold, whom she had not
seen for over four years, was also to be staying in the town at the Albion
Hotel.* 'What happiness it was for me to throw myself in the arms of
that *dearest* of Uncles, who has always been to me like a father, and
whom I love *so very* dearly,' she wrote in her diary. 'I look up to him as
a Father with confidence, love and affection. He is the best and kindest
adviser I have . . . I have such great love for him and such *great* confidence
in him.' 'I love him so *very* much,' she added later. 'Oh, my love for him
approaches to a sort of adoration. He is indeed *"il mio secondo padre"*,
or rather *"solo padre"*, for he is indeed like my real father, as I have
none.' His young wife, Queen Louise, daughter of Louis-Philippe, King
of the French, whom he had married when she was twenty a bare three
years before, was also 'quite delightful', 'an Angel' who behaved towards
her in the most friendly manner, playing games with her in the evenings,
praising her drawings, sending her hairdresser to rearrange her light
brown hair and pressing upon her all kinds of presents from her own

---

* When on holiday at Ramsgate the Princess and her mother usually stayed at Townley House
near East Cliff Lodge which belonged to Moses Montefiore, the philanthropist, who gave her a
key to the private gate to his grounds. Soon after her accession she knighted the London sheriffs
at a ceremony in the Guildhall and noted in her diary: 'One of [them] was Mr Montefiore, a Jew,
an excellent man [who lived to be over a hundred years old]; and I was very glad that I was the
first to do what *I* think quite right, as it should be' (RA Queen's Journal, 9 November 1837).

wardrobe which were followed by boxes of dresses and hats sent to her when Queen Louise had returned home.[1]

Yet the Princess was still feeling unwell; and when she returned to Ramsgate from Dover, where she had said goodbye to King Leopold and Queen Louise, she found life 'terribly *fade* & dull without them' and tired herself out with crying. She was, indeed, really '*very* ill'. The Duchess's doctor, James Clark, was called but did not stay long. The Duchess considered that her daughter's indisposition could largely be attributed to the girl's 'childish whims' and Baroness Lehzen's imagination.[2] Conroy hinted that it was all brought about by the Princess's childishness and he hinted that it was a mere *maladie imaginaire*, further evidence of the fanciful girl's inability to reign without her mother's constant guidance. One day he took advantage of her indisposition to endeavour to induce her to sign a paper authorizing his appointment as her Private Secretary. 'They (Mama and John Conroy) attempted (for I was still very ill) to make me promise [to do so],' she later said. 'I resisted in spite of my illness and their harshness, my beloved Lehzen supporting me alone.'[3]

When Dr Clark had returned to London, it was clear that his patient was now seriously ill, suffering perhaps from severe tonsillitis or typhoid fever exacerbated by mental stress: she was feverish with a racing pulse. Lehzen proposed that Dr Clark should be sent for again; but the Duchess accused her of making an unnecessary fuss. 'How can you think I would do such a thing?' she said. 'What a noise that would make in town; in short we differ so much about this indisposition that we had better not speak of it at all.'[4]

When the Princess grew worse, however, both Conroy and the Duchess agreed that Dr Clark must be summoned immediately; and when he replied to the effect that he could not come until late that night, a local doctor was called in. But by now the patient was recovering. Even so, after his return, Dr Clark thought it as well to remain in Ramsgate for over a month, while Lehzen, the 'most affectionate, devoted, attached friend' the Princess had ever had, nursed her 'as attentively as ever'.

On 3 November 1835 Princess Victoria felt strong enough to report to King Leopold that she was 'much better', but she had to admit that she had grown '*very* thin' and her hair was falling out 'frightfully'; she was 'litterally now getting bald'.[5] Dr Clark advised a new regime for her at Kensington: she should be moved to apartments on a higher floor; she should go for regular walks, not sit too long at her lessons, exercise her arms with Indian clubs, and chew her food thoroughly, curbing her inclination – reproved by Baroness Lehzen as well as King Leopold and Princess Feodora – to eat too fast, even though of late she had not been eating much at all: a dose of quinine had been followed by potato soup for luncheon, and a thin slice or two of mutton with rice and orange jelly for dinner.[6]

By the end of January 1836 she had settled once more into the tedious routine of life at Kensington Palace, longing 'sadly', as she put it, 'for some gaiety', but for days on end seeing no one of her own age from the outside world and having to endure the company of 'the usual party' including Sir John Conroy, now more detested than ever, the boring Lady Conroy, the '2 Miss Conroys', Victoire and Jane, and the friend of the Conroys, the clever and incompatible Lady Flora Hastings. She was still convalescent, living on a spare diet which now included bread and butter, performing exercises to strengthen her legs and arms and taking drives to the villages north of Kensington, Hampstead, Finchley and Harrow, and to places she was taken to on her mother's charitable rounds. She went one August evening to St George's Chapel at Windsor and stood looking mournfully at the tombs, one of which was her 'poor dear Father's', sadly reflecting how cruel it was to lose those whom we loved and to be 'encumbered' by those we disliked.

There were, of course, breaks in this boring and frustrating existence: there was her first drive down the course at Ascot during race week; there were rare visits to Windsor Castle for dinners and dances, and even rarer appearances at St James's on drawing-room days; there were walks on Hampstead Heath with Dash, 'DEAR SWEET LITTLE DASH', whom not so long ago she had been in the habit of dressing up like one of her dolls. There were singing lessons with the amusing, good-humoured and wholly delightful bass, Luigi Lablache, of whom she was so much in awe at first that no sound came out, though she later grew so fond of him that she would have liked to have had lessons every day instead of once a week. She eagerly discussed music with him in French and could not agree with his high estimation of Mozart. 'I am a terribly modern person,' she wrote in her journal, 'and I must say I prefer Bellini, Rossini, Donizetti, etc., to anything else; but Lablache who *understands* music *thoroughly* said, "*C'est le Papa de tous.*" '[7]

'Oh!' she wrote in her diary of Lablache's birthplace, 'could I but once behold *bella Napoli* with its sunny blue sky and turquoise bay dotted with islands!'[8]

There were, above all, exciting evenings at the theatre and the opera, where she delighted in the performances of the half-Italian, half-Swedish ballerina, Marie Taglioni, who 'danced quite exquisitely', of Taglioni's brother, Paul, 'the most splendid man-dancer [she] ever saw', of the tenor Rubini, the baritone Tamburini, her hero, Luigi Lablache, and the lovely soprano Giulia Grisi, 'a most beautiful singer and actress' whom she saw in her favourite opera, Bellini's *Puritani*, and in Donizetti's *Anna Bolena* by which she was 'VERY MUCH AMUSED INDEED'.[9]

There were interesting afternoons at the Zoological Gardens in Regent's Park; and evenings when she was brought downstairs by Lehzen to be introduced to distinguished guests, on one occasion to Sir Robert Peel, on another to Lord Palmerston who was 'so very agreeable, clever, amusing & gentlemanlike' and with whom, a year or two later, she had 'much pleasant and amusing conversation'. There were birthday parties and birthday presents including, one year, a print of Marie Taglioni from Lehzen, earrings from the King, a brooch containing a strand of her mother's hair, a writing-case from Sir John Conroy, a paper-knife from Lady Flora Hastings and a prayer book from 'a bookseller of the name of Hatchard'. There were occasional balls at Kensington Palace; and above all, there were very occasional visits by German cousins whose departure, as she lamented in her diary, made her 'quite *wretched*', grieved and sad, missing them '*dreadfully*', feeling that it was 'like a dream that all our joy, happiness and gaiety should thus suddenly be over'. King Leopold wondered in his cautious way if these bursts of excitement were good for her. Might they not undermine her health? But no; it was the tedium of life at Kensington and the stress of the relationships there that upset her and made her ill. 'Merriment and mirth' were a tonic. 'I can assure you,' she wrote to him, 'all this dissipation does me a great deal of good.'[10] So did a change of air at King Leopold's house at Esher, and a subsequent few days at Buxted Park in Sussex, the family home of her friend, Lady Catherine Jenkinson, daughter of the Earl of Liverpool.

Yet even away from Kensington Palace the tensions of life there followed her about like inescapable shadows. Lady Catherine got on well with Lehzen, so was *persona non grata* with the Conroy faction, and was soon to leave the Duchess of Kent's household, ostensibly on the grounds of ill health. The Duchess of Northumberland had also fallen out with Conroy who considered she was undermining his authority, since she had written to Princess Feodora requesting her to approach her uncle, King Leopold, and ask him to do what he could to protect Baroness Lehzen, who was still being treated 'with contempt and incredible harshness' in an attempt to get rid of her and replace her with someone of Conroy's own choosing. At the same time there was no love lost between Princess Victoria and the Conroys' sharp-tongued friend, Lady Flora Hastings. As for the Duchess of Kent's relations with the King they went from bad to worse.

There was trouble when the King declined to receive the Duchess's daughter-in-law, the wife of Charles, Prince of Leiningen, on the grounds that she was not of royal blood and therefore by tradition barred from the Closet at St James's Palace.[11] Then there was further trouble when the King required the gentlemen of the Duchess of Kent's household to leave the Throne Room during the course of a drawing room there because, so he said, only gentlemen of the King's and Queen's household enjoyed the privilege of attendance at such a reception in such a place, the households of other members of the Royal Family being limited to ladies only.[12]

These, however, were relatively minor incidents when compared with an outrageous and distressing contretemps at Windsor Castle on 21 August 1836. This was the King's birthday. He had invited the Duchess of Kent and Princess Victoria to come to Windsor for the Queen's birthday party on 13 August and then to stay on for his own on the 21st. The Duchess, rudely taking no notice of the invitation to the Queen's birthday party, replied that she intended to be at Claremont for her own birthday celebrations on 17 August but would bring her daughter to Windsor on the 20th.

> This put the King into a fury [Charles Greville was informed by one of the King's illegitimate sons, Adolphus FitzClarence, who was living in the Castle at the time]. He made, however, no reply, and on the 20th he was in town to prorogue Parliament, having desired that they would not wait dinner for him at Windsor. After the prorogation He went to Kensington Palace to look about it; when He got there He found that the Duchess of Kent had appro-

priated to her own use a suite of apartments, seventeen in number for which She had applied last year, and which he had refused to let her have. This increased his ill-humour, already excessive. When he arrived at Windsor [suffering from the effects of sleepless nights and asthmatic attacks] and went into the drawing-room (at about ten o'clock at night), where the whole party was assembled, he went up to the Princess Victoria, took hold of both her hands, and expressed his pleasure at seeing her there and his regret that he did not see her oftener. He then turned to the Duchess and made her a low bow, almost immediately after which he said that 'a most unwarrantable liberty had been taken with one of his Palaces; that He had just come from Kensington, where He found apartments had been taken possession of not only without his consent, but contrary to his commands, and that he neither understood nor would endure conduct so disrespectful to him.' This was said loudly, publicly, and in a tone of serious displeasure. It was, however, only the muttering of the storm which was to break the next day. Adolphus went into his room on Sunday morning, and found him in a state of great excitement. It was his birthday, and though the celebration was (what was called) private, there were a hundred people at dinner, either belonging to the Court or from the neighbourhood. The Duchess of Kent sat on one side of the King and one of his sisters on the other, the Princess Victoria opposite. Adolphus sat two or three from the Duchess, and heard every word of what passed. After dinner, by the Queen's desire, 'His Majesty's health, and long life to him' was given, and as soon as it was drunk He made a very long speech, in the course of which he poured forth the following extraordinary and *foudroyant* tirade: – 'I trust in God that my life may be spared for nine months longer, after which period, in the event of my death, no Regency would take place. I should then have the satisfaction of leaving the royal authority to the personal exercise of that Young Lady (pointing to the Pss.), the Heiress presumptive of the Crown, and not in the hands of a person now near me, who is surrounded by evil advisers and who is herself incompetent to act with propriety in the station in which She would be placed. I have no hesitation in saying that I have been insulted – grossly and continually insulted – by that person, but I am determined to endure no longer a course of behaviour so disrespectful to me. Amongst many other things I have particularly to complain of the manner in which that young Lady has been kept away from my Court; she has been repeatedly kept from my drawing-rooms, at which She ought always to have been present, but I am fully resolved that this shall not happen again. I would have her know that I am King, and that I am determined to make my authority respected, and for the future I shall insist and command that the Princess do upon all occasions appear at my Court, as it is her duty to do.' He terminated his speech by an allusion to the Princess and her future reign in a tone of paternal interest and affection, which Adolphus told me was excellent in its way.

This awful philippick (with a great deal more which I forget) was uttered with a loud voice and excited manner. The Queen looked in deep distress, the Princess burst into tears, and the whole company were aghast. The Duchess of Kent said not a word. Immediately after they rose and retired, and a terrible scene ensued; the Duchess announced her immediate departure and ordered her carriage, but a sort of reconciliation was patched up, and she was prevailed upon to stay till the next day.[13]

The Duke of Wellington's comment upon all this was characteristically laconic: 'Very awkward, by God!'

The Princess's distress was alleviated by the thought that her beloved Uncle Leopold was coming to England to stay at Claremont in three weeks' time. Her delight in his company was as profound as ever: 'He is *so* clever,' she recorded in her diary, 'so mild and *so* prudent; he alone can give me good advice on *every thing*.' She loved Queen Louise, too, she protested, and 'very much regretted' that she was unable to come to England with her husband as she was expecting a second child. Louise sent 'lovely' presents, however, a silk dress and a satin bonnet, the dress 'made by Mlle Palmyre, the first dressmaker of Paris'.

Her uncle's visit was soon over, however; and thereafter week after week passed at Claremont with 'the usual society', including that of Conroy's daughter, Victoire, whom she increasingly grew to dislike the more she hated the girl's father, and she longed to return to London for the season, yearning for the opera and the theatre and 'for some merriment after being so very long in the country' with such companions as she was obliged to live with there. Yet, when she did return to Kensington, life there was far from gay: Conroy was as detestable as ever and more than ever determined not to lose his influence in the Duchess of Kent's household when her daughter came of age. The Duchess herself was just as much under Conroy's influence as she had ever been.

*   *   *

Shortly before her eighteenth birthday Princess Victoria received a letter from the King in which he told her that he proposed applying to Parliament for a grant of £10,000 a year to be entirely at her own disposal. He intended her also to have the right to appoint her own Keeper of the Privy Purse, suggesting Sir Benjamin Stephenson whom the Duchess much disliked, for this post. The Princess was, in addition, to have the right to form her own household. When the Lord Chamberlain brought this letter to Kensington, Sir John Conroy insisted upon its being delivered to the Princess in the Duchess's presence. Once the Princess had read it she handed it to her mother who was, of course, appalled by its contents. Having satisfied herself that the King had consulted the Cabinet before writing the letter, she wrote an extremely angry reply to Lord Melbourne, the Prime Minister, then, having summarily dismissed suggestions by her daughter that her tutor, the Revd George Davys, now Dean of Chester, might be appointed her Keeper of the Privy Purse, and that the Princess might have a private conversation with Lord Melbourne, the Duchess, with Conroy's help, wrote a letter to the King which the Princess, who had felt 'very miserable' the evening before and had refused to go down to dinner, was required to copy. 'I wish to remain in every respect as I am now in the care of my Mother,' ran this letter which the Princess had for a time resisted in copying. 'Upon the subject of money I should wish that whatever may be necessary to add, may be given to my dear Mother for my use, who always does everything I want in pecuniary matters.'[14]

When he read this letter the King commented, before laying it aside, that Victoria had not written it.[15] To a later letter, offering a compromise – £4,000 a year for the Princess and £6,000 for herself – the Duchess replied curtly, rejecting it without even consulting her daughter who by now no longer spoke to her when they were alone together.

By this time the King was clearly very ill. He had arranged to give a ball on the evening of 24 May when the Princess came of age; but he was not well enough to greet his niece who drove to St James's through streets crammed with people whose anxiety, so she wrote, 'to see poor stupid me was very great, and I must say I am quite touched by it, and feel proud, which I always have done of my country and the English nation'.[16] At the Palace she was told that His Majesty had directed that she should occupy his own chair of state. She did not greatly enjoy the ball, though. She felt Sir John Conroy's eyes on her the whole evening, like those of a disapproving hawk; and when it was over she wrote resignedly in her diary: 'Today is my eighteenth birthday! How old! And yet how far am I from being what I should be.'[17]

It was a sentiment which both Sir John Conroy and her mother did all they could to endorse. 'You are still very young,' the Duchess, with Conroy clearly at her shoulder, wrote to her, 'and all your success so far has been due to your *Mother's* reputation. Do not be *too sanguine* in *your* own *talents* and *understanding*.' Conroy himself asserted that Victoria was 'younger in intellect than in years' and that she had too flippant a mentality to dispense with the guidance of those who knew her best.

The day after her birthday her uncle Leopold's friend and counsellor Baron Stockmar, a Coburger of Swedish descent, arrived in London. Then forty-nine years old, Christian Frederick Stockmar was a qualified physician who had been head of the military hospital in Coburg. Having come across him there, Prince Leopold had been impressed by his honesty and knowledge of the world, and he had asked him to become his personal physician. When Princess Charlotte died, Prince Leopold had begged Stockmar never to leave him. Stockmar had promised never to do so and thereafter he spent more time with Leopold and on various missions for him than he did with his wife and children. Small, rotund, hypochondriacal, trustworthy, sardonic, moody, obsessively moral, and with a rather too high opinion of his understanding of political manoeuvres and psychological insights, he was to become a familiar figure at the English court, where, until his retirement to Coburg in 1857, he was to be seen walking into dinner of an evening without decorations and wearing ordinary trousers instead of the regulation knee-breeches.

He soon grasped the realities of the imbroglio at Kensington. On previous visits to England he had got on quite well with Sir John Conroy who spoke of him with the 'greatest respect'; but as he came to understand the extent of the man's ambition and of his influence over the Duchess of Kent – an influence which King Leopold was later to describe as 'witchcraft' – Stockmar began to agree with his master that Conroy's conduct was 'madness' and 'must end in his own ruin'.

Certainly Conroy's machinations became almost desperate as King

William's health rapidly deteriorated and the accession of Princess Victoria as Queen grew ever closer.

On 22 May Sir Henry Halford, the King's doctor, reported that his 72-two-year-old patient was 'in a very odd state and decidedly had the hay fever and in such a manner as to preclude his going to bed'. Four days later Lord Palmerston, the Foreign Secretary, wrote of the King being in 'a very precarious state' and, 'though he would probably rally', it was not likely he would last long. 'It is desirable he should wear the crown some time, however,' Palmerston added, 'for there would be no advantage in having a totally inexperienced girl of eighteen, just out of strict guardianship, to govern an Empire.'

In the meantime, Conroy was doing all he could to ensure that his guardianship was maintained, while the Princess, supported by Baroness Lehzen and Baron Stockmar, was doing all she could to break free from her guardian's control. He again proposed to her that he be appointed her Private Secretary, a proposal which she naturally again rejected. After a conversation with her on 9 June, Stockmar reported to King Leopold:

> I found the Princess fairly cool and collected, and her answers precise, apt and determined. I had throughout the conversation, the impression that she is extremely jealous of what she considers to be her rights and her future power and is therefore not at all inclined to do anything which would put Conroy into a situation to be able to entrench upon them. Her feelings seem, moreover, to have been deeply wounded by what she calls '*his* impudent and *insulting* conduct' towards her. Her affection and esteem for her mother seem likewise to have suffered by Mama having tamely allowed Conroy to insult the Princess in her presence, and by the Princess having been frequently a witness to insults which the poor Duchess tolerated herself in the presence of her daughter ... O'Hum [Conroy] continues the system of intimidation with the genius of a madman, and the Duchess carries out all that she is instructed to do with admirable docility and perseverance ... The Princess continues to refuse firmly to give her Mama her promise that she will make O'Hum her confidential adviser. Whether she will hold out, Heaven only knows, for they plague her, every hour and every day.[18]

The Princess also managed to have a private conversation with the moderate Tory, Lord Liverpool, of whom she was so fond. Like Stockmar,

Lord Liverpool urged her not to consider for a moment appointing Conroy her Private Secretary, a post for which he was quite unsuited. She must rely on the Ministers at present in office, particularly Lord Melbourne, the Prime Minister, to advise her. Of course for the moment she must continue to live with her mother. To all this the Princess agreed. With Lord Liverpool, Baron Stockmar and King Leopold all supporting her, she now felt quite capable of resisting Sir John Conroy's threats and blandishments. Lord Liverpool suggested that, as a compromise, the Princess might consider appointing Sir John her Privy Purse, provided he did not stray from that department. But, primed by Lehzen, the Princess protested that Lord Liverpool 'must be aware of many slights & incivilities Sir John has been guilty of towards her, but besides this she knew things of him which rendered it totally impossible for her to place him in *any* confidential position near her ... She knew things which entirely took away her confidence in him, & that she knew this of herself without any other person informing her.'[19]

Before parting from Lord Liverpool she suggested he spoke to Baron Stockmar who would tell him many things she did not like to talk about herself. Also, Lord Liverpool's daughter, Lady Catherine, would confirm what she had told him about Sir John Conroy's intolerably rude behaviour towards herself.

The day after this conversation with Lord Liverpool, Baron Stockmar reported that 'the struggle between the Mama and daughter' was still going on and that the Duchess was 'being pressed by Conroy to bring matters to extremities and to force her Daughter to do her will by unkindness and severity'. Conroy claimed he had been advised by James Abercromby, a former Judge-Advocate-General and the future Lord Dunfermline, that the girl must be 'coerced', if she would not listen to reason. But, so he later maintained, he decided not to go to such lengths because he 'did not credit the Duchess of Kent with enough strength for such a step'.[20]

The King was now very close to death. When told this on 19 June the Princess 'turned pale and burst into tears'. The next morning, her mother woke her at six o'clock to tell her that the Archbishop of Canterbury and the Lord Chamberlain, Lord Conyngham, whose horses had galloped all the way, had come to the Palace and wished to see her. She got out of bed and went downstairs, the Duchess holding her hand and carrying a candle in a silver candlestick, Lehzen following with a bottle of smelling salts. 'I went into my sitting room (only in my dressing gown) and *alone*', she wrote in her diary, 'and saw them. Lord Conyngham then acquainted me that my poor Uncle, the King, was no more, and had expired at 12 minutes past 2 this morning and consequently that *I* am *Queen*.'[21]

7

THE YOUNG QUEEN

'Got *such* a letter from Mama, oh, oh *such* a letter.'

'I CANNOT RESIST TELLING YOU,' Thomas Creevey wrote to his step-daughter, Elizabeth Ord, 'that our dear little Queen in every respect is *perfection*.'[1]

A few weeks later Creevey gave an example of the little Queen's good nature by relating a story of her encounter with one of her ladies, Lady Charlemont, well known to be a bluestocking, who had asked Lady Tavistock, the Queen's Lady of the Bedchamber, if she might take books out of the library at Windsor. '"Oh yes, my dear," said Lady Tavistock, not knowing what reading means, "as many as you like."'

> Upon which Lady Charlemont swept away a whole row, and was carrying them away in her apron. Passing thro' the gallery in this state, whom should she meet but little Vic! Great was her perturbation, for in the first place a low curtsy was necessary, and what was to come of the books, for they must curtsy too. Then to be found with all this property within the first half hour of her coming and before even she had seen Vic! ... But Vic was very much amused with the thing altogether, laughed heartily and was as good humoured as ever she could be.[2]

Creevey's good opinion of the Queen was commonly shared. Charles Greville, never a man to pay an idle or ill-considered compliment, had an opportunity to study her closely when, acting in his office as Clerk to the Privy Council, he attended a meeting of the Council in the Red Saloon at Kensington Palace soon after eleven o'clock on the morning of her accession, and was much impressed by her behaviour.

She had already had a conversation with 'good, faithful' Baron Stockmar over breakfast, written to her uncle, King Leopold, signing herself for the first time 'your devoted and attached Niece, Victoria R.' and to Princess Feodora, assuring her that she would 'remain for life' her 'devoted attached Sister, V.R.'.* She had also written a letter of condolence to her aunt, Queen Adelaide, whom she addressed as 'Her Majesty the Queen, Windsor Castle' and, when it was intimated to her that she should have written 'Her Majesty, the Queen Dowager', she replied, 'I am quite aware of Her Majesty's altered status, but I would rather not be the first person to remind her of it.'[3] In her letter she assured her that she must remain at Windsor Castle just as long as she liked.

At nine o'clock she had received the Prime Minister, Lord Melbourne, talking to him 'of COURSE *quite* ALONE' as she intended 'always' to do with all her Ministers, and assuring him, as King Leopold had advised her to do, that she intended to 'retain him and the rest of the present Ministry at the head of affairs and that it could not be in better hands than his'.[4] She had had another brief conversation with him before entering the Red Saloon for the Council meeting, going into the room by herself 'quite plainly dressed, and in mourning'.† She had been asked if she would like to be accompanied by the Great Officers of State, but she had decided to go in 'quite alone'.[5]

> There never was anything like the first impression she produced [Charles Greville wrote in his diary], or the chorus of praise and admiration which is raised about her manner and behaviour, and certainly not without justice. It was very extraordinary, and some-

---

* She had been officially proclaimed 'our only lawful and rightful liege Lady Alexandrina Victoria', but she never considered the possibility of being known as Queen Alexandrina. She had that name omitted from all the documents which she was required to sign.
† In Sir David Wilkie's painting of this Council meeting, the artist portrayed the Queen in white rather than in mourning to provide a contrast to the black clothes of those Councillors who were not in uniform and to emphasize Her Majesty's youthful innocence. Since the paintings she really liked were those that reproduced their subject with photographic accuracy, she did not approve of Wilkie's licence. Indeed, after examining this picture in later years she maintained that it was one of the worst she had ever seen (RA Journal, 12 November 1847). She far preferred the work of Landseer – although she described his *Swan attacked by Eagles* as 'not pleasing' – and, later, of Winterhalter and Angeli. As for George Richmond's portraits with their 'green flesh and blue lips', they were beyond the pale. The work of G. F. Watts was largely unintelligible, that of the Impressionists 'a joke in rather bad taste' (Frederick Ponsonby, *Recollections of Three Reigns*, 1951, 52).

thing far beyond what was looked for. Her extreme youth and inexperience, and the ignorance of the world concerning her, naturally excited intense curiosity to see how she would act on this occasion, and there was a considerable assemblage at the Palace, notwithstanding the short notice which was given.[6]

She bowed to the company, took her seat, read a short speech written for her by Lord Melbourne in 'a clear, distinct' voice 'without any appearance of fear or embarrassment', then offered her hand to be kissed by the Privy Councillors who came forward to be sworn one after the other, following her two uncles, the Dukes of Cumberland and Sussex,* and blushing 'up to the eyes', so Greville noticed, as these 'two old men' knelt before her to swear allegiance.

> Her manner to them was very graceful and engaging; she kissed them both and rose from her chair and moved towards the Duke of Sussex, who was farthest from her and too infirm to reach her. She seemed rather bewildered at the multitude of men who were sworn ... [But] she went through the whole ceremony (occasionally looking at Melbourne for instruction when she had any doubt what to do, which hardly ever occurred) and with perfect calmness and self-possession, but at the same time with a graceful modesty.[7]

She was 'perfectly composed and dignified', 'though a red spot on either cheek showed her mental agitation', Lord Dalmeny confirmed; while the Duke of Wellington declared that 'if she had been his own daughter he could not have desired to see her perform her part better': her personality not only filled her chair, 'she filled the room'. It was noticed with satisfaction that not by a smile or gesture did she indicate partiality, favour or disapproval for any of the Councillors who came forward to kiss her hand.

> Her voice [one of the Tory Councillors, John Wilson Croker, said] which is naturally beautiful, was clear and untroubled and her eye was bright and calm, neither bold nor downcast ... There was a blush on her cheek which made her look both handsome and

---

* Her other uncle, the Duke of Cambridge, was in Hanover where he had been Viceroy, representing his brothers, George IV and William IV – who were also Kings of Hanover – for twenty-one years. On the death of William IV, the eldest of his surviving brothers, the Duke of Cumberland, became King Ernest of Hanover since the Salic law, prohibiting the throne passing to a woman, applied there and prevented Victoria from becoming Queen of Hanover as well as of Great Britain and Ireland.

interesting; and certainly she *did* look as interesting and handsome as any young lady I ever saw.[8]

Such praise of her modest yet regal demeanour could be heard all over London during the next few days as she fulfilled one engagement after another. When the Council meeting was over on the first day of her reign (and she was seen through the glass door rubbing her hands and skipping away like a schoolgirl) she saw both Lord Melbourne and Baron Stockmar again; she also saw the Archbishop of Canterbury, the Home Secretary, Lord John Russell, and the Master of the Horse, Lord Albemarle. She appointed Dr James Clark her physician and created a special office in the Household, that of Attendant on the Queen, for Baroness Lehzen who wisely declined accepting an official position for fear of arousing jealousy but who, the Queen said, must 'ALWAYS remain' with her as her 'friend'.[9] She dismissed Sir John Conroy from her Household and would have liked to have had him dismissed from her mother's also, but this she could not yet contrive to do. She had her bed removed from her mother's room and arranged for a doorway to be made between Lehzen's bedroom and the room where she herself was to sleep. Before going to bed that night, she went downstairs to say 'good-night to Mama etc'.[10]

In her long diary entry for that day this was the first mention of the Duchess since she had been awakened by her at six o'clock that morning. It was immediately apparent that the relationship between her mother and Conroy and herself was now to be transformed. On this the first night of her reign she had her dinner alone, and was clearly determined to demonstrate her independence: her mother was not to presume to come to her whenever she liked. 'I had to remind her,' she told Lord Melbourne, '*who* I was.' 'Quite right,' Melbourne commented, 'disagreeable but necessary.'

Lord Melbourne advised her not to answer the notes the Duchess sent her and to let him reply to them formally on her behalf. 'My appeal was to *you* as my daughter,' the Duchess replied crossly, ignoring the Prime Minister's missives, 'not to the Queen.'

When the Queen and her mother did dine together for the first time there was trouble over the precedence accorded to the Duchess who was placed at table below the Queen's aunts. 'Oh! what a scene did she make.' Then there was trouble over the Duchess's demand for the rank and precedence of Queen Mother which her daughter rejected immediately. 'It would do my mother no good,' she said, 'and would no doubt, offend my aunts.' Frequently she discussed her relationship with the Duchess with Lord Melbourne to whom she admitted her dislike of her. Melbourne advised her to be patient and polite, however much her mother exasperated her by her constant complaints and criticisms, her protestations that she ate too much or went to the theatre too often: it would never do if the Queen were held responsible for a formal break in their relationship. All the same, Melbourne made no secret of his own opinion of the Duchess in his talks with the Queen. She was 'a liar and a hypocrite'; he had never known 'so foolish a woman'. This was 'very true', the Queen agreed and they both laughed. For her daughter's nineteenth birthday the Duchess pointedly presented her with a copy of *King Lear*.[11]

It was all the more galling to the Duchess because her daughter was, by contrast, especially respectful and affectionate in her dealings with Queen Adelaide, the Queen Dowager, and generous towards the late King's bastard children whose existence her mother continued to ignore as completely as she could.

The antipathy between mother and daughter was also exacerbated by the Duchess's insistence that Sir John Conroy and his family should be received at Court and the Queen's determination that they should certainly not.

> I thought you would not expect me to invite Sir John Conroy after his conduct towards me for some years past [she told her mother in one characteristic letter], and still more so after the unaccountable manner in which he behaved towards me, a short while before I came to the Throne.[12]

The Queen also declined to grant permission for the Duchess to take Sir John and their friend, Lady Flora Hastings, to the proclamation ceremony, on the advice, so she said, of Lord Melbourne; a refusal which provoked an angry protest from her mother: 'Take care, Victoria, you know your prerogative! Take care that Lord Melbourne is not King.'[13]

Yet another angry letter from the Duchess was prompted when Conroy was refused an invitation to a banquet at the Guildhall. In this 'extraordinary' letter the Duchess maintained that not to invite him would 'look like the greatest persecution'. 'The Queen should forget what displeased the Princess,' her mother added. 'Recollect that I have the greatest regard for Sir John, I cannot forget what he has done for me and for you, although he had the misfortune to displease *you*.'[14]

The Queen, however, was not to be moved: she could not, she said, depart from the line of conduct she had adopted, upset though she was by the scenes her mother made and the letters she received from her. She was soon to decide that her mother never had been very fond of her.

There was also trouble over the Duchess's debts which by the end of 1837 were to amount to well over £50,000. Prompted by Conroy, she had asked her daughter to contribute £30,000 towards the repayment of this sum. She herself would find the rest of the money, provided her income was suitably increased. After the matter had been considered by the Cabinet, the Chancellor of the Exchequer, Thomas Spring-Rice, was authorized to say that they were prepared to recommend to Parliament the payment of those debts which had been incurred before the Queen came to the throne. This offer the Duchess promptly and indignantly rejected, declaring at the same time that she would not in any case negotiate with her Majesty's servants: she would rather state her case directly to Parliament.

Ministers then proposed increasing the Duchess's income from £22,000 to £30,000 a year, and this was accepted. At the same time the Queen's income was settled at £385,000 a year, including £60,000 for her Privy Purse and £303,760 for the salaries and expenses of her Household. In addition she enjoyed the revenues of the duchies of Lancaster and Cornwall at that time worth about £30,000 a year.

The Queen, who had been taught to be careful with her pocket money as a girl, had frugal instincts; but, now that she was so well provided for, she was generous with her new-found wealth, continuing pensions to those who had received them in her predecessor's time and offering, for instance, £300 to her relatively poor half-sister, Feodora, for her expenses whenever she was able to come over to England to visit her. She also settled her father's debts as she had long had in mind to do; but finally settling her mother's was a much more difficult and vexatious problem and led to the Queen's receiving further angry letters from the Duchess who had soon overspent the increase in her allowance, even though she had been most generously helped by Coutts & Co., the bankers, both before and after her daughter's accession.[14]

'Got <u>such</u> a letter from Mama, oh, oh <u>such</u> a letter,' the Queen was later to write in her diary on 15 January 1838.[15] She and Conroy really ought to remember, she added, 'what incalculable falsehoods they have told about these debts. During the King's [William IV's] life they said there were no debts and that it was all a calumny of the King's – which is really infamous'. She was 'much shocked' by it all, and even more so when she heard that her mother's debts had appreciably increased despite the additional income she was receiving. She was likely to get into 'a dreadful scrape', Lord Melbourne observed. The Queen said that she really ought to be able to manage on the handsome income now allowed her. 'Yes, if her income really were well managed,' Melbourne said, 'but not if *he* makes money by it.'[16]

8

MELBOURNE

'It has become his province to educate, instruct and form the most interesting mind and character in the world.'

AS THE DAYS PASSED people spoke of the new Queen with mounting enthusiasm. A large crowd stood in the courtyard of St James's Palace and cheered her loudly as she stood by an open window to hear the heralds proclaim her Queen and it was 'most touching' to see the colour drain from her cheeks and the tears well up in her eyes. She was cheered again quite as vociferously when she drove to the House of Lords for the dissolution of Parliament for the first time on 17 July 1837 and, later, when she went to the Lord Mayor's dinner in Guildhall. It really was 'most gratifying', she told Princess Feodora, 'to have met with such a reception in the *greatest* capital in the *World* and from thousands and thousands of people. I really do not deserve all this kindness for what I have yet done.'[1]

Charles Greville said that at her second Privy Council meeting she presided 'with as much ease as if She had been doing nothing else all her life.' 'She looked very well, and though so small in stature, and without any pretension to beauty, the gracefulness of her manner and the good expression of her countenance give her on the whole a very agreeable appearance, and with her youth inspire an excessive interest in all who approach her.'[2]

Princess Lieven, not the most indulgent of critics, was much impressed by the contrast between her childish face and sometimes rather diffident smile and the dignity of her queenly manner. Lord Palmerston, the

Foreign Secretary, said that 'any Ministers who had to deal with her would soon find that she was no ordinary person'.

Many of those who saw her now for the first time were surprised to see how very small she was, surely no more than five feet in height if that. She herself told Lord Melbourne that the 'worry and torment' of the 'Kensington System' had stunted her growth. She said as much to King Leopold whose letters frequently referred to her diminutive size and who wrote to her teasingly as though she could do something about it if she put her mind to it: in one letter he told her that he had heard reports that she was growing at last and expressed the hope that she would 'persist in so laudable a measure'. He had, however, he later regretted, 'not been able to ascertain that she had really grown taller lately'; he felt he 'must recommend it strongly'. In a subsequent letter, thanking her for sending him a portrait of her, he commented that 'she shone more by her virtues than by her tallness'.

It was generally agreed that, as well as being very short, she was a little too plump and really, it had to be admitted, rather plain with the protuberant blue eyes and receding chin of her Hanoverian grandfather, George III. Within a few weeks of Victoria's accession, the wife of Andrew Stevenson, the American Minister in London, watched her at a dinner. 'Her bust, like most English women's is very good,' Mrs Stevenson wrote, 'hands and feet are small and very pretty . . . Her eyes are blue, large and full; her mouth, which is her worst feature, is generally a little open; her teeth small and short, and she shows her gums when she laughs, which is rather disfiguring.'[3] The laugh itself, however, Mrs Stevenson decided on a later occasion, was 'particularly delightful', 'so full of girlish glee and gladness'. Others also spoke of this pleasing, uninhibited laugh and a voice which was, and remained, exceptionally clear and melodious. Her smile, too, was described as enchanting, and her deportment at once graceful and impressive.

Thomas Creevey, who was invited to dine at Brighton Pavilion in October, said that 'a more homely little being you never beheld, *when she is at her ease*, and she is evidently dying to be always more so. She laughs in real earnest, opening her mouth as wide as it can go, showing not very pretty gums . . . She eats quite as heartily as she laughs, I think I may say she gobbles . . . She blushes and laughs every instant in so natural a way as to disarm anybody. Her voice is perfect, and so is the expression of her face, when she means to say or do a pretty thing.'[4]

After a conversation with her, Lord Holland, Chancellor of the Duchy of Lancaster, came away 'quite a courtier' and 'a bit of a lover'. 'Like the rest of the world', he later decided, he was both 'captivated and surprised'.*[5]

Although shy and often uncertain of herself in the presence of people whom she took to be intellectually superior to herself, she was already capable of assuming an alarming hauteur and fixing those who had offended her in a glare of disapproval from faintly hooded eyes, the disconcerting gaze of the basilisk. She had not been Queen for long when her Mistress of the Robes, the grand, young and beautiful Duchess of Sutherland, was half an hour late for dinner. She did not hesitate to give her 'a very proper snub', telling her she 'hoped it might not happen another time'. She had occasion to reprimand her Maids-of-Honour also. She did not like doing this, she told Lord Melbourne; but, he said, she must start as she meant to go on, otherwise they would take advantage of her. She was determined not to let them do that.

As Charles Greville observed, the young Queen had already begun to exhibit 'signs of a peremptory disposition, and it is impossible not to suspect that, as she gains confidence, and as her character begins to develop, she will evince a strong will of her own'.

She could also be self-centred, apparently quite unaware of the difficulties and discomforts she was imposing upon others. In September that year she was riding in her carriage at Windsor when, feeling the cold, she had got out to walk. 'Of course, all her ladies had to do the same,' Lady Tavistock told Thomas Creevey, 'and the group being very wet, their feet soon got into the same state. Poor dear Lady Tavistock, when she got back to the Castle, could get no dry stockings, her maid being out and her cloathes all locked up . . . I am sure [she] thinks the Queen a resolute little tit.'[6]

So did some of her other ladies who were inconsiderately required to stand in the drawing room until the gentlemen came up after dinner,

---

* There were those, of course, who were not captivated by the young Queen. The Revd Sydney Smith wrote to one of his radical friends: 'Victoria has had a very fine day for her visit to the City [on 9 November 1837]. It disgusts me to see a million of people busying themselves about the foolish ceremonies of a dumpy little girl of eighteen – America for ever' (Alan Bell, *Sydney Smith: A Biography*, 1980, 164).

which they were required to do soon after the ladies had withdrawn. 'I hear the Duchess of Kent first remonstrated and has since retired from the drawing-room for half an hour every evening to repose herself in her own room, till she can return and *sit* by her daughter or at the Whist table in the Evening,' Lord Holland related. 'It was droll enough to see the Ladies, young and old, married or unmarried with all their *rumps* to the wall when we came from the dining room and eagerly availing themselves of their release when the Queen took her seat on the sofa.'[7]

Nor did most guests find the evenings very lively thereafter. Charles Greville, invited to dine one day in March 1838, described a characteristic large dinner party attended by, amongst others, Lord Rosebery and his wife, Lord and Lady Grey, Lord Ossulston and the Hanoverian Minister, Baron Münchhausen. Just before dinner was announced the Queen entered the room with the Duchess of Kent, preceded by the Lord Chamberlain, Lord Conyngham, and followed by her six ladies.*

> She shook hands with the women, and made a sweeping bow to the men, and directly went in to dinner, conducted by Münchhausen, who sat next to her, and Conyngham on the other side ... After the eating was over the Queen's health was given by [her Chief Equerry] who sat at one end of the table: a vile, vulgar custom, and, however proper it may be to drink her health elsewhere, it is bad taste to have it given by her Officer at her own table ... However it has been customary in the last two reigns...[8]
>
> When we went into the drawing-room, and huddled about the door in the sort of half-shy, half-awkward way people do, the Queen advanced, and spoke to everybody in succession ... As the words of Kings and Queens are precious, and as a fair sample of a royal after-dinner colloquy, I shall record my dialogue with accurate fidelity.
> Q. 'Have you been riding to-day Mr Greville?'
> G. 'No, Madam, I have not.'
> Q. 'It was a fine day.'
> G. 'Yes, Ma'am, a very fine day.'
> Q. 'It was rather cold though.'
> G. (like Polonius). 'It *was* rather cold, Madam.'
> Q. 'Your sister, Ly. Francis Egerton, rides I think, does not She?'

---

* Dinner was served at eight o'clock, later than in most houses. Middle-class families generally dined at about six o'clock, as did the Carlyles. Lord and Lady Holland and Lord and Lady John Russell dined at seven (*Early Victorian England*, 1830–65, ed. G.M. Young, 1932, i, 98).

G. 'She does ride sometimes, Madam.'
(A pause, when I took the lead through adhering to the same topic.)
G. 'Has your Majesty been riding to-day?'
Q. (with animation). 'O yes, a very long ride.'
G. 'Has your Majesty got a nice horse?'
Q. 'O, a very nice horse.'

– gracious smile and inclination of head on part of Queen, profound bow on mine, and then She turned again to Lord Grey. Directly after I was deposited at the whist table to make up the Duchess of Kent's party, and all the rest of the company were arranged about a large round table (the Queen on the sofa by it), where they passed about an hour and a half in what was probably the smallest possible talk, interrupted and enlivened, however, by some songs which Ossulston sang. We had plenty of instrumental music during and after dinner.

Nobody expects from her any clever, amusing, or interesting talk, above all no stranger can expect it. She is very civil to every-body, and there is more of frankness, cordiality, and good-humour in her manner than of dignity. She looks and speaks cheerfully: there was nothing to criticise, nothing particularly to admire. The whole thing seemed to be dull, perhaps unavoidably so, but still so dull that it is a marvel how anybody can like such a life. This was an unusually large party, and therefore more than usually dull and formal; but it is much the same sort of thing every day. Mel-bourne was not there, which I regretted, as I had some curiosity to see Her Majesty and her Minister together.[9]

Had Melbourne been of the company that evening, Greville would have seen the Queen in a far more lively mood.

The Queen's relationship with Melbourne was of the closest and most trusting kind. He was fifty-eight when she came to the throne, still attrac-tive though rather portly now, sophisticated and urbane. She delighted in his conversation, rejoiced in his celebrated epigrams, aphorisms and paradoxes, his well-told reminiscences, his brilliant table-talk and anec-dotes which were full of irreverent, heterodoxical and sometimes flippant asides but usually contained information 'of the most *interesting* kind'. It became 'a source of great amusement' to her to 'collect his "sayings"'. 'He has *such* stores of knowledge,' she wrote; 'such a wonderful memory; he knows about everybody and everything; *who* they were and *what* they did.' He remembered things 'from *thirteen months old!*' and his days at Eton in great detail.[10] She delighted in the stories he told her about Napoleon and Byron, Pitt and Charles James Fox, her wicked uncles, and was very pleased that he did not include their brother, her father, as being of their naughty company. 'From all what I heard,' she wrote, 'my father was the best of all.'[11]

His conversation was not only unfailingly interesting, it made her laugh. He would plead, for example, that he rarely went to church 'for fear of hearing something very extraordinary'. Besides, his 'father and mother never went. People didn't use to go so much formerly; it wasn't the fashion.' Or he would protest that it was almost worthwhile for a woman to be beaten by her husband, 'considering the exceeding pity she excites'. In the world of Whiggery, in which Whigs were 'all cousins', people used never to change their lives when they married: 'they were very fond of their wives, but did not take care of them, and left them to themselves'. Chastity was not prized and there was 'great licence'. In any case, the wife was 'always in the wrong'.

Whig families like his also emphasized their separateness from the rest of society by bestowing nicknames which were recognized only by the cognoscenti and they pronounced words in a peculiarly Whiggish way. When Queen Victoria was once asked if Lord Melbourne had been a proper Whig she replied that he must have been because he spoke in a recognizably Whiggish manner, pronouncing Rome as 'room' and gold as 'goold'.*[12]

Talking of children he said that 'almost everybody's character was formed by their mother and that if children did not turn out well, their mothers should be punished for it'. Talking of doctors he would say that the English variety killed you while the French merely let you die; and commenting on horse racing he would express the opinion that the Derby was 'not perfect without somebody killing himself'. Yet at heart he was 'such a good man', 'excellent and moral with such a strong feeling against immorality and wickedness'. One day when she remarked that there were

---

* This Whiggish talk was a development of the eighteenth-century Cavendish drawl as adopted by the Devonshire House circle, and, in particular, by Georgiana, Duchess of Devonshire. In this strange – and, to outsiders, tiresome – language hope, for instance, was pronounced as 'whop', yellow as 'yaller', cucumber as 'cowcomber', spoil as 'spile'. Emphasis fell on unexpected syllables, as in the word balcony, the stress in which fell on the 'cony' rather than the 'bal' (Amanda Foreman, *Georgiana, Duchess of Devonshire*, 1998, 30, 45–6).

so few good preachers in the Church, he agreed with her and added, 'But there are not *many very good* anything.' That was very true, the Queen thought. She was equally sure, though, that *he* was one of the '*very good*'.[13]

Having so high an opinion of Melbourne's talents and virtues, she basked in his skilful flattery. Her shyness, he assured her, was not only appealing, it was indicative of a sensitive and susceptible temperament; her smallness, of which she was continually conscious, was a positive advantage in a queen; her inexperience was all to the good: she came to her duties fresh and unprejudiced. Upon her complaining of the great difficulty she had in keeping her temper when she was 'very much irritated and plagued' and how 'very sorry' she was when she 'let it out' towards her servants, he comforted her by observing that a person who had rather a choleric disposition might control it, never wholly got over it and could not help letting it out at times.

He endeavoured to curb her tendency to intolerance and to a truthful directness which verged on tactlessness; but the advice was given in such a 'kind and fatherly' way she never resented it. Nor did she mind when he warned her that, having inherited the Hanoverian tendency to plumpness, she was liable to grow 'very fat'.

The Queen was well aware of Melbourne's past amours, of the divorce cases in which he had been involved, of his late, unbalanced wife, Lady Caroline Ponsonby, who had been so much in love with Byron, and of his pathetic, infantile son, also dead. These misfortunes made him all the more fascinating in her eyes, all the more to be pitied, loved and indulged. She soon concluded 'that he was, in fact, the best-hearted, kindest and most feeling man in the world ... straightforward, clever and good', a 'most truly honest and noble-minded man'. She esteemed herself 'most fortunate to have such a man at the head of the government', a man in whom she could 'safely place confidence'. There were 'not *many* like him in this world of deceit'.*[14]

Drawn to Melbourne by their common experience of loneliness, the

---

* 'For most of the first three years of her reign, Victoria's watercolour box and pencils lay idle. But when she did take up her pencil, very often her subject was Lord Melbourne. His handsome rumpled face appears again and again, on loose sheets of blotting paper, in the margins of unfinished letters, sometimes in the scarlet and blue Windsor uniform in which Victoria specially admired him, sometimes playing with one of her dogs' (Marina Warner, *Queen Victoria's Sketchbook*, 81).

Queen spoke to him of her past life, as well as the problems and business of politics, talking to him for three or four hours a day and writing to him on the occasions when they could not meet. These occasions were rare enough since he now virtually lived at Court where their intimacy was plain for all to see. 'I have seen the Queen with her Prime Minister,' wrote Princess Lieven. 'When he is with her he looks loving, contented, a little pleased with himself; respectful, at his ease, as if accustomed to take first place in the circle, and dreamy and gay – all mixed up together.'[15]

Charles Greville, who suspected that the Queen's feelings for him were '*sexual* though she [did] not know it', thought that no man was more formed to ingratiate himself with her than Lord Melbourne.

> He treats her with unbounded confidence and respect, he consults her tastes and her wishes, and he puts her at her ease by his frank and natural manners, while he amuses her by the quaint, queer, epigrammatic turn of his mind, and his varied knowledge upon all subjects . . . [He is] so parental and anxious, but always so respectful and deferential . . . She is continually talking to him. Let who will be there, he always sits next to her at dinner, and by arrangement, because he always takes in the Lady-in-Waiting which necessarily places him next to her, the etiquette being that the Lady-in-Waiting sits next but one to the Queen. It is not unnatural, and to him it is peculiarly interesting. I have no doubt he is passionately fond of her as he might be of his daughter if he had one, and the more because he is a man with capacity for loving without having anything in the world to love. It is become his province to educate, instruct, and form the most interesting mind and character in the world . . . Melbourne thinks highly of her sense, discretion, and good feeling.[16]

Content as she was to listen to his advice, to be instructed in such simple matters of propriety as the inadvisability of receiving divorced women at Court, of allowing maids-of-honour to walk unchaperoned on the terraces at Windsor Castle and of accepting the dedication of novels until he had read them to ensure that they contained nothing 'objection-able', the Queen was always ready, having formed her own views, to express her own opinions.[17]

While the Queen's feelings for Melbourne may have been subconsciously sexual, as Charles Greville suggested, she herself said that she loved him like 'a father'. She forgave him when he fell asleep after dinner and when he snored, as he did even in chapel, or became 'very absent' and began talking to himself, 'loud enough to be heard but never loud enough to be understood'. 'I am now, from habit,' she wrote, 'quite accustomed to it; but at first I turned round, thinking he was talking to me.' By way of apology, and then with welcome regularity, bouquets of flowers would arrive at the Palace from Brocket Hall, Melbourne's house in Hertfordshire.

Although he was conscientious in instructing the young and, in many respects, naive Queen about the political problems of the day, the workings of Parliament and the Cabinet, and the mysteries of the Constitution – leaving Lord Palmerston, the Foreign Secretary, to acquaint her with international relations – Lord Melbourne cannot be said to have aroused the Queen's social conscience, or to have made her more aware of the pitiable conditions in which so many of her people lived and which she had briefly glimpsed in her travels in the Midlands and in the North before her accession to the throne. Melbourne was far from being an idle man. That acute observer, the Revd Sydney Smith, commented: 'Our Viscount is somewhat of an impostor ... I am sorry to hurt any man's feelings and to brush away the magnificent fabric of levity and gaiety he has reared, but I accuse our Minister of honesty and diligence.'[18] Yet Melbourne's suspicion of reform and of the motives of reformers, his not altogether flippant suggestion that one should 'try to do no good' and then one wouldn't 'get into any scrapes', undoubtedly had their effect on the still developing sensibilities of the young Queen Victoria. He maintained that Sir Walter Scott was quite right to suggest that it was not worthwhile bothering with the poor; it was better to 'leave them alone'. Melbourne was quite convinced that the attempts by his niece's husband, Lord Ashley, later Lord Shaftesbury, to improve the conditions of children working in mines and factories were quite unnecessary and doomed to failure: since education of such children would never 'do any good'; parents should be free 'to send them under a certain age to work'.

One day the Queen mentioned that she had just read *Oliver Twist* and had been much affected by its 'accounts of starvation in the Workhouses'. But Melbourne dismissed the book as one of Dickens's own blinkered characters might well have done: 'It's all among Workhouses, and Coffin Makers, and Pickpockets ... It's all slang; just like the Beggar's Opera ... I don't like these things; I wish to avoid them; I don't like them in *reality* and therefore I don't wish to see them represented.'[19] As for railways, which were built by Irishmen – 'who mind neither lord nor laws' – and which he refused to have within fifteen miles of his house at Brocket, he didn't 'care about them'. 'None of these modern inventions,' he told the Queen, 'consider human life.'[20]

9

✶✶✶✶✶✶✶✶✶✶✶

CORONATION

'What was *called* an Altar
was covered with sandwiches, bottles of wine, etc.'

AFTER A DISTURBED NIGHT in which she had 'a feeling that something awful was going to happen tomorrow', the Queen was woken up at four o'clock in the morning in her bedroom at Buckingham Palace by the sound of guns in the Park, and 'could not get much sleep afterwards on account of the noise of the people, bands etc. etc.'. It was Thursday, 28 June 1838 and she was to be crowned that day in Westminster Abbey. Thousands of people had travelled to London the day before until, as the diarist Mary Frampton told her mother, there were 'stoppages in every street ... Hundreds of people waiting ... to get lifts on the railway in vain ... Not a fly or cab to be had for love or money. Hackney coaches £8 or £12 each, double to foreigners.'[1]

'The uproar, the confusion, the crowd, the noise are indescribable,' Charles Greville confirmed. 'Horsemen, footmen, carriages squeezed, jammed, intermingled, the pavement blocked up with timbers [for the spectators' stands], hammering and knocking and falling fragments stunning the ears and threatening the head ... The town all mob, thronging, bustling, gaping and gazing at everything, at anything, or at nothing. The Park one vast encampment, with banners floating on the tops of tents and still the roads are covered, the railroads loaded with arriving multitudes.' He found the racket 'uncommonly tiresome', yet he had to concede that the 'great merit of this Coronation is that so much has been done for the people [the theatres, for example, and many other places of entertainment were to be free that night]. To amuse and interest *them* seems to have been the principal object.'[2]

While not prepared to spend as much as the lavish sum of £243,000 which Parliament had voted for the coronation of King George IV, the Government were prepared to ensure that the ceremony in the Abbey and its attendant processions and celebrations were conducted with appropriate grandeur and an eye to the enjoyment of the people. £70,000 was deemed a reasonable sum, £20,000 more than had been spent on the coronation of King William IV.

Much attention was paid to the pretty dresses of the Queen's eight young, unmarried trainbearers, the Queen's own three different robes, the new uniforms of the Warders of the Tower and the Yeomen of the Guard, the regalia to be used in the various rites of the Abbey service, and the crown which had been used for the coronation of George IV but which had to be modified for Queen Victoria's much smaller head before being reset with diamonds, pearls, rubies, emeralds and sapphires.

'It was a fine day,' the Queen, having been up since seven o'clock, wrote in her journal, recalling the long ride to the Abbey in the state coach drawn by eight cream horses, down gravelled streets lined with policemen and soldiers, up Constitution Hill to Hyde Park Corner, then down Piccadilly, St James's and Pall Mall to Trafalgar Square and Whitehall, accompanied by the Duchess of Sutherland, her Mistress of the Robes, and the Earl of Albemarle, the Master of the Horse.

'The crowds of people exceeded what I have ever seen,' the Queen continued her account. 'Many as there were the day I went to the City, it was nothing – nothing to the multitude, the millions of my loyal subjects, who were assembled in *every spot* to witness the Procession. Their good humour and excessive loyalty was beyond everything, and I really cannot say how proud I feel to be the Queen of *such a Nation*. I was alarmed at times for fear that the people would be crushed and squeezed on account of the tremendous rush and pressure.'[3] But she kept smiling and bowing from side to side.

Preceded by the Royal Huntsmen, the Yeomen Prickers and Foresters and the Yeomen of the Guard, and followed by an escort of cavalry, the state coach drew up outside the Abbey door to be greeted by thunderous cheers. Inside the Abbey there were more cheers for the Queen and clapping, too, for Lord Melbourne and for the Duke of Wellington and for Wellington's opponent in the Peninsular War, Marshal Soult, created

Duke of Dalmatia by Napoleon and appointed French Ambassador Extra-ordinary to the Court of St James's by Louis-Philippe, King of the French. 'Soult was so much cheered, both in and out of the Abbey,' commented the dandiacal merchant, Thomas Raikes, 'that he was completely over-come. He has since publicly said, "*C'est le plus beau jour de ma vie.* It shows that the English believe I have always fought loyally." In the Abbey he seized the arm of his aide-de-camp, quite overpowered, and exclaimed, "This is truly a great people." '[4]

Wellington was predictably not so pleased by his own reception, the 'great shout and clapping of hands'. He looked down the aisle 'with an air of vexation', his friend, Lady Salisbury thought, as if to say, 'This should be for the Queen.'[5] She fully deserved the acclamation, the Duke considered: she carried herself with such charm, dignity and grace, never more so than when the frail and ancient Lord Rolle tripped up as he approached her to make his homage. 'It turned me very sick,' the writer, Harriet Martineau, recorded. 'The large, infirm old man was held by two peers, and had nearly reached the footstool when he slipped through the hands of his supporters, and rolled over and over down the steps, lying at the bottom coiled up in his robes. He was instantly lifted up; and he tried again and again, amidst shouts of admiration of his valour.'[6] 'May I not get up and meet him?' the Queen asked in anxious concern; and, since no one answered her, she outstretched her hand as he manfully rose to his feet and attempted to climb the steps once more as the congregation's vociferous cheers echoed round the Abbey walls.[7]

Wellington's high opinion of the Queen's demeanour was commonly shared. As she caught her first glimpse of the brilliant assembly in the Abbey she was seen to catch her breath and turn pale, clasping her hands in front of her. One of her trainbearers, Lady Wilhelmina Stanhope, believed 'her heart fluttered a little' as they reached the throne; 'at least the colour mounted to her cheeks, brow, and even neck, and her breath came quickly';[8] and there were those who regarded with some disapproval the smile she exchanged with Baroness Lehzen when, while sitting on the throne, she caught sight of that 'most dear Being' in the box above the royal box.

But to most observers she was a model of dignity and composure as she received the welcome accorded by the boys of Westminster School, whose traditional privilege it was to shout a Latin greeting to the monarch on such occasions. She was equally dignified as she turned from side to side to acknowledge the congregation's shouts of 'God Save Queen Victoria', and as she undertook to 'govern the people of this United Kingdom ... according to the statutes in Parliament ... to cause law and justice, in mercy, to be executed in all [her] judgements ... [and] to maintain the laws of God, the true profession of the Gospel and the Protestant Reformed religion established by law.'

'All this,' she replied to the Archbishop of Canterbury in a clear and steady voice, 'I promise to do.'[9]

She appeared undaunted by the solemnity of the occasion, the blaze of diamonds, the glittering gold plate on the altar, the splendid uniforms of foreign dignitaries, the magnificent robes of the peeresses, the hundreds of faces peering down at her from the specially erected galleries draped with red cloth fringed with gold, and the solemn moment when – as she sat in St Edward's Chair with four Knights of the Garter holding a canopy of cloth of gold over her head – she was anointed by the Archbishop with holy oil, 'as Kings, priests and prophets were anointed'.

She appeared equally composed when the crown was placed upon her head and the peers and peeresses put on their coronets and the bishops their caps to cheers and drum beats, to the notes of trumpets and the firing of guns at the Tower and in the royal parks. Indeed, although in doubt from time to time as to what she was expected to do, she seemed far more calm than the clergy, who, as Charles Greville said, 'were very imperfect in their parts and had neglected to rehearse them'.[10] She was also far calmer than Lord Melbourne who was, she noticed, 'completely overcome and very much affected' when the crown was placed on her head and who, kneeling down to kiss her hand, could not hold back his tears as she 'grasped his with all [her] heart'.[11]

Lord John Thynne, who, as his deputy, took the place of the elderly, infirm Dean of Westminster, admitted that 'there was a continual difficulty and embarrassment, and the Queen never knew what she was to do next'. She whispered to Thynne, who appeared to know more than his colleagues did, 'Pray tell me what to do, for they don't know!' Certainly Edward Maltby, the scholarly, 'remarkably maladroit' Bishop of Durham, who had an important role in the ceremony, 'never could tell [the Queen],' so she complained, 'what was to take place'. At one point he lost his place in the prayer book and began the Litany too soon. When the time came for the ring to be placed on her little finger, the Archbishop endeavoured to place it on her fourth. She told him it was too small; but he persisted, pressing it down so hard that she had 'the greatest difficulty' in getting it off again in the robing room afterwards and had to apply iced water to her fingers for half an hour. When she was given the extremely heavy orb she asked what she was meant to do with it. She was told that she was to carry it; but it then transpired that she had been given it too soon. By this time the Archbishop '(as usual) was so confused and puzzled and knew nothing' that he went away. She, too, was sent away to St Edward's Chapel and had to be summoned back from it when it was discovered that George Henry Law, Lord Ellenborough's brother, the Bishop of Bath and Wells, had turned over two pages at once, thus omitting an essential part of the service.[12]

Nor were the lay peers and trainbearers any more adroit than the clergy. The peers gave the Queen a headache, so her Mistress of the Robes said, by 'very unceremoniously' knocking her crown instead of touching it gently in their act of homage. One of them 'actually clutched hold of' it, while others might well have knocked it off altogether had she not 'guarded herself from any accident or misadventure by having it made to fit her head tightly'.[13] As for the bearers of the Queen's train, they carried it 'very jerkily and badly', one of them admitted, 'never keeping step as she did, even and steadily and with much grace and dignity, the whole length of the Abbey'.[14] Two of them could be heard chattering to each other throughout the service as animatedly as they might have done had they been at a ball.[15] And, when the coronation medals were thrown about in the choir and lower galleries by Lord Surrey, the Treasurer of the Household, everybody scrambled 'with all their might and main to get them, and none more vigorously than the maids-of-honour!'

All in all, Benjamin Disraeli, one of the recently elected Members of Parliament for the borough of Maidstone, told his sister, 'the want of rehearsal' was very obvious: 'Melbourne [who, feeling ill, had dosed himself with laudanum and brandy] looked very awkward and uncouth, with his coronet cocked over his nose, his robes under his feet, and holding the great Sword of State like a butcher ... The Duchess of Sutherland ... full of her situation ... walked, or rather stalked up the Abbey like Juno ... Lord Lyndhurst [the former and future Lord Chancellor] committed the *faux pas* of not backing from the presence ... I saw Lord

Ward after the ceremony ... drinking champagne out of a pewter pot, his coronet cocked aside, his robes disordered, and his arms akimbo.'[16]

Nor were Melbourne and Ward the only peers to appear dishevelled in their robes. Indeed, only two of them apparently knew how to wear them properly, both of these being practised performers in amateur theatricals. If Disraeli had gone into St Edward's Chapel – 'a small dark place behind the altar', as the Queen described it – he would have seen what Melbourne represented as being 'more *unlike* a Chapel than anything he had ever seen; for, what was *called* an Altar was covered with sandwiches, bottles of wine, etc.'

It was almost five hours before the ceremony was over; but conscious that she deserved Lord Melbourne's words of praise – 'You did it beautifully – every part of it, with so much taste; it's a thing that you can't give a person advice upon; it must be left to a person' – the Queen did not yet appear to be tired. After an hour spent changing into her purple robe of state in the robing room, then waiting there until half past four, she was taken back through crowds as dense as ever, carrying her sceptre and, heavy as it was, the orb, her close-fitting crown on her head, and the people cheering her all the way to Buckingham Palace where she dashed upstairs to give a bath to her beloved dog, Dash.[17]

After dinner she went into the Duchess of Kent's room; but it was not so much to see her mother – who had burst into tears at the sight of her daughter kneeling alone in the Abbey to receive the Sacrament – as to go out on to the balcony to watch the fireworks in Hyde Park where the next day a grand fair was to be held until the following Monday night. She remained on the balcony until after midnight, when she admitted at last to feeling rather weary. 'You may depend upon it,' Melbourne told her solicitously, 'you are more tired than you think you are.' She herself, she decided, would 'ever remember this day as the *proudest*' of her life.[18]

IO

✷✷✷✷✷✷✷✷✷✷✷

THE HASTINGS AFFAIR

'I at length expressed to her my uneasiness respecting her size,
and requested that at my next visit, I might be permitted
to lay my hand upon her abdomen with her stays removed.'

ONE DAY IN THE WEEK after the coronation the Queen recorded in her diary that she was '*quite cross . . . annoyed and put out*'. Irritated as she often was by other people's illnesses, she was particularly exasperated by Lord Melbourne who had taken to his bed. He had obviously been exhausted by the service in the Abbey where he had appeared quite worn out by the weight of the Sword of State which it had been his duty to carry. 'It was *most provoking and vexatious*', the Queen complained, that she should be deprived of the 'agreeable daily visit' of her Prime Minister, who would talk to her so amusingly, sitting beside her so comfortingly and protectively, letting Dash, or another of her dogs, a Scotch terrier called Islay, lick his hand. 'All dogs like me,' he said complacently.

The Queen was also put out whenever he did not come to dinner. 'Lord Melbourne dines with Lady Holland,' she wrote after one of these Melbourneless evenings. 'I wish he dined with me.' She was jealous and admitted it. She was also jealous of the beautiful Duchess of Sutherland, who often sat next to Lord Melbourne at dinner and made it almost impossible for him to talk to anyone else.

His absence was particularly tiresome at this time, as she had a meeting of the Privy Council to attend on 4 July; and there she must be without the person who made her 'feel safe and comfortable'.

She was not feeling very well herself. A rash had broken out on her hands; and, as the summer turned into autumn, she grew increasingly prone to headaches, outbursts of irritation and bouts of lethargy during which she found it an effort to get out of bed in the morning, get dressed, or even brush her teeth. Her handwriting suffered: she wrote indistinctly, misspelling words and leaving others out.

Lord Melbourne, by then recovered from his illness, told her she ate too much, was too fond of highly spiced food, drank too much ale and not enough wine; and did not take enough exercise: she ought to walk more in the open air. She protested that walking made her feel tired as well as sick, and she got stones in her shoes and her feet got swollen. As for Lord Melbourne's contention that she should eat only when she was hungry, she was always hungry, she retorted, so, if she followed his advice, she would be eating all day long. In any case, the Queen of Portugal was always taking exercise, yet she was very fat. It was certainly true that Victoria was putting on weight: she was weighed on 13 December and, to her consternation, discovered that she was only one pound under nine stone.[1] Her skin had taken on a yellowish tinge; her eyes were sore and troublesome – she once showed Melbourne a stye which rather disgusted him – and she feared she might be going blind, as her grandfather, George III, had done. Moreover, her hands were always cold in winter and her fingers red and swollen. She admitted herself that she was 'cross and low'. By the end of the year she was given to lamenting that she was 'unfit for [her] station'; and it took all Melbourne's tact and powers of persuasion to get her to think otherwise.

Baron Stockmar reported to King Leopold that she had become rather difficult of late, over-conscious of her exalted position, quick to take offence, impatient of advice and thoroughly out of sorts. By the beginning of the next year she was still far from being as lively and happy as she had been in the months immediately following her accession, and quite unprepared to deal rationally with a scandal concerning Lady Flora Hastings that now engulfed the Court.

She had never liked Lady Flora, known to her friends as 'Scotty'. The woman was an 'amazing spy who would repeat everything she heard', an 'odious' person. It was 'very disagreeable having her in the house'.[2] The Queen was quite ready to believe the worst of her when it appeared from her distended figure that she might be pregnant. Both the Queen and Baroness Lehzen, who much resented Lady Flora's teasing of her, became convinced that she was pregnant. So did others; and 'the horrid cause' of this condition, so the Queen decided, was undoubtedly that 'Monster and demon Incarnate', Sir John Conroy, who, so it was believed, had travelled back from Scotland overnight in a post-chaise alone with his friend, the 'amiable & virtuous' Lady Flora, after spending the Christmas holidays with her mother, at Loudon Castle.[3] Conroy had taken the opportunity – 'to use plain words' – to get her 'with child'.[4] Lady Tavistock – who, as senior Lady of the Bedchamber, had been approached by other ladies to protect their purity from this contamination – was authorized to consult Lord Melbourne.

Melbourne had already heard something about Lady Flora's supposed condition from Sir James Clark, who had been appointed Physician in Ordinary to the Queen in 1837, and predictably gave the advice that he was wont to do when faced with a difficult problem that had no easy solution. He had once told the Queen, 'All depends on the urgency of a thing. If a thing is very urgent, you can always find time for it; but if a thing can be put off, well then you put it off.' So, on this occasion, he advised that the 'only way' was 'to be quiet and watch it'.[5] If no fuss was made it would no doubt all blow over. Similar advice was later given to Lord Hastings, Lady Flora's young brother, by the Duke of Wellington, who was generally consulted, and loved to be consulted, in such *tracasseries*: the wisest plan, the Duke advised, was to hush the whole matter up.[6]

Unfortunately, Lady Flora, concerned about her condition, consulted Sir James Clark who, as a man who had started his professional life as a surgeon in the Navy, was not as well qualified as he might have been to give advice on female complaints. He did not 'pay much attention' to her ailments, Lady Flora said, or, perhaps, he 'did not understand them'. He prescribed rhubarb and ipecacuanha pills and a liniment largely composed of camphor and opium.[7] However, having felt her stomach over her dress, he discovered a 'considerable enlargement of the lower part of her abdomen'. But 'being unable to satisfy myself as to the nature of the enlargement,' he reported, 'I at length expressed to her my uneasiness respecting her size, and requested that at my next visit, I might be permitted to lay my hand upon her abdomen with her stays removed. To this Lady Flora declined to accede.'[8] Clark then said, according to Lady Flora's own account, that Lady Portman and others of the Queen's ladies were talking about her; he considered that they did so with justification; he thought no one could look at her and doubt that she was pregnant; he urged her to confess as 'the only thing' to save her; nothing but a thorough medical examination 'could satisfy the ladies of the Palace, so deeply were their suspicions rooted'.[9]

After this unpleasant conversation Clark consulted the Duchess of Kent, who refused to believe that her lady-in-waiting was pregnant. However, Lady Portman, who also went to see the Duchess, insisted that it was 'impossible that the honour either of the Court or of the Lady can admit of the least doubt or delay in clearing up the matter'.[10]

So the Duchess, rather than allow Lady Flora to leave Court under unwarranted suspicion, advised her to agree to what Sir James Clark had proposed.

And so Lady Flora changed her mind about submitting to a proper medical examination. She consented to undergoing one, provided Sir Charles Clarke, an experienced accoucheur and leading practitioner in midwifery, who had known the Hastings family for years, was present in the room with Sir James Clark. The two doctors accordingly conducted their examination in the presence of Lady Portman, who stood by the window with her head in her hands, and Lady Flora's maid, who was in tears throughout.[11] After this examination a formal declaration was issued in both the doctors' names:

> We have examined with great care the state of Lady Flora Hastings with a view to determine the existence, or non-existence, of pregnancy, and it is our opinion, although there is an enlargement of the stomach, that there are no grounds for suspicion that pregnancy does exist, or ever has existed.[12]

This report was expected to settle the matter. But in a conversation with Lord Melbourne, Sir Charles Clarke remarked that there were cases when, despite appearances of virginity, pregnancies had occurred. Sir Charles had observed such cases himself.[13] Melbourne reported this conversation to the Queen and was evidently persuaded that Lady Flora's condition was one of those which Sir Charles had mentioned. When the Queen remarked that Lady Flora had not been seen in the Palace for some time because she was so sick, Melbourne repeated, 'Sick?' with what the Queen described as 'a significant laugh'.[14]

Having read the doctors' report, the Queen agreed with Melbourne that the whole matter was getting 'very uncomfortable' and she thought that it would be as well that she should see Lady Flora and conciliate her. So she sent a message of regret to her through Lady Portman, who had already apologized herself, and offered to see her immediately. Lady Flora replied that she was too ill to see the Queen at present. A few days later, however, she appeared in the Queen's sitting room. 'She was dreadfully agitated,' the Queen wrote, 'and looked very ill, but on my embracing her, taking her by the hand, and expressing great concern at what had happened, and my wish that all should be forgotten, she expressed herself exceedingly grateful to me, and said that, for Mama's sake, she would suppress every wounded feeling and would forget it, etc.'[15]

The Hastings family were not prepared to forget it, though; nor was Lady Flora's friend, Sir John Conroy, who was quick to seize this opportunity to make trouble for those who had thwarted his ambition; nor were certain Tory propagandists who recognized in this scandal at Court a useful stick with which to beat Melbourne and the Whigs whom the Queen so openly supported; and nor, on reflection, was Lady Flora herself who wrote to her uncle by marriage, Captain Hamilton Fitzgerald, then living in Brussels, informing him that her honour had been 'most basely assailed'.

Fitzgerald left for London immediately. Lord Hastings, Lady Flora's brother, was equally determined to avenge this slur on his family's good name. Having seen his sister, he was convinced that Lord Melbourne was responsible for promoting the scandal, and he announced that he would challenge him to a duel. But, having talked to him, he was forced to conclude that the Prime Minister had tried to keep everything quiet and that he must look elsewhere for a culprit. His sister generously maintained that the Queen herself was not responsible. She was quite sure, she said, 'that the Queen does not understand what they have betrayed her into. She has endeavoured to show her regret by her civility to me, and expressed it most handsomely with tears in her eyes.'[16] Even so, her brother demanded an audience with the Queen which Lord Melbourne tried to prevent, thereby provoking an outraged letter from Lord Hastings:

> Having waited two days in the hope of having an audience with Her Majesty which I requested (if not as a matter of right as a Peer, at least as one of feeling), my patience being exhausted, and

being anxious to return to the bosom of my afflicted and insulted family, I am forced to resort to the only means now left in my power, of recording my abhorrence and detestation of the treatment which my sister has lately sustained.[17]

He shared his sister's belief that the Queen was not directly responsible for this treatment, declaring that responsibility rested with the 'baneful influence' which surrounded the throne and declaring that if he discovered any more relevant facts about the whole affair he would return to Court from whose 'polluted atmosphere' he for the time being retired.

The 'baneful influence' Lady Flora herself identified in her letter to Hamilton Fitzgerald as 'a certain foreign Lady', Baroness Lehzen, whose 'hatred of the Duchess of Kent [was] no secret'. Lady Flora also blamed Lady Portman, her 'accuser' in this 'diabolical conspiracy'. 'Good bye, my dear uncle,' her letter ended. 'I blush to send you so revolting a letter, but I wish you to know the truth, and nothing but the truth – and you are welcome to tell it right and left.'[18]

Excerpts from this letter were accordingly sent to the press;* so were letters written to both the Queen and Lord Melbourne by Lady Flora's mother, the Dowager Marchioness of Hastings, who praised the behaviour of the Queen's 'admirable mother', contended that Her Majesty's honour demanded that 'the criminal inventor' of the falsehoods spread about her daughter should not 'remain without discovery', and demanded as a 'mark of public justice' the removal of Sir James Clark from the Queen's Household. To this last request Melbourne replied, 'The demand which your Ladyship's letter makes upon me is so unprecedented and objectionable that even the respect due to your Ladyship's sex, rank, family and character would not justify me in more, if indeed it authorizes so much than acknowledging the letter for the sole purpose of acquainting your Ladyship that I have received it.' This letter, with the rest of the correspondence, was published in the *Morning Post*.[19]

By now Lady Flora's humiliation, the Queen's supposed failure to make a proper apology for it, as well as her failure to dismiss her Scottish doctor, Sir James Clark, from her Household as he had been dismissed

---

* 'Ly F. by her letter to Mr Fitzgerald had done herself no good,' Lady Holland commented. 'It is a gross, indelicate disclosure which shocks people. The mischief is to her; but the rebound is bad for the Court. The young, innocent Queen should never have had her ears polluted by such filthy stories' (The Earl of Ilchester, ed. *Elizabeth, Lady Holland to Her son, 1821–1845*, 175).

from her mother's, were the subject of intriguing gossip in almost every drawing room in London.

Lord Melbourne characteristically advised the Queen to take no notice of such gossip, nor of the letters which were appearing in the newspapers. But the Queen could not bring herself to ignore them; and the more she fretted about them the more she worked herself up into a fury with Lady Hastings, that 'wicked, foolish old woman', and with 'that wretched Ly. Flo.'.[20] She would like to see the whole Hastings family hanged alongside the editor of the *Morning Post*. As for her mother, who had taken Lady Flora's side and was reported to have looked after her when she was ill as though she had been her own child, her behaviour had been unforgivable. Indeed, it was her mother's behaviour which angered the Queen quite as much as that of the Hastings family. She confessed to Lord Melbourne that she felt 'a growing dislike for Mama', and that it was like 'having an enemy in the house'.

Day after day she spoke in these terms, week after week the atmosphere in the Palace became more charged, and the coolness between the rival households of the Queen and the Duchess became more marked. Lady Tavistock, fearful that Lord Hastings would challenge her husband to a duel, followed Lady Flora about in an effort to make amends. 'Won't you speak to me? Won't you shake hands?' she pleaded. 'That is quite impossible,' Lady Flora said.[21]

She became increasingly ill, while the Queen, dismissive as usual of other people's complaints and always most reluctant to change an opinion once formed, continued to deny the seriousness of Lady Flora's illness which she felt sure was just 'a billious attack'. Her mother insisted that, on the contrary, the poor woman was gravely ill; she was 'in a dreadful state' about her; indeed, she thought Lady Flora was dying. The thought that she might die greatly alarmed Lord Melbourne. That would certainly lay the Queen open to reproach; it would be wise to send to enquire after her. 'First of all,' he said, 'because she is under your roof, and then because it shows feeling.'

But the Queen's dislike of the woman had become so intense that she could not show such feeling. While her mother, who now refused to sit next to Lady Tavistock at the whist table, kept crying and insisting that Lady Flora was mortally ill, her daughter attended a ball and enjoyed herself 'excessively'.

There then, however, came very grave reports from Sir William Chambers, one of the leading physicians in London, who had succeeded Sir James Clark as the Duchess of Kent's physician. The Queen was advised to postpone another ball which was due to be held on 26 June. This she did and sent word that she would go to see Lady Flora that afternoon. But the dying woman felt too ill to see her then. Chambers advised her to go to her as soon as she could the next day.

> I went in alone [the Queen recorded of this distressing visit]. I found poor Lady Flora stretched on a couch looking as thin as anybody can be who is still alive; literally a skeleton, but the body *very* much swollen like a person who is with child; a searching look in her eyes, a look rather like a person who is dying; her voice like usual, and a good deal of strength in her hands; she was friendly, said she was very comfortable, and was very grateful for all I had done for her, and that she was glad to see me looking well. I said to her, I hoped to see her again when she was better, upon which she grasped my hand as if to say 'I shall not see you again.' I then instantly went upstairs and returned to Lord M. who said, 'You remained a very short time.'[22]

Four days later Lady Flora was still clinging weakly to life. The Queen said to Lord Melbourne that she found it very disagreeable and painful 'to think there was a dying person in the house'.[23] On 5 July in the early hours of the morning, over a week since the Queen had last seen her, Lady Flora died. A post mortem was conducted by the distinguished surgeon, Sir Benjamin Brodie, who discovered a large tumour on the liver: 'the uterus and its appendages presented the usual appearances of the healthy virgin state'.

The Queen felt *no* remorse, she told Lord Melbourne defiantly. She had 'done nothing to kill her'. However, much of the Press, led by the *Morning Post*, and many of the public at large considered that she should have felt remorse. At Ascot that summer, as her open carriage was driven up the course, two ladies in a private stand, one of them a duchess (two 'foolish, vulgar women' in the Queen's opinion, who ought to be flogged), hissed her loudly. Other voices could be heard shouting, 'Mrs Melbourne'. She was hissed and booed also in the streets of London, as she had been at the opera in Lady Flora's lifetime; and insults such as 'Whose belly up now?' were hurled at her as she rode by. Few men troubled to raise their hats at sight of her as they had done in the recent past. In fact, as Greville commented, it seemed that nobody cared for the Queen any more; loyalty was a dead letter; the scandal had played the devil with her popularity.

The *Morning Post* continued to upbraid her, attacking *The Times* for the excuses it offered for her behaviour. Pamphlets, assailing the 'evil counsellors' by whom she was surrounded, the 'stranger harboured in our country' (Baroness Lehzen) and the 'court physician with his cringing back' (Sir James Clark), were hawked about the streets. At a dinner in Nottingham, so General Sir Charles Napier said, his was the only voice to respond to the royal toast. Lord Ilchester believed the Queen would be well advised to leave London for a time to avoid further insult. Lord Melbourne suggested that a body of police should be made available on the day of Lady Flora's funeral in case the Queen's mourning carriage, which he thought should be sent as a token of respect, was stoned by demonstrators.

The family disdainfully returned the £50 which the Queen had sent to Lady Flora's maid; and for many years thereafter the blinds of Loudon Castle were drawn whenever Queen Victoria went to Scotland.

Not long after the funeral which, in fact, was conducted without serious interruption though, as Melbourne feared, a few stones and jeers were directed at the Queen's coach, Her Majesty was riding in Hyde Park where, although the crowd was 'very great', there was '*not one hiss*'. In fact a few people cheered her as she rode through the gate into St James's Park. This, she wrote with complacent satisfaction, 'is a *good* answer to those fools who say that the public feeling – a few paid Wretches – was displayed on Thursday by hooting at Ministers'.[24]

She was, however, far from as content and relieved as her protestations suggested. The Lady Flora Hastings affair had upset her deeply, and induced in her that malaise and inappetence so often consequent upon her emotional distress. She was 'disgusted with everything' and would have left the country immediately had she been a private individual. She was even, so she told Lord Melbourne, 'tired of riding'. As for Melbourne himself, he was conscious of not having guided the young Queen in the way he should have done: he certainly should not have shuffled the blame on to her ladies during his interview with Lord Hastings. He felt penitent. So did the Queen at last. When she got a stone in her shoe while walking with him, he told her it was a penance. She did not contradict him.[25]

✳✳✳✳✳✳✳✳✳✳✳✳

II

'A PLEASANT LIFE'

'If Melbourne ever left the room
her eyes followed him, and ...
she sighed when he was gone.'

FOR ALL VICTORIA'S occasional withering disapproval and what Lady
Paget called her 'commanding look', and for all the criticism levelled at
her in the immediate aftermath of the Lady Flora Hastings affair, it was
generally conceded that the Queen was a young woman of charm and
character, self-willed and pertinacious admittedly but determined, as she
confided to her journal, to do her utmost to fulfil her duty to her country.
'I am very young,' she wrote with unconscious pietism, 'and perhaps in
many, though not in all things, inexperienced, but I am sure, that very
few have more real good will and more real desire to do what is fit and
right than I have.'

Certainly she was relishing her new role as Queen and was scarcely
in need of the sympathy expressed for the 'poor little Queen' by Thomas
Carlyle who said that she could hardly be expected to choose a bonnet
for herself let alone undertake a task 'from which an archangel might
shrink'.[1] She said that sometimes when she woke up in the morning she
was 'quite afraid that it should all be a dream'. It was such 'a pleasant
life', she said. 'Everybody says that I am quite another person since I
came to the throne,' she told Princess Feodora. 'I look and am so very
well ... I [lead] just the sort of life I like. I have a good deal of business
to do, and all that does me a world of good.'[2]

She had left Kensington Palace with mixed feelings: she had had days
of great unhappiness there; but she had pleasing memories of it too, most

particularly of the earlier days of her childhood. But she had been anxious to move into Buckingham Palace as soon as possible, even though it was scarcely habitable yet, builders still having much work to complete at the time of King William IV's death. She had insisted on moving within three weeks of her accession; and so she had done. She was delighted with it. Thomas Creevey thought it a dreadful building which really ought to be called The Brunswick Hotel: it displayed 'every species of infirmity', its costly ornamentations exceeding 'all belief in their bad taste', its raspberry-coloured pillars enough to 'quite turn you sick to look at'.[3] The Queen, however, having no pretensions to taste in the design and decoration of rooms, was delighted with the Palace, its 'high, pleasant and cheerful' interiors, and its garden of forty-five acres laid out by the botanist, W. J. Aiton. It was just the place for parties, she thought, for balls and for concerts given by her own band.

Her first state ball had been given in the Palace in May 1838. She had 'felt a little shy in going in' but had soon been caught up in the excitement of the music, the galops and quadrilles. She 'had not danced for *so* long & was so glad to do so again'. She felt 'so happy and so merry'. Her cousin, Prince George of Cambridge, 'thought she danced really very nicely and seemed to be very much amused'.[4] She did not leave the ballroom until ten minutes to four and by the time she climbed into bed the sun was up.[5] She had shocked some of her guests, including old Lady Ilchester, by eating her supper standing up in the ballroom, breaking with the custom of King William IV who, as Mary Frampton said, was 'quite Citizen King enough' but who 'always supped with the Queen in his private apartments with a select party'.[6] Charles Greville, however, was much struck by Queen Victoria's 'exceedingly graceful manners', blended with 'dignity and cordiality, a simplicity and good humour, when She talks to people, which are mighty captivating. When supper was announced She moved from her seat, all her officers going before her – She, first, alone, and the Royal Family following; her exceeding youth strikingly contrasted with their mature ages, but She did it well.'[7]

She was not so taken with the Marine Pavilion at Brighton, that remarkably exotic structure which John Nash had created for her uncle, George IV, 'a strange, odd, Chinese-looking thing, both inside and out-side', the 'most extraordinary Palace' that she had ever seen.[8] But, although she felt too much on display there, she grew to be less censorious of the place. Her sitting room was 'pretty & cheerful' and from her bedroom she had 'a nice little peep of the sea'.[9]

To begin with she was not much taken with Windsor Castle either. She had first arrived there as Queen towards the end of August 1837 on a rainy day when the great stone towers and terraces, haunted by the cawing of rooks, looked particularly gloomy. She had felt that she did not belong there, that she was not mistress of the place, that at any moment she might 'see the poor King and Queen'.[10] Memories of the King's quarrels with her mother, and of herself being 'terribly scolded' by her mother in the Tapestry Room in the Lancaster Tower because of her wish to be on good terms with her uncle, had come back to depress her. It was not long, however, before the atmosphere of the place captured her imagination. She even grew to like the tolling of the bells and the striking of her grandfather's numerous clocks. She enjoyed the games of battledore and shuttlecock she played with her Ladies in the immensely long Great Corridor beneath the Canalettos and the family portraits. Ministers whose company she enjoyed came to stay. So, to her 'inexpressible happiness', did King Leopold and Queen Louise; and when they had gone she wrote to Queen Louise to say that the late summer she had spent at Windsor was the 'pleasantest summer she had *EVER* passed in her life'.[11]*

Back in London she settled down to the routine of her life with perfect contentment, much enjoying, indeed 'delighting' in her work. She had been advised to be methodical about this by King Leopold who told her 'the best plan is to devote certain hours to [business]; if you do that, you will get through it with great ease. I think you would do well to tell your Ministers that for the present you would be ready to receive those who should wish to see you between the hours of eleven and half-past one.' He went on to suggest that 'whenever a question of some importance' arose with these Ministers 'it should not be decided on the day it [was] submitted'.[12]

Although her obedience to this advice sometimes annoyed her Ministers, none of them could deny that she was extremely conscientious in

---

* After her husband's death there, however, her earlier distaste for the Castle returned: in a letter to her eldest daughter in 1867 she referred to it as 'that dungeon', and in 1884 she described it as 'this dreary, gloomy old place' (*Beloved Mama: Private Correspondence of Queen Victoria and the German Crown Princess, 1878–85*, ed. Roger Fulford, 1971, 172).

her consideration of the matters put to her; and when King Leopold suggested that she ought to spend more time at Claremont and less in London she retorted that she could not possibly do so: she had to see her Ministers '*every* day'. She did 'regular, hard but delightful work with them' and 'never felt tired or annoyed' by the hours she had to devote to it.[13]

She got up promptly at eight o'clock and dealt with papers until it was time for breakfast at which her mother usually joined her, but not until she had received a formal invitation. At eleven o'clock she saw Lord Melbourne, not only as her Prime Minister but also as a kind of private secretary and confidential adviser. After luncheon she went out riding with various ladies and gentlemen of her Household, Melbourne on one side, an equerry on the other. She was usually dressed in a black velvet riding habit, sometimes galloping ahead of the others on her lively horse, displaying her skill and grace as a horsewoman. 'She has a small, active, safe but very fleet horse,' Lady Holland told her son, 'nor does she undervalue the last quality, or allow it to rust for want of using: the pace at which she returns is tremendous ... I am startled by the thinness of Lord Melbourne. It is too much; but it may be partly ascribed to the hard riding of those who are attendants of the Queen.'[14]

Before dinner at eight, the Queen took up her sketchbook or her music; and, after dinner, there were those dutiful, stilted conversations with her guests which Charles Greville had described, followed by more intimate talk with a few friends, games of chess and draughts, jigsaw puzzles and spillikins. Or she might look into books of prints, Lord Melbourne at her side, making comments pertinent or wry, paradoxical, funny or facetious, occasionally reducing both her and himself to helpless laughter, the loud hoots of Melbourne's laugh, like those of the Duke of Wellington, being heard all over the room. He told her, for instance, when talking of cannibalism, of the old woman ill in bed who was asked if there was anything she would like to have and who replied, 'I think I could eat a little piece of the small bone of a boy's head.' He defended Henry VIII's treatment of his wives by declaring, 'Oh, those women bothered him so.' He recommended the employment of Dissenters as gardeners because they wouldn't take time off to go hunting or to the races. He read out 'so funnily' a printed paper which he had come across in a packet of Assam tea and which contained a commendation of the product by one Dr Lun Qua, a name that 'put him into paroxysms of laughter, from which he couldn't recover for some time, and did one good to hear'. She herself, she said, would sometimes almost 'die with laughing' in his company.[15]

The Duke of Wellington, while admitting that he liked Melbourne and thought that he was 'the best Minister' the Queen could have, was 'afraid he joked too much with her, and made her treat things too lightly which are very serious'.[16] When Melbourne told the Queen of this criticism, which he had heard about through Lord Clarendon, he conceded that there was some truth in it. She protested, however, that it was not so. Nor would she have agreed with the earnest and upright Lord Ashley, later Lord Shaftesbury, who, while recognizing that the Prime Minister had 'a sincere and even ardent affection for the Queen', suggested that he did not possess the 'courage to act and advise her according to her real interests'. 'His society and conversation are pernicious to a young mind,' Ashley believed. 'His sentiments and manner blunt the moral sense . . . [His cynicism] and 'reckless language' were a 'perpetual source of poison to her mind'.[17]

The Queen would have none of this. As for the confidence of the Crown, she insisted, 'God knows, No *Minister*, no friend EVER possessed it so entirely, as this truly excellent Lord Melbourne possesses mine!'

It was noticed that when Lord Melbourne was not by her side after dinner, she glanced repeatedly in his direction; Lord Hatherton observed that 'she could not bear that he should be out of her sight . . . if Melbourne even left the room her eyes followed him, and . . . she sighed when he was gone';[18] and when he was not at Court she was jealous of the hostess who had attracted his presence elsewhere. More often than she liked this was Lady Holland; and once, when she knew he had gone to Holland House, she lamented in her diary, 'I WISH he dined with me.' She told him that Lady Holland, who was old enough to be her grandmother, did 'not care for him *half* as *much* as she did, which made him laugh'. Indeed, she said, 'I am sure none of your friends are as fond of you as I am.'[19]

12

✳✳✳✳✳✳✳✳✳✳

'A HEADSTRONG GIRL'

*'They wished to treat me like a girl,
but I will show them that I am Queen of England.'*

HE WAS, SAID THE QUEEN, capable of 'every villainy'. She and Lord Melbourne were once again, on 21 January 1839, talking about Sir John Conroy. Melbourne had remarked, apropos of the man's intimacy with the Duchess of Kent, Princess Sophia and Lady Flora Hastings, not to mention his wife, 'What an amazing scape of a man he must have been to have kept three ladies at once in good humour.'[1]

Conroy, that 'Devil incarnate', had been giving trouble ever since she had come to the throne. On the very morning of the late King's death, as Lord Melbourne came out of the Privy Council meeting, he was handed a paper listing the sacrifices Conroy had made, both professionally and financially, to serve the Duchess so selflessly and the conditions which he required before he could consider retirement: they were a peerage, the Grand Cross of the Order of the Bath, and a pension of £3,000 a year.[2] 'This is really too bad! Have you ever heard such impudence,' exclaimed Lord Melbourne as the paper fell from his hands.[3] Soon, however, he came to agree with Baron Stockmar that the man's retirement was the 'only measure' which might help to improve the Duchess of Kent's relationship with her daughter who was, indeed, prepared to promise almost anything to the dreadful fellow provided he left the country; and, since Conroy protested that he was far from content with the mere baronetcy accorded him, he was given an undertaking that, if Melbourne 'should continue as her Majesty's adviser', he would be raised to an Irish peerage as soon as a new creation could be made. Melbourne had hoped that this offer would induce Conroy to leave the country; but Sir John declined to fulfil his part of the bargain until the Queen had fulfilled hers. So he and his family remained at Kensington where, so Princess Lieven heard, he bullied the Duchess as vigorously as ever. All this, Lord Liverpool observed to Baron Stockmar, was 'the result of Lord M.'s careless way of doing things'.

As the months went by, however, Conroy's position and reputation in England became increasingly insecure. He felt obliged to lodge an action for libel when *The Times* in a prominent article hinted at gross mismanagement of the Duchess of Kent's financial affairs by 'a certain newly created baronet' who had also been enabled to buy 'a certain estate in Wales' with money not his own. Then there were complaints from the Duchess of Kent's Coburg relations that the sitting room which had been made available to them on their visits to England was insolently invaded by this Irish interloper who was accustomed to come in and sit there as if he, too, were a member of her family. Following upon these complaints came a letter from James Abercromby, by now the highly respected Speaker of the House of Commons, who bluntly informed Conroy that it was 'everywhere boldly asserted' that his 'remaining in the family of the Duchess of Kent' was the main if not the only cause of the sorry state of the relationship between the Queen and her mother. If he withdrew from London he would be doing a service of the 'greatest public importance'.[4]

At length the Duke of Wellington, always delighted to be involved in such delicate situations, was called upon for help as, indeed, he had been in the Lady Flora Hastings case upon which both the Duchess of Kent and the Marquess of Hastings had sought his advice.

After a conversation with Wellington, Conroy agreed to leave the country, a decision for which the Duke with evident satisfaction took full credit, telling Charles Greville that he had persuaded the man to go by means of cajoling and flattery, using 'plenty of butter', and assuring Conroy that his decision to leave was 'an honourable and manly course'.[5]

Unfortunately the departure of Sir John Conroy for Italy did not improve relations between the Queen and the Duchess who, having assured Conroy that she still retained for him 'the most unshaken esteem', was kept quite as much at arm's length at Buckingham Palace as she had ever been at

Kensington. She was required to seek permission before visiting her daughter in her apartments and was not infrequently told that Her Majesty was too occupied with affairs of state or other matters to receive her. One day the Queen was talking to Lord Melbourne in the Blue Closet when her mother 'unceremoniously opened the door, but on [the Queen's] holloaing out, begged pardon and retired'.

The ill feeling between mother and daughter was exacerbated by complaints from the Duchess that the apartments allowed to her and her household were uncomfortably small when compared with those of the Queen who slept in a large bedroom between those of her maid and Baroness Lehzen, her 'ANGELIC, dearest *Lehzen*. . . the most estimable & precious treasure' she possessed and 'EVER SHALL POSSESS'.[6]

The comfort of having Lord Melbourne to talk to, and support her when plagued by such problems as were posed by her mother, made life so much more agreeable than it might otherwise have been; and when, at the beginning of May 1839, the Queen learned from the Home Secretary, Lord John Russell, that their Government was facing defeat on a colonial issue in the House of Commons and that her beloved Prime Minister would have to resign, she received the news with horrified dismay. Some weeks earlier the possibility of his Government's defeat had distressed her beyond measure: 'I am but a poor helpless girl who clings to him for support and protection, & the thought of ALL ALL my happiness being possibly at stake, so completely overcame me that I burst into tears and remained crying for some time.'[7]

Now, distressed as she already had been by the Lady Flora Hastings affair and the presumptuous demands of the now mercifully departed Conroy, she was even more distraught: 'The state of agony, grief and despair into which this [defeat of the Government] placed me may be easier imagined than described!' she wrote in her diary. 'That happy peaceful life destroyed, that dearest kind Lord Melbourne no more my minister . . . I sobbed and cried much.'[8]

'I really thought my heart would break,' she added after Melbourne had been to see her to confirm the terrible news himself and she had begged him 'ever to be a father to one who never wanted support more than she does now', 'He was standing by the window; I took that kind dear hand of his in both mine and looked at him and sobbed out, "Don't forsake me." I held his hand for a little while, unable to leave go; and he gave me such a look of kindness pity and affection, and could hardly utter for words, "Oh! no!" in such a touching voice.[9] We then sat down as usual and I strove to calm myself . . . After a pause he said, "You must try and be as collected as you can and act with great firmness and decision" . . . I went on crying and feeling as thoroughly wretched as human mortal can be.'[10]

When he had gone she wrote him three letters beseeching him to come to see her again and to stay for dinner. He would not come to dinner, he replied: it would not be proper to do so while negotiations for a new Government were in progress; but he would come to see her that afternoon.

In the meantime Lord John Russell called to see her; but she could not stop crying and she was still in tears when Lord Melbourne returned with a paper in which he recommended her sending for the Duke of Wellington who would probably suggest that she send for Sir Robert Peel, who had been Prime Minister in the Tory administration of 1834–5. If the Duke did so, she must try to make allowances for Peel's stiff, shy, awkward manner.[11] Certainly Peel was 'an underbred fellow' for all his time at Harrow and Christ Church. He was, after all, 'not accustomed to talk to Kings and Princes' as Melbourne himself was, yet he was 'a very able and gifted man'.[12]

'I burst into tears and said, "You don't know what a dreadful thing it is for me,"' the Queen continued in her diary entry. 'He looked really so kindly at me and seemed much affected . . . I sobbed much, again held his hand in both mine . . . as if I felt in doing so he could not leave me . . . He then got up . . . and he kissed my hand, I crying dreadfully.' When he had gone she wrote to beg him to ride tomorrow in the Park so that she could 'just get a glimpse' of him; it would be 'such a comfort'. 'Ld. Melbourne may think this childish but the Queen *really* is so *anxious* it might be; & she wld bear thro' all her trials so much better if she did just see a friend's face sometimes . . .'

That evening she 'could not touch a morsel of food' and spent a restless night. The next morning the Duke of Wellington called. He told her that he was really too old at seventy, too deaf, too out of touch with the House of Commons to think of becoming Prime Minister again. He recommended, as Melbourne had supposed he would, that she should send for Sir Robert Peel.

The prospect of Peel as Prime Minister depressed her still further: he was so difficult to talk to, his shyness made her shy too, his nervous mannerisms were so distracting. Her uncle, George IV, had been driven in his presence to complain of his irritating habit of thrusting out his arms as he talked; the Queen herself said that the way he pointed his toes and shook down his cuffs reminded her of a dancing master. Charles Greville compared him to a 'dapper shopkeeper': 'he eats voraciously and cuts cream jellies with his knife.'

Although Peel seemed 'embarrassed and put out' when he came into the Queen's presence that afternoon – and was 'such a cold, odd man . . . oh, how different, how dreadfully different, to that frank, open, natural and most kind, warm manner of Lord Melbourne' – the interview was not as painful to her as she had feared it might be.[13] Melbourne had advised her to express the hope that none of her Household except those engaged in politics would be removed. 'They'll not touch your ladies,' he had said, to which she had replied that they would not dare: she 'never would allow it'. She mentioned the subject of her Household to Peel, 'to which at present he would give no answer, but said nothing should be done without the Queen's knowledge and approbation'.[14]

The next day the Queen received a letter from Lord Melbourne in which he suggested that she ought to 'urge this question of the household strongly as a matter due to yourself and your own wishes'. But, if Sir Robert Peel insisted upon certain changes she should not refuse them, nor break off negotiations upon the point.

That, however, was precisely what she intended to do. During Peel's second audience that day, he came more firmly and directly to the question uppermost in both their minds. 'Now, Ma'am,' he said, 'about the Ladies.' The Queen, bridling at the implied question, replied that she could never give up any of her ladies, that she 'had never imagined such a thing'.

Did she intend to retain *all* of them? Peel asked

'All.'

The Mistress of the Robes and the Ladies of the Bedchamber?

'All.'[15]

But some of these ladies were married to his Whig opponents, protested Peel, who, so the Queen noted with satisfaction, began to look 'quite perturbed'. It did not matter whom they were married to, she riposted: she never talked politics with her ladies. He would not ask her to change her younger ladies, Peel persisted; it was only some of the more important, senior ladies whom he would like to see replaced. But these, she countered, were just the ones she could not spare; besides, queens had not been asked to make such sacrifices in the past. Comparisons with past queens did not really apply, Peel pointed out; they had been queen consorts, *she* was a reigning queen: that made all the difference. 'Not here,' the Queen declared sharply, resolutely standing her ground.[16]

'I never saw a man so frightened,' she reported triumphantly to Lord Melbourne. 'He was quite perturbed . . . I was very calm but very decided, and I think you would have been pleased to see my composure and great firmness . . . the Queen of England will not submit to such trickery. Keep yourself in readiness for you may soon be wanted.'[17]

Some three hours later Peel returned to the Queen. He had already reassured her when she had asked him that he surely could not expect her to give up the society of Lord Melbourne. Nothing could be further from his thoughts, he had said: he would always 'feel perfectly secure in the honour of Lord Melbourne'. He was also perfectly agreeable to the appointment of the Queen's friend, Lord Liverpool, as Lord Steward. But the question of the ladies was a different matter. He tentatively suggested that some changes might be desirable to show that the new Government enjoyed Her Majesty's confidence but he again assured her that nothing would be done without her knowledge and approval. The Queen quickly rejoined that the only members of the Household with whom she could be expected to part were those gentlemen who were also in Parliament. Taking childish pride in her stiff demeanour, she remained, she said, 'very much collected, civil and high' throughout the interview. She found the man 'cold, unfeeling' and 'disagreeable' and took no trouble to disguise her distaste as Peel put forward the names of the men he proposed to her as Ministers. When he awkwardly took his leave and the door closed behind him she gave vent to her feelings in further floods of tears.

Forced to conclude that he could do nothing more to persuade her to be less intransigent, Peel enlisted the support of the Duke of Wellington who found that the Queen had worked herself up into a state of 'high passion and excitement'.

'Well,' he began, 'I am sorry to find there is a difficulty.'

'Oh, he began it not me,' she replied. 'It is offensive to me to suppose that I talk to any of my ladies upon public affairs.'

'I know you do not . . . But the public does not know this.'[18]

The discussion continued for some time; but the old Duke was powerless in the face of the young girl's stubborn pertness. As Charles Greville observed, the Queen, 'a clever but rather thoughtless and headstrong girl', was 'boldly and stubbornly' using her ladies as a pretext to fulfil her 'longing to get back her old Ministers' and she was not prepared to abandon that pretext however unconstitutional it might be.

Soon after Wellington had withdrawn from the battle, Peel returned to the Palace to say that unless there was *some* demonstration of her confidence in a Tory administration, and if she insisted on retaining all her ladies, his colleagues had concluded 'unanimously that they could not go on'. Having tartly observed that her '*Ladies* were *entirely* her own affair and not the Ministers'' and that 'Sir Robert must be very weak if *even* the *Ladies* were required to share his political opinions', she wrote in triumph to Melbourne, 'This was *quite* wonderful! . . . What a blessed and unexpected escape.'[19]

Most of the senior members of the Cabinet were far readier than Melbourne himself to believe the Queen had done well to stand firm against Peel's demands. Melbourne noted with some concern that Peel had asked for *some* changes not a complete replacement of the entire household as was widely believed. But this did not much concern Lord John Russell, who considered it unthinkable to desert the Queen in her stand against the Tory demands, nor Lord Grey, the former Prime Minister, who believed Her Majesty had 'the strongest claims' to the Government's support 'in the line which she [had] taken'. So Lord Melbourne, not unwillingly, allowed himself to be persuaded. He read out to his colleagues a summary of two letters he had received from the Queen in which she sounded a highly triumphant note: 'Do not fear that I was not calm and composed. They wanted to deprive me of my Ladies, and I suppose they would deprive me next of my dressers and my housemaids; they wished to treat me like a girl, but I will show them that I am Queen of England.'[20] That evening she gave a ball for the Tsarevich, the future Tsar Alexander II, noting in her diary afterwards that both Peel and the Duke of Wellington looked 'very much put out . . . I left the ballroom at ¼ to 3, much pleased, as my mind felt happy.'[21]

There was, however, a feeling in the country, and not only amongst Tories, that the Queen, as she herself was later to admit, had behaved unwisely and impetuously in this the first constitutional crisis of her reign.

Charles Greville, as was so often the case, well expressed the view of these critics of the Queen's behaviour:

> It is a high trial of our institutions when the caprice of a girl of nineteen can overturn a great Ministerial combination, and when the most momentous matters of Government and legislation are influenced by her pleasure about the Ladies of the Bedchamber ... The origin of the present mischief may be found in the objectionable composition of the Royal Household at the accession. The Queen knew nobody, and was ready to take any Ladies that Melbourne recommended to her. He ought to have taken care that the female part of her Household should not have a political complexion, instead of making it exclusively Whig as (unfortunately for her) he did. The simple truth in this case is that the Queen could not endure the thought of parting with Melbourne, who is everything to her ... In the course of the transaction She thought She saw the means presenting themselves of getting Melbourne back, and She eagerly grasped at, and pertinaciously retained them. Nothing else would have emboldened her to resist the advice and opinion of the Duke of Wellington and to oppose so unbendingly her will to his authority. There is something which shocks one's sense of fitness and propriety in the spectacle of this mere baby of a Queen setting herself in opposition to this great man ... She has made herself the Queen of a party.[22]

Baron Stockmar, too, was concerned that a 'great Ministerial combination' had been overturned by 'the caprice of a girl of nineteen'. He wondered if, like her grandfather, King George III, she was mentally unbalanced. 'How could they,' he asked, 'let the Queen make such mistakes, to the injury of the Monarchy?'[23]

13

✳✳✳✳✳✳✳✳✳✳✳

GERMAN COUSINS

'Cousins are not very good things ... Those Coburgs
are not popular abroad; the Russians hate them.'

IT IS RUMOURED and confidently believed in the highest circles
[*The Watchman* had informed its readers on 4 May 1828] that Prince
George, Son of His Royal Highness, the Duke of Cumberland, will
speedily be betrothed to his royal Cousin, the Princess Victoria,
daughter of the late Duke of Kent; the Prince is a fine healthy boy,
in his tenth year, and the Princess, a lovely child, within a few days
of the same age.[1]

Wild as was this surmise, it was scarcely more improbable than some
other conjectures about Princess Victoria's future husband which were
to appear in newspapers over the next few years. Indeed, the French press
suggested that she was to be married to her uncle Leopold, ignoring the
fact that the Church of England's Table of Kindred and Affinity prohibited
such a marriage in her own country. She was also, at one time or another,
rumoured to be intended as a bride for the Duke of Nemours's brother,
the Duke of Orléans, for the Duke of Brunswick, nephew of King George
IV's unbalanced wife, Queen Caroline, for Prince Adelbert of Prussia, for
Prince Christian of Schleswig-Holstein, the future King Christian IV of
Denmark, and for the eldest son of the Prince of Orange who, to the
fury of King Leopold, had been invited to England by King William IV,
a warm advocate of the match. 'Really and truly I never saw anything
like it,' expostulated King Leopold, who had other plans for his niece. 'I
am really *astonished* at the conduct of your old Uncle the King; this
invitation of the Prince of Orange and his sons, this forcing him upon

others is very extraordinary ... I am not aware ... of the King's even having *spent a sixpence for your existence*'.[2]

Fortunately the Princess did not at all like the look of the young men from Holland. 'The boys are both very plain,' she reassured her uncle, 'moreover they look heavy, dull and frightened and are not at all prepossessing. So much for the *Oranges*, dear Uncle.'[3]

King Leopold's opposition to the Orange match was prompted not only by the troubles he foresaw as King of the Belgians but also by his having a candidate of his own. This was Prince Albert, son of King Leopold's eldest brother, Ernest, Duke of Saxe-Coburg and Gotha, whom his family had long destined for the role of consort to the English Queen.

Born on 24 August 1819 at the Schloss Rosenau, his father's modest Gothic castle on the edge of the forest of Thuringen a few miles from Coburg, Prince Albert had been an exceptionally good-looking child, 'superb, extraordinarily beautiful', in the words of his mother, though the Dowager Duchess of Coburg considered him 'too slight for a boy'. Certainly he was rather feminine, sensitive and shy, far from robust and often in tears.

His early years had been overcast by the departure of his mother who, when he was no more than five years old and in bed with whooping cough, had left her profligate and much older husband, whom she had married at sixteen, for an army lieutenant two years younger than herself. He never saw her again; and his character, introspective, and given to melancholy, was for ever scarred by this painful separation from a beautiful woman who had petted and indulged him.

Yet his childhood was far from being as unhappy as he was later to describe it to his eldest daughter. He was much attached to his elder brother, Ernest; his father, stern with others, was not unkind to him, bestowing upon him an affection which was warmly returned; his good-natured grandmothers did their best to take the place of his mother; his tutor, Herr Florschütz, was sympathetic and understanding, his Swiss valet attentive and protective. He was an intelligent and painstaking pupil, preternaturally conscientious. At the age of eleven he wrote with earnest precocity in his diary, 'I intend to train myself to be a good and useful man.' And this assiduous determination to do well marked his every activity: he applied himself to sport and games with as much diligence as he brought to his lessons. When walking in the lovely countryside around the Rosenau, he made detailed and exact observations of all the natural objects he came across and formed comprehensive collections of stones and shells, stuffed birds, insects and butterflies, all neatly labelled and categorized.

After ten months studying in Brussels, where his uncle, King Leopold, kept a close eye on his protégé's progress, he and his brother were sent, in April 1837, to undergo more advanced studies at Bonn University where Prince Albert was described as a model student, getting up at five o'clock to read his books and write his essays, diligently attending lectures, taking careful notes, fencing and skating with skill and grace. But it was felt that he did not yet display those social graces, that ease of manner which would be expected of him at the English Court: with strangers he was inclined to be distant, formal and stiff. So in October 1838 he was sent with Baron Stockmar on a continental tour, following the route which so many young gentlemen had taken before him through Florence, Rome and Naples. In Italy he was as conscientious in his studies as he had been in Germany, getting up early to read and to learn Italian, walking round galleries, museums and churches, studying paintings and sculpture.*[4] He sketched; he played the piano; he went for long walks. Baron Stockmar could not fault his industry; but there was, it had to be admitted, more than a whiff of pedagogic pedantry in the evident pleasure he took in the dissemination of his knowledge, in his categoric pronouncements upon the merits or faults of whatever came under his observation, his readiness to correct the misapprehensions of others, to score points. In Rome, for example, he was granted an audience with Pope Gregory. 'The Pope asserted,' recorded the Prince, 'that the Greeks had taken their models from the Etruscans. In spite of his infallibility, I ventured to assert that they had derived their lessons in art from the Egyptians.'[5]

---

* The Prince was much attracted to the art of the early Renaissance which was not then fashionable. When he could afford to do so, and with the help and advice of Ludwig Gruner, the painter and engraver, who was with him in Italy, he began to collect early Italian, German and Flemish pictures. The Queen was later to give him, as birthday presents, Daddi's *Marriage of the Virgin*, the *Coronation of the Virgin*, attributed to the school of Jacopo di Cione, and Cima da Conegliano's *Four Saints* and the *Annunciation*.

The Prince was to encourage Sir Charles Eastlake, Director of the National Gallery from 1855, to purchase early Italian pictures when the Trustees still preferred to buy works of the High Renaissance. The National Gallery was extended partly to accommodate the acquisitions which the Prince induced it to buy.

The Prince's humour, too, was of a rather heavy and ponderous kind. He was said to be a fairly convincing mimic but no one could have called him witty; and he had a distressing fondness for rather childish jokes; he was fond of one about a short-sighted man who came into a room and, mistaking a fat woman for a stove, turned his back on her with his coat tails turned up. He also enjoyed catching people out on April Fool's Day and perpetrating practical jokes such as that which he and his brother played upon the inhabitants of a small German town through which they drove. Prince Albert held up the head of his dog at the window, while he and Prince Ernest crouched down in the bottom of the carriage out of sight of the people who had gathered to see them pass by.[*6]

With the example of his parents and his brother – who was twice to contract a venereal disease – ever before his eyes, he had a horror of sexual irregularities. He was also subject to an occasional nervous irritability and a tendency to express opinions, in the words of his brother, 'which are wont to arise from contempt of mankind in the abstract'.

What concerned Stockmar as much as anything else in Prince Albert's character was his awkward manner with women, a gaucherie which the Baron attributed principally to his 'having in his earliest years been deprived of the intercourse and supervision of a mother, and of any cultivated woman. He will always have more success with men than with women. He is too little *empressé* with the latter, too indifferent and too reserved.'[7]

When he had first arrived in England aged sixteen with his brother, Ernest, in May 1836, Prince Albert had been an undeniably handsome and prepossessing boy. His constitution was, however, not well adapted to the bustle and festivities, the dinners and balls, the concerts and levees

---

* According to Lord Granville, the Queen's family also appreciated this kind of joke. Wit was wasted on them, Granville said, since nothing made them laugh as much as hearing 'one had trapped one's finger in the door'. The Queen was herself much amused by such mishaps as a man squashing his hat by sitting on it or by a misfortune such as experienced by the wife of the Secretary of the Office of Works who, 'when she rose from her curtsy, her dress gave a loud crack like a pistol shot, much to the Sovereign's amusement' (James Lees-Milne, *The Enigmatic Edwardian: Life of Reginald Brett, Viscount Esher*, 1986). With the Queen, however, it was not always easy to know whether or not she was being intentionally funny, as, for instance, when she gently instructed a 'décolletée' granddaughter before going into dinner: 'a little rose in front, dear child, because of the footmen'.

which he was expected to attend. He was not accustomed to late nights: one evening he had felt compelled to go to bed at what the lively Princess Victoria considered an absurdly early hour; the next evening at a ball attended by over 3,000 guests to celebrate the Princess's seventeenth birthday, after having danced only twice, the Prince had turned 'as pale as ashes' and looked as though he were going to faint. He had been obliged to take to his bed for two days. 'I am sorry to say,' the Princess had reported to her uncle Leopold the next day, 'that we have an invalid in the house in the person of Albert.'[8] Frequently in the future she was to refer in her journal to Prince Albert's 'delicate stomach'. Unlike the Queen, he had not been able to build up natural resistance to infections consequent upon the appallingly insanitary conditions which he encountered in England, having become used in his childhood and early manhood to the far more hygienic conditions of his native land.[9]

The ceaseless round of entertainments in England, so he had complained to his stepmother, were all too much for him: one concert had lasted until one o'clock in the morning, another had gone on until two. However, in letters to her uncle and his wife, Princess Victoria had assured them that she found Albert and his brother most agreeable, though it had to be said that Albert was rather fat:

> They are both very amiable, kind and good. Albert is very handsome which Ernest is not, but he has a most good-natured countenance ... I thank you, my beloved Uncle, for the prospect of great happiness you have contributed to give me in the person of dear Albert. Allow me, then, my dearest Uncle, to tell you how delighted I am with him, and how much I liked him in every way. He possesses every quality that could be desired to render me perfectly happy. He is so sensible, so kind, and so good, and so amiable too. He has, besides, the most pleasing and delightful exterior and appearance you could possibly see.[10]

'The charm of his countenance is his expression, which is most delightful,' she had written in her diary, 'full of goodness and sweetness and very clever and intelligent.'

Prince Albert had been less enthusiastic. 'Dear Aunt [the Duchess of Kent] is very kind to us, and does everything she can to please us,' he had added in his letter to his stepmother, 'and our cousin is also very amiable.'[11] That was all. He had later expressed certain reservations about his cousin: they shared a love of music, but did they have much else in common? He was told she was 'incredibly stubborn', that she delighted in 'ceremonies, etiquette' and the 'trivial formalities' of court life, that she did not share his love of nature, that her pleasure in balls that went on all night was not in the least abated and that after these balls she liked to lie late in bed. Besides, he feared that he would be dreadfully homesick in England.

Princess Victoria herself, much as she had liked Prince Albert upon this brief acquaintance, had not wanted to marry so soon, not until 1840 and perhaps not even then; and she had grown rather annoyed with King Leopold for pressing the marriage upon her. She was 'not yet quite grown up'; and Prince Albert was still a boy really: she would not want him as a husband until he was at least twenty years old. Besides, he 'ought to be perfect in the English language; ought to write and speak it without fault, which is far from being the case now: his French too is . . . unfortunately . . . not good enough yet in my opinion.' She had also been concerned by his habit of falling asleep after dinner. Had Lord Melbourne been told about that? Lord Melbourne, who disapproved of the Queen's passion for dancing into the small hours of the morning, had merely replied that he was *very* glad to hear it.

After Prince Albert had gone home and she herself had become Queen, there was another reason for her not wanting to be married just yet. Once the Flora Hastings affair was in the past and she had contrived to retain Lord Melbourne as Prime Minister, she was much enjoying herself as a young, unattached queen. On her twentieth birthday the Grand Duke Alexander of Russia, the 21-year-old son and heir of the Tsar Nicholas I, came to Windsor where a grand dinner in St George's Hall was followed by a ball which did not finish until nearly two o'clock in the morning. 'I never enjoyed myself more,' she wrote in her journal. 'We were all so merry'; and the Grand Duke was 'a dear, delightful man'. She had loved dancing the mazurka with him: he was 'so very strong, that in running round you must follow quickly, and after that you are whisked round like in a *Valse*, which is very pleasant . . . I really am quite in love with him . . . He is so frank, so really young and merry, has such a nice open countenance with a sweet smile and such a manly figure.' After the Grand Duke, no one else was 'seen to advantage'. When she went to bed on the night of that exciting ball she could not get to sleep until five o'clock.[12]

From time to time she and Melbourne discussed the question of her marriage and one day they considered all those of royal blood who might be considered as a husband for her. There was not one whom they thought suitable. Yet she did not think she ought to marry a commoner: it would not do, she thought, to make a subject one's equal. There were, however, those who thought she might, even so, consider marriage to her equerry, Lord Alfred Paget, son of the cavalry commander, the Marquess of Anglesey, one of the most handsome young men at Court who wore her portrait on a chain round his neck, tied another portrait of her round the neck of his retriever, Mrs Bumps, and who took pains to ingratiate himself with Baroness Lehzen, calling her 'mother' as the Queen did.[13]

Lord Melbourne did not altogether approve of King Leopold's choice of Prince Albert. 'Cousins are not very good things,' he said. 'Those Coburgs are not popular abroad; the Russians hate them.' The Duchess of Kent was a fair example of the breed. The men of the family were not so bad, the Queen objected, laughing. Melbourne, laughing too, said he hoped so. But what if the Prince were to take the side of his aunt, the Duchess, against her? In any case a marriage with a German cousin would not go down well in England. It would not go down well with himself, come to that: Germans never washed their faces and were always smoking, and he hated tobacco, the very smell of it made him swear for a good half hour. On the other hand marriage into an English family would not go down well, either, except with the particular family honoured. Indeed, if one were to create a man specifically for the purpose of marrying the Queen it would be 'hard to know what to make'. It might be better 'to wait for a year or two'. It was a 'very serious question'. An early marriage was '*not* NECESSARY'.[14]

The more she thought about it the more she found the whole subject 'an odious one'. She really 'couldn't understand the wish of getting married' merely for the sake of it. She 'dreaded the thought of marrying'. She was so accustomed to getting her own way that she 'thought it was 10 to 1 she wouldn't agree with anyone'. When she spoke, as she often did, of her unhappy relationship with her mother, who made it plain that she would never leave her daughter until she was married, Lord Melbourne had commented, 'Well, then, there's *that* way of settling it.' To this solution of her troubles with her mother she strongly objected:

she thought the idea of marrying for that reason a quite 'shocking alternative'. Yet she was tired of living with people so much older than herself. When her young relations came to stay she realized how much she liked living with young people, for after all she was young herself, which she 'really often forgot'.

In September some other young Coburg cousins came to stay, her uncle Ferdinand's sons Augustus and Leopold, their sister Victoire, and yet another cousin, Alexander Mensdorff-Pouilly, son of Princess Sophia of Saxe-Coburg. Queen Victoria enjoyed their company immensely, their family jokes and high spirits, Victoire's carefree gaiety, Alexander's striking looks and pretty hair, his endearing habit of shaking hands at every fresh meeting. 'We were *so* intimate, *so* united, *so* happy,' she wrote after they had gone and she had been to Woolwich to wish them a tearful farewell aboard the *Lightning* before clambering down the ship's ladder and calling out to an officer who offered his assistance, 'No help, thank you. I am used to this.'[15]

Before having her young cousins, Albert and Ernest, to stay again, however, she thought it as well to make it quite clear that the visit must not be seen as compromising her in any way. Albert must understand that 'there was no engagement between us'. She had never made any definite promise to marry him and would not do so now. She might like him as a friend and a relation but no more than that; and even if she did come to like him more than that, so she told her uncle Leopold, she 'could make no final promise this year for, at the *very earliest*, any such event could not take place till *two or three years hence*'.[16]

Disturbed that Prince Albert might be put off by this apparent reluctance on the Queen of England's part, King Leopold had already asked his nephew to come to see him in Brussels. The Prince was reassuring: he was prepared to wait on the understanding that the marriage would take place in the end. 'I am ready,' he said, so the King reported to Baron Stockmar, 'to submit to this delay if I have some certain assurance to go on. But if after waiting, perhaps for three years, I should find the Queen no longer desired the marriage, it would place me in a very ridiculous position and would to a certain extent ruin all the prospects of my future life.'[17]

The King was reassuring in turn. All would turn out well when Prince Albert made his next visit to England.

* * *

This visit took place in October 1839. In anticipation of it the Queen was on edge, snappy with her servants and disinclined to concentrate on her paperwork. When she was told that her cousins were not able to leave quite as early as they had hoped, she wrote a sharp letter to King Leopold: 'I think they don't exhibit much *empressement* to come here, which rather shocks me.'[18] She was also unusually sharp and impatient with Lord Melbourne who was more than ever liable to fall asleep after dinner and during the sermon in church on Sundays, snoring loudly. She wondered how he could do so before so many people. When he drank wine in an effort to stay awake, she told him it would make him ill. She was annoyed with him, too, for not telling her about some changes in the Home Office – she was 'the last person' to be told about what was done in her name – and for pressing her, as King Leopold had done, to invite some Tories to meet them when Albert and his brother came. She abruptly marched out of the room; and when she returned she looked more cross than ever. A fortnight or so before her cousins were due to arrive she was again 'sadly cross to Lord Melbourne when he came in, which was shameful'. 'I fear he felt it,' she wrote in her diary, 'for he did not sit down of himself as he usually does, but waited until I told him to do so.' 'I can't think what possessed me', she continued, 'for I love this *dear excellent* man who is kindness & forbearance itself, *most* dearly.'[19]

A young person like her, who 'hated a Sunday face', 'must *sometimes* have *young* people to laugh with'. She had missed that sadly in the lonely days at Kensington when she had longed 'for some gaiety', some 'mirth', and when she had looked admiringly at handsome young men at parties and had made lists of the prettiest girls in the room. 'Nothing so natural', commented Lord Melbourne with apparent unconcern yet with tears in his eyes.[20]

14

✶✶✶✶✶✶✶✶✶✶✶

PRINCE ALBERT

'I believe that Heaven has sent me an angel
whose brightness shall illumine my life.'

ON THE MORNING of 10 October 1839 Queen Victoria awoke in her bedroom at Windsor with a headache and feeling rather sick: the pork she had had for dinner the night before had disagreed with her. It was not a propitious beginning to her cousins' visit; nor was the news that some lunatic had smashed a few of the Castle's windows. She went out to get some fresh air, and was walking along a path when a page ran towards her with a letter. It was from King Leopold who told her that her cousins would arrive that evening.

Accordingly, at half past seven, she was standing at the top of the stairs to greet them. She watched them as they climbed up towards her, pale after a tempestuous Channel crossing in a heaving paddle-steamer, and she was immediately overcome by a *coup de foudre* – Prince Albert was 'beautiful'. His blue eyes were 'beautiful'; his figure, too, was 'beautiful', no longer rather too fat as she had thought when they first met but broad in the shoulders with a 'fine waist'. All in all, he was so 'excessively handsome', his moustache was so 'delicate', his mouth so 'pretty', his nose 'exquisite'. He really was 'very fascinating'. He set her heart 'quite going'. Everything about him seemed perfect. He was just the right height, attractively tall as she liked men to be but not so tall as to emphasize her own diminutive size.[1]

On further acquaintance he proved to be so 'aimiable' and 'unaffected', so clever, so graceful in his movements, so elegantly dressed. His voice was charming, his manner delightful, his red leather topboots so unusually smart, his beautiful greyhound, Eos, so splendidly groomed, obedient and picturesque.

Unfortunately his trunks had not yet arrived and so he and Prince Ernest felt unable to appear at dinner, which Lord Melbourne thought they ought to have done. They did appear after dinner, however, and the Queen was further entranced by Prince Albert who danced 'so beautifully', holding himself so well with that 'beautiful figure of his'. Two days later she learned, as she listened to him playing Haydn symphonies with Ernest in a nearby room, that he played the piano as well as he danced. He did not enjoy dancing as much as she did, however. He seemed happier on Sunday evening as he looked through an album of drawings by Domenichino while the Queen sat by his side.

She recited his praises to Lord Melbourne who listened patiently and kindly, endeavouring to suppress the sadness and anxiety he felt at the prospect of the changes in his life which now seemed inevitable. Yes, Prince Albert was 'certainly a very fine young man, very good looking'; and handsome looks, as he well knew, were important to her. She had readily admitted when he had teased her about her admiration for Prince Alexander Mensdorff-Pouilly that she was 'not insensible to beauty'. She had made a good choice in Prince Albert, Lord Melbourne assured her. His 'strong Protestant feelings' would be an additional asset, provided he was not bigoted. Oh, no, the Queen replied, he was certainly not bigoted. Well then, Melbourne assured her in so 'fatherly' a way, with tears yet again in his eyes, 'I think it is a very good thing and you'll be much more comfortable; for a woman cannot stand alone for long, in whatever situation she is.'[2] He suggested only that she should take a week before she definitely made up her mind. But she did not need a week; she could not wait so long:

'I said to Lord Melbourne, that I had made up my mind (about marrying dearest Albert) – "You have" he said; "well then, about the time?" Not for a year, I thought; which he said was too long . . . Then I asked if I hadn't better tell Albert of my decision soon, in which Lord Melbourne agreed. How? I asked, for that in general such things were done the other way – which made Lord Melbourne laugh.'[3]

On the afternoon of 15 October, five days after Prince Albert's arrival, having accepted the fact, as she told her Aunt Gloucester, that Albert 'would never have presumed to take such a liberty to propose to the

Queen of England', she sent him a note asking him to come to her in the Blue Closet. He arrived nervous and trembling. She too was trembling, although the squeeze he had given her hand when they had parted the night before gave her hope that all would be well. At first they talked self-consciously in German of other things, though both knew what was to be said. At length, she said in a rush that it would make her *'too happy'* if he would consent to what she wished. The quickly spoken words ended their nervousness. Before she had finished uttering them he took her hands in his, covering them with kisses and murmuring in German that he would be very happy to spend his life with her. 'He was so kind, so affectionate,' the Queen wrote when she was alone again. 'Oh! to *feel* I was, and am, loved by *such* an Angel ... He is *perfection*; perfection in every way – in beauty – in everything ... Oh! How I adore and love him ... We embraced each other over and over again.'[4]

That evening, after Prince Albert had appeared at dinner in the Windsor uniform of blue and red designed for the Royal household by George III, the Queen was handed a letter before she went to bed addressed to 'Dearest greatly beloved Victoria'. 'How is it,' she read, 'that I have deserved so much love, so much affection? ... I believe that Heaven has sent me an angel whose brightness shall illumine my life ... In body and soul ever your slave, your loyal ALBERT.' After reading it the Queen burst into tears.[5]

It was clear to all at Court that she was blissfully happy. Her passion was plain to see: her eyes followed Prince Albert round the room as they had once followed Lord Melbourne. Victoria and Albert sang duets together; they walked and rode together; they gave each other rings and locks of hair; he sat beside her while she signed papers, blotting the ink; he accompanied her when she reviewed a parade of soldiers in Hyde Park, wearing, she noted with admiration, a pair of white cashmere breeches with *'nothing under them'*.[6] They gazed at each other longingly, obviously dying for the moment when they could be alone together, to hold each other and to kiss; and, when they were alone, tears of happiness and pleasure poured down her cheeks as he took her face in his hands, whispering endearments, kissing her mouth 'repeatedly'.

'I love him more than I can say,' she wrote to King Leopold that same day. 'These last few days have passed like a dream to me, and I am so much bewildered by it all that I hardly know how to write. But I *do* feel *very, very* happy.'[7] When they had to say goodbye on his return to Coburg she 'cried much, wretched, yet happy to think we should meet again so soon! Oh! how I love him, how intensely how devotedly, how ardently!'[8]

Prince Albert's affection for her was already deep and unfeigned. 'I need not tell you that since we left all my thoughts have been with you and your image fills my whole soul,' he wrote to her from Calais. 'Those days flew by so quickly, but our separation will fly equally so.'[9]

'Dearly beloved Victoria, I long to talk to you,' he told her a fortnight later, 'otherwise the separation is too painful. Your dear picture stands on my table and I can hardly take my eyes off it.'[10] 'Victoria is so good and kind to me,' he told Baron Stockmar, 'that I am often at a loss to believe that such affection should be shown to me. I know the great interest you take in my happiness, and therefore pour out my heart to you.' 'Love of you fills my heart,' he wrote to the Queen herself. 'Where love is there is happiness ... Even in my dreams I never imagined I should find so much love on earth.' He wished to walk through the whole of life, 'with its joys and its storms' with Victoria at his side.

Prince Albert's letters to his friend, Prince von Löwenstein, and to his tutor and family in Germany, however, reveal that he did not view the future, and its expected 'storms', without concern. He spoke of the 'firm resolution' and 'courage' he would need in the position he would have to occupy, of the tribulations that marriage to the Queen of England would be bound to bring, of his 'dread of being unequal' to his position. He ended a letter to his grandmother: 'May God be my helper.' His future lot was 'high and brilliant but also plentifully strewn with thorns'.[11] To his stepmother he wrote that Victoria was 'good and amiable'; and he was sure that heaven had not given him into evil hands; but the skies above him would 'not always be blue and unclouded'. Life, wherever one was, had its storms. It was consoling to contemplate the future opportunity for 'promoting the good of so many'. He would be untiring in his efforts on behalf of the country to which he was to belong; but he would never cease to be 'a true German, a true Coburg and Gotha man'. Soon after his return to Coburg, he had a foretaste of the difficulties that lay ahead.

LEFT Princess Victoria aged two with her mother, the Duchess of Kent. A portrait by Sir William Beechey.

BELOW The four-year-old Princess Victoria. A portrait by Stephen Poyntz Denning.

Princess Victoria with her beloved spaniel, 'Dash'. A portrait by Sir George Hayter.

RIGHT Queen Victoria
aged twenty. A portrait
by Sir Edwin Landseer.

BELOW The Duchess of
Kent's devious friend,
John Conroy, painted by
Alfred Tidey in 1836.

BELOW RIGHT One of
the only two water-
colours by Queen
Victoria of Prince
Albert's 'beautiful face'.

Prince Albert. A portrait by the prolific miniature-painter, Sir William Charles Ross.
OPPOSITE Queen Victoria portrayed in her wedding dress by Franz Xaver Winterhalter.

Windsor Castle in Modern Times: Queen Victoria, Prince Albert and Victoria, Princess Royal by Sir Edwin Landseer. A scene overlooking the East Terrace at Windsor Castle showing Prince Albert stroking his favourite greyhound, Eos, and wearing the scarlet boots which the Queen thought so 'very picturesque'.

LEFT Queen Victoria aged twenty-four in 1843, by Franz Xaver Winterhalter. This was Prince Albert's favourite portrait of her.

ABOVE *La Filatrice Addormentata* (The Sleeping Spinner) by Julius Froschel – a birthday present given by Prince Albert to the Queen on her thirtieth birthday in 1849.

Florinda by Winterhalter, a riot of naked flesh, described by the Queen as 'splendid and delightful'. It was a present from her to Prince Albert, and hung opposite their desks in her sitting room at Osborne

15

※※※※※※※※※※※※

THE BRIDEGROOM

'You Tories shall be punished. Revenge! Revenge!'

ON 23 NOVEMBER 1839 the Queen made her Declaration of Marriage at Buckingham Palace before an assembly of Privy Councillors. She appeared before them in a simple dress and wearing a miniature of Prince Albert in a bracelet on her wrist. It was 'rather an awful moment', she confessed; and her hands were so fluttering that she nearly dropped the paper on which the Declaration was written.[1] But, as at her first Council meeting, her voice was clear and true. J. W. Croker, the politician and essayist, thought her 'as interesting and handsome as any young lady' he had ever seen.[2]

News of the engagement had already reached Coburg and Gotha where it had been received with great pleasure. In Coburg the sounds of gunfire and pistol shots in the streets could be heard throughout the night; and in Gotha cannon thundered as the Prince, standing in the throne room before the ladies and gentlemen of the Court, was invested with the Order of the Garter by his father, the Duke, and Queen Victoria's half-brother, Prince Charles of Leiningen, both Knights of the Garter themselves. At the subsequent banquet the band of the Coldstream Guards, which had sailed from England for the occasion, played 'God Save the Queen'.[3]

In England, where the Prince landed at Dover on 7 February after a stormy, five-hour crossing, crowds gathered to cheer him on his way through Kent in the pouring rain, escorted by the Earl of Cardigan's 11th Light Dragoons, henceforth known as the 11th Prince Albert's Own

Hussars[4]. At Canterbury, where he and his brother stayed the night and attended a service in the Cathedral, the city was illuminated in his honour.[5]

The enthusiasm of the populace was not, however, universally shared at Queen Victoria's Court or in Tory aristocratic circles, though it was generally conceded that, 'if her political partisanship were to be limited, she undoubtedly needed a husband's guidance and support'. Yet this husband was only twenty, the same age as herself; and, so *The Times* observed, 'one might without being unreasonable, express a wish that the Consort selected for a Princess so educated and hitherto so unfairly guided as Queen Victoria – should have been a person of riper years, and likely to form more sound and circumspect opinions.'[6]

The Queen's uncles were scornful of the match; so were many of the prosperous middle classes. Newspapers reported it with lukewarm approbation or with unconcealed disapproval. Versifiers proposed that Prince Albert had come to England to marry the Queen for money:

> He comes the bridegroom of Victoria's choice
> The nominee of Lehzen's Voice;
> He comes to take 'for better or for worse'
> England's fat Queen and England's fatter purse.[7]

The question of money had, in fact, already arisen as one of the first problems to blight the Queen's happiness. Lord Melbourne had assured her that there would be no difficulty in getting Parliament to agree that the Prince should receive the same provision of £50,000 a year which Prince Leopold had received upon his marriage to Princess Charlotte, and which Prince George of Denmark had had when he married the future Queen Anne in 1683. But there *was* difficulty. The Radical, Joseph Hume, protested that, having regard to the financial state of the country and the distress of the poor, £21,000 would be quite sufficient. The House of Commons did not think so; but when a Tory Member proposed that £30,000 a year would be a fair compromise this amendment was accepted by a large majority.[8]

The Queen was furious: she said she hated the Tories more than ever. She had long decided that, like insects and turtle soup, they were among the things she most disliked in all the world. The Prince, who greatly regretted that he would not now be able to do so much as he had hoped for poor scholars and artists, was also much put out. 'I am surprised that you have said no word of sympathy to me about the vote of the 28th,' he wrote to the Queen in a letter far sharper than any he had yet sent her, 'for those nice Tories have cut off half my income . . . and it makes my position not a very pleasant one. It is hardly conceivable that anyone could behave as meanly and disgracefully as they have to you and me. It cannot do them much good for it is hardly possible to maintain any respect for them any longer. Everyone, even here [Coburg], is indignant about it.'[9]

The Queen became even angrier with the Tories, and with their standard bearer the Duke of Wellington, when it was suggested that Prince Albert, like many of his Coburg relations, had 'papistical leanings'. In Victoria's Declaration of Marriage to the Privy Council, the Prince had not been specifically described as a Protestant prince and therefore able to receive Holy Communion in the form prescribed by the Church of England, since Lord Melbourne had thought it best not to mention religion at all. He did not want to upset the Irish Catholics, who supported him in the House of Commons, and he could not employ the usual formula about 'marrying into a Protestant family' because a large number of Coburgs were either Roman Catholics themselves, or, like King Leopold, had married into Catholic families.

The Duke of Wellington – who, while not really caring a fig about it, according to his private secretary, had expressed the opinion that the annual income of £30,000 was quite sufficient for Prince Albert – now rose in the House of Lords to declare that the people ought to know something about the Queen's future husband other than his name, that they should be given the satisfaction of knowing that he 'was a Protestant – thus showing all the public that this is still a Protestant State'.[10]

'Do what one will,' the Queen protested to King Leopold, 'nothing will please these most religious, most hypocritical Tories whom I dislike (I use a very soft word), most heartily.' It was absurd of them to make this fuss, seeing that, by the law of the land, she could not 'marry a Papist' anyway. Sir Robert Peel was 'a low hypocrite', a 'nasty wretch'; as for that 'wicked old foolish' Duke of Wellington, she would never speak to him or look at him again; she would certainly not ask him to her wedding. 'It is MY marriage,' she protested when Melbourne endeavoured to dissuade her from slighting the Duke in this way, 'and I will only have those who can sympathize with me.' Nor would she send a message to Apsley House when it was reported that the Duke was ill. Charles Greville called there and found 'his people indignant that, while all the Royal Family have been sending continually to enquire after him, and all London has been at his door, the Queen alone has never taken the slightest notice of him'. Greville immediately sent Melbourne a note 'representing the injury it was to *herself* not to do so'. Melbourne asked Greville to come to see him without delay and told him when he arrived that the Queen was 'very resentful, but that people pressed her too much, did not give her time'. To this Greville replied that it 'really was lamentable' that she did the things she did, that she would get into a great scrape. The people of England would not endure that she should treat the Duke of Wellington with disrespect. Greville had no scruple in saying so to Melbourne since he knew that he was doing his utmost to keep her straight. 'By God!' Melbourne said, 'I am moving noon and night at it.'

He wondered, though, if it were not too late now for the Queen to send a message to Apsley House. 'Better late than not at all,' Greville advised him; so Melbourne sat down and wrote to the Queen. 'I suppose she will send now?' Greville asked. 'Oh, yes,' Melbourne replied. 'She will send now.'[11]

Then there was trouble over the precedence to be granted the Prince. King Leopold, who regretted not having accepted the offer of an English peerage as Duke of Kendal himself, had suggested that Prince Albert should be created an English peer so that his 'foreignership should disappear as much as possible'. But the Queen dissented. 'The whole Cabinet agrees with me in being strongly of the opinion that Albert should *not* be a Peer,' she replied to her uncle. 'I see everything against it and nothing for it.' She told the Prince why:

> The English are very jealous of any foreign interference in the Government of the country and have already in some of the papers ... expressed a hope that you would not interfere: – now, tho' I know you never would, still, if you were a peer they would all say the Prince meant to play a political part – I am sure you will understand.[12]

The Prince himself had no wish to be an English peer: 'It would be almost a step downwards, for as a Duke of Saxony, I feel myself much higher than as Duke of Kent or York.' He was quite content to have no title other than his own. 'As regards my peerage and the fears of my playing a political part, dear, beloved Victoria,' he wrote, 'I have only one anxious wish and one prayer: do not allow it to become a matter of worry to you.'[13]

Though Albert had expressed his own opposition to receiving a peerage, the Queen was strongly of the view that he should have precedence over all other peers in the country, including the royal dukes. If she had her way he would be King Consort.

Once again the Duke of Wellington, now recovered from his illness, opposed her: the precedence of the Royal Family, he pointed out, was fixed by Act of Parliament. It was well known that he held no brief for the royal dukes; but it would be unfair to ask them to support a change in the law to interfere with their rights. When Charles Greville asked the Duke what he thought should be done about the Prince's precedence, he answered emphatically, 'Oh, give him the same which Prince George of Denmark had: place him next before the Archbishop of Canterbury.' 'That will by no means satisfy her,' Greville objected. At this the Duke 'tossed his head and with an expression of extreme contempt said, "Satisfy her! What does that signify?" '[14]

Upon hearing Tory objections to her granting the Prince the precedence she had in mind for him, the Queen was quite as cross as Melbourne had feared she would be. She 'raged away', perfectly 'frantic', in her own words, railing at her uncles and the vile, confounded, 'infernal Tories' responsible for this 'outrageous insult'. They were 'wretches', 'scoundrels' 'capable of every villainy [and] personal spite'. 'Poor dear Albert, how cruelly they are ill-using that dearest Angel! You Tories shall be punished. Revenge! Revenge!'[15]

In her anger she turned upon Melbourne himself. She was forced to concede that the state of feeling in the country, the unemployment and the unrest – the plight of the poor which he usually did not care to think or talk about – made the reduction of Albert's allowance at least tolerable. But there could be no excuse for this cruel slight over the matter of precedence. Lord Melbourne really ought to have foreseen the trouble that there might be. He should not have led her 'to expect no difficulties'.

Melbourne unwisely commented that there would not have been such difficulties were Prince Albert not a foreigner: foreigners always caused trouble, particularly from Coburg. They had been through all this before, the Queen crossly rejoined. She could never have married one of her own subjects, and she was not marrying Albert because he was a Coburg but because she loved him and he was worthy of her love. Later Melbourne tactlessly stumbled into trouble again when the Queen remarked that one of the things she most loved about Albert was his indifference to the charms of all women other than herself. 'No,' said Melbourne carelessly, 'that sort of thing is apt to come later.' It was 'an odd remark to make to any woman on the eve of marriage, let alone the *Queen*', Lord Clarendon observed when Melbourne told him of this gaffe, chuckling 'over it amazingly'. Certainly the Queen took it very ill. 'I shan't,' she said, 'forgive you for that.'

She did, of course, and she came close to forgiving the Duke of Wellington when, having read a pamphlet prepared by Charles Greville, he changed his mind about Prince Albert's precedence. The Queen, he now declared, much to the annoyance of the Duke of Cambridge, had 'a perfect right to give her husband whatever precedence she pleased'. So, the Lord Chancellor and the Attorney General concurring, Letters Patent granting the Prince the precedence she had wanted to give him were issued by the Queen. From then on the Queen's attitude to the Duke of Wellington softened. He had, after all, supported her when she had expressed a wish to be accompanied only by her mother and one of her ladies in the state coach on her way to St James's Palace to be proclaimed. Her Master of the Horse, Lord Albemarle, insisted that he had a right to ride with her as he had done with William IV. 'The point was submitted to the Duke of Wellington as a kind of universal referee in matters of precedence and usage. His judgement was delightfully unflattering to the outraged magnate – "The Queen can make you go inside the coach or outside the coach or run behind it like a tinker's dog." '[16] The Queen decided to ask the Duke to her wedding after all. She drew the line, however, at inviting him to the wedding breakfast. She had not entirely forgiven him yet. 'Our Gracious,' Wellington concluded, was still 'very much out of Temper.'[17]

A problem which concerned the Prince far more than his title or his precedence was the composition of his Household which he hoped would be of perfect respectability, unlike the Queen's which comprised a number of men whose morals were highly questionable, including the Lord Chamberlain, the Marquess of Conyngham, whose mistress was employed as

Housekeeper at Buckingham Palace, and the Earl of Uxbridge, the Lord Steward, whose mistress had also been found a position in Her Majesty's household. Indeed, there were so many Pagets living at Court, in addition to Lord Alfred Paget, the Clerk-Marshal, that it was known as 'the Paget Club House'.

Prince Albert had assumed that he would be allowed to choose his gentlemen himself and that some of them might be German and all, of course, 'well educated and of high character'. Believing as he did that the Crown should not display a preference for any political party, that King William IV had been much misguided to favour the Tories and Queen Victoria was equally in error to demonstrate her support of the Whigs, he had hoped that his own household would indicate his impartiality. 'It is very necessary,' he wrote, 'that they should be chosen from both sides – the same number of Whigs as of Tories.'[18]

The Queen, encouraged by Melbourne, did not agree. 'As to your wish about your Gentlemen, my dear Albert,' she told him severely, 'I must tell you quite honestly that it will not do. You may entirely rely upon me that the people who will be round you will be absolutely pleasant people of high standing and good character ... You may rely upon my care that you shall have proper people and not idle and not too young and Lord Melbourne has already mentioned several to me who would be very suitable.'[19]

It was useless for the Prince to protest. 'I am very sorry,' he had replied, 'that you have not been able to grant my first request, the one about the Gentlemen, for I know it was not an unfair one ... Think of my position, dear Victoria, I am leaving my home with all its associations, all my bosom friends, and going to a country in which everything is new and strange to me ... Except yourself I have no one to confide in. And it is not even to be conceded to me that the two or three persons who are to have the charge of my private affairs should be persons who already command my confidence.'[20]

The Queen was not softened by this appeal, although Lord Melbourne thought that it might now be better to give way, and King Leopold wrote what the Queen described as 'an ungracious letter' urging the Prime Minister to persuade the Queen to take a 'correct view'. But, so she wrote to Prince Albert, that was just like Uncle Leopold: he was 'given to believe that he must rule the roast [sic] everywhere ... I am distressed to be obliged to tell you what I fear you do not like but it is necessary, my dearest most excellent Albert . . . I only do it as I know it is for your own good.' It was conceded that a German whom the Prince did know, Herr Schenk, should be appointed to a minor post which did not entitle him to a place at the equerries' table; but the appointment of Private Secretary, the principal post in his Household, was to be filled by George Anson who was not only a confirmed Whig and Secretary to the Whig Prime Minister, Lord Melbourne, but whose uncle, Sir George Anson (chosen for an appointment as Groom of the Bedchamber), was also a Whig. In vain the Prince protested to his 'dearest love' that taking the Secretary of the Prime Minister as his own Private Secretary would surely from the beginning make him 'a partisan in the eyes of many'. The Queen, however, was 'very much in favour' of the appointment: Mr Anson was 'an excellent young man, very modest, very honest, very steady, very well informed' and would be 'of much use' to him. Further objection was clearly useless: advised to do so by Baron Stockmar, the Prince gave way, on condition that Anson resigned as the Prime Minister's Secretary before he became his own.[21]

The Prince submitted with a good grace, much to the relief of the Queen who had been warned by King Leopold that Prince Albert had seemed 'pretty full of grievances' when he had passed through Brussels on his way back to England. She had, in fact, been so worried that he would be resentful that she was feeling ill when he returned. But all was well. 'Seeing his *dear dear* face again' put her 'at rest about everything'.[22]

Almost at once she spoke to him about Anson's appointment and the 'little misunderstandings' that had arisen because of it. He accepted the fait accompli and was, so the Queen said, 'so dear and *ehrlich* [honest] and open about it'. She 'embraced him again and again'.[23] Her recent peevishness evaporated in her love for him, in her pleasure at his having given way to her demands and in excited anticipation of their marriage. Yet she felt it impossible to agree with his suggestion that her bridesmaids must be selected only from those young ladies whose mothers were of unblemished character. Lord Melbourne had been aghast at this suggestion. As he told Greville, the Prince was 'a great stickler for morality' and 'extremely strait-laced'. He did not seem to appreciate that the lower orders should, of course, be judged by moral standards but those of high birth must be deemed above such considerations. The Queen at first objected that there surely could not be one set of moral standards for the humble poor and another for the aristocratic rich; but she acknowledged the impossibility of submitting to Prince Albert's severe proscriptions; and among the twelve tall, plain bridesmaids there were several whose mothers could not have passed his test.

'I always think one ought always to be indulgent towards other people,' the Queen explained to Prince Albert, 'as I always think, if we had not been well brought up and well taken care of, we might also have gone astray.'[24]

The evening before the wedding the Queen and Prince Albert went through the marriage service together and, mindful of the painful embarrassment at the coronation, tried on the ring. The Prince, who had endured yet another fearful Channel crossing, seemed tired and rather nervous, still suffering from the effects of severe seasickness which had left his face, so he said, more the colour of a wax candle than that of a human visage. But the Queen was in high spirits and serenely happy. She went to bed excitedly conscious that it would be, as she wrote in her journal, the last time she would sleep alone. She slept peacefully, quite untroubled by the agitation she had noticed in her dear bridegroom's manner, worried only by the thought that she might have a lot of children.

16

✸✸✸✸✸✸✸✸✸✸✸

HONEYMOON

'I am only the husband, and not the master of the house.'

THE QUEEN AWOKE on Monday, 10 February 1840 to a blustery morning with torrents of rain splashing against her bedroom windows; but the clouds soon cleared and, as was so often to happen on important days in her life, the sun came out for an afternoon of what was to become known as 'Queen's weather'. After breakfast – in defiance of the traditional belief (in her opinion a 'foolish nonsense') that it was unlucky to do so – she went to see the bridegroom to whom she had already written a note: 'Dearest, How are you today and have you slept well? I have rested very well, and feel very comfortable . . . What weather! I believe, however, the rain will cease. Send one word when you, my most dearly loved bridegroom, will be ready. Thy ever faithful, Victoria R.'[1] Then, with a wreath of orange flower blossoms on her head, wearing a white satin dress and a sapphire brooch set with diamonds, a present from the Prince, and accompanied by her mother and the Duchess of Sutherland, she was driven to the Chapel Royal, St James's, where the marriage was to be celebrated, much to the annoyance of the Queen who thought it a 'shocking locale'. She would have had a private ceremony had not Melbourne spoken strongly against it, for she had, so she said, 'a horror' of being married before a large congregation. She would have far preferred a simple ceremony in a room at Buckingham Palace, a small room which would afford her an excellent excuse not to ask people she did not want.

The Duke of Sussex, wearing the black skullcap he so often affected, and close to the tears he was to shed throughout the ceremony, gave her away, quite ready as always, so it was said of him, to give away what did not belong to him.[2] He led her to the altar where Prince Albert, looking pale in the uniform of a British field-marshal, and decorated with the Order of the Garter, stood waiting for her. Albert's nervousness, so it was supposed, was increased by the loud whispers of Queen Adelaide and of his aunt, the Duchess of Kent, who was plainly annoyed by the fact that once again she had been given a place that did not accord with what she conceived to be her precedence.

The Queen's progress up the aisle was much impeded by the brides-maids who, since her train was far too short to allow them all to grasp it while walking normally, had to trip forward as though walking on ice in order not to tread on each other's ankles.[3] But the Queen 'only felt so happy'. She was pale and rather nervous – the congregation could see the orange flower blossoms quivering on her head. But she made her responses in confident tones, and remained perfectly patient when the Duke of Norfolk, insisting that as Earl Marshal it was his privilege and duty to sign the register first, could not find his spectacles in order to do so and kept all the others waiting while he went through one pocket after another in a laborious attempt to locate them.

Unlike her coronation, the marriage service passed off without too many untoward incidents, although the Queen's uncle, the Duke of Cam-bridge was – by contrast with the 'disconsolate and distressed' Duchess of Kent – 'decidedly gay, making very audible remarks from time to time'; while the bridegroom himself was 'certainly a good deal perplexed and agitated in delivering his responses'.[4]

The bride, however, had behaved 'with much grace and propriety', according to Charles Greville, 'not without emotion, though sufficiently subdued'. She had been seen to tremble as she entered the Chapel and as the congregation applauded her as she stood before the altar. But her voice had been clear and confident and her 'eye bright and calm'. As she left the Chapel it was noticed that she paused to kiss her aunt, Queen Adelaide; but that she merely shook hands with her mother.[5]

It was also remarked that of the three hundred or so people in the Chapel, very, very few were Tories. Indeed, Charles Greville said that, apart from the Duke of Wellington and Lord Liverpool, there were only three Tories there, Lord Willoughby de Eresby and the Marquess of Cholmondeley, whose presence was required as joint Lord Great

Chamberlains, and Lord Ashley, who was there because he was married to Lord Melbourne's niece, Lady Emily Cowper. The Queen 'had been as wilful, obstinate and wrong-headed as usual about the invitations,' Greville said, 'and some of her foolish and mischievous Courtiers were boasting' about the pointedly small number of Tories invited. 'The D. and Dss of Northumberland [her former governess] were not there and She did worse than not invite them . . . for the invitation was sent so late that they could not have got it in time to come; and the truth is that it was intended not to invite them at all. Nothing could be more improper and foolish than to make this a mere Whig party, and if She *was* to make a selection, She might with great propriety have invited all those, such as the D. of Rutland and [the Marquess of] Exeter, who had formerly received and entertained her at their houses. But She would not, and stuffed in a parcel of Whigs taken apparently at haphazard, in preference to any of these.'[6]

The Queen returned with her husband for the wedding breakfast to Buckingham Palace where, awaiting them, was an enormous wedding cake, three yards in circumference, which needed four men to carry in.[7] Lord Melbourne came up to congratulate her. 'Nothing could have gone off better,' he assured her. She pressed his hand and 'he said, "God bless you, Ma'am" most kindly, and with such a kind look'.[8] He, too, had done well, carrying the Sword of State with far more ease and confidence than he had shown at the coronation and wearing a magnificent dress coat which, to the Queen's delighted amusement, he had claimed would be the 'Thing most observed' at the marriage ceremony.

During the half hour which the Queen and Prince spent alone together before the wedding breakfast, the Queen gave her husband a wedding ring; and he said there must never be a secret which they did not share. After the breakfast, so the Queen recorded, 'Dearest Albert came up and fetched me downstairs, where we took leave of Mamma and drove off at near 4, Albert and I alone which was SO *delightful*'.[9]

> Upon leaving the Palace for Windsor She and her young Husband were pretty well received [Charles Greville reported], but they went off in a very poor and shabby style. Instead of the new chariot in which most married people are accustomed to dash along, they were in one of the old travelling coaches, the postillions in undressed liveries, and with a small escort, three other coaches

with post horses following. The crowds on the roads were so great that they did not reach the Castle till 8 o'clock.[10]

'Our reception was most enthusiastic and hearty and gratifying in every way,' the Queen confirmed. 'There was an immense crowd of people outside the Palace, and which I must say never ceased until we reached Windsor Castle ... the people quite deafening us; and horsemen and gigs etc. driving along with us. We came through Eton where all the Boys ... cheered and shouted. Really I was quite touched.'[11]

On arrival at Windsor she inspected the apartments which had been prepared for them, changed her dress, then went into the Prince's room where she found him playing the piano and wearing the Windsor uniform with which, as a clothes-conscious man, he had replaced the travelling outfit he had worn in the coach, this in turn having replaced the field-marshal's uniform. He stood up, put his arms around her and was 'so dear and kind'.

> We had our dinner in our sitting room [the Queen recorded], but I had such a sick headache that I could eat nothing, and was obliged to lie down in the middle blue room for the remainder of the evening on the sofa; but ill or not, I NEVER, NEVER spent such an evening!! MY DEAREST DEAREST DEAR Albert sat on a footstool by my side, and his excessive love and affection gave me feelings of heavenly love and happiness I never could have *hoped* to have felt before! He clasped me in his arms, and we kissed each other again and again! His beauty, his sweetness and gentleness – really how can I ever be thankful enough to have such a *Husband*! ... to be called by names of tenderness, I have never yet heard used to me before – was bliss beyond belief! Oh! this was the happiest day of my life! – May God help me to do my duty as I ought and be worthy of such blessings![12]

It was also bliss beyond belief to wake up next morning, after having, so she said, not slept very much, and to find that 'beautiful angelic face' by her side. 'It was,' she wrote, 'more than I can express.' 'He does look so beautiful in his shirt only, with his beautiful throat seen.'[13] It was bliss also to have him with her at breakfast and to gaze again upon his naked throat, exposed above the black velvet collar of his jacket, to walk with him arm in arm upon the Terrace where her grandfather King George III had paraded with Queen Charlotte and their several daughters, to write letters in her sitting room while he, exhausted and still suffering from the effects of his dreadful seasickness, dozed on a sofa, then rested his 'darling head' on her shoulder. It was delightful, too, to watch him shave in the morning and to have him put on her stockings for her.[14]

On that first day of her honeymoon she wrote to Lord Melbourne to assure him how 'very very happy' she was; she 'never thought she could be so loved' as she was by 'dearest, dear Albert'. And she told King Leopold that she was 'the happiest, happiest Being that ever existed'. Really she did 'not think it possible for anyone in the world to be happier'. Her husband was 'an Angel'.[15]

The Prince grew more and more tired as the days of the short honeymoon progressed; for, as Melbourne commented, it was quite 'a whirl'. The first evening was the only one they spent alone. On Tuesday there was a dinner party for ten. The Queen thought it a 'very delightful, merry, nice little party'; but the Prince was obviously still exhausted. The next evening she 'collected an immense party . . . for a dance which she chose to have at the Castle'. This is 'a proceeding quite unparalleled,' Charles Greville wrote in high disapproval. 'Even her best friends are shocked at her not conforming more than she is doing to English customs, and not continuing for a short time in that retirement, which modesty and native delicacy generally prescribe and which few Englishwomen would be content to avoid. But She does not think any such constraint necessary . . . Lady Palmerston said to me last night that she was much vexed that She had nobody about her who could venture to tell her that this [ball on Wednesday] was not becoming and would appear indelicate. But She has nobody who dares tell her, or She will not endure to hear such truths. [Lord] Normanby [the Home Secretary] said to me the same thing. It is a pity Melbourne did not tell her . . . He probably did not think about it.'[16]

Prince Albert had, in fact, already suggested before their marriage that 'it might perhaps be a good and delicate action not to depart' from what he had been told was the 'usual custom in England for married people to stay up to four to six weeks from the town and society'. Since this was so, he ventured diffidently, might they not retire from the public eye for 'at least a fortnight – or a week'?

The Queen had replied to this suggestion as sharply as she had done when the Prince had proposed being allowed to choose his own household:

My dear Albert, [she had written] you have not at all understood the matter. *You forget, my dearest Love, that I am the Sovereign, and that business can stop and wait for nothing. Parliament is sitting and something occurs almost every day for which I am required and it is quite impossible for me to be absent from London; therefore two or three days is already a long time to be absent. . . I must come out after the second day. . . I cannot keep alone. This is also my wish in every way.*[17]

While refusing to prolong the honeymoon, the Queen was determined to make the most of the three days she had allocated to it. On the Wednesday evening she stayed up dancing until after midnight when she went upstairs to find her husband fast asleep. She woke him up and they went to bed. On Thursday there was another dance at which she bounced around the floor with Prince Albert in a lively, graceful galop.

Late nights did not preclude early rising. On the morning after their first night together it was 'much remarked', so Greville said, 'that she and P A were up very early walking about [in fact, they were up at half past eight, and did not go out until the early afternoon] which is very contrary to her former habits. Strange that a wedding night should be so short; and I told Lady Palmerston that this was not the way to provide us with a Prince of Wales.'[18]

The days, even so, the '*very, very* happy days', were too short for the Queen. Prince Albert's 'love and gentleness' were 'beyond everything': to 'kiss that dear soft cheek, to press [her] lips to his' was 'heavenly bliss'. On her return to London, Melbourne commented that she seemed very well. 'Very,' she said, 'and in very high spirits.' She 'never could have thought there was so much happiness in store.'[19]

She delighted in walking with her husband in the grounds of Buckingham Palace when he would tell her the names of the trees and flowers. She obviously loved it when he would display his affection for her as he came into her room, as Lady Lyttelton, a Lady of the Bedchamber, saw him do one day, his cheeks flushed after riding in the Park, taking her hand in his. She was so pleased that he always got up from the dinner table as soon as he could, requiring the other gentlemen to follow him presently, having finished their wine. He then joined her in the drawing room where he would play and sing duets with her, or occupy himself with double chess, leaving her to talk to Lord Melbourne. Sometimes they would all play games together. One evening the whole court 'took to playing spillikins and puzzling with alphabets'; another evening they 'learnt a new round game', and they 'all grew quite noisy over it' – it was called *main jaune* and they liked it better than *mouche*. When they played *vingt-et-un* or Pope Joan the stakes were never high, and it was rather tiresome always to have to remember to carry new coins so that court etiquette should not be broken by passing used money to the Sovereign, but the maids-of-honour, 'all wearing their badge of the Queen's picture surrounded with brilliants on a red bow, looked so cheerful when they were gambling and a haul of even threepence excited them.'[20]

Once they played a letter game in which Melbourne was given the word 'pleasure' to guess. The Queen gave the Prime Minister a hint: it was a common word, she said. But not, said the Prince, 'a very common *thing*'. Melbourne suggested, 'Is it truth or honesty?' They burst out laughing.[21]

Prince Albert could not fully share his wife's contentment. He confided in Baron Stockmar that he considered her 'naturally a fine character but warped in many respects by wrong upbringing'. She was wilful and thoughtless, and while kind at heart, given to outbursts of temper and moods of sulky pettishness. There could be no doubt that he loved her; but he was deeply concerned not only to be denied her confidence in what he termed the 'trivial matters' of the running of their households, but also by her strong disinclination to allow him to take any part in political business. He was not asked into the room when she was talking to the Prime Minister; nor did she discuss affairs of state with him, changing the subject when he tried to talk to her about political matters. Nor did she allow him to see the state papers which were sent to her by the various government departments, whereas he learnt from his brother that Prince Ferdinand of Saxe-Coburg-Kohary, the husband of Maria da Gloria, Queen of Portugal, was King Consort and as such vetted all her visitors before they were allowed to see her and then to do little more than to kiss her hand. The English, however, so Victoria reminded her husband, were 'very jealous of any foreigner interfering in the government of this country'.[22]

'My impression,' Lord Melbourne told George Anson, 'is that the chief obstacle in Her Majesty's mind is the fear of difference of opinion and she thinks that domestic harmony is more likely to follow from avoiding subjects likely to create difference.'[23] A greater obstacle, no doubt, was her reluctance to share her authority with anyone, even her adored husband.

'The Prince ought in business as in everything to be necessary to the Queen,' King Leopold advised, 'he should be to her a walking dictionary for reference on any point which her own knowledge or education have not enabled her to answer. There should be no concealment from him on any subject.'[24] There was concealment, though; and there was much resentment when Prince Albert presumed to offer his advice. When, for example, a box of official papers arrived labelled tersely, 'sign immediately', he suggested she show her displeasure at receiving such peremptory instructions by not signing for a day or two. She signed at once.[25]

She was, in fact, prepared to limit the Prince's role as partner to what she herself ingenuously called a little 'help with the blotting paper'. He told his friend, Prince William of Löwenstein, 'In my home life I am very happy and contented; but the difficulty in filling my place with the proper dignity is that I am only the husband, and not the master of the house.'[24]

There were other problems, too. He could not share his wife's passion for excitement, merriment and late nights. He preferred the peace of the countryside to the bustle of the town, and he liked to go to bed early. He told his brother that he sometimes wished he were back at Coburg 'in a small house' instead of living the life that his sense of duty had imposed upon him.[27]

When he was feeling tired or particularly frustrated, he became irritable over matters of little importance. Often he was seen to be asleep in the evening, and then the Queen would nudge him to wake him up, as Guizot, the French Ambassador, noticed her do at a concert soon after their marriage: 'Prince Albert slept. She looked at him, half smiling, half vexed. She pushed him with her elbow. He woke up, and nodded approval of the piece of the moment. Then he went to sleep again.'[28] He was often bored in the evenings, constantly disappointed that he was unable to fulfil his ambition to bring scientific and literary people about the Court, to make it a more general reflection of the life of the country.[29]

He was far from being a morose man: he did take pleasure in life, but his pleasures were far more restrained, less hectic than hers. He found it difficult to get used to the food and the climate in England, and a strain to have to speak English most of the time. The ordinary people of the country seemed quite happy to accept him; but the upper classes remained extremely wary of him, while several members of the old Royal Family were still openly antagonistic, the Duke of Cambridge making a ridiculous fuss when his Garter banner in St George's Chapel, Windsor, was moved a few inches to make way for that of the 'young foreign upstart'. The Duchess of Cambridge went so far as to remain seated when the Prince's health was drunk at a dinner.

The quarrel between the Duchess of Cambridge and the Prince became more heated than ever when her son, that 'odious' boy as the Queen had described him, was rumoured to have made Lady Augusta Somerset pregnant. Prince George of Cambridge was a highly flirtatious though rather timid young man and Lady Augusta, eldest daughter of the Duke of Beaufort, a 'very ill-behaved girl, ready for anything that her caprice or passions excite her to do'. So there were some grounds for the rumour, false though it was, and Prince Albert firmly believed it to be true. Both he and the Queen refused to speak to Lady Augusta when she appeared at Court and ordered the ladies there not to do so either. And when solemnly assured that the stories were unfounded, the Prince's reply – that he supposed, therefore, 'they must believe that it was so' – left the Cambridges 'by no means satisfied' and the Beauforts 'boiling with resentment and indignation'.[30]

The Prince was now more unpopular with the aristocracy than ever. His prudery, his obvious cleverness, his enterprise on the hunting field, his graceful accomplishment on the ballroom floor and as a skater on frozen lakes, his vigour as a swimmer, his talents as a musician and singer, all aroused dislike and jealousy rather than admiration. At dinner parties his competence, his conscientiousness, his intelligence and his honesty would alike be grudgingly conceded but then, as Baron Stockmar remarked, someone would be sure to add, 'Look at the cut of his coat, though, and the way he shakes hands' with his elbow held stiffly at his side. Even the way he rode a horse appeared determinedly, even arrogantly, German. With women, it was often observed, he was particularly ill at ease, concealing his shyness in their presence beneath a veneer of stiff formality or avoiding their eyes altogether as though aware of some grave fault of character that would not allow him to recognize their existence. When walking in the park at Windsor or in the gardens at

Buckingham Palace, with his sleek greyhound at his heels, he would pass them by without a word. Later, in the drawing room, he would make it painfully plain that he was totally unmoved by their charms. He had 'never feared temptation with regard to women', he admitted to his secretary, having 'no inclination in that respect': such 'species of vice disgusted him'. The Queen was far from displeased by this obvious 'utter indifference to the attraction of all ladies'; but the ladies themselves naturally found his impassivity disconcerting, not to say demeaning; nor did the maids-of-honour like the manner in which the Prince walked out of the door in front of them and would not allow them to sit down in his presence: once when the pregnant Lady John Russell seemed to be overcome by fatigue the Queen whispered to her to sit down but took the precaution of placing Lady Douro in front of her so that the Prince should not notice this breach of etiquette.[31]

Well aware of his unpopularity among the upper classes and at Court, Prince Albert felt increasingly homesick. And on the return of his father to Coburg after a brief visit to England the Queen found her husband weeping bitterly in the hall. Embarrassed to be found in so unmanly a state, he ran upstairs to his room. She hurried after him, anxious to comfort him; but he was, for the moment, inconsolable: she had never known her father, he reminded her, and her childhood had been a miserable one in comparison with the past with which he had had so suddenly to break.

The Queen was moved by his nostalgia. 'God knows,' she wrote in her diary, 'how great my wish is to make this Beloved being happy and contented.'[32]

17

✖✖✖✖✖✖✖✖✖✖✖✖

ROBERT PEEL

'I cannot understand how anyone can wish for such a thing,
especially at the beginning of a marriage.'

WITHIN A FEW WEEKS of her marriage the Queen discovered herself
to be pregnant; and this event was to mark a profound change in the
Prince's career as Consort. The Queen, however, was dismayed. It was
'the ONLY thing' she dreaded. She was 'furious'. It was 'too dreadful',
she told Prince Leopold. She 'could not be more unhappy', she confessed
to the Dowager Duchess of Saxe-Coburg-Gotha. 'I am really upset about
it and it is spoiling my happiness; I have always hated the idea and I
prayed God night and day to be left free for at least six months . . . I
cannot understand how anyone can wish for such a thing, especially at
the beginning of a marriage.'[1] And if her 'plagues' were to be 'rewarded
only by a nasty girl', she told King Leopold that she would drown it.[2]

Shortly before the birth she was to consult Charles Locock, the obstetrician, who confessed to his friend, Lady Mahon, that he 'felt shy and
embarrassed' but that she 'very soon put him at his ease'.

> She had not the slightest reserve & was always ready to express
> Herself, in respect to her present situation, in the very plainest
> terms possible [Locock confided in Lady Mahon who told her
> friend, Charles Arbuthnot, who, in turn, passed the account on to
> his friend, the Duke of Wellington]. She asked Locock whether she
> would suffer much pain. He replied that some pain was to be
> expected, but that he had no doubt Her Majesty would bear it very
> well. 'Oh yes,' said the Queen, 'I can bear pain as well as other
> People.' . . . Locock left Her Majesty without any very good impres-
> sions of Her; & with the certainty that She will be very ugly &

enormously fat. Her figure now is most extraordinary. She goes without stays or anything that keeps Her shape within bounds; & that she is more like a barrel than anything else.[3]

Dr Locock went on to say that there would be nobody at the delivery except himself, Prince Albert and a maid. Lady Mahon commented that no doubt the Queen would be very relieved at this privacy, 'upon which [Locock] remarked that he verily believed from Her manner as to delicacy, She would not care one single straw if the whole world was present.'

For Prince Albert, the pregnancy was a blessing. First of all it was considered necessary to provide for the contingency of the Queen dying and leaving a baby as heir to the throne. A regency was required; and after some proposals that a council of regency or, at least, a co-regent, should be appointed, Parliament passed a Regency Bill entirely to the Prince's satisfaction and to that of the Duke of Wellington who had gained further favour with the Queen by declaring that the regent 'could and ought to be nobody but the Prince'.[4]

'In the event of Victoria's death and her successor being under eighteen years of age, I am to be Regent – alone – Regent without a Council,' the Prince told his brother with the utmost satisfaction. 'You will understand the importance of this matter and that it gives my position here in the country a fresh significance.'[5]

The next month when Parliament was prorogued he rode with the Queen to the Palace of Westminster and there sat in a chair next to her throne; in September his writing table was moved next to hers, both at Buckingham Palace and Windsor Castle. That month also he was appointed a Privy Councillor. By then he had also been made a Freeman of the City of London and had made his first public speech as President of the Anti-Slavery Society; and, although extremely nervous, he had delivered it very well. Lord Holland reported that it was 'now all the fashion to praise Prince Albert'; while Lord Melbourne remarked to the Queen, commenting upon the readiness with which it had been agreed that Prince Albert should be appointed sole Regent in the event of her death, 'Three months ago they would not have done it for him. It is entirely his own character.'[6]

The Prince complacently reported to Stockmar that he was now 'constantly provided with interesting papers', and to his brother he wrote that he had 'come to be extremely pleased with Victoria during the past few months. She had only twice had the sulks ... Altogether she puts more confidence in me daily.'[7]

A lingering source of trouble, however, was the continued and unwelcome presence of Baroness Lehzen who, now that she was no longer the most important person in the Queen's life, attempted to exert with all the more authority her influence over her. This influence was still profound, for although the Queen loved Lehzen she was also rather frightened of her and was reluctant to stand firm against what her husband took to be her gross importunities and reprehensible delight in gossip. Time and again when the Queen and Prince were alone together, the sharp nose of the Baroness would appear round the door and, with the smell of caraway seeds on her breath, she would summon the Queen away to some business connected with the household, the nature of which was not divulged to the Prince whose dislike of the woman – the 'old hag' as he called her, or, in allusion to the jaundiced appearance of her skin, the 'Yellow Lady' – began to deepen into an almost obsessive hatred. He knew that she had opposed his being appointed Regent in case of the Queen's death; he knew, too, that she had also opposed his being permitted to accompany her when she went to open the new Parliament and to sit beside her while she read the speech from the Throne. She told the Queen that her husband really ought to have no position of real power in the state, to fade into the background with no high official status, as she had done. Yet that hesitancy in his nature, which Stockmar had condemned, induced the Prince not to tackle the problem firmly but, as he himself put it, to 'remain on his guard, and patiently abide the result'. He was also, so Stockmar thought, inhibited by his concern not to provoke the Queen's anger which might bring on symptoms of that distressing, hereditary malady of mental derangement which had afflicted her grandfather, King George III, and, on occasions to a lesser degree, her uncle, King George IV.

So, in the meantime, according to Stockmar, the Queen continued to be 'influenced more than she [was] aware of by the Baroness'.[8]

The Queen's baby, a girl, to be christened Victoria Adelaide Mary Louisa and to be known in the family as 'Pussy', was born at Buckingham Palace, a fortnight before she was expected, on 21 November 1840, a 'dark, dull, windy, rainy day with smoking chimneys', after a labour of twelve hours during which the mother 'suffered severely' but was 'not at all nervous once it began'.[9] The Duchess of Kent and the Prince, holding his wife's hand, were both in the room at the time with the obstetrician, Dr Locock, and a midwife. In the next room, the door to which was left open, were three other doctors; and, in a room beyond that, were various Ministers and dignitaries, including the Prime Minister, the Archbishop of Canterbury, the Bishop of London and the Lord Steward of the Household, Lord Errol, who claimed that he could see the Queen plainly the whole time and hear what she said. The baby was brought into their room and placed, 'stark naked', upon a table for their inspection.

The Queen admitted to being 'sadly disappointed' it was not a boy. Her husband, too, was disappointed; but when Dr Locock had called out, 'Oh Madam it is a princess', the mother had cheerfully replied, 'Never mind, the next will be a Prince.'[10]

She fervently hoped, however, that there would not be too many more babies of either sex; and when King Leopold tactlessly wrote to say that he hoped that the little Princess Victoria would be the first of several children, she responded crossly:

> You cannot *really* wish me to be the Mamma *d'une nombreuse famille* for I think you will see with me the great inconvenience a large family would be to us all, and particularly to the country, independent of the hardship and inconvenience to myself; men never think, at least seldom think what a hard task it is for us women to go through this *very often*.[11]

Throughout her confinement, and during the fortnight in which she was kept in bed after the birth, Prince Albert was 'just like a mother' to her; 'nor could there be a kinder, wiser or more judicious nurse'. 'He was content to sit by her in a darkened room, to read to her, or write for her. No one but himself ever lifted her from her bed to her sofa, and he always helped to wheel her on her bed or sofa into the next room. For this purpose he would come when sent for instantly from any part of the house.' In the evenings he dined with the Duchess of Kent.[12]

He had his rewards. On the day of Princess Victoria's birth he represented the Queen at a Privy Council meeting and ten days later he wrote contentedly to his brother, 'I have my hands very full as I also look after Victoria's political affairs.'[13] According to his Private Secretary, George Anson, with whom the Prince was now (and would remain) on the best of terms, this advance in his status 'had been brought about by the fact of the Prince having received and made notes of all the Cabinet business during the Queen's confinement, this circumstance having evinced to the Queen his capacity for business and power to assist'. To the Duke of Wellington the Prince confessed that his aim was, in fact, to be far more than a kind of assistant to the Queen. He intended to be 'the natural head of the family, superintendent of her household, manager of her private affairs, her sole *confidential* advisor in politics, and only assistance in her communication with the officers of the Government . . . her private secretary and her permanent Minister'.[14]

The satisfaction which the Prince felt at his growing influence was, however, soon overcast by his concern about the Queen's political sympathies. Her dear friend Melbourne's Government had been in trouble for some time when in the summer of 1841 the Tories won a decisive victory in a general election. During this election the Queen, choosing not to tell him of arrangements of which he was sure to disapprove, took the Prince on a tour of various Whig magnates to whose houses she had been introduced during those 'royal progresses' which had so exasperated King William IV. They went to Chatsworth and Woburn Abbey, to Panshanger, the house of Lord Melbourne's nephew, Earl Cowper, and to Lord Melbourne's own house, Brocket Hall. The Prince did not appear to advantage in any of them. He disapproved of the rivalries of adversarial politics which set 'families by the ears', 'demoralised the lower classes' and 'perverted many of the upper'.[15] The Crown should be above such partisanship; and he told the Queen that it really was her duty to be so.[16]

Yet when the Tories won their resounding victory she could not disguise her disappointment; nor did she attempt to do so. She declared that she would never send for 'that bad man Peel who had behaved so wickedly in the past'. She declined to attend the opening of the first session of the new Parliament; and did not conceal her strong reluctance to accept Sir Robert Peel as her Prime Minister in place of Lord Melbourne whom she had seen almost every day for four years. 'Eleven days was the longest I was ever without seeing him,' she told King Leopold, 'so you may imagine what this change must be.' She had grown so very accustomed to him, whereas Peel was always so shy and awkward with her. Charles Greville thought she would get on better with him if only he could keep his legs still.[17]

Melbourne tried to comfort and reassure her: he agreed to write to her regularly as what she termed a *'very* useful and valuable friend out of office'; and so he did for some time, much to the concern of both Peel and of Baron Stockmar who spoke about it to Melbourne who burst out angrily, 'God eternally damn it!' But when Stockmar warned him that Peel was threatening to resign and that Melbourne's old friend, Mrs Norton, was entertaining dinner parties with stories based on what she was told of the correspondence, Melbourne wrote far less frequently and then not on delicate political matters.

Certainly, as Melbourne admitted to the Queen, he hated the idea of not seeing her regularly and did not at all relish the thought of losing office; but he was tired, he told her, and the rest would do him good. Besides, he was leaving her in excellent hands. 'The Prince understands everything so well,' he said, 'and has a clever able head.' She could rely upon his advice and assistance with confidence. He had, so he said, formed 'the highest opinion of HRH's judgement, temper and discretion'.[18]

To ease the way for them both, he had advice to give to Peel in his dealings with the Queen. Rather than give it to Peel himself, he asked Charles Greville, whom he met at a dinner at Stafford House, to pass it on for him.

> Whenever he does anything, or has anything to propose [Melbourne said] let him explain to her clearly his reasons. The Queen is not conceited; she is aware there are many things she does not understand, and she likes to have them explained to her elementarily, not at length and in detail, but shortly and clearly; neither does she like long audiences, and I never stayed with her a long time.[19]

Some time later, on this occasion through George Anson, Melbourne added another piece of advice for Peel: Don't irritate her by 'talking *at* her about religion'.

Urged to recognize his merits by the Prince, who had much more in common with the serious, stiff, happily married Peel than he had with the easy-going, amusing Melbourne, the Queen was more accommodating and gracious with her new Prime Minister than he had reason to expect and, at Prince Albert's urging, was prepared to be more accommodating than she had been in 1839 about the ladies of her Household.

At the Council meeting at which the new Ministers were appointed and took over from their predecessors, she conducted herself, so Greville said, in a manner which excited his 'greatest admiration' and was 'really touching to see'. 'She looked very much flushed, and her heart evidently brim full, but she was composed, and throughout the whole of the proceedings, when her emotion might very well have overpowered her, she preserved complete self-possession, composure and dignity.'[20]

'There was not one of the new Government who did not place the fullest confidence in Her Majesty's intended fairness towards them,' W. E. Gladstone, who had been appointed Vice-President of the Board of Trade, told George Anson. 'They admired the extreme dignity of the Queen . . . It was evidently painful to her but her conduct was beautiful.'[21] W. B. Baring, the new Secretary to the Board of Control, and Sir George Grey, Chancellor of the Duchy of Lancaster, were seen to be in tears. Lord Erroll dashed out of the room before he, too, broke down.[22]

'Peel told me she had behaved perfectly to him,' Greville continued, 'and that He had said to her that He considered it his first and greatest duty to consult her happiness and comfort; that no person would be proposed to her who could be disagreeable to her . . . I asked him if She had taken this well, and met in a corresponding spirit and he said, "Perfectly." In short, he was more than satisfied; he was charmed with her.'

18

✷✷✷✷✷✷✷✷✷✷✷✷

THE PRINCE
AND THE HOUSEHOLD

'But you see, properly speaking, it is not our fault;
for the Lord Steward lays the fire only
and the Lord Chamberlain lights it.'

'REALLY WHEN ONE IS SO HAPPY, blessed in one's home life, as I am,' the Queen wrote not long after Sir Robert Peel came into office, 'politics (provided my country is safe) must take only 2nd. place.' Already George Anson had noted that 'Her Majesty interests herself less and less about politics' and that 'her dislike is less than it was to her present Ministers'.[1]

Victoria soon came to regard Peel far less unkindly and was able to recognize his great qualities. To be sure he was still rather stiff and irritating on occasions; but he could talk 'very interestingly' and strongly recommended himself to her by entertaining a high opinion of Prince Albert's character and attainments. He saw to it that the Prince, who now had keys to Cabinet boxes, was sent all important Government papers so that he could go through them with the Queen and explain to her any points she did not understand. Peel also made it possible for the Prince to be present when Ministers had audiences with her; indeed, on occasions, the Prince saw Ministers alone on the Queen's behalf, with her approval, and held receptions for her since, so she said, 'presentations to *him* should be considered the same as to me'.

He wrote memoranda for her, drafted letters, took decisions, became, in effect, not only a highly competent and extremely hard-working private secretary, but an adviser of exceptional, indeed unique influence, intent, as Anson put it, upon 'reforming' the Queen's mind and 'drawing out her Powers'.[2] Also, much to the annoyance of the old Royal Family who still considered him a meddlesome interloper, the Prince began to assume an importance in fields beyond the spheres of government and the Court. He was, for example, appointed to the chairmanship of an Arts Commission 'to take into consideration the promotion of the Fine Arts in connection with the rebuilding of the Houses of Parliament' which had been almost destroyed by fire in 1834.

On his own initiative he set about reforming the Royal Household, an immense organization consisting of an astonishing variety of courtiers, attendants and servants.

The Housekeeper was one of numerous senior servants and specialist officials, many of whose offices had been established centuries before and some of whose duties had long since been forgotten. There were Pages of the Presence and Pages of the Backstairs, Resident Bedchamber Women, Body Linen Laundresses and Linen Women, Fire Lighters, Livery Porters, Butlers, Under Butlers, Footmen, Cooks and Kitchen Boys, a Rat Killer and a Chimney Sweep. The large medical establishment included four Physicians to the Person, two Sergeant Surgeons, the Physician, Surgeon and Apothecary to the Household, the Dentist, the Chemist and Druggist to the Person.[3]

The archaic administration of this large Household was examined by Baron Stockmar in one of those lengthy memoranda which poured from his busy pen. He explained the difficulties of running the royal palaces when daily life was ruled by three separate departments, those of the Lord Steward (consisting of no fewer than 445 persons), the Lord Chamberlain and the Master of the Horse, all of which changed with every administration. The heads of these departments no longer lived at Court but delegated their authority to 'servants very inferior in rank', none of whom was sure how far they might trespass upon the customary preserves of another department and all of whom went through an elaborate procedure before anything worthwhile was done. If, for instance, a pane of glass required replacing in the kitchen or a cupboard door mending, a requisition had to be prepared and signed by the Chief Cook; it had then to be countersigned by the Clerk of the Kitchen; then taken to be signed by the Master of the Household; then taken to the Lord Chamberlain's office, where it was authorized and passed on to the Clerk of the Works who was responsible to the Department of Woods and Forests. The consequence of this rigmarole was that many a window remained broken for months while many others were permanently opaque since the Lord Chamberlain was responsible for the inside and the Department of Woods and Forests for the outside and their cleaners very rarely worked simultaneously. One day Baron Stockmar, always susceptible himself to the cold at Windsor, was asked by the Queen to complain to the Master of the Household that the dining room was often icy. 'But you see,' he was told, 'properly speaking, it is not our fault; for the Lord Steward lays the fire only and the Lord Chamberlain lights it', the Lord Chamberlain being responsible for the numerous housemaids, while the porters, like the cooks, came under the Lord Steward's department, and the footmen, who slept 'ten and twelve in each room', under the Master of the Horse.[4]

When guests arrived it was difficult to find anyone to show them to their apartments. It was often equally difficult for them to find the way down to the drawing room; and at night, if they happened to forget which corridor led to their rooms, they might wander about for minutes on end, helpless and unassisted. Once a visitor got lost on his way to bed and was forced to spend the night on a sofa in the State Gallery adjoining the Waterloo Gallery where a housemaid found him and, supposing him to be drunk, fetched a policeman.[5] Another guest, who got lost one night, 'spent nearly an hour wandering about the corridors to try and identify his bedroom'. At length he opened a door which he imagined led to it and came upon the Queen having her hair brushed by a maid.*[6]

Vast amounts of money were squandered in all the royal palaces and the system was frequently abused: it was discovered, for instance, that of the tens of thousands of people who were provided with dinners every year, only a proportion were actually entitled to them; that, when carriages were needed, the signatures of ladies-in-waiting would be forged in order to obtain them; that an under-butler was still being paid £1. 15s a week for 'Red Room Wine', a legacy from the days when officers on guard in George III's time were allowed this sum for wine served in a room hung

* The same embarrassments were occasioned at Osborne where one evening in 1900 'just as dear old Lady Erroll had taken off her hair and picked out her teeth someone knocked at the door. She said "Come in!"' Then she opened it and there stood A. J. Balfour, the future prime minister, in the passage. He could not find his room and was at his wit's end. He had tried Aline's [the Hon. Aline Majendie, a maid-of-honour] and was trembling with bashfulness (Victor Mallet, *Life with Queen Victoria: Marie Mallet's Letters from Court 1887–1901*, 1968, 199).

with red wallpaper; and that all the candles were replaced every day in the principal rooms whether or not they had been used, the candles removed being appropriated by the staff as a traditional perquisite. Nor was it only candles that were appropriated or mysteriously disappeared. At Windsor, in one single representative quarter, no fewer than 184 new brushes, brooms and mops were purchased together with twenty-four new pairs of housemaid's gloves, twenty-four chamois leathers and ninety-six packing mats. At any one time there were between three and four hundred dozen dusters 'scattered all over the Castle'.[7]

At Buckingham Palace drains were faulty; there were no sinks for the chambermaids on the bedroom floors; few of the lavatories were properly ventilated; the bells would not ring; some of the doors would not close; and many of the thousand windows would not open. The waste from a newly installed lavatory was discharged on to a roof outside the Queen's dressing room window.[8] Yet officials and servants alike in the royal residences were far from poorly paid. In the first year of the Queen's reign – when in more modest households a domestic servant might earn about twelve pounds a year – the lowest of the four grades into which the Palace housemaids were divided received £15 15s. a year, the highest £45 10s. And these wages were increased by the Queen, who was always a tolerant and generous mistress to her domestic servants. Linen women received £60 a year, the First Page of the Backstairs £320; even the Fourth Page of the Presence, Second Class had £140. The Mistress of the Robes received £500 a year, the Lord Chamberlain £2,000.

Nor were their wages and perquisites all that the lower servants received, for they were paid, in addition, 2s. a day board wages, and when they became too old or ill to perform their duties they might expect a pension which in 1837 was between £30 and £40 a year for twenty years' service. Apart from their regular emoluments they were often also given tips by foreign visitors to the Castle and these were usually liberal. In 1842, for example, the King of Prussia left £500 for distribution and the share of a housemaid of the First Class was £5 15s. 0d. Tsar Nicholas I left £2,000, gave the Housekeeper a diamond parure worth another thousand pounds, and 'freely bestowed rings, watches and brooches'.[9]

Having, with Baron Stockmar's help, come to realize the immense waste of money involved in the running of the Royal Household, Prince Albert methodically set about its reform. The Master of the Household was made responsible for the co-ordination of the activities of all the departments involved; and excessive manning was reduced to such an extent that savings were made of some £25,000 a year.

Naturally the activities of the Prince, never the most tactful of men, did nothing to make him better liked in the Household, nor did they endear him to those outside it who were predisposed to dislike and distrust him. Caricaturists depicted him counting scrubbing brushes and ferreting for candle ends at Windsor where, it was said, he had given instructions that the servants must provide themselves not only with their own soap but with their own mops and brushes and that they must no longer be offered tea as an alternative to cocoa.[10] Servants in the royal service had grown accustomed to their perquisites, official and assumed; while guests did not take kindly to being allowed only two candles in their rooms and on ringing for more being told by a maid, as Thérèse Tietjens was when she was summoned to Windsor to sing to the Queen, 'that the allowance to each room was just two candles and no more. "But," added the maid considerately, "there is no regulation which would prevent you cutting those two candles in halves and making four." '[11]

As with candle ends so with lavatory paper. Sir Arthur Ellis, an equerry, was disconcerted to discover that the lavatories at Windsor were supplied with 'NEWSPAPER'.

With some order and economy imposed upon the household as well as upon the nursery and the royal farms, parks and gardens, life at Court assumed a quiet, dignified, respectable formality conformable to the Prince's taste.

On being presented to the Queen, gentlemen went down on one knee and raised the right arm with the back of the hand uppermost. The Queen would then lay her hand on theirs so that they could brush it with their lips. They must not speak. On rising they were required to bow to Her Majesty, then to His Royal Highness. Ladies, on approaching the Queen, had to drop the trains of their dresses which were then spread out behind them by attendants armed with wands. Having made their curtseys, they had to retreat several paces backwards, contriving not to fall over their trains as they gathered them up over their arms.[12]

The Queen, who ultimately became quite as inflexible as the Prince regarding the procedure to be observed at presentations, was most particular over the clothes to be worn: married ladies wore lappets; unmarried ladies wore veils; both wore a headdress of three white feathers. Anyone who wanted, for reasons of health, to wear a dress cut higher in the neck than was customary had to obtain permission to do so from the Lord Chamberlain. The permission was usually granted but the Queen insisted on the veils, lappets and feathers. A Mrs Sebastian Gassiot who, being unable to fasten her plumes in the usual way because ill health had obliged her 'to have all her hair cut quite short', wanted to know whether she might appear in a 'Dolly Varden cap with the plumes and lappets fastened to it', was told that the Queen, who had been 'much amused' by the request, had replied to it – 'decidedly no'.[13]

Gentlemen, if they were not entitled to wear a uniform, had to appear in court dress with a claret-coloured coat, knee breeches, long white stockings, and buckled shoes and sword, although later on in her reign old men were allowed to wear breeches which came down to the ankle and buttoned there. They were meant to 'give the same impression as stockings'.

The problem facing American Ministers abroad was settled by William Marcy, Secretary of State, who ruled that they should appear 'in the simple dress of an American citizen'. At that time the American Ambassador in London was James Buchanan, who later became President. Sir Edward Cust, the Queen's Master of the Ceremonies, told Buchanan that although the Queen would no doubt receive him whatever he wore, an ordinary suit would be disagreeable to her, so he appeared in a black coat and pantaloons, white waistcoat and cravat. The Queen greeted him with an 'arch but benevolent smile'.[14]

If the Queen's views on court dress called forth a good deal of satirical comment in the Press, her views on the uses and scope of the *Court Circular* aroused much more. Every day, in the most ponderous and humourless way, her own and her family's activities were recorded under this heading in the newspapers. Every time the Queen left Windsor for 'the Paddington Terminus of the Great Western Railway', every time she and the Prince 'promenaded in the pleasure grounds adjacent to the Castle', every time he went 'shooting in the royal preserves', every time she invited an honoured guest to 'partake of a collation', the facts were recorded and detailed.

'The Marmosets, pretty little dears, are in good health,' an apposite parody ran in a comic journal. 'The severe frost has not in any way injured the turtle-doves in the new dovecote. The tailless cats have been slightly affected owing to their having been indulged with a tête-à-tête on the Castle walls.'[15] Sometimes there was no need of parody. Once 'Her Majesty was most graciously pleased during her stay at Windsor to enjoy most excellent health and spirits.' And later 'Her Majesty, attended by Viscountess Jocelyn, went riding in the Park on two ponies.'[16]

> I don't know why [one of the Queen's maids-of-honour wrote home to her father in the 1840s], but the dullness of our evenings is a thing impossible to describe. The Queen and Ladies sit at the round table and make conversation; and Flora and I sit at our own table and work; and the Prince generally stays in the other room talking with the Gentlemen till near bed-time; then he comes in with one or two big-wigs who sit at the Queen's table, where they sit till she gives the move at half-past ten, then the other gentlemen make a rush, from the whist table or from the other room, and we gladly bundle up our work, and all is over.[17]

Visitors to Windsor Castle frequently complained of the lack of the 'sociability which makes the agreeableness of an English country house'. There was no room in which the guests could 'assemble, sit, lounge, and talk as they please'. The billiard room was so inaccessible it might as well have been in the town of Windsor; the library, 'although well stocked with books', was cold and unfurnished, 'offering none of the comforts of a habitable room'.[18] If the 'most agreeable people in the world' were invited one hardly saw them, as the 'chacun chez soi system' was the fashion of the place.[19]

Of course, some guests preferred to be left on their own, to do as they pleased throughout the day until dinner time; and Lord Clarendon told the Duchess of Manchester that he always liked Windsor better than any other country house because 'One is left to one's own devices and nobody does anything to *amuse* one.'[20] But, for most, the lack of even the pretence of gaiety, the need to observe 'a continual air of deference and respect', was depressing and enervating.

At dinner, when the guests met for the first time during the day, a military band usually 'covered the talk', as Lord Macaulay discovered, 'with a succession of sonorous tunes'.[21] He found himself next to a 'foreign woman who could hardly speak English intelligibly'.[22] Lord Ashley found that the band was very necessary to fill up the long 'pauses of conversation'. Even during Ascot races when a splendid banquet was given in St George's Hall, which appeared 'very magnificent, blazing with gold plate and light', it was, Charles Greville thought, despite the splendour, all 'very tiresome'.[23] It could be particularly tiresome when the Duke of Wellington was one of the guests since he was so fearfully deaf and shouted so. '*Very good-looking man*,' he once bawled in Lady Lyttelton's ear, referring to the Tsar, Nicholas I, who sat immediately opposite and understood English perfectly. 'Always was so – scarcely altered since I saw him last – rather browner – no other change – very handsome man now. Don't you think so?' Lady Lyttelton felt compelled to shout an answer, 'Yes, very handsome, indeed.' On occasions the Duke would talk 'as loud as thunder' about some matter of delicate state importance which should have been mentioned only in Cabinet; and the Queen would blush 'over and over' and at last succeed in interrupting him by 'screaming out upon some other subject'.[24]

After dinner there was sometimes a concert by the Castle band or by distinguished musicians invited to Windsor for this purpose. Occasionally there was an opera, the performers and orchestra being brought down to Windsor by special train and sent back afterwards. The performance was given in the Waterloo Gallery where the acoustics were not very good and where Francesco Tamagno, not having arrived in time to try out his voice there, once let himself go with such force that the Queen, who was as usual sitting in the front row, was quite stunned by the blast.[25]

Occasionally, too, there was a play with a cast brought down from the West End. More often the play was performed, rather nervously, by members of the household and sometimes there was a presentation of tableaux in which all the members of the Royal Family joined and this was 'very wearying for the audience, who had to sit for two and a half hours with very long intervals between the tableaux'.[26]

But boring as these performances usually were, it was better to have something to do after dinner, Charles Greville decided – having sat through a series of declamations by Mlle Rachel in French which he could not understand – for otherwise there was nothing at all with which to occupy the evening. And getting through the evening was always the 'great difficulty in Royal society'.[27]

*   *   *

The Queen was at her most contented when there were no guests whom she did not know very well to entertain; or when there were only a few close friends staying the night or, best of all, when she and Prince Albert were alone together. Later, after the birth of their children, she confessed to her eldest daughter that she begrudged the time she had to be with them, when she 'longed to be alone with dearest Papa'. The times spent with him were 'always her happiest moments'.[28]

She described them in great detail, providing a vivid account of the early mornings when the wardrobe maid came into their bedroom at seven o'clock to open the shutters and, usually, the window too. The Prince, who slept in long white drawers enclosing his feet, would get up and put on his quilted dressing gown. He then went to his sitting room where 'his green German lamp was lit'.

'He brought the original one from Germany,' the Queen recorded, '& we always have 2 on our tables which everywhere stand side by side (& shall ever do so) & wrote letters, read etc. & at a little after eight . . . he came to tell me [in German] to get up.' He usually brought with him letters which he had written in English for her to read through for him in order to check his spelling and grammar. After his last child was born and was able to walk and talk she went into his dressing room to watch him dress and see him put on the blue ribbon of the Order of the Garter which he always wore under his waistcoat. When she arrived to find him dressed already she would 'make dearest Albert laugh so by saying, "What a pity"!' The child 'stopped with him till he' came out of his room. He then walked down the passage to breakfast with her, holding her hand.[29]

In the evenings when the Queen and Prince were once more alone together they often read to each other. 'I sit on a sofa, in the middle of the room with a small table before it, on which stand a lamp & candle-stick,' she wrote contentedly, 'Albert sitting in a low arm-chair, on the opposite side of the table with another small table in front of him on which he usually stands his book.'

'I have been so happy there,' she wrote another day in the summer of 1843, when expressing regret at having to leave one royal residence for another, 'but *where* am I not happy *now*?'[30]

The Prince seemed contented now, too, when there were no difficult guests or intimidating women to put him ill at ease. Long gone were the evenings when he would play double chess alone while the Queen talked to the Prime Minister, and the ladies and gentlemen of the Household were bored to death. The Prince now played more rowdy games and even joined in Blind Man's Buff with the ladies, made puns, invented riddles, took part in charades, danced the 'wildest, merriest' dances, played games with the children, gave them magic lantern shows, arranged presents for them on their birthdays in the 'present room', and once built a house for the Princess Royal with her wooden bricks, a house so tall that he had to stand on a chair to put the roof on and even then to reach above his head. 'Such a fall it made! He enjoyed it much the most.'

He was even capable of laughing at himself now and had a large collection of caricatures, some of which lampooned him mercilessly.[31] One evening after dinner he showed some of these to the Queen and her ladies, 'running from one to the other, and standing over us to see how we laughed,' Lady Lyttelton wrote, 'and laughing so loud himself as to be quite noisy and boyish. But' – and there was so often this 'but' – 'his voice! It is sadly disenchanting.'[32]

One evening the ladies and gentlemen of the Household danced 'the reel *con amore* which was very amusing', so the Hon. Georgiana Liddell, one of the Queen's maids-of-honour, said, and 'made the Queen laugh heartily'. On another evening, after quadrilles and Roger de Coverley, the Queen proposed that everyone who could dance at all should join in a country dance. 'The obedience was like the effect of a magical horn,' Lady Lyttelton thought. 'Lord Aberdeen [the Foreign Secretary in Peel's cabinet] looked more like a scarecrow than ever, quite as stiff as timber, and the countenance of Sir Robert Peel, so mincing on his legs and feet', was 'full of the funniest attempt to look unconcerned' while in reality he was 'very naturally, both shy and cross'.[33]

But the Queen watched Albert, so beautiful, so kind, so good. He had the grace of a ballet dancer and once performed like one when the Queen was criticized for looking grumpy. She had been very tired, she said, and might have looked cross, 'What am I to do another time?' she asked him. The Prince advised her, so Lady Lyttelton said, 'to behave like an opera dancer after a pirouette, and always to show all her teeth in a fixed smile ... He accompanied the advice with an immense pirouette and prodigious grin of his own, such as few people could perform after dinner without being sick, ending on one foot and t' other in the air.'[34]

In later years the Queen remembered with particularly wistful pleasure the evenings in her dressing room before she and Prince Albert went to bed. She pictured him leaning against the fireplace, 'talking over the company – and what had passed – such a pleasure; sometimes my maids would come in and begin to undress me – and he would go on talking, would make his observations on my jewels and ornaments and give my people good advice as to how to keep them or would occasionally reprimand if anything had not been carefully attended to . . . He would then go to his dressing-room . . . I undressed quickly – but alas! I dawdled and often read while my hair was doing afterwards . . .'[35]

19

✳✳✳✳✳✳✳✳✳✳✳✳

ROYAL QUARRELS

'Victoria is too hasty and passionate for
me to be able often to speak of my difficulties.'

IN FEBRUARY 1841, six months before the formation of Sir Robert
Peel's administration, the Queen and Prince Albert asked the Duke of
Wellington – now considered by the Queen the 'best friend' that she and
her husband had – to represent the Duke of Saxe-Coburg at the christening of their first child, Victoria.

'I was never so well received,' the Duke had recently written after a
visit to Windsor. 'I sat next to the Queen at dinner. She drank wine
repeatedly with me; in short, if I was not a Milksop, I should become a
Bottle Companion.'[1] He went out of his way to please her. At a military
review in Windsor Park he gave orders that the guns should remain
silent until she had left the parade ground, knowing that she hated
the noise of artillery. There would be no firing, he assured her; but
some mistake had been made and no sooner were the words out of
his mouth than 'bang went the guns all down the line!' It was so
irresistibly funny that the Queen 'burst into an uncontrollable fit of
laughter'. But the Duke was furious; he positively 'blew up'; no one
could appease him; and he gave orders for the gunners to leave the field
immediately.[2]

He was more successful in his attentions to the Queen at a concert
at Buckingham Palace. She had a bad cold and ran out of handkerchiefs
before the performance was over. The Duke, who was sitting immediately
behind her, noticed her plight; and, since he always carried a reserve
supply in his pocket, was able to help her. 'I immediately slipped one of

mine into her hand,' he related contentedly, 'then a second, then a third; and whispered I had a fourth at her service should she require it.'[3]

The Queen's daughter, Princess Victoria, behaved with great propriety and like a 'Christian' at her christening, so the child's father reported. 'She was awake but did not cry at all and seemed to crow with immense satisfaction at the lights and brilliant uniforms, for she is very intelligent and observing.'[4]

The child's mother, however, was in no such contented mood; for she was already pregnant again and exasperated and depressed as a result. 'What made me so miserable,' she later declared, 'was to have the first two years of my married life utterly spoilt by this occupation. I cld enjoy nothing, not travel about or go about with [my husband]. If I had waited a year . . . it wld. have been very different.' As it was, she had to 'suffer aches and sufferings . . . miseries and plagues'; she had to 'give up enjoyments', take 'constant precautions'. She felt 'so pinned down', with her 'wings clipped'. In short, the female sex was a 'most unenviable one'.[5]

A 'poor woman' was 'bodily and morally the husband's slave,' she complained. When heavily pregnant she felt more like a cow or a dog, a rabbit or a guinea-pig than a human being – women who enjoyed being pregnant were 'disgusting'. Besides, she got so depressed and ill-tempered, and then she had terrible quarrels with the Prince as, for instance, when he rebuked her for not paying proper attention when they were cataloguing prints together. She lost her temper on such occasions. He would leave the room; she would follow him 'to have it *all* out'. He would retreat to his room to write her a letter, pained and reasonable, which would exasperate her; and then, in the end, she would be filled with remorse and pity and resolve to curb that hasty temper which she so often lamented in the pages of her journal.

Twice in October 1841, she feared she was going to give birth prematurely, and for days on end she felt 'wretched . . . low and depressed'. While quite fond of children she did not at all care for babies, when all they were capable of was what she called 'that terrible frog-like action'. An ugly baby was a 'very nasty object, and the prettiest was frightful when undressed'. She would certainly not breast-feed the object as her mother had breast-fed her.

The thought of having another of these creatures filled her with dismay and disgust. She gave birth to it on the morning of 9 November; and it was as she feared it might be. 'My sufferings were really very severe, and I don't know what I should have done, but for the great comfort and support my beloved Albert was to me during the whole time.'[6] The baby, 'a large boy', appeared at twelve minutes to eleven and was, as the mother recorded, 'taken to the Ministers for them to see'. He was to be given the names Edward, after his grandfather, and Albert, after his father; and what a pleasure it was to his mother that he was to have that '*dearest name!*'

For their part, the Ministers were delighted to see so obviously robust a baby, and so was the country at large. No heir had been born to a reigning monarch since the appearance of George III's first child, almost eighty years before; and this new birth led royalists to hope that the monarchy, which the young Queen was now making more respectable and popular, was secure from a decline into its recent disrepute. Salutes were fired, crowds gathered in the streets to cheer and sing 'God Save the Queen', and the Prime Minister made reference to the nation's enthusiasm in a speech at the Guildhall, which was decorated for the occasion with illuminated letters spelling 'God save the Prince of Wales'. *The Times* described the 'one universal feeling of joy which ran throughout the kingdom'. 'What a joy!' wrote the boy's grandmother, the Duchess of Kent, expressing a common opinion. 'Oh God, what a happiness, what a blessing!'[7]

The relief the Queen herself felt at having given birth to a prince did not for long revive her spirits. For although Prince Albert Edward, known at first as 'the Boy' and afterwards as Bertie, was as 'strong and robust a baby as you could hope to see', his sister, 'Pussy', so healthy at first, 'so strong and fat' in the summer, was now sickly and pale and losing weight, and this, so her mother said, 'fusses and worries me much'.[8] In this anxiety she and the Prince had their first serious quarrel.

The source of the mischief was Baroness Lehzen who felt her position increasingly threatened by the Queen's deepening love for her husband and her reliance upon him. There were those who found the Baroness an agreeable and interesting woman; among them were Charles Greville, Lady Lyttelton and, at first, Baron Stockmar. Certainly there could be no question of her devotion to the Queen whose diary entries – which in earlier times the Baroness had read with the satisfaction they were no doubt intended to give – were filled with references to the love which Victoria felt for her and the gratitude she owed her for her protection and care during their days at Kensington. But Lehzen had become crotchety and ever more jealous, convinced that 'no one but she could take proper care of the Queen as she had done in the past', arousing suspicion by the close access she had to the Queen's private finances, hostility amongst Tories because of her outspoken support of the Whigs, and resentment in Prince Albert whom, in George Anson's opinion, she was 'constantly misrepresenting'. She exaggerated the Prince's every little fault', tried 'to undermine him in the Queen's affections and [made] herself a martyr, ready to suffer and put up with every sort of indignity for the Queen's sake'. With the Baroness, Anson concluded, 'we must always be subject to troubled waters'.

Anson wrote a memorandum of an interview he had had with the Baroness on 21 June 1842. He had gone to see her about an unbalanced army officer who had been making crazy protestations of love for the Queen. She had reported this to the Lord Chamberlain but had not let the Prince know of the officer's pestering as Anson thought she should have done. The Prince's conduct, she said, 'with great agitation and earnestness', had 'rendered it impossible for her to consult him. He had slighted her in the most marked manner and she was too proud not to resent it ... He had once told her to leave the Palace, but she replied he had not the power to turn her out of the Queen's house.'

Lord Melbourne agreed with her about this. The Prince had 'no right to ask the Queen to make such a sacrifice'; and if he were to say that he would go if the Baroness did not, the Queen might well reply, 'In this alternative you have contemplated the possibility of living without me. I will show you that I can contemplate the possibility of living without you.'

In his growing frustration the Prince raged with uncharacteristic passion against the 'crazy, stupid intriguer' who was 'obsessed with the lust of power', and 'regarded herself as a demi-God and anyone who [refused] to recognise her as such [was] a criminal'.[9] 'Victoria, who on other questions is just and clear-sighted,' he complained to Stockmar, 'does not see this because she has never been away from [Baroness Lehzen] and, like every good pupil, is accustomed to regard her governess as an oracle. Besides this, the unfortunate experience they went through together at Kensington has bound them still closer, and Lehzen, in her madness, has made Victoria believe that whatever good qualities she possesses are due to her ... There can be no improvement until Victoria sees Lehzen as she is.' She would '*really* be happiest without her'.[10]

The quarrel spread to the nursery which Lehzen proposed should be handed over to her control. The Prince, however, was convinced that Lehzen, the nurses and the doctor were all incompetent and that his little daughter's weakness was their fault. He said as much one day to a nurse who was spitefully impertinent in her reply. 'That is really malicious,' he complained to the Queen who, in turn, flared up in fury, accusing him of wanting to drive the child's mother out of the nursery and shouting that he could murder the baby if he wanted to. Endeavouring to control his own anger, the Prince murmured, 'I must have patience.'[11] He went down to his room where he gave vent to his anger in a passionately angry letter to his wife which he sent to Stockmar, asking him to send it on to her when he thought the right moment had come for her to receive it. 'Dr Clark has mismanaged the child and poisoned her with calomel,' the letter ran, 'and you have starved her. Take the child away and do as you like and if she dies you will have it on your conscience.'[12]

'All the disagreeableness I suffer comes from one and the same person,' the Prince wrote in another of his long letters to Stockmar, 'and that is precisely the person whom Victoria chooses for her friend and confidante ... Victoria is too hasty and passionate for me to be able often to speak of my difficulties. She will not hear me out but flies into a rage and overwhelms me with reproaches and suspiciousness, want of trust, ambition, envy etc. etc. There are, therefore, two ways open to me: (1) to keep silence and go away (in which case I am like a schoolboy who has had a dressing-down from his mother and goes off snubbed), (2) I can be still more violent (and then we have scenes ... which I hate because I am so sorry for Victoria in her misery ...)'[13]

There was no doubt that these scenes did make the Queen miserable, and that she deeply regretted that she was 'so passionate when spoken to'. 'I feel so forlorn and I have got such a sick headache,' she told Stockmar after Prince Albert had stormed out of the nursery. 'I feel as if I had had a dreadful dream. I do hope you may be able to pacify Albert. He seems so very angry . . . I don't wish to be angry with him.'

She feared that her flashes of temper were 'irremediable as yet, but [she] hoped in time [they] would be got over'. 'There is often an irritability in me which . . . makes me say cross and odious things which I don't myself believe and which I fear hurt A., but which he should not believe . . . like being miserable I ever married and so forth which come when I am unwell . . . I have often heard Albert own that everybody recognised Lehzen's former services to me and my only wish is that she should have a quiet home in my house and see me sometimes . . . I assure you *upon my honour* that I see her very seldom now and only for a few minutes, often to ask questions about papers and *toilette* for which she is the greatest use to me. A. often and often thinks I see her when I don't . . . I tell you this as it is true, as you know me to be . . .'[14]

'Our position is very different from any other married couple. A. is in my house and not I in his . . . Dearest Angel Albert, God only knows how I love him. His position is difficult, heaven knows, and we must do everything to make it easier.'[15]

It was made rather easier after the nursery had been reorganized. When Princess Victoria had been its only infant occupant it had been under the supervision of the widow of an admiral, Mrs Southey, a worthy, old-fashioned fogey who declined to make any concessions to modern ideas and still wore a wig. Although warmly recommended by the Archbishop of Canterbury, she had never been very satisfactory as Superintendent of the nursery and was even less so when there were two children to look after. She had not liked living at Windsor Castle, though she enjoyed gossiping in overheated rooms with Baroness Lehzen; and she went out too often, leaving her charges in the care of nursemaids inclined to squabble. She was not sufficiently firm or vigilant to ensure that the strict rules of the nursery were observed: that the two children must never be left alone for an instant; that no unauthorized person must ever be permitted to see them; that there must not be the slightest variation in the daily routine without prior consultation with the parents, who were to be regularly informed of the children's progress and any treatment recommended by their doctors. When consulted by the Queen – who complained that Mrs Southey was 'totally unfit' and that the children were 'quite left in the hands of low people – the Nursery and Nursery Maids [who] were vulgar and constantly quarrelling' – Lord Melbourne gave it as his opinion that the nursery ought to be entrusted to the care of a lady of rank who could command more authority, control the tantrums of the stubborn and wilful Princess, and report intelligently upon the development of the little Prince. This was also the opinion of Baron Stockmar who, with characteristic industry, provided the children's parents with a memorandum on the subject over thirty pages long, concluding that 'a Lady of Rank & Title' should be appointed in Mrs Southey's place. After discussions with various advisers, this most important post of Superintendent of the royal nursery was offered to one of the Queen's ladies of the bedchamber, Lady Lyttelton, eldest daughter of the second Earl Spencer, widow of the third Baron Lyttelton, and mother of five children. She was not well off and was thankful to have employment at Court where she was most regular in her religious observances, rather to the disapproval of the Queen who looked askance upon her High Church tendencies, all the more so because Lady Lyttelton's brother, George, an occasional visitor to Windsor, was a priest of the Church of Rome and Superior of the Order of Passionists.[16]

The choice of Lady Lyttelton as Superintendent was a highly fortunate one. She was a gifted woman; understanding, good-natured, calm and sensible. She had managed the occasionally flighty maids-of-honour with firmness and tact. Besides, she loved Windsor, greatly admired Prince Albert, and thought most highly of the Queen who never lied or dissembled and through whose 'extraordinary character' she detected a 'vein of iron'.

Lady Lyttelton considered that the Queen was unnecessarily anxious about her daughter, known to Lady Lyttelton as 'Princessy' and to the Queen as 'our fat Vic or Pussette', who was over-watched and over-doctored and 'always treated with what [was] most expensive'. 'Cheaper and commoner food and ways', in Lady Lyttelton's opinion, were 'often wholesomer'.[17]

'Princessy' did not take to Lady Lyttelton at first, screaming with 'unconquerable horror' when she arrived; and thereafter, though bawling less, treating her with a kind of irritable reserve which was finally overcome by Lady Lyttelton's patience and tact. With the little Prince there were no such problems. He continued to flourish, remaining constantly 'in crowing spirits' and in the best and calmest of tempers. When he was two years old Lady Lyttelton said that his 'worst crime' was 'to throw his cows and his soldiers out of the windows'; but this she considered was unlikely to 'furnish a dangerous precedent' for his future life.[18]

With peace in the nursery restored by Lady Lyttelton, who was in the Queen's opinion 'perfection', life became much easier for Prince Albert, all the more so when it was agreed that Baroness Lehzen must go. She had brought it upon herself, Stockmar thought. 'She was foolish enough to contest [Prince Albert's] influence, and not to conform herself to the change in her position . . . If she had done so and conciliated the P., she might have remained in the Palace to the end of her life.'[19] Having already succeeded in removing from the household the objectionable Pagets who, in his opinion, had gravely compromised the Court's moral tone and who had been prominent in Baroness Lehzen's support, the Prince had by now acquired what Stockmar termed 'unbounded influence'. He made arrangements, at the end of September 1842, for the woman's departure. She left England to live with a sister at Bückeburg with the generous pension of £800 a year.

The Queen, who gave her a carriage as a leaving present, felt that her departure was for 'her and our best' and was relieved when Lehzen herself said that her removal to Hanover was 'necessary for her health' and that, 'of course', Victoria did 'not require her so much now'. When the time came for her to leave, the Queen decided that rather than go to say goodbye, she would write to her which would be 'less painful'. 'I am much relieved,' she wrote in her diary, 'at being spared the painful parting [although] I so regret not being able to embrace her once more.'[20]

On her future visits to Germany the Queen saw Lehzen upon only two occasions, but regularly and affectionately she wrote to her until she died at the age of eighty-six in 1870. Between the Queen and Prince Albert, however, her name was rarely mentioned after her departure and, when it was, the Queen was contrite, ready to sympathize with her husband and to take responsibility upon herself for the quarrels which her presence in the Castle had provoked.' I blame myself for my blindness,' she wrote in her journal. 'I shudder to think what my beloved Albert had to go through . . . It makes my blood boil.'

She conceded, though, that Lehzen had been 'an admirable Governess'. 'I owed her much,' she wrote, 'and she adored me . . . I adored her, though I also feared her ... She devoted her life to me, with the most wonderful self-abnegation, never ever taking one day's leave.' She did, however, the Queen added, get to be 'rather trying at the end'.[21]

The departure of Baroness Lehzen was a watershed in the Queen's life.

20

✾✾✾✾✾✾✾✾✾✾✾

OSBORNE

'Albert and I talked of buying a place of our own.'

'OH! IF I COULD ONLY DESCRIBE our dear happy life together,' the Queen wrote in her diary at the beginning of November 1844. Even the prospect of having other babies did not so much daunt her now. Her only wish was that her 'great happiness' should last, her most fervent prayer that God would grant 'His protection of us *together*'. Two years previously, soon after Lehzen's departure, she had 'looked over & corrected' some comments she had made in her old journals which 'did not *now* awake very pleasant feelings'. The life she had led then 'was so artificial'. She was ashamed to remember some of the things she had done and said and written, the pain she had allowed Lehzen to inflict upon Albert, the 'unbounded admiration and affection' she had felt for Lord Melbourne in her need to cling to someone, her working herself up into something which Albert thought 'became at last quite foolish'. 'I thought I was happy,' she wrote. 'Thank God! I now know what real happiness means!'[1]

Albert was all in all to her, 'such a perfection, such an angel'. She hated to be parted from him, regretted so much that he was always so busy that she could not see more of him; no one, she was to tell her eldest daughter, could be as blessed as she was with such a husband: he was her father, protector, guide, 'adviser in all and everything; she might even say her mother as well as husband'. She supposed 'no-one was ever so completely altered in every way' as she had been by her dearest husband's 'blessed influence'.[2]

Her diary is filled with references to him, praise of his goodness, his kindness, his perfection – Albert playing the organ with a baby on each knee, Albert pushing the children round the nursery in a basket and playing hide and seek with them, helping them to chase butterflies and making them laugh by turning somersaults in a haystack. 'He is so kind to them,' their mother wrote contentedly in her journal, 'and romps with them so delightfully, and manages them so beautifully and kindly.' 'It is not every papa,' commented Lady Lyttelton after seeing him helping one of them to get dressed, 'who would have the patience and kindness to do so.'[3]

At Christmas time he could be seen building snowmen twice as tall as himself, playing ice hockey, driving a sledge across the snow and setting up a Christmas tree.*

Each Christmas, the chandeliers were taken down in the Queen's sitting room at Windsor where trees, hung with candles and toffees, took their place; the dining room tables were piled high with food and on the sideboard stood an immense baron of beef. In the Oak Room there was another Christmas tree surrounded by presents for the members of the household, and on each present was a card written by the Queen. 'Everything,' so the Prince told his brother, 'was totally German.'

When Albert's father died Victoria abandoned herself to the grief her husband felt in recalling the days of his lost childhood, disregarding the manifold faults of the old reprobate who had plagued her with demands for money, and giving vent to an extravagance of uncontrolled mourning, 'all on the Prince's account', as Lady Lyttelton said.[4]

---

* Prince Albert is often said to have introduced the custom of the Christmas tree from Germany to England. But the credit for this properly belongs to his wife's grandmother, Queen Charlotte. 'The Queen [Charlotte] entertained the children here, Christmas evening, with a German fashion,' recalled the Hon. Georgina Townshend, state housekeeper at Windsor Castle. 'A fir tree, about as high again as any of us, lighted all over with small tapers, several little wax dolls among the branches in different places, and strings of almonds and raisins alternately tied from one to the other, with skipping ropes for the boys, and each bigger girl had muslin for a frock, a muslin handkerchief, a fan, and a sash, all prettily done up in the handkerchief, and a pretty necklace and earrings besides. As soon as all the things were delivered out by the Queen and Princesses, the candles on the tree were put out, and the children set to work to help themselves' (*Memoirs and Correspondence of Field-Marshal Viscount Combermere*, 2 vols., London, 1866, ii, 419).

As a child Queen Victoria regularly had a Christmas tree, and her aunt, Queen Adelaide, always set one up at her Christmas parties for children in the Dragon Room at Brighton Pavilion. (Olwen Hedley, 'How the Christmas tree came to the English Court', *The Times*, 22 December 1958).

God has heavily afflicted us [she told King Leopold]. We feel crushed, overwhelmed, bowed down by the loss of one who was so deservedly loved, I may say adored, by his children and family ... You must now be the father of us two poor bereaved heart broken children ... I loved him and looked on him as my own father; his like we shall *not see again*. I have never known real *grief* till now, and it has made a lasting impression on me.[5]

'My darling stands so alone,' she added in a letter to Baron Stockmar, 'and his grief is so great and touching ... He says (forgive my bad writing, but my tears blind me) I am now *all* to him. Oh, if I can be, I shall be only too happy.'[6]

She dreaded the thought that Albert would now have to go to Germany to help his brother see to their father's confused affairs. But, when he did go, he made his absence less unbearable by writing to her often and with real, if rather stilted, affection, beginning a letter, written on the day of his departure from Dover, 'My own dear darling, I have been here about an hour, and regret the lost time which I might have spent with you. Poor child! you will, while I write, be getting ready for luncheon, and you will find a place vacant where I sat yesterday. In your heart, however, I hope my place will not be vacant ... You are even now half a day nearer to seeing me again; by the time you get this letter you will be a whole one – thirteen more, and I am again within your arms. Your most devoted, Albert.'[7]

On the day of his return the Queen had the 'immense joy' of being 'clasped in his arms'. He himself wrote, 'I arrived at six o'clock in the evening at Windsor. *Great joy*.'[8]

Both the Queen and Prince had at this time grown fond of Windsor, despite its many disadvantages and occasional whiffs of noxious smells (although the Queen was in later years to dislike it much, describing it as 'prison-like, so large and gloomy', an 'undesirable and unenjoyable residence'). But it could scarcely be described as cosy, or, to use a favourite word of both the Queen's and Prince's, *gemütlich*.[9] Nor could Buckingham Palace which, when King George IV rebuilt the less grandiose house his father had bought as a London retreat from St James's, had never been intended as a family home. The Queen complained to Peel of its 'total want of accommodation for our own little family which is fast growing up ... If [alterations] were to be begun this autumn [1845] it could hardly be occupied before the spring of 1848 when the Prince of Wales would be nearly seven and the Princess Royal nearly eight years old and they cannot possibly be kept in the nursery any longer. A provision for this purpose ought therefore to be made this year. Independent of this, most parts of the Palace are in a sad state and will ere long require further outlay to render them *decent* for the occupation of the Royal Family or any visitors the Queen may have to receive . . . *Something* must absolutely be done during this Session.'

The Queen was supported in her views by Edward Blore, the architect employed by William IV to complete the work which had been started by John Nash for George IV but had been left unfinished at King William's death. Blore contended that there were no rooms in the Palace which could be converted into day and night nurseries except poky attics designed for use as servants' quarters. Moreover, the state apartments were inadequate and the kitchens a disgrace. Nor were there any suites suitable for distinguished guests from abroad. Indeed, Prince Albert was quite right to consider the whole Palace 'a disgrace to the Sovereign and the Nation'.[10]

Blore proposed enclosing Nash's courtyard by a completely new east front with a central balcony facing down the Mall and removing the Marble Arch which stood in front of the courtyard to a position at the top of Park Lane, where it remains today. It was estimated that this would cost £150,000 – a sum subsequently voted by Parliament – and it was hoped that at least part of this would be covered by the sale of the Marine Pavilion at Brighton.

The Queen had decided that the lack of privacy at Brighton was intolerable. During a visit there in the winter of 1845 the crowds 'behaved worse' than she had ever seen them do before, like 'a pack of ill-bred dogs', in the words of *Punch*, hunting their quarry 'to the very gates of the Pavilion'.[11] 'We were mobbed by all the shopboys in the town, who ran and looked under my bonnet,' the Queen complained, 'treating us just as they do the band, when it goes to the parade. We walked home as fast as we could.'[12]

Fortunately by then she and Prince Albert had found a place which would afford them the seclusion they could never hope to enjoy at Brighton or in London, or, indeed, at Windsor.

*   *   *

'During our usual morning walk,' the Queen had written one day in 1843, 'Albert & I talked of buying a place of our own, which would be so nice; perhaps Norris Castle might be something to think of.'[13] She had been much taken with the Isle of Wight as a girl; and now that she could afford it, she thought how wonderful it would be to have a place there of one's own, quiet and retired. 'God knows *how willingly* I would *always* live with my beloved Albert and our children in the quiet and retirement of private life and not be the constant object of observation and of newspaper articles,' she told King Leopold; and later she made the same observation to one of her German relations: 'Every year I feel less and less desire for the so-called "worldly pleasures", and if it were not my duty to give receptions and banquets, I should like to retire to the Country with my husband and children.'[14]

The Isle of Wight seemed to offer an ideal sanctuary, secluded from the outside world, yet not too remote from London, in fact less than three hours' journey away by rail and steamer.

Sir Robert Peel encouraged the Queen and the Prince in their plans and brought to their attention a Georgian house overlooking the Solent near Cowes with some 800 acres. Here, at Osborne House, Prince Albert could be free from the circumlocutory delays and restrictions of the Office of Woods and Forests and of those 'other charming departments' which really were, as the Queen put it, 'the plague of one's life'.[15] At Osborne he could look forward to becoming, as he told the Dowager Duchess of Coburg, 'partly forester, partly builder, partly farmer and partly gardener'.[16]

The estate belonged to a daughter of the Duke of Grafton, Lady Isabella Blatchford, who was asking £30,000 for it. This was considered too high; so the Prince gave Lady Isabella the impression that he and the Queen were not all that keen to buy it. He would, however, consider renting it for a year to see how they liked it. A figure of £28,000 was then offered and accepted. But then Lady Isabella changed her mind and demanded the original asking price. Eventually a figure of £26,000, excluding the furniture and farm crops, was agreed between the parties; and a further £18,600 was spent on additional farmland purchased from Winchester College. By the end of 1847 a total of £67,000 had been spent on an estate of 1,727 acres.[17]

Charles Greville, who went to Osborne House for a Council meeting four months after the Royal Family moved in, did not think much of it. 'A miserable place,' he considered it, 'such a vile house' that, before the meeting, 'the Lords of the Council had no place to remain in but the entrance hall . . . Fortunately the weather was fine' so they walked about in the grounds. The Queen 'will spend first and last a great deal of money there,' Greville commented, 'but it is her own money and not the nation's. I know not where she gets it, but Graham [Sir James Graham, the Home Secretary] told me She had money. He also told me she is naturally inclined to be generous, but the Prince is fond of money.'[18]

Greville might think it 'very ugly'; but the Queen was entranced by Osborne House and its surroundings: it was 'so snug and nice' – a description, given in a letter to King Leopold, which Theodore Martin thought it as well to replace in his printed version with the more queenly 'pleasant'.[19] 'It is impossible to see a prettier place,' she told Lord Melbourne, 'with woods and valleys and *points de vue*, which would be beautiful anywhere, but all this near the sea . . . is quite perfection. We have a charming beach quite to ourselves. The sea is so blue and calm that the Prince said it was like Naples. And then we can walk about anywhere by ourselves without fear of being followed and mobbed.'[20] She could go down to the sea undisturbed:

> Drove down to the beach with my maid [she wrote in her journal one summer's day in 1847] and went into the bathing machine, where I undressed and bathed in the sea (for the first time in my life), and a very nice bathing woman attending me. I thought it delightful till I put my head under the water, when I thought I should be stifled.[21]

In a letter to Peel she was equally enthusiastic: 'We are more and more delighted with this lovely spot, the air is so pure and fresh, in spite of the hottest sun which oppresses one so dreadfully in London and even at Windsor . . . The combination of sea, trees, woods, flowers of all kinds . . . make it, to us, a perfect little Paradise.'[22]

She thought the original house, 'our dear little Home', 'all our *very own*', quite large enough; but Prince Albert did not agree.[23] So it was demolished and a much bigger house, an Italianate villa with two campanile – the Clock Tower and the Flag Tower – was built in its place. There was a central Pavilion for the Royal Family, a guest wing containing apartments for the Duchess of Kent, as well as rooms for visitors, and another wing for members of the Household who were also to be accommodated in cottages in the grounds. It was designed by Prince Albert himself with the help of his artistic adviser, the painter and engraver Ludwig Gruner, and the master builder Thomas Cubitt, a former ship's carpenter who had made a fortune building houses in Clapham Park as well as Belgravia (one of these George Anson's). The Queen laid the foundation stone of the new building with its much criticized stucco façades on 23 June 1845, and the family moved in just over a year later.[24]

'Nobody caught cold or smelled paint,' Lady Lyttelton recorded. 'Everything in the house is quite new [much of the furniture, including the painted billiard table with slate legs, was designed by Prince Albert himself] and the dining room looked *very* handsome.* The windows, lighted by the brilliant lamps, must have been seen far out to sea'; and, when the shutters were closed, the looking-glass fixed to their inner sides brilliantly reflected the bright light from the chandeliers.[25]

As the Queen formally entered the house for the first time a Scottish maid-of-honour threw a shoe in after her in the traditional belief of her countrymen that this would bring good luck; and, after dinner that night, in accordance with a tradition of the country of his own birth, Prince Albert quoted two lines of German meaning 'entering a new house is a solemn thing to do'. 'It was dry and quaint', being a quotation from Luther, Lady Lyttelton commented on his rendition, 'but we all perceived that he was feeling it.'[26]

From the beginning, the Queen loved Osborne, to which more land was eventually added until the estate extended to over 2,000 acres. She was to come here twice a year, from the middle of July until the end of the third week in August and for Christmas from 18 December to 23 February. She took great pride in the handsome rooms which owed so much to Albert's discernment and taste, the intertwined letters V and A which celebrated their ideal partnership, the arrangement of the pictures, of William Dyce's *Neptune Entrusting Command of the Sea to Britannia* which was placed at the top of the Pavilion staircase, and Winterhalter's

---

* The billiard room, drawing room and dining room all open into each other round three sides of the staircase, with screens of scagliola columns to make the divisions. 'The advantage of this open plan was that all the necessary equerries and ladies-in-waiting could be in attendance without the rooms seeming too large, and that they could be conveniently on call round the corner without having to stand because they were in the royal presence' (Mark Girouard, *The Victorian Country House*, 80).

Florinda, her birthday present to him (another riot of naked flesh, described by the Queen as 'splendid and delightful'), which was hung opposite their desks in her sitting room.*[27]

She was delighted by the lovely grounds which the Prince had planned and drained, levelled and planted; the avenue of cedars leading to the main entrance like the approach to a Tuscan villa, the model farms, the children's garden plots. She loved it all the more because Albert liked it so.† It did her heart good, she said, to see how he enjoyed it all. He was so full of enthusiasm for the place and for 'all the plans and improvements' he meant to carry out. He was 'hardly to be got at home for a moment'. For the rest of her life she recalled with pleasure standing on the balcony outside her sitting room on summer evenings listening to the hiss and patter of the fountains and the song of the nightingales in imitation of which Albert used to whistle so well on their walks together through the woods. 'Never do I enjoy myself more or more peacefully,' she wrote, 'than when I can be so much with my beloved Albert – follow him everywhere.'[28]

---

* Unlike most of her ladies and many of her other contemporaries, the Queen was not in the least shocked by such paintings of naked women. The directors of an art school, where William Mulready's nude studies were on display in 1853, were warned against letting her see them. She not only clearly and openly admired them but expressed a wish to buy one (*Early Victorian England*, ed. G. M. Young, ii, 113).

† Not all her family were so impressed, although her grandson's wife, Princess May of Teck, the future Queen Mary, who went there in 1892, was fond of the 'large, white airy house with its great sheet-glass windows looking out to sea, its dining-room decorated with Winterhalter portraits, its pungent and beautiful arboretum, and the newly completed Indian wing', the Durbar Corridor and the Durbar Room, the decoration of which was then nearing completion (James Pope – Hennessy, *Queen Mary*, 1959, 228). 'Even as a child I was struck by the ugliness of the house, which has been described as "a family necropolis",' wrote Queen Mary's son, King Edward VIII. 'The floors of the corridors and passages were inlaid with mosaic; let into the walls were numerous alcoves each displaying in life size a white marble statue of a dead or living member of "Gangan's" large family. It had long been Queen Victoria's ardent wish that her eldest son would make it his home. But by this time my grandfather's affections had been too long rooted in Sandringham. He had long since made up his mind to get rid of Osborne when it fell to him; and shortly, in spite of the mild protestations of some of his sisters, he handed the property over to the State as a convalescent home for disabled officers of the Boer War' (*A King's Story: The Memoirs of HRH. The Duke of Windsor*, 14).

21

✳✳✳✳✳✳✳✳✳✳✳

TRAVELLING

'Her Majesty travels at the rate of forty miles an hour.'

IT WAS THE OPPORTUNITY of being so much with Prince Albert that made her travels with him so enjoyable for the Queen. At Windsor Castle and Buckingham Palace he was so preoccupied with work that there were days when he seemed to have no time to spare for her. 'I have a great deal to do,' he had complained to his brother in November 1840, 'and hardly ever get out into the open air'; while, some two and a half years later, Stockmar described him as 'well and contented', but 'pale, fatigued and exhausted'. When he was away from the cares and the duties he imposed upon himself, however, the Queen could enjoy more of his company and attention and have him to herself for hours on end.

In the summer of 1843, four months after the birth of their third child, Princess Alice, the Queen and Prince Albert had gone abroad together for the first time. They had been invited to France by Louis-Philippe, King of the French, whose Foreign Minister and dominant figure in his Government was François Guizot, formerly French Ambassador in London and a warm advocate of closer Franco-British relations. Not only was it the first time the Queen had been abroad, it was the first time that any English sovereign had visited a French monarch since 1520 when Henry VIII met François I at the 'Field of the Cloth of Gold'.

The Queen and Prince sailed from England on 25 August in the royal yacht, the *Victoria and Albert*, which had been launched earlier that year and was commanded by one of King William IV's bastards, Lord Adolphus FitzClarence. The Prince, as usual, was dreadfully seasick; but the Queen relished the voyage. 'The sailor-gypsy life' at sea, she thought, was 'very delightful'. She enjoyed her breakfast with the King's son, the Prince de Joinville, who came aboard off the French coast. Despite his deafness, she found him 'an amiable, agreeable companion', 'amusing and full of anecdotes'. 'The good, kind' King was very pleasant, too. He was standing up in his barge, she said, as the royal yacht approached Le Tréport and was so impatient to greet his visitors that 'it was very difficult to prevent his getting out of the boat before it was close enough. Then he came up as quickly as possible and warmly embraced me.' Assuring her repeatedly how delighted he was to see her, he helped her into the barge which was rowed ashore with the 'Royal Standards of England and France floating side by side over the two sovereigns' heads'. On the shore large crowds welcomed the Queen with shouts of 'Vive la Reine d'Angleterre.'[1]

'We then,' the Queen recorded, 'got into a curious old carriage, a sort of char à banc with a top to it in which we sat with the King and Queen [Marie-Amélie, daughter of Ferdinand, King of the Two Sicilies] and all the ladies of the family', including the Princess of Joinville, the Duchess of Orléans, and Louis-Philippe's daughter, Louise, Queen of the Belgians.[2]

It was a most uncomfortable journey to the King's residence, the Château d'Eu. Charlotte Canning, the Queen's lady-in-waiting, described the coach as 'a mixture between one of Louis XIV's time and a marketing cart from Hampton Court'. The driver almost overturned the unwieldy contraption as he was endeavouring to negotiate a gateway, and the passengers, in Lady Canning's words, were 'taken for some miles along a very narrow field road, in deep dust and over stones, and ruts and holes'.

Nor, when at last they arrived, did Lady Canning much enjoy her stay at Eu. Admittedly the dinner on the first evening, served at the early hour of seven o'clock, was excellent, but it was served oddly. The Queen, wearing what Lady Canning thought a most unsuitable dress of scarlet crêpe de chine trimmed round the bottom with three rows of lace, did not know what to do with the 'great French loaf' which was placed beside her on an untidy table with 'everybody's bread and crumbs and dirt' remaining on the cloth 'all through the dessert'.

The evening in general, like subsequent evenings, was 'dullish'. The

French ladies were 'all rather tiresome' as well as 'dowdy'; while having to listen to Lord Liverpool, who accompanied the visitors from England as Lord Steward of the Household, talking incessantly 'in disagreeable French', was tedious beyond measure. After dinner one evening, in the middle of a performance by a man playing the French horn in a most eccentric manner, the King's son, the Duke of Montpensier, 'had the giggles and it caught from one person to another till all were in tears and the poor performer's sounds became stranger and stranger'. 'I kept grave very long indeed,' Lady Canning said, 'but my lips shook and some very deep notes vanquished me at last. I am very sorry for the poor man, but his back was partly turned and I hope he did not find out, and between each spasm every good-natured person called out "*C'est étonnant! Merveilleux!*"'

Whether or not Queen Victoria joined in the general merriment, Lady Canning did not say; but she did record the fact that a band of fifty men played under Her Majesty's window and 'almost deafened her'.[3]

For her part, however, the Queen enjoyed herself greatly. She felt as though it were a dream that she was at Eu, her 'favourite castle in the air of so many years', a fine château begun by Henry of Guise in 1578, enlarged by Mademoiselle de Montpensier in the seventeenth century and restored by Louis-Philippe. She got on very well with Queen Marie-Amélie with whom she was 'very merry and laughed a good deal'. Indeed, the whole French royal family was delightful: she felt 'so at home with them all', as though she were 'one of them'. It was so pleasant to be in 'a family circle with persons of [her] own rank with whom [she] could be on terms of equality & familiarity'. She felt 'so gay and happy with these dear people' and was, in Lady Canning's words, 'as amused as a child could be'. When she was obliged to leave Eu she did so 'with very great regret', recalling with pleasure the clear blue skies of Normandy, the meals *al fresco* or in large tents, the kind attentions of Louis-Philippe, who had English beer and English cheeses specially imported for his English guests, the sight of Albert swimming in the sea.[4]

Albert, also, had been charmed by his hosts. He did not much care for French people generally; but these, he told Stockmar, 'received us with a heartiness, I might say affection, which was quite touching'.[5]

Before setting out for France the Queen had been advised by the

Prime Minister to take care that the visit did not 'get mixed, either in reality or in appearance, with politics', while the French King's daughter gave similar advice to her mother: 'My excellent father should be natural, patriarchal, without ceremony, as he is always,' Queen Louise had advised. 'But unless she begins the subject, which she certainly will not ... he should not enter into politics and avoid everything which could suggest he was trying to influence her.'[6]

The Queen was thankful that this advice had been followed, that, according to an official report, 'no exchange of views on political subjects took place', and the visit had gone off without any political differences to disturb the happy atmosphere.

Having returned to spend a few days with her children at Brighton, she and Prince Albert returned to the Continent in the royal yacht to stay with King Leopold. Prince Albert was seasick once more as a matter of course; but the Queen was unaffected by the choppy waters of the Channel and she could not help laughing, so Lady Canning reported, at the sight of Prince Albert, followed by Lord Liverpool, then Lord Aberdeen, the Foreign Secretary, 'all vanishing in haste'.[7]

Once again, Lady Canning did not enjoy herself during the few days the royal party spent in Belgium. To the Queen, on the other hand, they were a delight. It was 'such a joy' for her to be 'once again under the roof of one who [had] ever been a father to [her]'. She was taken to Bruges, and Ghent, Brussels and Antwerp; and everywhere she was met with 'cordiality and friendliness', even though her clothes came in for what Lady Canning considered to be well-deserved criticism. The bonnet she wore at Ghent 'would do for an old woman of seventy and her pink petticoat was longer than her muslin gown'.[8] In Brussels, Charlotte Brontë, then studying French at M. and Mme Héger's school in the rue d'Isabelle, described her as 'very plainly dressed' as she drove through the streets, a 'little, stout, vivacious lady' of twenty-three.[9]

Little and stout though she was, she might at least, Charlotte Canning thought, have made some sort of effort to appear more elegant. Lady Canning had looked through her dresses while waiting for her in her cabin in the ship sailing for Ostend. 'They are decidedly very badly chosen,' she had thought, 'and quite unlike what she ought to have. Her dresser never ceased sighing and lifting up her hands and eyes all the time I looked at them and lamenting how little she cared about her dress.'*[10] Some of her clothing, indeed, was bought at Caley's, the drapers in Windsor High Street. One black silk dress was described by Lady Wolseley as being made 'anyhow and nohow'.[11]

The Queen enjoyed staying in country houses in England with Prince Albert as much as she did travelling with him on the Continent. She asked for lists of proposed fellow-guests to be submitted to her; but she very rarely objected to a name. She was not always a welcome guest, however: when she paid a short visit to the Duke of Wellington at Walmer Castle with the intention of giving her children a taste of the bracing air of the Kentish coast after an outbreak of scarlet fever had prevented them going to Brighton, the Duke complained that he had had to 'pull the building to pieces' to suit her convenience and that when she arrived late – her carriage having got stuck in the Castle entrance – the place was a scene of the most utter confusion with trunks and baggage in every room and 'Abigails, Maids, Nurses of all ages and descriptions running about'.[12]

The visit, however, was a success, even though the wind howled through the rattling windows. The Queen, so she claimed, formed quite an affection for the place.† A subsequent visit by the Queen and Prince Albert to the Duke's country house in Hampshire, Stratfield Saye, was also a success. There were only nine guest bedrooms in the house and the reception rooms were by no means large. The Duke had protested that the house was quite inadequate to receive Her Majesty. But she 'smiled and continued to be very gracious but did not give a hint of postponing the Visit'. So 'bells had to be hung from H.M. Apartments into those for Her attendants, Walls broken through, etc.'. 'You recollect Poor Mrs Apostles the Housekeeper,' the Duke reported to Lady Wilton, 'I thought that she would have burst out crying while I was talking to

---

* Before Prince Albert's death she was, however, interested in the clothes of others. In her journal she often gave detailed descriptions of them. 'We were received . . . by Lady Bulkeley whose dress I shall describe,' a characteristic entry runs (RA Queen's Journal, 9 August 1832). When her eldest daughter left home Victoria pressed her to tell her exactly what she was wearing in Germany: 'What bonnet did you wear on landing? And what bonnet the next two days . . . What also did you wear on the road . . . No one has told me what your toilette was to be these next days! . . . I see by the papers you wore a green dress at the Cologne concert: was that the one with black lace? I am so anxious to know . . . how all my toilettes succeeded . . . I am particularly vexed at hearing nothing, about your dresses. Let your German ladies give me an account of them' (Roger Fulford, ed., *Dearest Child: Letters between Queen Victoria and the Princess Royal, 1858–61*, 32, 34–5, 38).

† However, she later told Lady Salisbury that Walmer Castle was 'the most uncomfortable house she ever was in' (Kenneth Rose, *The Later Cecils*, 44).

Her of the Honour intended and the preparations to be made. She said to me, "My Lord, Your House is a very comfortable Residence for yourself, your family and your friends. But it is not fit for the reception of the Sovereign and her Court." I answered, "Very true." '[13]

The Duke proved himself to be a most attentive host, showing the Queen to her room and returning to escort her down to dinner, where he amused her by helping her to the dishes himself, 'rather funnily giving such large portions & mixing up tarts and puddings, but being so kind and attentive about it'.[14] After dinner he sat near to the Queen on the sofa where the conversation was 'certainly rather to the benefit of the whole society'. But he was 'very well and in very good spirits', she told her mother; and he went upstairs before her 'in the eveg: with two candles in his hand'.[15]

She had a 'nice little sitting room', a 'snug bedroom', and she and Albert both had dressing rooms. If she was to be critical, she had to confess that the Duke's central heating system made the rooms too hot. The Duke might have known that she would have found them so, her objection to warm rooms being well known: he confided in Lady Salisbury, he was 'never warm at Windsor, excepting in bed!'[16]

The Duke took Albert shooting and into the tennis court and the billiard room. Family prayers were said in the morning which had never been done before; and when, 'thank God!', the visit was concluded, the Duke attended 'Her Majesty on Horseback to the Borders of the County'.[17]

Some two years before this, in 1843, the Queen and Prince Albert had gone by train to stay at Drayton Manor near Tamworth, Staffordshire, a house in the Elizabethan style which Sir Robert Smirke had designed for Sir Robert Peel in the early 1830s.*

Still travelling by train, they went on to Chatsworth where the Duke of Devonshire, so Charles Greville said, 'would have willingly dispensed with her visit'. Nevertheless, 'all the people who have been at the Royal

---

* The train went along 'very easily though not quite as fast as the Great Western' (Queen Victoria's Journal, 28 November 1843). The Queen had made her first railway journey on the Great Western from Slough to Paddington the year before. The seventeen-mile journey had taken just twenty-three minutes, at an average of forty-four miles an hour. Prince Albert had thought this rather dangerous. 'Not so fast next time, Mr Conductor, if you please,' he is often said to have requested. The Queen's Private Secretary, when arranging a journey to Scotland with the Secretary of the Great Northern Railway in August 1854, gave the instruction: 'Her Majesty travels at the rate of forty miles an hour.' (Public Record Office, RAIL 236/6061, quoted in Jack Simmons, Railways, 253).

progress,' Greville continued, 'say there never was anything so grand as Chatsworth ... The Duke treats the Queen right royally. He met her at the station and brought her in his own coach and six, with coach and four following, and eight outriders. The finest sight was the illumination of the garden and the fountains; and after seeing the whole place covered with innumerable lamps and all the material of the illuminations, the Guests were astonished and delighted when they got up the following morning not to find a vestige of them left, and the whole garden as trim and neat as if nothing had occurred.'[18]

The Queen knew the house well, having been to stay there as a girl as well as during the elections of 1841, but on this later occasion there was something new and remarkable to see apart from the illuminations. This was a huge conservatory, 'the most stupendous and extraordinary creation imaginable', in the Queen's own words.[19] Over sixty feet high and nearly three hundred feet long, 'the whole entirely of glass', it had been designed by the remarkable man who had organized the illuminations, Joseph Paxton, a farmer's son, appointed superintendent of the gardens at Chatsworth in 1826 by the Duke who was himself President of the Horticultural Society of London.

From Chatsworth, where, so the Queen said, she would have liked to stay on for another day, the royal party went on to Belvoir Castle in Leicestershire which had not long since been restored for the fifth Duke of Rutland after a fire.

The Duke had arranged a day's fox hunting for the Prince and 'to the surprise of everybody', so Greville said, 'he acquitted himself in the field very creditably. He was supposed to be a very poor performer in this line, and as Englishmen love manliness and dexterity in field sports, it will have raised him considerably in publick estimation to have rode well after the hounds in Leicestershire.'[20]

The Queen was much put out that the Prince's dash and skill should have created such a stir. 'One can hardly credit the absurdity of people here, but Albert's riding so boldly and hard has made such a sensation that it has been written all over the country, and they make much more of it than if he had done some great act! It rather disgusts one, but still it has done, and does good, for it has put an end to all impertinent sneering for the future about Albert's riding.'[21]

The Queen would also have been annoyed had she known about the stories that were circulating in society about the possible reasons for her travelling about so much in England and abroad, rumours that she might have inherited a form of the mental disturbance which had afflicted her grandfather, George III. Charles Greville 'heard a whisper . . . that the Queen had been in a restless state – always wanting to go somewhere and do something, and that it was thought advisable to let the excitement find a vent in these excursions. It is certainly remarkable that from the time Parliament broke up till now [December 1843] she has been, with only short intervals, in a constant state of locomotion, first in France, then in Belgium, then at Cambridge [where they stayed in the Master's Lodge at Trinity College and the Prince received the honorary degree of Doctor of Civil Law]* and now these recent visits.'[22] At the beginning of 1844 Greville heard that it was 'reported in the City that the Queen's mind [was] not in a right state . . . slight appearances [indicated] restlessness, excitement, nervousness'.[23]

The travelling could not be resumed in 1844, first because of one of those frequent occurences of family mourning and then because of the Queen's pregnancy with her fourth child, Prince Alfred, 'Affie', who was born on 6 August. But in the summer of 1845 the Queen and her husband were free to go abroad again, this time once more to Belgium to see King Leopold and Queen Louise, then on to Bonn, where the Prince showed the Queen the small house where he had lodged as a student, then to the palace of the King of Prussia where the Queen was extremely annoyed, and made no attempt to disguise her annoyance, that her husband was not given the precedence she considered was due to him, the Archduke Frederick of Austria, an uncle of the Emperor, being placed above Prince Albert at a banquet at the Prussian Court. For days after this slight, so it was reported at home, the Queen remained grumpy. 'We hear of nothing but the dissatisfaction which the Q. gave in Germany,' Charles Greville recorded, 'of her want of civility and graciousness, and a great many stories are told which are probably exaggerated or untrue. It is clear, however, that the general impression was not favourable.'[24]

Once they had crossed over the border into Coburg, however, the Queen's annoyance was forgotten in her pleasure at the reception she

---

* At Cambridge, 'both in going and returning,' the Queen recorded in her journal, 'the scholars threw down their gowns for us to walk over, like Sir Walter Raleigh' (RA Queen Victoria's Journal, 25 October 1843).

and the Prince were accorded by the crowds that lined their route to the town, this 'dear old place' as the Queen called it, as though it had been her childhood home as well as her husband's. 'If I were not who I am,' she wrote the next day after a visit to Albert's birthplace, the Rosenau, '*this* would have been my real home, but I shall always consider it my second one.' She climbed the stairs to the small bedrooms which had been Albert's and his brother, Ernest's. The view was beautiful; the wallpaper, she noted, with her eye for such details, was 'still full of holes from their fencing'.[25]

Regrettably their German hosts, in an effort to entertain their visitors, laid on a grand *battue* in the Thüringen Forest which Lady Canning described with strong distaste:

> Three hundred men had been employed beating the woods for ten days to drive the deer [into a canvas enclosure] . . . The shooters were stationed in different little turf forts, four or five guns together. Then a signal was given and an army of *chasseurs* instantly threw down the canvas wall . . . Then everybody fired at the poor things who were driven in and out of the wood and up and down the hill till all were killed – it was a piteous sight, much the worse from the bad shooting, for most of the poor beasts were dreadfully wounded long before they were killed.[26]

The Queen also condemned the *battue* which, she maintained, was 'hardly real sport', amounting to 'a kind of slaughter'. But what distressed her quite as much was the fact that Albert was condemned in England for having taken part in it. The prestige he had won for riding so well to hounds in Leicestershire was largely dissipated by his massacring deer in the Thüringer Wald.

She herself was also much criticized at home.

> Nothing can exceed the universal indignation felt here by people of every description at the brutal and stupid massacre of the deer which Albert perpetrated and at which she assisted [commented Greville].* It has been severely commented on in several of the

* The Queen did not take part in the shooting herself. Indeed, she was opposed to ladies shooting at all. When she heard that her granddaughter, Princess Victoria of Hesse, had gone out shooting with her father, she wrote to her: 'I was, darling Child, rather shocked to hear of your shooting at a mark but far more so at your idea of going out shooting with dear Papa. To look on is harmless but it is not lady like to kill animals & go out shooting – and I hope you will never do that. It might do you gt harm if that was known as *only fast* ladies do such things' (*Advice to a Grand-daughter: Letters from Queen Victoria to Princess Victoria of Hesse*, ed. Richard Hough, 26).

papers, and met by a very clumsy (and false) attempt to persuade people that She was shocked and annoyed. No such thing appeared and nothing compelled her to see it. But the truth is [added Greville] her sensibilities are not acute, and though she is not at all ill-natured, perhaps the reverse, she is hard-hearted, selfish and self-willed.[27]

22

×××××××××××

BALMORAL

'They live [at Balmoral] not merely like private
gentlefolks, but like very small gentlefolks.'

SOON AFTER THE QUEEN AND PRINCE ALBERT moved into their
new house at Osborne they considered the possibility of buying another
retreat, farther from London and far more remote. They had first been
to Scotland in 1842, sailing from Woolwich to Edinburgh in the *Royal
George* and staying with the Duke of Buccleuch and Queensberry, one
of her aides-de-camp and Captain-General of the Royal Company of
Archers, at Dalkeith Palace, Midlothian, and then with the Marquess of
Breadalbane, a future Lord Chamberlain of the Household, at Taymouth
Castle in Perthshire. They were enchanted by all that they saw as they
travelled to Loch Leven and Scone, Stirling Castle and Linlithgow, the
Prince constantly reminded of the Coburg he loved and missed: even the
people of the Highlands seemed to him to look like Germans.[1]

'Scotland has made a most favourable impression upon us both,' he
told his grandmother. 'The country is full of beauty . . . perfect for sport
of all kinds, and the air remarkably pure and light . . . The people are
more natural, and are marked by that honesty and sympathy, which
always distinguish the inhabitants of mountainous countries, who live far
away from towns. There is, moreover, no country where historical tra-
ditions are preserved with such fidelity . . . Every spot is connected with
some interesting historical fact, and with most of these Sir Walter Scott's
accurate descriptions have made us familiar.'[2]

Two years later, in the autumn of 1844, the Queen and Prince were
back in Scotland as guests of Lord Glenlyon, shortly to succeed his uncle

as sixth Duke of Atholl, at Blair Castle in Perthshire. Again they were enchanted by both countryside and people. The Queen was 'quite delighted' with Blair Atholl, Charlotte Canning said, and in such 'very high spirits, full of jokes and fun', while the Prince was 'in ecstacies'. 'We are all well,' he told the Dowager Duchess of Coburg, 'and live a somewhat primitive, yet romantic, mountain life, that acts as a tonic to the nerves, and gladdens the heart of a lover, like myself, of field-sports and of Nature.' Lady Canning disapproved of their going to a Church of Scotland service in the Kirk on Sunday when they might well have joined the 'poor little episcopal congregation'. This was also the view of the *Morning Post* which condemned the Queen for going to a service in the 'meeting-place of the Calvinists or Presbyterians, to whom Prelacy – the Prelacy Her Majesty has sworn to maintain – is the object of implacable hate and abhorrence'. But Prince Albert was perfectly satisfied with the Kirk, the service there being quite like what he had been used to in Germany.[3]

'I can only say that the scenery is lovely,' the Queen wrote in her diary, 'grand, romantic, and a great peace and wilderness pervades all, which is sublime.' 'Blair itself and the houses in the village looked like little toys from the great height we were on,' she continued, having climbed the hill of Tulloch, guided by one of Lord Glenlyon's servants in his Highland dress. 'It was quite romantic. Here we were with only this Highlander behind us holding the ponies, not a house, not a creature near us, but the pretty Highland sheep with their horns and black faces.' 'It was really the most delightful, most romantic ride and walk' she had ever had. Indeed, the whole short holiday had been a delight and the Highlanders she had encountered were such 'chivalrous, fine, active people'. When she got home she found it difficult to reconcile herself to being at Windsor again as she pined for her 'dear, dear Highlands, the hills, the pure air, the quiet, the retirement, the liberty – *all*'.[4]

Three years passed. Another child was born, the Queen's third daughter, Helena, to be known as 'Lenchen', on 25 May 1846. Then in the summer of 1847 the Queen was able to spend another holiday in Scotland to which she had so much been looking forward, this time as a guest of the second Marquess of Abercorn, Groom of the Stole to the Prince Consort, who lent the royal party a remote fishing lodge at Ardverikie on the shore of Loch Laggan, Inverness. Even though it poured with rain for much of the time, the Queen was again enchanted by Scotland and the Scottish people; and when they got home they decided they must have a place in the Highlands themselves.

They were encouraged in this decision by Sir James Clark, still the Queen's Physician-in-Ordinary, who had been born at Cullen in Banffshire and who, as author of 'The Influence of Climate in the Prevention and Cure of Chronic Diseases' and of a 'Treatise on Pulmonary Consumption', entertained a high opinion of the curative and prophylactic effects of pure fresh air, Highland air in particular. He was acquainted with Sir Robert Gordon who lived at Balmoral, a turreted castle of white-washed granite with slit windows, a high-pitched roof and round towers with cone-shaped roofs. It stood not far from Ardverikie, where the air and climate were, in Sir James's opinion, particularly beneficial. Fortuitously, Sir Robert died suddenly over his breakfast table on 8 October 1847; and the Queen, pressed by Sir James Clark to do so, bought what remained of the lease from Sir Robert's brother, Lord Aberdeen, who had inherited it. She did so without having seen it but she was satisfied that it was presentable enough for their purpose by a set of watercolours commissioned from the Scottish landscape painter, James Giles, a friend of Lord Aberdeen.[5]

Early the following year the Queen and Prince went to see Balmoral, 'a pretty little Castle in the old Scotch style', and were not disappointed. 'All seemed to breathe freedom and peace,' the Queen wrote, 'and to make one forget the world and its sad turmoils.' The pure air was 'most refreshing', the soil 'delightfully dry', and all was 'so calm and so solitary', so reminiscent of the Thüringer Wald. It was 'wonderful not seeing a single human being, not hearing a sound excepting that of the wind, or the call of the blackcock or grouse'. And then the Highlanders were so intelligent and warm-hearted, so well bred, so polite without being in the least subservient.

She and Albert, she felt sure, could both be very happy and healthy at Balmoral; and so they were. Charles Greville, who went there in September 1849 to attend a Council 'to order a Prayer for relief against the cholera', painted a picture of the most perfect contentment. Leaving on a Monday by the five o'clock train, he spent the first night at Crewe, the second at Perth and arrived at Balmoral at half past two on Wednesday afternoon just in time for the meeting.

'I am glad to have made this expedition,' he wrote in his diary, 'and to have seen the Queen and Prince in their Highland retreat, where they certainly appear to great advantage. The place is very pretty, the house very small.' So small was it in fact that there were no sitting rooms for guests; and Ministers might well find themselves discussing state affairs with Her Majesty while she was sitting on the edge of their bed on which, as Lord Malmesbury discovered, they had to write their despatches, their secretaries being lodged three miles away. The billiard room had to serve also as a drawing room and the ladies had to keep moving about to dodge the players' cues.

> They live here without any state whatever [Greville continued]. They live not merely like gentlefolks, but like very small gentlefolks, small house, small rooms, small establishment. There are no Soldiers, and the whole guard of the Sovereign and the whole Royal Family is a single Policeman, who walks about the grounds to keep off impertinent intruders or improper characters. They live with the greatest simplicity and ease. He shoots every morning, returns to luncheon, and then they walk and drive. She is running in and out of the house all day long, and often goes about alone, walks into the cottages, and sits down and chats with the old women. I never before was in society with the Prince, or had any conversation with him. On Thursday morning John Russell and I were sitting together after breakfast, when he came in and sat down with us, and we conversed for about three-quarters of an hour. I was greatly struck with him. I saw at once (what I had always heard) that he is very intelligent and highly cultivated, and moreover that he has a thoughtful mind, and thinks of subjects worth thinking about. He seemed very much at ease, very gay, pleasant, and without the least stiffness or air of dignity. After luncheon we went to the Highland gathering at Braemar ... We returned as we came, and then everybody strolled about till dinner. We were only nine people, and it was all very easy and really agreeable, the Queen in very good humour and talkative; he still more, and talking very well; no form, and everybody seemed at their ease. In the evening we withdrew to the only room there is besides the dining-room, which serves for billiards, library (hardly any books in it), and drawing-room. The Queen and Prince and her Ladies and Gordon [the Prince's equerry, Alexander Hamilton Gordon] soon went back to the dining-room, where they had a Highland dancing-master, who gave them lessons in reels. We (J. R. [Lord John Russell] and I) were not admitted to this exercise, so we played at billiards. In process of time they came back, when there was a little talk, and soon after they went to bed.[6]

Everyone agreed with Greville that the Queen was in exceptionally good humour when she was in Scotland, a country superior to all others, in her opinion, there being, as a rather exasperated Lady Lyttelton said, nothing to compare with 'Scotch air, Scotch people, Scotch hills, Scotch rivers, Scotch words'. Lady Lyttelton added that she herself could 'never see, hear or witness these various charms'.[7]

Mary Ponsonby described the Queen as being 'so easy to satisfy' when she was in this country so beloved by her, 'so warmly genial', 'so completely charming'.[8] Indeed, according to Lord Clarendon, the Queen was 'quite a different person' when in Scotland. She was always loath to leave it and its 'wild, simple and peculiar charms' in order to go back to Windsor, to return to the formal life she was required to live there. 'Altogether I feel so sad … at the bitter thought of going from this blessed place,' she wrote to the Princess Royal, 'leaving these hills – this enchanting life of liberty – these dear people – and returning to tame, dull, formal England and the prison life of Windsor!'[9]

She relished her days out with Albert, setting off on ponies with the ghillies through the 'wildest and finest scenery', past burns with water 'as clear as glass', taking out her sketch book while Albert crept off to stalk stags or shoot ptarmigan, fishing for trout with him on the loch, entering the cottages on the estate with little presents for the women who spoke to her in their 'curious Highland English' which she liked so much, sitting down with them to share a simple meal and making purchases in the shape of butter and eggs, going up to the granite hut at Allt-na-Guibhsaich for a picnic above Loch Muich, attended by a lady-in-waiting, servants and ghillies, meeting women who did not know who she was, one who presented her with a bunch of flowers, another who offered her milk and a bit of bread.[10]

To their great pleasure the Queen and Prince were eventually able to buy the freehold of Balmoral with its 17,400 acres for £31,500 from the trustees of the Earl of Fife in 1848 and afterwards to extend the property by acquiring the adjacent 6,000 acres of the Birkhall estate, which was bought by the Duchy of Cornwall for the Prince of Wales, as well as by taking a lease of another neighbouring estate, Abergeldie. Then in 1852 they fulfilled their plans to build a completely new house, as they had done at Osborne.

The following year the Queen laid the foundation stone of the new

Scottish baronial Balmoral Castle which Prince Albert had himself designed with the help of William Smith, an architect and builder from Aberdeen. It was, the Queen said, 'a beautiful' building, her 'dearest Albert's *own* creation', his 'own work, own building, own laying out as at Osborne'. His 'great taste' and the 'impress of his dear hand' was 'stamped everywhere'.

It was certainly eclectic in style, incorporating ideas gleaned in Germany and Bruges as well as from the turreted style of his Scottish baronial neighbours. In its design there was, as Lady Augusta Bruce, the Duchess of Kent's lady-in-waiting, observed with reticence, 'a certain absence of harmony of the whole'.

Since it was Albert's creation the Queen, of course, would have nothing said against either its architecture or its interior decoration. The whole place was 'charming', the rooms were 'delightful, the furniture, papers, everything perfection'.

The rooms admittedly were bright and cheerful, the large windows commanding lovely views; but many visitors were by no means favourably impressed by the general ambience of the place, the tartan curtains and tartan chair coverings, the tartan wallpaper and tartan carpets, the thistle motifs which were in such abundance that Lord Clarendon thought they would 'rejoice the heart of a donkey if they happened to *look like* his favourite repast, which they don't'.[11] Lord Rosebery was to say that he thought the drawing room at Osborne was the ugliest in the world until he saw the one at Balmoral. 'The ornaments are strictly Scotch,' Rosebery wrote, 'and the curtains and the covers are of "dress Stuart" tartan. The effect is not very pretty.'*[12]

The owners of the place were as 'Scotchified' as their habitat: the Queen even came to adopt a kind of Scottish accent to suit her surroundings, once saying, as she sat down to dinner, what one of her ladies

---

* 'Dear Grand-Mama's taste in wallpapers was rather sad and very doubtful!!!' her daughter-in-law, Queen Alexandra, had to concede in a letter to Queen Mary in 1910. 'That washed out pink moiré paper in the sitting-room is *sickly* and the one in the bedroom appalling but I never liked to touch anything of hers so I left it exactly as she had it ... I wonder if you have made any alterations' (RA/CC/42/81, quoted in Georgina Battiscombe, *Queen Alexandra*, 1969, 220).

Queen Mary did, indeed, in the words of her biographer, 'make radical changes' at Balmoral, 'for she had inherited all her father's [Francis, Duke of Teck's] passion for re-hanging pictures and re-arranging rooms. One of her first steps was to have the panelling stripped and lightened, and it is now only in the back passages that one can find traces of the dark marmalade-coloured paint' (James Pope-Hennessy, *Queen Mary, 1867–1953*, 205).

transcribed as 'I a do*a*nt know why the candles give no*a* light now, it is so d*aa*rk.'[13] Her family had taken to wearing kilts; and Prince Albert, who had bought a huge Gaelic dictionary, had designed their own tartans, a white 'Victoria tartan' and a red 'Balmoral tartan'. The food served in the dining room had a distinctive Scottish bias: oatmeal porridge and smoked haddock were served at breakfast; and around the table during dinner marched Highlanders playing bagpipes, the loud skirls of which, so a maid-of-honour said, were enough to blow your head off. In time the place acquired its own distinctive, somehow Scottish smell, a 'special smell', described by one of the Queen's granddaughters as of a combination of 'wood fire, stags' heads, rugs and leather'.[14]

Lord Clarendon also complained that the house was so fearfully cold that his toes were frost-bitten as he was having dinner, while in the drawing room the two little sticks in the fireplace hissed at the man who was trying to light them and the Queen, thinking, Clarendon supposed, that they were in danger of catching fire, had a large screen placed between the royal nose and the unignited wood.

Tsar Nicholas II expressed the opinion that Balmoral was colder than the Siberian wastes; while Mary Ponsonby, like the Duke of Wellington at Windsor, was never warm there except in bed. Other guests were distressed to observe that the Queen, being notoriously impervious to cold herself, had the big windows opened on all but the iciest days and, here as elsewhere, had thermometers placed in all the principal rooms so that she could ensure that they never became what she herself considered overheated by the reluctantly permitted fires of beechwood, almost always beechwood since the Queen had 'the same rooted objection to coal as to gas'.*[15]

The Marchioness of Dalhousie, who had become accustomed to the heat of India while her husband was serving as Governor-General there, 'never saw anything more uncomfortable' than Balmoral Castle, nor

---

* She was later persuaded to tolerate the installation of gas lighting at Buckingham Palace and Windsor Castle. But candles remained the preferred lighting at Balmoral since she considered 'this old-fashioned style cosier'. Towards the end of the Queen's life, Sarah Tooley was told that 'she does not take to the electric light and will not have it introduced into the royal palaces' (*The Personal Life of Queen Victoria*, 1901, 266). In fact, it was introduced, even at Balmoral, in the 1890s. 'It brightens up one's bedroom very much,' wrote Lady Lytton, 'but the Queen does not like it and feels the glare very much for her eyes, and in the sitting room it is not very skilfully done' (*Lady Lytton's Court Diary*, 1961, 142).

anything she coveted less. 'The Queen in her own house is far from a Constitutional Sovereign,' commented Lord Rosebery. 'She allows her family (at least, and I think the whole household) no fires at this time of year [September].'[16]

Ministers abhorred the place, not only because they wasted so much of their time travelling there when they were required to attend upon the Queen, but also because they were so uncomfortable when they did get there. 'Carrying on the Government of a country six hundred miles from the Metropolis' doubled the labour involved in being Prime Minister, Disraeli was later to complain, though not, of course, to the Queen herself who was deaf to all appeals not to spend so much of her time in Scotland.[17]

Lord Salisbury, who made 'no attempt to conceal his disgust with the place', was always 'heartily glad' to get away from it. Both he and Disraeli had to obtain doctors' orders to have their rooms heated to a reasonable temperature – while the Queen's Private Secretary, Sir Henry Ponsonby, was to lament, 'Every private house strikes me as comfortable, after the severe dreariness of our palatial rooms *here*.'*[18]

* The domestic staff at Balmoral had far more reason to complain of their accommodation than ministerial guests and members of the household. 'The under servants are so fearfully crowded at Balmoral in their rooms,' Lady Lytton wrote in her diary in the 1890s. 'Four laundry maids have to sleep in one bed in a tiny room' (*Lady Lytton's Court Diary, 1895–99*, 77).

23

✳✳✳✳✳✳✳✳✳✳✳✳

THE PRINCE OF WALES

'He was afraid of his father.'

WHEN THE QUEEN laid the foundation stone of the new Balmoral Castle on 28 September 1853, her heir was eleven years old. The placid equanimity he had displayed in the earliest years of his infancy had not survived his fifth birthday. Lady Lyttelton, now known as 'Laddle', had had cause to complain of his being 'uncommonly averse to learning' and requiring 'much patience from wilful inattention and constant interruptions, getting under the table, upsetting the books and sundry other *anti-studious* practices'.[1]

His father, neither then nor later, did not try to conceal the fact that Victoria, the Princess Royal, was his favourite child. When he came into the nursery, as he often did – once, to the Princess Royal's indignation, sitting in 'Laddle's' chair – his eye alighted upon her with pleasure; but in the contemplation of her brother his countenance became troubled and apprehensive. Edward's mother also seemed to prefer her sharp and quick-witted daughter to her difficult son and spent far more time with her. It was already rumoured in society that the Queen did not much care for her eldest son, that, as Charles Greville put it, 'the hereditary and unfailing antipathy of our Sovereigns to their Heirs Apparent [was] already taking root'.[2] Lady Beauvale was quoted as saying that the Queen had observed that the Prince was 'a stupid boy'. He began to stammer; and his sister teased him for it, imitating him, driving him to fury. One afternoon the two children had 'a tremendous fight' when brought down to their parents' room; so the next day they were brought down separately but, the one being taken into the room before the other was taken away, they fell to quarrelling again.

It was worse when other children were born and they, too, proved to be brighter than the Prince of Wales. By the time he was six he had already been overtaken by Princess Alice, who was not only more than eighteen months younger than himself but who was 'neither so studious nor so clever as the Princess Royal'.

The Queen could but hope that in time the boy would improve; and in the meantime she was not a neglectful mother, although, as Lady Lyttelton said, she was certainly a strict one, more ready to find fault than to praise. She was also determined to ensure that the children were never indulged and were given object lessons in the virtues of thrift and simplicity, that they were brought up 'as simply and in as domestic a way as possible' and that they grew to be 'fit for *whatever station*' they might 'be placed in, *high or low*', since the 'bane of the present day was pride, vulgar, unchristian pride'. They had to make do with simple fare such as the boiled beef and semolina pudding which a member of the household once saw being carried up to the nursery; and the younger ones had to be content with clothes handed down to them from their older siblings who had grown out of them.

Strict though she was, she sometimes played games with the children, rowdy games like blind man's buff and fox-and-geese, and quieter ones like beggar-my-neighbour. She danced quadrilles with the Prince of Wales as her partner, and on summer evenings she went for little walks with him and helped him to catch moths. She watched him rehearse plays with his brothers and sisters under the direction of their conscientious father who made them 'say their parts over and over again'. Occasionally she would announce a special day's holiday and they would all go sailing or have a picnic. 'Children,' the Queen decided, 'though often a source of anxiety and difficulty are a great blessing and cheer and brighten up life.' She had to admit, however, that she found 'no special pleasure' in the company of her own children 'and only very exceptionally' did she find 'intimate intercourse with them either agreeable or easy'. On occasions she would play with them out of a sense of duty rather than inclination. When her husband was away 'ALL the children' [were] as *nothing* to her. It 'seemed as if the whole life of the house and home were gone'.

The two elder children were at first taught separately from the others, particular attention being paid to English, arithmetic, history, writing and geography, and an hour a day being devoted to both German and French. The Queen undertook to give religious instruction to her daughter, though not to her son, and to supervise her prayers. But she found it difficult to spare the time to do so, delegating this task to others who were told to ensure that the child had 'great reverence for God' but that she should be encouraged to feel 'devotion and love' for Him rather than 'fear and trembling'. As to whether or not the children should say their prayers kneeling or in bed, she consulted Princess Feodora, who considered it 'absurd that kneeling could have anything to do with making prayers acceptable to the Almighty'. So did Prince Albert, who considered kneeling to be a 'peculiar feature of English religiosity'. Lady Lyttelton, however, thought it was 'highly irreverent' not to kneel. So Prince Albert gave way since the children were to be brought up as Anglicans and therefore 'their prejudices must be those of the English Church'.[3]

If any alterations in the syllabus were considered necessary, or if any exceptional awards or punishments were proposed, the parents had to be consulted. Lady Lyttelton herself did not believe in the severe punishment of young children; but Prince Albert considered that physical chastisement was occasionally necessary to secure obedience. Even his daughters were whipped on his instructions and were subjected to lengthy admonitions with their hands tied together. At the age of four Princess Alice received 'a real punishment by whipping' for telling a lie. The Prince of Wales and his brothers received even harsher treatment.[4]

Doubts were expressed about the efficacy of this harsh treatment, not, however, by Lord Melbourne, who was deeply interested in flagellation, showed his mistresses pictures of women being beaten and seems to have given Caroline Lamb 'practical lessons upon whipping'. He himself had been flogged at Eton and thought he had not been flogged enough: it 'would have been better' if he had been 'flogged more', since the floggings had 'an amazing effect on him' and had been 'of no inconsiderable service'. But he advised the Queen not to set too much store by the whole process of education: it might 'mould and direct the character' but rarely altered it.[5]

Neither the Queen nor Prince Albert subscribed to this view; nor did Baron Stockmar, who, needless to say, provided them with long memoranda on the subject and gave them the alarming warning that the parents 'ought to be thoroughly permeated' with the truth that 'their position is a more difficult one than that of any other parent in the kingdom'.[6]

Insisting that discipline must continue to be strict, the parents believed that the children's syllabuses must remain exacting, particularly that of the Prince of Wales, so that 'the grand object' of his education might be fulfilled. This object, declared the Bishop of Oxford, one of those numerous experts consulted by the parents, must be none other than to turn the Prince into 'the most perfect man'.[7]

In furtherance of this ambitious scheme, it was decided that the Prince should be 'taken *entirely away* from the women', provided with a valet and handed over to a male tutor, Henry Birch – who was employed for this purpose in April 1849 at a salary of £800 a year – while still, in the Queen's words, growing 'truly under his father's eye and guided by him so that when he has reached the age of sixteen or seventeen he may be a real companion to his father'.

Birch found his charge extremely disobedient, impertinent to his masters and unwilling to submit to discipline. He was also exceedingly selfish and unable even 'to play at any game for five minutes, or attempt anything new or difficult without losing his temper'; and when he did lose his temper his rage was uncontrollable.[8]

He could not bear to be teased or criticized; and though he flew into a tantrum or sulked whenever he was teased, Birch thought it best, 'notwithstanding his sensitiveness, to laugh at him . . . to ignore his dislike of chaff' and to treat him as boys would have treated him in an English public school. His parents thought so, too; and they caused him anguish by mocking him when he had done something wrong or stupid. 'Poor Prince,' commented Lady Lyttelton one day when he was derided for asking, 'Mama, is not a pink the female of a carnation?'[9]

Mr Birch did not disguise his belief that the policy of keeping the Prince so strictly isolated from other boys was one of the reasons for his tiresome behaviour. It was Birch's 'deliberate opinion' that many of his pupil's 'peculiarities' arose from the effects of this policy, 'from his being continually in the society of older persons, and from his finding himself the centre round which everything seems to move'.

But his father did not agree, considering it advisable to safeguard him as far as possible from the company of boys of his own age who might well corrupt him. It would be far better, Prince Albert thought, to concentrate upon his son's education rather than upon his need for companionship. There were lessons to be learned every weekday, including Saturday. Holidays, except on family birthdays, were rare, though the Queen did insist that Sundays should, as Prince Albert put it, be treated as 'days of recreation and amusement'; and when Birch protested to Stockmar that he had never heard of a family in which games like cricket were allowed on a Sunday, the Queen, who had strong views on the question, protested that Sundays had 'always been treated as a holiday': she was set against 'the extreme severity of the Sunday in this country when carried to excess'. A tutor who took her third son, Prince Arthur, who had been born in 1850, to two church services on a Sunday was reprimanded for his zealotry. Similarly the Prince of Wales was enjoined to take Holy Communion only twice a year, even though the Prayer Book specified a minimum of three attendances.

When the Prince went away with his parents, Birch went with them. In August 1849 he accompanied the Queen and Prince Albert on a visit to Ireland and, dressed in a sailor suit, he was driven about the streets with them; but as soon as he got back to Vice-Regal Lodge or aboard the royal yacht, *Fairy*, he had to settle down to his books again. When he went with his parents to Balmoral, he was quickly disabused of the hope that he was to have a short holiday. His tutor thought a little deer stalking or some other outdoor activity 'such as taking the heights of hills' would not come amiss. But Prince Albert said that 'it must not be supposed that [the visit to Balmoral] was to be taken as a holiday'. The tutor was required to send regular reports on his pupil's progress to the boy's father, who was rarely comforted by what he read. The boy's German was quite good: by the age of five he could read a German book without much difficulty and carry on a conversation in German without undue hesitation, though this ability seemed to interfere with his mastery of English. Despite all the efforts of the actor, George Bartley, who was employed to give him elocution lessons, the Prince never altogether lost his slight German accent and to the end of his life there was a noticeably Germanic guttural burr in his pronunciation of the letter 'r'. His French was not as good as his German, and it was not until later in life that he acquired the accent and vocabulary on which he was to pride himself.

In his anxiety Prince Albert consulted the eminent phrenologist, George Combe, one of the seventeen children of a Scottish brewer, who, having examined the boy's cranium, 'pointed out the peculiarities of his temperament and brain'.

'The organs of ostentativeness, destructiveness, self-esteem, combativeness and love of approbation are all large,' Combe gloomily concluded. 'Intellectual organs are only moderately well developed.'[10]

'I wonder whence that Anglo-Saxon brain of his has come,' Prince Albert commented, on receiving Combe's report. 'It must have descended from the Stuarts, for the family has been purely German since their day.'

As time passed the Prince became increasingly dissatisfied with Mr Birch, who, conscious of the disapproval and resentful at being required to spend 'morning, noon and night in the company of a child' without holidays, offered to resign at once if his employers 'knew of anyone who would be more likely to succeed in the management of so young a child'. Relations between Birch and the parents were further strained by his wish to become ordained. The Queen, who had so strongly disapproved of Lady Lyttelton's High-Church views, thought that Birch's 'Puseyism' might well render him an unsuitable tutor once he had taken Holy Orders. She agreed to his remaining on condition that he promise not to be 'aggressive' in his religion, that he attend Presbyterian services when the royal family were in Scotland, and that he did not forswear 'innocent amusements' such as dancing and shooting. Although assured that Birch was 'plain straightforward Church of England', Prince Albert could not agree to his retaining his appointment should he be ordained. It was settled, therefore, that he would not respond to his vocation for the time being. He continued as tutor until January 1852 when, having entered Holy Orders, he resigned.[11]

By then he had become attached to his charge and did his best to reassure the boy's father that his progress was not as disappointing as his parents were inclined to believe. Certainly his writing and spelling left much to be desired, but 'we must not forget', Birch reported, 'that there are few English boys who know so much French and German or know so much general information'. The pupil's regard for the tutor was reciprocated; and the Prince was much distressed by his father's refusal to keep him on. 'It has been a terrible sorrow to the Prince of Wales who has done no end of touching things since he heard he was to lose him,' wrote Lady Canning. 'He is such an affectionate dear little boy; his little notes and presents which Mr Birch used to find on his pillow were really too moving.'[12]

Birch's successor was Frederick Waymouth Gibbs, a rather staid, unhumorous, unimaginative, fussy and opinionated barrister of twenty-nine who had been a Fellow of Trinity College, Cambridge. His mother being insane and his father bankrupt, he had been brought up with the sons of his mother's friend, Sir James Stephen, Professor of Modern History at Cambridge and grandfather of Virginia Woolf. He was to receive a salary of £1,000 'with any addition to that sum which Baron Stockmar [might] decide to be just and reasonable', and to remain with the Prince until his seventeenth birthday.

Gibbs soon learned that his task would not be an easy one. On his arrival the Queen summoned him for an interview at which, so he recorded in his diary,

> She spoke a good deal about the Princes and bade me notice two peculiarities in the Prince of Wales. First, at times he hangs his head and looks at his feet, and invariably within a day or two has one of his fits of nervous and unmanageable temper. Secondly, riding hard, or after he has become fatigued, has been invariably followed by outburst of temper.[13]

He had been 'injured by being with the Princess Royal who was very clever and a child far above her age,' the Queen continued. 'She puts him down by a look – or a word – and their natural affection [has been] impaired by this state of things.'

The new tutor's early contacts with the Prince himself, however, were pleasant enough. The day after his predecessor's departure he went for a walk with both the Prince of Wales and Prince Alfred, and the elder boy, now ten years of age, politely apologized for their silence. 'You cannot wonder if we are somewhat dull today,' he said. 'We are sorry Mr Birch has gone. It is very natural, is it not?' Mr Gibbs could not deny that it was, indeed, very natural. Gibbs no doubt expected in his self-satisfied way that in time the Prince would develop the same kind of affection and respect for himself. But the Prince never did. On the contrary, he grew to detest him, and was soon as unruly and unpredictable as he had ever been in the worst days of Mr Birch.

The Prince's other tutors ventured to express the opinion that the boy was being overworked. On the orders of his father, who continued to believe in the efficacy of a sound boxing of the ears or a few sharp raps across the knuckles with a stick, there was no relaxation in the length and frequency of the boy's lessons which began at eight o'clock in the morning and ended at six o'clock at night, seven days a week.

Between his intellectual pursuits he was taught riding, gymnastics and dancing, and – under the instruction of a drill sergeant – military exercises. In winter he was taught to skate; in summer to swim and play croquet. He learned about forestry and farming, carpentry and brick-laying.

His tutors were instructed to ensure that he was exhausted by the end of each day, when a report upon his progress and conduct was submitted to his parents.

The product of this regimen was not an appealing child. The Prince of Wales's sense of frustration and inferiority, combined with the strain of exhaustion, led him not only to seek relief in outbursts of furious violence, but also to be aggressively rude to those few boys of his own age whom he was ever allowed to meet.

The Queen admitted in confidence to her eldest daughter that 'Papa ... momentarily and unintentionally [could sometimes be] hasty and harsh', but she did not question the necessity for severity with the Prince of Wales.

The Prince responded to this severity with fear as well as with violence. 'He was afraid of his father,' wrote Charles Wynn-Carrington, one of those few Etonians allowed into Windsor Castle, who did not find it surprising that this was so, for Prince Albert seemed to him 'a proud, shy, stand-offish man, not calculated to make friends easily with children. Individually I was frightened to death of him, so much so that on one occasion [when] he suddenly appeared from behind some bushes, I fell off the see-saw from sheer alarm at seeing him, and nearly broke my neck.'[14] The Prince was never allowed to forget that he was being con-stantly and anxiously watched by his father, and that by others he was for ever being compared – of course, unfavourably compared – with him. The Queen once informed her son in one of many similar letters:

> None of you can ever be proud enough of being the child of such a Father who has not his equal in this world – so great, so good, so faultless. Try ... to follow in his footsteps and don't be discour-aged, for to be really in everything like him none of you, I am sure, will ever be. Try, therefore, to be like him in some points, and you will have acquired a great deal.[15]

Hard as he was kept at his lessons, there were occasional days of pleasure for the Prince. He afterwards remembered how much he had enjoyed going out hunting and deer stalking, fishing and shooting with his father, though hard as he practised he never learned to shoot very well. He remembered, too, the delight he had experienced at being taken with his brothers and sisters to the zoo and the pantomime, to Astley's Circus, and the opera at Covent Garden; the excitement when Wombwell's menagerie visited Windsor Castle, when General Tom Thumb, the American dwarf from Barnum's 'Greatest Show on Earth', came to Buckingham Palace; and when Albert Smith, who related so vividly his adventures while climbing Mont Blanc, gave a lecture at Osborne. He remembered also the plays which Charles Kean and Samuel Phelps put on at Windsor before presenting them in London at the Princess's Theatre and Sadler's Wells; and the performances at Balmoral of the marvellous conjuror, John Henry Anderson, the 'Wizard of the North' – of course, so the Prince confided to one of his father's guests, 'Papa [knew] how all these things [were] done'.[16]

The more practical part of the children's education, including the making of bricks and the erection of tents, took place at Osborne where their father, a knowledgeable gardener himself, arranged for them to have their own gardens, complete with shed and tools marked with their initials and suitable for their respective sizes. Here in neat rows in individual plots they grew vegetables as well as flowers; and nearby were shrubs, planted by the four eldest children, all with labels bearing their names painted by the Prince of Wales on outlines pencilled for him by one of his mother's ladies-in-waiting.[17]

Facing these gardens was a Swiss cottage similar to one in the grounds of the Rosenau, a wooden structure made from prefabricated parts and looking so authentic, as the Queen said, that one could 'fancy oneself suddenly transported to another country'. The foundation stone was laid on 5 May 1853 in one of those family celebrations dear to Prince Albert's heart, with all the children, including his third son and seventh child, the three-year-old Prince Arthur, heaping on mortar with a trowel and tapping the stone with a hammer. The two elder boys helped with the construction of the stone plinth, their father paying them wages and their mother – while not mentioning the handiwork of the Prince of Wales –

commending his younger brother, Alfred, who 'worked as hard and steadily as a regular labourer'.

In this cottage the girls learned to cook on the range in the brightly tiled kitchen, using a great variety of pans and utensils which, after use, were hung in neat, shining rows on the dresser. Upstairs, as well as a dressing room and a dining room, in which stood a piano, there was a small museum containing all manner of objects – shells, butterflies, pressed flowers, fossils – collected by the children, with the help of their father, and supplemented by donations (such as the scorpions, tarantulas and stick insects) presented by Lady Canning, their mother's former lady-in-waiting, by then Vicereine of India.[18]

Outside, there was a miniature earthworks constructed by the two elder boys under the direction of a young officer in the Royal Engineers, Lieutenant John Cowell, who was later to spend twenty-eight years as Master of the Household, even though he was 'rather too much of a John Bull', with 'unreasonable likes and dislikes', for the Queen's taste, and despite the fact that soon after his appointment he had earned her profound displeasure by presuming to criticize one of her Highland servants, Archie Brown.*[19]

---

* Cowell was once the recipient of one of the Queen's celebrated sharp retorts. He had written her a long letter to complain of a clergyman, the son of a peer, styling himself 'the Rev. and Hon.' This letter was returned to Cowell with the words scrawled across it: 'It is a matter of perfect indifference to the Queen what he is called' (quoted in Elizabeth Longford, Victoria R.I., 576).

24

PALMERSTON

[He felt] 'Like a man restored to life after his funeral sermon had been preached'.

'My relations with Her Majesty are most satisfactory,' wrote Sir Robert Peel soon after his appointment as Prime Minister in September 1841. 'The Queen has acted towards me not merely (as everyone who knew Her Majesty's character must have anticipated) with perfect fidelity and honour, but with great kindness and consideration. There is every facility for the despatch of public business, a scrupulous and most punctual discharge of every public duty and an exact understanding of the relation of a constitutional Sovereign to her advisers.'[1]

For her part, the Queen could scarcely have been more content with Sir Robert's subsequent behaviour. She warmly supported his policies and strongly condemned those who opposed them. His decision to increase the grant to Maynooth, the training college for Roman Catholic clergy in Ireland, was eminently sensible, 'one of the greatest measures ever proposed'; and she blushed for the narrow-minded, bigoted Protestants who opposed it, 'so void of all right feeling, & so wanting in Charity'.[2] As for Mr Gladstone, who felt that he must resign over the grant since he had once written a book condemning subsidies to Roman Catholics, she quite agreed with the Foreign Secretary, Lord Aberdeen, who was alleged to have said to Gladstone, 'No one reads your book and those who do, don't understand it.'[3]

She also shared Peel's belief that the time had come to reform the Corn Laws, and was outraged by those in his own party, including the Duke of Wellington, Lord Stanley and Benjamin Disraeli, who would not support him. 'Oh,' she cried, 'for a little true, *disinterested patriotism.*' She well understood the truth that lay behind the popular riddle:

'Why are the Tories like walnuts?'
'Because they are troublesome to Peel.'[4]

They were troublesome to Prince Albert, too; and when the Prince appeared in the House of Commons to hear Peel speak, Lord George Bentinck rose to attack him for having been 'seduced by the First Minister of the Crown to come down to this House to usher in, to give *éclat*, and, as it were, by reflection from the Queen, to give the semblance of a personal sanction of Her Majesty to a measure which . . . a great majority at least of the landed aristocracy of England, of Scotland and of Ireland, imagine fraught with deep injury, if not ruin to them'. The Prince never appeared in the House of Commons again, while the Queen expressed her fury with these diehard Tory gentlemen who 'did nothing but hunt all day, drink Claret or Port wine in the evening, & never studied or read about any of these questions.'[5]

Lord Melbourne, who condemned Peel's support of the free trade he had once opposed as being 'damned dishonest', was, the Queen thought, quite as bad as these gentlemen on the opposite side of the House. Indeed, Melbourne, in the Queen's opinion, had become rather tiresome of late, eating enormous dinners after breakfasts of grouse and mutton chops, living in a dirty house staffed by sixteen servants, talking to himself more loudly than ever and 'making fierce faces', upsetting himself with thoughts that filled his eyes with tears, believing himself to be on the verge of bankruptcy, though his fortune was still considerable, and applying to the Queen for money which she advanced to him and for a pension which she was advised not to grant. In October 1842 he had a stroke from which he never completely recovered.

Under the influence of Prince Albert, who entertained a low opinion of Whigs and was not a man to overlook the failings of Lord Melbourne, the Queen's attitude to her former much-admired mentor had already begun to change. Although no longer in office, Melbourne was reluctant to withdraw from her life; and an attempt by Stockmar and Anson to put a stop to his continuing correspondence with the Queen, and his offering of unsolicited advice, met with but little success.

While Melbourne described his time as the Queen's Prime Minister as the 'happiest part of his life', she wrote of the dream being past. She was sure she 'did not wish those times back' in the way that he did.

Earl Granville's son, Frederick Leveson-Gower, a fellow-guest at Chatsworth in 1843, was grieved to see them together: 'Lord Melbourne was so much broken in health that he was nearly in a state of second childhood. I believe he had not met Her Majesty since he ceased to be her Minister. Her manner to him was kind; still, he bitterly felt the change in the situation, and it was sad to see him with tears frequently in his eyes.'[6]

Scarcely aware, as a young woman in her new-found happiness, of the depth of the grief which Melbourne, as an ill and lonely man, felt at his exclusion from her life, Victoria was not deeply moved by his death in November 1848. Certainly, as she said, she 'sincerely regretted' it, 'for he was truly attached to [her] and was a noble kind-hearted generous being', 'tho' not a good or firm Minister'.

Rereading parts of her journal which covered those years when she had been in thrall to him, she wrote, 'I cannot forbear remarking what an artificial sort of happiness mine was *then*, and what a blessing it is that I have now in my beloved Husband *real* and solid happiness, which no Politics, no worldly reverses can change.'[7]

Three years before Lord Melbourne's death, to the Queen's great distress, Peel had been forced to resign over a contentious Irish Bill, and, with a reluctance she took no trouble to conceal, she had had to send for Lord John Russell.

Peel had gone to Osborne to tender his resignation. He was 'visibly much moved', Prince Albert wrote, 'and said to me it was one of the most painful moments of his life, to separate himself from us'.[8] To his friend, Sir Thomas Fremantle, however, two days after his secretary had been shot in the back by Daniel MacNaghten, a mad Scotsman, Peel declared that 'on every personal and private ground' he 'rejoiced at being released from the thankless and dangerous post of having the responsibility of public affairs'.[9] Nevertheless, when Lord John Russell failed in his first attempt to form a government and Peel was asked by the Queen to withdraw his resignation, he did so without hesitation, feeling, as he told Princess Lieven, 'like a man restored to life after his funeral service had been preached'. The Queen had been suitably grateful to her 'worthy

Peel' who, by agreeing to continue as Prime Minister, had shown himself 'a man of unbounded loyalty, courage, patriotism and high-mindedness'.[10]

Peel, however, did not survive for long: defeated in the House of Commons in the summer of 1846, he tendered his resignation for the second time and was succeeded as Prime Minister by Lord John Russell, who appointed Lord Palmerston Foreign Secretary.

Lord Palmerston at this time was sixty-one years old. The elder son of the second Viscount Palmerston, he had been born on the family's estate, Broadlands in Hampshire, and had passed much of his childhood in Italy – where he learned to speak Italian fluently – before going to Harrow, then to Edinburgh to board with Dugald Stewart, the philosopher, before entering St John's College, Cambridge and taking the degree of Master of Arts without examination as at that time noblemen were permitted to do. Vivacious, self-confident and even-tempered, walking into rooms with brisk and jaunty step, he was a handsome man, very attractive to women and well meriting his nickname 'Cupid'. At Windsor one night he had entered the bedroom of one of the Queen's ladies in the unfulfilled hope of seducing her. George Anson, putting a slightly different interpretation on Palmerston's visit, suggested that, having been accustomed to sleeping with another lady in that bedroom, he had 'probably from force of habit floundered in'. Whatever his motives and intentions, the Queen found it difficult to forget Palmerston's conduct, while Prince Albert found it impossible to forgive.[11]

Before her marriage, however, when Palmerston had been Foreign Secretary in Melbourne's Cabinet, the Queen had been won over by Palmerston's charm and the trouble he took to instruct her in the intricacies and formalities of foreign politics, the supervision of which Prince Albert, like Baron Stockmar, was to persuade her to believe was 'peculiarly within the Sovereign's province'. Palmerston had taught her how to address her fellow sovereigns and how to end letters to them in her own hand, writing the appropriate endings for her in pencil so that she could write over them before the pencil marks were carefully rubbed out. He had also advised her as to what kinds of presents to give to these fellow sovereigns and to their most distinguished subjects. He gave her tutorials on foreign relations and provided her with specially drawn maps and an annotated *Almanac de Gotha*. She had found these lessons both instructive and enjoyable and Palmerston's company most agreeable: he was, she considered, both clever and amusing. After sitting next to him at dinner one evening she had told the King of the Belgians how 'pleasant and amusing' she had found Palmerston's conversation. They had subsequently had so much talk regarding Middle Eastern problems when she was pregnant with her first child that she had agreed the forthcoming baby would have to be called 'Turko-Egypto'. When Palmerston had left office upon Melbourne's resignation, the Queen had written of his 'valuable services', which he had performed in 'so admirable a manner' and which had 'so greatly promoted the honour and welfare of this Country in its relations with foreign powers'.

But slowly her attitude towards Palmerston had begun to change. In December 1839 he married Lord Melbourne's beautiful sister, Emily, whose first husband had been the fifth Earl Cowper; and the Queen, who disapproved of widows remarrying, had confided to an amused Lord Melbourne that 'somehow or other' she did not thereafter like Lord Palmerston as much as she had done in the past.

As Lord John Russell's Foreign Secretary he gave her constant cause for irritation. It could not be denied that the man was extremely knowledgeable and extraordinarily hard-working. Yet he was too impetuous in his determination to strengthen Britain, to assert the country's rights and maintain her influence, too prone to bluster and threaten, too highhanded. On occasions, he was astonishingly rude and undiplomatic. He sent despatches before the Queen had time to approve of them; he delayed sending boxes of papers for days on end and then sent so many at once that she could not get through them all; when obliged to do so he would apologize, blaming unnamed subordinates in the Foreign Office – over which he exercised what Charles Greville described as 'an absolute despotism' – and then carry on just as before.

The Queen was all the more annoyed at being sidetracked by Palmerston because not only had she been taught to believe by Baron Stockmar that it was the Crown's inalienable right to supervise foreign policy, but she believed also that Prince Albert had a far clearer grasp of the realities of foreign politics than any British politician, particularly such a politician as she now found Palmerston to be, with his insouciant, arrogant manner, his manipulation of the press, and his facile excuses. While she and

Prince Albert were inclined to sympathize with the various monarchies of Europe, being related by blood or by marriage to so many of them, Palmerston was openly sympathetic towards the liberal movements striving to undermine them. Prince Albert's lengthy memoranda setting out his views on foreign relations were either completely ignored, or glanced at and set aside as though of no interest or account – a manifestation of disdain which the Queen found unforgivable. A case in point was the revolutionary movement for a united Italy. Whereas Palmerston could not regret the expulsion of the Austrians from Italy, as he told King Leopold, since their rule was 'hateful to the Italians', the Queen sympathized with the Emperor and felt ashamed of the policy which 'we are pursuing in this Italian controversy'. By the summer of 1848 she was so exasperated by what she took to be the overbearing conduct of the Foreign Office that she wrote to Lord John Russell to say that she was 'highly indignant' and 'would have no peace of mind' so long as Lord Palmerston remained at its head, the cause of 'no end of troubles'. Later, in September at Balmoral, she told Lord John that she could 'hardly go on with' Palmerston; she was 'seriously anxious and uneasy for the welfare of the country and for the peace of Europe in general'. Russell had to agree with her; yet, mindful of the undoubted fact that his Government could scarcely survive if Palmerston were to be dismissed, he assured the Queen that the Foreign Secretary was 'a very able man', 'entirely master of his office'.[12]

Europe was in turmoil that year. Twelve months before, the Queen had expressed herself as being '*very* anxious for the future', while Prince Albert had written to Stockmar, 'The political horizon grows darker and darker.' Greece, Spain and Portugal were all 'in a state of ferment'. Now the Austrian Empire and Germany, as well as Italy, were in uproar too; while in Ireland the sufferings of the poor were, in the Queen's words, 'too terrible to contemplate'.

In France, King Louis-Philippe was forced to abdicate and to seek refuge in England where he and his Queen, having assumed the titles of the Count and Countess of Neuilly, were given shelter at Claremont. They, together with other refugees from France, were so welcomed and so generously treated by the Queen that the Government felt it necessary to hint that she might be in danger of antagonizing the provisional government of republican France. It seemed in April that revolution might break out in England, too.

25

✻✻✻✻✻✻✻✻✻✻✻✻

CHARTISTS

'Working people met in their thousands
to swear devotion to the common cause.'

RADICALS HAD LONG had cause to complain that the progress of reform in England was not proceeding fast enough. Lord Ashley's Factory Act of 1833 had limited the hours which children could be made to work and made it illegal to employ them under the age of nine in most textile mills, while the Mines and Collieries Act of 1842 had gone some way towards dealing with the exploitation of women and children in coal mines. But the Poor Law Amendment Act of 1834 had done little to ameliorate the miseries of the destitute who, by the abolition of outdoor relief, were obliged to seek shelter in workhouses as squalid as the one described in Charles Dickens's *Oliver Twist*. There was also widespread dissatisfaction with the Reform Act of 1832 which, while welcomed by the propertied middle class, was a profound disappointment to radicals and the militant working class. There was dissatisfaction also with the failure of attempts to develop trade unionism; and this general discontent ensured that unrest had continued throughout the 1830s and well into the 1840s and helped to increase support for the movement for political reform known as Chartism.

The movement took its name from a People's Charter drawn up by a group of radicals who demanded of the Government universal male suffrage, annual parliaments, equal electoral districts, voting by ballot, an end to property qualifications for Members of Parliament, and the introduction of salaries for them. Support for these demands was loudly voiced at meetings held both day and night all over the country. One such gathering at Halifax attracted a crowd of 200,000. 'It is almost impossible to imagine the excitement caused,' one Chartist wrote of these rallies. 'Working people met in their thousands to swear devotion to the common cause.'[1]

The Queen, as an impressionable young woman, had been urged by Melbourne to believe that the country was in a far better state than some would have her believe and that, in any case, social reform was not to be encouraged. All change was likely to be for the worse and to be advocated by hypocrites. Why, look at Lord Ashley (later Lord Shaftesbury) and his concern for little workers: he disliked his own children! Discontent was being aroused by a few troublesome malcontents, particularly in Ireland. The Queen, who was inclined to pity 'the poor Irish' who had been so 'ill treated', had once been amused by Melbourne's flippant remarks, but in later life she refused to dismiss hardship with merriment. Influenced by Melbourne she had once referred to a Bill intended to set further limits upon the hours spent by workers in factories as 'undesirable'; yet after a later visit to a workhouse she felt she would like to devote her life to the poor and downtrodden.

When alarmed by the violence on the Continent in 1848 which threatened to overthrow the established order, she did, to be sure, talk of the 'insubordination of the poor'; and when told of a family that slept seven in a single bed, she commented in her matter-of-fact way that she would have chosen to sleep on the floor. But she was capable of being moved to pity and grief by distress; and she maintained, without undue exaggeration after Prince Albert's death, that 'more than ever' did she 'long to lead a private life tending the poor and the sick'. She was also generous in her charities and did not shrink from facing the unpalatable as Lord Melbourne had done.* She was concerned that her children should show a sympathy for the poorer of her subjects. She was pleased when Prince Albert became President of the Society for Improving the Condition of

---

* Throughout her reign, following the example of her grandfather, King George III, the Queen was generous in her contributions to charities as well as to needy members of her family and to retired servants. A patron of about 150 institutions, she gave money to many if not most of them; and in one representative year, 1882, she was to distribute £12,535 to 230 charities. 'There were also donations for the relief of victims of earthquakes and storms, fires and shipwrecks, famines and colliery disasters. Temperance interestingly hardly figured . . . All told, her patronage books show that she gave away something in the order of £650,000 to charitable purposes during her reign, excluding cash handouts to the poor and pensions to retired servants' (Frank Prochaska, *Royal Bounty: The Making of a Welfare Monarchy*, 77).

the Labouring Classes; she encouraged him in his interest in Working Men's Clubs, Public Libraries and Reading Rooms, was proud of his designs for artisans' dwellings, two of which were built as models; and she encouraged him in his efforts to improve the lot and housing of the people who lived and worked on their estates at Osborne and Balmoral. If all the cottage property in the United Kingdom were to be kept in the same condition as that of Her Majesty and the Prince Consort, Sir Edwin Chadwick, the social reformer, declared, the death rate would be reduced by nearly one half.[2] After the Prince's death, the Queen remained faithful to his example. 'The Queen has been much distressed by all that she has heard and read lately of the houses of the poor in the great towns,' she was to write to the Prime Minister in 1883. 'The Queen will be glad to learn . . . whether the Government contemplate the introduction of any measures, or propose to take any steps to obtain more precise information as to the *true* state of affairs in these overcrowded, unhealthy and squalid' houses.[3]

Yet there was always a firm line to be drawn between sympathy and charity for the poor and the kind of agitation proposed on their behalf by the Chartists, both those who were prepared to work within the law and those who advocated the use of violence in pursuit of their aims. 'I maintain that Revolutions are always bad for the country,' she declared, 'and the cause of untold misery to the people . . . Obedience to the laws & to the Sovereign is obedience to a higher Power.'[4]

She feared that violence might be unleashed upon London when the Chartists announced that on 10 April 1848 a petition, listing their demands and said to contain almost five million signatures, would be presented to Parliament by 150,000 demonstrators marching to Westminster from Kennington Common.

Intimidated by the prospect of enormous crowds of menacing people marching through the streets, a number of noblemen summoned servants and retainers from their country estates to defend their London houses; while the Commander-in-Chief, the Duke of Wellington (whom Charles Greville on a visit to Apsley House found 'in a prodigious state of excitement' as he formulated plans to deal with the menace), advised the Queen and her family to leave for Osborne before the demonstration took place.[5]

The Queen had recently given birth to her sixth child, Princess Louise, and was suffering from what, in years to come, would be diagnosed as post-natal depression, from time to time dissolving into tears and clearly frightened. She readily agreed to go. Already the lamps outside Buckingham Palace had been smashed to shouts of '*Vive la République!*' and who could tell what might happen when immense crowds marched past on their way to the Palace of Westminster, organized by a leadership which Prince Albert described as 'incredible', having 'secret signals' and corresponding 'from town to town by means of carrier pigeons'?

On the morning of 8 April the Royal Family were driven to Waterloo Station which had been cleared of spectators and surrounded by special constables. As soon as they had all boarded it, the train steamed off for Gosport, the Queen lying on her sofa, worrying about the three-week-old Princess Louise, but no longer crying. 'I never was calmer & quieter & less nervous,' she told King Leopold without her usual strict regard for the truth. '*Great* events make me quiet & calm; it is only trifles that irritate my nerves.'[6]

The Duke of Wellington arranged that the nine thousand troops called upon to deal with troublemakers should be kept out of sight, concerned that there might possibly be riots if they were seen, while 170,000 special constables were enrolled to ensure that the march did not get out of hand.

All the 'enormous preparations' were unnecessary, however. The day of the march 'passed off with surprising quiet' and the 'intended tragedy was rapidly changed into a ludicrous farce,' Charles Greville commented. 'Feargus O'Connor [the Irish orator and journalist, a leading figure in the Chartist movement] harangued his rabble, advising them not to provoke a collision, and to go away quietly – advice they instantly obeyed, and with great apparent alacrity and good-humour. Thus all evaporated in smoke . . . But everybody rejoices that the defensive demonstration was made, for it has given a great and memorable lesson which will not be thrown away, either on the disaffected and mischievous, or the loyal and peaceful; and it will produce a vast effect in all foreign countries, and show how solid is the foundation on which we are resting. We have displayed a great resolution and a great strength, and given unmistakeable proofs that if sedition and rebellion hold their heads in this country, they will be instantly met with the most vigorous resistance, and be put down by the hand of authority, and by the zealous co-operation of all classes of the people.'[7]

The Queen expressed her profound relief that the workmen, misled by professional agitators and the 'criminals and refuse of London' ('such wanton & worthless men'), remained loyal after all. Five months later, in her speech from the throne at the prorogation of Parliament on 5 September 1848, after several Chartist leaders (whose meetings had been infiltrated by Government agents) had been arrested on charges of sedition, she declared, 'The strength of our institutions has been tried, and has not been found wanting. I have studied to preserve the people committed to my charge in the enjoyment of that temperate freedom which they so justly value. My people, on their side, feel too sensibly the advantages of order and security to allow the promoters of pillage and confusion any chance of success in their wicked designs.' Some four months later she wrote to King Leopold, 'I write to you *once* more in this *old & most dreadful* year ... But I must not include myself or my country in [its] misfortunes ... On the contrary I have nothing but thanks to offer up for *all* that has happened here.'[8]

Yet the Queen was more than ready to agree with Prince Albert that there were those amongst her people, poor and distressed, who were deserving of help. Within a fortnight of the collapse of the Chartist protest in April 1848, Lord Ashley was invited to Osborne where, during a walk in the grounds with Prince Albert, the condition of the poor was discussed. Some years earlier, the Prince had written to Ashley to congratulate him on a speech he had made denouncing the employment of young children in coal mines, and to assure him that the Queen supported him in his views for which she had the 'deepest sympathy'. Now Ashley urged him to demonstrate the interest which the Royal Family took in the welfare of the working classes by visiting such London slums as those by the river south of the Strand. This Prince Albert did; and afterwards at Exeter Hall he made a speech which the Queen had helped him to rehearse and in which he stressed the importance of the more affluent and better-educated classes of society supporting and contributing to plans to ameliorate the hardships of the less fortunate, calling upon the Government to care for those who were in no condition to care for themselves.[9]

The Queen considered it unlikely that the Prime Minister, who had opposed the Prince's visit to the slums, would respond with any enthusiasm to her husband's plea. Indeed, the more she saw of Lord John Russell, the deeper was her sorrow at losing her 'kind and true friend', Sir Robert Peel.

26

✳✳✳✳✳✳✳✳✳✳✳

'PAM IS OUT'

'The levity of the man is really inconceivable.'

LORD JOHN RUSSELL, third son of the sixth Duke of Bedford, was an emaciated little man, not noticeably taller than his dumpy monarch who found him stubborn, opinionated and graceless. He would be better company, she said, 'if he had a third subject; for he was interested in nothing except the Constitution of 1688 and himself'.[1] Worse than this, he was either incapable or unwilling to curb the excesses of his tiresome Foreign Secretary, Lord Palmerston.

Month after month the Queen and Prince had cause to complain of Palmerston's behaviour, his continued habit of sending her drafts of his despatches after the despatches themselves had been sent, his agreeing to alterations and then taking no notice of them, the intemperate language in which some of them were framed, in one case so annoying the Spanish government that they expelled the British Ambassador from Madrid, in another wording a despatch which the Queen described as being 'unworthy of a gentleman'.[2] It made her feel ill, she told her doctor, to read such things. In January 1849 the tiresome man went so far as secretly to supply Garibaldi's rebels in Sicily with arms for use in an uprising against their legitimate sovereign, King Ferdinand II. It really was too bad, the Queen complained: it was she, after all, who had to bear the responsibility for such activities.[3]

She told the Prime Minister, not for the first time, that the day might well come when she would have to insist upon having the man dismissed. Could not some other appointment for him be found? Could he be sent to Ireland as Lord Lieutenant? Russell toyed with the idea, considering the possibility of offering him an earldom and the Order of the Garter as an inducement. But then Palmerston said he was willing to apologize fully for any problems he may have caused; and so he was still Foreign Secretary when the country was brought to the brink of war after the house of a Jewish merchant of Portuguese descent, Don David Pacifico, Portugal's Consul-General in Athens, had been burned down by an anti-semitic mob of Greek Orthodox rioters. Don Pacifico sent an absurdly inflated bill for damages of £80,000 to the King of Greece. The Greek government naturally rejected it; and, since he had been born in Gibraltar and was accordingly a British subject, Don Pacifico appealed for help to London.

Palmerston was quite ready to intervene and a fleet was despatched to blockade Piraeus and seize ships of a sufficient value to meet Don Pacifico's claims. This was too much for both France and Russia to tolerate. Palmerston had provoked another diplomatic crisis, though he seemed quite unconcerned by all the fuss. The Queen, who had given birth to her seventh child, Prince Arthur, on 1 May 1850, wrote in her diary a fortnight later, 'The levity of the man is really inconceivable.'[4] She told Lord John Russell that he really must be forced to leave the Foreign Office.

The next month, however, Palmerston made his position virtually unassailable by a speech in the House which even the Queen felt obliged to describe as 'most brilliant'. For nearly five hours, 'without stopping for one moment even to drink a little water', he justified his actions with a peroration which delighted the nationalist sentiments of his countrymen and was worthy of a man who, after Prince Albert's death, the Queen decided had, 'with all his many faults, the honour and power of his country strongly at heart':

> As the Roman in days of old held himself free from indignity when he could say *Civis Romanus Sum*, so also a British subject, in whatever land he may be, shall feel confident that the watchful eye and the strong arm of England will protect him against injustice and wrong.[5]

The debate lasted four days but the issue could not be in doubt. The week before, the Conservative leader, Lord Stanley, had moved a vote of censure on the Government in the House of Lords which had been carried by thirty-seven votes; now, in the House of Commons, Palmerston had ensured that the Government would survive; and so, by forty-six votes, it did.

The Queen, much as she could not help but admire the Foreign Secretary's speech, could not condone his actions. With Prince Albert to help her, she composed a memorandum to be sent to the Prime Minister setting out what was in future to be expected from Lord Palmerston, and making clear that if he 'arbitrarily altered or modified' measures to which the Queen had given her royal sanction she would 'exercise her constitutional right of dismissing' him. He was, she recognized, an 'able, sagacious, patriotic and courageous' man, but 'his modes of proceeding were often too violent and corrupt', while the language of his despatches 'was often less calculated to conciliate than to mortify and offend'.[6]

Lord John sent this memorandum to Palmerston who asked to be granted an interview with Prince Albert. The Prince was, as he confessed, moved by the demeanour of the Foreign Secretary who appeared before him 'much agitated' and with tears in his eyes. He undertook to mend his ways. He had promised to do so before, however; and neither then nor now did he do so.[7]

A month after Palmerston's interview with Prince Albert there arrived in London on a tour of Europe a retired Austrian general with a most unsavoury reputation. This was Julius, Freiherr von Haynau, known to the public in England as 'Hyena', a man who had suppressed nationalist uprisings in Hungary and in Brescia in Italy with notorious brutality and who was alleged to have had a woman flogged almost to the point of death. Soon after his arrival in London, where his evil reputation had been broadcast by Hungarian refugees, he visited Barclay and Perkins's Brewery. Immediately recognized by his martial bearing and by the prominent nose, deep-set eyes and enormous yellow moustache which had been featured in caricatures of him in the popular press, he was set upon by draymen who knocked 'the Austrian butcher' down, beat him with broom handles and dragged him along Bankside by his hair and whiskers. An apology for this degrading treatment of one of the Emperor of Austria's generals was drafted by Palmerston for despatch to the Emperor's

Winterhalter's portrait of the Duchess of Kent which the Duchess later gave to the Queen as a birthday present.

Princess Victoria's uncle, Leopold, who was elected King of the Belgians in 1831.

Victoria's sketch of Louise Lehzen, a profound influence on her childhood, who devoted herself to the Princess with possessive intensity.

Princess Victoria's sketch of her much-admired singing master, Luigi Lablache, who began giving her regular lessons at Kensington Palace in 1836.

The young Queen Victoria riding with Lord Melbourne at Windsor (detail), after a painting by Sir Francis Grant exhibited at the Royal Academy in 1840.

Victoria's skilful portrait of her first Prime Minister, Lord Melbourne.

Baron Stockmar, from the painting by John Partridge.

LEFT An early photograph by B. E. Duppa of the 35-year-old Queen Victoria, holding a portrait of Prince Albert, taken at Buckingham Palace on 13 July 1854.

RIGHT Prince Albert aged thirty-four, a photograph taken by B. E. Duppa in May 1854.

The Great Exhibition of 1851 with which, so the Queen believed, her 'dearest Albert's name' would for ever 'be immortalized'.

ABOVE LEFT The Queen's sons, the Prince of Wales and Prince Alfred, with the unimaginative barrister, Frederick Waymouth Gibbs, their tutor; a photograph by Roger Fenton taken in 1854.

ABOVE The Princess Royal (with butterfly net and collecting box), Albert Edward, Prince of Wales, Princess Alice and Prince Alfred at Osborne in August 1853.

LEFT Princess Victoria, 'Vicky', with the Crown Prince of Prussia, Frederick William, 'Fritz', photographed at Windsor four days after their wedding in 1858.

Napoleon III, Emperor of the French, from a sketch by Queen Victoria based on a medallion of the Emperor.

BELOW The Royal Family on the Lower Terrace at Osborne in May 1857. (*Left to right*) Prince Alfred, Prince Albert, Princess Helena, Princess Alice, Prince Arthur, Queen Victoria holding Princess Beatrice, the Princess Royal, Princess Louise, Prince Leopold, Albert Edward, Prince of Wales.

LEFT The mourning Queen and Princess Alice with a bust of Prince Albert, from a photograph taken in 1862, the year after his death.

BELOW The Blue Room at Windsor preserved as a memorial to the Prince Consort with a bust of him by William Theed.

Ambassador in London, but it was accompanied by some aspersions on the regime for which General Haynau had fought and a suggestion that he had been ill-advised to come to England at a time when he was likely to be unwelcome here. Sent this draft, the Queen asked for some alterations to be made to it, only to be told, as she had been so often told in the past, that the text had already been despatched.[8] As though it were excuse enough for this breach of his undertaking not to send unapproved despatches, Palmerston assured the Queen that he had 'good reason to know that General Haynau's ferocious and unmanly treatment of the unfortunate inhabitants of Brescia and of other places and towns in Italy . . . and his barbarous acts in Hungary excited almost as much disgust in Austria as in England'.[9]

The next year a leader of those Hungarian revolutionaries against whom Haynau had acted with such brutality, Lajos Kossuth, also arrived in London where he addressed several mass meetings, speaking in excellent English which he had taught himself in prison from a study of the Bible and Shakespeare.

The welcome accorded to this enemy of Austria – the 'stupid Kossuth fever', as she referred to it – exasperated the Queen; and, when she learned that her Foreign Secretary intended to receive the revolutionary, she threatened to dismiss him if he presumed to do so. The Prime Minister warned him not to be so provocative. Palmerston replied that he would not be told whom he could and whom he could not receive in his own house.[10] But, as he had done in the past, he climbed down rather than be dismissed. 'Oh wonder,' wrote the Queen who had reason to believe that he had seen Kossuth anyway. 'Lord Palmerston yielded to the general will . . . He lowers himself more and more.'[11]

He had, however, survived only to make more trouble. Having first caused offence by officially receiving a deputation of radicals who thanked and praised him for his support of Kossuth and who referred to the Emperors of Austria and Russia as 'odious and detestable assassins', he then entangled himself with the politics of France where Prince Louis Napoleon, the Austrian Emperor's nephew, who had been elected President of the French Republic in December 1848, staged a *coup d'état* at the beginning of December 1851 and later declared himself Napoleon III, Emperor of the French.

On hearing of this coup, the Queen wrote to the Prime Minister asking him to tell Lord Normanby, British Ambassador in Paris, to do nothing for the moment. Normanby was consequently instructed that 'nothing should be done ... which would wear the appearance of an interference of any kind in the internal affairs of France'.[12] When Normanby next called on the French Minister for Foreign Affairs, however, the Minister told him that he had heard from Count Walewski, Napoleon I's illegitimate son and the French Ambassador in London, that Lord Palmerston had already expressed to him the British Government's full approval of the French Emperor's *coup d'état*.

The Queen, who had hoped that one of her Orléans relations might perhaps become King of France one day, was extremely angry when she learned of this latest example of Lord Palmerston's infuriating independence.

Lord John Russell agreed that this time Lord Palmerston had gone too far and must be required to resign, popular though he was in the country. It was no good his making the excuse that what he said to the French Ambassador was his own private view and not the Government's official opinion. His lack of 'decorum and prudence' was such that he could no longer be trusted with the Ministry for Foreign Affairs. The Queen and Prince Albert had been most concerned by Palmerston's friendly reception of the radicals who came to thank him for his support of Kossuth. But this fresh contretemps provided a more satisfactory excuse to get rid of him. Lord John offered him the Lord Lieutenancy of Ireland, an offer which he rejected with the observation that he could scarcely be considered lacking in 'decorum and prudence' since these were qualities which surely were required in Ireland as much as anywhere else.[13]

> Palmerston is out! actually, really and irretrievably out [Charles Greville recorded in his diary on 23 December 1851]. I nearly dropt off my chair yesterday afternoon, when at five o'clock, a few moments after the Cabinet had broken up [Lord Granville, a favourite at Court] rushed into my room and said 'Pam is out, the offer of the F. Office goes to Clarendon to-night, and if he refuses (which of course he will not) it is to be offered to me!! ... December 24th. To my unspeakable astonishment Granville informed me yesterday that Clarendon had refused the Foreign Office and that he had accepted it.[14]

'Our relief was great,' wrote the Queen in her journal, 'and we felt quite excited by the news, for our anxiety and worry during the last five years and a half, which were indescribable, was mainly, if not entirely, caused by [Lord Palmerston]. It is a great and unexpected mercy.'[15]

27

✳✳✳✳✳✳✳✳✳✳✳

THE GREAT EXHIBITION

'Dearest Albert's name is for ever immortalized.'

'IT WAS the *happiest, proudest* day in my life, and I can think of nothing else,' the Queen wrote of 1 May 1851. 'Albert's dearest name is for ever immortalized with this *great* conception, *his* own, and my *own* dear country *showed* she was *worthy* of it.'[1]

At the beginning of the previous year, the Prince, as President of the Royal Society of Arts, had presided over the first meeting of the Commissioners for the Great Exhibition which had been conceived as a means of demonstrating that the progress of mankind depended upon international cooperation, that the prosperity of one country depended upon the prosperity of others, and that Britain's mission was 'to put herself at the head of the diffusion of civilization'.

The idea had been discussed in the summer of 1849 at a conference in Buckingham Palace attended by, amongst others, Thomas Cubitt, the builder, John Scott Russell, the civil engineer, who was Secretary of the Royal Society of Arts, and the versatile Henry Cole, soon to be the Society's Chairman. Cole was a remarkable and astonishingly versatile man. At one time or another an assistant keeper of the Public Record Office, closely concerned with the inauguration of the penny post, exhibitor at the Royal Academy, newspaper and magazine editor, writer of children's books, associated with the establishment of schools of music and cookery, ceramic designer, Secretary of the Anti-Corn-Law League, friend of the novelist Thomas Love Peacock, whose collected works he edited, and of W. M. Thackeray, Cole was a man not only of extraordinary

resource and energy, but also of unfailing good temper. The Prince –
making one of those rather heavily humorous plays on words which so
much appealed to him – would say, when faced with some difficulty or
delay, 'We must have steam, send for Cole.'[2]

The difficulties were, indeed, formidable. There were problems in
finding a suitable site for the Exhibition: Battersea Fields, Regent's Park,
Primrose Hill, the Isle of Dogs, Leicester Square, and the courtyard of
Somerset House were all suggested before it was decided to settle upon
Hyde Park, much to the displeasure of people whose houses overlooked
it or were in the habit of riding there, as well as of *The Times*, which
forecast that the whole of the park would become 'a bivouac of all
vagabonds'. Kensington and Belgravia would be uninhabitable and the
Season would be ruined. 'The annoyance inflicted on the neighbourhood
will be indescribable ... We can scarcely bring ourselves to believe that
the advisers of the Prince cared to connect his name with such an outrage
to the feelings and wishes of the inhabitants of the metropolis.'[3]

Other Jeremiahs forecast food shortages caused by the crowds of
foreigners who would come to see the Exhibition, as well as riots, robberies
and an influx of 'bad characters at present scattered over the country'
which would make it advisable for all 'wise persons residing near the
Park to keep a sharp look out over their silver forks and spoons and
servant maids'.[4] Engineers, so Prince Albert told the King of Prussia in
a facetious letter, had warned that the galleries would collapse killing the
visitors beneath; doctors that the Black Death would break out again;
'theologians that this second Tower of Babel would draw upon it the
vengeance of an offended God'.[5]

Henry Manning, the future Cardinal, who had been received into
the Roman Catholic Church in April that year, did, indeed, condemn the
project as a potential danger to faith and morals, while the King of
Hanover, as ready to cause trouble in England as he had been as Duke
of Cumberland in the past, warned the Crown Prince William of Prussia
and his wife and son not to accept the Queen's invitation to 'this rubbishy
Exhibition'. 'I am not easily given to panicking,' King Ernest added, 'but
I confess to you that I would not like anyone belonging to me exposed
to the imminent peril of these times. Letters from London tell me that
the Ministers will not allow the Queen and the great originator of this
folly, Prince Albert, to be in London while the Exhibition is on.'[6]

When it became known that, after 230 entries proposing ideas for the Exhibition hall had been rejected, a huge glass building, designed by Joseph Paxton, the superintendent of the Duke of Devonshire's gardens at Chatsworth, was to be erected in the Park, the alarmists became more vociferous than ever: the Crystal Palace, as *Punch* was the first to call it – 'a cucumber frame between two chimneys', in John Ruskin's description – would be blown down in the first strong gale; the galleries would collapse; hailstones and thunder would smash the glass; the sparrows in the tall elm trees which were to be enclosed in the edifice would spatter visitors and exhibits alike.*

The Prime Minister, concerned by talk of riots and assaults, consulted the Commander-in-Chief, the Duke of Wellington, who considered that soldiers, largely cavalry, should be employed but kept out of sight, as he had suggested at the time of the Chartist demonstration in 1848. But Prince Albert did not like this talk of soldiers: he argued that the presence of the military would not be in keeping with the tone and purpose of the Exhibition. So the Prime Minister suggested enlisting policemen from Paris. The Duke might as well have been asked to send for bashi-bazouks or Zulu warriors. He replied to Lord John Russell's proposition in a letter which made the Prime Minister hastily and apologetically explain that he was only trying to be helpful. 'I feel,' the Duke protested, 'no want of confidence in my own powers to preserve the public peace and to provide for the general safety without requiring the assistance of French officers.'[7]

Colonel Charles Sibthorp, the anti-Catholic, anti-Reform, ultra-Tory Lincolnshire landowner, who was Member of Parliament for Lincoln, forecast all manner of evils likely to result from a needless exhibition of foreign paraphernalia which was no less than an advertisement for free trade and all its attendant threats to landed society. The whole concept, Sibthorp declared in the House in his usual wild manner, was 'the greatest trash, the greatest fraud and the greatest imposition ever attempted to be palmed upon the people of this country. The object of its promoters is to introduce among us foreign stuff of every description.'[8]

* The well-known story that the Duke of Wellington, asked for his advice as to how to solve this problem which had foxed everyone else, suggested to the Queen with typical directness and brevity, 'Try sparrow hawks, Ma'am', is, sad to say, apocryphal. It owes its origin to a fictitious story printed in a provincial newspaper (Norman Gash, *Wellington Anecdotes: A Critical Survey*, 8–9).

The Queen dismissed all fears and prejudiced opinions out of hand. Like Prince Albert, she was greatly impressed by the proposal for a vast glass edifice almost two thousand feet in length and sixty-four feet high – containing 4,500 tons of iron and nearly 300,000 panes of glass, thirty miles of guttering, two hundred miles of wooden sash bars – which would provide space for some 14,000 displays from every corner of the world. Of course, it would withstand the noise and tramping feet of any number of visitors: it had been tested by three hundred workmen jumping up and down in the galleries, by soldiers marching heavily along the central aisle and trundling trolleys of cannon balls across the pine floor. The Queen made numerous visits to the Park to see the Crystal Palace – 'one of the wonders of the world' as she called it. When it was finished, she took her five eldest with her, and was amused and touched to hear the Duke of Devonshire exclaim in admiration and wonder, 'Fancy one's gardener having done all this.'[9]

The Queen, of course, took even greater pride in Prince Albert's part in it. 'I *do* feel proud,' she wrote, 'at the thought of what my beloved Albert's great mind has conceived.' On the day of the opening ceremony she left Buckingham Palace soon after eleven o'clock in a procession of nine state carriages.

> The Green Park & Hyde Park were one mass of densely crowded human beings in the highest good humour & most enthusiastic [she recorded in her journal]. I never saw Hyde Park look as it did, being filled with crowds as far as the eye could reach. A little rain fell, just as we started, but before we neared the Crystal Palace, the sun shone & gleamed upon the gigantic edifice upon which the flags of every nation were flying.[10]

When she appeared in the building she found 'the Nave was full of people, which had not been intended, & deafening cheers and waving of handkerchiefs continued the whole time of our long walk from one end of the building to the other'. Wearing a small crown, she had her husband on one side of her with the Princess Royal – who had 'a small wreath of pink wild roses in her hair & looked very nice' – and, on her other side, holding her hand, was the Prince of Wales in Highland dress. Trumpets blared, organs and orchestras played, a choir of six hundred voices sang, a military band played the march from Handel's *Athalia* as they approached the canopied dais, and the 'myriads of people filling the galleries and seats around cheered and cheered'.

It was 'a day to live for ever', far more moving and exciting than her coronation. 'God bless my dearest Albert,' she wrote later. 'God bless my dearest Country, which has shown itself so great today! One felt so grateful to the great God, who seemed to pervade and to bless all.'

There were moments to touch the heart as well as stir the emotions. She saw the two old warriors, the Duke of Wellington and the Marquess of Anglesey, walking up and down a trifle unsteadily, arm in arm between the exhibits; the Duke, over eighty now, bent with arthritis, Anglesey limping on his artificial leg, both talking in the loud voices of the deaf as they did so often in the House of Lords. The Queen also saw what she took to be a Chinese member of the diplomatic corps, looking most picturesque in blue tunic and black-and-red cap, approach the royal dais to kowtow beneath the canopy. It mattered not at all that the supposed oriental envoy was, in fact, the captain of a junk moored in the Thames who charged a shilling a head for people to look over his strange craft. His obeisance appeared quite as sincerely meant as the cheers of the French visitors who shouted, '*Vive la Reine!*' and as those of the crowds who acclaimed her and the Prince when they appeared together on the balcony overlooking the Mall after their return to Buckingham Palace.[11]

The Queen went back to the Exhibition time after time, clearly fascinated by the extraordinary variety of the thousands of exhibits from forty different countries, the engines of every description, the jewels, including the largest pearl ever found and the Koh-i-Noor diamond which she had worn at the opening ceremony, the electric telegraph, the Persian carpets, the Indian silks, the Spanish mantillas, the Swiss embroideries, the German porcelain, the French Sèvres, Aubusson and Gobelins, the leather goods and textiles, the china, glass and cutlery, the assorted clocks and watches, a knife with three hundred blades, a garden seat made of coal, a doctor's walking stick with the equipment for an enema in the handle, a machine which could turn out fifty million medals a week, another machine that printed 10,000 sheets an hour, a stuffed frog holding an umbrella, a collapsible piano, an alarm bed that threw its occupant out at the chosen time, a fine arts section displaying the works of living artists and of those who had died within the past three years.

Unusually for a monarch, the Queen took a particular interest in the machinery. 'Some of the inventions were very ingenious,' she wrote, 'many of them quite Utopian.' The Exhibition, she concluded, 'has taught me so much I never knew before – has brought me in contact with so many clever people I should never have known otherwise, and with so many manufacturers whom I would scarcely have met unless I travelled all over the country and visited every individual manufactory which I never could have done.'[12]

By the time the Exhibition closed to the strains of the National Anthem on 15 October, over six million people had visited it, including a woman of eight-four who had walked from Cornwall; and enough money had been made for the purchase of some thirty acres of land in South Kensington on which were built those museums, colleges and other institutions, including the Victoria and Albert Museum and the Royal Albert Hall, on and near to Exhibition Road, of which the Queen was to have due cause to be proud.

The whole enterprise had been 'a complete and beautiful triumph,' she observed with the utmost pleasure and pride, 'a glorious and touching sight, one which I shall ever be proud of for my beloved Albert and my Country . . . The absurd reports of dangers of every kind & sort, set about by a set of people – the "*soi-disant*" fashionables & the most violent protectionists – are silenced.'[13]

On 9 July that year the Lord Mayor and the Corporation of the City had given a ball to celebrate the continuing success of the Great Exhibition. On their way to the Guildhall, the Queen and Prince were cheered as loudly as she and her children had been on their way to Hyde Park on the opening day; and, on their return from the Guildhall, they were greeted again by crowds of people who had waited for hours for their reappearance. 'A million of people,' the Prince told Stockmar, 'remained till three in the morning in the streets and were full of enthusiasm towards us.'[14]

Some five years before, having opened the new Royal Exchange, the Queen had assured King Leopold of her popularity: 'They say no Sovereign was ever more loved than I am (I am bold enough to say), & *this* is because of our domestic home, the good example it presents.' Now her beloved husband was at last taking some of his own share of the popularity which the monarchy enjoyed.

28

✺✺✺✺✺✺✺✺✺✺

'SCENES'

'If you are violent
I have no other choice but to leave you.'

THE QUEEN'S HAPPINESS in her marriage was still on occasions darkly clouded by quarrels with her husband. No one doubted that she still adored him, that the tired-looking man, paunchy and pale though only thirty-two years old when the Great Exhibition closed, remained for her the paragon of beauty and goodness she had married. Yet she could fly into sudden rages with him, accuse him of all manner of faults and selfishness, of being indifferent to the distress and pain and disgusting degradation which she, as a woman, had to endure when bearing and giving birth to babies and which he, as a man, evaded.

Pregnancy followed pregnancy and with the pregnancies there came bouts of depression. Her 'poor nerves', so she had told King Leopold shortly before the arrival of Princess Alice in April 1843, 'were so battered last time' that she 'suffered *a whole* year' from it. Still, she had continued stoically, 'those nerves were incidental and I am otherwise so strong and well, that if only my happiness continues I can bear everything else with pleasure'.[1]

An exceptionally violent altercation erupted soon after the birth of her fourth son and eighth child, Prince Leopold, on 7 April 1853. The birth itself had been rendered relatively easy by the presence of Dr John Snow, a Yorkshire farmer's son who had made a name for himself in London by his improvements in the methods of administering ether and chloroform as anaesthetizing agents. The Queen, who surprised medical opinion as expressed in the *Lancet* by agreeing to make use of

so unconventional an anodyne, found 'that blessed chloroform . . . soothing and delightful beyond measure'; and, when her next and last child,
Princess Beatrice, was born in April 1857, she insisted that Dr Snow should
again attend her.*

Soon after Prince Leopold's birth, however, as so often in the past,
she suffered from post-natal depression and an agitation of nerves as
upsetting as any she had undergone after previous births. The baby was not
strong, so delicate, indeed, that his baptism had to be postponed: it was
later discovered that he was suffering from haemophilia, a rare hereditary
disorder characterized by a tendency to uncontrollable haemorrhaging
after even the slightest injury.†

Anxiety about the baby exacerbated the Queen's distress which her
husband himself increased by treating her as though she were a wilful
child. It was, in fact, as 'Dear Child' or 'dear, good little one' that he
often addressed her in writing her one of those long letters, partly in
German, mostly in English, which, having retreated from her presence,
he composed when her hysterical outbursts became as insupportable to
him as his infuriating Olympian calm was to her.

> Dear Child [he wrote to her on 2 May 1853]. Now it will be right
> to consider calmly the facts of the case. The *whole* offence which
> led to a continuance of hysterics for more than an hour, and the
> traces of which have remained for more than 24 hours more, was:
> that I complained of your turning several times from inattention

---

* The Queen's use of chloroform did not find universal approval. Protests followed; some were
religious (the Bible taught women were to bring forth in pain) but most were medical, on grounds
of safety. 'In no case,' boomed the *Lancet*, 'could it be justifiable to administer chloroform in
perfectly ordinary labour' (Roy Porter, *The Greatest Benefit to Mankind: A Medical History of
Humanity from Antiquity to the Present*, 367–8).
† The gene which was transmitted to Prince Leopold must have come from his mother rather
than Prince Albert, since haemophiliac fathers cannot have haemophiliac sons. And, as there are
no known haemophiliacs among Queen Victoria's ancestors, the brothers D. M. and W. T. W.
Potts, one an embryologist, the other a professor of biology, have argued that either the gene was
a new mutation – 'the probability of a mutation for haemophilia is 1 in 25,000 to 1 in 100,000' –
or Victoria was not the child of Edward, Duke of Kent. They contend that if the Duchess of Kent,
'keen to produce a child who might well be heir to the British throne, had suspected the fertility
of her husband [who seems not to have had any children by Madame de St Laurent or from other
liaisons] she might have tried to improve her chances with another man . . . There is nothing in
the character of the Duchess of Kent to suggest that she would have baulked at sleeping with
another man if she had decided the Duke was unable to give her a child, and several aspects of her
character would fit with a secret knowledge that Victoria was illegitimate.' There is no suggestion, in
this rather improbable theory, as to who this other man might have been (D. M. Potts and
W. T. W. Potts, *Queen Victoria's Gene: Haemophilia and the Royal Family*, 55–65).

the wrong leaves in a Book which was to be [used] by us as a Register . . . of prints . . . This miserable trifle produced the distressing scene . . . in which I am accused of making things worse by my false method of treatment. I admit that my treatment has on this occasion as on former ones signally failed, but I know of no other . . . When I try to demonstrate the groundlessness and injustice of the accusations which are brought against me I increase your distress . . . But I never intend or wish to offend you . . . If you are violent I have no other choice but to leave you . . . I leave the room and retire to my own room in order to give you time to recover yourself. Then you follow me to renew the dispute and to have it all *out*. . . Now don't believe that I do not sincerely and deeply pity you for the sufferings you undergo, or that I deny you do really suffer very much, I merely deny that I am the *cause* of them, though I have unfortunately often been the occasion . . . I am often astonished at the effect which a hasty word of mine has produced . . .

In your candid way you generally explain later what was the real cause of your complaint . . . It appears now that the apprehension that you might be made answerable for the suffering of the Baby (occasioned by the milk of the Wet nurse not agreeing on account of your having frequently expressed a wish to have a Nurse from the Highlands of Scotland) was the real *cause* of your distress which broke out on the occasion of the Registration of the prints . . .[2]

Over the years such quarrels would suddenly erupt. Months passed in complete harmony; and during these months the Queen would congratulate herself on her 'great progress', her efforts in 'trying energetically to overcome' her faults. How could she thank her dearest Albert for his unchanging love and wonderful tenderness? She had to acknowledge that she had 'little self control'. 'I feel how sadly deficient I am,' she confessed, 'and how over-sensitive and irritable, and how uncontrollable my temper is when annoyed and hurt . . . Have I improved as much as I ought? I fear not . . . Again and again I have conquered this susceptibility [to irritation] – have formed the best of resolutions and *again* it returns [to the] annoyance of that most perfect of human beings, my adored Husband.'[3]

After months of harmony, generally without warning and usually on some trivial pretext, there would be a furious outburst. The Prince would retreat; the Queen would follow him from room to room, upbraiding him; the Prince would find sanctuary at last; the Queen would be filled with remorse; letters between them would be exchanged.

At such times, Sir James Clark felt 'uneasy'. 'Regarding the Queen's mind,' he wrote, 'unless she is kept quiet, the time will come when she will be in danger ... Much depends upon the Prince's management.'[4]

Alternately lecturing her as a father might have done, drawing attention to her faults and follies, and congratulating her on weeks of 'unbroken success in the hard struggle for self control', the Prince's letters charted the volcanic upheavals in a generally placid and contented relationship.

He considered it a 'pity' that she could 'find no consolation' in the company of her children, that she had a mistaken notion that 'the function of a mother [was] to be always correcting, scolding, ordering them about and organizing their activities'. It was 'not possible to be on happy, friendly terms with people you have just been scolding'. She must try to control her 'fidgety nature' which made her 'insist on entering, with feverish eagerness', into details and orders which, in the case of a queen, are commands to whomever they may be given. 'Like everyone else in the house', he made 'the most ample allowance for her state' when pregnant; but he could not bear her 'bodily sufferings for her': she must 'struggle with them alone – the moral ones [were] probably caused by them'. It would be better if she were 'rather less occupied' with herself and her feelings and took 'more interest in the outside world'. She must not make a display of her sufferings before him as if to say 'This is all your work'. Such accusations were not calculated to make him wish to take any steps 'towards reconciliation'.

He was not yet ready to forgive, that was not how he felt, he told her in one of their quarrels; but he was ready to 'ignore all that [had] happened, take a new departure', and 'try in future to avoid everything' which might make 'her unhappy state of mind worse'. He was trying to keep out of her way until her 'better feelings' returned and she had 'regained that control' of herself which she had 'again lost quite unnecessarily'. He had not said a word which would wound her, and had not begun the conversation, but she had followed him about and continued it from room to room. It was 'the dearest wish of [his] heart to save [her] from these and worse consequences, but the only result' of his efforts was that he was 'accused of want of feeling, hard heartedness, injustice, hatred, jealousy, distrust etc, etc.'

'I do my duty towards you,' he wrote in yet another letter, 'even though life is embittered by "scenes" when it should be governed by love and harmony. I look upon this with patience as a test which has to be undergone, but you hurt me desperately and at the same time do not help yourself.'

When one of these scenes was over and all was quiet and contented again, his letters would strike a different note: he had not realized the extent to which her nerves were shaken; he promised never in future to 'express a difference of opinion' until she was better; he had noticed 'with delight' her efforts to be 'unselfish, kind and sociable' and her success in being so. His 'love and sympathy' were 'limitless and inexhaustible'.

29

CRIMEAN WAR

'I regret exceedingly not to be a man
and to be able to fight in the war.'

A FEW WEEKS after the birth of Prince Leopold, there was a riot in Bethlehem where a fight over custody of the Church of the Nativity had broken out between monks of the Roman Catholic Church supported by France, and monks of the Orthodox Church supported by Russia. Bethlehem was at that time within the immense and crumbling Turkish empire which, stretching from the Adriatic to the Persian Gulf, from the Black Sea through Syria and Palestine to the deserts of Arabia, was ready for conquest and division.

Turkish police, Tsar Nicholas I complained, had connived at the murder of those Orthodox monks who had been killed in the rioting; and within a matter of days a Russian army was marching towards the Danube on a crusade to protect the Holy Places from Islam. Notes, memoranda, despatches and threats flew from St Petersburg to Paris, from Constantinople through Vienna to London, and crackled uncertainly over the electric telegraph.

By October 1853 Turkey was at war with Russia. England for the moment remained neutral. And then on 30 November the Russian Black Sea fleet under Admiral Nachimoff sailed out of Sebastopol, found a Turkish flotilla off the south shore of the Black Sea at Sinope and sank its every ship. Nearly four thousand sailors were lost, and many of them, so it was widely reported in the press, were shot by Russian gunners as they floundered in the water.

British opinion was outraged by what was commonly referred to as a 'massacre' and a massacre perpetrated by a Russian fleet when Britannia ruled the waves. Those voices previously crying caution and restraint were stilled by shouts for the destruction of Sebastopol. No one listened to talk of Turkish atrocities any more.

Lord Aberdeen, who had taken over as Prime Minister after the resignation of Lord John Russell's successor, the Earl of Derby, did not want war. Nor did Lord Clarendon, his Foreign Secretary. But Lord Palmerston, now Home Secretary and a more influential man than either of them, was a strong Russophobe; and Lord Aberdeen felt obliged to give way to Palmerston's views which were shared by *The Times*, by the country at large, and by the Queen who, a few weeks earlier, had doubted that England ought to go to war for the defence of 'so-called Turkish independence', but who concluded that she was now bound to do so.

On 27 March 1854 war was therefore declared on Russia, France having done so the previous day; and British soldiers went marching down to Portsmouth with their bands playing and the shouts and cheers of the crowd in their ears, while the Queen, with Prince Albert and their children, stood on the balcony of Buckingham Palace, appearing 'much affected', bowing and smiling 'most graciously', waving them goodbye.

But in the xenophobia which so frequently attacks countries upon declaration of war, the popularity which Prince Albert had briefly enjoyed at the time of the Great Exhibition was swept away. All the old prejudices against his stiff formality, his foreign clothes and rigid handshake, his prudish morality, his supposed misogyny, his Germanic tastes, his assumption of regal authority, his unwarranted interference in military affairs, were once more aired in the press and in the houses not only of the rich and aristocratic, but increasingly in those of the middle classes. It was said that he was sympathetic towards the Russians, that he attempted to persuade the Queen to be so too, and that he adopted a highly unconstitutional role at the audiences with Ministers which he regularly attended with her. It was even rumoured that he was involved in some traitorous activity for which he was to be sent to the Tower. Lord Derby said thousands of people gathered there to watch His Royal Highness go in, while some said it was certain he would have been sent there had not the Queen announced her intention to go with him.

It was also rumoured that the Prince spoke German more often than English and that he and the Queen always conversed in his native tongue, a story that she strongly denied. 'The Prince and Queen speak English quite as much as German,' she protested, and she went on to deprecate 'that continual and unbounded dislike (in England) of foreigners and *everything foreign* which breaks out continually, and is *very* painful to the Queen – whose Husband, Mother and all her dearest relations and friends are foreigners'. Both she and her husband took these aspersions on the Prince 'greatly to heart'.[1]

'In attacking the Prince, who is one and the same with the Queen herself,' she wrote to the Prime Minister, 'the throne is assailed, and she must say that she little expected that any portion of her subjects would thus requite the unceasing labours of the Prince.'

At the end of January 1855 the Government agreed to act. In Parliament, Ministers affirmed their complete trust in the Prince and their gratitude for his hard work in furthering the interests of the Queen and the country. Their declaration of trust was echoed in the House of Lords by Lord Derby.

The Queen was delighted by this 'triumphant refutation' of all 'the atrocious calumnies' and 'mad delusions' that had been voiced about the Prince: the position of her 'beloved lord and master', she reported to Stockmar, 'had been defined for once and for all'.

Neither the Prince nor the Queen provided any valid excuse for adverse criticism of their behaviour during the war. The Prince occupied himself with formulating detailed plans – rejected by the Government – for the raising of a force of fifteen thousand foreigners, and with writing memoranda, letters and papers of all kinds so voluminous in number that they now fill some fifty volumes in the Royal Archives. The Queen, often accompanied by her husband, reviewed regiments and naval squadrons on their departure for the Dardanelles. She set an example by knitting woollen socks, mittens and scarves. She wrote letters of condolence to the bereaved, and this she found 'a relief', since she could express 'all that she felt'. She inspected hospitals, including Chatham Hospital where, so she complained to Lord Panmure, the Secretary for War, the wards were 'like prisons' or 'robbers' dens', the beds being so closely packed together that there was 'hardly space to walk' between them. The sight of the wounded, she wrote, 'such fine, powerful frames laid low and prostrate with wounds and sickness on beds of suffering or maimed in the prime of life, is indescribably touching to us *women* who are born to suffer and can bear pain more easily'.² She spoke to each man in turn, questioning them about their wounds, and had intended 'to make some kind of general speech', but she was 'so agitated that it all stuck in [her] throat'.³

She offered the royal yacht as a troopship, money to buy artificial limbs for disabled soldiers, and pensions for the wounded. She urged that they should all be told that '*no one*' took a warmer interest in them or felt more for them than she did. She took a particular interest in the quick distribution of medals, a subject which is mentioned in almost every one of her letters to Lord Panmure during the three months before she was able to award them herself to her wounded Guards. 'At first I was so agitated I could hardly hold the medal,' she recorded of this occasion. 'Many of the privates smiled, others hardly dared look up . . . Many said, "Thank you, your Majesty", and all touched my hand, the first time that a simple Private has touched the hand of his Sovereign and that – a Queen! – I am proud of the tie which links the lowly brave to his Sovereign. Nothing could exceed the good manners of the men.'⁴

'Day and night' she thought of 'her beloved troops'; and this was quite true. 'What an awful time!' she wrote in her journal. 'I never thought I should have lived to see & feel all this. If only there was more reliable news from the front. If only,' she exclaimed, 'one knew the details!' She did hear of a victory on the Alma river, 'and never,' she wrote, 'in so short a time, has so strong a battery, so well defended, been so bravely & gallantly taken'. Then came news of the heroic charge and destruction of the Light Brigade under the command of the brave and dreadful Lord Cardigan, then of the fearful losses suffered in the battle fought on 5 November 1854 in the fog at Inkerman. 'The victory is no doubt a very brilliant one,' she wrote. 'But I fear dearly bought . . . what suffering from cold and what privations are already being endured . . . The Russians lost in killed, wounded and prisoners, 15,000!! The Guards, however, lost fearfully! The anxiety and uncertainty increase sadly.' It was all so 'heart-breaking'.⁵

She '*never* regretted more' that she was a woman and could not go to war with her brave soldiers who were suffering such appalling hardships. 'I assure you,' she told Princess Augusta, 'that I regret exceedingly not to be a man and to be able to fight in the war. My heart bleeds for the many fallen, but I consider that there is no finer death for a man than on the battlefield.'[6] Particularly did she feel so in a war against the Russians who shamefully abandoned their wounded, did not bury their dead, and shot at 'our soldiers as they were tending' their own wounded men.[7] Albert might not think so; but she agreed with General Bentinck, the Guards Brigade commander, that the Russians were 'so cruel and savage and fighting in a stupid, dogged way'. With enemies like these it was foolish of the Government to propose a Day of Humiliation and Prayer – prayer, perhaps, but humiliation, certainly not.

She envied Florence Nightingale who had gone out with thirty-eight nurses to organize a military hospital in Scutari. She herself would have liked to 'do so much good and look after the noble brave heroes whose behaviour [was] admirable. Dreadfully wounded as many [were] there [was] never a murmur or a complaint'.[8]

She sent Miss Nightingale a letter of warm thanks with an enamelled and jewelled brooch designed by Prince Albert; and after the war was over she invited her to Balmoral where, in the Prince's words, 'she put before us all that affects our present military hospital system and the reforms that are needed. We are much pleased with her. She is extremely modest.'[9]

So long as the war lasted, the Queen signed the commissions of every officer so that the 'personal connection between the Sovereign and the Army should be preserved'; and she was often to be seen, despatches in hand, studying maps of the theatre of war. General Canrobert, the French commander-in-chief, who met her in August 1855, said that she seemed as familiar with the allied positions in the Crimea as he was himself. Despite her grief at the losses her army suffered, her imagination was stirred by the drama and excitement of war, an emotion which her husband could not share. 'You never saw anyone,' said Lord Panmure to the British commander, Lord Raglan, 'so entirely taken up with military affairs as she is.'[10] 'Whenever any instructions of any importance are sent to Lord Raglan,' she told Panmure, 'the Queen would wish to see them, if possible *before* they are sent.' She wanted to be '*told everything*'.[11]

For this reason she invited Lord Cardigan, a notorious adulterer, to Windsor three weeks after his return to England to give her a first-hand account of the charge of the Light Brigade and of the general situation in the Crimea. He described the charge 'very simply and graphically –

very modestly as to his own wonderful heroism – but with evident & very natural satisfaction'.* He repeated his account the next day for the benefit of the royal children and other members of the family.[12]

At the beginning of the war the Queen had had every confidence in Lord Raglan, a kindly, patrician officer who had served as an aide-de-camp to Wellington at Waterloo and had been close to the Duke ever since. She had written grateful and friendly letters to him. 'The Queen's letter is most gracious. It is impossible to be more so,' he had written home to his daughters upon his promotion to field marshal after the battle of Inkerman, 'and Lord Aberdeen's expressions towards me are most flattering.'[13] But later everything had changed. The Queen's letters were still polite and gracious, but there was in them an undertone of accusation. Writing from Windsor on New Year's Day in 1855, she briefly acknowledged his previous letter, then, without further preliminaries, came straight to the purpose of her own.

> The sad privations of the Army, the bad weather and the constant sickness are causes of the *deepest* concern and anxiety to the Queen and the Prince. The braver her noble Troops are and the more patiently they bear all their trials and sufferings the more *miserable* we feel at their long continuance.
>
> The Queen *trusts* that Lord Raglan will be *very* strict in seeing that *no unnecessary* privations are incurred by any negligence of those whose duty it is to watch over their wants. The Queen heard that their coffee was given them green instead of its being roasted and several other things of the kind. It has distressed the Queen as she feels so conscious that they should be made as comfortable as circumstances can admit of. The Queen earnestly trusts that the larger amount of warm clothing has not only reached Balaclava but has been distributed and that Lord Raglan has been successful in procuring the means of hutting for the men. Lord Raglan cannot think how much we suffer for the Army and how painfully anxious we are to know that their privations are *decreasing* . . .[14]

Raglan replied at length; but the Queen was not satisfied; and when Lord Panmure sent her a copy of a highly censorious despatch he had written on behalf of the Government, categorizing the Commander-in-

---

* A picture of him doing so was painted by James Sant, who portrayed Prince Albert standing next to the Queen. The Queen, however, is not in the finished picture. She is said to have had her likeness painted out after having heard some particularly unpleasant story about Cardigan's private life (Saul David, *The Homicidal Earl: The Life of Lord Cardigan*, 326).

Chief's perceived failings, she expressed herself as being 'much pleased with it'. 'Painful as it must be to have to write or receive it,' she wrote to Panmure, 'the truth of everything stated there is undeniable.'[15]

At the end of the week the Queen wrote again to return the 'Morning State of the Army in the Crimea' which Panmure had sent her, and to agree with him in expressing 'astonishment at the meagre and unsatisfactory reports from Lord Raglan which contain next to nothing'.[16] This reluctance of Lord Raglan's to use expressions of either enthusiasm or alarm, and his reliance on the bare figures of the 'Morning States' to give the Government the information it required, were a source of real anxiety to the Queen. Her patience, 'indeed she might say *nerves*', were 'most painfully tried' by it.[17]

By this time Lord Aberdeen had resigned as Prime Minister. Before war had been declared he had struggled to keep the peace, endeavouring, in the Queen's words, 'to obtain more from the Emperor of Russia than he is justified in hoping'. And, when war seemed inevitable, he suggested to the Queen that Palmerston would be a far better leader of the Government than he could hope to be. But the Queen objected: she would not feel safe with Palmerston.

'If it comes to being safe,' Lord Aberdeen observed, 'I fear Your Majesty would not be safe with me during war, for I have such a terrible repugnance for it.'

'This will never do,' said the Queen.

'I'm all for patching up, if we can.'

'This is unfortunate.'[18]

Lord Aberdeen struggled on for about a year until, in the early hours of 30 January 1855, the House of Commons divided on a heatedly debated motion, moved by John Roebuck, the radical Member for Sheffield, 'that a Select Committee be appointed to enquire into the condition of our Army before Sebastopol, and into the conduct of those Departments of our Government whose duty it has been to minister to the wants of that Army.'[19]

Sydney Herbert, the Secretary-at-War, in replying for the Government in the Commons, clearly implied that the whole responsibility for what was happening in the Crimea lay with that 'collection of regiments which called itself the British Army and not with the Government'. 'When you come to the staff,' he said, 'can you expect men who have not only never seen an army in the field but have never seen two regiments banded together, to exhibit an acquaintance with the organization of an army?'[20]

The House was not impressed by this determined effort to shuffle the whole of the blame on the Army. Mr Roebuck's motion was carried by a two-thirds majority. The next day Lord Aberdeen resigned. The Government had fallen with 'such a whack', as Gladstone, Chancellor of the Exchequer, put it, that 'they could hear their heads thump as they struck the ground'.[21]

Although he was over seventy, Palmerston was the obvious choice as Lord Aberdeen's successor. But the Queen was determined not to have the rude old man whom she and the Prince, translating his name into German, called 'Pilgerstein' as her Prime Minister if she could possibly help it. Having consulted the elderly Lord Lansdowne, a former Lord President of the Council, she sent for Lord Derby; but he refused to take office. She even sent for Lord John Russell, whose resignation from the Government as soon as he had heard of Roebuck's motion had filled her with 'indignation and disgust'. Russell accepted, but he could not find sufficient support. So she was obliged to send for 'Pilgerstein'.

He was deaf and short-sighted, he dyed his hair and had 'false teeth wh[ich] w[ould] fall out of his mouth when speaking if he did not hesitate & halt so much in his talk'.[22] But he still had much life and vigour and sound sense in him. And he knew a good deal about the Army. He had been Secretary-at-War when he was twenty-four, and he had worked hard and well in this appointment for nearly twenty years, though earning the dislike of practically all his colleagues and of everyone connected with the Horse Guards. 'It is quite extraordinary,' Mrs Arbuthnot had said, 'how he was detested.'[23]

To her surprise and relief the Queen did not find 'Pilgerstein' nearly as troublesome and high-handed as she had expected. He was even quite accommodating: when he proposed that he should appoint Henry Layard, the archaeologist and outspoken liberal Member for Aylesbury, as Under-Secretary for War the Queen objected. Her cousin, the Duke of Cambridge, who had commanded the 1st Division without notable authority at the battle of the Alma, warned her that Layard's appointment would be most unpopular in the Army; while she herself objected to him on the grounds that he was not 'a thorough gentleman'. Evidently prepared to make amends for his tiresome behaviour as Foreign Secretary in the past, Palmerston gave way.

In her relief at finding him so accommodating, the Queen grew quite fond of him. Eventually, indeed, she and the Prince agreed that, of all the Prime Ministers they had had, Lord Palmerston was the one who gave the least trouble. 'He is most amenable to reason,' she added, '& most ready to adopt suggestions. The great danger was foreign affairs, but now these are conducted by an able & impartial man [the Earl of Clarendon] & that [Lord Palmerston] is responsible for the *whole*, everything is quite different.'[24] It was particularly gratifying to her that Palmerston came to have a very high opinion of Prince Albert's talents. 'I had no idea,' Palmerston declared, that he possessed 'such eminent qualities'. He was 'an extraordinary man'; how fortunate it was that the Queen had married 'such a Prince'. In July 1856 she was to reward her reformed and valued Minister with the Order of the Garter.[25]

30

NAPOLEON III

'His lovemaking was of a character to flatter
her vanity without alarming her virtue.'

SOON AFTER Lord Palmerston's appointment as Prime Minister, it was decided to invite Britain's ally, the Emperor Napoleon III, to make a state visit to England. He had announced his intention of going to the Crimea himself to take command; and in both London and Paris it was considered necessary to do all that could be done to prevent him undertaking a mission which would be as much of an annoyance to the British Army as it would to the French generals.

Before operations had begun in the Crimea, Prince Albert had been to Boulogne to see the Emperor and had dictated a memorandum about the visit to his secretary. Surprisingly, Napoleon spoke French with a German accent, the result of his having been educated at a gymnasium in Augsburg after his mother had been banished into exile upon the defeat of his uncle, Napoleon I, at Waterloo in 1815. Prince Albert found him humorous and lazy, rather quiet, not very well informed, but quite without pretence. His entourage was undistinguished and seemed afraid of him. He was certainly the 'only man' who had 'any hold on France, relying on the "nom de Napoléon". He does not care for music,' the Prince added with some disapproval, 'smokes a great many cigarettes [which the Prince refused], was proud of his horsemanship in which [the Prince] could discover nothing remarkable'.[1]

The Queen – who had confessed that she was 'really upset' at having to part with her husband, though he was away for only three days – was reassured by her husband's report. She had heard other far less favourable

230

accounts of the Emperor, and had been horrified when the French Ambassador, Count Walewski, had made it known that his master wished to marry the seventeen-year-old Princess Adelaide of Hohenlohe, daughter of Queen Victoria's beloved half-sister, Princess Feodora. Relieved beyond measure when Princess Adelaide refused the Emperor's offer, the Queen wrote to her half-sister:

> Now that this terrible affair about our dear Ada has been decided by herself – I can write to you what I have felt . . . Your dear child is *saved* from *ruin* of every possible *sort*. You know what *he* is, what his moral character is – (without thinking him devoid of good qualities and even valuable ones) what his entourage is, how thoroughly immoral France and French society are – hardly looking at what is wrong as more than fashionable and natural – you know how very insecure *his* position is – you know his age, that his health is indifferent, and naturally his wish to marry Ada [is] merely a political one, for he has never seen her . . . I ask you if you can imagine for a moment anything more awful than the fate of that sweet innocent child.[2]

Ten days after this letter was written the Emperor announced that he was to marry instead a Spanish lady of twenty-seven, Eugénie de Montijo, who lived in Paris for much of the year. This, in the Queen's opinion, was a much more suitable match. The woman was beautiful by all accounts and, while not born or brought up to be an Empress, she was said to have charm and intelligence. When her engagement to the Emperor was announced, one of her admirers had committed suicide and she herself had attempted to kill herself when another suitor had proposed marriage to her sister instead of to herself. Yet, if she was an adventuress, so was he an adventurer. 'Had the lady been unexceptionable in character and conduct and had she been French,' Lord John Russell, at that time Foreign Secretary in Lord Aberdeen's Administration, had observed to the Queen, 'it would perhaps have been the best decision the Emperor could take. As it is, the character of the Court will not be improved, and the best part of France will keep away from it.'[3]

There were those who thought the English Court would have been well advised to keep clear of both the Emperor and Empress. But the Queen was determined to ensure that his visit to her country was a success. The day before their arrival she inspected the suite of rooms in

Windsor Castle which had been prepared for them, noting with approval the new carpets, the regilded furniture, the bright colours, the embroidered monograms on the bed curtains, the dressing table on which her own gold toilet set was to be placed.

The next day, 16 April 1855, she awaited their arrival with anxiety. 'These great meetings of sovereigns,' she thought, were 'always very agitating'. But once the Emperor had walked into the Castle her nervousness began to disappear. She received him at the State Entrance while a band played the music of a song, made popular by the French Army, which had been written by the Emperor's mother, Hortense de Beauharnais Bonaparte, step-daughter of Napoleon I. 'I cannot say what indescribable emotion filled me,' the Queen recorded, having overcome her nervous apprehension, 'how much all seemed like a wonderful dream. I advanced and embraced the Emperor, who received two salutes on either cheek from me ... I next embraced the very gentle graceful and evidently very nervous Empress.' She then presented her two eldest children, first Vicky, the Princess Royal, who, 'with very alarmed eyes', made 'low curtsies', then Bertie, the Prince of Wales, whom the Emperor embraced.[4]

At dinner in St George's Hall – before which the Empress's high-spirited ladies could be heard laughing and shouting to each other through their open doors and across the corridors – the Emperor lost no time in bringing up the subject of his proposed visit to the Crimea, blaming his generals for their reluctance to assume the responsibility which he would take when he got there. But what a long way to go from France, the Queen observed, and what of the dangers when he arrived? As to that, he replied, there were dangers everywhere.

Dinner was followed by a ball in the Waterloo Chamber, tactfully known that evening as the Picture Gallery. And how it excited the Queen to think that she, 'the granddaughter of George III, should dance with the Emperor Napoleon, nephew of our great enemy, now my nearest and most intimate ally!'[5] Making one of his rather heavy jokes, Prince Albert had said that he would have to see that the necessary precautions were taken in the crypt of St George's Chapel in case, upon the arrival of a Bonaparte as guest at Windsor, George III should turn in his grave.[6]

Over the next few days there were concerts and operas and military reviews, drives in the sunshine through the London streets to cheers for the Queen and cockney shouts of 'Vive le Hemperor!', and a ceremony at which Prince Albert seemed to take 'longer than usual' to tie the Garter round the leg of the Emperor, who put his wrong arm through the Order's ribbon. With every hour she spent in his company, the deeper the Queen fell under the insinuating charm of her seductive guest. It had to be conceded that his appearance was far from prepossessing; his head was too big for a very short body; a small, black, rather disconcerting tuft of hair grew beneath his lower lip, a style of beard already known as imperial. Yet he went out of his way to please her, to flatter her, to address her in an excitingly bewildering manner that stopped just carefully short of outright flirtation. It was 'very extraordinary and unaccountable', she told Lord Clarendon with naivety, that he seemed to know so much about her. 'He even recollects how I was dressed,' she said, 'and a thousand little details it is extraordinary he should be acquainted with.' On hearing this, Clarendon said to himself, '*Le Coquin!* He has evidently been making love to her.'[7] His 'lovemaking was of a character to flatter her vanity without alarming her virtue'.[8]

The Emperor's voice was 'low & soft', his manner 'easy, quiet and dignified', 'so very good natured and unassuming and natural'. There was 'something fascinating, melancholy and engaging' about him which drew you to him. He made her feel that she was physically attractive to him in a manner to which she was quite unaccustomed; yet, at the same time, she felt that she could say anything she liked to him because, as she put it, 'I felt – I do not know how to express it – safe with him.'[9]

He was, indeed, she was soon to decide, a 'very *extraordinary* man with great qualities . . . wonderful *self-control*, great *calmness*, even *gentleness*' and a 'great *power of fascination*. . . as *unlike a Frenchman* as possible, being much more *German* than French in character'. She might almost say he was 'a mysterious man . . . possessed of *indomitable courage, unflinching firmness of purpose, self-reliance, perseverance and great secrecy*; to which should be added a great reliance on what he called his *star* and a belief in omens and incidents as connected with his future destiny'.[10] He observed, for example, that the initials of his host and hostess and their guests spelled N E V A, the river that flows through St Petersburg, but what exactly this was intended to indicate he did not say.[11]

The Queen was much taken also by the Empress, a 'charming lovable creature', so 'lively & talkative', so good-looking, so demure, so graceful, so elegant in her crinoline that even Albert admired her. 'Altogether I am delighted to see how much he likes and admires her,' the Queen wrote, 'as it is so seldom I see him do so with *any* woman.'[12] The Empress and the Queen found they could talk to each other in the friendliest way, so the Queen was able to bring up the vexed question of the Emperor's proposed command in the Crimea and to suggest, as she already had suggested to the Emperor himself, that his life should not be endangered by such an adventure. She was able to make the same point at a meeting at Buckingham Palace following one at Windsor attended by Prince Albert, the French and British Ambassadors and various Ministers and generals, all of whom, as Lord Panmure said, 'seemed to arrive at one opinion as to the inexpediency of the Emperor's going' to the Crimea.

A few days later, after his return to Paris, the Emperor wrote to thank the Queen for her kindness and to tell her that 'in view of the difficulties' which he found there, he was on the point of abandoning his plans to take over the command of his army. He added that he was looking forward to welcoming the Queen and the Prince to Paris in August during the Paris Exhibition.

The Queen, too, was looking forward to this visit. Since the Emperor's departure, she confided in Stockmar, she had been able to '*think* and talk of nothing else other than his visit to England'. He was such a 'wonderful and remarkable man ... The Prince, tho' less enthusiastic than I am, I can see well, shares this feeling. It is very reciprocal on the Emperor's part.'[13]

The Queen and the Prince and their two elder children, the Prince of Wales, then aged thirteen, and the Princess Royal who was fourteen, arrived in Paris at the Gare de Strasbourg on the evening of 18 August 1855, two days after the French army, acting independently of the British, had decisively defeated the Russians on the banks of the Tchernaya. The streets from the railway station to the Champs Elysées were lined with thousands of soldiers, amongst them a regiment of Zouaves in their splendid uniforms with baggy red trousers, friends, so the Queen noted, of her 'dear Guards'. As the crowds shouted their welcome, bands played and cannon roared in the darkening distance. The Queen felt 'quite bewildered but enchanted'. It was 'like a fairy tale, and everything so beautiful'.[14]

She was driven to the royal château of Saint Cloud, where the rooms prepared for her use had been redecorated in white and gold and the legs of a table which had been made for Queen Marie Antoinette had been specially cut short so that she could sit at it comfortably. There were Gobelin tapestries on the walls; beneath her balcony fountains played in the garden. She was '*delighted, enchanted*': Paris was more '*beautiful*' than any other city she had seen.[15]

She was taken to the Tuileries, the Palais de l'Elysée, the Hôtel de Ville, to the Sainte Chapelle and Notre Dame, Malmaison, the Palais de Saint Germain and to the Louvre, marching from one treasure to the next, for once untroubled by the heat which made a member of the Emperor's suite declare that he would give everything, everything '*la Vénus de Milo incluse, pour un verre de limonade*'. Her determination to miss nothing led Lord Clarendon, the Foreign Secretary, to observe resignedly that no royal personage ever known to history rivalled her 'indefatigability'.[16]

She was taken to Versailles to luncheon at the Petit Trianon, that delightful little *pavillon* of honey-coloured stone designed for Madame de Pompadour, King Louis XV's entertaining mistress. She was driven through the city incognito in a fiacre, passing houses and cafés outside which people sat drinking and talking in the sunshine. She heard a voice cry out '*Celle-la ressemble bien â la Reine d'Angleterre*', and was quite put out that she was not recognized. 'They do not seem to know who I am,' she said rather huffily. There was no mistaking her, though, despite the black veil that covered her face. As in Brussels, so in Paris, she was dressed as if in defiance of fashion. On occasions she wore an unsightly gown with a straw bonnet perched on her head, carrying a huge handbag, 'a voluminous object like one of our grandmother's', as General Canrobert described it, 'made of white satin or silk on which was embroidered a poodle in gold'. 'When she put her foot on the steps she lifted her skirt which was very short (in the English fashion I was told) and I saw that she had on small slippers tied with black ribbons which were crossed round her ankles.' At other times she appeared in a 'shocking toilette', a white flounced gown topped with 'a crude green' mantle, and, 'in spite of the great heat, a massive bonnet of white silk . . . with streamers behind and a tuft of marabout [sic] feathers on top . . . Her dress was white and flounced; but she had a mantle and sunshade of a crude green which did not go with the rest of her costume.'[17]

The Emperor, however, contrived to appear quite impervious to the Queen's dowdiness. At a grand ball at Versailles at which the Empress appeared, tall and radiant in a white crinoline brilliant with diamonds, he went up to the Queen and murmured admiringly 'Comme tu es belle!' He danced a waltz with her, so she said, 'very quietly'. It was an extraordinary evening. There were flowers everywhere, hanging from the ceilings, draped across the looking-glasses, covering the music stands of the hundreds of musicians. The fireworks display, the most brilliant the Queen had ever seen, had for its finale a set piece of the towers and walls of Windsor Castle exploding into light. At the splendid supper afterwards, 'The whole stage was covered in,' the Queen recalled, 'and four hundred people sat down at forty small tables.'[18]

A most moving scene was enacted in the Hôtel des Invalides where the ashes of Napoleon I, brought back from exile on the island of St Helena, lay in a coffin in the Chapel of St Jérôme awaiting burial in the crypt. As thunder roared and rain poured down in the Place Vauban outside, the Queen was deeply moved by the solemnity of the occasion. She told the Prince of Wales to kneel down by the coffin; and the sight of the small boy paying homage in the candlelight to his country's former enemy as a band played 'God Save the Queen', brought tears to the eyes of the French generals in attendance. 'Strange and wonderful indeed,' commented the Queen. 'It seems as if in this tribute of respect to a departed foe, old enmities and rivalries were wiped out, and the seal of Heaven placed upon that bond of unity, which is now happily established between two great and powerful nations.'[19]

The Prince of Wales had never enjoyed himself more, even though Lord Clarendon, who had been instructed to keep an eye on him and tell him how to behave, thought his mother's severity was 'very injudicious'.[20] Certainly the boy was constantly asking questions while rarely giving his full attention to the answers; but his manners and behaviour were perfectly respectable, though on occasions rather pert and opinionated. One day, as they were riding together in a carriage, Clarendon had been obliged to contradict something the Prince had said; but the Prince, quite unabashed, had riposted, 'At all events that is my opinion.' To this Clarendon had sharply replied, 'Then your Royal Highness's opinion is quite wrong.' The rebuke had seemed to surprise the Prince a good deal.[21]

For most of the time, however, the Prince had been serenely happy, intoxicated by the sight of a city he was to grow to love, the pretty, beautifully dressed ladies in the Tuileries, the brilliant fireworks at Versailles. He hero-worshipped the romantic and mysterious Emperor to whom he had confided one afternoon, 'You have a nice country. I should like to be your son.'[22] He adored the Empress Eugénie, too, and pleaded with her to let him and his sister stay behind in Paris for a few days on their own. The Empress replied that she was afraid that the Queen and Prince Albert could not do without them. 'Not do without us!' the Prince protested. 'Don't fancy that, for there are six more of us at home, and they don't want *us*.'[23]

When it was time for them to leave, the Contesse d' Armaille noticed the way the Prince looked intently all around him at the Gare de Strasbourg 'as though anxious to lose nothing' of his last moments in the city. As for the Queen, she had also relished every minute of the visit, obviously '*delighted, enchanted, amused* and *interested*' in all and by all that she had seen and done. She had made sure that it was a great diplomatic success, while returning to England with 'feelings of *real* affection for and interest in France'. Skittishly, she told the Emperor that she would come back next year as an ordinary traveller. Bag in hand, she would jump out of the train, catch a cab and arrive at the Tuileries in time for dinner.[24]

The Princess Royal also had much enjoyed herself and, like her brother, she had conceived a passion for the Empress who was so elegantly dressed by the English-born fashion designer, Charles Frederick Worth; and, having seen for herself on her earlier visit to England that Queen Victoria had no dress sense, the Empress had had a number of dresses sent to Windsor for Vicky to wear in Paris, all made to the measurements of a life-size doll belonging to the Princess, and sent in parcels to Windsor addressed to the doll. Before Vicky left, she was given a bracelet of rubies and diamonds containing strands of the Empress's hair. The Princess, sent into 'ecstasies' by the present, burst into tears.[25]

31

✳✳✳✳✳✳✳✳✳✳✳✳

THE PRINCESS ROYAL

'I felt as if I were being married over again,
only much more nervous.'

'I MUST WRITE DOWN AT ONCE *what* has happened – what I *feel* &
how grateful I am to God for *one* of the happiest days of my life!' the
Queen wrote at Balmoral on 29 September 1855, soon after her return
from Paris.[1] For days past she had been expecting to hear the news which
so much excited her, since on the twentieth of the month Prince Frederick
William of Prussia had asked Prince Albert if he might propose to the
Princess Royal. The Queen had feared he might not do so, that he would
not find her daughter sufficiently attractive: as Lord Clarendon said, she
was 'always finding fault with her daughter's looks, and complaining of
her being ugly and coarse'.[2]

Prince Albert had no hesitation in giving his permission for the proposal to be made. Long harbouring a distrust of France, he had consist-
ently advocated closer ties with what he hoped would one day soon be
a liberal Germany, unified under the leadership of Prussia. Besides, Prince
Frederick – Fritz, as he was known in the family – was a pleasant, well-
intentioned young man, 'unaffected and amiable' in the Queen's words
and moreover (always a strong recommendation to her) handsome, as
well as tall and broad-shouldered. Of course, Vicky could not marry until
she was at least seventeen and that would not be for another three years;
but there could be no harm in an engagement. Prince Frederick was
twenty-four and had, he said, hoped that he would be able one day to
marry Vicky ever since he had first seen her when she was no more than
ten.

At Balmoral that autumn of 1855, having made his hopes formally known to her parents, he said that his 'great wish' was to belong to their family by a marriage to their 'so sweet and charming, so clever and natural' eldest child. The Queen, overcome with emotion, could only squeeze Prince Frederick's hand, while Prince Albert assured him that they would give their child to him with 'complete confidence'.[3] For the moment nothing was to be said publicly, only a few members of their families being told and no Ministers officially being informed other than Lord Palmerston and the Foreign Secretary, Lord Clarendon, both of whom warmly approved of a union which they thought 'politically of great importance'. The London newspapers and periodicals did not, however, all agree with them when the engagement became known. Prussia, a relatively insignificant power, and the Hohenzollerns, one of many 'paltry German dynasties', were unworthy of an English Princess.[4] Moreover, Prussia had close ties with Russia and had shown no sympathy for England over the war in the Crimea. The Princess Royal might well find herself in a position in which devotion to her husband might be treason to her country. *Punch* wrote of a 'very suspicious looking eagle', a 'bird of ill-omen', having been seen hovering about Balmoral and having an eye on Her Majesty's dovecote.[5]

The eagle had fluttered rather than swooped down upon the dove during a ride on ponies to Craig-na-Ban. Fritz declared his love for Vicky, after having picked her a sprig of white heather which he said was an emblem of good luck. 'He began to speak of Germany', the Queen was told, 'his hope that she would come there and stay there . . . She answered that she would be happy to stay there for a year; he added he hoped that always, always – on wh. she became very red – he continued, he hoped he had said nothing which annoyed her – to which she replied "oh! no," – he added might he tell her Parents, wh. she then expressed a wish to do *herself*. He then shook hands with her – said this was one of the happiest days of his life'.[6]

When Vicky rejoined her parents, Fritz, so the Queen said, 'gave me a wink, implying that he had said something to Vicky, and she was extremely agitated and nervous'. Later, in her room, the Queen asked Vicky if she felt the same about Fritz as he did about her. "Oh, yes," she said eagerly, with an indescribably happy look . . . "I am very fond of the Prince." . . . Albert came in to say that Fritz was there – & I took her in. She was nervous but did not hesitate or falter in giving her very decided answer ... He kissed her hand twice and ... she threw herself into his arms, & kissed him with a warmth which was responded to by Fritz again and again & I would not for the world have missed so touching and beautiful a sight ... It is his first love! Vicky's great youth makes it even more striking but she behaved as a girl of 18 would ... To witness that dear child's innocent joy – to see the happiness of two such dear, pure young Beings – is more happiness than I cd. ever have expected.'[7]

Prince Frederick's happiness was somewhat marred, however, by the Queen's insistence that when he and the Princess Royal were alone together – and this did not often happen – she herself should sit in the next room and the door between them should be left open. She later decided that perhaps she had been 'severer than she ought to have been'.[8]

While the Royal Family were at Balmoral that September, a telegraphic despatch arrived with news from General Simpson, who had succeeded to the command of the British Army in the Crimea on the death there of Lord Raglan. The message read, 'Sevastopol is in the hands of the Allies.'

> Albert said they should go at once and light the bonfire which had been prepared when the false report of the fall of the town arrived last year, and had remained ever since, waiting to be lit ... In a few minutes Albert, and all the gentlemen, in every species of attire, sallied forth, followed by all the servants, and gradually by all the population of the village – keepers, gillies, workmen – up to the top of the cairn. We waited, and saw them light it, accompanied by general cheering. The bonfire blazed forth brilliantly, and we could see the numerous figures surrounding it – some dancing, all shouting ... Albert came down and said the scene [which he described as a 'veritable Witch's dance'] had been wild and exciting beyond everything – The people had been drinking healths in whiskey, and were in great ecstasy.[9]

It was a French victory, though, not an allied one. The British soldiers, mostly raw recruits or old soldiers whose nerve had long since been shattered, had come to a halt at the foot of the defensive works and, under intensive fire, had refused to go forward; while the French, whose losses were almost three times as heavy, seized and clung on to the

Malakoff redoubt until the Russian commander decided he could no longer hold Sebastopol which was by then a smoking ruin.

When she heard the details of her army's failure and disgrace, the Queen expressed her deep regret that the war should end on so shameful a note, while Palmerston, well aware that France, having vindicated her military honour, now longed for peace, declared that he would rather continue fighting with no other ally than Turkey than agree to unsatisfactory terms. 'I own that peace rather sticks in my throat,' the Queen confessed, '& so it does in that of the *whole* Nation.'[10]

She liked to think of herself as a soldier's child; and while the peace negotiations were making laborious progress, she kept as closely in touch as she could with her army, welcoming home soldiers returning from the Crimea, visiting the wounded, reviewing parades of recruits. She attended a field day at Aldershot and found it '*so* exciting', never having been 'so completely *in* anything of this kind before'. A few weeks later, she reviewed a parade of troops, appearing before them in a new military tunic of scarlet and gold, a crimson and gold sash, a blue skirt with white piping and a hat with a red and white plume and golden tassels, and looking far smarter than ever she did in civilian clothes. The following month she was in military attire again, sitting on a horse named Alma and reviewing the largest force of British soldiers 'assembled in England since the battle of Worcester' in 1651.

By then the protracted peace negotiations had at last been concluded by the Peace of Paris of 30 March 1856, a treaty so generally unpopular in England that the heralds who announced it in London were hissed at Temple Bar. Relations between France, whose army had so single-handedly secured the final victory, and Britain, whose military reputation had been so shamefully besmirched, went from bad to worse until, on 14 January 1858, there was an outrage in Paris which threatened to break them off altogether.

As the Emperor and Empress were driving to the opera on the evening of that day, three bombs were hurled at their carriage and in the explosion, which sent the glass canopy of the Opera House crashing into the rue Lepelletier, extinguishing all its lights, ten people and two horses were killed, the Emperor and Empress escaping with cut faces.

'The noise and cries were dreadful, as well as the rush of the crowd, many bleeding,' Queen Victoria wrote, having been told what had happened by Prince Albert's brother, Ernest, who was in the Emperor's box waiting for the performance to begin. 'The Empress's dress was splashed with blood from the wounded around her . . . [She was] wonderfully composed and courageous, even more so than the Emperor. [She told the police, 'Don't bother about us, such things are our profession. Look after the wounded.'] They remained throughout the performance.'[11]

Several attempts on the Emperor's life had already been made. 'You know,' he had said to his friend, Lord Malmesbury, when he had been in England three years before, 'I am neither fanciful, nor timid, but I give you my word of honour that three men have been successively arrested within fifty yards of me armed with daggers and pistols . . . These men all came straight from England, and had not been twelve hours in France. Your police should have known it and given me notice.'[12]

He now had further cause for complaint, since the man responsible for this latest attempt on the Emperor's life was an emotionally disturbed Italian count, Felice Orsini, who had been welcomed in England as a champion of his country's freedom from Austrian control, a cause which he believed might be furthered by provoking a revolution in France that would spread to Italy.

The French were outraged to learn that not only had Orsini been greeted as a hero in England – where his published accounts of his life as agent of the revolutionary, Giuseppe Mazzini, had been widely read and admired – but also that the bombs which he and two accomplices had hurled at the Emperor's carriage had been manufactured in Birmingham. Count Walewski, the French Foreign Minister, complained of such dangerous men as Orsini being harboured in England, while there were calls from French army officers for an invasion of England to prevent such protection of revolutionaries in the future. Lord Granville observed, 'The accounts from France are very bad. A war with France would not surprise me.'[13] Palmerston ignored the French Ambassador's letter; but his Government did introduce into the House of Commons a Bill intended to strengthen the law relating to conspiracy. Resentment in England about anti-British sentiments in France led to the Conspiracy to Murder Bill being defeated, however, and to the fall of the Government.[14]

Ten days before Orsini's attempt on the Emperor Napoleon's life, the Princess Royal had been married to Prince Frederick of Prussia in the

Chapel Royal, St James's, where the Queen herself had been married. 'I felt as if I were being married over again,' the Queen wrote, 'only much more nervous.'[15] So nervous was she, indeed, that in a daguerreotype of the bride and her parents taken before the ceremony her features were reduced to a blur by her trembling. She feared that she might break down in the Chapel. Once there, however, she recovered her composure; and, having noted that the bridegroom was very pale and seemed as nervous as the Archbishop of Canterbury as he waited at the altar, she was proud to see 'our darling flower' looking 'very touching and lovely with such an innocent, confident and serious expression' as she approached him, 'her veil hanging back over her shoulders, walking between her beloved father and dearest Uncle Leopold'.[16]

Afterwards, when the Princess went up to the Throne Room to sign the register, dry-eyed and holding her husband's hand, as Mendelssohn's 'Wedding March' was played on the organ, the Queen was 'so moved, so overjoyed and so relieved' that she felt she could have 'embraced everybody'. The next day, having watched her child acknowledging the cheers of the crowd from the balcony of Buckingham Palace – and having enjoyed the wedding breakfast even though the Princess was hidden from her view behind a gigantic wedding cake – she felt quite sad that 'all was over': it had all been 'so brilliant, so satisfactory'.[17]

That evening, after the bride and bridegroom had driven off for a brief honeymoon at Windsor Castle, where, on the first evening after dinner, they sat 'almost too shy to talk to one another', the Queen felt 'so lost without Vicky'. She was, therefore, much relieved to receive a letter from her to which she replied immediately, telling her how well she had behaved and how happy her parents were to think that she was now 'in other but truly safe and loving hands'. It had been difficult for the Queen, possessive as she was, to accept that she must now put her 'maternal feelings aside' if she was 'not to be very jealous'. It was an 'awful moment to have to give one's innocent child up to a man', knowing 'all that she must go through'.[18]

'That thought – that agonizing thought ... of giving up your own child, from whom *all* has been so carefully kept & guarded, to a stranger *to do unto her as he likes*, is to me the most torturing thought in the world,' she wrote to her daughter years later. 'While I feel *no* girl could go to the altar (and would probably refuse) if she *knew* all, there is something VERY DREADFUL in the thought of the sort of trap she is being *led into*.'[19]

Four days after the wedding, the parents had to say goodbye to their child. The prospect of parting on that 'dull, still, thick morning' made the Queen feel quite 'sick at heart'. The night before, when she and Prince Albert had gone with her to her room, Vicky had 'cried so much'; and her mother had said to her husband on their way back to their own room that it was 'like taking a poor lamb to be sacrificed'. 'It really makes me shudder,' she later told Vicky, 'when I look round at all your sweet, happy, unconscious sisters, and think I must give them up too – one by one.' Now, her 'breaking heart gave way'; and she wept helplessly as they stood at the carriage door. Vicky who, in her own words, loved her parents 'so passionately, so intensely', cried too, holding her mother in her arms; and there were tears also in Fritz's eyes.[20]

The next day Vicky, who had told her mother that she thought it would kill her 'to take leave of dear Papa', wrote him a loving letter:

> My beloved Papa,
> The pain of parting from you yesterday was greater than I can describe. I thought my heart was going to break . . . I miss you so dreadfully, dear Papa, more than I can say; your dear picture stood near me all night, it was a comfort to me to think that I had even that near me. I meant to have said so much yesterday, but my heart was too full for words. I should have liked to have thanked you for all that you have done for me. To you, dear Papa, I owe most in this world. I shall never forget the advice it has been my privilege to hear from you at different times, I treasure your words up in my heart . . .
> I feel that writing to you does me good, dear Papa; I feel that I am speaking to you, and though the feeling that I cannot see you or hear your dear voice in return makes the tears rise to my eyes, yet I am thankful that this is left to me. Goodbye, dearest Papa – I must end. Your most dutiful and affectionate daughter, Victoria.[21]

That same day her father had written to her, his favourite child:

> My heart was very full when yesterday you leaned your forehead on my breast to give free vent to your tears. I am not of a demonstrative nature, and therefore you can hardly know how dear you have always been to me, and what a void you have left behind in my heart: yet not in my heart, for there assuredly you will abide

henceforth, as till now you have done, but in my daily life, which is evermore reminding my heart of your absence.[22]

In the lessons he had given her after her engagement he had made it plain what his daughter's duty as the Crown Princess – and, no doubt, eventually *Kaiserin* – was to be the gradual liberalization of Prussia and the unity of the German states under Prussia and in alliance with the England which she loved. 'I feel I am serving you both,' she told her parents a few days after her arrival in what was to be her new home, 'and that I am proving my deep gratitude to you. In doing my duty here, and in imitating your great and glorious example, I may I hope be of real use to you.'[23]

This is just what Otto von Bismarck, the future German Chancellor, feared. 'You ask me . . . what I think of the English marriage,' he replied to a letter from General Leopold von Gerlach. 'The "English" in it does not please me . . . If the Princess can leave the Englishwoman at home and become a Prussian, then she may be a blessing to the country . . . But . . . if our future Queen remains even only partly English, I can see our Court in danger of being surrounded by English influence.'[24]

'Poor dear child,' the Queen wrote, 'I often *tremble* when I think *how* much is expected of her . . . I do not like the idea now of *our Child* going to Berlin, more or less the *enemy's den.*'[25]

She comforted herself by writing to her at least twice a week, and receiving in return letters which, nearly as long, arrived in England almost as frequently. In the years between 1858 and 1901, a total of almost eight thousand surviving letters passed between them.[26] The Queen's letters, affectionate, candid, detailed, are replete with unsolicited advice and occasional reprimands, as though her daughter remained the seventeen-year-old girl who had left home so soon after her marriage. 'You have not written me one single word, for more than a week!!' one letter begins. 'Now let this not happen again promise me and answer this.'[27] 'I asked you several questions,' another letter reminded her, 'and you have not answered one! You should just simply and shortly answer them one by one and then there could be no mistake about them. My good dear child is a little unmethodical and unpunctual.'[28]

She must always be tidy in appearance and avoid loud laughter; 'remember never to lose the modesty of a young girl towards others (without being a prude)'; she should protest against the rude jokes of the King's brother, Prince Charles, 'or at least not speak to him, if he gets on such abominable subjects, but be very stiff and reserved'; she must avoid high-heeled boots and 'fearfully full sleeves – for God's sake take care or you will set yourself on fire'. Repeatedly, she is also warned against over-heated, unwholesome rooms, so bad for the health, and against being too lazy to look at thermometers and to open windows. Her mother hoped that she was 'not getting fat again' – 'do avoid eating soft, pappy things or drinking much' – and that she would consult an English dentist – 'German dentists are not famous and German teeth so bad.'

She was to take no notice of the 'extraordinary' German convention that pregnant women should not stand as godmothers; nor was she to follow the German custom of 'lying in a dressing gown on a sofa at a christening'; she must promise her mother 'never to do so improper and indecorous a thing . . . Let German ladies do as they like but the English Princess must not.'

Vicky must not try to paint in oils – 'you remember what Papa told you on the subject. Amateurs never can paint in oils like artists and what can one do with all one's productions? Whereas water colours always are nice and pleasant to keep in books or portfolios.' Vicky must correct her careless spelling and her use of unnecessary capital letters as well as remember to number her letters properly. Also, when writing at her desk, she must sit up straight – 'remember how straight I always sit, which enables me to write without fatigue at all times.' She was 'almost angry' when her daughter referred to 'dear, dear Windsor' when she herself was in residence there and 'struggling with homesickness' for her 'beloved Highlands'. She could not, she said, 'feel the slightest affection for this old dull place, which please God shall never hold my bones, I think I dislike it more and more . . . You don't say a word about all the affectionate speeches of those dear people at Balmoral, which I write to you about.'[29]

In another letter she wrote of her surprise on learning that her daughter had been to see *The Merry Wives of Windsor*: she herself had 'never had courage to go to see it'. She had, she said, 'always been told how very coarse it was – for your adored Shakespeare is dreadful in that respect and many things have to be left out in many of his plays'. The Queen had also been surprised to read in one of her daughter's previous letters that she thought Ada, the daughter of Princess Hohenlohe, must be 'glad' at being pregnant again.

> How can anyone, who has not been married above two years and three quarters rejoice at being a third time in that condition? [she continued, warming to a favourite and perennial theme] I positively think those ladies who are always enceinte quite disgusting; it is more like a rabbit or a guinea-pig than anything else and really it is not very nice ... Let me repeat once more, dear, that it is very bad for any person to have them very fast – and that the poor children suffer for it even more, not to speak of the ruin it is to the looks of a young woman – which she must not neglect for her husband's sake, particularly when she is a Princess.[30]

32

INDIAN MUTINY

'We are in sad anxiety about India
which engrosses all our attention.'

HOSTILITIES IN THE CRIMEA had not long been formally concluded
when news reached London of renewed fighting; this time in India, where
for some time now unrest had been fostered by the agents of princes
dispossessed by the British, and by agitators, troublemakers, fakirs,
maulvis, and men who had cause to resent the rule of the subcontinent
by the East India Company, the British Government's representative in
the civil administration of India, which was also responsible for the armies
of native infantrymen and cavalrymen, sepoys and *sowars*, maintained by
the three Presidencies: Bengal, Madras and Bombay. Villagers collected
to hear warnings of the designs of the *firinghis* (the foreigners who, so
they were told, were bent on destroying their faith), and to listen to
prophecies that the British would be forced to leave India in 1857, the
hundredth anniversary of the defeat of Sirāj-ud-Dawlah's forces by the
East India Company's army under Robert Clive at Plassey. Sepoys were
assured that the British were not invincible; that, following the Crimean
War, Russia had conquered and annexed England; and that, since their
country's population was less than a hundred thousand, the English could
not – even if the Russians let them – reinforce their own regiments,
known as the Queen's Regiments, in India. They were told that Lord
Canning, the recently appointed Governor-General, had been sent out
with the express purpose of converting them to Christianity, and that the
widows of soldiers killed in the Crimean War were being shipped out to
India where the principal land-holders would be compelled to marry

them so that their estates would eventually fall into Christian hands. Sepoys were also told that the new cartridges issued for their rifles were greased with beef fat or pig fat and thus intended to defile them and destroy their caste.

These fears erupted into violence on 10 May 1857 at Meerut where men of a native regiment, the 3rd Light Cavalry, had refused to handle the new cartridges and had consequently been sentenced to imprisonment with hard labour, for ten years. After this punishment had been pronounced upon them at a parade of all the troops at Meerut, their uniforms were stripped from them, their boots removed and their ankles shackled. The next day the native troops mutinied; British officers and their wives were killed either by sepoys or by *budmashes* from the bazaar; and soon the uproar spread all over the Ganges valley: Delhi and nearby towns were seized by the mutineers.[1]

The Queen, who had long been fascinated by India and proud of it as the 'jewel in her crown', was appalled to read reports of what was happening there. 'We are in sad anxiety about India, which engrosses all our attention,' she told King Leopold. 'I know you feel much for us all. There is not a family hardly who is not in sorrow and anxiety about their children, and in all ranks – India being *the* place where everyone was anxious to place a son!'

Her thoughts, she told Lady Canning, were 'almost *solely* occupied with India'; and she urged Palmerston and his Government to display a more urgent sense of the gravity of the mutiny. 'The Queen *must* repeat to Lord Palmerston,' she wrote soon after learning of the murders at Meerut, 'that the measures taken by the Government are *not* commensurate with the magnitude of the crisis.' She and the Prince, so he said, had to be 'constantly digging [their] spurs' into the Government's side.[2]

The Queen read of such tragedies as the massacre of the women and children at Cawnpore with horror: they made 'one's blood run cold'; they haunted her '*day* and night'. 'The horrors' of Cawnpore 'surpass all belief', she wrote, '& it was a great *mercy all* were killed!' Yet, 'It shd. never have been made known, for that no good can be done any more, & it can only distract for life the unhappy relations'.[3]

She read with equal horror of the reprisals exacted upon the rebels, the mass executions, the firing of mutineers' bodies from the mouths of cannon, the cries for more and more bloody revenge, the disgraceful attacks upon Lord Canning, now derisively known in India as 'Clemency' Canning, who refused to give way to persistent demands that even harsher punishments should be imposed upon captured rebels, that, in the words of one Assistant Commissioner, they should 'all be shot like dogs'.[4]

'There is a rabid and indiscriminate vindictiveness abroad, even among men who ought to set a better example, which it is impossible to contemplate without a feeling of shame for one's own countrymen,' Lord Canning wrote to the Queen. 'Not one man in ten seems to think that the hanging and shooting of forty thousand or fifty thousand men can be otherwise than practicable and right.'[5]

The Queen was entirely in agreement with the Governor-General. She considered the shouts for a bloody revenge 'too horrible and really quite shameful'. There must, of course, be suitable punishment for the perpetrators of these 'awful horrors', but the 'greatest kindness' should be shown to the 'many kind and friendly natives' who had helped the British. 'They should know that there is no hatred to a brown skin – none; but the greatest wish on the Queen's part to see them happy, contented and flourishing.'

'Justice, and that as stern and inflexible as law and might can make it, I will deal out,' Canning told Lord Granville, Lord President of the Council. 'But I will never allow an angry or indiscriminate act or word to proceed from the Government of India as long as I am responsible for it.'[6]

In this spirit he firmly refused to agree to accept a petition suggesting that martial law should be proclaimed throughout Bengal; and, to the satisfaction of the Queen and the Prince, he passed a resolution to ensure that captured sepoys should not be punished without regard to the gravity of their offences. Such compassion seemed misplaced to most Europeans in Calcutta; they petitioned the Queen for the recall of the Governor-General who, they contended, was no fit person to deal with the monsters who had perpetrated the horrors witnessed in India. But the Queen was not impressed by the petition. She knew that Canning was well aware of the dangers of racial animosity and she recognized that stern justice for the rebels had to be tempered with understanding of their fears. 'I think that the greatest care ought to be taken not to interfere with their religion,' she told Lady Canning, 'as once a cry of that kind is raised among a fanatical people – very strictly attached to their religion – there is no knowing what it may lead to and where it may end.'[7]

She was entirely in agreement with the Governor-General and his supporters that what was needed now was a spirit of reconciliation, not retribution, and that the friendship of the Indian people was to be sought, not their enforced submission. After all, the rebellion had affected only a small part of the country and the mutiny had been largely confined to various regiments in Bengal; many disarmed sepoys had returned quietly to their homes; and thousands of Indian soldiers and camp followers had fought with the British, who could not have survived without their support.

On 1 November 1858, preceded by military salutes and followed by thanksgiving services and firework displays, a proclamation had been read out at every military cantonment in India. The document declared that the East India Company had been abolished, that the Queen and her Government now ruled India directly, that religious toleration would be observed and ancient customs respected, and that the Queen offered pardon to all rebels who had not taken part in the murder of Europeans.

She and Prince Albert had played a significant part in the wording of the proclamation. They had objected to certain passages in the Government's draft which seemed to them too severe and unsympathetic. They particularly objected to a passage which referred to the Queen's power to 'undermine native religions and customs'. The proclamation, Prince Albert decided, 'cannot possibly remain in its present shape'.[8] 'Such a document,' the Queen wrote, 'should breathe feelings of generosity, benevolence and religious toleration.' It should endeavour to 'draw a veil over the sad and bloody past', to remove the fear of so many Indians that the British wanted to interfere with their religion, and endeavour to persuade them that the 'deep attachment which Her Majesty feels to her own religion, and the comfort and happiness which she derives from its consolations, will preclude her from any attempt to interfere with the native religions'.[9]

Within a fortnight of the proclamation of peace in India, the Prime Minister of Piedmont, Count Camillo Cavour, wearing dark glasses and carrying a passport in the name of Giuseppe Benso, crossed the French frontier and was driven to Plombières to discuss with the Emperor Napoleon III the reopening of conflict in Europe.

Having recovered from the shock of his attempted assassination, the

Emperor had come to believe that Orsini's plot was a sign that the decisive moment had come for him to fulfil a long-held ambition 'to do something for Italy'. As a young man, he had belonged to the Carbonari, a secret society dedicated to the ultimate unity of the various kingdoms, duchies and republics into which Italy was then divided. He had risked his life fighting against the misgovernment of the Papal States. And it was as though his former doubts and speculations, concealed as always behind an atmosphere of contrived mystery, had suddenly been swept away by a brilliant vision of his preordained path.

He could find it in his heart to admire Orsini, and for a time considered the possibility of reprieving him. In the words of the British Ambassador in Paris, Lord Cowley, the Emperor was 'regularly bitten with this miscreant'. He had always remained a conspirator himself at heart and in Mazzini, Orsini's former master, he recognized a fellow spirit. So it was that he and Cavour came to be driving together in the hot sun at Plombières, discussing war and the fate of Italy.

Cavour's master, King Victor Emmanuel II, was a squat man with enormously strong, thick legs and an immense moustache which swept up towards his little grey eyes in a ferociously intimidating crescent. Untidy in his dress and blunt in his speech, he was coarse in his habits. Detesting official banquets, through which he would sit glaring about him, his eyes rolling alarmingly, his hand on his sword, he preferred to eat huge peasant dishes of steaming ragout smothered in garlic and hot onions. His appetite for women was equally voracious and uninhibited.

As an ally in the Crimean War – in which his army had fought, on Cavour's advice, in order to obtain a say in the peace negotiations – King Victor Emmanuel had been invited to England in 1855. Charles Greville described him as being 'frightful in person, a great, strong, burly, athletic man, brusque in his manners, unrefined in his conversation, very loose in his conduct, and very eccentric in his habits'.[10] But, although he was expected to behave as he had done in Paris – where he had terrified everybody and enquired of the Emperor as to the price of a dancer who struck his fancy at the Opera – he was on his best behaviour at Windsor. Indeed, he became quite a favourite at Court where the Queen seemed intrigued by him, though she was given a hint of what was to come when he told her that he did not like 'the business of a King'. He would become a monk if he could not make war; there was no need to worry about that, though: another war was inevitable.

Kings had to make sure that wars were just, the Queen observed. They would have to answer to God for men's lives.

Yes, one had to aim for a just war, the King conceded. But God would always pardon a mistake.

'Not always.'[11]

He seemed like a character in an *opera buffa* as he showed the Prince of Wales his sword which, he told him, could cut an ox in half at a single stroke. The Duchess of Sutherland felt sure he could easily wield it for such a purpose. King Victor Emmanuel seemed to her to be the only Knight of the Garter she had ever seen who 'looked as if he would have the best of it with the dragon'.[12]

He took what seemed to be an unconscionable time before he consented to bend down when the Queen held up her face to be kissed; then, having planted a kiss upon her cheek, 'he began upon her hand, and bestowed upon it three kisses that resounded throughout the room'. When he was installed as a Knight of the Garter, he put forward one leg, then the other until 'at last he asked the Queen in his loud voice, "*Laquelle?*" She nearly let fall the Garter from laughing, the Prince was in fits and all the KG's at the table began to titter.'[13]

The Queen was in no such jolly mood, however, when she heard that, in accordance with the agreement reached at Plombières in July 1858, Europe was to be 'deluged with blood', as her Foreign Minister, Lord Malmesbury, put it, 'for the personal ambition of an Italian attorney and a tambour major, like Cavour and his master'.

The conduct of King Victor Emmanuel, with whom she had felt herself to be on such good terms, and of the French Emperor, whom she had once so greatly admired, produced, so she said, 'universal indignation amongst all right-thinking people'. She believed that, although her people for the most part approved of the idea of Italian independence, they disapproved strongly of the Emperor of the French attacking another Empire 'without rhyme or reason'.

She and Prince Albert went to France again in August to meet the Emperor at Cherbourg, where the Prince was 'conscious of a change' in him and worried by the obvious indications that France was preparing for another war.[14] There were hundreds of workmen labouring in the port where the breakwater was being extended, the harbour was being fortified and warships were under construction in the docks. The Queen could not but feel concerned about the identity of the enemy the Emperor had in mind, but he was unforthcoming, '*boutonné*' and evasive.[15]

A year earlier, when he and the Empress had been guests at Osborne, their relations with the Queen and the Prince had been perfectly friendly. They had enjoyed a pleasant outing together to Carisbrooke Castle; and the Emperor had intrigued the Queen by his account of the strange powers of a spiritualist medium, Daniel Dunglass Home, the inexplicable phenomena of whose séances had so mystified guests at the Tuileries and at Fontainebleau.

Now the former, easy atmosphere had become clouded by suspicion. The Queen made it clear that she disapproved of the Emperor's liaison with Madame Walewska, the beautiful, ambitious, Florentine wife of the French Foreign Minister, while the French were suspicious of a gentle-man-in-waiting in the visitors' entourage, a man who was suspected of being – and who, indeed, was – an officer in the Royal Engineers. The Emperor complained of his military and naval rearmaments being reported in English newspapers as intended for a possible onslaught on England: would not Her Majesty take steps to correct these misrepresentations in the London press? The Queen replied that, as a constitutional monarch, she had no power to do so.

On her return home, the Queen spoke to the Prime Minister, Lord Palmerston's successor, Lord Derby, about the Emperor's clear intention of going to war; but Derby did not seem much concerned. Prince Albert, whose distrust of the French was much increased by what he had seen in Cherbourg, was exasperated. 'The war preparations in the French marine are immense!' he told his mother-in-law. 'Ours despicable. Our Ministers use fine phrases, but they do nothing. My blood boils within me.'[16]

Prince Albert was still more disturbed when Cavour succeeded in provoking Austria to declare war and the Emperor Francis Joseph's forces were defeated by the French and Piedmontese at Magenta on 4 June 1859, then at Solferino three weeks later. By the Peace of Villafranca, Parma and Lombardy were ceded to France for subsequent cession to Piedmont.

Throughout the war the Queen and Prince had found themselves at odds with public opinion in their country. They saw the French Emperor as 'the universal disturber of the world' and the Emperor Francis Joseph as the legitimate ruler of those lands in northern Italy which had been dominated by Austria since the eighteenth century and which had been confirmed as Austrian by the Congress of Vienna after the Napoleonic wars. To make matters worse, the Government of Lord Derby – who had personally been much abused in the press for his supposed support of Austria – resigned in June 1859 after the introduction of a contentious Reform Bill; and the Queen, obliged to recall Lord Palmerston, whose support of the movement for Italian unity was well known, had also to accept the unappealing Mr Gladstone as Chancellor of the Exchequer and Lord John Russell as Foreign Secretary.

33

THE GERMAN GRANDSON

'You say no one is perfect but Papa.
But he has his faults too.'

POLITICAL PROBLEMS and the war in Italy, England's unpreparedness
for war herself, and the immense amount of work which Prince Albert
undertook with such ceaseless assiduity that he could often be seen actually running down the corridors at Buckingham Palace and Windsor
Castle with papers in his hands and files under his arm, had taken sad
toll of the Prince's health. He looked increasingly worn; his trim figure
had thickened; he had long been going bald; he wore a wig and fur-lined
coat in winter in the rooms which his wife insisted on keeping so cold;
and, before he could hold his pen, he had to warm his hand over the
flame of his lamp.

He was Prince Consort now, having been granted that title by the
Queen by letters patent in 1857; but the title had given him scant pleasure.
As he told his brother, it should have been granted at the time of his
wedding but prejudice against him had prevented that and now it came
too late. In fact, it might not have come at all had there not been a fear
that 'wicked people might later on succeed in bringing up the Prince of
Wales against his father, and tell him that he should not allow a *foreign*
prince to take a place before him'.[1]

It was, however, concern for the happiness of his beloved daughter,
whose presence he missed every day, which occupied his thoughts more
than the possible future behaviour of his son. And in his anxiety about
the child, and his longing for her responsive, affectionate, stimulating
company, he came close to quarrelling again with his wife. Already before

their daughter's marriage, following some difference of opinion about Prince Frederick, the Queen had received an angry and unjust letter, dated 5 November 1856:

> Fritz is prepared to devote his whole life to your child whom you are thankful to be rid of – and because of that you turn against him ... This is not a question of bickering but of attitudes of mind which will agree as little as oil and water and it is no wonder that our conversation on the subject cannot end harmoniously and I am trying to keep out of your way until your better feelings have returned and you have gained control of yourself.[2]

Within a short time of her marriage Vicky was pregnant as she had much hoped to be.* It was an ambition which much distressed her mother who, when she learned of her daughter's pregnancy, wrote to say how the 'horrid news' upset her 'dreadfully'. 'I am so sorry about you,' she added a day or two later. 'It is well Fritz is not in sight just now or he would not have been graciously received.'[3] 'I own I cannot enter into that,' she continued in the same vein when Vicky wrote to say how proud she was to be giving birth to an immortal soul. 'I think much more of our being a cow or a dog at such moments.'[4]

She wanted to go to see Vicky and to take her other daughters, Alice, by then fifteen years old, and Helena, twelve, with her. But there was opposition to this plan: 'Papa says that I should be fidgeting myself about your sisters all the time, which would be very unpleasant as it would take my mind from you.'[5] There was also opposition to a suggestion that the two sisters might go to Germany later: Papa, who was 'very hard-hearted and a great tyrant on all such occasions', would not hear of it. It was disappointing, Vicky agreed; but her Papa was an oracle, she thought, and what he decided 'must be right'.[6]

Then there was trouble over the Queen's correspondence with her daughter. Before the Princess left home it was understood between them that letters would be exchanged most regularly as they were, indeed, to

---

* She told her husband that she was 'counting on having a dear baby at my breast every 2 years' or she would 'not be happy'. 'To have a baby at one's breast' was 'the *greatest* joy of womanhood'. This was 'something a man cannot understand but it is nonetheless true ... So please, my dearest man, *lots more* sweet little things – it is simply *too* lovely.' The Crown Prince obliged her: they were to have eight children in thirteen years. Yet when in 1870 she came across an English family with fifteen children she was ashamed because by then she had borne only six (John C. G. Röhl, *Young Wilhelm: The Kaiser's Early Life, 1859–1888*, Cambridge, 1998, 97–8).

be. The Prince considered this correspondence excessive; and he told his wife so: it would be quite enough, he said, if she wrote no more frequently than once a week. So her mother wrote to her to suggest that when she next wrote to her father she should tell him what she herself wanted. 'Just tell him what you feel,' the Queen suggested, 'for I assure you – Papa has snubbed me several times very sharply on the subject and when one writes in spite of fatigues and troubles to be told it bores the person to whom you write, it is rather too much.' Nor was this all. Not only did his wife write too often, so did his daughter in reply: 'Papa says you write too much ... If you knew how [he] scolds me for (as he says) making you write ... He is sure you make yourself ill by it, and constantly declares (which I own offends me much) that your writing to me at such length is the cause of your often not writing fully to him.'[7]

By this time the Queen was further aggrieved by the Prince's insistence that her second son, Prince Alfred, although no more than thirteen years old, should go to sea after he had taken the usual navy examination; and for months on end she would be deprived of the sight of his 'dear face which shed sunshine over the whole house, from his amiable, happy, merry temper'.

I have been shamefully deceived about Affie [she complained to Vicky]. It was promised me that the last year before he went to sea, he should be with us, instead of which he was taken away and I saw but very little of him, and now he is to go away for many months [in the frigate *Euryalus* to the West Indies by way of the Cape of Good Hope] and I shall not see him God knows when!, and Papa is most cruel upon the subject. I assure you, it is much better to have no children than to have them only to give them up! It is too wretched ... I look forward with horror to the separation ... Two children in one year. It is horrible.[8]

The Queen found relief in her sadness at Prince Alfred's departure in the arrangements she was busily, not to say officiously, making for the birth of her first grandchild. She insisted that the prospective mother's layette as well as her nurse must be British. So must the nursemaids and the child's nanny, Mrs Hobbs being chosen for this post.

The Princess must also have British doctors, since, while '*German Oculists & even Surgeons*' were cleverer than British, there was 'not a doubt that in the particular line of *childbirth & women's* illnesses the

English are the *best* in the World, more skilful & *much* more *delicate'.*[9]

The Queen therefore arranged for Sir James Clark to go to Germany, followed by another of her own physicians, Dr Edward Martin, as well as an English midwife, Mrs Innocent, having already required that her daughter's German physician, Dr Wegner, should be sent to England to be present at the birth of her own last child, Princess Beatrice, on 14 April 1857, so that he could see how well things were managed there.

If only she could be there herself, she told her daughter; she only wished she could 'go through' it all on her behalf and save her 'all the annoyance'. Now that she had got used to the idea she was, she said, delighted by the thought of being a grandmother at only thirty-nine: 'to look and feel young [was] great fun'. Yet, even so, the thought that she could not herself be in Germany to see her daughter through her confinement drove her 'almost frantic'. All she could do was give advice, which she did in letter after letter, urging her not to talk to her ladies about her condition and its consequences; they would only alarm her; but, of course, there was no need for alarm; she must not 'dread the denouement'; there was no need for that.[10]

As well as advice came parcels of medicines and baby clothes, camphor lozenges for insomnia, tincture for toothache, details of her own confinements, complaints about the selfishness of men 'who would *not bear* for a *minute* what *we* poor *slaves* have to bear', and warnings not to indulge in 'baby worship', 'since *no lady*, and still less a Princess is fit for her *husband* or for her *position* if she does THAT.' 'With your great passion for little children (which are mere little plants for the first 6 *months*) it would be very natural for you to be *carried away* by your pleasure in having a child.'[11]

As her pregnancy advanced, the Princess felt sure it was not progressing as it should. The experienced Mrs Innocent thought so too. But Dr Wegner disagreed with them, though he was scarcely in a position to judge since his patient was too embarrassed to discuss her symptoms with him, communicating with him through her husband.[12]

Sir James, whose opinion might well have been considered unreliable in view of his faulty diagnoses years before in the case of Lady Flora Hastings, agreed with Wegner. So did another German doctor in attendance, Professor Eduard Arnold Martin.

The baby, a boy, the future Kaiser Wilhelm II, was born on 27 January

1859 in the Kronprinzenpalais, Unter den Linden, after the agonizing labour of a breech birth which necessitated the rotation of the child in the birth canal. Quantities of chloroform, administered by Clark, made the pain suffered by the eighteen-year-old mother scarcely more bearable. 'Vicky's pain, as well as her horrible screams and wails, became ever more severe,' the Crown Prince reported to his mother-in-law. 'However, whenever she was granted a respite from her suffering she would ask for forgiveness from everyone for her screaming and impatience, but she could not help herself. When the final stages of labour began, I had to try with all my might to hold her head in place, so that she would not strain her neck over much. Every contraction meant a real fight between her and me, and even today [29 January] my arms still feel quite weak ... With the strength of a giant, she was at times able to hold off 2 people, & thus the awful torture escalated until the moment of birth was so near that complete anaesthesia with chloroform was undertaken ... Vicky was laid at right angles on the bed; she let forth one horrible long scream, & was then anaesthetized.'[13]

The life of the child 'lay in the balance' for a time as he was slapped and slung about by the German midwife, Fraülein Stahl, who, in her own opinion, 'saved the Prince from the grave for which he had been intended' by ignoring court etiquette and the grumbles of the shocked doctors and slapping the child 'first softly then more vigorously, slap, slap, slap', until at last 'a weak cry escaped his pale lips'.[14] Later it was noticed that his 'poor little left arm', which was to remain withered for the rest of his life, 'hung helpless at his side'.[15]

'My precious darling, you suffered more than I ever did,' the Queen wrote to her daughter, having received a report from Sir James Clark. 'How I wish I could have lightened [the pain] for you!'[16]

'I am *so* happy, *so* thankful he is a boy,' the Princess wrote in reply. 'I longed for one, more than I can ever describe ... You need not be afraid I shall be injudiciously fond of him, although I *do* worship him ... and I feel he is my *own* and he owes me so much, and has cost me so much.'[17]

By May, Princess Frederick had recovered sufficiently to make the journey to Osborne to see her parents who had missed her so much ever since she had left home. 'I can assure you,' her mother had written to her a few months before, 'that there is not an hour in the day, not a picture or any object of any kind which I look at – when I do not think of you.'[18]

The Princess was 'so very happy' to be at Osborne once again. When in Germany it had made her cry to think of the 'dear view out of the windows, the darling Swiss cottage', her little garden, the trees she had planted. And 'such happiness' it was, too, for her mother to have her daughter back at home for a time, 'to be at last together again'.[19]

In September 1860, eighteen months after the birth of her first grandson, the Queen and her husband went to Germany for a holiday. Overwhelmed by work and worry, the Prince had not been able to spare the time to go before, though he was longing to see his daughter again. He would also be able to see his grandson, Wilhelm, and another grandchild, Wilhelm's sister, Charlotte, who had been born without complications two months before. Moreover, he would have an opportunity of discussing the disturbing state of European affairs with his much missed mentor, old Baron Stockmar, who had recently left England for the last time and had settled in retirement in Coburg.

The Queen could hardly speak, she 'felt so touched' at the sight of her daughter who was in deep mourning for the Prince Consort's stepmother, the Dowager Duchess of Saxe-Coburg and Gotha, who had died the day before.

'Our darling grandchild was brought,' the Queen wrote. 'Such a little love! He came walking in at Mrs Hobbs's hand in a little white dress with black bows, and was so good. He is a fine, fat child, with a beautiful white soft skin . . . and a very dear face . . . He has Fritz's eyes and Vicky's mouth and very curly hair . . . such a darling, so intelligent . . . We felt so happy to see him at last.'[20]

A week later the Prince Consort, having gone out shooting, left his wife and daughter sketching near the Kalenberg castle while he returned to Coburg, making the excuse that he had people to see. Before he reached Coburg, however, the horses drawing his carriage bolted and were careering towards a closed railway crossing when he saw his danger and threw himself from the carriage, cutting his nose, arms and legs and suffering bruises. He was, however, not injured so badly that he was unable to go to help the coachman, to whose wounds he told the doctors to attend when they were hurriedly brought to the scene.

The Prince's equerry, Colonel Henry Ponsonby, went to report the accident to the Queen who, carrying her sketches, was walking back towards Coburg with Vicky, much amused by a bossy peasant woman who told the Princess the skirts of her dress were getting dusty and why didn't she pick them up. The Queen rushed home and hurried up to her 'dearest Albert's rooms and found him lying quietly on [his valet's] bed with lint compresses on his nose, mouth and chin. He was quite cheerful, had not been in the least stunned.' But 'oh! God! What did I not feel!' she wrote that evening. 'I could only, and do only, allow the feelings of gratitude, not those of horror at what might have happened, to fill my mind ... I must thank God for having preserved my adored one! I tremble now on thinking of it ... The escape is very wonderful, *most merciful*! God is indeed most gracious.'[21]

Although he had not been badly injured, the Prince's nervous system, as his brother, Ernest, the Duke of Coburg, observed, was far more shaken than the Queen realized. When Baron Stockmar saw how deeply despondent the Prince had become, he said to the Duke, 'God have mercy on us! If anything serious should ever happen to him, he will die.'[22]

The Prince himself had a premonition of death. Ten days after his carriage accident he went for a walk with his brother in the countryside outside Gotha and, 'in one of the most beautiful spots, Albert stood still and suddenly felt for his pocket handkerchief.' The Duke 'went up to him and saw that tears were trickling down his cheeks ... He persisted in declaring that he had been here for the last time in his life.'[23] He had expressed a similar despondency to the Queen at Osborne after planting some saplings which, he said, he would never see grow into trees. Why ever not, she had protested: he was only forty and that was not 'so very old'. No, he persisted mournfully, 'I shall never see them grow up.'

His melancholy persisted on his return home in November 1860. At Balmoral in early December he was 'seriously unwell'; and on the 5th the Queen reported in her journal that he was 'very weak'. The next day he wrote to tell Vicky that he had felt too ill and 'too miserable' to hold his pen the day before, suffering from violent sickness and bouts of shivering.[24] When he had recovered sufficiently to go back to his work, he told his daughter that he had been suffering from what he called 'the real English cholera'.[25]

Scarcely had he recovered from that than he was ill again with swollen glands, 'inflammation of the nerves of the upper part of the cheek', and dreadful toothache which his dentist said was the severest attack he had ever known. His sufferings he described as 'frightful' and two operations performed by the dentist afforded no relief.[26] The Queen told Vicky that she wished she could bear it all for him, since, as she often said, women were born to suffer and bore it 'so much more easily'. 'Our nerves,' she said, 'don't seem so racked, so tortured as men's are.'[27] It was 'a most trying, wearing and distressing time', for she 'could not bear to see him suffer so much and to be so despondent and weak and miserable'. Nor could she disguise from her daughter her occasional exasperation with the gloom into which his concern for his health was inclined to sink him, the irritability to which overwork reduced him, as when, for instance, reading documents, letters and newspapers spread before him on a table after breakfast, he would dismiss any interruption with a curt, '*Störe mich nicht, ich lese das fertig* ('Don't disturb me. I am busy reading').'[28]

> Dear Papa never allows he is any better or will try to get over it, but makes such a miserable face that people always think he's very ill. It is quite the contrary with me always; I can do anything before others and never show it, so people never believe I am ill or even suffer. His nervous system is easily excited and irritated and he's completely overpowered by everything . . .[29] You say no one is perfect but Papa. But he has his faults too. He is often very trying – in his hastiness and over-love of business – and I think you would find it very trying if Fritz was as hasty and harsh (momentarily and unintentionally as it is) as he is![30]

34

DEATH OF THE DUCHESS

'I kissed her dear hand and placed it next my cheek.'

ON 15 MARCH 1861 the Queen went to see her 75-year-old mother at Frogmore where she had been suffering from intermittent attacks of erysipelas for several months. Her close friend and secretary, Sir George Couper, who had brought order to the chaos in which Sir John Conroy had left her affairs, had died a fortnight before and the Duchess was not expected to survive him for long.

She and her daughter had long since overcome the antagonism of earlier years. 'Poor woman,' Lord Holland had written at the beginning of the Queen's reign. 'The importance of her actions and opinions are gone by. She will count for little or nothing in the new court.' This was true and she had much resented it. She had often been told that her daughter was too busy to see her. 'This was neither a happy nor a merry day for me,' she had written on Victoria's birthday in 1837. 'Everything is so changed.' Her apartment at Windsor was 'very far from the room' to which her daughter had moved. There had been constant grumbles, 'unhappy scenes', 'extraordinary letters'. Lord Liverpool had told Stockmar, 'It is a hard and unfair trial for the Queen, whose mind and health should not be exposed to such absurd vexation and torment . . . Although I should be very sorry to see Mother and Daughter separated, yet anything I am sure is better than the present state of things.' Her mother had 'seemed delighted', the Queen thought, when she had told her that she was to marry Prince Albert; but she had, in fact, complained bitterly that she had not been informed about the engagement earlier – why, even the Prince's valet had known before she did! This was not true, said the Queen. Then the Duchess had grown extremely grumpy when told she could not move into Buckingham Palace with her daughter and nephew, and had expressed her dissatisfaction with Ingestre House in Belgrave Square which the Queen had taken for her at £2,000 a year and which, so she complained, was too small. Upon the death of George III's daughter, Princess Augusta, she had grudgingly accepted not only Clarence House, St James's but also Frogmore House at Windsor.[1]

Since then, relations between mother and daughter had slowly improved. The Queen had written to her when Sir John Conroy died in 1854 to say:

> I quite understand your feelings on the occasion of Sir John Conroy's death . . . I will not speak of the *past* and of the many sufferings he entailed on us by creating divisions between you and me which could never have existed otherwise, they are buried with him. For his poor wife and children I am truly sorry. *They are now free* from the *ban* which kept them from ever appearing before me![2]

'Yes,' the Duchess had replied, 'Sir John Conroy's death was a most painful shock. I shall not try and excuse the many errors that unfortunate man committed, but it would be very unjust if I allowed all the blame to be thrown on him. I am in justice bound to accuse myself . . . I *erred* in *believing blindly*, in *acting without reflexion*. . . I allowed myself *unintentionally* to be led to hurt you, my dearest child, for whom I would have given at every moment my life! Reflexion came always too late, but not the *deserved punishment*! My sufferings were *great, very great*. God be praised that those terrible times are gone by and that only death can separate me from you My beloved Victoria.'[3]

Now death for the Duchess was coming and her daughter gave way to that heartrending, almost hysterical grief which her family and attendants had learned to dread. She had been overwhelmed with grief when King Leopold's Queen Louise died in 1850;[4] the sudden death of Prince Albert's Private Secretary, George Anson, 'almost the only intimate friend he had in this country', made her 'wretched'.[5] When Sir Robert Peel – a 'very bad and awkward rider', in Charles Greville's opinion – had died in July 1850 after falling from his horse on Constitution Hill, the Prince felt the loss '*dreadfully*', while she herself deeply lamented the passing of 'our truest friend and trustiest counsellor'.[6] The death of the Duke of

Wellington in September 1852 had distressed her even more; and as the coffin of the 'GREATEST man this country ever produced', rolled by on its immense and unwieldy black and gold funeral car towards St Paul's, while bands played dirges chosen by the Prince, she 'wept unrestrainedly'; and she wept again when she saw the Duke's old groom leading his horse beneath the Palace balcony, a pair of Wellington boots reversed hanging from its side.[7]

But no death yet had called forth lamentations quite as desperate as her mother's. 'Oh, what agony, what despair was this,' she wrote, having knelt before her as she lay, breathing heavily, on a sofa in her room.

> I kissed her dear hand and placed it next my cheek; but, though she opened her eyes, she did not, I think, know me. She brushed my hand off . . . I went out to sob . . . I asked the doctors if there was no hope. They said, they feared, none whatever . . .
>
> As the night wore on into the morning I lay down on the sofa, at the foot of my bed. I heard each hour strike. At four I went down again. All still – nothing to be heard but the heavy breathing, and the striking, at every quarter, of the old repeater, a large watch in a tortoiseshell case, which had belonged to my poor father, the sound of which brought back all the recollections of my childhood.[8]

Feeling faint and exhausted she went upstairs again and lay down 'in silent misery'. At half past seven she returned to her mother's room where she sat on a stool to hold her hand. The breathing grew fainter and fainter. 'At last it ceased . . . The clock struck half past nine at the very moment . . . The dreaded terrible calamity has befallen us, which seems like an awful dream . . . oh God! how awful . . . The constant crying was a comfort and relief . . . But oh! the agony of it.'[9]

For days on end her emotions were in turmoil as she abandoned herself to 'fearful and unbearable outbursts of grief' with an alarming intensity. 'It is *dreadful, dreadful* to think we shall never see that dear kind loving face again,' she wrote, 'never hear that dear voice again . . . The *dreadful* thing, as I told Albert yesterday, is the certainty that the loss is irrevocable.' The day of her death was 'the most dreadful day' of her own life.[10] She felt 'so stupefied', 'stunned'. 'The relief of tears' was great: they came 'again and again everyday.' 'I do not want to feel better,' she told the Crown Princess Frederick. 'I love to dwell on her . . . and not to be roused out of my grief.'[11] Lord Clarendon thought that she was actually 'determined to cherish' it. 'She never ceases crying,' he told the Duchess of Manchester, '& always went morning and evening, to Frogmore [where her mother was buried] as if it was a satisfaction to feed her grief.' 'I hope this state of things won't last,' he added, 'or she may fall into a morbid melancholy to which her mind has often tended and which is a constant source of anxiety to P[rince] A[lbert].'[12]

She ate all her meals alone; she sat by herself in her mother's 'dear room', despite the awful stillness of the house. Going through the Duchess's papers, she was 'wretched to think how, *for a time* two people [Conroy and Lehzen] wickedly estranged us', and she was deeply moved to read how her mother and her 'beloved Father *loved* each other' and how much she herself was loved: it was '*too* touching'.[13]

She took the Prince of Wales, who had arrived at Windsor, to see the 'beautiful peaceful remains' of his grandmother. But, embarrassed by his mother's excessive lamentations, he could not bring himself to behave as she wished; and she accused him of being heartless and selfish. Writing on paper with black edges which she considered insufficiently broad, her son replied that, 'since [his] sisters were sympathizing with her so warmly and affectionately', he had not liked to intrude, fearing that he would be in the way and believing that they would be 'a greater support' to her than he could possibly be.[14]

Prince Albert, who had himself been in tears on leaving the Duchess's room shortly before she died, could not comfort the Queen either. Having her work to do as well as his own, he was, as he said, 'well nigh overwhelmed' by business. He took the Queen to Osborne in the hope that she would recover there more quickly than at Windsor; but she was so nervous there that she could not bear to be with the children whose talk disturbed her so, none more so than the voice of the Prince of Wales.

35

✳✳✳✳✳✳✳✳✳✳✳

THE DISAPPOINTING HEIR

'The systematic idleness, laziness –
disregard of everything is enough to break one's heart,
and fills me with indignation.'

'BERTIE CONTINUES such an anxiety,' the Queen had written to the Crown Princess Frederick in April 1859 when the Prince of Wales was seventeen years old.

> I tremble at the thought of only three years and a half before us – when he will be of age and we can't hold him except by moral power! I try to shut my eyes to that terrible moment! He is improving very decidedly – but Oh! it is the improvement of such a poor or still more idle intellect. Oh! dear, what would happen if I were to die next winter. It is too awful a contemplation. His journal is worse a great deal than Affie's [Prince Alfred's] letters. And all from laziness! Still we must hope for improvement in essentials; but the greatest improvement I fear, will never make him fit for his position. His only safety – and the country's – is his implicit reliance in everything, on dearest Papa, that perfection of human beings.[1]

'I feel very sad about him,' she told her daughter on another occasion, 'he is so idle and so weak. God grant that he may take things more to heart and be more serious for the future.' He was such 'a very dull companion' compared with his brothers, who were 'all so amusing and communicative'. 'When I see [Affie] and Arthur and look at . . . ! (You know what I mean!) I am in utter despair! The systematic idleness, laziness – disregard of everything is enough to break one's heart, and fills me with indignation.'[2] Even his physique depressed her. She complained of his small head, his big Coburg nose, his protuberant Hanoverian eyes, his shortness, his receding chin, his tendency to fat, 'the effeminate and girlish' way he wore his hair.[3]

When he was created a Knight of the Garter in November 1858 she noticed how knock-kneed his legs appeared in court dress. Later she commented disapprovingly upon his 'pallor, dull, heavy, blasé look'. His heart was warm and affectionate, she had to admit; but 'O, dear . . . Oh Bertie alas! alas!'[4]

Part of the trouble was that she considered him to be a 'caricature' of herself; she saw her own failings magnified in him.[5] So, in fact, had Baron Stockmar, who considered that the boy was 'an exaggerated copy of his mother'. But whereas she had tried to improve herself, he appeared incapable of the effort.

The Prince Consort expressed quite as deep a concern, particularly after receiving far from encouraging reports from Colonel Robert Bruce, the Prince's Governor, who had to admit that, while his charge could undoubtedly be charming, he was still far too prone to outbursts of temper, to egotism and to the adoption of domineering attitudes. He exaggerated the importance of etiquette and dress; had little or no respect for learning; possessed small powers of reflection and was 'prone to listlessness and frivolous disputes'. He took no interest in anything but clothes, his father lamented, 'and again clothes'. Even when out shooting 'he [was] more occupied with his trousers than with the game'.[6]

He was certainly 'lively, quick and sharp when his mind [was] set on anything, which [was] seldom . . . But usually his intellect [was] of no more use than a pistol packed in the bottom of a trunk if one were attacked in the robber-infested Apennines.'[7]

The Queen was equally exasperated. 'Poor Bertie! He vexes us much.' 'There is not a particle of reflection, or even attention to anything but dress! Not the slightest interest to learn, on the contrary, *il se bouche les oreilles*, the moment anything of interest is being talked of.'[8]

To encourage his appreciation of art and to acquire 'knowledge and information', the Prince was sent to Rome immediately on his return from a visit to his sister in Berlin. Colonel Bruce was once more in charge of the party and was provided by the Prince Consort with a detailed itinerary together with the most exact instructions as to the Prince's behaviour and course of study. At the same time Bruce was instructed by the Queen to be present whenever the Prince talked to any 'foreigner or stranger'. It was 'indispensable that His Royal Highness should receive no foreigner or stranger alone, so that no report of pretended conversations with such persons could be circulated without immediate refutation.'

Having failed to derive much profit from his tour of Italy, the Prince was sent to Edinburgh for three months' intensive work before embarking on the next stage of his education, a period of study first at Oxford, then at Cambridge. The reports from none of these seats of learning did much to comfort the Prince's parents.

'Bertie's propensity is indescribable laziness,' the Prince Consort wrote to his daughter in Germany. 'I never in my life met such a thorough and cunning lazybones ... It does grieve me when it is my own son, and when one considers that he might be called upon at any moment to take over the reins of government in a country where the sun never sets.'[9]

Having so much to condemn and criticize, the Queen and Prince Consort were all the more surprised to learn that their son had done quite well in the first of the examinations which he was required to undergo at the end of each term. The Dean of Christ Church, who thought the Prince 'the nicest fellow possible, so simple, naif, ingenuous and modest', was 'quite satisfied' with the results.

The Prince Consort received further favourable reports about his son from Germany, where he was sent for part of his Easter holidays in 1860 and where the ageing Baron Stockmar was much impressed by the great improvement he detected in him. 'That you see so many signs of improvement in the young gentleman is a great joy to us,' his father replied to Stockmar's letter of commendation. 'For parents who watch their son with anxiety, and set their hopes for him high, are in some measure incapable of forming a clear estimate, and are apt at the same time to be impatient if their wishes are not fulfilled.'[10]

In the summer of that year the Prince of Wales was sent out to represent his parents in Canada and on that occasion they acknowledged the compliments paid to him with less grudging satisfaction, as they did the good reports they received of his behaviour and reception in the United States where, so Bruce said, he 'created everywhere a most favourable impression'.

His mother was delighted with these reports and, for once, gave him credit unreservedly. 'He was immensely popular everywhere,' she told Princess Frederick as the Prince was on his way home, 'and he really deserves the highest praise, which should be given him all the more as he was never spared any reproof.' The Prince Consort, too, was prepared to recognize that much of the credit for the resounding success of what King Leopold called this 'tremendous tour' must rest with his son,[11] though the Queen chose to suppose that 'when Bertie was received in the United States as no one ever has been received', this was 'principally owing to the (to me incredible) liking they have for my unworthy self'.[12]

The young hero arrived home and was welcomed at Windsor with warm congratulations. Although he was 'a little yellow and sallow' and his hair looked so fair when he stood next to Affie (who was 'very dark and very handsome'), the Queen thought that he looked well, had grown a little taller and was 'decidedly improved'. Yet she felt constrained to add, with more than a hint of disapproval, that he had become 'extremely talkative'. He had also taken, she later noticed, to lounging about with a cigar stuck in his mouth.

Soon after his return from the United States, the Prince was sent to the Curragh military camp near Dublin to gain some experience of army life. The experiment was not a success: he found it impossible to keep pace with the demanding programme his father had drawn up for him; and when his parents came to watch a review on the Curragh, all that the Queen could find to say of Bertie's part in it was that he did not look 'so very small'.[13]

For the Prince, however, his time on the Curragh had its compensations. There were several convivial and congenial young Guards officers at the camp; and one evening, after a noisy and rather drunken party in the mess, some of these persuaded a young actress to creep into his quarters and wait for the Prince in his bed. This was Nellie Clifden, a vivacious, cheerfully promiscuous and amusing girl who was also unfortunately most indiscreet. The Prince was much taken with her. On his return to England, he continued seeing her when he could, and, on one occasion at least, she seems to have gone to Windsor. Delighting in her company, the Prince felt more than ever disinclined to concentrate upon a subject to which his parents had urged him to lend his mind – his marriage.

*   *   *

The subject had first been broached soon after the Prince's return from America. But he had not been in the least responsive, maintaining that he was determined to marry only for love. When the Queen wrote to him about his duty to get married to a suitable bride, he replied to her, so she complained to Bruce, 'in a confused way'. Eventually, however, he agreed to consider marrying Princess Alexandra of Schleswig-Holstein-Sonderburg-Glucksburg, the daughter of Prince Christian of Denmark, a distant relative of the drunken, divorced King Frederick VII and recognized as his heir. Her mother was Princess Louise, daughter of the Landgrave William of Hesse-Cassel. There were thus two strong objections to this match which the Queen and Prince Consort had initially dismissed out of hand. In the first place, they much disapproved of the Hesse-Cassel family, whose castle at Rumpenheim near Frankfurt was said to be the scene of the wildest and most indecorous parties; and in the second place they were most reluctant to become entangled in the complicated question of the Duchies of Schleswig and Holstein, which had been ruled for years by the Kings of Denmark but which the Germans considered they had a good right to annex.

As opposed to these objections, however, Princess Alexandra herself was wholly unexceptionable. The reports of her from Copenhagen were enthusiastic. She was only just seventeen and still at school; but, though so young, she displayed a remarkable grace of movement and manner. And when the Queen saw the photograph sent to her by Walburga Paget, the German wife of the British Minister in Copenhagen, who had once been Princess Frederick's lady-in-waiting, she had to admit that Alexandra was, indeed, '*unverschämt hübsch*', 'outrageously pretty'. The Princess was not in the least intellectual and had rather a quick temper, but few other faults could be found in her. If she occasionally displayed a lamentable ignorance, she was never tactless; and if she was sometimes a little stubborn, she was never unkind. 'She is a good deal taller than I am,' the Crown Princess told her parents, 'has a lovely figure but very thin, a complexion beautiful as possible ... You may go far before you find another Princess like Princess Alix ... Oh, if only she was not a Dane ... I should say yes – *she* is *the* one a thousand times over.'[14] So the Queen allowed herself to be convinced that Princess Alexandra must 'be charming in every sense of the word'. She seemed all the more desirable because not only was the Russian court also interested in her as a bride for Tsar Alexander's heir, but so was the Queen of Holland on behalf of the Prince of Orange. Evidently she was a 'pearl not to be lost'. 'May he be only worthy of such a jewel,' the Queen wrote to the Crown Princess, 'there is the rub.'[15]

The Prince Consort shared the Queen's high opinion of Princess Alexandra and when he heard that his brother, Ernest, Duke of Coburg, was raising objections to the match on the grounds that it would not be in the best interests of Germany, he wrote him a furious letter: 'What has that got to do with you? . . . Vicky has racked her brains to help us to find someone, but in vain . . . We have no choice.'[16] To his son, the Prince Consort wrote, 'It would be a thousand pities if you were to lose her.'

So, in September, without marked enthusiasm, the Prince of Wales embarked for the Continent with General Bruce to see the girl whom his sister, having contrived a meeting with her at Strelitz, now described as 'the most fascinating creature in the world'. When the Prince met her at Speyer he gave his parents a report as flat and unrevealing as they had come to expect.

> We met Prince and Princess Christian, and the young lady of whom I had heard so much . . . I must ask you to wait till I see you, and then I will give you my impression about her. Princess Christian seems a very nice person, but is, unfortunately, very deaf. The Prince is a most gentlemanlike, agreeable person. After having thoroughly seen over the cathedral we lunched at the hotel and then proceeded here [Heidelberg].[17]

The Prince of Wales was little more forthcoming when he arrived home and reported in person to his parents at Balmoral. The Queen gathered that he was 'decidedly pleased with Pcss. Alix' and thought her face and figure pretty, but he 'seemed nervous about deciding anything yet'.[18] 'As for being in love,' she added in a letter to her daughter, 'I don't think he can be, or that he is capable of enthusiasm about anything in the world . . . Poor boy – he does mean well – but he is so different to darling Affie!'[19] The Crown Princess had rallied to the Prince of Wales's defence when their mother had been particularly critical of him before the meeting with Princess Alexandra. She had been brave enough to write then: 'One thing pains me, and that is the relation between you and Bertie! . . . His heart is very capable of affection, of warmth of feeling and I am sure that it will come out with time and by degrees. He loves his home and feels happy there and those feelings must be nurtured.'[20]

The Prince Consort considered the whole situation thoroughly unsatisfactory; and he decided to put the whole problem down on paper in an effort to bring some clarity into his son's mind which, at the moment, appeared to be 'a little confused'. If the Princess and her parents were to be invited to England before the Prince made up his mind, he must '*thoroughly understand*' that this would be in order that he might propose to the young lady if she pleased him on further acquaintance, and if she did not please him he must say at once that the matter was at an end.[21]

The Prince assured his father that he understood the position perfectly well, and agreed to do as he suggested. But he remained as unenthusiastic as ever; and the Prince Consort was quite baffled by the 'unsolved riddle' of his son's reluctance to marry since his time on the Curragh, as he had earlier expressed a 'desire to contract an early marriage' as soon as he was of age. The next month, however, the Prince Consort did solve the riddle at last; and he sat down to write to his son 'with a heavy heart upon a subject which [had] caused him the greatest pain' he had ever felt in his life, and which, so the Queen afterwards decided, proved too much for him to bear.[22]

He had been forced to recognize that there could be no doubt of the appalling fact that the Prince of Wales had had sexual experience with a woman who was a known *habituée* of the most vulgar dance halls in London. Sparing her the 'disgusting details', the Prince Consort broke the news to the Queen, then wrote an enormously long and anguished letter to his son in which he elaborated the likely consequences of his terrible sin, the possibility that the woman might have a child by him or get hold of a child and pretend that it was his.

He was too heartbroken to see his son at present, he said, but he 'assured him that he would do his best to protect him from the full consequences of his evil deed'. The Prince must, therefore, confess everything.

The Prince did confess everything in the most abjectly apologetic and contrite manner. He declined to name the officers responsible for his degradation; and his father accepted his refusal as right and proper, telling him that it would have been cowardly for him to have done so. But everything else was admitted and regretted.[23]

The Prince Consort was thankful to recognize that the letter displayed a sincere repentance, and he was prepared to forgive his son for 'the terrible pain' which he had caused his parents. But forgiveness could not restore him to the state of innocence and purity which he had lost for ever, having 'sunk into vice and debauchery'. An early marriage was now essential.

Two days after writing this letter of forgiveness and exhortation, on 22 November 1861, the Prince Consort went to Sandhurst to inspect the buildings for the new Staff College and the Royal Military Academy. It was a cold wet day and he returned to Windsor tired out and racked by rheumatic pains. The next day he caught a cold and this, combined with his continuing anxiety over his son, aggravated his insomnia. 'Albert has such nights since that great worry,' the Queen wrote anxiously. 'It makes him weak and tired.'

Ill as he was, however, he felt he must go up to Cambridge to talk to his son, to try to make him understand the disgrace he had brought upon himself and his family, and the urgent need to get married. He left on 25 November, feeling 'greatly out of sorts', having scarcely closed his eyes at night for the last fortnight. It was another cold, wet day; but he went out for a long walk with his son, who lost the way in his unhappiness and embarrassment so that when they arrived back at Madingley Hall, where the Prince was living, the Prince Consort was utterly exhausted. 'I am at a very low ebb,' he told the Crown Princess, a few days later. 'Much worry and great sorrow (about which I beg you not to ask questions) have robbed me of sleep during the past fortnight. In this shattered state I had a very heavy catarrh and for the past four days am suffering from headache and pains in my limbs which may develop into rheumatism.'[24]

36

✖✖✖✖✖✖✖✖✖✖✖

DEATH OF THE PRINCE

'I must tell you, *most confidentially*, that
it requires no little management to prevent
her breaking down altogether.'

'DEAREST PAPA... is not well, with a cold [and] neuralgia – a great depression,' the Queen confirmed to their daughter, 'The sad part is – that this loss of rest at night (worse than he has ever had before) was caused by a great sorrow and worry, which upset us both greatly – but him especially – and it broke him quite down. I never saw him so low.'[1]

Soon after the Prince Consort's return from Madingley there arrived at Windsor the draft of despatches which caused him grave concern. A British mail steamer had been stopped by an American warship off the coast of the United States where the first shots of the Civil War had been fired at Charleston earlier that year, in April 1861. On this ship were two Confederate envoys representing the southern states which had seceded from the Union. These envoys, who were on their way to Europe, were seized and taken to New York, much to the indignation of the British people. The British Government proposed to seek reparation for this breach of international law in words so provocative that the Prince considered that they might well lead to war between Britain and the northern States. Ill as he was, the Prince got up at seven o'clock as usual after a restless night to write a memorandum for the Queen suggesting that a less truculent despatch be sent so that the Americans might be given an opportunity to release 'the unfortunate passengers' without loss of face. The Cabinet accepted the Queen's amendments as suggested by the Prince and war was averted. On her copy of the document the Queen later noted in the margin, 'This draft was the last the beloved Prince ever wrote. He was very unwell at the time & when he brought it to the Queen he said, "I could hardly hold my pen."'

It was a Sunday. He forced himself to go to chapel; but he could eat nothing either before or after the service, and, having gone early to bed, spent another sleepless night. The next day in her diary the Queen described herself as being 'terribly nervous and depressed'. 'My dearest Albert did not dress,' she wrote, 'but lay on his sofa in his dressing-gown ... He kept saying ... he should not recover! which we all told him was too foolish & [he] must never speak of it.' 'I do not cling to life,' he had once told her. 'You do; but I set no store by it ... I am sure if I had a severe illness I should give up at once. I should not struggle for life. I have no tenacity of life.'

Deeply distressed by the Prince's fatalism, the Queen was 'dreadfully annoyed' to receive a letter from Lord Palmerston in which he proposed calling upon the advice of Dr Robert Ferguson, a highly respected physician, who had attended Her Majesty at the birth of all her children. There was no need for further medical advice, she told Palmerston crossly: Sir James Clark was still in attendance; so was Dr William Jenner, 'a most skilful Physician', who had been appointed Physician Extraordinary to the Queen on the death in a railway accident of Dr William Baly, Sir James's colleague. The Prince had had 'a feverish cold the last few days, which disturbed his rest at night' but he had been 'similarly affected' before and there was every reason to hope that in a few days it would 'pass off'. 'Her Majesty would be very unwilling to cause unnecessary alarm, where no cause exists for it, by calling in a medical man who does not upon ordinary occasions attend at the Palace.'[2]

'Good kind old Sir James', concerned as he so often was for the Queen's mental state, assured her that 'there was no cause whatever for alarm – either present or future'. Yet, despite her letter to Palmerston, she was herself 'in an agony of despair', 'crying much', she recorded in her journal, 'for I saw *no* improvement & my dearest Albert was so listless and took *so* little notice and hardly smiled'.[3]

That night and the next he was 'utterly restless', wandering about from room to room, the Queen in tears in his wake. 'The Prince, when ill, is extremely depressed and low,' Sir Charles Phipps, his Privy Purse and Treasurer, reported to Palmerston, 'and the Queen becomes so nervous and so easily alarmed that the greatest caution is necessary . . . I must tell you, *most confidentially*, that it requires no little management to prevent her from breaking down altogether . . . The suggestion that it would be desirable to call in another Medical Man would I think frighten the Queen *very much*, and the Prince already is annoyed with the visits of the *three* who attend him. Sir J. Clark is here daily [alternating his visits with those to his wife who was dangerously ill at Bagshot Park, the house which had been lent to them by the Queen], Dr Jenner remains here permanently, and Mr Brown the Windsor Apothecary, who knows the Prince's constitution better than anybody also sees him . . . The mere suggestion [of further advice] agitated the Queen dreadfully . . . As cheerful a view as possible should be taken to her of the state of the Prince.'[4]

By 6 December he seemed so much better that the Queen was almost cheerful herself. He asked for the latest news; he looked over the plans of the house which his second daughter, Princess Alice, and her future husband were to occupy; he smiled fondly at his wife. 'I found dearest Albert quite himself,' the Queen wrote, 'so dear and affectionate when I went in with little baby [Princess Beatrice] whom he kissed, and he quite laughed at some of her new French verses, which I made her repeat.'[5]

The next day, however, her hopes of a recovery were dashed. A rash on his stomach developed, suggesting that he was suffering from typhoid fever, though his illness might well have been caused by cancer of the stomach. The Queen's journal entry for that day recorded:

> I went to my room & cried dreadfully and felt Oh! as if my heart must break – oh! such agony as exceeded *all* my grief this year. Oh God! help and protect him . . . I seem to live in a dreadful dream. My angel lay on the bed in the bedroom & I sat by him watching him & the tears fell fast.[6]

On Sunday, after a restless night during which he again wandered about in his dressing gown from one room to another with 'a strange wild look', his mood alternated between affection for the Queen, whose face he stroked, smiling and calling her by his pet names for her, *Fräuchen* and *Weibchen*, and irritation and impatience, such impatience that when she tried to help in explaining something to Dr Jenner he 'quite slapped' her hand, 'poor dear darling'. When calmer he asked to be moved into the Blue Room, where the winter's sun was streaming through the windows, and for music to be played for him. A piano was brought up to the next room and there Princess Alice played *Ein Feste Burg ist Unser Gott* for him; and tears came into his eyes.[7]

His tongue was 'dreadful' now, 'dry and with a thick furred coat'. The doctors told Palmerston that they would like to call in further advice, even though the Queen was 'disinclined' to it and the Prince might well be alarmed. 'He is *extremely low* himself,' Sir Charles Phipps wrote. 'There is no doubt that the death of the King of Portugal [Pedro V, a young favourite cousin who had recently died of typhoid fever] not only grieved him very deeply, but would make him exceedingly nervous if he had any idea that his illness bore any similarity to that of which the King died. Any alarm or further depression might have a *very injurious* effect upon the Prince in his present state, and it will therefore require some tact and judgement to announce the arrival of fresh medical advice.'

It was decided, even so, that further opinions should be sought. So Dr Watson, a respected Physician Extraordinary to the Queen, was called in as well as Sir Henry Holland, although Lord Clarendon would no more have trusted Holland than he would have trusted Sir James Clark: neither was capable of looking 'after a sick cat'.

Soon after his arrival at the Castle, Dr Watson reported to the Prime Minister that the Prince was '*very ill*': it was 'impossible not to be very anxious'.[8] Nor had the Prince any doubt now as to just how ill he was. When Princess Alice told him that she had written to Vicky to say his illness had taken a serious turn, he said, 'You did wrong. You should have told her I am dying.'[9]

The next day, however, he seemed slightly better. 'He wanders frequently,' the Queen wrote, '& they say it is of no consequence tho' very distressing, for it is so unlike my own Angel ... Oh! it is an anxious, anxious time.' But, although confused, he behaved affectionately now towards the Queen who, going to him on the morning of 11 December, found him sitting up. 'He laid his dear head (his beautiful face, more beautiful than ever, has grown so thin) on my shoulder and remained a little while, saying, "It is very comfortable so, dear child."'[10] She was so relieved by his apparent improvement that on the afternoon of Friday 13th she decided that she could go out for a walk.

But no sooner had she gone than Dr Jenner appeared in the room of the Queen's Bedchamber Woman, Lady Augusta Bruce, sister of the

Prince of Wales's Governor, with the alarming report that 'such sinking had come on that he had feared the Prince would die in his arms'.[11]

When the Queen returned he decided it was necessary to break to her the distressing tidings of what had taken place in her short absence. So Lady Augusta went down to the Queen's room. 'I was alone with her and most touching it was,' Lady Augusta told her sister. 'The words "The country, oh the country. I could perhaps bear my own misery, but the poor country" were constantly recurring.'[12]

After breaking down again in tears, the Queen – having struggled to compose herself as she usually contrived to do in his presence – returned to the Prince's room where she 'found him very quiet & comfortably warm, and so dear & kind'. He 'called her *gutes Fräuchen*' and kissed her 'so affectionately & so completely like himself'. 'He folded his arms and began arranging his hair just as he used to do when well and he was dressing. These were said to be bad signs. Strange! As though he were preparing for another and greater journey.'[13] She held his 'dear hands' between hers. He kissed her, then gave a piteous sigh, not of pain, 'but as if he felt he was leaving me, and laid his head upon my shoulder'.

The following morning she went to his room at seven o'clock as she usually did, having been given rather more favourable reports during the night.

> It was a bright morning [she recalled when she could bring herself to think of it], the sun just rising and shining brightly . . . Never can I forget how beautiful my darling looked lying there with his face lit up by the rising sun, his eyes unusually bright gazing as it were on unseen objects and not taking notice of me . . . Sir James was very hopeful, so was Dr Jenner, & said it was a 'decided rally', – but that they were all 'very, very, anxious'. Sir H. Holland was very anxious. All constantly there or in the next room & so was I. I asked if I might go out for a breath of fresh air. The doctors answered 'Yes, just close by, for half an hour!' . . . I went out on the Terrace with Alice. The military band was playing at a distance & I burst out crying and came home again . . . Sir James was very hopeful, he had seen much worse cases. But the breathing was the alarming thing – so rapid . . . I was crying in despair saying, how should and could I ever get on.[14]

The Prince of Wales had been sent for and he and the other children came into the room. He smiled at them but did not speak. The Queen bent over him and said to him '*Es ist kleines Fräuchen*' ('It is your little wife'). He bowed his head. She asked him if he would give her '*ein Kuss*' and he did so. He seemed 'half dozing, quite quiet'.

'I left the room for a moment and sat on the floor in utter despair,' she continued. 'Attempts at consolation from others only made me worse.' Inside the room Princess Alice turned to Lady Augusta Bruce and whispered, 'This is the death rattle.' The Princess went to fetch her mother who, upon entering the room exclaimed, 'Oh, this is death. I know it. I have seen *this* before.'[15]

> I took his dear left hand which was already cold ... and knelt down by him ... *All, all* was over ... I stood up and kissed his dear heavenly forehead & called out in a bitter and agonizing cry, 'Oh! my dear darling!' and then dropped on my knees in mute distracted despair, unable to utter a word or shed a tear! ... Then I laid down on the sofa in the Red Room, & all the gentlemen came in and knelt down & kissed my hand, & I said a word to each.[16]

One of the gentlemen, Sir Howard Elphinstone, Prince Arthur's Governor, described the scene – the Queen lying on the sofa, Princess Alice kneeling on the floor beside her, holding her in her arms, Princess Helena sobbing violently, the Prince of Wales standing in front of the sofa, 'deeply affected but quiet'. Elphinstone hesitated, unable to speak, until the Queen held out her hand to clutch his own and 'with a violent effort' brought out the words, 'You will not desert me? You will all help me.'

'I was deeply moved,' Elphinstone wrote in his diary, 'and answered a few words and retired, not forgetting to return the gentle pressure of the Prince of Wales's "Handdruck". The Prince was lying in the next room; his face calm, peaceful. He had gone without a struggle, but likewise without saying a word ... He died in the same room as King William IV ... About a week before he told Princess Alice that he would die ... He never even tried to rally from the moment the illness commenced ... And then in that feeble state recurred to him the scenes of childhood, which he wished to see again, to hear the birds twittering about the woods at Coburg, and be again in his warm-hearted home, away from the frigidity of England.'[17]

PART TWO

✳✳✳✳✳✳✳✳✳✳✳✳

1861–1901

37

✳✳✳✳✳✳✳✳✳✳✳

THE GRIEVING WIDOW

'There is no one left to hold me in their arms
and press me to their heart.'

THE PRINCE CONSORT had once said of the Queen that she 'lived much in the past and in the future, perhaps more than in the present'. After his death she certainly abandoned herself to the past and to her memories of him with a passionate intensity. She could never forget him; no one else should. Even her youngest son, then only eight years old and staying in Cannes for the sake of his precarious health, was told: 'You will therefore sorrow when you know & think that poor Mama is more wretched, more miserable than any being in this World *can* be! I pine and long for your dearly precious Papa so dreadfully ... You will, my poor little Darling, find Mama old – & thin – & grown weak – & you must try & be a comfort (*tho that none* can be – for none *can* replace the *All* in *All* I have lost).'[1] She sent the boy two photographs of his father which he was to have framed, 'but *not* in black', and 'a Locket with beloved Papa's hair' which he was to wear 'attached to a string or chain round [his] neck & a *dear* pocket handkerchief of beloved Papa's' which he must keep 'constantly with him'.[2]

Everyone at court had to wear mourning on all social occasions until the end of 1862; and, after 1864, although her maids-of-honour were allowed to wear grey, white, purple and mauve – the last of these colours later being forbidden in its 'fashionable pink tints' – the lady-in-waiting who was in personal attendance upon the Queen was required to wear mourning as deep as Her Majesty's own. All the ladies were, of course, in the words of one of them, 'plunged back into the deepest mourning with jet ornaments' whenever one of the frequent court mournings occurred.[3] Even the royal servants were obliged to wear a black crêpe band on their left arm until the end of 1869; while the Queen's daughter, Princess Alice, wore a black trousseau at her marriage in July 1862 to Prince Frederick William Louis of Hesse, which was, the Queen herself said, more like a funeral than a wedding. Her mourning writing paper was discarded for a fresh supply with even wider black edges into which the ends of words would disappear, to the exasperation of her secretaries and correspondents, for the rest of her life.*

On the first morning of her widowhood she went into the Blue Room to gaze upon her beloved husband's features. Warned by her doctors not to kiss them, she kissed his clothes instead. She had every part of the room photographed so that it could be preserved exactly as it had been at that moment of the night, ten minutes to eleven on 14 December 1861, when her own life had been shattered. At her command a memorandum was issued by the Lord Chamberlain decreeing that the room 'should remain in its present state and not be made use of in the future'.[4]

She gave orders for Albert's dressing gown and fresh clothes to be laid each evening on his bed and for a jug of steaming hot water to be placed on his washstand. Between the two beds in the room a marble bust of him was placed; above it she had his portrait hung, wreathed with evergreens; and almost every day fresh flowers were strewn beneath it on the pillows. The glass from which he had taken his last dose of medicine was kept on the table beside it where it remained for more than

---

* The Queen had always had an almost obsessive predilection for the observance of mourning, far more so even than was commonly accepted as appropriate at the time. When her distant relation, the Tsar, had died during the Crimean War, she had caused 'IMMEDIATE search to be made for Precedents as to the Court going or not going into mourning for a sovereign with whom at the time of his decease England was at war'. And when her half-brother, Prince Charles of Leiningen, died, 'the Queen put on a black gown immediately,' recorded one of her maids-of-honour. 'We have no orders yet about it, but of course it will be silk and crape; and a six months' mourning' (Eleanor Stanley, *Twenty Years at Court*, London, 1916, 320). Even the Queen's youngest child, Princess Beatrice, was dressed in a black silk and crêpe dress during a period of court mourning when she was barely three years old (Roger Fulford, ed., *Dearest Child*, 249).

The serious attention which the Queen gave to the obligations of mourning is reflected in a rather touching note addressed to her private secretary in 1892: 'Does Sir Henry Ponsonby think it possible for her to go *privately* to see *Venice*? [a spectacular production staged at Olympia]. She hears it is really admirably done. Pss Beatrice is delighted with it & it is a real success. In the day of course & it is not a theatre or a play & it will be 5 months & ½ since her dear grandson's [Prince Albert Victor's] death & 3½ after her dear son-in-law's [the Grand Duke of Hesse's] & she wd very much like to see it' (Arthur Ponsonby, *Henry Ponsonby*, 83).

forty years. On his writing table his blotting book lay open with his pen upon it as though it were waiting for him to pick up. Guests at Windsor were required to write their names in his visitors' book as well as in the Queen's, 'as before', Disraeli commented, 'calling on a dead man'.[5]

A notice was fixed to the Blue Room door informing those who passed it that everything within was just as the Prince had left it, although, in fact, the ceiling had been redecorated and much of the china and several of the pictures, as well as the Prince's marble bust, had not been there before. Similar notices were placed outside all the other rooms at Windsor and in the other royal residences to the effect that their contents had been arranged by him.[6] She had herself photographed gazing up at his bust; and she went to bed each night clasping one of his nightshirts and with a cast of his hand close enough for her to touch it with her fingers. Each morning the four-year-old Princess Beatrice was brought into her room and encouraged to chatter about her father. 'What a pity,' the child once said, 'that I was too little to be at your marriage.'[7]

As at Windsor, so it was at Osborne: in March 1862, Lord Clarendon, during a visit to Osborne, found it 'difficult to believe' that the Prince would not, at any moment, walk into his room where the Queen received him, since 'everything was set out on his table and the pen and his blotting-book, his handkerchief on the sofa, his watch going, fresh flowers in the glass'.[8]

Numerous monuments were erected to his memory: a marble effigy, supported by the wings of four bronze angels, was placed in St George's Chapel, Windsor, in King Henry VIII's tombhouse which was lined with marble, roofed in copper and renamed the Albert Memorial Chapel. A huge statue by Joseph Durham was erected in the Royal Horticultural Gardens in South Kensington where, to the Queen's annoyance, her husband had spent so much time in the last months of his life; and an equestrian bronze by Charles Bacon was unveiled at Holborn Circus.* Commemorative stones were laid at Balmoral and in Windsor Park. The first of several municipal tributes, an equestrian statue by Thomas

---

* The equestrian bronze at Holborn Circus was unveiled by the Prince of Wales in January 1874. A stone statue by Thomas Earle, also unveiled by the Prince of Wales, which originally stood at the Licensed Victuallers' Association Asylum in Old Kent Road, was moved in 1958 to the Victuallers' retirement home in Denham Garden Village. In provincial towns all over the country, and in Edinburgh and Glasgow, memorials were erected, to the Queen's great satisfaction.

Thornycroft, was unveiled at Wolverhampton in 1866; and Lord Clarendon apprehended the appearance not only of many other statues of 'the late Consort in robes of The Garter upon some curious and non-descript animal that will be called a horse', but also of numerous 'Albert Baths & Washhouses'. The Queen would not object to such memorials, Clarendon added, since she had 'no more notion of what is right and pure in art than she [had] of the Chinese grammar'.[9]

A committee was appointed to discuss a national memorial in London and the Queen chose George Gilbert Scott's Gothic design for what was unveiled ten years later in July 1872 as the Albert Memorial. By then the Royal Albert Hall of Arts and Sciences had already been declared open by the Prince of Wales at Kensington Gore. In the grounds of Frogmore, near the Duchess of Kent's mausoleum, a plot of land was chosen for a far more elaborate royal mausoleum in which Prince Albert was to be buried and she herself would join him when the time came. Inspired by Hawksmoor's mausoleum at Castle Howard which she had seen during her visit to Yorkshire in 1850, by the Gothic mausoleum at Claremont built in memory of Princess Charlotte, and by the family mausoleum at Coburg, which she described in 1860 as being 'beautiful and so cheerful', the Frogmore mausoleum, an Italian Romanesque building with an interior ornamented in the style of Raphael, whom Prince Albert considered the greatest artist of all time, was to cost some £200,000.[*10] Completed almost a year to the day after the Prince's death, it was designed by his artistic adviser, Professor Ludwig Gruner, and the architect, A. J. Humbert. It was consecrated by Samuel Wilberforce, the Bishop of Oxford, who considered the sight of the grieving Queen and the file of her fatherless children as one of the most touching he had ever witnessed in his life. The next day the Prince's coffin was brought here from St George's Chapel and, later, an effigy of the Prince by Carlo Marochetti was laid above the sarcophagus, a huge block of grey Aberdeen granite.

The Queen was only forty-two but she expected and hoped that soon, perhaps within a year, her own body would be brought here to rest beside

---

* Some time earlier the Queen had been left about £250,000 by an eccentric miser, John Camden Nield, who had lived in squalor in Cheyne Walk, Chelsea. He had not vouchsafed any reason for his generous bequest but the Queen, reassuring herself with the thought that he had known she would not waste it, increasing the sums he had left to his executors, and donating a sum to his parish church, gratefully accepted it. Part of the bequest was assigned to the cost of the mausoleum.

her husband's. She was 'naturally much occupied with leaving this world'.

People at court marvelled at her apparent self-possession in the early days of her widowhood, her submission to the divine will. It was as though she were doing all she could to follow the Prince's advice, 'to take things as God sent them', to remember that her 'great task in life' was 'to control [her] feelings'. Sir Charles Phipps reported to Gladstone, the Chancellor of the Exchequer, on the night of the Prince's death, 'The Queen, though in an agony of grief, is perfectly collected, and shows a self control that is quite extraordinary.' The next day Phipps wrote again to say that 'except in the paroxysms of grief' she was 'perfectly composed': she was 'determined to do Her duty to the Country'.[11] And so she did for a time, conscientiously signing papers within three days of the Prince's death. 'Alas,' Phipps added, 'she has not realized her loss – and when the full consciousness comes upon her – I tremble . . . What will happen – where can She look for that support and assistance upon which She has leaned in the greatest and least questions of her life?'

When the full consciousness did come to her, her misery and desolation were painful to witness. She went into 'every detail of the illness', Lord Clarendon said, 'his appearance after death, etc. etc.', which threw her into fresh 'paroxysms of grief'.[12]

'How am I alive after witnessing what I have done?' she asked the Crown Princess. 'Oh! I who prayed daily that we might die together & I never survive Him! I who felt when in those blessed Arms clasped & held tight in the sacred Hours at night – when the world seemed only to be ourselves – that nothing could part us! I felt so vy secure – I always repeated: "And God will protect us", though trembling always for his safety . . . It cannot be possible . . . Oh! God! Oh! God . . . I don't know what I feel.'[13] Her own death would be the 'greatest blessing', since 'pleasure, joy – all is for ever gone'.

'The poor Q[ueen] does not seem to improve,' Lord Clarendon told the Duchess of Manchester in the middle of March 1862, 'her only relief in thinking of her desolate future is the conviction that She shall & must die soon. She is worse off than ordinary persons with relations & friends who in time bring changes & comfort – but she is isolated.'[14]

She contemplated suicide, but, so she wrote to her daughter in Germany, 'a Voice told me for *His* sake – no, still endure.' The Princess herself was in an agony of grief. 'Why has the earth not swallowed me up?' she asked. 'He was too great, too perfect for Earth that adored Father whom I worshipped with more than a daughter's affection.'[15] Night after night she dreamed of him and in one dream she 'took his dear hand and kissed it so long and so often and cried over it and did not like to let it go'.[16]

Three months after her father's death, in March 1862, she was granted permission to visit her mother in England. 'Mama is dreadfully sad,' she told her husband. 'She cries a lot; then there is always the empty room, the empty bed, she always sleeps with Papa's coat over her and his dear red dressing-gown beside her and some of his clothes in the bed! ... [She is] as much in love with Papa as though she had married him yesterday ... She feels the same as your little *Fräuchen*. . . and is always consumed with longing for her husband.'[17]

'Truly the Prince was my entire self,' her mother wrote, 'my very life and soul ... I only lived through him My heavenly Angel! Surely there can never have been such a union, such trust and understanding between two people ... I try to feel and think I am living on with him, and that his pure and perfect spirit is leading and inspiring me ... There is no one left to hold me in their arms and press me to their heart ... Oh! how I admired Papa! How in love I was with him! How everything about him was beautiful and precious in my eyes. Oh! how I miss all, all! Oh! Oh! the bitterness of this.'[18]

In her misery it distressed her to see the happiness others enjoyed in their marriages and, with characteristic honesty, she admitted it. She was '*less glad*' than she ought to have been to 'see people happy – so *odd* and wrong! I *can't bear* to look at a man and his wife walking together.' She could not even now bring herself to show enjoyment of the plays the younger children staged for her. She watched them attentively, reviewing them in her journals; but she explained to Elphinstone that 'if she appeared *listless* and did *not* applaud, it was only because the recollections of the *happy past* when the beloved Prince arranged everything ... weighed her down and it was ALL she could do to sit thro' it.'*

When she left for Balmoral her suffering was worse. She was constantly

---

* Nearly two years after Prince Albert's death, the Queen was still lamenting her misery to Elphinstone: 'As time goes on and *others* feel *less*, *her* deep settled melancholy – her ever increasing helplessness and loneliness are *more keenly* and acutely felt. The struggle gets daily worse, the want *hourly more felt*' (Mary Howard McClintock, *The Queen Thanks Sir Howard*, 51).

expecting to hear his footsteps, his voice. 'Oh, darling child,' she wrote to the Crown Princess, 'the agonizing sobs ... the stags' heads – the rooms – blessed, darling Papa's room – then his coats – his caps – kilts – all, all convulsed my poor shattered frame.'[19] The next year she told Queen Augusta that the 'wild, grim, solitary mountains' comforted her. 'The mountains, the woods, the rocks' seemed to 'talk of him'. She wanted to do nothing but 'sit and weep and live only with Him in spirit and take no interest in the things of this earth'. Her misery was becoming 'a necessity'; she 'could not exist without it'.[20]

The Royal Household began to fear she was going mad. 'The poor Queen,' they would say to each other in nervous concern, while she herself was wont to tap her forehead with the tips of her chubby white fingers as though concerned for her sanity. She confessed to Lord Clarendon that more than once she thought she was indeed going mad. 'My reason, my reason,' she would say. Clarendon himself told Lord Stanley that Prince Albert had once said to him that it was his 'business to watch that mind' of the Queen's 'every hour and every minute – to watch as a cat watches at a mousehole'.[21]

The Queen was often seen to glance at a bust of the Prince before signing an official document; and, it was said, she would sometimes ask softly if he approved of it. 'She believes that his eye is now constantly upon her,' Clarendon commented, 'that he watches over every action of hers & that, in fact, She never ceases to be in communication with his spirit!'[22] The Prince had done so much for her in the past, guided her in every way, that she did not know how she could survive without him; and, in her misery, anxiety and irritability, she blamed his fatalistic resignation, his gloomy acceptance of his destiny, for his own death. 'He would die,' she told Lord Derby in her grief. 'He seemed not to care to live.' 'Then she used the words, "He died from want of what they call pluck." '[23] As if in reproach at his abandonment of her, she called herself 'a deserted child'.[24]

Her physical health, so robust in the recent past, suffered grievously in her psychoneurotic state. She felt so listless she could not bring herself to take any exercise, yet she lost weight. She complained of *violent* nervous headaches; her pulse raced and, almost for the first time in years, she felt the cold. Her memory was failing, she complained; she was 'wasting away'; she was 'a wreck'. Her complete prostration, she told King Leopold, was caused by overwork, over-anxiety and the weight of responsibility and '*constant* SORROW and *craving* for the ONE absorbing object' of her love. She tried to comfort herself by recalling the happiness of the years of her marriage; and she remembered, too, with wry affection, his faults and foibles, his reluctance to abandon conversation with men for the company of ladies in the drawing room, his habit of eating too fast, his practice of falling asleep before she came to bed, his disinclination to talk to her when he was busy reading the newspapers. 'Dear Darling,' she commented, 'I fear I tried him sadly.'

38

※※※※※※※※※※

SEANCES AND SERVICES

'I like the man but *not* the Bishop.'

THE QUEEN wrapped herself in her grief and longed for the day when her spirit would meet Prince Albert's in a future life after death. She dismissed ill-conceived attempts to comfort her as impatiently as she dismissed the words of a clergyman, who said that she must now consider herself a bride of Christ, as so much 'twaddle': the man 'must have known that he was talking nonsense'. Occasionally, so she told Randall Davidson, the Dean of Windsor, she was assailed by doubts as to whether or not there was, indeed, an afterlife; but these thoughts did not trouble her for long: she spoke more often of her faith in an 'eternal reunion hereafter'; and, in this later life, she was to be rather concerned to reflect what her husband might have to say to her. 'Do you know, my dear,' she was to tell one of her granddaughters, 'I sometimes feel that when I die I shall be just a little nervous about meeting Grandpapa for I have taken to doing a good many things that he would not quite approve of.'

'I feel now to be so acquainted with death,' she wrote to the Princess Royal soon after her mother died, '& to be much nearer that unseen world.'[1] She felt sure that her husband was watching her and that she was in communion with his spirit, though she did not know what other spirits she might encounter and did not care for the thought of meeting some of them. She was said to have objected to the idea of King David being presented to her because of his disgraceful treatment of Uriah the Hittite; and when one of her ladies remarked that they would soon all meet in Abraham's bosom she haughtily replied that she herself would 'not meet Abraham'.[2]

In the afterlife in which the Queen would encounter those 'dear ones waiting', there was no hell and no Devil – belief in these was 'unutterably horrible and revolting'. She was, however, tempted to believe in the occult, in second sight, psychic phenomena, the power of magnetism – she had tried table-turning one evening at Osborne where the table had spun about most convincingly, and she even conducted séances with such members of the household who could be persuaded to take part in them. She also, like Napoleon III, was much struck by coincidences and was superstitious about luck. May was an unlucky month; marriages should not take place in May; and 14 December, the day upon which Prince Albert died, was always for her a day approached with apprehension. The birth of one of her great-grandsons, the future King George VI, on that day consequently caused the family much concern; and the child's grandfather, the Prince of Wales, announced the news of the birth with a kind of apology. His mother was, indeed, 'rather distressed that this happy event should have taken place on a darkly sad anniversary for us';[3] but she was mollified on being invited to become godmother to the 'dear little Boy born the day when his beloved great grandfather entered on a new and greater life', and she was additionally pleased to be told he was to be named Albert ('a byeword for all that is great & good'). She gave him a bust of Prince Albert as a christening present.[4]

So far as Christian worship was concerned, the Queen was quite down-to-earth. She was pleased when the Franciscan monks at Cimiez said they would pray for her; but for the rites of their Church – 'strange observances repugnant to all the simplicity of our Saviour's teaching' – she had no taste or inclination, although she did once go to a Roman Catholic service in Switzerland and found it an agreeable experience. Nor could she 'bear to hear the violent abuse of the Catholic religion which is so painful and so cruel towards the many innocent and good Roman Catholics'. She did, however, think that the 'atrocious Catholic clergy' at King Leopold's funeral were 'nasty Beggars'.[5]

She was inclined to reserve her censure for Mr Gladstone's friends, the Tractarians of the Oxford Movement who rejected the Protestant element in Anglicanism in favour of its pre-Reformation Catholic tradition and who aimed at restoring the High-Church ideals of the seventeenth century. Tractarians, she believed, were 'R. Catholics at heart and very insincere as to their professions of attachment' to the Anglican Church.

She disliked evangelicals, too, once remarking to Disraeli that 'the extreme Evangelical School' did 'the Established Church as much harm as the High Church'. She considered their tirade against theatres and dancing and their strict Sabbatarianism particularly distasteful. 'I am not at all an admirer or approver of our very dull Sundays,' she once remarked to the Princess Royal, 'for I think the absence of innocent amusements for the poor people a misfortune and an encouragement of vice.' She strongly supported the opening of art galleries and museums on a Sunday and when it was proposed to prohibit by law bands playing in parks on that day she protested to the Prime Minister about the 'incomprehensible blindness' of the proposer of such a ridiculous measure. Going to church on a Sunday was, however, a duty not to be neglected. 'Let me add one word wh. as your *Godmother* as well as your Grandmother I may,' she once concluded a letter to Princess Victoria of Hesse. 'It is not to neglect going to Church or to *read* some good & serious religious work, *not materialistic & controversial* ones – for they are very bad for everyone – but *especially* for *young* people.'[6]

Episcopalians came in for the same sort of strictures as Sabbatarians. 'You know,' she remarked one day to Gladstone, 'I am not much of an episcopalian.' 'No, Ma'am,' he replied mournfully, 'I know that well.' Indeed, the Queen went so far as to say that she did not like bishops. She made the remark to Lady Lytton after she had attended a reception for a large number of them, 'a very ugly party', at Lambeth Palace. 'But your Majesty likes *some* bishops,' Lady Lytton protested, 'for instance, the Bishop of Winchester [Randall Davidson, a clever, persuasive man, "singularly pleasing in both appearance and manner", in the Queen's opinion, who had left the Deanery at Windsor to become Bishop of Rochester before being translated to Winchester] and the Bishop of Ripon [William Boyd Carpenter].' 'Yes,' conceded the Queen, 'I like the man but *not* the Bishop.'[7]

Indeed, she thought it as well to write to Davidson when he went to Rochester, having previously written very crossly to the Prime Minister for not having done what she had asked him to do and appointed him Bishop of Winchester: 'The Queen must honestly confess that she has never found people promoted to the Episcopate remain what they were before. She hopes and thinks that will not be the case with the Dean.'

If she did not much care for bishops and was a tireless critic of church dignitaries generally, the Queen, with a few notable exceptions, did not much take to many humbler Anglican clergymen either. She once remarked of a man, a 'really most talented person' and 'good looking besides' who was appointed tutor to her youngest son, that the 'only objection' she had to him was that he was a clergyman;[8] and on another occasion she wondered 'why the clergy should go fussing about the poor or servants . . . The servants are very good people. Why can't they be left alone?'*[9]

Her journal contains many references to 'terribly long services' and tediously long sermons of which she grew increasingly intolerant in her old age. The Duke of Portland recorded that A. V. Baillie, later to be Dean of Windsor, but then a young curate, once asked Sir Henry Ponsonby for his advice about a sermon he was to preach in the Queen's presence. 'It doesn't much matter *what* you say,' Ponsonby told him, 'because her Majesty is too deaf to hear; but on no account let it last for more than five minutes.'[10]

All in all she felt more at home in a Scottish kirk – 'the real and true stronghold of Protestantism' – than in any other place of worship. 'I have always,' she once declared to a deputation from the Church of Scotland, 'been devoted to Scotland and to the Church.' 'I am nearly a Dissenter,' she confessed, 'or rather more a Presbyterian.' She found the simplicity of the services at Crathie and the quiet devotion of the congregation there most moving; and she caused some consternation among the members of her household by declaring that she intended to take communion at Crathie and expected them, as well as the servants at Balmoral, to do the same. When her youngest son objected she was furious. 'Let me now more strongly and emphatically point out to you, that it is your sacred *duty* to take the sacrament with me,' she told him . . . 'I have *never* known *any one refuse* to take the *Sacrament* with a Parent – and especially the Head of the Country – if asked to do so.'[11]

She wrote gratefully of the 'admirable' sermons of her 'dear friend' and chaplain the Revd Norman McLeod, listening to which she would sometimes nod in agreement and approval. 'Every one came back delighted,' she wrote after one service conducted by McLeod whose prayers, she said, 'gave me a lump in my throat. How satisfactory it is to come back from church with such feelings.'[12]

---

* She asked the same question about missionaries, shocking Lady Lytton by saying that she wished they would leave the Mohammedans alone (Mary Lutyens, ed., *Lady Lytton's Court Diary*).

She was equally impressed by another sermon, preached the following year by the Revd John Laird, parish minister of Errol, who 'electrified all present by a most admirable and beautiful Sermon, which lasted nearly an hour, but which kept one's attention rivetted.'[13] This was in 1855. It was very rarely thereafter that she would sit patiently through a sermon half as long. She did not, as Queen Elizabeth I was known to do, interrupt the parson's discourse; but she would make it quite clear from her expression when he had said enough.

39

※※※※※※※※※※※

PRINCESS ALEXANDRA

'May he be only worthy of such a jewel,
there is the rub.'

ALTHOUGH SHE HAD BEEN reluctant to depart from the place where
her beloved husband lay awaiting his funeral, the Queen left for Osborne
five days after his death. She looked utterly miserable during the crossing,
according to her lady-in-waiting, the Duchess of Atholl, who described
the 'desolate look of that young [42-year-old] face in Her *Widow's* cap!
for somehow the Queen looked like a child'. She held the Duchess in a
'passionate embrace'; and the older woman thought '*What* was there that
I would not do for her.'[1]

At Osborne she tried to deal with papers and despatches, determined,
as she said, to do her duty, struggling to understand the difficulties which
the Prince would so carefully have explained to her, the words seeming
to swim before her eyes. As at Windsor and, later at Balmoral, she could
not escape from the fear that she might go mad.

She felt she could not bear to see her Ministers alone; and she told
the Prime Minister, Lord Palmerston, that they would have to conduct
their business either through Princess Alice or General Grey, George
Anson's successor as the Prince's Private Secretary and now her own.

When the Prime Minister pressed her to accept the fact that this
method of conducting business was impossible she gave way with clearly
stated reluctance. But she insisted that she was not up to the strain
of attending meetings of the Privy Council. In this difficulty a strange
compromise was reached. The recently appointed Clerk of the Council
was Arthur Helps, an astute, cultivated and tactful man whom the Queen

came to like and to trust; and it was agreed that he and the requisite number of councillors should stand in one room while the Queen should sit in the next with the door between them open. She would then authorize Helps to give her consent to the matters laid before the councillors for their approval.

She was to be a similarly remote presence on the occasion of the Prince of Wales's marriage to Princess Alexandra which was to take place on 5 March 1863.

In the months immediately following her husband's death, the Queen had made no bones of her conviction that – as she said to Lord Hertford one day – the Prince Consort had been 'killed by that dreadful business at the Curragh'.[2] She asked Vicky to tell Stockmar so: 'There must be no delusion about that – it was so; he was struck down . . . Oh! that cross.'[3]

She found it impossible to look at her eldest son 'without a shudder'. She could scarcely bear to be in the same room with him, she confessed to her daughter, the Crown Princess. 'He does not know that I know all – Beloved Papa told him that I could not be told all the disgusting details . . . Tell him [the Crown Prince Frederick, who had made an appeal to the Queen on his brother-in-law's behalf] that I try to employ him, but I am not hopeful.'[4]

The Prince Consort's friend, Colonel Francis Seymour, encouraged the Queen to believe that the Prince of Wales's 'fall' was, in reality, no more than 'a youthful error that very few young men escape', that it was 'almost impossible' to hope that the Prince would be one of them, and that the father's 'extraordinary pureness of mind' had led him to exaggerate the seriousness of what most other men would consider a venial fault. But the Queen would not be persuaded, and when the Crown Princess urged her not to be so hard upon the boy – to accept the fact that he knew he was 'neither like you nor Papa'; he could not help it – she replied:

> All you say about poor Bertie is right and affectionate in you; but if you had seen what I saw, if you had seen Fritz struck down, day by day get worse and finally die, I doubt if you could bear the sight of the one who was the cause; or if you would not feel as I do, a shudder. This dreadful dreadful cross kills me![5]

Her distress was made all the more difficult to bear because the contemplation of her son's future enjoyment of his young and attractive wife made her own loss so painful to remember. She confessed to her daughter that Bertie's 'prospect of opening happiness of married life' wrung her 'poor heart' which seemed 'transfixed with agonies of longing!' 'I am alas! not old,' she wrote to her, 'and my feelings are strong and warm; my love is ardent.'[6]

The Prince did what he could to heal the breach between himself and his mother, writing letters for her, letting her know that he shared her grief for the loss of 'one of the best and kindest fathers'. But it was all to no avail; and relations between mother and son became so bad that the Prime Minister came to see the Queen to tell her that the country was 'fearful [they] were not on good terms'. The Prince was so much away from home there was talk of a serious estrangement. The Queen protested that this was not so and the Prince was 'a very good and dutiful son'. Certainly he was much away from home, but this was 'unavoidable, as Bertie's living in the house was not a good thing'.

In writing to her daughter, the Queen was more open. Contact with her son was 'more than ever unbearable' to her, she admitted. She had decided it would be best if he left the country again for a time. His father had planned that his education ought to be completed by a tour of Palestine and the Near East, and now was a suitable time for him to embark upon it.

So, in February 1862, accompanied by General Bruce, he set out for Venice by way of Vienna. The 'poor Boy' was 'low and upset' when he wished his mother goodbye. So was she; and he returned for a moment after he had left her room, close to tears. He had felt his father's death far more deeply that she had supposed, and was distressed to leave her, knowing that in her misery she had almost grown to hate him.

> The Q: and the P: of W: are as bad as ever if not worse [Lord Clarendon told the Duchess of Manchester on the authority of King Leopold shortly before the Prince's departure]. And all his efforts to improve them have been fruitless – it seems an antipathy that is incurable but quite justifiable – it is entirely her fault as the poor boy asks nothing better than to devote himself to comforting his Mother & with that object would be delighted to give up his foreign expedition but she wouldn't hear of it & seems only to wish to get rid of him. The Q:'s conduct in the matter is hardly

sane but, as we know, it has never been otherwise, the eccentricity cannot be attributed to her misfortune but if it goes on & she lives it will produce a most painful state of things.[7]

On his return from his tour in June 1862 the Prince was profoundly relieved to find that his mother appeared to have overcome those feelings of deep resentment and dislike which had so distressed him at the time of his father's death. Indeed, she seemed actually glad to have him home again. She confessed that she was at first 'much upset at seeing him' because 'his beloved father was not there to welcome him back'. But he was so much improved, she thought, looking 'so bright and healthy' and being 'most affectionate: the tears came into his eyes' when he saw her. His time away had 'done him so much good', his mother continued a few days later; and he went on 'being as good, amiable and sensible' as anyone could have wished. Improved 'in every respect', he was 'so kind and nice to the younger children, more serious in his ways and views'. She was especially pleased to note that he was 'very distressed about General Bruce' who, having contracted a fever in the marshes of the Upper Jordan, had died soon after his return to England in his sister's rooms in St James's Palace.

The Prince was now twenty-one years old and his mother was anxious that there should be no further delay in his marriage. He, too, she was thankful to say, seemed 'most anxious' to make his formal proposal to Princess Alexandra, for whom he had bought a 'number of pretty things' on his travels. The Queen, however, thought that before any proposal was made, Princess Alexandra's family should be told that the Prince of Wales was a '*mauvais sujet*'. So the Crown Princess was instructed to let the Princess's mother, Princess Christian, know that '*wicked wretches*' had led the 'poor innocent Boy into a scrape' which had caused his parents the 'deepest pain'. She was told to add that both his parents had 'forgiven him this (*one*) *sad mistake*', that his mother was very confident that he would make 'a steady Husband', and that she looked to his wife 'as being HIS SALVATION'.[8]

This message was accordingly passed on to Princess Christian who was further assured, without too strict a regard for accuracy, that the Prince was 'very domestic and longed to be at home'. So arrangements for the marriage went ahead, and the Queen meanwhile used a journey to Coburg to revisit the places where her husband had lived as a child as an excuse to meet Princess Alexandra and her parents at King Leopold's palace at Laeken.

She was immediately taken with her proposed daughter-in-law whom she found as lovely as the Crown Princess had said she was, 'with such a beautiful, refined profile and quiet lady-like manner'. The Queen was accordingly gratified to receive a letter from her son saying that he had proposed to her.

> She immediately said *yes* [the Prince reported] ... I then kissed her hand and she kissed me. We then talked for some time and I said I was sure you would love her as your own daughter and make her happy in the new home, though she would find it very sad after the terrible loss we had sustained. I told her how *very* sorry I was that she could never know dear Papa. She said she regretted it deeply and hoped he would have approved of my choice. I cannot tell you how happy I feel.[9]

'May he be only worthy of such a jewel,' the Queen commented apprehensively. 'There is the rub!' She let it be known that, although they were engaged, there must be no question of their being left alone together, except 'in a room next to the Princess's mother's' and then 'with the door open and for a short while'. This is how her own courtship had been conducted after she herself had proposed to the Prince's father. Also, Princess Alexandra must come over to England by herself before the marriage so that she could be warned 'not to use her influence to make the Prince a partisan in the political questions now unhappily in dispute' between her country and Germany, since this would 'irritate all the Queen's German connections and create family feuds – destructive of all family comfort and happiness'.

The Princess was reluctant to come, not wanting it to appear that she was being summoned on approval and 'terribly frightened' of being left alone with the Queen for long. Both the Prince of Wales and the King of the Belgians tried rather diffidently and wholly unsuccessfully to persuade the Queen not to subject the Princess to such embarrassment; but the Queen was adamant. 'I should see the girl,' she said, 'so that I could judge, before it is too late, whether she will suit me.'[10]

So, while the Prince was sent abroad again, Princess Alexandra came to England and listened to the Queen's lectures with tactful acquiescence. She concealed the resentment which she subsequently admitted she had felt that her father, who had brought her over to England, had – for want of an invitation to stay at Osborne – been obliged to put up at a hotel; and that her mother, from whom she had never been parted before, had not been asked to come to England at all. She was polite, charming, understanding, affectionate; and the Queen was more delighted with her than ever, particularly when, after listening to many stories about the Prince Consort, the Princess burst into tears at an account of his death. 'How He would have doted on her and loved her,' the Queen wrote, paying her the highest compliment she could.[11]

She certainly adored her now herself. 'I can't say how I and we all love her!' she told the Crown Princess. 'She is so good, so simple, unaffected, frank, bright and cheerful, yet so quiet and gentle that her [companionship] soothes me. Then *how* lovely!'[12]

When Princess Alexandra, now known as Alix, returned to England three days before the wedding it was clear, however, that the sad memories aroused by what was to take place in St George's Chapel were to cast their gloom over what the Queen professed would be 'the only ray of happiness in her life since her husband's death'. She was too 'desolate' to come down to dinner, which she had served to her and a lady-in-waiting in a different room; and was 'much moved' when, to show her sympathy with the Queen's distress, 'Alix knocked at the door, peeped in and came and knelt before [her] with that sweet, loving expression which spoke volumes.' The Queen kissed her 'again and again'.[13]

Princess Alexandra was 'much moved' herself, so the Queen recorded, when, the day before the wedding, she took the bride and bridegroom to the mausoleum at Frogmore. 'I opened the shrine and took them in . . . I said, "*He* gives you his blessing!" and joined Alix's and Bertie's hands, taking them both in my arms. It was a very touching moment and we all felt it.'[14]

The Queen, 'very low and depressed', according to Lady Augusta Bruce, remained preoccupied with thoughts of her husband even on the day of the wedding. She had herself photographed sitting down in front of the bridal pair, looking at neither of them but gazing instead at a marble bust of the Prince Consort.

She had decided that she could not bring herself to take part in the procession to the chapel, nor to discard her mourning for the day. She would continue to wear the black streamers of widowhood and her black widow's cap with a long white veil. She put on the badge of the Order of the Garter that her 'beloved one had worn' and a miniature of 'his noble features.' She proceeded to the Chapel from the deanery by a specially constructed covered way and entered directly into the high oak closet on the north side of the altar which Henry VIII had built so that Catherine of Aragon could watch the ceremonies of the Order of the Garter.[15]

Sitting in this closet, she was 'agitated and restless', Lady Augusta Bruce recorded, moving her chair, putting back her long streamers, asking questions of the Duchess of Sutherland. Her expression was 'profoundly melancholy'. When the organ played the first anthem and Jenny Lind sang the chorale which had been composed by Prince Albert, she looked across at the new East window and reredos which the Dean and Canons had erected in his memory and seemed 'transfixed', suffering indescribably. Charles Kingsley, one of the Queen's Chaplains in Ordinary, who was 'exactly opposite to her the *whole* time', saw her throw back her head and look 'up and away with a most painful' expression on her face. Norman McLeod, Dean of the Chapel Royal, who was standing next to Kingsley, touched him on the arm, and, with tears in his eyes, whispered in his 'broad Scotch', 'See, she is worshipping him in spirit!'[16]

In the congregation below the Queen's closet, her daughters were in tears; the Archbishop of Canterbury made rather heavy weather of announcing the bride's six Christian names; the bridesmaids were, in Lady Geraldine Somerset's opinion, 'eight as ugly girls as you could wish to see'; the Knights of the Garter hurried down the aisle in a kind of gaggle instead of proceeding decorously two by two; and Benjamin Disraeli was seen to receive a frigid glance from the Queen for having raised his eye-glass in the direction of her closet: he 'did not venture', so he told a friend, to use his glass again.[17] There was only one really embarrassing moment, however; and that was when the bridegroom's four-year-old nephew, the future Kaiser Wilhelm II, who was wearing Highland dress, decided to enliven the proceedings by trying to throw the cairngorm from the head of his dirk across the choir. He had already caused great consternation by hurling his aunt's muff out of the carriage window and by addressing the Queen familiarly as 'Duck'.[18] He now created further disturbance by turning on his uncles, Prince Alfred and Prince Leopold, who tried to restrain his bad behaviour in the chapel, and by biting them both as hard as he could on their legs.

After the ceremony a luncheon was held for the royal guests, but the Queen did not attend it, again preferring to eat alone. Afterwards, at about four o'clock, from a window in the Grand Corridor, she watched the bridal carriage set off for Windsor station. She then walked down the path to the mausoleum at Frogmore, to pray alone, 'by that blessed resting-place'.[19]

On their return to Windsor after a week's honeymoon at Osborne, the Queen was pleased with the look of them both. 'Alix looked so sweet and lovely at luncheon,' she recorded the day they arrived back at the Castle, 'and Bertie so brightened up.'

She was not pleased with either of them, however, when they, like most people in the country, made clear their support of Denmark in that country's quarrel with Germany over the Duchies of Schleswig and Holstein which had been ruled for years by the Kings of Denmark but which the Germans considered they had every right to annex. The problem was an extremely complicated one, so complicated, in fact, that Lord Palmerston observed in a celebrated comment that there were only three people who had ever understood it, the Prince Consort, who was dead, a German professor who had gone mad, and he himself who had quite forgotten what it was all about. What was certain, at least, was that the Queen, having regard to the fact that the inhabitants of the Duchies were of largely German stock, supported German claims, as she had no doubt Prince Albert would have done. Indeed, she had recently declared that the 'German element' was the one which she wished 'to be cherished and kept up' in the 'beloved home' which she had shared with her husband; and she had told her daughter, the Crown Princess, that she much regretted that the Prince of Wales never wrote to Princess Alexandra in 'anything but English'. 'I hope,' she wrote to her daughter after the Prince of Wales had visited her in Berlin, 'that you have Germanized Bertie as much as possible.'[20]

Princess Alexandra, naturally sympathetic towards Denmark when German armies invaded the country of her birth, was, on the other hand, outspokenly anti-German. Her attitude was warmly endorsed by her husband. 'This horrible war will be a stain for ever on Prussian history,' the Prince of Wales wrote in a letter to Mrs Bruce, his late

Governor's widow, 'and I think it is *very* wrong of our government not to have interfered before now.'

'The dreadful war in Denmark causes both the Princess and myself great anxiety,' the Prince wrote in a letter to Lord Spencer, his Groom of the Stole, 'and the conduct of the Prussians and the Austrians is really quite scandalous.'[21] Such remarks were not only addressed to his friends. The Prussian Ambassador, the disagreeable Count Bernstorff, felt constrained to register a formal complaint about the Prince's behaviour which was matched by that of the Princess, who pointedly refused to speak to Bernstorff after she had observed him declining to raise his glass in a toast to the King of Denmark.[22]

The Prince and Princess were resolved not to be silenced. Nothing the Queen could do prevented them from speaking out. So strongly did the Prince feel, in fact, that he even discussed what he considered to be the pusillanimous policies of the Government with the leading members of the Opposition after his offer to act as an intermediary between London and Copenhagen had been treated – as the Queen instructed that it should be treated – '*with extreme* caution'. 'Oh,' the Queen lamented to her daughter in Germany, 'if Bertie's wife were only a good German and not a Dane! ... It is terrible to have the poor boy on the wrong side, and aggravates my sufferings greatly.'[23]

With her eldest son being so troublesome, with his wife expecting a baby (a weak thing born prematurely as a result, so it was said, of her distress over her country's plight), with her daughter, the Crown Princess, writing angry letters about England's attitude towards Prussia, with the Crown Prince fighting in the Prussian army – and, to his brother-in-law's disgust, wearing on his Prussian uniform 'a most objectionable ribbon which he received for his *deeds of valour* ???' – and with Palmerston and Lord Russell, those 'two dreadful old men' in open sympathy with Denmark, the Queen prohibited all further mention of the Schleswig – Holstein business at Windsor and everywhere else.

40

✳✳✳✳✳✳✳✳✳✳✳✳

THE RECLUSE

'We must all try, *gently*, to get her
to resume her old habits.'

ACTIVE AS SHE HAD BEEN in attempting to guide her Government's foreign policy and priding herself on having 'the eyes of Argus in spite of [her] broken heart', the Queen continued to live, so far as the outside world was concerned, in impenetrable and mournful seclusion.

A few months before Prince Albert's death, the poet, A. J. Munby, had seen her on her way to and from Parliament, 'in ermine robe and diamond coronet, looking well and young. Great crowd and more cheering than I have heard before – one workman near me very enthusiastic, shouting, "England's Crown for ever!" as he held his hat up.'[1]

Now the months went by and neither Household nor Ministers could persuade her to show herself in public. Charles Grey, her Private Secretary, was blamed by the Cabinet for not doing more to urge her to do so, since he was known to be as close to her as any member of her Household. Indeed, she herself had written to him to say that she could not deny he was her '*main* support'; and when he was away, she added, 'she always feels *additionally anxious*. She is *not* worrying herself now [January 1863], & is calmer; but her constant & ever increasing grief – added to a terribly nervous temperament by nature (which her precious Husband knew but too well & often had to suffer . . .) – prevents her taking anything calmly.'[2]

Grey did what he could to persuade her to emerge from her seclusion, knowing quite well that, as her second daughter, Princess Alice, assured him, and as he himself observed at a ghillies' ball at Balmoral, the Queen's health was not really as delicate as she claimed it was. 'Princess Alice also says that the Queen owned to her that she was afraid of getting too well – as if it was a crime ... She is so nice & touching in her manner that it is difficult to find the heart to urge her to do anything she does not like – but after the next anniversary, we must all try, *gently*, to get her to resume her old habits.'[3]

Grey was reluctant to press her too hard, since he knew this would make her all the more determined to cling to her privacy, and that when she was urged to make a public appearance she would, as likely as not, turn to her doctors for a reason for refusing. The Queen's physician, William Jenner, who was created a baronet in 1868, was much criticized for not giving Ministers a more accurate account of his patient's state of health. When pressed on this point by Lord Halifax, the Lord Privy Seal, he protested, 'But how can I? Isn't it better to say the Queen can't do so and so because of her health – which is to a certain extent true – than to say she won't?' It was much easier, in fact, to agree with her own diagnoses than to antagonize her by dissent.[4]

Lord Halifax, commenting on the Queen's obstinacy and nervousness, spoke of some 'evidence of insanity'. However, since she had 'always been much the same in these matters', there was no need to fear that her mind would grow worse.[5] Yet she herself instructed Jenner to tell Lord Derby that 'any great departure from her usual way of life, or more than ordinary agitation, might produce insanity'.

Jenner agreed that the Queen's nerves were 'a species of madness' against which it was 'hopeless to contend'.[6] Her insistence on seclusion was due to 'nervousness'. He pointed out how hard she worked at her papers, how diligently she went through her despatch boxes even in Scotland where it was really necessary she should go for periods of relaxation, since she needed an 'entire change of air at least twice a year'. The Scottish writer and biographer, Sir Theodore Martin, confirmed how hard she worked at her papers. Martin had sprained his leg while skating on the Isle of Wight and the Queen had sat by him and read to him every day 'as if she had been his mother'. 'They had been daily in close intercourse at Osborne' so Martin had had an opportunity of 'seeing her in her room surrounded by the despatch boxes which [came] to her twice a day from London'.

'From 7.30 a.m. when she gets up, to twelve at night or 12.30,' so Martin told A. J. Munby, 'she is continually at work, except the hours of meal & exercise, and half an hour after dinner, when someone reads to her.'[7]

Even so, as Jenner knew, she was inclined to overstate her case, talking and writing of 'constant incessant labour' and being 'overwhelmed with business', protesting, as she did to the Crown Princess, how impossible it was for her to bear the 'noise and excitement' of public appearances 'without feeling really ill'. It was all very well for General Grey to refer in private to the 'Royal Malingerer', and for Lord Clarendon to speak of 'Eliza' as being 'roaring well' and able to do 'everything she likes and nothing she doesn't'. Jenner remained convinced of the real distress which lay behind her almost hysterical outbursts, her wild protests against being 'driven to desperation by the want of consideration shown by the *public* for her health and strength', against her being required to work and drudge 'from morning to night' in total disregard of the danger of a '*complete breakdown* of her nervous system', against her – 'a poor weak woman shattered by grief and anxiety and by nature terribly nervous' – being 'dictated to by public clamour into doing what she physically CANNOT', against all 'unreasonable demands from which she [expected] Ministers to protect her'.

The people of the country began to grumble about a Queen who might just as well be dead for all they heard about her. Lord Torrington, one of her lords-in-waiting, complained to General Grey that there was a 'considerable danger' of the public ceasing to take any interest in the monarchy, while the 'ignorant mass' might well come to believe that 'Royalty [was] of no value'. 'There is not a tradesman in London,' so Torrington thought, 'who does not believe he is damaged by the Queen not coming to London.'[8] Newspapers took up and endorsed these complaints. The *Globe* and *The Times* criticized her for retreating to Balmoral when she should have been available to her Ministers six hundred miles further south – comments which induced her to instruct General Grey to 'tell her when such articles *are* in the papers, as then she won't read them'.[9] A Member of Parliament went so far as to ask in the Commons 'whether it is the intention of Her Majesty's Government, out of consideration to Her Majesty's health, comfort and tranquility . . . to advise Her Majesty to abdicate'.[10]

This drew forth from the Queen a characteristic protest:

She thinks it vy important that the question of her *state* of health *once* for *all* shld be understood – It is simply this: The Queen's health – & nerves – require in the spring time a *short interval* of bracing mountain air & comparative quiet – or she must break down completely & *if* the public will *not* take her – as she is – she must *give all up* – & give it to the Pr of Wales – No doubt they wld wish her to be always in London for *their* convenience . . . but the Queen *can't*. . . The Queen's looks belie her & *nobody* believes *how* she suffers.[11]

In March 1864 a large poster, fixed to the railings of Buckingham Palace, announced to passers-by that 'these commanding premises' were 'to be let or sold, in consequence of the late occupant's declining business'.

That spring the Queen was persuaded to make an appearance at a flower show in the Royal Horticultural Gardens; and in June she steeled herself to take a drive from Buckingham Palace to Paddington in an open carriage and, although the experience was 'very painful', she was deeply gratified to see how pleased people were to see her again. A fortnight before this rare excursion she had received a letter from King Leopold urging her to show herself more in this way. Well knowing the effect it would have upon her, he reminded her that the Prince of Wales and his wife – now living in grand style at Marlborough House with a household of over a hundred persons, including scarlet-coated and powdered footmen, pages in blue and black, and innumerable maids – were '*constantly before the public* in EVERY IMAGINABLE SHAPE and CHARACTER', filling 'entirely *the public mind*'.[12] Having taken her uncle's advice not to let her heir and his wife overshadow her, she noted complacently how the people stopped to look at her and ran after her carriage when she did bring herself to appear in public, this, 'naturally', they did not do for them.

The Queen drew the line, however, at opening Parliament. When this was proposed to her in 1864; she told the Prime Minister that such a function was '*totally out of the question*'. It had been difficult enough to do so when she had had '*the support* of her dear husband, whose presence alone seemed a tower of strength, and by whose dear side she *felt safe* and *supported* under *every* trial'. Even with that support she had been 'always terribly nervous on *all* public occasions, but *especially* at the opening of Parliament, which was what she *dreaded for days*, and hardly ever went through without suffering from headaches before or after the ceremony.'[13]

This was true: she had once told Prince Albert that on every such occasion she was so nervous it was as though it were the first time she had endured it; and Lady Lyttelton had once noticed at a prorogation ceremony how uncontrollably she was trembling. Now that her husband's support had gone, no child could feel 'more shrinking and nervous than the poor Queen' when she had to '*do* anything'.

Apart from an appearance at Wellington College – the public school founded as a memorial to the great Duke, with which her husband, as President of the Governors, had been closely associated and to which one of her grandsons was sent – the Queen was very rarely seen beyond the walls of Windsor Castle, Buckingham Palace and Osborne in 1864. Nor was she in 1865 when, in the spring of that year, her life, so she lamented to her eldest daughter, was still 'bereft of joy', still – as she wrote to the widow of Abraham Lincoln who was assassinated in April – 'utterly broken-hearted' by the loss of her 'own beloved husband', 'the light of [her] life'.[14] But during the next year she brought herself to appear in public rather more often: she went to the Royal Academy, the South Kensington Museum – where she was intrigued by an exhibition of porcelain painted by 'ladies or at least women' – and to the Zoological Gardens. She went to inspect a parade of troops at Aldershot; she walked round the workhouse at Old Windsor – where she was sorry to see men and their wives housed in separate quarters in their old age – and was shown over the prison at Parkhurst on the Isle of Wight where some prisoners knelt before her in tears, 'sobbing for pardon', and others, mostly Roman Catholic and Irish women, were 'so unmanageable & excited that nothing could be done with them'.[15]

She drove over from Balmoral to attend the Highland Gathering at Braemar and to open a waterworks at Aberdeen where she was actually induced to make a speech. She went to Wolverhampton in the royal train from which she alighted with 'trembling knees' to unveil a statue of Prince Albert; and, anxious to obtain a dowry for Princess Helena, who was to marry the impecunious Prince Christian of Schleswig-Holstein-Sonderburg-Augustenburg that year, as well as an annuity for Prince Alfred, shortly to be created Duke of Edinburgh, who had celebrated his twenty-first birthday the year before, she actually agreed to open Parlia-

ment in February 1866 for fear lest the House of Commons made difficulties about granting money for the children of a Queen neglecting her
duty. But it would, she protested, be a terrible experience to be 'ALONE
in State' and exhibited as though she were an oddity or attraction in
some kind of show, 'the spectacle of a poor, broken-hearted widow,
nervous and shrinking dragged in deep mourning' to what she 'could
only compare to an execution'.[16] She would force herself to go, however,
though definitely not in the state coach.

In the event she was quite as nervous as she had expected to be,
unable to eat most of her luncheon and afraid that she was going to faint
as she entered the Chamber and felt 'all eyes fixed' upon her in the
intimidating silence. She was clothed all in black with a black veil and
black widow's cap surmounted by a small coronet of diamonds and
sapphires.

> Today the Queen opened Parliament [A. J. Munby recorded in his
> diary] ... Very stout, very red in the face, she looked, bowing at
> the carriage window. She was well received, but not so warmly as
> the Princess of Wales who followed ... It was a good humoured
> crowd.[17]

'When I entered the House [which was very full],' she wrote in her
journal that night, 'I felt as if I should faint. All was silent and all eyes
fixed upon me, and there I sat alone.' The robes she had worn before
her widowhood were draped over the throne, next to which stood an
empty chair. While the Lord Chancellor read the speech which she could
not bring herself to deliver, she stared ahead, motionless, her face like a
mask, willing herself not to break down.[18]

On the way back to Buckingham Palace she gave vent to her relief in
a stream of talk to her daughters, Princesses Louise and Helena, who
were sitting opposite her in the carriage. Later Princess Alice wrote to
congratulate her mother on her 'great effort' which would bring its
reward. 'Think of the pride and pleasure it would have given darling
Papa,' she said, 'the brave example to others not to shirk their duty.'[19]

The Queen steeled herself to open Parliament again in February the
next year. But afterwards she wished she had not done so:

> Yesterday was a wretched day, and altogether I regret I went [to
> open Parliament] – for that stupid Reform agitation has excited
> and irritated people, and there was a good deal of hissing, some

groans and calls for Reform, which I – in my present forlorn position – ought not to be exposed to [the Parliamentary Reform Act extending the suffrage was passed in August that year]. There were many, nasty faces – and I felt it painfully. At such times the Sovereign should not be there. Then the weather being very bad – the other people could not remain to drown all the bad signs. Of course it was only bad people.[20]

41

✳✳✳✳✳✳✳✳✳✳✳

DISRAELI

'He is full of poetry, romance & chivalry. When he knelt down
to kiss my hand wh[ich] he took in both his – he said:
"In loving loyalty and faith."'

ONE OF THE ORDEALS which the Queen found most trying was the inescapable and constant tribulation of having to grow accustomed to new men in her Cabinet, for she had always hated change and clung to old friends with an almost passionate intensity. Six months after her husband's death she had asked Lord Clarendon to warn Lord Derby, the Leader of the Opposition, that her mind was so strained that a change of Government might well be 'more than her reason could stand'.

She also contrived to ensure that her Household remained comparatively stable, even though this eventually entailed being served by increasingly elderly men, several of whom were deaf. General Grey, the Queen's Private Secretary, was still in office when he died aged sixty-six in 1870. Henry Ponsonby, who succeeded him, remained Private Secretary until he suffered a stroke in 1895 in his seventieth year. Sir Thomas Biddulph, Keeper of the Privy Purse, was also in his seventieth year when he died at Abergeldie Mains near Balmoral; and Sir James Clark was well over seventy when he was treating the Prince Consort in his last illness. Sir Arthur Bigge, Ponsonby's successor, later Lord Stamfordham, remained the Queen's Private Secretary until her death.

Changes in her household were nearly always opposed, often successfully. When at the age of forty-one, in November 1863, Lady Augusta Bruce decided to marry – and had accepted the 48-year-old Canon Arthur Penryn Stanley of all people – the Queen did not trouble to hide her displeasure and mortification: 'Lady Augusta has most unnecessarily decided to marry (!!!)' she told King Leopold, 'I thought she never would leave me!*. . . It has been my greatest sorrow and trial since my misfortune! . . . She will remain in my service and be often with me, but it cannot be the same, for her first duty is now to another.'†

When a far less valued lady left to get married, the Queen admitted that she grudged 'any change in [her] Household now'. Fortunately most of her ladies were widows and there could be no question of their remarrying: she was firmly opposed to any such union and her ladies were left in no doubt as to where their duty lay – to the memories of their late husbands and to herself. She could scarcely prevent Lady Augusta's marriage; but she did manage to postpone for three years the marriage of one of her equerries, Henry Ponsonby's son, Frederick, to a colonel's pretty daughter with whom he had fallen deeply in love, on the grounds that a man 'always told his wife everything and therefore all her private affairs would get known all over London'. When the Queen's opposition to the marriage was at last overcome, Ponsonby was made to understand that he could never expect to be given a house.[2]

Over government changes the Queen could exercise no such control as she endeavoured to exercise in her Household; and the prospect of having to deal with a new Minister always filled her with the utmost

---

* The marriage of middle-aged or elderly women was always severely frowned upon by the Queen. When the philanthropist Angela Burdett-Coutts, with whom she had been on friendly terms, married William Ashmead Bartlett, a man of American descent, '40 years younger than herself', the Queen was appalled. 'The poor foolish old woman . . . looked like his grandmother and was all decked out with jewels – not edifying' (RA, Queen Victoria's Journal, 3 May 1881). In an attempt to prevent what she called the 'mad marriage' she had written to Lord Harrowby, the bride's cousin, to say that she trusted 'that Lady Burdett-Coutts had given the fullest consideration to this step . . . It would grieve her much if Lady Burdett-Coutts were to sacrifice her high reputation and her happiness by an unsuitable marriage' (RA A 15/544, 18 July 1880).

Lord Harrowby sent the letter to his cousin with a covering note: 'You may suppose that I have been much startled by the receipt of the enclosed letter – what answer am I to give?' 'I think you had better say (what is true),' the Baroness replied, 'in reply to the enclosed rather singular letter that you have no information on the subject alluded to' (Harrowby MSS. quoted in Edna Healey, *Lady Unknown: The Life of Angela Burdett-Coutts*, 1978, 198).

† Princess Beatrice, then aged six, was almost as surprised as her mother to learn of 'Guska's' engagement and she dictated letters to both the intended bride and bridegroom to say so: 'I hope you are quite well, dear Guska. I find it very extraordinary that you are going to be married . . . I suppose you are going to dress in a low white gown, or are you going to have a high white gown? . . . I think you will look very funny as a *Deanness*.'

'I hope you are quite well, Canon. It is very funny that you are going to be Dean of Westminster . . . It is very funny that you are going to be married. Goodbye.' (*Letters of Lady Augusta Stanley*, 316–7).

alarm and foreboding. When Lord Palmerston died in October 1865 and Lord Russell succeeded him as Prime Minister she was distraught, dreading the change more than words could express, although, so she now told King Leopold, she had never really liked Palmerston any more than she did Russell. 'He had many valuable qualities,' she wrote of 'Pilgerstein', 'though many bad ones, and we had God knows! terrible trouble with him . . . I never could the least respect him, nor could I forget his conduct on certain occasions to my Angel.'[3]

No sooner had she found Russell not nearly as difficult as she had feared he might be than his Government was defeated. Aghast at the thought of having to accept a Conservative Government under Lord Derby, she at first refused to accept Russell's resignation; and, when she was persuaded that she would have to do so, she gave way with a decidedly ill grace, complaining that all these changes were '*very* trying'. It was trying even having to accept Benjamin Disraeli, a man whom Prince Albert had described as being 'without one single element of the gentleman in his composition', as Chancellor of the Exchequer once again, though she had recently had cause to modify her earlier view that Disraeli was 'detestable, unprincipled, reckless, & not respectable'. He had certainly paid a most admirable public tribute to her husband whose acquaintance, he privately assured her, was 'one of the most satisfactory incidents of his life'. The Prince was, he had said, 'the only person' whom he had 'ever known who realized the Ideal . . . There was in him an union of the manly graces and sublime simplicity of chivalry with the intellectual splendour of the Attic Academe.'[4]

Mr Disraeli had also spoken most movingly about the Albert Memorial, and, when he had become Chancellor of the Exchequer and Leader of the House of Commons for the first time under Derby, he had impressed the Queen by the clarity and vividness of the parliamentary reports which it was his duty – his 'pleasure', he said – to send her. But he was a very odd person; so was his wife; and, while she felt assured of his devotion to herself and the Crown, she had never been quite at ease in his presence. This was soon to change.

In February 1868, after Lord Derby's resignation, Disraeli became Prime Minister. It was, the Queen thought, 'a proud thing for a Man "risen from the people" to have obtained!'[5] And if he was scarcely 'a man of the people', his father being a distinguished and well-to-do man of letters and his mother descended from one of the most ancient of Jewish families, it was certainly a remarkable achievement for Disraeli to have reached, as he put it himself, 'the top of the greasy pole'. For he was undoubtedly an outsider in the hierarchy of his party. Not only his race and tastes and manner but even his education separated him from his colleagues: apart from the Lord Chancellor, Lord Chelmsford, who had been educated at a naval school at Gosport, he was the only member of his Cabinet who had not attended a well-known public school: two had been to Rugby, one to Shrewsbury, the remaining nine to Eton.

From the beginning he set out to woo and flatter the Queen with an infallible instinct for the phrase, the gesture, the compliment, the overture that would most delight her. He was later to tell a colleague who had asked for advice as to how to handle the Queen, 'First of all, remember she is a woman.' He never forgot this himself. She responded by sending him a valentine card depicting cherubs lying on clouds.

'The present Man will do well,' she told the Crown Princess with complacent satisfaction, 'and will be particularly loyal and anxious to please me in every way.[6] He is vy peculiar . . . most singular – thoroughly Jewish looking, a livid complexion, dark eyes and eyebrows and black ringlets. The expression is disagreeable, but I did not find him so to talk to. He has a very bland manner, and his language is very flowery . . . but he is vy clever and sensible and vy conciliatory, He is full of poetry, romance & chivalry. When he knelt down to kiss my hand wh[ich] he took in both his – he said: "In loving loyalty and faith." '[7]

It would, he assured Her Majesty, 'be his delight and duty to render the transaction of affairs as easy as possible'. In 'smaller matters', he hoped he would succeed in this endeavour; but he ventured to trust that, in the great affairs of state, Her Majesty would deign not to hold from him the benefit of her wise guidance. 'Your Majesty's life has been passed in constant communion with great men,' he continued in the same tone of complimentary blandishment, 'and the knowledge and management of important transactions. Even if Your Majesty were not gifted with those great abilities, which all must now acknowledge, this rare and choice experience must give Your Majesty an advantage in judgement, which few living persons, and probably no living prince, can rival.'*[8]

---

* The compliment, if rather high-flown, was not an altogether idle one. Her knowledge of foreign courts was indeed, remarkable; and amongst her progeny were, or were to be, heirs to the thrones of Russia, Germany, Greece, Romania, Spain and Norway.

Disraeli himself recognized that he did lay it on 'rather thick' with her. When he received a box of primroses from Windsor, for example, he told her that 'their lustre was enhanced by the condescending hand which [had] showered upon him all the treasures of Spring'. As he said to Matthew Arnold, 'you have heard me called a flatterer, and it is true. Everyone likes flattery; and when you come to royalty, you should lay it on with a trowel.'[9] But he never underestimated the Queen's astuteness; he grew genuinely fond of her; in treating her with elaborate courtesy and deferential flirtatiousness he was behaving towards her as he did towards all women he liked. In writing those long, amusing, informative, gossipy letters which meant so much to her, he was indulging a whim to please her rather than performing a necessary and arduous duty.

Disraeli's letters certainly delighted her. She told Lady Augusta Stanley that she 'had never had such letters in her life', that she 'never before knew *everything*'.[10] 'No Minister,' she wrote, 'since Sir R. Peel (excepting poor dear Lord Aberdeen) has ever shown that care for my personal affairs, or that respect and deference for me which he has.'

There were, of course, things she was not told; but Disraeli was always anxious to ensure that she was given the impression of constantly being consulted except on trivial matters not worth her consideration. On suggesting, for example, that the Duke of Atholl might be appointed a Knight of the Order of the Thistle, he wrote, 'Your Majesty is a much better judge of these matters than himself; and indeed there are very few public matters on wh[ich] he feels more and more every day Your Majesty is not much more competent to advise than be advised.'[11] 'I never deny,' he once said, explaining his method of dealing with her. 'I never contradict, I sometimes forget.'[12]

Attentive towards her in his fulsome correspondence, Disraeli was as careful to charm her whenever they met. He did not much like going to Windsor, that 'castle of the winds' as he called it, remembering with a shudder the icy draughts that blew under doors and through ill-fitting window frames; but he never showed his discomfort to her. He resented having to go to Balmoral, being forced to travel so many miles from London to a place where it rained almost continuously throughout his first visit and where he caught a cold on his second: he never paid a third. But he displayed no irritation. He 'seemed delighted with his visit,' the Queen wrote of the first occasion, '& made himself most agreeable'.[13]

On a subsequent visit to Osborne it was the Queen who made herself most agreeable to him.

> Osborne was lovely [Disraeli told his friend, Lady Bradford], its green shades refreshing after the fervent glare of the voyage, and its blue bay full of white sails.
>
> The Faery [Disraeli's less mocking than affectionate nickname for the Queen] sent for me the instant I arrived. I can only describe my reception by telling you that I really thought she was going to embrace me. She was wreathed with smiles, and, as she tattled, glided about the room like a bird. She ... said, 'To think of your having the gout! How you must have suffered! And you ought not to stand now! You shall have a chair!'
>
> Only think of that! I remember that Lord Derby after one of his severest illnesses, had an Audience of her Majesty, and he mentioned it to me, as a proof of the Queen's favour, that Her Majesty had remarked to him, 'how sorry she was she could not ask him to be seated'.[14]

Disraeli was Prime Minister, however, for less than a year. In December 1868 she was obliged to part with him and to accept a Liberal Government under the leadership of the 59-year-old William Ewart Gladstone.

When she had first met Mr Gladstone, whose character Prince Albert had held in high regard, she had esteemed him too. 'He is very agreeable,' she had written at that time, 'so quiet & intellectual, with such a knowledge of all subjects, & is such a *good* man.' But since then she had changed her mind about him, comparing his 'cold loyalty' to the throne with the 'warm devotion' of Disraeli and agreeing with the Hon. Emily Eden that Gladstone did not converse, he harangued: 'and the more he says,' Miss Eden added, 'the more I don't understand ... if he were soaked in boiling water and rinsed until he was twisted into rope, I do not suppose a drop of fun would ooze out.'[15]

He spoke to the Queen at great length with what Henry Ponsonby described as that 'terrible earnestness', which he brought to the most trivial activities, even to the rattling of dice, giving the impression that, while he revered the monarchy, he did not set great store by the intelligence of its present representative who, he considered, had to have everything explained to her in the most exhaustive and exhausting detail. Yet, when the Queen made some comment, so she complained, he would merely say, 'Is that so? Really?' 'He does not care what you say. It makes no difference.'

The Queen grudgingly recognized Gladstone's talents, granted that he had a fine, commanding presence and a sonorous voice; yet she could not bring herself either to like or to respect him. Lacking Disraeli's ingratiating tact and sensitivity, he addressed her, as she said herself, as though she were a public meeting rather than a woman and was quite incapable of following the advice of his wife who sensibly said to him, 'Do pet the Queen, and for once believe you can, you dear old thing.' Similar advice was given to him by Dean Wellesley who had been at Eton with him: 'Everything depends upon your manner of approaching the Queen ... You cannot show too much regard, gentleness, I might say, even tenderness towards her.' But it was not in Gladstone's nature to 'pet' her; nor could he bring himself to flatter her. On the contrary, he gave her the impression that he did not think her worthy of such attentions. 'The Queen,' she once told her Private Secretary, 'must complain bitterly of the want of respect and consideration of her views which ... ought to be regarded on the part of the Government ... She feels hurt and indignant.'[16] She often felt humiliated as well as exasperated by Gladstone's clever, tedious, high-minded discourses and took refuge in the conclusion that he was a humbug. She would have concurred both with Mary Ponsonby, who complained that, marvel of erudition though Mr Gladstone might be, he could 'never understand a man, still less a woman', and with Henry Labouchere who said that he did not object to Gladstone's always having the ace of trumps up his sleeve, but only to his pretence that God had put it there. Mr Gladstone, the Queen eventually decided, was 'a mischievous firebrand', 'arrogant, tyrannical and obstinate'.

One of Gladstone's principal preoccupations on coming into office was how best to deal with what he termed the 'Royalty question', how to persuade the Queen to appear more often in public, a problem which gave him what he called 'the blue devils'.

42

✳✳✳✳✳✳✳✳✳✳✳

JOHN BROWN

'She is really doing all in her power to create suspicions
which I am persuaded have no foundation.'

THE FEELINGS RUNNING HIGH against the Queen – despite her
occasional public appearances in the late 1860s – and what was perceived
as her selfishness and greed as well as her wilful refusal to perform more
public duties, were fanned by certain newspapers and magazines which
brought up other more scurrilous charges against her: she was showing
exceptional partiality to one of her Highland servants. This 'great Court
favourite', as *John O' Groats Journal* referred to him, was said to be far
more than an indulged servant: he was the Queen's lover; she was 'in an
interesting condition'; they were secretly married; he was her medium in
spiritualist seances; he was her keeper, for she had gone mad. Curiosity
about the man consumed society. One day in March 1867 A. J. Munby
saw 'a long line of carriages near the Achilles statue in the Park waiting
to see the Queen go by to Windsor ... And then the Queen drove by,
with outriders & hussars, her younger children with her, looking plump
& matronly and pale, in widow's weeds; and that John Br n, of whom
there is so much foolish talk, sat behind, a big man in livery.'[1]

Most of the members of the Royal Household, although reputedly
referring to Brown as 'the Queen's stallion', were convinced, as Henry
Ponsonby told his brother, that while 'certainly a favourite', the man was
'only a Servant and nothing more'; and what Ponsonby supposed had
begun as a joke had been 'converted into a libel'.[2] Randall Davidson, who
saw much of her in his capacity as Dean of Windsor and her domestic
chaplain, said that 'one had only to know the Queen to realize how

321

innocent' her relationship with the man was.[3] Yet he was such an extraordinarily indulged favourite that it was not surprising that caricatures
depicted him standing proprietorially in front of an empty throne, that
defamatory pamphlets referred to the Queen as Mrs Brown, or that
parodies of the *Court Circular* appeared in the press:

> Balmoral, Tuesday.
> Mr John Brown walked on the Slopes. He subsequently partook
> of a haggis. In the evening, Mr John Brown was pleased to listen
> to a bag-pipe. Mr John Brown retired early.[4]

> She is really doing all in her power to create suspicions which I
> am persuaded have no foundation [Lord Stanley commented on
> the Queen's relationship with Brown]. Long solitary rides, in
> secluded parts of the park; constant attendance upon her in her
> room: private messages sent by him to persons of rank: avoidance
> of observation while he is leading her pony or driving her little
> carriage: everything shows that she has selected this man for a kind
> of friendship that is unwise and unbecoming in her position. The
> Princesses – perhaps wisely – make a joke of the matter, and talk
> of him 'as mama's lover'.*[5]

---

* The improbable notion that he was, indeed, her lover has since been given credence by such
books as *Queen Victoria's John Brown* (1938) by E. E. P. Tisdall who claimed to have seen a letter,
subsequently lost, which had been retrieved from a wastepaper basket by a footman and which
suggested that the Queen's relationship with Brown was far from platonic. The suggestion has
also been given credence by the release from its embargo in 1972 of the 'secret diary' of the
traveller, politician and poet Wilfrid Scawen Blunt, who was told by the courtesan, Catherine
Walters, known as 'Skittles', about conversations she had had with the sculptor, Edgar Boehm,
who gave Princess Louise lessons in sculpture and was widely believed to be her lover. For three
months Boehm had been at Balmoral working on a bust of Brown and accordingly had had ample
opportunities to witness the relationship between the Queen and her servant who 'had unbounded
influence' with her, treating her 'with little respect' and 'presuming in every way upon his position
with her'. According to Boehm, so 'Skittles' told Blunt, it was 'to be with him, where she could
do more as she liked, that the Queen spent so much of her time at Balmoral ... She used to go
away with him to a little house in the hills where, on the pretence that it was for protection and
to look after her dogs, he had a bedroom next to hers, the ladies-in-waiting being put at the other
end of the building ... Boehm saw enough of his familiarity with her to leave no doubt of his
being allowed "every conjugal privilege".' Boehm also told 'Skittles', who in turn told Blunt, that
'the Queen, who had been passionately in love with her husband, got it into her head that somehow
the Prince's spirit had passed into Brown' and that this was why, 'four years after her widowhood',
she had allowed him 'all privileges' (Wilfrid Scawen Blunt, 'Secret Diary' MS 9, Department of
Manuscripts and Printed Books, Fitzwilliam Museum, Cambridge, quoted in Theo Aronson, *Heart
of a Queen*, 1991, 159–61).
    More than twenty years after Brown's death it came to light that there was in existence a black
tin box containing over three hundred letters written by the Queen about Brown to Dr Alexander
Profeit, her factor at Balmoral. The Queen's former physician, James Reid, was asked by King
Edward VII's Private Secretary, Lord Knollys, to retrieve these letters from Dr Profeit's son, George
Profeit, who was threatening to blackmail the King about them. Reid managed to get hold of the

John Brown was a blunt, strong, good-looking and excessively self-assured man with thick curly hair and a beard that did not fully conceal a determined, emphatic chin. One of nine sons bought up on a small farm, he had started life as a stableboy at Balmoral and had later been employed by the Queen and the Prince Consort as a ghillie. Seven years older than Prince Albert and the Queen, he had treated them both without a trace of either subservience or disrespect. The Prince had liked him and had picked him out from the other ghillies as the one to be trusted with the special duty of watching over the Queen's safety and seeing to her comfort. He had performed his duties to her entire satisfaction, combining, as she put it herself, 'the offices of groom, footman, page and *maid*, I might almost say, as he is so handy about cloaks and shawls'.[6] Indeed, before her husband's death she had already come to regard him as indispensable. When Sir Howard Elphinstone proposed one day that Brown should accompany Prince Arthur on some expedition she quickly put a stop to that idea: 'Impossible. Why, what should I do without him? He is my particular ghillie.'[7]

Since her husband's death the Queen had come to rely on Brown more and more whenever she was at Balmoral and she had taken him and her pony-chaise with her on her visit to Germany in 1862. A link with her precious past, he had further recommended himself to the Queen by his presence of mind in two carriage accidents. He was so dependable,

---

letters, presumably after paying an agreed sum for them; and handed them over to the King who, as 'a great destroyer of papers', in all probability burned them. Before handing them over Reid read them and noted in his diary that 'many of them' were 'most compromising'. He confided the substance of them to a 'green memorandum book' which was burned on Reid's death by his son in 1923 (Michaele Reid, *Ask Sir James: The Life of Sir James Reid, Personal Physician to Queen Victoria*, 1987, 56, 227–8). Whatever these letters contained, it is most improbable that a sexual relationship was revealed in them. Frederick Ponsonby who, as the Queen's Assistant Private Secretary, came to know her intimately, wrote: 'The stories about John Brown were so numerous and so obviously made-up that it hardly seemed worthwhile to correct them ... Whether there was any quite unconscious sexual feeling in the Queen's regard for her faithful servant I am unable to say, but ... I am quite convinced that if such a feeling did exist, it was quite unconscious on both sides, and that their relations up to the last were simply those of employer and devoted retainer' (Frederick Ponsonby, *Recollections of Three Reigns*, 95).

In December 1998 it was reported in the press that photographs, papers and mementoes had been found in a trunk in the attic of a house at Ballater near Balmoral, 'the home of a descendant of Mr Brown'. The executive producer of the film *Mrs Brown*, Douglas Rae, who had been granted access to these papers, was quoted as saying that 'there is no doubt in my mind they were written by two people who were very, very close and shared an intimate friendship ... The family has decided that nothing will be made public while the present members of the Royal Family, particularly the Queen Mother, are still alive.' Mr Rae said that he had been unable to establish any truth in rumours that Queen Victoria had a child by Brown and that the couple married in secret' (*Daily Telegraph, The Times*, 28 December 1998).

so faithful, so comforting and so much at ease in her presence. He was also most generous, often contributing considerably more towards the cost of wedding presents to the Balmoral staff or to funds for servants in distress than the gentlemen of the Household. He was also habitually outspoken and not infrequently drunk. The Queen, however, seemed to take pleasure in his rough, masculine assertiveness – he was so unlike Arthur Stanley, the Dean of Westminster, who appeared to her to be 'of no sex' – and she affected not to notice Brown's inebriation or, when it was obvious, attributed it to 'bashfulness'. 'Hoots, then, wumman,' Brown had been heard to snap at her when he pricked her chin while fixing the strap of her bonnet, 'Can ye no hold yerr head up.' Or, if he did not approve of her dress, he would comment derisively, 'What's this ye've got on today, wumman?' When she made some complaint about her sketching table he told her to stop complaining, silencing her with the words, 'I canna mak one for ye.' Once a maid-of-honour, seeing him with a picnic hamper, asked him if it was tea he was taking out. 'Well, no,' he told her. 'She don't much like tea. We tak oot biscuits and spirits.'

As the months passed Brown became increasingly indulged, increasingly assertive and – with the other servants who were jealous of him and the courtiers who were exasperated by him – increasingly disliked. He was 'all powerful', so Lord Carlingford was led to believe. 'No servant had a chance of promotion except through him, and he favoured no man who didn't like his glass . . . Some of the courtiers were full of attention to J. B., gave him presents, etc. – and he despised them for it. He was, however, unwearied and devoted in his attention to the Queen.'[8] And since he was so, and since Her Majesty was so dependent upon him and refused to go out driving with any other servant, Dr Jenner and Sir Charles Phipps, with her immediate agreement, decided towards the end of 1864 to have Brown brought down from Balmoral to Osborne for her health's sake. At least he would get her out into the open air when no one else could.

By the beginning of 1865 Brown had been promoted to the office of 'The Queen's Highland Servant', with duties both indoors and out; and by the end of 1872, his salary having been raised to the most generous sum of £400 a year, the Queen was referring to him, in notes addressed to John Brown, Esq., as her *'friend'* and 'most confidential attendant', who had not had 'a *single day's holiday* or been absent for *a day* or a *night*' from his post. 'He comes to my room – after breakfast & luncheon to get his orders,' the Queen told the Crown Princess, '& everything is always right – he has such an excellent head & memory . . . is besides so devoted, & attached & clever . . . It is an excellent arrangement, & I feel I have here always in the house, a good, devoted soul . . . whose only object & interest is my service, & God knows how much I want to be taken care of . . . And in this house where there are so many people, & often so much indiscretion & no Male head now – such a person is invaluable.'[9] 'He is devoted to me,' she told King Leopold. 'It is a *real comfort*.'[10]

With most of the members of her Household, though, irritation with Brown and his domineering ways turned to detestation. He did not like being kept up late by smokers, so the smoking room had to be closed by midnight. Neither her sons nor her sons-in-law were permitted to smoke in her presence, but Brown puffed away on the solid cakes of tobacco he stuffed into his pipe. He did not like being sent for '*at all hours* for trifling messages', so the equerries were told that 'he must not be made "a man of all work" – besides, it loses his position'.[11]

He quarrelled with the Queen's chaplain; he quarrelled with her German librarian; he quarrelled with the factor at Balmoral; he quarrelled with Ministers, once causing astonishment by stopping Gladstone in mid discourse with the injunction, 'Ye've said enough'.[12] He quarrelled with Prince Alfred, the Duke of Edinburgh, and when he was at last prevailed upon to apologize and was told that His Royal Highness seemed satisfied, he declared loftily, 'I am satisfied, too.'[13] He quarrelled with the Queen's Assistant Private Secretary, Arthur Bigge, who was disturbed in his room at Balmoral one day by Brown who came in 'with a stern countenance' to say, 'You'll no be going fishing. Her Majesty thinks it's about time ye did some work.'[14]

While not actually quarrelling with the Queen's daughters, he was resented by them not least because, in Princess Alice's words, 'he alone talks to her on all things, while we, her children, are restricted to speak on only things which do not excite her, or of which she chooses to talk.'

There were those who believed that the Queen was sometimes rather frightened of Brown, particularly when he was drunk.* Once he was

---

* He was certainly not frightened of her – this was, for her, a large part of his appeal. The Prince of Wales once said to Margot Tennant that, when she met his mother, he hoped she would not be afraid of her, 'adding, with a charming smile, that with the exception of John Brown, everybody was' (*The Autobiography of Margot Asquith*, ed. Mark Bonham-Carter, 1962, 50).

discovered by Henry Ponsonby lying inebriated on his bed when the Queen was waiting in her carriage for him to take her on her afternoon drive. Ponsonby locked Brown in his room, went downstairs, 'mounted the box and drove off'. 'The Queen knew what it was and knew that he knew. But on this, as on other occasions, she turned a blind eye.'[15]

In 1867 Brown's attendance upon the Queen, who had been most reluctantly persuaded to be present at a review in Hyde Park, was insisted on by Her Majesty as a condition of her own appearance. When the Ministers protested against the man's being with her upon so important a public occasion – which was fortunately cancelled in the end for other reasons – the Queen declared angrily that she would 'not be dictated to' nor '*made to alter*' what she had found answered 'for her comfort'. It was absurd to suggest, she told one of her equerries, that her carriage might have been attacked had she appeared in the Park with 'poor, good Brown'. The feeling against him was fostered by '*ill-natured* gossip in the highest classes, caused by dissatisfaction at *not forcing* the Queen *out* of her seclusion'.

So Brown's influence continued, and visitors to Balmoral and Osborne were astonished at its extent. At Osborne, a royal son-in-law, on going out to shoot one morning, found that Brown had been there before him and there were no birds left in the coverts. At Balmoral, so a member of the Royal Household related, 'he sends up to find out how the fish are. If he hears a bad report he does not go out and the Queen then offers the [fishing] to [one of her doctors].' His brusqueness was legendary. 'When the Mayor of Portsmouth came to ask the Queen to go to a Volunteer review, the Private Secretary sent in the request to her and hoped to get the reply privately so that he might convey it civilly to the Mayor,' Ponsonby recorded. 'As they both sat in the Equerries' room waiting, Brown put his head in and only said, "The Queen says saretenly not." '[16] He was equally blunt when informing members of the Household which of them were to dine with the Queen, on occasions putting his head round the door, glancing from one face to the next, then announcing, 'All what's here dines with the Queen.'

Brown's behaviour during the ghillies' balls was particularly objectionable. 'What a coarse animal that Brown is,' the Lord Chancellor once complained. 'Oh yes, I know the ball could not go on without him. But I did not conceive it possible that anyone could behave so roughly as he does to the Queen.'[17] Lord Ribblesdale, a lord-in-waiting, described one of these rowdy balls which the Queen attended, 'following the revolutions of the dancers with a benevolent but critical eye':

> We had what seemed to be incessant reels, Highland schottisches, and a complicated sustained measure called the 'Flowers of Edinburgh'. Even with proficiency this dance requires constant attention, if not actual presence of mind, to be in the right place at the right moment - anyhow, more than I possessed in the mazy labyrinth. I was suddenly impelled almost into the Queen's lap with a push in the back and 'Where are you coming to?' It was Mr John Brown exercising his office as Master of Ceremonies. After a good many Caledonians, Mr Brown came to ask the Queen, 'Now, what's your Majesty for?' Mindful of her English subjects the Queen suggested a country dance. This did not find favour. 'A country dance,' he repeated, turning angrily on his heels.[18]

Henry Ponsonby, who had joined the household as the Prince Consort's equerry in 1856, found these ghillies' balls as tiresome as did Lord Ribblesdale. He did not enjoy the company of the ghillies at the best of times. He found deer stalking extremely boring and, when compelled against his will to take part in the sport, he stuffed his pockets with newspapers and the *Fortnightly Review* so as to render the long waits less wearisome. At the end of the day there was sometimes a gruesome torch-lit dance round the slaughtered animals during which the ghillies absorbed torrents of whisky and sang songs. Further quantities of whisky were drunk around the huge granite cairn which had been erected to the memory of Prince Albert and which still bears the legend: 'Albert the Great and Good, raised by his broken-hearted widow.'

Still more whisky was drunk at the ghillies' balls from which Ponsonby stole away whenever he could with the excuse that he had important work to do. But his absence was always noticed and remarked upon with 'some asperity'. Should he return, he was obliged, as a punishment, to dance a particularly rowdy sort of reel which was one of John Brown's favourites.[19]

The Queen attended these balls regularly and appeared to enjoy them to the full, even insisting that they were not cancelled when the Court was officially in mourning: on the death of the Grand Duke of Hesse she declined to postpone the forthcoming ball for more than three days, giving as an improbable excuse that she did not 'regard it as gaiety'.[20]

Exasperating as the gentlemen of the Household found John Brown's behaviour, they could not but agree that the man, 'exceedingly trouble-some', though he was, had his uses.

'I believe he was honest,' wrote Henry Ponsonby after Brown's death, 'and with all his want of education, his roughness, his prejudices and other faults he was undoubtedly a most excellent servant to her ... He was the only person who could fight and make the Queen do what she did not wish.'[21]

He reminded her of 'former happy days', and knew well how to comfort her in the present with his rough and simple sympathy and loyalty. It meant so much to her, she said, to have 'one faithful friend' near her whose 'whole object' she was and who could 'feel so deeply for her' and 'understand [her] suffering'.

Just as he felt perfectly at ease with her, so she did with him, quite without that shyness which so often overcame her in the presence of others. She also felt protected. When she was working in her tent in the garden he would march about outside to make sure she was not disturbed; and when out in her carriage he would drive off anyone who came too close. 'I wish to take care of my dear, good mistress till I die,' he once said to her by her own account. 'You'll never have an honester servant.' She then 'took and held his dear kind hand' and said that she hoped he might long be spared to comfort her.

Concerned that her pleasure in the company of John Brown was helping her to overcome the worst of her continuing grief at the loss of her husband, the Queen consulted the 'tender hearted' Gerald Wellesley. Wellesley reassured her: God sometimes placed sympathetic people in the path of those who mourned to comfort them; it was only right that the bereaved should turn to them for consolation.[22]

Improbable as they were, the rumours of the Queen's supposedly passionate love affair with her ghillie continued to circulate, while she did nothing to conceal her reliance upon him and her affection for him. Regularly she sent him greetings cards at Christmas and New Year inscribed 'to my best friend J. B. from his best friend V. R.', 'to my kind friend from his true & devoted one', 'from a devoted grateful friend'.[23] And at least one of her communications to him was addressed to her 'darling'.

Edwin Landseer's painting, *Queen Victoria at Osborne*, showing her reading a letter as she sits side-saddle on a black horse whose rein is held by John Brown, was exhibited at the Royal Academy in the 1860s and sold engraved copies in large numbers. One of these engravings – in which at her insistence Brown's beard was shortened – she gave to Sir Howard Elphinstone with a note: 'It is beautifully engraved and the likeness of herself (rather a portly elderly lady) [in fact portrayed as a rather attractive 46-year-old one] and her good faithful attendant and friend are both, she thinks, *very* good.'[24]

Soon after this picture was shown at the Royal Academy, there appeared the Queen's *Leaves from the Journal of Our Life in the Highlands* in which John Brown figured prominently. In a long footnote devoted to Brown in this book, he is described as having 'all the independence and elevated feelings peculiar to the Highland race, and is singularly straightforward, simple-minded, kind-hearted and disinterested; always ready to oblige; and of a discretion rarely to be met with'. 'His attention, care and faithfulness cannot be exceeded,' the Queen added, 'and the state of my health, which of late years has been sorely tried and weakened, renders such qualifications most valuable and indeed most needful.'[25]

John Brown is shown leading ponies up mountain tracks, rowing boats across lochs, speaking in praise of Prince Albert's patience, sitting on the box of the sociable, causing amusement by calling the Queen 'Your Majesty' when she was travelling incognito as Lady Churchill, being 'too bashful' to wait at table when the royal party were on one of their expeditions from Balmoral, being 'very merry' in the commercial rooms of the hotels where they stayed the night.

The Queen's *Leaves from the Journal of our Life in the Highlands* first appeared in a privately printed edition; and there were many who thought that it should have remained in that edition if it were to be printed at all. Lady Augusta Stanley, for example, considered that it would 'do great harm to our dear One'. It was all very well for Arthur Helps – the Clerk of the Privy Council, who edited the book and wrote a preface to it – to claim that there was no one who wished 'more ardently than her Majesty that there should be no abrupt severance of class, but rather a gradual blending together of all classes'.[26] Lady Augusta deplored the footnotes devoted to mere servants as though 'on the same footing' as gentlemen.[27] Others regretted that the book gave the impression that the Queen's life was one long holiday. Yet others criticized the naivety of the writing, its ingenuousness, its occasional banalities and unintentional humour. Yet its very simplicity, the 'homeliness' which the author herself feared might prevent it being taken seriously, the atmosphere of happy enjoyment which pervades it, all contributed to its great success. When it was published by Smith, Elder & Co., one hundred thousand copies were sold within three months: it was estimated that the author eventually received more than £30,000 in royalties; and, while it was much parodied in such publications as *John Brown's Legs or Leaves from a Journal in the Lowlands*, it was not altogether undeserving of the high-flown praise which Disraeli cast upon it as possessing 'a freshness and fragrance like the heather amidst which it was written'. It gave him the opportunity to delight the Queen with his celebrated flattery – 'We authors, Ma'am!'

So the Queen dismissed the objections of her critics. 'From all and every side,' she said, 'the feeling is the same, the letters flow in, saying how much more than ever I shall be loved now that I am known and understood.' 'It is very gratifying,' she wrote to the Crown Princess who, like most of the family, disapproved of the publication, 'to see how people appreciate what is simple and right and how especially my truest friends – the people – feel it. They have (as a body) the truest feelings for family life.' 'You have also never said one word about my poor little book,' the disgruntled Queen complained, 'my only book. I had hoped that you and Fritz would have liked it.'[28]

'I know,' she told the Prince of Wales, 'that the publication of my book did me more good than anything else.'[29]

43

✖✖✖✖✖✖✖✖✖✖✖✖

'THE ROYALTY QUESTION'

'It is impossible to deny that H. M. is drawing too
heavily on the credit of her former popularity.'

DESPITE THE OCCASIONAL CHEERS that greeted the Queen when
she did appear in public, both her Household and the Government grew
increasingly concerned by the resentment occasioned by the infrequency
of those occasions on which she agreed to emerge from her purdah.

In the summer of 1869 General Grey decided that the time had come
to make a forceful effort to persuade the Queen to appear in public more
often. He was not convinced that she was as ill as William Jenner said
she was when there was some unwelcome duty to perform. She must be
reminded by the Prime Minister in a peremptory manner of her duty.
She was, with difficulty, persuaded by Gladstone to leave Osborne a few
days before she had intended to do so in order to be in London to deal
with important matters of state, though she insisted that this must on
no account be considered a precedent. Also – performing both ceremonies
on the same day that year – she opened Holborn Viaduct and Blackfriars
Bridge; but these occasions were not a success: as she drove down the
Strand her carriage was hissed.

A few months later, in February 1870, she flatly refused to open
Parliament. It was an unfortunate beginning to a most troublesome year.
That same month the Prince of Wales was required to appear in court to
give evidence in an unsavoury divorce case involving a pretty, unbalanced
woman, Harriet Mordaunt, who had confessed to her husband that she
had committed adultery 'often and in open day' with several men, including His Royal Highness. The Prince strongly protested his innocence; but

he could not deny that he had written Lady Mordaunt several, fortunately quite innocuous, letters. Sir Charles Mordaunt's petition was dismissed on the grounds that since his wife was insane, and was by then consigned to a lunatic asylum, she could not be a party to the suit.

The Queen was convinced of her son's innocence of the charge of adultery; but she did not hesitate to condemn his 'intimate acquaintance with a young married women' which could not fail 'to damage him in the eyes of the middle and lower classes'. She also strongly condemned the society in which he led his fast life, the 'frivolous, selfish and pleasure-seeking' rich. As Sir Charles Dilke observed, the Queen's Court was 'singularly dowdy by the side of the Prince of Wales's'. 'But on the other hand', Dilke added, 'though her servants are shabby, the people about the Queen are more *uniformly* gentlemen and ladies than those about the Prince.'[1]

The Prince, booed at Ascot races and at the theatre, attacked in pamphlets and ridiculed in magazines, countered the Queen's criticisms of his conduct by tentatively admonishing her for hers. 'If you sometimes came to London from Windsor,' he wrote to her, 'and then drove for an hour in the Park (where there is no noise) the people would be overjoyed ... We live in radical times, and the more *People see the Sovereign* the better it is for the *People* and the *Country*.'[2] This was precisely the view of the Royal Household; and, in particular, of Henry Ponsonby.

Henry Ponsonby, who had been appointed one of the Queen's equerries after the Prince Consort's death, had often helped General Grey with his work, and, as a reticent, intelligent man with a fluent pen and a bold clear hand, he had for some time been recognized as his most likely successor. Ponsonby's appointment was not made, however, without considerable opposition from the Queen's family who objected to what they supposed to be his 'extreme radical tendencies'. General Grey had been a Liberal and had once sat in the House of Commons in the Liberal interest for High Wycombe. But Ponsonby's views were supposed to be far more extreme than those of Grey, while his wife's political opinions were notorious. Mary Ponsonby was condemned as being 'clever', a dreadful failing – she actually wrote articles for the *Pall Mall Gazette* – and she had, as even her devoted husband had to admit, 'peculiar views on everything'. Consequently both the Duke of Cambridge, the Queen's cousin, and her son-in-law, Prince Christian, were rigidly opposed to

Ponsonby's appointment. But the Queen, as Ponsonby wrote, 'disregarded the remonstrances and was pleased to appoint me, sending me at the same time a hint through the Dean of Windsor that I was to be cautious in expressing my opinions and not to permit my wife to compromise me in her conversation' – a hint which, when conveyed to Mary Ponsonby, elicited the response that *she* herself had no intention of being compromised 'by being supposed to agree for an instant with the opinions of Court Officials'.

Although Ponsonby's untidy clothes and far too long trousers were a disgrace, and although the Queen had occasion to rebuke him more than once for causing too much rowdy laughter in the Equerries' Room, she liked him from the beginning and recognized in him the kind of qualities which were to make him an exceptional private secretary. He had the ability to get to the root of a problem without wasting time with irrelevancies; he had a good knowledge of the world and of men; he was understanding, patient and industrious. While witty and possessed of a fine sense of the ridiculous, he was also capable of listening carefully to what was said to him by even the most tedious and stupid people without revealing a trace of irritation or boredom. He could express himself well in conversation and also in writing; and he had a lively sense of humour. He did not consider himself a gifted linguist, but he could converse and write letters in French, had a working knowledge of Italian and, though correspondence in German had to be left to the German secretary, he was usually capable, as he used to claim with some pride, of starting a German visitor off in his own language and then receiving 'the resultant prolonged monologue with sufficiently appropriate interjections' to put him at his ease.

Most important of all, Ponsonby understood as well as anyone the Queen's contradictory character. She did not, he said, 'belong to any conceivable category of monarchs or of women. She bore no resemblance to an aristocratic English lady, she bore no resemblance to a wealthy middle-class Englishwoman, nor to any typical Princess of a German court. She was not in the least like the three queens regnant her predecessors ... Moreover she reigned longer than the three other queens put together. Never in her life could she be confused with anyone else, nor will she be in history. Such expressions as "people like Queen Victoria" or "that sort of woman" could not be used about her.'[3]

It was Henry Ponsonby's understanding of the Queen's character that made him so useful a private secretary. Like General Grey he knew just how far he could go on any particular occasion in persuading her to act against her own wishes, and he refused to jeopardize his influence over her by pressing her too hard when he well knew such pressure would merely result in her refusing to discuss the subject again. 'When she insists that 2 and 2 make 5,' he wrote, 'I say that I cannot help thinking they make 4. She replies there may be some truth in what I say, but she knows they make 5. Thereupon I drop the discussion. It is of no consequence and I leave it there.' He contrasted this method with that of a colleague who pursued such controversies, bringing in proofs, arguments and, worst of all, former sayings of her own. 'No one likes this,' Ponsonby added. 'No one can stand admitting they are wrong, women especially; and the Queen can't abide it. Consequently she won't give in.'

Ponsonby's way of dealing with the Queen, in contrast to that of the unnamed colleague, frequently did result in her giving in, or, more often, quietly allowing a matter to drop rather than admitting that she had been wrong.

One trivial, if time-consuming, incident well illustrates Ponsonby's way of dealing with a mistress to whom, he said, advice had always to be given 'in a most gingerly way'. It concerned the arrangements for a holiday abroad, every trifling detail of which had to be submitted for the Queen's approval. Taking the register of servants who were to accompany her she struck all but one off the list of housemaids, maintaining that one housemaid would be quite enough. The staff objected and, as usual, asked Ponsonby to intervene. He did so, and thus recorded the result:

> Of course quite right that only one housemaid should go. I would send to her [another] girl from the Hotel. But stray girls were not always very honest. So I hoped the Queen would not leave things about to tempt her. I got the answer that another housemaid should go from here.[4]

Towards the end of her life, when Ponsonby had become rather forgetful and his handwriting, so she complained, had become difficult to read, she began to find his circuitous way of approaching problems rather irritating. 'He has no backbone,' she complained to her doctor, James Reid, 'is always placid and easily talked over by anybody. He has

Winterhalter's portrait of the Queen with the Prince of Wales in 1846.

The Swiss Cottage at Osborne. A watercolour by William Leighton Leitch.

BELOW LEFT A drawing by the Queen of the Prince of Wales just before his ninth birthday.

BELOW RIGHT The Queen's watercolour of her youngest child, Princess Beatrice, in a smart purple frock covered by a washable dress-saver.

Winterhalter's painting of the Queen holding Prince Arthur, who is being presented by the Duke of Wellington, his godfather, with a casket on the occasion of the child's first birthday on 1 May 1851. In fact the Duke's present was a cup and a model of the throne, but Prince Albert, who stands behind the Queen in the picture, thought the casket, which belonged to the Queen, a more appropriate offering.

Queen Victoria opening the Great Exhibition in 1851. An illustration by André & Sleigh, after a painting by H. C. Selous in Cassell's *History of England*.

Following the German custom of his wife's grandmother, Queen Charlotte, Prince Albert had fir trees put up at Windsor at Christmas 'lighted all over with small tapers'.

Princess Alice in 1861. A portrait by Winterhalter.

Sorrow by Landseer, with Osborne House in the background. When this picture was shown at the Royal Academy in 1865 it prompted salacious speculation about the Queen's relationship with her servant, John Brown.

The Queen's dressing room at Balmoral, relatively free of the tartan furnishings and decoration of other rooms in the house which prompted Lord Rosebery to observe that he thought the drawing room at Osborne the ugliest room in the world until he saw the one at Balmoral.

The Queen's bedroom at Balmoral.

no courage, but agrees with me, and then is talked over by others and agrees with them. He agrees with everybody.'[5]

As General Grey had done, Ponsonby tackled Sir William Jenner about the Queen's refusal to perform her royal duties in the way Ministers required.

> Jenner said he had charge of her health and would do his duty [Ponsonby recorded in a memorandum] ... He would not advise her to do things against her health for a political object. If Ministers did not believe him [when he maintained she was ill] there was nothing he could do about it ... 'But,' I said, 'you could ask her to try – perhaps it would not do her harm. Besides which, it is not for the good of the Government but the existence of the Queen.' No, he would not hear of that.

'People ask how can she attend Gillies' Balls at Balmoral [which she did, staying up until one o'clock in the morning] and not stand a little of London balls?' Ponsonby protested.

'He said (which is very true) that at Gillies' Balls she speaks to none but at London Balls she would be expected to speak to many.'

'But why shouldn't she live more in town and drive about there?'

'Because it makes her head ache.'

'Well, if she is ill how can it be good for her to travel so far to Balmoral?'

'Of course, it is. When people are ill they are often ordered off to a distance at once.'

So, while Jenner stood firm, maintaining that 'his care was her health and not her actions', Ponsonby could do nothing. Nor could her children. Jenner 'positively refused the Crown Princess, Princess Louise and Prince Arthur's entreaties, saying he could be of no use.' Nor could Ministers persuade her to do what she did not want to do. She told the Lord Chancellor that 'she had seen from long experience that the more she yielded to pressure and alarm ... it only encourages further demands and that she is then teased into doing what is bad for her health.'[6]

When she was asked to open Parliament in January 1866 she wrote the Prime Minister a letter of extravagant but not atypical protest:

> The Queen must say that she does feel very bitterly the want of feeling of those who ask the Queen to go to open Parliament . . . Why this wish should be of so unreasonable and unfeeling a nature, as to long to witness the spectacle of a poor, broken-hearted widow, nervous and shrinking, dragged in deep mourning, alone in State as a Show, where she used to go supported by her husband, to be gazed at, without delicacy of feeling, is a thing she cannot understand, and she never could wish her bitterest foe to be exposed to! . . . She owns she resents the unfeelingness of those who have clamoured for it. Of the suffering which it will cause her – nervous as she now is – she can give no idea, but she owns she hardly knows how she will go through it.[7]

'It is impossible to deny that H. M. is drawing too heavily on the credit of her former popularity,' Lord Halifax, the Lord Privy Seal, wrote to Ponsonby, 'and that Crowned Heads as well as other people must do much that was not necessary in former days to meet the altered circumstances and altered tone of modern times . . . The mass of the people expect a King or a Queen to look and play the part. They want to see a Crown and Sceptre and all that sort of thing. They want the gilding for the money. It is not wise to let them think . . . that they could do without a sovereign who lives at Osborne and Balmoral as any private lady might do.'[8]

Referring to 'the Royalty question', Gladstone lamented that 'a meaner cause for the decay of thrones cannot be conceived. It is like the worm which bores the bark of a noble oak tree and so breaks the channel of its life.' One of the Queen's own equerries observed to Gladstone, 'There is only one great capital in Europe where the Sovereign is unrepresented and that capital is London.'[9] Joseph Chamberlain, the Radical politician and future Cabinet Minister, expressed the view in 1871 that 'The republic must come, and at the rate at which we are moving, it will come in our generation.'[10] Charles Bradlaugh, proprietor of the republican weekly periodical, the *National Reformer*, expressed the view that 'the experience of the last nine years [since 1861] proves that the country can do quite well without a monarch and may therefore save the extra expense of monarchy.'[11]

The Queen's seclusion was a recurring topic in almost every newspaper. 'The living have their claims as well as the dead,' a characteristic article in *The Times* averred. 'Every honour that affection and gratitude could pay to the memory of the Prince Consort has been offered [and the time had now come] for the Queen to think of her subjects' claims and the duties of her high station, and not postpone them longer to the indulgence of an unavailing grief.'

The general public agreed. Lady Amberley, Lord John Russell's daughter-in-law, noted in her journal, 'Everyone is abusing the Queen very much for not being in London or Windsor ... No respect or loyalty seems left in the way people allow themselves to talk of the Queen, saying things like, "What do we pay her for if she will not work?" and "She had better abdicate if she is incompetent to do her duty."'[12]

Occasional support came to the Queen both from expected and unexpected quarters. John Bright, the Radical orator and Member of Parliament for Birmingham, in a speech at St James's Hall on 4 December 1866, had declared that he was 'not accustomed to stand up in defence of those who are the possessors of crowns. But I think there has been, by many persons, a great injustice done to the Queen in reference to her desolate widowed position'; and he 'ventured to say this, that a woman – be she the Queen of a great realm, or be she the wife of one of your labouring men – who can keep alive in her heart a great sorrow for the lost object of her life and affection is not at all likely to be wanting in a great and generous sympathy for you.'[13]

The Queen was so touched by this declaration in her favour by Bright, the death of whose first wife had left him 'in the depths of grief, almost of despair', that, when Bright agreed to become President of the Board of Trade in Gladstone's cabinet, the Queen proposed that, as an old man and a Quaker, he should not be required to kneel and kiss hands at the formal ceremony of acceptance of office. Bright accordingly did not kneel but, wearing knee breeches especially made for the occasion, he did kiss the Queen's hand, something Quakers 'in general never do'.*[14]

But Bright's views were shared by few others. Most of his fellow-politicians, of both left and right, agreed with *The Times* and those other newspapers which voiced the same opinions.

---

* Having gone down to 'bask in the Osborne fog of royalty' soon after Bright's appointment as President of the Board of Trade, Lord Clarendon, the Foreign Secretary, reported to the Duchess of Manchester, 'Bright seems to have made a very good impression ... "Eliza" spoke to me of his gentle, kind manner wh: is quite true when he is in the company of ladies. The Maids of Honour made him play Blind Hookey with them & Heaven knows what other traps they set for Quaker virtue ... "Eliza" so far from being afraid of Bright has quite a predilection for him as he has several times defended her in a manner for wh: she is grateful & *can never forget*' (A. L. Kennedy, ed. *My Dear Duchess: Social and Political Letters to the Duchess of Manchester*, 247–8).

44

✹✹✹✹✹✹✹✹✹✹✹✹

'THE PRINCELY PAUPER'

'She must solemnly repeat that unless
her Ministers *support* her . . . she *cannot* go on.'

THE REPERCUSSIONS of the Mordaunt divorce case had scarcely died
away when in the summer of that year of 1870 war broke out between France
and Prussia. At first France was seen in England as the aggressor; but, later,
the Queen was once more in trouble for her widely reported sympathy for
the Germans which flew in the face of the sympathies of her people who
became, as she put it, 'very French'. At a meeting of republicans in October,
after Napoleon III's army had been beaten at Sedan, a French border fortress
on the Meuse, and France had been declared a republic, the Queen's Court
was described, not for the first time, as constituting a mere 'pack of Germans'. Even so, when the defeated French Emperor arrived in England in
March 1871 the Queen greeted him warmly:

> I went to the door with Louise and embraced the Emperor '*comme
> de rigueur*'. It was a moving moment, when I thought of the last time
> he came here in '55, in perfect triumph, dearest Albert bringing him
> from Dover, the whole country mad to receive him, and now! He
> seemed much depressed and had tears in his eyes, but he controlled
> himself and said, '*Il y a bien longtemps que je n'ai vu vôtre Majesté.*'
> He led me upstairs and we went into the Audience Room. He is grown
> very stout and grey and his moustaches are no longer curled or waxed
> as formerly, but otherwise there was the same pleasing, gentle, and
> gracious manner. My children came in with us. The Emperor at once
> spoke of the dreadful and disgraceful state of France.[1]

The month before the Emperor's arrival the Queen had consented to
open Parliament and she agreed to wear a new crown; but it was said

that once again she was stirring herself only because she wanted more money: Prince Arthur, soon to be created Duke of Connaught, was twenty-one that year and in need of an annuity, while, on 21 March, Princess Louise was to marry the Marquess of Lorne, son of the Duke of Argyll, and had to have a dowry.

Yet, having opened Parliament in February, the Queen was most reluctant to delay her departure for Balmoral to prorogue it in August, in spite of a plea from Gladstone and hints from her eldest daughter who composed a letter which was signed by all the Queen's children and children-in-law but which, in the event, was never delivered to her. 'No one has prompted us to write,' this letter ran. 'No one knows except we ourselves ... It is we your children, whose position in the world had been made so good by the wisdom and forethought, and the untiring care of yourself and dear Papa, who now feel how utterly changed things are, and who would humbly entreat you to enquire into the state of public feeling, which appears to us so very alarming.'[2]

The Queen had not prorogued Parliament in person since 1852, she protested. 'What killed her beloved Husband?' she asked in a letter to the Lord Chancellor, Lord Hatherley. 'Overwork & worry – what killed Lord Clarendon [Gladstone's Foreign Secretary who had died suddenly the year before]? The same ... & the Queen, a woman, no longer young [she was now fifty-two] is supposed to be proof against all and to be driven and abused till her nerves and health will give way with hurry and agitation ... She must solemnly repeat that unless her Ministers *support* her ... she *cannot* go on & must give her heavy burden up to younger hands. Perhaps then those discontented people may regret that they broke her down when she might still have been of use.'[3]

Four days after this letter was written the Queen developed a sore throat. She was, she said, feeling 'extremely unwell'. The Household had so often been told that she was poorly when an unwelcome duty was to be performed that few believed her. But when she left for Balmoral on 17 August she really did look ill; and at Balmoral for the whole of the rest of the month and the beginning of the next she filled her diary with accounts of a very painful arm, sleepiness during the day, a 'choking sensation with violent spasms', rheumatic pains and gout. She had never felt so ill 'since typhoid at Ramsgate in 35'. She 'reluctantly agreed' that Joseph Lister, at that time Professor of Clinical Surgery at Edinburgh, should be sent for. On 4 September Lister lanced an abscess in her arm, an operation which, she confessed, made her 'dreadfully nervous' because, so she said, contradicting an earlier assertion, she bore 'pain so badly'. That night she could 'hardly turn over' in her bed, while the next day she could not walk because her gouty foot was so painful. John Brown was required to carry her to bed because she was too heavy for the maids to lift – Lord Stanley had recently described her as 'very large, ruddy and fat'. On 18 October she recorded in her journal:

> A most dreadful night of agonizing pain. No sedative did any good
> ... Had my feet and hands bandaged. My utter helplessness is a
> bitter trial, not even being able to feed myself ... Dictated my
> Journal to Beatrice, which I have done most days lately ... Was
> unable all day hardly able to eat anything.[4]

By the time she was on the way to recovery towards the end of the month she had lost two stone.[5]

Meanwhile, attacks upon the invisibility of the grasping miser, the 'princely pauper', continued apace. A copy of an anonymous pamphlet, attributed to the historian G. O. Trevelyan, Liberal Member for the Border Burghs, entitled *What does she do with it?*, reached Balmoral. In it the author condemned the Queen's parsimony and hoarding of money and calculated that she was squirrelling away no less than £200,000 a year. On 6 November, another Member of Parliament, Sir Charles Dilke, delivered a loudly cheered speech in which he declared that the cost of the Royal Family to the nation had risen to £1,000,000 a year – ten times, so another speaker claimed, the income of the President of the United States – and Dilke suggested that this enormous expense was 'chiefly not waste but mischief'. Even the middle classes, he said, would welcome a republic if it were to be 'free of the political corruption that [hung] about the monarchy'. When, referring to the extravagant number of officials at Court, which still included a salaried Lord High Falconer and a Lithographer-in-Ordinary, Dilke said that one of them was a Court undertaker, a man in the crowded audience called out that it was a pity there was not more work for him to do.*[6]

---

* When he was a boy, Dilke had been presented to the Queen at the Great Exhibition with which his father, Sir Charles Wentworth Dilke, the first baronet, had been closely connected. Years later the Queen said that she remembered stroking his head and that 'she supposed she must have rubbed the hairs the wrong way' (Dilke Papers, quoted in Roy Jenkins, *Sir Charles Dilke*, 20).

A fortnight after Dilke's speech was delivered, on 21 November 1871, a telegram arrived at Balmoral from the Prince of Wales's country house at Sandringham in Norfolk which led the household to fear that this man's wishes might soon be fulfilled. The Prince, at the age of thirty, was dangerously ill with typhoid fever contracted during a visit to Lord Londesborough's house near Scarborough where the noisome drains were soon to be responsible for the deaths of the Earl of Chesterfield as well as the Prince's groom.

45

✳✳✳✳✳✳✳✳✳✳✳

TYPHOID FEVER

'They were suddenly nearly carried away by a stampede
of royalties, headed by the Duke of Cambridge and
brought up by Leopold, going as fast as they could.'

THE QUEEN – while still declining to allow her heir to play any part
in the business of government on the grounds that he was both irrespon-
sible and indiscreet – had at last come to view the Prince of Wales in a
less disagreeable light, even though it continued to rile her that her eldest
son was now so much more popular in the country at large than her far
worthier husband had ever been. He was really 'so full of good and
amiable qualities'. She could not help wishing that he was not always
'gadding about' all over the country and on the Continent; but, when he
was at home, she was sure 'no heir apparent ever was so nice & unpre-
tending as dear Bertie'. 'I am always glad & happy to have him a little
with me,' she wrote, '& I only wish I could see him oftener.'[1] The news
of his serious illness shocked her deeply; and on 29 November 1871 she
hurried to Sandringham to be with him.

Princess Alice was already there, a severe trial to her sister-in-law, the
Princess of Wales, who found her bossy and unsympathetic. Prince Alfred
was also there. His brother, Prince Leopold, was soon to come. So was
the Duke of Cambridge. When the Prince of Wales's two youngest sisters,
Princess Louise and Princess Beatrice, arrived as well, they were obliged
to sleep in the same bed, so crowded had the house become with courtiers,
servants, visiting Ministers and anxious members of the patient's family.
And what 'an extraordinary family' they were, thought Princess Alexandra's Lady of the Bedchamber, Lady Macclesfield. She found it 'quite

342

impossible to keep a house quiet as long as it is swarming with people and really the way in which they all squabble and wrangle and abuse each other destroys one's peace'. The one exception, Lady Macclesfield decided, apart from the Princess of Wales, was the Queen who remained 'charming, so tender and quiet',[2] though not so quiet as to refrain from objecting to her son's habit of keeping all the clocks at Sandringham half an hour fast because of the Princess of Wales's chronic unpunctuality. 'She had them all put back. She thought it a ridiculous habit and a "lie" – so characteristic of her!'[3]

Calm as she contrived to be at Sandringham, however, the Queen could not disguise her apprehension. 'Somehow,' she wrote in her journal on 6 December, 'I always look for bad news & have not much confidence.' Her son had rallied a little soon after her arrival and she had felt able to leave Sandringham for a time; but grave reports had brought her hurrying back and by the 7th he was reported to be 'as bad as ever or worse'. Lady Macclesfield reported to her husband: 'The doctors say that if he does not rally within the next hour a very few more must see the end.'[4] That night Prince Leopold was called to his brother's dressing room and on his way there passed numerous relations and servants and members of the Household, all in their night clothes. 'It was,' he wrote, 'too dreadful to see the poor Queen sitting in the bedroom behind a screen listening to his ravings. I can't tell you what a deep impression it made on me.'[5]

The doctors' subsequent bulletins, five of which were issued during the course of a single day, inspired a poet – generally thought, though probably mistakenly, to be Alfred Austin, later to be appointed Poet Laureate – to write those lines that were to confer upon him an immortality which all Austin's later writings would certainly have denied him:

> Across the wires the electric message came:
> 'He is no better; he is much the same.'

On 12 December the Queen, who was in fearful dread that the Prince would die on the anniversary two days later of his father's death, went to bed 'with the horrid feeling' that she would 'be called up'. The next day the end seemed imminent: her son's temperature had risen to 104°. 'In those heart-rending moments,' she wrote, 'I hardly knew how to pray aright, only asking God if possible to spare my Beloved Child.'[6]

She did not often leave the house, though all the windows were kept tightly closed against the snow and there was such a fusty smell in the crowded rooms that the Duke of Cambridge became convinced that they were all in danger of catching typhoid fever, too. He rushed about the house, sniffing in corners, and jumping up with a startled cry of, 'By George, I won't sit here!' when the Prince of Wales's Private Secretary said that he also had noticed a bad smell in the library. For days the Duke remained 'wild on the subject', insisting on examining all the drains of the house until a man came from the gas company and discovered a leaking pipe.[7]

Fearful as he was of catching typhoid fever, the Duke seemed quite as much alarmed by the Queen. So apparently were the rest of the family. One day Henry Ponsonby was walking in the garden with Prince Alfred's equerry when they 'were suddenly nearly carried away by a stampede of royalties, headed by the Duke of Cambridge and brought up by Leopold, going as fast as they could'. Ponsonby thought that a mad bull must be on the rampage. But the stampeding royalties 'cried out: "The Queen! The Queen!" and [everyone] dashed into the house again and waited behind the door until the road was clear.'[*8]

The Queen herself continued to endeavour to keep calm and controlled, but distress at her son's plight and concern for her daughter-in-law sometimes proved too much for her. One day she burst into tears and cried out, 'There can be no hope!' Indeed, for days on end there seemed little reason to expect that the Prince could recover as he lay tossing and sweating in his bed, frequently in delirium, making all kinds of wild remarks, revealing guilty secrets of his past.

But then the crisis passed. On 14 December he was, as his mother said, brought back from the 'very *verge* of the grave'. The next day, when she went into his room, he smiled, kissed her hand, and said, 'Oh! dear Mama, I am so glad to see you. Have you been here all this time?'[9]

Two months later the Prince, 'quite himself again', went to recuperate at Osborne. He was 'gentler and kinder than ever', the Queen contentedly told his eldest sister. 'And there is something different which I can't exactly express. It is like a new life – all the trees and flowers give him

---

* This was by no means the only example of her family's fear of the Queen. In March 1900, the Duke of York spoke to Lord Esher about 'the impropriety of the Queen going to Italy at this moment. I thought he talked a good deal of sense. They none of them dare, however, to tackle H. M.!' (*Journal and Letters of Reginald, Viscount Esher*, 1934, i, 258–9).

pleasure, as they never used to do, and he was quite pathetic over his small wheelbarrow and little tools at the Swiss Cottage. He is constantly with Alix, and they seem hardly ever apart.'[10]

The Queen was naturally much against the sort of public thanksgiving which Gladstone suggested would be appropriate to the occasion. But the Government, sensing the mood of the people, insisted that a procession through London followed by a service in St Paul's Cathedral would satisfy a universal demand for some such celebration. Princess Alexandra agreed with them. So the Queen gave way; and having done so, she saw to it that 'the *show*', as she sardonically termed it, was carried out properly. There would be an open carriage; there would be banners and flags in the streets; the bells would ring in the church towers and steeples. Of course, John Brown would be sitting on the box of her carriage 'in his vy handsome full dress'.

The subsequent celebration, so Gladstone gratefully declared, was perhaps the most satisfactory that London had ever witnessed. It was a quite 'extraordinary manifestation of loyalty and affection'. The royal carriage, an open landau drawn by six horses, was greeted by deafening cheers all along the route. The Queen, her black dress trimmed with miniver and a white feather in her bonnet, obligingly entering into the spirit of the occasion, waved and nodded to the crowds and, raising her son's hand up in her own, kissed it with fond tenderness.[11] 'People,' she said, 'cried.' It was 'a day of triumph ... Everywhere troops lined the streets, and there were fifteen military bands stationed at intervals along the whole route, who played "God save the Queen" and "God bless the Prince of Wales", as the carriage approached which evoked fresh outbursts of cheering. I saw the tears in Bertie's eyes ... It was a most affecting day.'[12]

The enthusiasm was nearly universal. The feelings of the country towards the monarchy had changed almost overnight. Republicanism as a significant force in British politics, already damaged by the excess of the Paris Commune, had suffered a blow from which it was never to recover. As the Prince of Wales's friend Lord Carrington said, the monarchy was now safe. When Charles Dilke again brought up the question of the Queen's expenditure in the House of Commons, he was shouted down.[13]

Despite her cheerful demeanour on that day of thanksgiving, however, the Queen was still not yet ready to show herself in public or to grant audiences to her Ministers more often than was strictly necessary. When in the summer of 1872 Edward Cardwell, the Secretary for War, enraged her by paying a tribute to the troops in his own name rather than in hers, Henry Ponsonby was brave enough to suggest that she must be prepared to accept that such things were bound to happen so long as her Ministers saw her so rarely.

Nor was the Queen yet prepared to allow – even after twelve years of widowhood – any more of those splendid entertainments that had formerly been given to such royal visitors as Tsar Nicholas I, the King of Saxony, King Louis-Philippe, Napoleon III and King Victor Emmanuel II. Before the Prince Consort's death, in 1841 alone, no fewer than 113,000 people had been entertained to dinner at Windsor. But after 1861 the Queen had persistently declined to have strange foreign royalties to stay at Windsor. She was, she said, 'UTTERLY incapable of entertaining any Royal personage as she would wish to do, except those who are very nearly related to her, and for whom she need not alter her mode of life.'[14]

To welcome the Sultan of Turkey, who had come to England in 1867, she had permitted some appropriate celebrations and had allowed her band to play for 'the first time these 6 sad years'. But she had done so reluctantly; she had declined to come down from Balmoral a single day early – even though warned that English influence, which was then paramount at Constantinople, might well be damaged if the Sultan were shown less respect than he had been in Berlin and Paris – and she was very glad when it was time to say goodbye to her 'oriental brother' whose visit was concluded by a naval review in a turbulent sea at Spithead during which he had to go repeatedly below deck to be sick.[15]

The Queen of Hawaii, a 'peculiarly civilized ... savage', who later arrived on an official visit, was asked to come to Windsor at three o'clock in the afternoon so that the Queen, who gave her no more than a few minutes of her time, would not have to ask her to luncheon.

She had been equally unwelcoming towards the King of Sweden, who had had to stay at the Swedish Legation, Prince Humbert of Italy, who was told there was no room at Windsor Castle and had been put up at the White Hart in the town, and Khedive Ismail of Egypt who was grudgingly granted a night's hospitality at Windsor (provided his entourage was small) with a strong protest 'against the pretension raised that she should at her *own expense*, in the *only Palace* of her own ... entertain all Foreign Potentates WHO *choose* to come here for their own amusement'.[16]

In 1873 the Queen was with great difficulty persuaded to welcome the Shah of Persia for reasons which Gladstone assured her were of the utmost political importance. She was very irritable and fidgety before his visit, so Henry Ponsonby recorded, insisting that the Government must contribute to the cost of the entertainment of the Shah's entourage, asking crossly why he was termed 'Imperial'. 'Because he is the Shah-in-Shah,' Ponsonby replied. 'Well, that's no reason!' she snapped and had the title removed from the programme.[17] Then she twice changed her mind about the date of a military review to be held in the Shah's honour in the Park.

The Queen, Ponsonby had to admit, had some reason for her agitation. Reports had reached London of the Shah's 'uncivilized notions and habits', his custom of 'wiping his wet hands on the coat-tails of the gentleman next to him without compunction', of sacrificing a cock to the rising sun, of his clumsiness with knife and fork and his habit of drinking out of the spout of a teapot. It was rumoured that he intended to leave three of his wives behind but that several other ladies would be included in his suite to console him in their absence, that he generally dined alone and preferred to have his meals, which usually included roasted lambs cooked on tripods, served on a carpet. 'For this purpose,' the Household were warned, 'a movable carpet [which, after he had gone, was found to be severely burned] should be kept ready whereupon *his* servants will put the dishes etc. brought to the door by the English servants ... The Shah does not like to have his meats cut up. Rice, lamb, mutton, fowls are favourite dishes. The cuisine should be somewhat *relevée*.' It must be expected, the British Ambassador in Berlin added, that the Shah might throw his arm round the Queen's chair at formal dinners, 'put his fingers into dishes, or take food out of his mouth to look at it after it has been chewed, or fling it under the table if it does not suit his taste'.[18] He might also make improper suggestions to the Queen's ladies; and might well be rude to them: when Baroness Burdett-Coutts was presented to him he looked in her face and, summing up two of the few words of French he knew, exclaimed, '*Quelle horreur!*'[19]

As it happened, however, the Shah turned out to be not as *outré* as the Queen had expected. He was 'fairly tall and not fat', with a 'fine countenance and very animated', dignified and pleasant. At first she felt 'very shy' with him as they sat next to each other in full state in the middle of the White Drawing Room, surrounded by English and Persian Princes and Princesses; but since he was not in the least shy with her, she soon overcame her embarrassment. He showed no inclination to eat strangely in her presence, contenting himself mostly with fruit and iced water handed to him by his cup-bearer. He was covered with jewels, with immense rubies serving as buttons in his diamond-studded coat, with epaulettes of emeralds, and an aigrette of diamonds in his astrakhan hat. But she, too, wore splendid jewels, the largest of her pearls and the Koh-i-Noor diamond; so she did not feel overshadowed. On the advice of the Prince of Wales she invested him with the Order of the Garter, although he was a Moslem; and, having kissed her hand, he presented her with two orders in return while the Grand Vizier helped to save her headdress from falling off. She also gave him a miniature of herself set in diamonds which, so she heard with profound satisfaction, he had kissed publicly 'with reverence' before his departure from Windsor railway station. Most gratifying of all, at luncheon in the Oak Room, as bagpipers marched up and down, he had told her that he had had her *Leaves from the Journal of Our Life in the Highlands* specially translated into Persian.[20]

46

✳✳✳✳✳✳✳✳✳✳✳

MAIDS-OF-HONOUR

'I was more than astonished, I was rather *angry*.
I did not expect my Maids-of-Honour to be
snapped up before *my very nose*.'

SUCH EXCITEMENTS AS WERE AFFORDED by the visits of the Sultan
and the Shah to Windsor were still very rare. Yet by the time of the
Shah's visit in 1873 the Queen had at last outgrown the worst of her grief.
She was seen to smile more often, and to laugh. She began once more
to record in her diary incidents that had amused her; her letters became
more cheerful; she brought herself to play nostalgic tunes on her piano,
and she began to dance again – she was still dancing ('like a pot', a
German prince whose English was not strong enough for the compliment
informed her) at Windsor when she was seventy – she told funny stories
about herself and was fond of relating how one clear and starlit night
she had opened her bedroom window to look out into the dark sky and
a sentry at the foot of the Castle wall, thinking she must be a housemaid,
'began to address her in most affectionate and endearing terms. The
Queen at once drew her curtains but was simply delighted at what had
happened.'[1] She was still capable of exercising an undoubted charm which
Randall Davidson described as 'irresistible'.[2]

There was no relaxation, though, in the propriety that the memory
of Albert's strict moral sense had emphasized. The Queen, as her husband
had required of her, demanded impeccable discretion in conduct as well
as in conversation. To satisfy her sense of decorum people whose birth
or duties brought them into her presence must not merely be innocent,
they must never have appeared to be guilty. They must also conform to

those rules of conduct she had established for her household. Gentlemen, for instance, must wear black frock coats in her presence, even at Balmoral; maids-of-honour must never receive any man, even their brothers, in their own rooms; they must entertain them as best they could in the waiting room downstairs; and they must always be ladylike in their demeanour and conversation: one of them who was indelicate enough to complain of rheumatism in her legs was coldly informed by the Queen that, in her own youth, ladies 'did not have legs'. Another was considered to be wearing too much make-up. 'Dear General Grey' will tell her so, the Queen commanded. But the General himself bravely objected when Her Majesty's message was conveyed to him. 'Dear General Grey,' he said, 'will do nothing of the kind.'

Much was required of the eight maids-of-honour besides propriety of behaviour. Paid £300 a year, they were divided into pairs and expected to be on duty a month at a time for three months of the year. When she was appointed, Marie Adeane had to answer the following questions:

'1. Could I speak, read and write French and German?

2. Play the piano and read easily at sight in order to play duets with Princess Beatrice?

3. Ride?

4. Was I engaged or likely to be engaged to be married?'[3]

It was also understood that maids-of-honour would additionally be competent at needlework and sketching and be familiar with the rules of card games. They would be expected to converse amiably and intelligently to their neighbours at dinner, to be agreeable companions to the Queen when required to accompany her in her morning or afternoon rides, and, at all times, to be models of discretion. They must not keep diaries.[4]

It was also taken for granted that neither the maids-of-honour nor any other member of the Household would get married without the risk of incurring the Queen's strong disapproval. When James Reid, who was appointed her Resident Medical Attendant in 1881 and knighted in 1895, had the audacity to become engaged to one of her maids-of-honour, Susan Baring, Lord Revelstoke's daughter, the Queen was 'dumbfounded'. For weeks she refused to allow the engagement to be announced, while Reid complained to his fiancée that it was '*ridiculous* to have to submit to be treated like children'.[5]

I must tell you of a marriage wh. annoys me vy. much, [the Queen wrote to her eldest daughter] Sir J. Reid !!! and my M. of H. Susan Baring. It is incredible. How she cld. accept him I cannot understand! If I had been younger I wld. have let him go rather – but at my age it wld. be hazardous & disagreeable so he remains!! ... It is too tiresome and I can't conceal my annoyance. I have never said a word to her yet. It is a gt. mesalliance for her but he has money of his own.[6]

To another of her maids-of-honour, Elizabeth Bulteel, the Queen remarked, 'I was more than astonished, I was rather *angry*. I did not expect my Maids-of-Honour to be snapped up before *my very nose*.'[7]

It was five weeks before the Queen could bring herself to offer Reid her good wishes and then she felt compelled to add that she thought their future position would present 'many difficulties'. She trusted that they would 'both do their utmost to lessen as much as possible the unavoidable inconvenience to the Queen' and that Reid would 'still faithfully devote himself to his duties as in the past', in accordance with a set of regulations which she had already submitted to him.[8]

It was said at the time that the Queen forgave Reid only when he amused her by apologizing for getting married and promising never to do it again.

Annoyed as she had been with Sir James Reid, she was equally so when Marie Adeane asked Princess Beatrice to tell the Queen that she 'hoped to be married' to Bernard Mallet, A. J. Balfour's Private Secretary. 'This raised such a storm,' Marie Adeane wrote after receiving a cross letter from the Queen accusing her of inconstancy and informing her: 'You will easily understand that *this* has disappointed me *very* much.' The Queen 'told Lady Churchill that she was terribly vexed'; and weeks later the matter was 'still a sore point'. Eventually, however, all was forgiven, and when Miss Adeane went to say goodbye the Queen was so kind that the young girl burst into tears. 'I really do love the Queen so much,' she told her mother, 'and it pains me to vex her.'[9]

Demanding as she was – thinking nothing of taking the maids-of-honour out driving on the bitterest of days and, not feeling the cold herself, oblivious to her companions' shivering – the older the Queen grew the more securely she commanded the affection as well as the respect of her ladies, for, inconsiderate as she so often was, she was also capable of great kindness and understanding sympathy. In the same contradictory way, she was alternately almost painfully honest and capable of the most devious machinations, prudish and tolerant, hard-headed and sentimental, artless and acute, combining sound common sense with outlandish prejudices, real and pretended.

While frequently expressing her wish to fight alongside her brave soldiers and her pleasure when women succeeded in what were supposed to be male preserves, she was firmly opposed to their entering the professions, particularly the medical profession – the prospect of young girls and men entering the dissecting room together was an 'awful idea'.[10] The campaign for women's suffrage was a 'mad wicked folly': Lady Amberley who supported it 'ought to get a good whipping'.[11] Education 'ruined the health of the higher classes uselessly' and rendered the 'working classes unfitted for good servants and labourers'.[12]

She was 'Coburgized from head to foot' and took 'the part of foolish foreign royalties with extraordinary zeal'. Yet, if on many occasions she was absurdly prejudiced and unreasonable, she was essentially, as Henry Ponsonby recognized, a woman of good sense. She was obstinate but rarely obtuse. When far cleverer people were wrong, she was often instinctively right. As Lord Salisbury observed, she had a deeper understanding of the passing moods of her people than many politicians who spent far more time among them than she did.[13] Both Lord Salisbury, her last Prime Minister, and Henry Ponsonby recognized that in dealing with her one had not only to take advantage of her mercurial moods, as well as what she felt to be the state of her health, but also to try to understand her complex and contradictory character.

47

SECRETARIES AND MINISTERS

'People were taken by surprise
by the sheer force of her personality.'

AMONG THE MANY RULES which the Household were required to observe was an edict that there must be no smoking in any room which the Queen might enter, or, indeed, in the grounds of any of her residences, though she herself had been seen at a summer picnic lighting a cigarette and 'puffing very delicately' to keep midges away.[1]

Nor were her secretaries allowed to smoke when handling papers she might have to touch. Before she was persuaded – apparently by John Brown – that a little tobacco smoke was 'no bad thing to have about the hoose', cards were framed and hung upon the walls of the royal residences calling attention to the prohibition against smoking; and visitors to Windsor waited until the Queen went to bed and they could go along to the billiard room, the only place in the Castle where smoking was tolerated.[2] But the atmosphere in the billiard room was scarcely more relaxed than it was in the drawing room, particularly when the Queen's second son Prince Alfred was there, since the Duke was a most loquacious and boring talker. 'The Duke of Edinburgh occupies the chair and talks about himself by the hour,' Henry Ponsonby told his wife. 'Those who go [to the billiard room] are quite exhausted. Prince Henry [of Battenberg] has given up smoking in consequence.'[3]

Once Count Hatzfeldt, who could not make the effort for the long journey to the billiard room, yet 'could not live without a cigar', was reduced to lying on his bedroom floor and blowing the smoke up the chimney.[4] The King of Saxony was less discreet and profoundly shocked the Court by having the audacity to walk up the grand staircase with a cigar in his mouth.[5] Courtiers who smoked secretly took to carrying peppermints in their pockets, for there was no telling when a summons to the Queen might come; and even to be in church was no excuse for being late in answering it.[6]

Much as her ladies grew fond of her, she undoubtedly became an increasingly difficult, capricious and demanding employer as the years passed, frequently cross when, having sought advice, the counsel offered did not coincide with her own wishes. Disliking interviews in which her opinions, requests or orders might be called into question, she required that all matters, even those of a most trivial nature, should be committed to paper. Her private secretaries accordingly had an enormous amount of paperwork to get through every day, some of it of the utmost importance to the successful conduct of the Government's affairs, much else of no importance at all, each particular point for her consideration having to be submitted on a separate sheet.

There were requests for her to accept books, to grant permission to copy pictures, to approve the details of Court functions, to confirm appointments and dismissals, to give her assent to Government policy, to select the names of clergymen suitable as preachers at Osborne, to decree the punishment to be inflicted upon a drunken footman at Windsor. There was one exchange of memoranda, which lasted for weeks, about the installation of a lift at Buckingham Palace; there was another, which continued for even longer, about the rights and duties of the Queen's band. The Queen's replies to Henry Ponsonby's submissions came back either in the form of terse minutes at the foot of the document concerned or in letters, written hurriedly and sometimes indecipherably. One of the Queen's letters, in which she complained of the 'atrocious & disgraceful writing' of a young nobleman in the Colonial Office, took Ponsonby a quarter of an hour to get through. But at least, when they had at length been deciphered, her decisions were concise and definite. For example, Sir Frederick Leighton, President of the Royal Academy, asked permission to have a copy taken of a portrait of the Queen by Sir Martin Archer Shee. The Queen's refusal ran: 'It is a monstrous thing no more like me than anything in the world.' Another artist asked leave to engrave one of the pictures he had painted for her: 'Certainly not. They are not good and he is very pushing.' A lady wrote to ask if her daughter might be granted permission to gain material for an article on the Royal Mews: 'This is a dreadful and dangerous woman. She better take the facts from the other papers.' Oscar Wilde sought leave 'to copy some of the poetry written by the Queen when younger': 'Really what will people not say & invent. Never cd. the Queen in her whole life write *one line of poetry* serious or comic or make a Rhyme even. This is therefore all *invention* & *a myth*.'* Would the Queen graciously assent to the new medical school at Edinburgh being named after her? 'Yes, on *one condition* viz: that *no* rooms for vivisection are included in it.'†

So, day after day, the ebb and flow of paper ceaselessly continued: Canon Dalton must not repeat grace in Latin. It was a mistake to say the chaplain at Hampton Court had given satisfaction; he never did so and was 'most interfering and disagreeable'. Neither the Dean of Westminster nor the Dean of Christ Church was to be allowed to preach at Osborne; the sermons of the first were far too long and those of the second like lectures. With infinite care and patience Ponsonby transmitted the Queen's instructions, tactfully altering the wording so as to give the least offence, writing all the letters himself, for up till 1878 he had no assistant.[7]

---

* The Queen was greatly offended when, after the death of her son-in-law, the Emperor Frederick III, in June 1888, Oscar Wilde arrived at Windsor to write a report for the *Telegraph* on the funeral service to be held in St George's Chapel. She did, however, allow him to look round the Chapel where, so Henry Ponsonby said, 'he was most affected'. Wilde entertained a high opinion of Queen Victoria. After his disgrace, when he was living in France, he gave a party to celebrate her Diamond Jubilee, inviting sixteen schoolboys who were regaled with an immense cake inscribed with the words *Jubilé de la Reine Victoria* in pink sugar and who sang 'God Save the Queen' as well as the Marseillaise. Wilde, who had previously declared that the three great personalities of the nineteenth century were Napoleon, Victor Hugo and Queen Victoria, was asked if he had ever met her. He replied that he had. He spoke admiringly of her appearance – 'a ruby mounted in jet' – her walk and her regal demeanour (Richard Ellmann, *Oscar Wilde*, 509).

† The Queen had always had a horror of cruelty to animals. When the Crown Princess wrote to tell her of a 'stupid jager' who had shot her 'dear little cat', hung her on a tree and cut off her nose, her mother wrote to tell her how 'horrified' and 'distressed' she was: 'It is monstrous. The man ought to be hung on a tree. I could cry with you as I adore my pets . . . We always put a collar with V R on our pet cats and that preserves them. Our keeper once shot a pet one of Beatrice's. Keepers are very stupid but none would dream of mutilating an animal here! I think it right and only due to the affection of dumb animals . . . to mourn for them truly and deeply' (*Beloved Mama: Private Correspondence of Queen Victoria and the German Crown Princess*, ed. Roger Fulford, 87). When the Windsor buck-hounds were about to be abolished in 1892 she was reported to be 'delighted': she had 'always disliked that form of sport' (*Journals and Letters of Reginald Brett*, i, 160). Lady Holland had been amused in December 1844 when the 'dear little Queen asked for the life of an ox to be spared' at the Cattle Show 'because it had licked the hand of Prince Albert!' (*Elizabeth, Lady Holland to Her Son, 1821–1845*, ed. the Earl of Ilchester, 1946, 221).

Reading and answering letters occupied a large part of the Queen's secretaries' time abroad as well as at home, though many of those received on the Continent – such as one offering for sale a red, white and blue cat, and another addressed to 'Madam and dear Mother', asking her 'to give a little thought' to the son whom she had 'abandoned in India' – were not deemed worthy of reply.[8]

The paperwork, burdensome as it was, constituted the least tiresome of Ponsonby's duties. He was constantly importuned by seekers after honours and titles, many of whose shameless petitions he did not trouble to pass on to the Queen. He was also constantly being called upon to take up the grievances and pass on the complaints of the numerous minor royalties who 'hovered at a distance round the Court', as well as to settle quarrels and to pacify the ruffled feelings of those within the Household who had been affronted either by their colleagues or rivals, or, as was often the case, by the Queen's lack of consideration. One such complainant was the Marchioness of Ely, a lady of the bedchamber, a timid, nervous and perpetually flustered widow suffering from some form of speech defect which compelled her to convey messages from the Queen in a kind of 'mysterious whispering' which Ponsonby did not always 'strain his ears to hear'. Her complaints – made to Sir Thomas Biddulph, Master of the Household, who passed them on to Ponsonby – were that the demands of the Queen were 'killing her' and that Her Majesty had refused permission for Lady Ely's son to go to see her. She was, however, reluctant to make a fuss. 'Perhaps,' she said, 'the Queen would not like it.' 'It shows,' Biddulph reported to Ponsonby, 'her absurd fear of the Queen.'[9]

Ponsonby's services were required not only as a mediator between the Queen and her family and intimidated ladies but also in the settlement of disputes occasioned either by the huffiness of the German Secretary, Hermann Sahl – who was frequently so put out by some real or imagined slight that he refused to come down to meals – or by the squabbles of the Household doctors, often provoked by Sir William Jenner, a Tory of the most extreme kind, much given to outbursts of wild invective against Gladstone's Government which may well have been approved by the Queen but which seemed outrageous to Ponsonby. 'He is good at repartee and roars at his success,' Ponsonby told his wife after one particularly rowdy dinner at Osborne. 'He roundly abused Carlingford [Gladstone's Lord Privy Seal] and Lord Cairns [the former Lord Chancellor who was

very deaf] because they could not understand him. I refuted an argument
of his which he said he did not use. "Why," I exclaimed, "you said so
just now." His eyes disappeared and in a calm voice he said, "I strongly
advise you to consult an aurist, the first aurist in London, there is something extraordinarily wrong about your ears." '[10]

Ponsonby was fond of Jenner, however, despite his loud cantanker-
ousness and reactionary views. He also liked James Reid who, on his first
arrival at Court, was informed that he could not, as an ordinary doctor,
dine with the gentlemen of the Household as this would be a breach of
the Queen's instructions for the social acceptance of members of his
profession. Not at all put out by this, Reid began to give dinners of his
own to which many members of the Household preferred to go rather
than to endure the dullness and constraints of their own dining room.[11]

It was to men like Reid that Ponsonby turned for relief from the
appalling dullness of court life. This dullness was never more oppressive
than it was at Balmoral, to which the Queen remained devoted because
of its association with her happy married days and which her Ministers
abhorred, not only because they wasted so much of their time travelling
there when they were required to attend upon the Queen, but also because
they were so uncomfortable when they did get there.

Sir Henry Campbell-Bannerman, who was there one winter as minister-in-attendance when the snow was thick on the ground, reported to
his wife:

> It is the funniest life conceivable: like a convent. We meet at meals,
> breakfast 9.45, lunch 2, dinner 9: and when we have finished each
> is off to his cell . . . In this weather, I spend the whole day reading
> alone in my room . . . The Castle . . . carpeted & curtained in tartan
> . . . is all intersected by long, narrow passages, ending in baize doors
> and I could not find my way . . . It has been a perfectly dreadful
> day. Snowing ever since 10 a.m. . . . I drove to church at Crathie
> . . . My companions envied me my nice fur coat . . .
>
> The amusing thing is the way [the Household] lament the
> dullness. Certainly the actual dinner is triste enough, every one
> half whispering to their neighbour . . . They are all so sick of each
> other they jump at a stranger.[12]

There were compensations, though: he 'got on very well' with both
Princess Louise and Princess Beatrice. It was 'really a different thing'

when Princess Louise was of the company; while Sir Henry Ponsonby was 'a perfect brick – so natural & unaffected through it all: he makes it endurable'. He was a fund of amusing stories. He told Campbell-Bannerman one of Mrs Gladstone writing a letter: 'Dear Lord Borthwick, will you let my son fish in your waters at Invercauld?' and receiving the reply, 'Dear Mrs Gladstone, I am not a Lord, I do not live at Invercauld, & I have no fish.'

The Queen, so Campbell-Bannerman heard, was 'always either very serious or all smiles'. When summoned to dine at her table one evening, he himself was 'quite fatigued' by 'a long & very animated conversation with her' while a band – '*quite* charming', 'so beautiful', in her opinion – played in the corridor outside. At a subsequent dinner, 'rather a more dégagé party altogether than usual', the Queen was 'very merry over some old Aunts of hers who when she was a girl used old-fashioned pronunciations – obleege, goold for gold, ooman for woman, ospital for hospital etc. etc.'*[13]

Life at Balmoral would not have been so tedious for members of the Household had they been allowed more freedom. But everything to do with the running of their lives was under the Queen's own strict control. She decided the precise time of their arrival and departure; she directed that they must never leave the house until she herself had gone out; when they did go out they must use only those particular ponies which, divided into five categories, were allocated to their use. Maids-of-honour must not talk to the gentlemen unless accompanied by a chaperone; on Sundays everyone had to go to church.

Demanding and difficult as she could be there were few members of her Household who were not eventually captivated by her capricious charm, the delightful smile which transformed the severity of the grumpy expression caught in the photographs of her that she so liked to have taken. The Dean of Windsor, Randall Davidson, attempted to define this charm:

---

* Gladstone was one of the few Ministers who enjoyed life at Balmoral. 'I bade farewell reluctantly to Balmoral,' he told his wife on leaving the place as minister-in-attendance in 1871, 'for it is as homelike as any place away from home can be, and wonderfully safe from invasions' (Roy Jenkins, *Gladstone*, 347). To Lord Rosebery life at Balmoral seemed like 'one perpetual and astounding meal . . . The luncheon . . . has two distinguishing features on Sunday. The first is that it begins with mutton broth; and the second is the introduction of an odious drink called birch wine. On tasting it I remarked that I thought the bottle was corked' (Robert Rhodes James, *Rosebery*, 66).

I think it was the combination of absolute truthfulness and simplicity with the instinctive recognition and quiet assertion of her position of Queen ... I have known many prominent people but with hardly one of them was it found by all and sundry so easy to speak freely and frankly ... I have sometimes wondered whether the same combination of qualities would have been effective in a person of stately or splendid appearance. May it have been that the very lack of those physical advantages, when combined with her undeniable dignity of word and movement, produced what was in itself a sort of charm? People were taken by surprise by the sheer force of her personality. It may seem strange, but it is true that as a woman she was both shy and humble ... But as Queen she was neither shy nor humble, and asserted her position unhesitatingly.[14]

48

REGINA ET IMPERATRIX

'Oh! that Englishmen were now what they were!!
But we shall assert our rights – our position –
& "Britons never will be slaves" will be our Motto.'

On 24 May 1874 Queen Victoria celebrated her fifty-fifth birthday. Three months previously she had been delighted when, in the general election of that year, the Conservatives were returned to power with their first clear majority over the Liberals since 1841 and Mr Gladstone, protesting that he 'deeply desired' what he called 'an interval between Parliament and the grave', decided to retire.

Released from the oppressive presence of the 'old hypocrite' and basking once more in the affectionate flattery of Disraeli, the Queen began to take a far more enthusiastic interest in public affairs than she had ever done before in her life and allowed herself to be persuaded by cajoling encouragement, sometimes with the support of John Brown, to do things no one else could have induced her to do. 'Disraeli has got the length of her foot exactly,' commented Henry Ponsonby. 'He seems to me always to speak in a burlesque . . . with his tongue in his cheek . . . He communicates . . . boundless professions of love and loyalty. He is most clever . . . In fact, I think him cleverer than Gladstone.'[1]

The Queen was well aware of the wiles and coaxing blandishments which Disraeli used in his attempt to impose his will upon her. 'He had a way when we differed,' she told Lord Rosebery wistfully after Disraeli's death, 'of saying, "Dear Madam" so persuasively', as he put his head on one side, his ringlets, dyed a deep black, falling over his temples.[2]

Persuasive as he was, however, he could not always get his way with her; and on occasions she contrived to get her own way with him. She did so, for example, with the Public Worship Regulation Bill which Disraeli would have liked to dispense with but which the Queen insisted was a necessary corrective to the extreme ritualists who were introducing papist practices into the Church of England. She also had her way over the Royal Titles Act which gave the Queen the right to style herself Empress of India at a politically inconvenient time. She had long wanted this imperial title which so many sovereigns like the King of Prussia had acquired and which enabled those who held it – as it enabled the Emperor of Russia whose designs in the Far East were notorious – to arrogate to themselves and their children dignities and precedence which she felt demeaning to herself and her own. 'I am an Empress,' she had announced one day in 1873 when she was certainly not, '& in common conversation am sometimes called Empress of India.' Why then, she wanted to know, had she never 'officially assumed this title?' She felt she ought to do so and desired to have 'preliminary enquiries made'.[3]

Disraeli, though he had no objection to the idea itself, did object to the introduction of the Bill at a time when the Liberal press would be able to make the most of the widespread opposition to it. But he did not want to disappoint 'the Faery'; and so he instructed the Lord Chancellor to put the announcement into the Queen's speech just after the paragraph referring to a forthcoming visit which the Prince of Wales was to make to India. 'What might have been looked upon as an ebullition of individual vanity' would then 'bear the semblance of deep and organised policy'.

The struggle to get the Bill passed was long and tiring; and Disraeli, who was suffering from gout, asthma and bronchitis, was seriously affected by the strain. But on 12 May 1876 the Queen was declared an empress and thereafter could sign herself with pride *Regina et Imperatrix*.[4]

Delighted with her new title, the Queen was reported to be 'in ecstasies', too, when Disraeli – borrowing £4,000,000 from Baron Rothschild while Parliament was in recess – bought the bankrupt Khedive of Egypt's shares in the Suez Canal on behalf of Her Majesty's Government. 'It is just settled,' Disraeli wrote to her triumphantly. 'You have it, Madam.'[5] Accepting it with gratitude, the Queen considered the purchase yet another example of her Prime Minister's '*very lofty views*' of her country's proper place in the world, besides being 'a blow against Bismarck'. She was confirmed in this opinion of him when troubles in the still huge though crumbling and ramshackle Turkish Empire showed how much 'greater' he was than Gladstone.

Never much concerned with the plight of oppressed nations and racial minorities struggling for freedom, Disraeli was disinclined to pay close attention to reports of the mistreatment of Christian subjects by their Turkish masters; and was concerned only lest the other great powers might profit from interference. When reports reached London that thousands of Bulgarian peasants had been murdered by Turkish irregular troops he affected to suppose that the stories of the massacre were mere 'coffee-house babble', referring to the 'atrocities' in inverted commas as though they were the figment of some inventive journalist's imagination. The Queen was rightly inclined at first to take the stories more seriously. 'She don't like the Turks,' Henry Ponsonby said, 'hates them more because of their atrocities.' But then Gladstone, equally outraged by the stories and sensing that the time had come to emerge from his premature retirement, helped to alter her view by giving voice to the horrified outrage of the British people in his famous pamphlet *The Bulgarian Horrors and the Question of the East*, which, castigating the Turks as 'the one great anti-human specimen of humanity', sold 200,000 copies within a month and brought large crowds of demonstrators to rallies all over London. Well aware that Gladstone's passionate protest was far more in tune with the nation's feelings than his own dismissive cynicism, Disraeli hotly denounced the pamphlet as 'contemptible', 'vindictive and ill-written', the product of an 'unprincipled maniac, perhaps the greatest ... of all the Bulgarian horrors'. The Queen was quite as condemnatory. Gladstone, that 'half-madman', was 'a mischief-maker and firebrand', whose conduct was 'shameful and most reprehensible'. The Turks, whose cruelty had previously been inexcusable, were now seen to have been reacting against the Russians, the Slavs' traditional protectors. And in her fury against the Russians on whose shoulders rested 'the *blood* of the murdered Bulgarians', and whose policies were seen as directed towards mastery in the East, the Queen became positively bellicose.[6] To demonstrate her support of her Prime Minister's 'Imperial policy' as against Gladstone's 'sentimental eccentricity', she not only opened Parliament in February 1877 but also went to a well-publicized luncheon with Disraeli at Hughenden Manor, his country house in Buckinghamshire, a visit which prompted a vehement supporter of Gladstone insultingly to jeer at 'the Jew in his drunken insolence' having had the Queen to eat with him 'ostentatiously ... in his ghetto'.[7]

As passions rose and quarrels grew ever more bitter in one of the fiercest political arguments that has ever erupted in England, Disraeli became increasingly anti-Russian. But while declaring that England's military resources were inexhaustible, and that once she entered into a war she would not stop fighting till right was done, he merely wished to threaten war rather than wage it, in the hope that peace might be preserved without loss of honour. The Queen, on the other hand, was less restrained. In music halls her people raucously sang the chorus to a popular song which added a new word to the English language, and she could not but sympathize with their sentiments:

> We don't want to fight, but, BY JINGO if we do,
> We've got the ships, we've got the men, we've got the money too.
> We've fought the bear before, and while we're Britons true
> The Russians shall not have Constantinople.

The Queen shared such emotions to the full. 'Oh, if the Queen were a man,' she told Disraeli, 'she would like to go & give those horrid Russians, whose word one cannot trust, such a beating.' To the Crown Princess, who was not so furious in her dislike of them as her mother, she wrote impatiently, 'I am sure you would not wish Great Britain to eat humble pie to those deceitful cruel Russians?'[8] Of those who suggested that Britain ought to be conciliatory towards the Russians, those 'horrible, wicked ... villainous, atrocious' Russians, she was dismissively scornful.[9] As for Lord Derby, the Foreign Minister, who was attempting to prevent a conflict by revealing Cabinet secrets to the Russian ambassador, 'words failed her'. Not trusting him to make her feelings plainly known to the Tsar, she wrote directly to St Petersburg without reference to him; and when Ponsonby expressed his concern at her indulging in so unconstitutional a practice she was quite unrepentant. It was a 'miserable thing to be a constitutional Queen,' she complained, '& to be unable to do what is right'.[10]

She threatened to 'lay down her crown' rather than 'submit to Russian insult'; and she admitted that she 'never spoke with such vehemence' as she did to the Colonial Secretary, Lord Carnarvon, who was far too pacific for her taste and had warned against a repetition of the Crimean War. 'Inspired by the British Lion', she 'pitched into him with vehemence and indignation,' she reported to the Crown Princess, '& he remained shrinking but still craven hearted! – wishing to say to the world we cld not act!!! Oh! that Englishmen were now what they were!! But we shall yet assert our rights – our position – & "Britons never will be slaves" – will yet be our Motto.'[11]

Nor did the Queen altogether spare from her strictures the Prime Minister who, pursuing a delicately balanced policy, was at one moment condemned by the Opposition for being too aggressive and at another berated at a banquet by a lady who angrily demanded to know what he was waiting for – to which question he replied with his customary suavity, 'At this moment for peas and potatoes, Madam.'[12]

When Russia imposed upon Turkey the secret conditions of the Treaty of San Stefano of March 1878 which was believed to require Turkey to pay an immense indemnity and to surrender several Aegean ports, thus providing the Russians with bases in the eastern Mediterranean, the Queen demanded forceful action. Lending her authority to the hawks in the Government and strongly advocating 'a bold and united front to the enemy', she reviewed troops, went to Spithead to inspect a naval task-force, and sent numerous telegrams to the Prime Minister as well as memoranda for him to read to his colleagues.

Faced with the prospect of further Russian aggression, the Cabinet – from which Lord Carnarvon and the Foreign Secretary, Lord Derby, both resigned – called up reserves, sent Indian troops to Malta and in June entered into a secret agreement with Turkey, undertaking to help to defend that country against further attacks. In return Britain was allowed to occupy Cyprus as what Disraeli called a *place d'armes* from which Russia's designs on the disintegrating Turkish Empire could be resisted.[13]

Having helped to ensure that the Treaty of San Stefano was submitted to a European congress, Disraeli left for Berlin where he so much impressed Bismarck that the Iron Chancellor was heard to observe, '*Der alte Jude, das ist der Mann.*'[14]

Much to the relief of the Queen who had been reluctant to allow him to go, Berlin being 'decidedly too far', Disraeli returned to London with what was claimed to be peace with honour. The Queen, while regretting that Russia 'had got anything', was quite satisfied with Disraeli's work. 'High and low are delighted,' she assured him happily, 'excepting Mr Gladstone who is frantic.'[15] She offered him a dukedom which he declined, having already gone to the House of Lords as the Earl of Beaconsfield. She then wrote to him to say, 'He *must* now accept the Garter. She must insist on it.' This he did accept, suggesting Lord Salisbury, who had succeeded Lord Derby as Foreign Secretary, should be given it too, and commenting when both of them received it, 'To become K.G. with a Cecil is something for a Disraeli.'[16]

The Queen listened with pleasure to his account of the successful negotiations. 'Bismarck, Madam,' he said, 'was enchanted to hear your Majesty had ordered the occupation of Cyprus. "That is progress," he said. His idea of progress is the occupation of fresh countries.' The Queen joined in the general laughter.[17]

She was well aware, though, that the occupation of fresh countries entailed the defence of them and that this would regrettably on occasions lead to war. From this she did not flinch. She had not done so during the Ashanti War of 1873; neither did she when the Afghan War broke out in 1878, nor yet in the Zulu War of the following year when a British force was all but annihilated at Isandhlwana and the Queen urged the Government 'not to be downhearted for a moment but show a bold front to the world' until the 'honour of Great Britain' had been restored. It much pained her, though, to have to approve of her soldiers fighting against such brave, black-skinned warriors as the Zulu King Cetewayo who should be treated well, so she told the Government when the war was over. It was almost equally painful to read of Mr Gladstone's maddening usurpation of her own right to champion the virtues and manliness of the African races, as well as his assumption of her authority to speak over the heads of parties and classes to the nation at large.

'If *we* are to *maintain* our position as a *first-rate* Power,' she wrote encouragingly to Lord Beaconsfield, 'we must, with our Indian Empire and large Colonies, be *Prepared* for *attacks* and *wars*, *somewhere* or *other* CONTINUALLY.'[18] And when wars did break out, it was folly, she contended, to make a premature peace after an early setback: this would only lead to difficulties in the future. It was also folly to give up territories once they had been acquired. When the Government proposed to make over the North Sea island of Heligoland – which had been seized by the

British navy in 1807 – to Germany in exchange for Zanzibar, she protested that it was 'always a bad thing' to 'give up what one has'.[19]

She was far from believing in war for war's sake. Yet there were occasions when conflict could not be avoided, when Britain would otherwise become 'the laughing-stock of the world'.[20]

49

✳✳✳✳✳✳✳✳✳✳✳

'THE HALF-MAD FIREBRAND'

'The Queen does not the least care but rather wishes it shd.
be known that she has the greatest possible disinclination
to take this half crazy & really in many ways ridiculous old man.'

WHEN DISRAELI'S CONSERVATIVES were defeated at the polls in
1880, the Queen did all she could to thwart the return to power of a man
who had followed such a '*blind* and *destructive* course' during the election
campaign. She had long since decided that she 'never COULD have the
slightest *particle* of confidence' in this awful man Mr Gladstone, 'a most
disagreeable person – half crazy, and so excited', who would become a
dictator if he could.[1] She would abdicate rather than have him back; she
would have the more tractable Lord Granville as Prime Minister, though
she did not rate his talents very highly; or she would, as Disraeli suggested,
send for Lord Hartington, even though she strongly disapproved of his
liaison with the Duchess of Manchester and his frequent appearances at
raffish parties at Marlborough House.[2]

Despite the advice which had been given to her by Prince Albert in
his efforts to guide her towards the creation of a new English monarchical
tradition which placed the throne above party, she had never fully grasped
the limits imposed upon a constitutional monarch. Indeed, Prince Albert,
who often overstepped the bounds of constitutional propriety by speaking
in the Queen's name, never completely comprehended these limits himself. He had seemed, on occasions, to share her endorsement of Baron
Stockmar's frequently expressed opinion that the Prime Minister was
merely the 'temporary head of the Cabinet', while the monarch was the
'permanent premier'.

When, for instance, in 1852 on the fall of his Conservative Government, Lord Derby had proposed that Lord Lansdowne should be sent for and Lord John Russell had maintained that his own claims should be considered more deserving, the Queen, after consultations with her husband, had rejected them both and had sent for the kindly, amenable, and 'safe' Lord Aberdeen to whom the Prince had gone so far as to hand a list of names considered suitable for inclusion in the Cabinet. Similarly, when faced six years later with the prospect of having to take back Palmerston, an eager proponent of a policy in Italy to which they had been opposed, the Queen and the Prince had done all they could to deny the 'old Italian Master' the premiership and had endeavoured to bring into being a government headed by Lord Granville.

Their efforts had been in vain, just as were those of the Queen in 1880 when she endeavoured to thwart the return to power of the dreadful Mr Gladstone, the 'most disagreeable' of all her Ministers, whom, *faute de mieux*, she was eventually obliged to accept as Prime Minister for the second time.

At his audience on 23 April, she treated him with what he loyally described as 'perfect courtesy', while comforting herself with the thought that the seventy-year-old '*half-mad firebrand*' would not be in office for long. Indeed, he told her as much himself, looking, so she thought, satisfyingly ill, old and haggard – though Henry Ponsonby considered he had never appeared more healthy.[3] In the meantime, to soften the blow of having to part with 'the kindest and most devoted as well as one of the wisest Ministers' she had ever had, she proposed to continue to correspond with Disraeli 'without anyone being astonished or offended, and even more without anyone knowing about it'. 'You can,' she told him, 'be of much use to me about my family and other things and about great public questions.' She would '*never* write, except on formal *official* matters, to the Prime Minister'.[4]

She asked Ponsonby to make it clear to Gladstone on his appointment that there must be 'no democratic leaning, no attempt to change [the previous Government's] foreign policy, no change in India, and *no* cutting down of estimates. In short *no lowering* of the *high position* this Country holds, and *ought always* to hold.'[5]

As she had feared, however, Gladstone's administration fell far short of the Queen's instructions and aspirations. It was, indeed, so she told the Crown Princess, the worst Government she 'had ever had to do with': the Foreign Secretary, Lord Granville, for instance, was 'absolutely *passé* and neglected things 'in a dreadful way', while the Colonial Secretary, Lord Derby, was 'a terrible Minister' who made 'dreadful messes'. As for Gladstone – struggling under the weight of the mountainous correspondence which the Queen imposed upon him – he thought that 'she alone [was] enough to kill any man'.

When in office Disraeli had always encouraged her to believe that her political role as monarch was far more important than any but the most monarchically inclined interpreter of the British constitution would have allowed it to be. He continued to do so in opposition. When the Queen strongly objected to the evacuation of Kandahar in Afghanistan and refused to announce it as part of the Government's programme in her Speech at the opening of Parliament in 1881, the Cabinet had to threaten to resign before she gave in to them. She surrendered most grumpily, making them only too conscious of her displeasure, speaking to none of them when they next came to Osborne, and noting with relish how they 'nearly tumbled over each other going out'. Before leaving the house, however, the Home Secretary had the courage to remind her that her Speech constitutionally did not express her own views but was 'only the speech of the Ministers'. Considering this opinion most distasteful, not to say demeaning, she instructed her youngest son, Prince Leopold, to enquire what Disraeli's views were on the subject. The Home Secretary's principle, Disraeli declared, with sublime indifference to the opinion of the leading constitutional theorists of the day, was quite unfounded: it was merely 'a piece of parliamentary gossip'.[6]

This was almost the last piece of advice which Disraeli gave her. In April 1881, weakened by bronchitis and asthma and by the deleterious medicines which his doctors had prescribed, he died and was buried beside his wife at his house, Hughenden. Throughout his illness the Queen had made anxious enquiries to which he had insisted on replying, the pencil shaking in his hand; but when he was asked if he would like her to visit him, he replied, making his last sad joke, 'No, it is better not. She will only ask me to take a message to Albert.'[7] His last authentically recorded words were, 'I had rather live but I am not afraid to die.'[8]

The Queen could 'scarcely see' for her 'fast falling tears' as she wrote to his friend and Private Secretary, Montague Corry. 'The loss is so *overwhelming*. . . Never had I *so* kind and devoted a Minister and very few such devoted friends. His affectionate sympathy, his wise counsel – *all* were so invaluable even out of office. I have lost *so* many dear and valued friends but none whose loss will be more keenly felt.' The blow was 'terrible', she told the Crown Princess; it made her feel quite ill, 'poorly and shaken'. Lord Beaconsfield was 'the truest, kindest friend and wisest counsellor'. And to Lord Barrington, who had acted as Lord Beaconsfield's Private Secretary when Corry had had to take his seriously ill sister abroad, the Queen wrote, 'Words are too weak to say what [she] feels; how overwhelmed she is with this terrible, irreparable loss . . . His kindness to the Queen on all and every occasion she never, never can forget and will miss cruelly.'[9]

The grief was deep and unfeigned; but it was not enduring; and she soon returned, more vigorous than ever, to her condemnation of her dead friend's political opponents. Not a single one of her Liberal Ministers, she decided, was worthy of his appointment, while their leader, as Gladstone himself gloomily recorded in his diary, was kept 'at arm's length', 'outside an iron ring'. The Queen did not trouble to disguise her hope that the tiresome old man would soon have to relinquish his office.

Her attitude towards him momentarily softened when he had paid a warm tribute to his erstwhile opponent in the House of Commons: she had actually asked him to sit down at his next audience. But it was only a short-lived *rapprochement*; and she grew increasingly exasperated by his unwillingness to submit to what he termed her 'intolerable' and 'inadmissible' claims to be fully informed about confidential discussions in Cabinet.[10] He much annoyed her by going abroad in 1883 without her permission and accepting hospitality from various foreign rulers, including the Tsar. He had irritated her even more when, standing as candidate for Midlothian, he had gone barnstorming through Scotland, making speeches about Reform, putting his head out of his railway carriage window to acknowledge the cheers of the crowd. She complained of these '*constant* speeches' and expressed her utter disgust at his 'stump oratory'; and when, in his curiously insensitive way, he sent her a press cutting which referred to his 'triumphal procession', she sent it on to Ponsonby by way of Lady Ely with a note to say she hadn't read it. As Henry Ponsonby observed, commenting on her 'jealousy', 'she feels aggrieved at the undue reverence shown to an old man of whom the public are being constantly reminded ... while HM is, owing to the life she leads, withdrawn from view ... She can't bear to see the large type which heads the columns of newspapers by "Mr Gladstone's movements" while down below in small type is the Court Circular.'[11]

The man angered her just as much when, in writing to congratulate her on Sir Garnet Wolseley's victory over the Egyptian nationalists led by Arabi Pasha at Tel-el-Kebir in September 1882, he totally neglected to note the part played in the battle by her son, Prince Arthur, the Duke of Connaught, commander of the 1st Guards Brigade, who had been described by Wolseley as 'a first rate Brigadier-General'.

This offence was followed by the Government's proposal to withdraw troops from the Sudan where a Muslim mystic, Muhammad al-Mahdi, rallying thousands of followers behind him, had proclaimed a mission to free Egypt from foreign domination. The Queen, convinced that the Mahdi must be overthrown, bombarded the Cabinet with messages urging the need for speedy and forceful action; and she was outraged when, belatedly and after ten thousand Egyptian soldiers had been killed by the rebels, General Charles George Gordon, who had been sent out to report on the situation there, found himself besieged in Khartoum.

Furious with Gladstone's Government for not acting sooner, she sent letter after letter requesting firm action. 'The Queen trembles for Gen. Gordon's safety,' she wrote to Gladstone. 'If anything befalls *him*, the result will be awful.'[12] But Gladstone was extremely slow in sending out troops to save Gordon, since the Mahdi's followers were 'rightly struggling to be free'; and when at last a relief force was despatched under General Wolseley, it arrived too late. General Gordon was stabbed to death near the gate of the palace in Khartoum on 26 January 1885. His head was then cut off and sent to the Mahdi and hung on a tree for three days. The Queen was aghast. She sent identical telegrams to Gladstone, Hartington, the War Minister, and Granville, the Foreign Secretary: 'These news from Khartoum are frightful, and to think that all this might have been prevented and many precious lives saved by earlier action is too frightful.'[13] All these telegrams were sent *en clair* so that there could be no doubt in the public mind what she thought of her Government. This highly unconstitutional act provoked Gladstone into declaring that he would 'never set foot in Windsor again';[14] while the Queen announced that her Prime Minister would 'for ever be-branded with the blood of Gordon, that heroic man'.[15]

The Queen was quite as cross with Hartington, who was 'very idle and [hated] business', as she was with Gladstone; and when the War Minister complained to Ponsonby of her communicating directly with generals in the field, she sent a blistering reply: 'The Queen always *has* telegraphed direct to her Generals, and *always will* do so . . . She thinks Lord Hartington's letter *very officious* and *impertinent in tone.* . . The Queen won't stand dictation. She *won't* be a *machine.*'[16]

She certainly intended to communicate with whomsoever she chose; and, having written to Gordon's sister to express her grief at her brother's death and the '*stain* left upon England' by the way it had come about, she wrote also to General Wolseley to warn him that the Government, some of whose members were 'very unpatriotic', might propose withdrawal from the Sudan. He was to resist such a proposal; he must also burn her letter as it was 'so *very* confidential'. She had already written to Lady Wolseley asking her to press her husband to 'THREATEN to resign if he does *not* receive strong support. *It must never appear* or Lord Wolseley *ever let out* the hint I give *you.* But I really think they *must be frightened.*'[17]

Nor did she intend to leave Gladstone in any doubt as to her views. It would be 'fatal' to the country's reputation and honour to withdraw from the Sudan, she told him. It would be seen as a humiliating surrender by British arms to 'savages'.

Despite the political crisis the Queen declined to come down from Balmoral. Gladstone must go to her: it was 'impertinent' of him to expect otherwise. The Prince of Wales was induced to add his voice to those pressing her to return to London or Windsor, hinting that her position as sovereign might be weakened if she did not. She remained obstinate and immovable. She could not 'rush about as a younger person and a man might do'. Mr Gladstone seemed to forget that she was a lady and an old lady at that whose strength had been severely taxed by forty-eight years of her arduous reign. 'He seems to think,' she wrote, 'that I am just a machine to run up and down as he likes.'[18] Besides, her journey by train could not be arranged without due notice. Moreover, it was Ascot week and there would be so many people milling around Windsor for the races that it would be 'extremely inconvenient and unpleasant' at the Castle.[19]

*　　*　　*

The reprimand which Gladstone had received from the Queen after she had heard the news of Gordon's death was handed to him by a station master on his way back to London from Lancashire; and it had induced him for a time to consider handing in his resignation.

To the Queen's profound relief he was soon afterwards forced to do so after a vote against the Budget. She declined to shake hands with him when he came with the other Ministers to deliver up the seals of their offices. He asked if he might kiss her hand. She held the tips of her fingers towards him with evident distaste, and was obviously much relieved when he had gone. General Wolseley, who went to Osborne soon after this uncomfortable interview, reported to the Duke of Cambridge that the Queen was 'so rejoiced and happy to be rid of Gladstone and his filthy lot!!' She was 'like a school girl set free from school'.[20]

The Conservative Government of Lord Salisbury which succeeded Gladstone's in June 1855 lasted but a few months, however; and in her efforts to avoid a further series of unwelcome meetings with Gladstone, the Queen once again overstepped the limits of her prerogative. At first she refused to accept the resignation of Lord Salisbury, to whom she had grown attached, then, having done so, and having given him a bronze bust of herself and offered him a dukedom, she made repeated efforts to prevent her 'dear great country' from falling into 'the reckless hands of Mr Gladstone' who would lead it to 'UTTER ruin'. Informed that the Liberals were severely critical of the delay, she sharply retorted, 'The Queen does not the least care but rather wishes it shd. be known that she has the greatest possible disinclination to take this half crazy & really in many ways ridiculous old man.'*[21]

In the end, of course, she was forced to take him and did so with such an ill grace that he was 'dreadfully agitated and nervous' at his first audience.[22]

'I have been forced to confide the formation of a Government to that old crazy man Merrypebble, as Louis calls him,' she told Princess Frederick. 'And I made it a condition that Pussy [Lord Granville] should not go to the FO [the Earl of Rosebery was appointed Foreign Secretary], as

---

* The Queen's opinion of Gladstone was not universally shared at Court. 'Mr Gladstone here,' wrote Lady Augusta Stanley, 'very agreeable, and oh! what a charming voice, and what beautiful English that is.' 'Mr Gladstone left today to our sorrow,' she wrote in another letter from Balmoral. 'He is most pleasant' (*Letters of Lady Augusta Stanley*, 206, 297).

well as that the foreign policy should not be changed. But the bother and nuisance is dreadful ... It is a great misfortune to lose such a man as Lord Salisbury who is one of the most intelligent and large minded and unprejudiced statesmen I ever saw.'[23]

Throughout the few months of this, Gladstone's third administration in 1886, she continually consulted Salisbury, seeking his advice as to the best method of ensuring that Gladstone's policies on Home Rule for Ireland were defeated and defying the convention that it was her constitutional duty to support the government in office.[24] In June 1886 Gladstone's Home Rule Bill was defeated, as she had hoped, believing Home Rule to be 'calamitous for Ireland, hazardous for England and tending towards separation'.[25] She accepted his resignation with unconcealed satisfaction and welcomed back Lord Salisbury who was so infinitely more understanding, who saw to it that she was not bothered unnecessarily and that, being an old lady, she was 'not to be overpressed', never dictated to. It was easy to see she was very fond of Salisbury, wrote a guest in his house, La Bastide, on the French riviera to which the Queen used regularly to go, often without warning, when she was on holiday near Nice at Cimiez. 'Indeed, I never saw two people get on better, their polished manners and deference to and esteem for each other were a delightful sight and one not readily to be forgotten.'[25]

'I cannot help feeling relieved,' the Queen wrote in her journal after the defeat of the Home Rule Bill, 'and think it is best for the country.' Surely now she would not have to deal with Mr Gladstone again. He was seventy-six years old, in failing health and, in her eyes, looking ill and agitated. In the elections which followed the dissolution, Gladstone's supporters took 276 seats, Salisbury's 394.

'The elections are beyond man's understanding,' a visitor remarked to Mrs Gladstone, 'the course of events can only be guided by the One above.'

'Oh, yes,' Mrs Gladstone replied, 'and if you wait he'll be down to tea in five minutes.'[26] Yet, even now the Queen had not seen the last of the 'abominable' old man who returned to power after a Liberal victory in the election of 1892, a victory won by a narrow margin which prompted the Queen to comment, 'These are trying moments & it seems to me a defect in our much famed Constitution, to have to part with an admirable

Govt like Ld Salisbury's for no question of any importance or any particular reason, merely on account of the number of votes.'[27]

She did not hesitate to announce in the *Court Circular* that she took leave of Lord Salisbury 'with regret'; nor did she trouble to conceal her reluctance to entrust the government of the country and the protection of her empire 'to the shaking hand of an old, wild, incomprehensible man of 82½'. When he came for his first audience he seemed quite as old as that, 'greatly altered & changed, not only much aged, walking rather bent, with a stick, but altogether; his face shrunk, deadly pale, with a weird look in his eye, a feeble expression about the mouth, & the voice altered'.[28] He forgot to kiss hands; and subsequently remembering the omission, he repaired it just before dinner. The Queen said coldly, 'It should have been done this afternoon.'[29]

At least, the man's frailty, so she hoped, would make it easier for her to refuse to accept as members of his Cabinet men of whom she disapproved, whatever the country's 'much famed constitution' might be supposed to say on the subject. She objected, for instance, to Henry Labouchere, the Radical Member for Northampton, both on moral grounds – he had lived with his wife, an actress, before marriage – and for political reasons – his attacks on the monarchy in his weekly journal, *Truth*, were unforgivable.[30] Labouchere complained to Ponsonby that it was unconstitutional of her to object to his appointment; but she said it did not matter what the man said: she would not agree to have him in the Cabinet. Gladstone gave way; and, with characteristic loyalty to the throne, took upon himself the responsibility of excluding Labouchere without mentioning the Queen's veto.[31] When the men whose appointment she did accept appeared before her, she found them 'a motley crew', particularly Sir William Harcourt, the Chancellor of the Exchequer, who had grown to resemble an elephant. She was studiedly distant with them all, and thought they looked too absurd when, instead of rising to their feet after having been sworn in, they crawled forwards to kiss her hand on their knees. As for Gladstone he was more didactic than ever, 'half crazy, half silly', as well as deaf. It was really 'a farce' having to deal with the 'deluded old fanatic' on such terms as they were. He truly was impossible. That winter at Balmoral she grew quite red in the face one Sunday with the effort of suppressing her laughter when the Minister in his thick Scottish accent prayed that the Lord would bestow His wisdom upon the Queen's Cabinet 'who sorely needed it'.[32]

At the wedding of the Prince of Wales's son, Prince George, to Princess May of Teck, in the summer of 1893, not long before his eighty-fourth birthday, Gladstone took it upon himself to sit down in the Queen's marquee even though she had declined to shake hands with him, merely giving him 'only a very stiff bow'. 'Does he perhaps think,' she asked a cousin indignantly, 'that this is a *public* tent?'[*][33]

Gladstone struggled on for another eight months until, at the end of February 1894, 'the deluded old fanatic', losing his sight and hard of hearing, felt obliged to tender his resignation. The occasion was painful for them both: she could not bring herself to express the sentiments which he longed to hear, nor even to thank him for his long service; and the letter she wrote to him afterwards was scarcely less formal than her manner. She would confer a peerage on him, she said; but she knew he would not accept it.[34]

To Mrs Gladstone she behaved less coldly. She asked her and her husband to stay at Windsor the night before his resignation. The next morning after breakfast Catherine Gladstone, in tears, assured the Queen that her husband had always been devoted to Her Majesty and to the Crown. 'She repeated this twice,' the Queen wrote, '& begged me to allow her to tell him that I believed it which I did; for I am convinced it is the case, though at times his actions might have made it difficult to believe. She spoke of former days & how long he had known me & dear Albert. I kissed her when she left.'[35]

Without asking for Gladstone's advice as to a successor, the Queen sent for Lord Rosebery.

She liked Rosebery; but his relationship with her, complicated by his acute shyness which sometimes brought out her own, was not an easy one. She treated him as though he were a small boy in constant need of advice and admonition, perpetually criticizing his speeches which ought to be 'less jocular', more 'serious' in tone, 'more befitting a Prime Minister'. A speech at Bradford in which he referred to the House of Lords, 'that permanent barrier against the Liberal Party' as 'a great national

---

* The Queen had been equally put out at a garden party some years before when the Duke of Cambridge had noticed 'the brute Gladstone' standing in the forefront of the circle before her tent while she had her tea, 'bang opposite her, hat in hand'. She said to the Duke, 'Do you see Gladstone? . . . There he has been standing this half-hour, determined to force me to speak to him! But I am as determined *not* to speak to him' (Giles St Aubyn, *The Royal George: The Life of Prince George, Duke of Cambridge*, 1963, 234).

danger', was particularly objectionable. She reprimanded him sternly for speaking in such a manner without consulting her, without 'obtaining her sanction'.[36] His policies, she objected, often seemed framed merely 'with the sole purpose of flattering useless Radicals'. His Government, weak and divided, was short-lived; and Rosebery, unhappy in office, was by no means sorry to see it disintegrate. The Queen welcomed back Lord Salisbury who remained in power for the rest of her reign.

When Gladstone died in May 1898 the Queen could not bring herself to feel the least regret and was much annoyed when the Prince of Wales, who had the greatest respect for Gladstone, a man utterly unlike himself, acted as pall-bearer at his funeral. What advice had he taken and what precedent had he followed for doing such a thing? his mother demanded to know. In a mood of rare defiance, the Prince replied shortly that he had not taken any advice and knew of no precedent.[37]

Nor could the Queen bring herself at first to write to Mrs Gladstone to express her regret at her husband's death. She had to concede 'he was a good & vy religious man', that he was 'full of ideas for bettering the advancement of the country', that he was always 'most loyal' to her personally and 'ready to do anything for the Royal Family'; but she could not agree that he was a great Englishman. He was 'a clever man, full of talent, but he never *tried* to keep up the *honour* and *prestige* of Gt Britain. He tried to separate England from Ireland and to set class against class.' The harm he did could not 'easily be undone'.[38] When Harriet Phipps asked her if she really was not going to write to Mrs Gladstone, she said, 'No, I did not like the man. How can I say I am sorry when I am not?'[39] All she could do was to tell the widow, in a tribute afterwards printed in *The Times*, that her husband was 'one of the most distinguished states-men of [her] reign' and that she would 'gratefully remember how anxious he always was to help and serve me and mine in all that concerned [her] personal welfare and that of [her] family'.[40]

She could never, however, bring herself to recognize fully Gladstone's great talents and virtues, either in his lifetime or after his death. His 'mixture of politics and religion' was objectionable; his tendency to treat her opinions and the information she was able to relay to him without apparent interest was exasperating; his appeal to the people and the respect which they felt for him aroused her deepest jealousy; the impression that he gave of being satisfied that he always knew best she found profoundly irritating. She was amused when Lord Salisbury told her that no one could understand how Gladstone managed to listen to a sermon without rising to his feet to reply.[41]

Yet Gladstone was almost pathetically grateful when the Queen's behaviour to him was gracious, when, most unusually, he and his wife were asked to Windsor, and when, on the occasion of their last meeting in France in March 1897, she was 'very decidedly kind' and actually shook hands with him, a privilege which he 'apprehended was rather rare with men' and which, so he said, 'had never happened with me during all my life'.[42]

Gladstone compared the Queen's attitude towards him to that of his own towards a mule which had carried him for miles when he had been on holiday in Sicily. 'I had been on the back of the beast for many scores of miles ... It had rendered me much valuable service. But ... I could not get up the smallest shred of feeling for the brute. I could neither love nor like it.'[43]

GOLDEN JUBILEE

'Never, never can I forget this brilliant year.'

'NEVER, NEVER CAN I FORGET this brilliant year,' the Queen wrote in her journal as 1887, the year of her Golden Jubilee, came to an end, a year 'so full of marvellous kindness, loyalty & devotion of so many millions which I really could hardly have expected.'[1]

She was not the only person to be surprised, since there had recently been a resurgence of criticism in the press of her continued avoidance of those appearances in public from which she still shrank; and at a Liberal parliamentary dinner a large number of the guests remained in their seats when the loyal toast was proposed, several of them not only declining to stand but even hissing.

She had at first refused to consider celebrating her fiftieth year on the throne in public, even though, apart from her grandfather, George III, only two other English monarchs, Henry III and Edward III, had reigned so long. She complained of rheumatism and backache and often felt unaccountably tired in the late afternoon. But the enthusiasm of the Prince of Wales, a master of the art of ceremony, eventually won her over, though she steadfastly refused to consider celebrating the event on the exact anniversary of her accession since that was also the day on which her uncle, William IV, had died; and she had always refused to perform any public duties which coincided with the anniversaries of the deaths of members of her family, almost all of which she remembered with distressing accuracy.

By March, preparations for the Jubilee were well in hand. Medals were struck and coins minted; designs approved for presents of Jubilee brooches and tie pins; convicts were released from prison and sentences remitted; arrangements were made for ladies who had been innocent parties in divorce proceedings to be admitted to Court. There were foundation stones to lay and buildings to open in commemoration of the great event: in March the Queen went to Birmingham to lay the foundation stone of the new red brick and terracotta Law Courts designed by Sir Aston Webb and Ingress Bell; after this there was another foundation stone to lay, that of T. E. Collcutt's Imperial Institute in South Kensington. In May she was driven to the East End of London to open the Queen's Hall of the People's Palace in the Mile End Road where she was annoyed to hear a 'horrid noise', booing, she believed it was called, an unpleasant sound which was '*quite* new' to the Queen's ears. She was assured that it did not reflect a general antipathy: socialists and the worst sort of Irish were responsible for it.[2]

On the morning of 20 June, a fine, sunny day, she drove to Windsor Station after breakfast at Frogmore, then from Paddington to Buckingham Palace which was crowded with royal relations. At the Palace she wrote in her journal, 'The day has come and I am alone, though surrounded by many dear children ... God has sustained me through many great trials and sorrows.'

At dinner that evening, a 'large family dinner', she sat between King Christian IX of Denmark and the Princess of Wales's brother, King George I of Greece. Opposite her was Leopold II, King of the Belgians, son of her beloved Uncle, who had died in 1865.[3]

All these royalties and many others, among them her son-in-law, the Crown Prince Frederick, resplendent in a white and silver uniform, accompanied her the next day to a thanksgiving service in Westminster Abbey, she herself being driven in an open landau, facing her daughter-in-law, the Princess of Wales, and her daughter, the Crown Princess. The noise of the cheering was deafening. Lady Geraldine Somerset, lady-in-waiting to the Duchess of Cambridge, wrote of the 'masses and *millions* of people thronging the streets like an anthill, and *every* window within sight and every roof of every house, men hanging on the chimneys! There was never anything seen like it ... And their enthusiasm! The Duke ... told us he had never seen anything like the enthusiasm anywhere!! It was one continuous roar of cheering from the moment [the Queen] came out of the door of her Palace till the instant she got back to it: Deafening.'[4]

She had been pressed to dress up for the occasion and wear a crown; but she had resolutely refused to do so, neither Ministers nor her family being able to change her mind, the Princess of Wales declaring that she had never been so snubbed when, as a 'special favourite' of the Queen, she had been asked to raise the subject with her.[5] The Queen did, however, agree to put on something rather out of the ordinary after the Duke of Edinburgh, who had obtained leave from his duties as Commander-in-Chief in the Mediterranean, had said to her coaxingly, 'Now, Mother. You must have something really smart.'[6] So she agreed to make some concession to the grandeur and celebratory nature of the occasion by donning a bonnet set off with white lace and diamonds and by wearing some of her many orders.

On her approach to the Abbey the congregation – alerted by particularly vociferous cheers that greeted the appearance of the Queen of the Sandwich Islands and the driver of a water cart passing the nearby church of St Margaret – hastily put away their newspapers and the wrapping of their sandwiches.

The Queen walked slowly up the aisle with the aid of her walking stick as the organist played a Handel march. She sat 'alone' thinking of her 'beloved husband, for whom this would have been such a proud day!' On her return to Buckingham Palace there was a late luncheon followed by a naval parade, then a gathering in the ballroom for the distribution of presents, then dinner for which she wore a new dress embroidered with silver English roses, Irish shamrocks and Scottish thistles, and after this there was a firework display which she watched from the Chinese Room, feeling 'half-dead with fatigue'.

During the next few days there were receptions and garden parties, naval and military reviews, a visit to the Albert Hall which had been taken over for the occasion by the Royal Society for the Prevention of Cruelty to Animals and the Battersea Dogs' Home, of which she was Patron, a tribute from the boys at Eton who sang the Eton Boating Song within the precincts of Windsor Castle and cheered her to the echo when she thanked them in her clear, melodious voice, and a special treat for tens of thousands of poorer children who were shepherded into Hyde Park where they were given buns and Jubilee mugs, sang 'God Save the Queen' ('somewhat out of tune', so Her Majesty thought) and watched in awe as an immense balloon rose into the sky and one little girl announced that the person in the basket was Queen Victoria being carried up to heaven.[7]

The celebrations ended with an immense garden party which the Duke of Cambridge described to his mother:

> He gave us a full account, how very pretty it was, and well done and well managed; the Queen doing her part admirably again; she spoke to great numbers, going about a great deal, right and left.[8]

Clouding the Queen's enjoyment of the celebrations was the presence of her grandson, Prince Wilhelm of Prussia. She had not wanted to invite him; but the Crown Princess had written to her to say that her son really '*ought* to be present' as her 'eldest Grand Child'. 'He need only stay for a very few days,' she added. 'He has behaved very badly to you – and to us – but I fear it would only do harm in every way to appear to take more notice of his behaviour than it is worth! It is well *not* to give him a handle for saying he is ill treated! . . . He fancies himself of immense importance & service to the State – to his country, thinks he is indispensable to Bismarck and the Emperor! As he has little heart or *Zartgefühl* [tact] – and as his conscience & intelligence have been completely *wharped* [sic] by the . . . people in whose hands he is, he is not aware of the mischief he does . . . His staying away would *only* be used by the Party against you & Fritz & me!'[9]

As it happened, Prince Wilhelm had already taken it for granted that he would be invited and, moreover – supposing that his father was too ill himself to travel – that he would represent his aged grandfather, the Kaiser, in London. Without consulting his father he wrote to the Queen to inform her of this arrangement. She was naturally much annoyed and when her son-in-law told her he was well enough to travel, she wrote to tell him how delighted she was, ending her letter: 'So fare well, beloved Fritz. God bless you and keep you for a *very very* long time to come in the best of health for the sake of the happiness and well-being of your country and Europe. Ever your faithful Mama, VRI.'[10] To her grandson she despatched a brief telegram: 'Am delighted dear Papa is quite able to come. You will therefore only bring 2 gentlemen.'[11]

Greatly irritated by this slight, Prince Wilhelm was even more outspoken than usual about his grandmother: it was 'high time the old woman died ... She causes trouble, more than one would think. Well, England should look out when I have something to say about things ... One cannot have enough hatred for England.'[12]

The Prince's reception in England exacerbated his anger. 'Pr. W and the Princess [Dona, his wife] were received with exquisite coolness, with bare courtesy,' commented a German lady-in-waiting. 'He only saw his grandmother a couple of times, at Court functions. *She* was always placed behind the black Queen of Hawaii!! Both returned not in the best of tempers.'[13]

Prince Wilhelm went straight to his grandfather to complain of his insulting treatment in London. He expressed his anger also to his father's court marshall who commented: Wilhelm 'opened his heart to me regarding his mother, and I saw that he hates her dreadfully. His bitterness knows no bounds. What will come of all this?'

✱✱✱✱✱✱✱✱✱✱✱

51

DIE ENGLÄNDERIN

'*That* was a woman! One could do business with her!'

IT HAD BEEN NOTICED before leaving the Abbey – when her sons and sons-in-law came forward to pay their homage to the Queen and to kiss her hand – that, as the Crown Prince Frederick took a step backwards having paid his homage, she held out her hand to him again, drew him towards her and for a moment held him in her arms.[1]

A month before, on 19 May 1887, a telegram had been received from the Crown Princess who had asked her mother to send to Germany the English surgeon, Morell Mackenzie, an acknowledged authority on diseases of the throat, the second volume of whose authoritative work on the subject had been recently published. He was required to attend the Crown Prince who, having caught a severe cold the previous autumn, had since been troubled with a hoarseness of voice which his German doctors believed might be caused by a cancerous lump on his larynx. Before an operation to remove it was performed, however, a specialist's opinion was required. Mackenzie had left Harley Street immediately for Germany, preceded by a warning to her daughter from the Queen that, while Mackenzie was 'certainly . . . very clever', he was greedy for money and honours and was disliked by others in his profession.[2] In Germany, Mackenzie cut away a small part of the growth which, sent for analysis, proved benign. All thoughts of a major operation had, therefore, been abandoned; and soon afterwards, the Crown Prince had left for London to attend his mother-in-law's Jubilee celebrations.

After the Jubilee the Crown Prince and Princess went to Scotland to stay near Balmoral at the Fife Arms, Braemar, where Morell Mackenzie again examined the Prince's throat and declared himself 'very pleased' with its condition. As though in reward for his encouraging diagnosis, the Prince wrote to his mother-in-law asking that Mackenzie be knighted. The Queen accordingly wrote to the Prime Minister with this request, adding 'he certainly saved the C. Prince's life & seems really to have cured him'.[3] Lord Salisbury replied, 'There can be no objection to the bestowal of Knighthood on the doctor who saved the life of Your Majesty's son-in-law. Perhaps it might be well to wait till the cure is generally known to be quite complete.'[4] Despite this cautionary advice Mackenzie was knighted a few weeks later.

From Scotland the Crown Prince was taken, via London, to Toblach in the Tyrol where Mackenzie once more examined him and, with an optimism which proved to be unfounded, declared himself, according to the Crown Princess, 'not unsatisfied about Fritz's throat in the *main*'.[5] From Toblach the Crown Prince went to Venice by way of Trent on the advice of Mackenzie who, so one of the German doctors declared, had 'developed a taste for "travel expenses"'[6]. Mackenzie's reports from Venice were rather less encouraging; but when his patient had been moved from there to Baveno on Lago Maggiore he was declared to be 'getting on very nicely', and he himself wrote to his mother-in-law to tell her that he was progressing quite well. At the beginning of November 1887, however, two days after he had moved again, this time to San Remo on the Riviera, an alarming swelling was discovered in a new place and Mackenzie now agreed with his German colleagues that their patient was suffering from cancer of the larynx.[7]

Meanwhile in Germany, where all manner of reports were circulating about the behaviour of the Crown Princess, *die Engländerin*, including a rumour that she was having an affair with her court marshal, Count Götz von Seckendorff, demands were being made that she should bring her husband home. Amongst the other attacks on her – which were described by her mother in a letter of protest to the British Ambassador in Berlin as 'shameful' – it was alleged that she was preventing an operation being carried out, preferring to risk the Prince's life rather than lose the chance of becoming Empress upon the death of her father-in-law, the Emperor Wilhelm I, who was himself expected to die quite soon. It was also suggested that, since the Prince was too ill to reign, the crown should pass to his son, Prince Wilhelm, when the Emperor died.

Prince Wilhelm arrived in San Remo with the intention of taking his father back to Berlin with him. But his mother refused to allow her husband to be moved.

'You ask how Willie was when he was here,' she reported to the Queen after her son's departure. 'He was *as rude*, as *disagreeable* as impertinent to me as possible when he arrived, but I pitched into him with, I am afraid, considerable violence, and he became quite nice and gentle and amiable (for him) . . . He thought he was to save his Papa fr. *my mismanagement*!! When he has not his head stuffed with rubbish at Berlin he is quite nice and "traitable" . . . but I will *not have* him dictate to me, the head on my shoulders is every bit as good as *his*.'[8]

The Queen was distressed to learn that her grandson had been persuaded that he should inherit the Kaiser's throne because his father was too ill to do so. It was a 'monstrous idea', she said. 'It must never be allowed – Fritz is capable of doing and directing anything and this must be stopped at once.' 'You have every reason to feel angry and annoyed,' she added in a subsequent letter when her daughter told her that her second son, Heinrich, was being as difficult as Wilhelm, maintaining, so she said, 'that his papa is lost through the English doctors and me . . . He is quite dreadful in this respect!! He is so prejudiced, and fancies that he knows better than his Mama and all the doctors here . . . He is as foolish as he is obstinate & pigheaded and . . . becomes so rude and impertinent that I can really *not* stand it.'[9]

On 10 March 1888 news reached San Remo that the old Emperor of Germany, Wilhelm I, had died and that, consequently, the Crown Prince was now the Emperor Frederick III. In a brief ceremony in the drawing room of the Villa Zirio, he took off his Order of the Black Eagle and, unable to speak, he drafted a note of thanks to Sir Morell Mackenzie for enabling him to live long enough to 'recompense the valiant courage' of his wife. As he placed the Order round her shoulders, she burst into tears.[10] Years before, she had told her mother that there was no one as blessed as she was in having such a husband and that there were 'great trials or sorrows awaiting' her. Now that time had come.[11] 'Poor Fritz succeeding his father as a sick and stricken man is so hard!!' she wrote to her mother, 'How much good he might have done!'[12]

'My OWN dear *Empress Victoria*,' the Queen replied, 'it does seem an impossible dream, may God bless her! You know *how* little I care for rank or Titles – but I cannot *deny* that *after all* that has been done and said, I own I am *thankful* and *proud* that dear Fritz and you should have come to the Throne.'[13]

They were not to occupy it together for long; and the Queen had 'no words to express' her 'indignation and astonishment' at the thoughtlessness which their son, the Crown Prince Wilhelm, displayed in his eagerness to succeed to it. His mother had expressed the hope that her husband might be spared long enough 'to be a blessing to his people and to Europe'; but it was clear when the Queen went to see him at Charlottenburg in April 1888 that he had but a short time to live.

Her Ministers had not wanted the Queen to go to Germany. Lord Salisbury warned her that Bismarck was 'in one of his raging moods' about the proposed marriage between the new Emperor's daughter, Victoria, known as 'Moretta', and Alexander of Battenberg, known as 'Sandro', a marriage which the Queen had at first promoted and the Chancellor had proscribed. Salisbury also warned her that there was likely to be trouble with her grandson, the Crown Prince Wilhelm, the impatient heir to the throne, who was now behaving in a more than usually obstreperous way. But the Queen had been determined to go. It was, she had insisted, a purely private visit. A telegram was despatched to the Empress: 'I shall bring my own matrass – leave it to you to say who I must see or *not*, besides my Grandchildren and Great Grandchildren, but beg not many.'[14]

When her train arrived at Charlottenburg station, her daughter and all her daughter's children were there to welcome her. She was taken to the Palace where she was shown up to rooms once occupied by Frederick the Great; and, after she 'had tidied [herself] up a bit', she was conducted to the Emperor's bedroom. 'He was lying in bed,' she wrote, 'and he raised up both his hands with pleasure at seeing me and gave me a nosegay. It was very touching and sad to see him thus in bed.'[15]

Afterwards, when she and her daughter were alone together, 'Vicky cried a good deal, poor dear'. 'Besides her cruel anxiety about dear Fritz,' she added, 'she has so many worries and unpleasantnesses', not least those occasioned by Bismarck's antagonism.[16]

When the Queen herself had a conversation with Bismarck the next day, however, she found him surprisingly friendly, not at all like the monster whom Vicky had described as 'the most mischievous and dangerous person alive'.[17] He had been much agitated before the interview, asking whereabouts the Queen would be in her room and would she be standing up or sitting; and, once in her presence, although the conversation was by no means contentious, he clearly found the old lady quite formidable, while she, for her part, had been 'agreeably surprised' to find him 'so amiable and gentle'. He came out of her room mopping his brow, according to her assistant private secretary, Arthur Bigge. *'Mein Gott! That* was a woman!' he declared. 'One could do business with her!' Later, he modified this impression by telling a colleague that 'Grandma behaved quite sensibly at Charlottenburg'.[18]

The next day the Queen returned to the railway station. Her daughter went with her and spent some time with her in her carriage. 'I kissed her again and again,' the Queen recorded in her journal that night. 'She struggled hard not to give way, but finally broke down, and it was terrible to see her standing there in tears while the train slowly moved off, and to think of all she was suffering and might have to go through. My poor child, what would I not do to help her in her hard lot.'[19]

A few weeks later the Emperor's illness took a turn for the worse. He had taxed his strength by insisting on attending the wedding of his son, Heinrich, to Princess Irene of Hesse; and by the middle of June he was finding it a struggle to swallow and had to be fed through a tube. It was considered advisable to send for Crown Prince Wilhelm who arrived with his wife, Augusta of Schleswig-Holstein, known as 'Dona', and immediately began bossing everyone about.

The day after her son's arrival the Empress, on entering her husband's room, realized that the end was near. Her one thought, she told her mother, was 'to help him over the inevitable end'. She asked him if he was tired; and he answered her in his hoarse whisper, 'Oh very, very.' 'Gradually his dear eyes took on a different look,' she wrote. 'We held a light up, but he did not blink at all ... He no longer seemed conscious, coughed hard once more, took a deep breath three times then gave an involuntary jerk and closed his eyes tight as if something was hurting him! Then everything was quiet.'[20]

'I am his widow,' she told her mother that same day, 'no more his wife. How am I to bear it? You did, and I will do.'[21]

'Darling, darling unhappy child,' the Queen wrote as soon as she heard of the Emperor's death. 'I clasp you in my arms, for this is a double, dreadful grief, a misfortune untold and to the world at large. You are far more sorely tried than me. I had not the agony of seeing another fill the place of my Angel husband wh. I always felt I never could have borne.'[22] 'I am broken-hearted,' she told the Crown Prince Wilhelm who had succeeded to his father's throne. 'Help and do all you can for your poor dear mother and try to follow in your best, noblest, and kindest of father's footsteps. Grandmama, V.R.I.'[23] None of her own sons, she confided to her journal, 'could be a greater loss'. Her son-in-law's death was a 'calamity' for the whole of Europe 'as well as for his own country'.[24]

Far from following his grandmother's advice, the young Kaiser – who even before his father's death had, in his mother's words, fancied himself 'completely the Emperor – and an absolute & autocratic one'[25] – behaved as though his father had been a traitor to his country, having the drawers of his writing desk emptied in a search for secret state papers, and marching about the room accusing his mother of hiding them.[26]

In fact she had already taken the precaution of asking her mother if she could bring all her private papers and those of her husband to England when they came over for the Jubilee celebrations in the summer of 1887. The Queen had readily agreed to this request and three wooden chests of papers had accordingly been handed over at Windsor Castle by the Crown Prince in July.[27] In May the next year a fourth chest containing further important documents had secretly been sent to Windsor, followed by yet another chest sent by way of the British Ambassador in Berlin who was led to believe that it contained jewels.[28]

Against his mother's wishes the new Kaiser now ordered a post-mortem of his father's remains and authorized the publication of a pamphlet which, while praising the behaviour of the late Emperor's German doctors, condemned the treatment of the British interlopers. 'An English doctor killed my father,' he stated publicly, 'and an *English* doctor *crippled* my arm – and this we owe to my mother who would not have Germans about her!'*[29]

---

* He had never made any secret of his dislike of the English. As a twenty-year-old lieutenant in the Guards, he had declared after a heavy nosebleed that it was 'good to be rid of this damned English blood'. The antagonism was, no doubt, exacerbated by his mother who, yearning for her 'own beloved England', thanking God that she was a 'regular John Bull' and hating her 'odious' life in Berlin, had urged him to remember that her own country was 'the most progressive, advanced, & liberal & the most developed race in the world, also the richest', as well as the greatest

The Queen concluded that, like Gladstone, her grandson was 'cracked'. His behaviour towards his mother made her 'blood boil'. It was, she told Lord Cranbrook, Lord President of the Council, 'abominable'. Her grandson 'seemed to think of himself as in some supernatural position'.[30]

---

naval power with the 'largest & most powerful Empire in the world in which the sun never sets', obviously more 'suited than any other to civilize *other* countries'. As General Count Alfred von Waldersee observed, this constant praise of England and belittling of Germany was counterproductive. 'If his parents intended to bring up a constitutional monarch who would obediently bow before the sovereignty of a parliamentary majority, they have been disappointed,' Count Waldersee said. 'It looks as if precisely the opposite has come about ... It is quite amazing that the Prince bears such a prejudice against England; to a great extent this is a very natural reaction to his mother's endeavours to make anglomaniacs out of the children.' The Crown Princess was eventually forced to recognize this herself and decided to 'keep silent on such issues'. 'Willy', she concluded, 'is *chauvinistic* and *ultra* Prussian to a degree & with a violence wh[ich] is often very painful to me ... Prussian princes have a certain "genre" & it runs in the blood' (John C. G. Röhl, *Young Wilhelm: The Kaiser's Early Life, 1859–1888*, Cambridge, 1998, 115, 267, 395, 409, 441).

52

✳✳✳✳✳✳✳✳✳✳✳

THE DAUGHTERS

'A married daughter I *MUST* have living with me, and
must *not* be left constantly to look about for help.'

WHEN PRINCESS ALICE, the Queen's second daughter, attempted to
persuade her mother to come out of her seclusion she caused quite as
much offence as the Queen's Ministers did when they suggested it. She
was sharply told that her mother must live the best way she found that
she could in order to get through all the work she had to do. 'I require,'
she said, 'to shape my own life and ways.'

Although she was no more than eighteen years old when her father
died, Princess Alice, a pretty, sympathetic girl, had more or less taken
over the running of the household while the Queen was in the first
agonies of her grief, sleeping in her mother's room, seeing Ministers on
her behalf, and doing all she could to comfort the grievously mourning
widow. The Queen, indeed, came so much to rely upon her that when,
less than six months after the Prince Consort's death, Princess Alice
married Prince Louis of Hesse-Darmstadt, her mother parted from her
with the utmost reluctance, comforting herself with the thought that she
and her husband would be able to spend much of their time in England,
'Louis not having any duties to detain him much at home at present'.[1]

For a long time the Queen – who had found the charming and graceful
Alice most 'obliging' – had insisted that she would not let the girl marry
so long as she could 'reasonably delay her doing so'. As she had told
King Leopold in April 1859, 'I shall not let her marry for as long as I
can.'[2] But then the Princess had met Prince Louis and, although Lord
Clarendon described him as a 'dull boy', coming from 'a dull family in

a dull country', she herself thought him delightful, while the Queen was also much taken with him: he was, if 'very shy and blushing when one talks to him about Alice', 'a dear, pleasant, bright companion, full of fun and spirits ... natural and unaffected – so quick-witted and taking an interest in everything and I think him so good-looking'.[3] The Duchess of Cambridge might well consider it 'an insignificant match'; but the Queen contended that 'great matches' did not 'make for happiness', often, in fact, causing great 'annoyance'. Better a thousand times not marry at all, she thought, 'than marry for marrying's sake'. This was advice she continued to press upon her children and their children for the rest of her life. 'I know full well,' she was to write to Princess Alice's daughter, Victoria, 'that *you* don't wish *to be married* for marrying's sake & to have a position. I know darling Child that you would *never* do this, & dear Mama had a horror of it; but it is a very *German* view of things ... I have told ... dear Papa that you were far too young to think of it, & that your 1st duty was to stay with *him*, and to be as it were the "Mistress of the House", as so many eldest daughters are to their Fathers when God has taken their beloved mother away.'[4]

As the day of Alice's 'wretched' wedding approached, the Queen had made it clear that she dreaded it. As at the Prince of Wales's wedding, she was almost hidden from view, this time by her four sons who surrounded her in the dining room at Osborne where the gloomy ceremony was conducted on 1 July 1862. After it was over the Queen broke down in floods of tears and was soon writing to Princess Alice to complain that she ought to spend more time in England than she evidently intended to do. There was, after all, nothing much for her to do in Darmstadt; it was selfish of Louis and his family to keep her there. She ought to be as much with her mother as possible. 'A married daughter,' she wrote, 'I MUST have living with me, and must *not* be left constantly to look about for help, and to have to make shift for the day which is too dreadful.'[5]

So, frequently complaining that Princess Alice spent far too much time in her husband's duchy, the Queen turned to her next daughter, Helena, 'Lenchen' as she was known in the family, to take her sister's place. At the time of Alice's wedding, Helena was sixteen years old, a kindly, sensible, but rather plain, dowdy and ungainly girl; and, as with Alice, her mother was possessively determined to keep her at home as long as she could, although she had no high opinion of her personality or deportment. 'Poor dear Lenchen,' the Queen wrote of her, 'though most useful and active and clever and amiable, does not improve in looks and has great difficulty with her figure and her want of calm, quiet, graceful manners.'

'I don't intend *she* should marry,' the Queen wrote the year after Alice's marriage,[6] 'till nineteen or twenty.' And, even then, her husband, as she had hoped of Alice's, must make England his 'principal home'. The husband chosen for her, Prince Christian of Schleswig-Holstein-Sonderburg-Augustenburg, was perfectly amenable in this respect. Unfortunately, he was not very desirable in any other: he smoked incessantly, which made him cough; his teeth were bad; he had very little hair and hardly any money; he had only one eye and at dinner parties would ask a footman to bring in a tray containing his glass eyes. 'He would explain the history of each at great length, his favourite being a blood-shot eye which he wore when he had a cold.'[7] He was fifteen years older than his intended bride and was generally acknowledged to be very boring. The Prince of Wales disapproved of the match; so did his wife who had hoped that Helena might marry her brother, the Crown Prince Frederick of Denmark; so did his sister, Alice, who was upbraided by her mother for interfering: it was 'monstrous' of her to do so when the Queen, her parent and sovereign, had settled the 'thing for Helena's good'.[8]

So Princess Helena was married on 5 July 1866 in St George's Chapel, Windsor, where, to general surprise, the Queen gave her daughter away, explaining, 'I was the only one to do it. I never could let one of my sons take their father's place while I live.'[9]

As agreed, the bride and her husband settled down at Windsor, first at Frogmore then, after Prince Christian's appointment as Ranger of Windsor Park, at Cumberland Lodge. The arrangement was not to prove a very satisfactory one: the Queen was to find Helena – who, like so many of her contemporaries, became addicted to laudanum – 'difficult to live with'; while Prince Christian proved quite as tedious in the Queen's opinion as he did in everyone else's. He was also very idle: one day the Queen, glancing out of her sitting-room window, saw him lounging about in the garden, smoking. She felt constrained to send him a note telling him to find something more constructive to do. In spite of his constant smoking he lived to be eighty-six.

Princess Helena's next sister, Louise, was considered no more satisfactory as a daughter than Princess Helena. A talented sculptress whose work was shown at the Royal Academy, she was good looking, outspoken, independent, indiscreet, often caustic and, in her mother's opinion, 'the most difficult' of all her daughters. There was never a question of her staying at home as a help and companion to the Queen who was perfectly ready to see her married when she came of age.

The candidate selected for her as a husband, although rumoured to be homosexual, was the Marquess of Lorne, heir to the eighth Duke of Argyll and grandson of the Queen's old friend, the Duchess of Sutherland, in happier years gone by her Mistress of the Robes. He was said to be a clever young man who wrote poetry. He had been found a seat in the House of Commons as Member for Argyllshire. Princess Louise was fond of him. So was the Queen who found him 'very pleasing, amiable and clever', though she did 'not fancy' him at first, complaining of his 'forward manner' and his unpleasant voice, the result of an injury sustained at Eton. Also there were grumbles from the Tories in the Household because Lorne sat in the Commons as a Liberal; and the Crown Princess did not approve, advocating a Prussian Prince, much to the annoyance of her mother who wrote to the Prince of Wales to protest against these 'foreign alliances' which, so often, meant that family feelings were 'rent asunder'. 'Beloved Papa' had advocated them, to be sure; but that was before Bismarck's Prussia had 'swallowed everything up'.[10]

There would be problems about precedence, of course, with Princess Louise married to a subject, the first time such a marriage had taken place in England since King Henry VIII's sister, Mary, had married Charles Brandon, Duke of Suffolk. And already the Queen considered that the Duke of Argyll was being rather too familiar as a future member of her family. 'I believe "Eliza" is a little nervous about the whole thing,' commented Henry Ponsonby. She 'is not accustomed to such intimacy with a subject'. He himself, however, was thankful that there was no 'talking now of this or that Seidlitz-Stinkinger', while the Queen eventually persuaded herself, or at least told Vicky, that the match had been greeted everywhere as the 'most popular act' of her reign. As for the future bride, she was not so concerned as others were about matters of precedence, about whether, for instance, she would be Princess Louise in her mother's houses and merely Lady Lorne in her husband's. At least, as she told

Ponsonby, with a side swipe at John Brown, she was quite sure she did not want 'an absurd man in a kilt' following her everywhere.[11]

Louise was married on 24 March 1871 at Windsor with far more ceremony than Alice and Helena had been. Her mother led the procession up the nave, to the strains of the bridegroom's family's marching song, 'The Campbells are Coming', the severity of her black dress offset by diamonds and rubies.[12] Soon afterwards the bride moved into apartments in Kensington Palace, outside which still stands the marble statue she created of her mother in her coronation robes.

She was often at odds with other members of her family and the Household. Marie Mallet found her 'fascinating, but oh, so ill-natured. I positively dread talking to her, not a soul escapes . . . Never have I come across a more dangerous woman, to gain her end she would stick at nothing.'* Mrs Mallet later decided, however, that she was 'at her best' when people were in trouble and this was 'a redeeming feature in her most complex character'. She trusted she would 'make up her quarrels and be a help to the Queen'.[13]

Louise was never of much help to the Queen though, and in long conversations with Dr Reid, with whom she was on the best of terms, she made no secret of her belief that her mother should abdicate in favour of the Prince of Wales. Her mother was, she said, no longer fit to reign and was 'reducing the future role of the Prince of Wales to a nonentity'.[14]

---

* She caused much consternation in the household in 1895 – after her marriage had broken down – by her relationship with Sir Arthur Bigge who succeeded Sir Henry Ponsonby as the Queen's Private Secretary in May that year. Princess Beatrice sent for Dr Reid in November 'to speak about Princess Louise's relations with Bigge and said that it was a scandal and something must be done. The Princess of Wales had written to her about it. Also Princess Christian, she said, was much exercised about it. Lady Bigge was in despair; she had ruined the happiness of others and would his. Prince Henry had seen Bigge drinking Princess Louise's health at the Queen's dinner. She had him in her toils. If the Queen knew all she would not keep Bigge.' It was over two years before the scandal finally subsided and relations between Princess Beatrice and Princess Louise improved at last (Michaela Reid, Ask Sir James: The Life of Sir James Reid, 102–4).

53

※※※※※※※※※※

THE SONS

'I agree with the Mohammedans that duty towards one's
Parents goes before every other but that is not taught as
part of religion in Europe.'

THE QUEEN EXERCISED as much control over her sons as over
her daughters. Prince Alfred, Duke of Edinburgh, like her eldest son,
Bertie, was alternately a source of great worry to her and an object of
affection. He was, she once regretted, 'reserved, touchy, vague and
wilful', a 'great, great grief'. Yet when he came home on leave, after
having been sent to sea at a tender age, so much against her wishes,
he was greatly improved. He was so like his 'dearest Papa', though
not, of course, so handsome, that she was delighted to see the 'good,
dear, clever' boy again. 'Bless him,' she wrote. 'He is such a dear,
dear boy ... We have not had a single fault to find with him since
he has been here.' He was 'very clever and intelligent' and talked 'so
sensibly and pleasantly' about all he had seen: everybody was pleased
with her 'dear darling'.[1] He had always had so many interests, unlike
that 'nameless youth', his elder brother. He collected stamps; he took
photographs; he played the violin though not very well, and wrote
music for it, though not very good music. He was a competent
draughtsman; he painted watercolours. Unfortunately, he did not always
observe her rule that servants should be treated in a kindly manner,
forgetting that 'civility and consideration for servants' was a thing
which the Queen was 'very particular about'.[2] On one occasion she
had cause to reprimand him severely: he must 'not treat servants etc.
as many do, as soldiers, which does great harm and which especially

in the *Queen's home* is totally out of place and she will not tolerate it.'*³

When Prince Alfred went back to sea again, however, there was another cause for complaint: he forgot the eighteenth anniversary of his parents' wedding and had to be sent a curt telegram demanding to know if he remembered what day it was.† Not only was he forgetful; when he came home again, he was grumpy and offhand, impatient with the servants and junior members of the Household whom he treated – though his mother repeatedly told him not to – like recalcitrant seamen. He also had a very quick temper and was notoriously avaricious. In 1862, the year after his father's death, while serving with the Mediterranean Fleet, he dealt his mother what she described as 'a heavy blow to her weak and shattered frame', proving himself 'both heartless and dishonourable', by becoming involved with a young woman on Malta just as his elder brother had disgraced himself in Ireland the year before. He was forgiven the following year, however, when he was described as being 'liker and liker to blessed Papa'. But the improvement was transitory. 'I am not as proud of Affie as you might think,' she wrote to the Crown Princess after he had been shot and wounded by a Fenian in Australia, 'for he is so conceited himself and at the present moment receives ovations as if he had done something – instead of God's mercy having spared his life . . .

---

* The Queen, in contrast, so Mary Ponsonby observed, was often more at ease with servants than with her guests, as the Prince Consort had also been. She would, she herself said, just as soon clasp 'the poorest widow in the land to her heart as she would any lady in high position'. Differences in rank must, of course, be supported; but one could never be 'sufficiently loving, kind and considerate to those beneath one'.

† She almost never forgot an anniversary herself. Her granddaughter, Princess Marie Louise, recalled how she invariably wore lockets containing mementoes of various members of her family on their birthdays: 'Her bracelets were gold chains from which hung various lockets containing the hair of her children and grandchildren . . . On birthdays and other family anniversaries, any special brooches or other pieces of jewellery given to her in commemoration of these events were always worn on the day itself' (Princess Marie Louise, *My Memories of Six Reigns*, 141).

Every year, from 1861 onwards, the anniversary of the Prince Consort's death was for her a day of mourning.

'This sad day,' she was to write a few weeks before her own death, 'so full of terrible memories, returned again.' The anniversary of his birth was always remembered and commemorated, too. 'This ever dear day has returned again without my beloved Albert being with me, who on this day, eighty one years ago, came into the world as a blessing to so many, leaving an imperishable name behind him,' she was to record in her journal on the last anniversary she was to live to see. 'How I remember the happy day it used to be, and preparing presents for him, which he would like . . . All, all is engraven on my mind and in my heart!' (Queen Victoria's Journal, 26 August 1900).

Yes, Affie is a great, great grief – and I may say a source of bitter anger for he is not led astray. His conduct is gratuitous.'[4] Then he gave further offence by his determination to marry the plain but extremely rich Grand Duchess Marie Alexandrovna, only daughter of Tsar Alexander II, who was head of a family which his mother particularly disliked as being 'false' and 'half-Oriental'. She wished to see the girl before the marriage took place; and was very cross when her father declined to bring her over for inspection. She was even more angry when Princess Alice supported the Tsarina's suggestion that the Queen herself should go over to the Continent to meet the girl at Cologne. 'You have entirely taken the Russian side,' she wrote to her daughter, 'and I do *not* think, dear child, that *you* should tell *me* who have been nearly *20 years longer* on the throne than the Emperor of Russia and am Doyenne of Sovereigns, and who am a *Reigning* Sovereign which the Empress is *not*, what I ought to do. I think *I* know *that*.'[5]

So the Queen did not meet the Grand Duchess Marie before the wedding, which took place in St Petersburg on 23 January 1874, the bridegroom appearing for the occasion in the uniform of a Russian naval captain, much to the Queen's displeasure. However, when she eventually did meet her new daughter-in-law she liked her very well. She seemed good-natured, natural and intelligent; not in the least shy or nervous in the presence of the Queen, who liked her all the more for that. The satisfaction was not mutual. Her family in Russia heard that the Duchess found her visits to Windsor and Osborne 'boring beyond belief', that English food was 'abominable', the late hours at Court 'very tiring', and London, where she and her husband lived at Clarence House, 'hideous'. As for her husband, it was obvious that she found his heavy drinking tiresome and his evil temper exasperating. She was relieved when he went back to sea as captain of the ironclad *Sultan* in the Mediterranean.

Prince Arthur, who was created Duke of Connaught and Strathearn in 1874, had never caused his mother the anxiety which his elder brothers had. Indeed, ever since Winterhalter had painted him on his first birthday receiving a present from his godfather, the Duke of Wellington, whose birthday it also was, Prince Arthur had given his mother little trouble at any time. She 'adored little Arthur from the day of his birth', she once told his governor. 'He has never given us a day's sorrow or trouble.' It was clear that he was her favourite son, dearer', she once confided in his father, 'than any of the others put together, thus *after you* he is the *dearest* and *most precious* object to *me* on Earth ... It gives me a pang if any fault is found in his looks and character, and the bare thought of his growing out of my hands and being exposed to danger – makes the tears come to my eyes.'[6] He was her 'precious love', really the 'best child [she] ever saw'.[7]

Well-behaved, polite, obedient, modest, he was a model child. He gave excellent performances in the children's plays when his younger brother, Prince Leopold, turned his back on the audience and General Grey's son was 'a stick'. Prince Arthur's one fault seemed to be that, as he grew older, he was rather too formal with servants. His mother urged him, as she had urged Prince Alfred, to remember that 'stiffness' was not requisite in her house 'This,' she said, 'applies especially to my excellent Brown, who *ought* to be treated by *all* of *you*, as he is by others, *differently* to the more ordinary servants (tho they should be treated with great friendliness).'

The Queen told Prince Arthur much else besides. His governor, Sir Howard Elphinstone, who had won a Victoria Cross at Sebastopol, was bombarded with instructions on all manner of points on the boy's upbringing. Notes, either delivered by a servant or screwed like *billets-doux* to be passed to him personally, perhaps as she went into dinner, were handed to him almost every day. The Prince was not to be allowed to mix with Eton boys of his age: the sons of courtiers could play with him if he needed companions. Eight to ten minutes were 'more than enough time for him to dress in'. 'As Prince Arthur has a little cold he had better not go out unless it clears up, and then not on the wet grass. Perhaps Major Elphinstone will take care he takes exercise at home and the rooms are kept cool as it is very mild.' 'Why did Prince Arthur *not* go out with his sister and brother this afternoon, and why did he come in so early?' He should 'write Mama with one M in the middle and Papa with a large P at the beginning'. Yet if the Queen wished to take the boy on an outing, the note took the form of a request rather than a command: 'May Prince Arthur go with his sister and little brother to the play with us tonight? Has he been good?'

Even when he had come of age the reprimands, instructions and admonitions continued: he must not keep his hands in his pockets; his father had hated the habit. He must not smoke too much; he must forswear racing and gambling; yachting attracted the worst kind of people and was also to be avoided; he must 'BREAK' with the higher classes. When his charge was nineteen, Elphinstone received a note to say that he looked rather poorly and should be 'dosed'. Every room at the Ranger's House, Greenwich Park, where Prince Arthur lived with his governor, his tutor and his valet, should be kept at a steady sixty degrees and 'never exceeded' – she usually stipulated fifty-six – and when its temperature rose higher than this one November day in Scotland, with the benefit of a fire in the room, she gave orders for a wash-basinful of water to be poured on the offending flames.[8]

As he had always wanted to do, Prince Arthur joined the Army, passing 'very well' in 1866 into the Royal Military Academy, Woolwich, but still living in the Ranger's House in Greenwich Park, separate from the other cadets. He obtained a commission in the Royal Engineers in 1868, transferring to the Rifle Brigade the following year. A conscientious soldier, he pleased his mother by telling her that, having worked his way up 'through every grade from Lieutenant to Lieutenant-Colonel [he] should not wish to skip the rank of Colonel'.* He subsequently gave her further pleasure by marrying Princess Louise of Prussia, daughter of Prince Frederick of Hohenzollern. At first she had opposed the match, disapproving of the girl's unpleasant father, as well as her ugly nose and mouth and her bad teeth: 'he should see others first.' But as soon as she saw the eighteen-year-old girl, she changed her mind. 'Had I seen "Louischen" before Arthur spoke to me of his feelings,' she wrote, 'I should not have grieved him by hesitating for a moment in giving my consent. She is a dear, sweet girl of the most amiable and charming character . . . I feel sure dear Arthur could not have chosen more wisely.'[9]

---

* Prince Arthur, who was created Duke of Connaught and Strathearn in 1874, was eventually promoted to field-marshal, but never achieved his ambition of becoming commander-in-chief, much to his mother's annoyance.

> She cannot [she protested] and will not submit to the *shameful principle* that Princes are to suffer for *their birth* in a monarchical country. Have a Republic at once, if that is the principle. She must *have an assurance* that such is *not* the case. Arthur was recommended *solely* on account of his peculiar *fitness*. It is very abominable that the Government, and a so-called Conservative one too, should wish to pander to the Radicals! (Quoted in Kenneth Rose, *Kings, Queens and Courtiers*, 53)

Prince Arthur felt so, too. He and his wife settled down happily together at Buckingham Palace.

The life of the Queen's youngest son was far less content. Rarely complimentary about her children when they were babies, she described Prince Leopold as being 'ugly' and 'very common looking', 'very plain in face'. He was also naughty and disobedient. Would it do to 'whip him well', she had once wondered in the presence of her mother. No, the Duchess had thought: the sound of a child crying was too distressing. 'Not when you have eight, Mama,' the Queen had said. 'That wears off. You could not go through that each time one of the eight cried.'[10]

Prince Leopold's looks improved somewhat as he grew older and he turned out to be cleverer and more studious than his brothers, a competent linguist, a capable musician with a pleasant singing voice, and with a precocious interest in early Italian painting and English literature. But he was certainly not prepossessing as a child: he suffered from a pronounced speech defect; he was, in his mother's words, 'very absurd' and 'dreadfully awkward'; and the more the Queen showed how concerned she was about his health, the 'constant fear' she felt about it, the more difficult, argumentative and pert he became.

'I heard your musical box playing most clearly this afternoon,' she once complained.

'Impossible. My musical box never plays.'

'But I know it was yours, as there was a drum in it I recognized.'

'That shows it wasn't my musical box. There is no drum in it.'[11]

The Queen compared Prince Leopold with her darling Arthur, who was 'so lovely & engaging, *so* sensible and so clever & such a very good little Child', whereas Leopold was '*quite* the reverse'.[12] Admittedly he was 'very clever' '& (when amiably disposed) amusing enough'. But he was very plain and difficult, constantly asking questions, 'excessively quizzical'.[13]

When he was five years old she told the Crown Princess, 'He is tall, but holds himself worse than ever, and is ... an oddity – and not an engaging child'. 'He walks shockingly,' she added the following year, 'and is dreadfully awkward ... His manners are despairing as well as his speech – which is quite dreadful ... His French is more like Chinese than anything else; poor child, he is really very unfortunate.'[14]

Lady Augusta Bruce, who thought him 'a dear', had to admit that he was 'passionate and always frightfully naughty in the presence of his parents, who think him quite a Turk! . . . I do not think they know how to manage him.'[15]

'However, it is very difficult,' Lady Augusta added, the symptoms of haemophilia having already appeared in the boy, 'for the battles are usually to avert some danger. He is perfectly restless and fearless.' He bruised himself with alarming frequency and became quite lame after falling over. 'Your poor little namesake is again laid up with a bad knee from a fall – w^h appeared to be of no consequence,' the Queen had written to the King of the Belgians not long after the boy's third birthday. 'It is very sad for the poor Child – for really I fear he will never be *able* to enter any active service. This unfortunate defect . . . is *often not* outgrown – & no remedy or medicine does it any good.'[16]

Before accepting the seriousness of her son's condition the Queen had been less sympathetic than irritated by his frailties and behaviour. But once she understood how incapacitating and dangerous the illness was, her attitude had changed. 'Poor Child,' she had told King Leopold, 'he is so very studious & so very clever but *always* meeting with accidents, which with another child would not be *mentioned* even, but which from the peculiar constitution of his blood vessels, which have no adhesiveness, become dreadful. He has now a bump on his forehead which is as big as a nut . . . Unfortunately all the "faculty" say *nothing* whatever can be done for it . . . He is very patient.'[17]

After suffering a coughing fit which made his nose bleed alarmingly, it was decided that he should be sent abroad to a warmer climate for a while; and so, on 2 November 1861, he left for France from Windsor where, on the Castle steps, he said goodbye to his 'dear Papa' whom he was never to see again. Upon his return his mother made it clear that, while he could never hope to replace him in her affections, he was to do what he could to take his father's place. She hoped that, if he was spared, he might grow up to 'resemble his precious father in character – in many of the qualities at least and . . . [might] go on with *His* work'.[18]

In order to ensure that he was, indeed, spared to fulfil this destiny, the Queen watched over the child, now eight years old, as diligently as she urged Elphinstone to watch over Prince Arthur. After an attack of internal bleeding brought on, so she thought, by riding, he was forbidden to ride again 'except at a foot's pace'; he was not to play games with other boys in which he might get hurt; he was not to be removed from the watchful eye of his mother and *'from his own Home'*. He was to be entrusted to the care of a Highland servant, John Brown's brother, Archibald, who could carry him about when he could not walk, and of a governor, a young officer in the Royal Horse Artillery, Walter George Stirling, who, his mother hoped, would 'take real care of our poor dear Boy'.[19]

Prince Leopold liked Stirling. So did the Queen at first. But he did not get on well with the Highlanders, particularly not with Archie Brown; and in the summer of 1866 she found an excuse for getting rid of him, much to the Highlanders' satisfaction. Stirling, she declared, was 'unsuited' to his post. 'He has not,' she told Major Elphinstone, 'enlarged views or knowledge enough to lead and develop so clever a boy as Leop^d – *without a father*.'[20]

Leopold was greatly distressed and angry with his mother. There was an embarrassing scene one day at luncheon when the thirteen-year-old boy appeared with 'a great gold ring on his *finger*'. His mother asked him what it was and who had given it to him. 'Someone,' he replied. Pressed, he 'grew very *red* & said "Mr Stirling"'.

'I cannot say how I miss you,' he wrote to Stirling. 'I always expect to see you coming in the morning as you always did, and as I was carried down to breakfast Louise and I missed you looking over the banister at the top of the staircase at us.'[21]

Having lost the company of Stirling, Leopold was also forbidden to spend so much time with his sister, Louise, who also disliked the 'dreadful Scotch servants', as her brother called them. 'I am no more allowed to stop with Louise as I used to do,' he told Stirling in one of several letters which he contrived to have delivered to him without the Queen's knowing. 'And this morning I got a message that I was never to ask anybody to come into the railway carriage in going to Scotland without first getting Mamma's permission.'

'Poor little fellow,' Princess Louise wrote to a friend, 'he is never allowed to come to me now, it is a great grief to us both. He said to me one day, "Lucy, I don't know what would happen to me if you ever went away, all would be over for me then."'[22]

Fortunately the boy's new tutor, the Revd Robinson Duckworth, a

Fellow of Trinity College, Oxford, was kind and understanding with his charge. He also took the trouble to be charming to the Queen, who was struck by both his manner and his good looks, and to establish satisfactory relations with the Highlanders, as his predecessor had failed to do.

Soon after Duckworth's appointment, Prince Leopold fell dangerously ill, bleeding from the bowel, and his mother sat anxiously by his bedside, fearing that he would die. When he began slowly to recover and the 'dear child' was given back to her 'from the brink of the grave', his mother decided that he must henceforth be the 'chief object' of her life, and that he and Princess Beatrice and their mother would be 'three inseparables'. The destiny of the two children was to be of help to her in her work. This was employment which Leopold at least seemed likely to become well qualified to do. 'He learns besides French and German, Latin, Greek and Italian,' the Queen told their eldest sister; 'is very fond of music and drawing, takes much interest in politics – in short in everything. His mind and head are far the most like of any of the boys to his dear Father.'[23]

This plan for his future was far from what Prince Leopold wanted. The thought of spending the rest of his life cooped up at Windsor and Osborne and that 'horrid', 'detestable', 'more vile and *most abominable*' place, Balmoral, appalled him, particularly as he would for so much of the time be in the hands of the detested Browns. 'I am rather in the grumps just now about everything,' he told Stirling in September 1868 when he was fifteen. 'The way in which I am treated is sometimes too bad (not Mr Duckworth, of course not, he is only too kind to me) but other people. Besides that "J.B." is fearfully insolent to me, so is his brother; hitting me in the face with spoons for fun, etc – you may laugh at me for all this; but you know I am so sensitive, I know you will feel for me.'[24]

'I am altogether very low about myself,' he wrote from Osborne in another letter to Stirling after a recurrence of his terribly painful illness in February 1870, 'as no sooner had I recovered from my last tedious illness ... than here I am laid up again ... This life here is becoming daily more odious & intolerable. Every inch of liberty is taken away from one & one is watched, and everything one says or does is reported.' He greatly feared, he added, that Mr Duckworth was going to be treated in the same way as Stirling himself had been, that his dismissal was soon to be engineered by the dreadful Browns who added so much to the misery of a life which was already 'so empty and idiotic' that he confessed to contemplating suicide.

'That *devil* Archie,' he told his new tutor, Robert Hawthorn Collins, after Duckworth's foretold departure, 'he does nothing, but jeer at, & be impertinent to me everyday, & in the night he won't do anything for me ... not even give me my chamberpot, & he is so insolent before the other servants, the *infernal blackguard*. I could tear him limb from limb I loathe him so.'[25]

'H.M. has grown more tyrannical over me & indeed over everybody than ever,' the Prince added in a letter the following year. 'I must say that I am getting heartily tired of my bondage & am looking forward to the day when I shall be able to burst the bars of my iron cage & fly away for ever.'[26]

He was eighteen now and saw a means of escape in persuading his mother to allow him to go to Oxford, writing her a skilful letter to point out the advantages of a university education, emphasizing that he wanted to follow in 'dear Papa's footsteps as much as possible' and that 'to meet with such companions of my own age as would be carefully selected would tend to take away that shyness of manner, & general dullness of spirit in conversation' of which she 'so naturally & so much' complained.

The Queen initially opposed this suggestion which she was greatly annoyed to discover had been discussed by others 'behind [her] back' before being proposed to her. His dear father would certainly have disapproved of the idea, she told the boy; and she herself had her own objections to both Oxford and Cambridge. St Andrews might have been considered but, of course, there could be no question of his going into residence anywhere. 'You fancy,' she told him, 'you are stronger than you really are.'

Eventually, however, she was persuaded or, as she put it, '*forced*' to give way and to allow Prince Leopold to study at Oxford, hedging her consent about with numerous conditions, on the clear understanding that it was '*merely* for *study* & *not* for amusement', that Leopold would return to Windsor at weekends when the Queen was there, go with her to Osborne at Easter and to Balmoral in May, even though this would mean missing most of the summer term, and that he realized how inconvenient it would be for her 'not having a grown up Child in the House in case of Visitors'.[27]

Leopold's happiness at Oxford was marred by what he called the 'bullying *letters* & *telegrams*' which he received from 'Home, *sweet* home', by the necessity of returning so frequently to 'headquarters' where, on one occasion at least, he and his mother had a '*screaming* row', and by the strict limitations placed upon his activities at Oxford so that he should not fall prey to temptation as his two eldest brothers had both done. He was limited in the number of men he could have to dinner and was forbidden to 'have any at all of the softer sex', which, as he told Stirling, 'is a great pity, as there are such *awfully* pretty girls here unmarried as well as married, & you know I am always a great admirer, & more than that, of fair females.'

He did, however, contrive to fall in love with one of the daughters of the Dean of Christ Church, the Revd Henry Liddell; and this made the wrench of leaving Oxford for Windsor, Osborne or the detested Balmoral all the more unpleasant. At Oxford he was, so Liddell's friend, Charles Dodgson, who wrote under the name of Lewis Carroll, said,' a universal favourite', whereas when required to be at 'headquarters' he was repressed and exasperated by his mother's anxious watching over him, her reluctance to allow him to do any public duties outside the house, her insistence that he must reconcile himself to remaining at home as a kind of private secretary.

After he came of age in April 1874, his mother, while continuing to fret and fuss about his health, allowed his life to become rather less restricted. Archie Brown was given other duties; the companionable and amusing Alick Yorke was appointed his equerry, and he was delighted to be able to tell his tutor, Robert Collins: 'Eliza found a servant for me, a *good one*! An *Englishman*!!! Oh Ye Gods! What a marvel!' After her son had recovered from an almost fatal attack of typhoid fever, the Queen even allowed him to rent a country house with Mr and Mrs Collins, Boyton Manor in Wiltshire, though she expressed her deep regret that he rejected the home that she had done all she could to make comfortable for him and declared that if he had talked about his plan of taking Boyton Manor to his brothers or sisters before discussing it with her, she would '*never* forgive it'.[28]

She still maintained that, because of his poor health, he must have no thoughts of a public role in life; and, when grudgingly granted permission to attend some public function, she took it upon herself to supervise the details. For instance, upon his accepting an invitation to become a Freeman of the City of London, she first of all tried to have the ceremony performed at Windsor, then instructed the Lord Mayor that 'everything should go thro' her'. And, upon his being appointed a Younger Brother of Trinity House, she not only told him not to stand too long during the ceremony but also directed him to wear Highland dress rather than the Trinity House uniform. Indeed, he was required to consult her about the clothes to be worn on all public occasions.[29]

Relations between the anxious mother and the wilful son grew progressively worse. Concerned about his moral as well as his physical well-being, she told him that he must not go to Cowes during the Regatta 'to lounge about or pay visits to fashionable ladies or indeed get familiar with people'. He must also, she insisted, be more polite and sociable when at Balmoral, visit the tenants more often, be more respectful to his mother and less quarrelsome with Beatrice.

In his determination to spend his time more profitably, to take on public responsibilities concerned with health, social issues, and the arts, he consulted Lord Beaconsfield. But Beaconsfield was not forthcoming and, after consulting the Queen, proposed that the Prince should be his mother's confidential assistant in her dealings with foreign affairs, in effect, that he should carry on with the work he was already doing.

> Of course I am very glad (& it interests me exceedingly) to see all the despatches which the Queen receives & to make 'précis' or analyses of them for the Queen, as I have been doing lately [Prince Leopold replied to Beaconsfield]. But then all this *is done, & much better done*, by her Private Secretary, & I feel that the Queen only gives me these things to do to keep me employed, & not because it is of any necessity to her ... Were my relations with the Queen more cordial, or could I ever hope that they might *become* more cordial, I should not be so very anxious as I am; but, as I fear, you are only too well aware, we are not on such terms as we ought to be, & we are never on such good terms as when we are absent from one another.[30]

As he might have expected, the Prince's complaint to Lord Beaconsfield was quite ineffective and, when his mother heard of it, it merely served to make her more angry with him than ever and, as she put it, 'grieved to see you still think you can *act* behind my back'.

When the Prince told Beaconsfield that the work he was given to do interested him, he was quite evidently speaking the truth; and, as relations between him and his mother gradually improved, she was grateful for his help. She allowed him to make use of a Cabinet key so that he could unlock boxes to consult confidential papers. 'Dizzy' had given him the key, his father's key, he told a friend: his brother, the Prince of Wales, was not allowed to have one.

The Queen's secretarial staff, however, were far from pleased that Prince Leopold should have been thus favoured, for they found him to be the highest of high Tories, opinionated, interfering and indiscreet, and they were thankful when in May 1878, to his mother's shocked concern, he told her, in a letter which Ponsonby described as 'respectful and dutiful in expression', that he declined to make the usual spring visit to Balmoral. Instead, he went to Paris for a fortnight.

On a subsequent visit to the Continent, Prince Leopold met Princess Helen of Waldeck-Pyrmont whom he was to marry.

He had been thinking of marriage for some time. Having fallen in love with the beautiful Alma, Countess of Breadalbane, he had hoped to marry the granddaughter and sole heiress of the third Viscount Maynard, who had been bequeathed estates worth £20,000 a year; but nothing came of this and soon afterwards she married Lord Brooke, heir to the earldom of Warwick. Nor did anything come of a proposed marriage to Mary Baring, daughter of Lord Ashburton, who had given him some encouragement to believe that she might accept his offer, but who soon decided that she was too young at nineteen to settle down, particularly with a young man who was so often ill.[31]

The Prince had then considered Princess Caroline Matilda of Schleswig-Holstein; but although the Queen liked her and was prepared to accept the girl to 'prevent a bad mistake being made' by his falling in love with someone less suitable, the girl's family raised objections, declaring that, before his death, her father had written a letter prohibiting the match.[32]

At last the Prince found a suitable bride in Princess Helen of Waldeck-Pyrmont. The Queen repeated her doubts that Leopold's health was up to marriage with any girl, at the same time expressing 'shock' at having to lose her son to a wife; yet, if he was determined to marry, she had to agree that, from all she had heard of her, Princess Helen was a good choice, even though the girl was reputed to be clever, perhaps too clever.[33] When her family arrived in England – with eighty trunks of luggage – for the wedding, the Queen was much taken with the bride whom she now saw for the first time. 'Helen is tall and "*élancée*"', she wrote in her journal, 'with a fine figure, rich colour, very dark hair, dark brown, deep-set eyes & a sweet smile. She has a charming, friendly manner & is very affectionate & warm hearted.'[34]

Even so, the thought of Prince Leopold's marrying was 'terrible'. He had recently slipped on a piece of orange peel, hurting his knee so badly that he had to hobble about with a stick, and on the wedding day he was 'lame and shaky'. It was 'a sad exhibition', she told the Crown Princess, 'and I fear everyone must be shocked at it and blame me! I pity her but she seems only to think of him with love and affection.'[35]

She certainly, like the Duke of Edinburgh's wife, pleased her mother-in-law by not being nervous in her presence. Indeed, she stood less in awe of the Queen than almost everyone else in the family. Soon after her marriage – at which the Queen appeared, for the first time in over forty years, wearing her white wedding lace over her black dress – she stormed into her mother-in-law's room to complain that a maid had been chosen for her without her being consulted in the matter. She wished, she said, to make her own appointments. After she had gone the Queen commented that she could do nothing with her; 'but unfortunately in this case she is quite right. It is what I should have done myself.'

To the astonishment of the Queen, who had doubted her son's ability to have children, her daughter-in-law became pregnant soon after the marriage and gave birth to a healthy daughter. The following spring the child's father, by then created Duke of Albany, decided to go to the south of France for the sake of his health, thinking, as his mother put it, that he required 'a little change and warmth'. 'But he is going alone,' she added, 'as Helen's health does not allow her to travel just now. I think it rather a pity that he should leave her.' And it was here at Cannes that, having fallen down on the tiled floor of a club house, he died in March 1884.[36]

The Queen was 'stunned, bewildered and wretched . . . utterly crushed' by the loss of one who, she now decided, had been the 'dearest' of her 'dear sons'. 'Oh! what grief,' she wrote. 'How dear he was to me, how I watched over him . . . He was such a charming companion, the "Child of the House" . . . and that poor loving young wife . . . Too, too dreadful! But we must bow to God's will and believe that it is surely for the best. The poor dear boy's life had been a very tried one.' His body was brought back to Windsor to be buried in St George's Chapel. His mother, blind as usual to the misdemeanours past and present of her favoured Highlanders, decreed that when the coffin was taken to the Chapel, Archie Brown should be present because he had, so she said, been such a devoted servant to the Prince in his lifetime.[37]

Less than four months later the Duchess gave birth to another child, a boy. This baby, the second Duke of Albany, was the Queen's thirty-second grandchild. She was to have six more. Four of these were the children of Princess Beatrice.

As the youngest daughter of the family, and a precocious and endearing child, Princess Beatrice had always been more indulged than her sisters. She had been allowed to behave in a way that would have been considered reprehensible in them. When told not to help herself to some delicacy on the table which would not have been 'good for Baby', she took it anyway with the characteristic comment, 'But she likes it, my dear.'[38] And when reproached, aged four, for being naughty she carelessly agreed that she had been: 'I was very naughty last night. I would not speak to Papa, but it doesn't signify much.'[39]

After the birth of Prince Leopold the Queen had told Sir James Clark that she thought that if she had yet another child 'she would sink under it'. Clark had thought that this was not improbable, though it was her mind that would give way, not her body.*[40] After the birth of Princess Beatrice she had soon regained her spirits, however. 'I have felt better and stronger this time than I have ever done before,' she wrote in her journal. She had quite thrown off her recent unhappiness when she had felt obliged to ask Prince Albert to support her in her dealings with their other children and not to scold her in front of them. 'I was simply rewarded and forgot all I had gone through when I heard dearest Albert say, "It is a fine child, and a girl!"'[41]

---

* In his book *Albert and Victoria* (London, 1972, 225) David Duff, citing 'private information', wrote, 'It has been passed down that he [Sir James Clark] revealed, to members of his own profession, the Queen's reply to his advice that she should have no more children. The reply was "Oh, Sir James, can I have no more fun in bed?"'

As the child grew up, her mother became even more reluctant to part with her than she had been to part with Princess Alice and Princess Helena. She made it quite clear that marriage would be severely frowned upon. She intended, so she admitted herself, to keep Beatrice 'young and childlike' for as long as possible, since she 'could not live without her'. This was for 'Baby's' good as well as for her own comfort. Besides, the shy girl had no wish to marry; nor had she ever had. When as a child she had watched Frith painting his picture of her eldest brother's wedding, the painter had asked her if she would have liked to have been one of his bridesmaids. 'No,' she replied much to her mother's satisfaction, 'I don't like weddings *at all*. I shall never be married. I shall stay with mother.'[42]

'I may truly and honestly say,' the Queen told the girl's eldest sister, 'I never saw so amiable, gentle, and thoroughly contented a child as she is. She has the sweetest temper imaginable and is very useful and handy ... She is my constant companion and hope and trust will never leave me while I live. I do not intend she should ever go out as her sisters did (which was a mistake) but let her stay (except of course occasionally going to theatres) as much as she can with me.'[43]

Years later the Queen still had the 'most violent dislike' of her 'precious Baby' marrying, and was still thanking God 'for such a devoted child who was really almost as much like a sister as a daughter'; and when Princess Beatrice's brother, Prince Leopold, died she was all the more indispensable. There must still be no question of marriage. 'I hate weddings,' the Queen said. 'They are melancholy things and cause the happiest beings such trials with them, bad health etc. etc.'[44]

Henry Ponsonby was reprimanded for having mentioned someone else's marriage at dinner: there must be no talk of such a thing in Princess Beatrice's presence.[45] Marriage, she often contended, was 'rarely' a source of 'real happiness'. She 'could never be enthusiastic about any marriage'. Indeed, she would go further: 'I hate marriages, especially of my daughters ... I detest them beyond words ... I often wonder,' she continued with increasing disregard for her grammar, 'that any mother can bear of giving up your own child, from whom all has been so carefully kept and guarded – to a stranger to do unto her as he likes is to me the most torturing thought in the world.'[46]

When she heard that Princess Beatrice had not only changed her mind about marrying but had actually chosen a man she wished to make her husband, the Queen flatly declined to talk about it. For weeks on end she refused to speak to her daughter, communicating with her by notes pushed across the breakfast table. Eventually, in 1885, she consented to the marriage, but only on the understanding that the man, Prince Henry of Battenberg, would come to live at Court, since it would have been '*quite out of the question*' for Beatrice to have left home. Indeed, she would surely 'never have *wished* it herself, knowing well how impossible it was for her to leave her mother'. After all, in twenty-two years, she had 'only been absent for 10 days once'.[47]

Even though her daughter was to remain at home, the Queen dreaded the approach of the wedding day when she would have to give up her 'own sweet, unspoilt, innocent lily and child' into the hands of another. She hoped and prayed there would be 'no results' for some time. At least she was thankful to say that there was 'no kissing (etc) which Beatrice dislikes' and which, so the Queen said, used to try her so 'with dear Fritz'. She had always considered there was 'gt want of propriety and delicacy . . . in treating your Bridegroom as tho (except in one point) – he were your Husband'. Young people were unfortunately 'getting vy American in their lives and ways'.[48]

The wedding day itself, the Queen expected, would be 'a gt trial' for her. But, in the event, the ceremony, held in the church near Osborne at Whippingham – the first time a royal bride had been married in a parish church in England – was, she thought, 'very touching'.

'I stood very close to my dear child, who looked very sweet, pure and calm,' the Queen wrote in her journal. 'Though I stood for the ninth time near a child and for the fifth time near a daughter, at the altar, I think I never felt more deeply than I did on this occasion . . . When the blessing had been given, I tenderly embraced my darling "Baby".'[49]

According to Labouchere's weekly journal, *Truth*, the ceremony was, however, not so pleasantly moving as the Queen's journal suggests. The Queen herself looked 'exceedingly cross', the Prince of Wales 'ill at ease and out of sorts'; the bridesmaids were remarkable for a 'decided absence of beauty'; the Archbishop of Canterbury gave a tedious address which made the Queen 'tap her foot in a very ominous way' and the Prince of Wales 'fidgety'; the Grand Duke of Hesse looked 'old and haggard', the Duke of Edinburgh 'even more sour and supercilious than usual', while his

Duchess's 'sullen expression which [had] become habitual . . . appeared to be accentuated for the occasion'. 'Princess Louise,' the report concluded, 'looked well but has a very flighty manner. Lord Lorne was in tartans, but certainly looked very common . . . Prince George of Wales seemed thoroughly well pleased with himself. He is a very ordinary looking lad but apparently has more go about him than his brother.'[50]

When the service was over and Princess Beatrice left for a villa a few miles away at Ryde for a honeymoon lasting a bare two days, it was 'horrid' for the Queen to have to say goodbye to her: it was like 'a punishment or a necessary execution'. She put her fingers in her ears to shut out the noise of the band. She then burst into tears and later commented, 'I agree with the Mohammedans that duty towards one's Parents goes before every other but that is not taught as part of religion in Europe.'[51]

Fortunately, the Queen grew fond of Prince Henry: he was 'so full of consideration for her' and became like a 'bright sunbeam' in the house, always so cheerful and helpful, as much at ease in her presence as she was in his; and, although there were in time to be four 'results' of his marriage to Princess Beatrice, the Queen was pleased to have these grandchildren always about the house.

54

✖✖✖✖✖✖✖✖✖✖

THE GRANDCHILDREN

'And there sat Grandmama not idol-like at all,
not a bit frightening, smiling a kind smile,
almost as shy as us children.'

IN HER LATER YEARS the Queen much enjoyed the company of young children. One of her ladies, Marie Mallet, described how delighted she appeared to be when her fetching little son, Victor Mallet, was presented to her, and pleased in particular by the interest he took in a portrait by Landseer of Eos, Prince Albert's favourite greyhound. The boy himself, who greeted her with a confident 'Good morning, Queen', was 'charmed at once by her beaming smile and great gentleness of voice and manner', and highly pleased with a miniature landau drawn by a pair of grey horses which she gave him as a present. On a later occasion she 'laughed till she cried' when the boy, by then three years old, having made a very low bow on entering the room, went up to kiss her hand, produced a little black and white toy pig and announced, 'Look at this pig. I have brought it all the way from London to see you.'[1]

Although she never outgrew her distaste for the whole concept and process of childbirth, the Queen endeavoured when she could to be present at the birth of her grandchildren, holding the hands of the mothers-to-be, murmuring words of sympathy and encouragement, and stroking their arms for hours on end. She nursed the babies on her knee when they were ill; and when they were a little older she allowed them into her room to play, preferably one at a time. 'Dear little things,' she said. 'I like to see them so at home with me.' She loved 'to hear their little feet & merry voices' when they came to stay with her. 'I must tell you *how* I enjoyed those 10 quiet days with your beloved ones!' she wrote after one such visit at Osborne in 1893. 'I don't know when I felt happier during the past few years.'

She had urged her daughters not to have too many children too soon. 'It is very sad,' she had told her eldest daughter, to become pregnant too often since it was 'ruin to the looks of a young woman'. Yet grandchildren, then great grandchildren, had nevertheless been produced at an astonishing rate.

When the Prince of Wales's fourth child was born in July 1868, the Queen wrote to her eldest daughter, 'The baby – a mere little red lump – was all I saw; & I fear the seventh grand-daughter & fourteenth grand-child becomes a very uninteresting thing – for it seems to me to go on like the rabbits in Windsor Park! The present large family is very far from enjoyable or good for me.' 'Unlike many people,' she told the Dean of Windsor, 'the Queen does *not* rejoice greatly at these constant additions to her family.'[2] In the end, however, she became reconciled to the process. On receiving in November 1896 a telegram which had arrived at Balmoral announcing the birth of twins to her granddaughter, Princess Margaret of Hesse, the eighth child of the Emperor Frederick, she 'laughed very much and [was] rather amused at the list of her great grandchildren being added to in such a rapid manner'.[3]

She was quite ready to condemn the behaviour of these descendants when in one of her cantankerous moods; and then the belief that they were 'sweet, dear, merry simple things' was quite forgotten. The Prince of Wales's sons, for example, were ill-bred and ill-trained when they were small, 'as wild as hawks'.[4] She 'could not fancy them at all'. Yet she grew to love them both; and they to revere her. The elder son of the younger of the two, the future Duke of Windsor, known in the family as David, well remembered being taken as a small boy to see her:

> Such was the majesty that surrounded Queen Victoria, that she was regarded almost as a divinity of whom even her own family stood in awe. However, to us children she was 'Gangan' ... She wore a white tulle cap, black satin dress and shiny black boots with elastic sides. What fascinated me most about 'Gangan' was her habit of taking breakfast in little revolving huts mounted on turntables so that they could be faced away from the wind. If the weather was fine, a small low-slung carriage ... would be at the front door. In this she would ride to one or other of the shelters

where her Indian servants would be waiting with her wheel-chair. They would serve her breakfast, which always began with a bowl of steaming hot porridge. Later she would call for her Private Secretary and begin the business of the day.

My great-grandmother always seemed to be surrounded by members of her immense family. She had nine children, forty grandchildren, numerous great-grandchildren [she was survived by thirty-seven] and countless nephews, nieces, and cousins by marriage . . .

From the time I learned to walk, one of my strongest recollections of these visits to 'Gangan' was of my being pushed forward to say 'how do you do' to Uncle Ernie or Aunt Louischen. Their greeting would be affectionate, but more often than not the words, though in fluent English, would be pronounced in the guttural accents of their mother tongue.[5]

The Queen was particularly fond of this boy, David, a 'most attractive little boy, and so forward and clever'. 'He always tries at luncheon time to pull me up out of my chair,' she wrote in her journal, 'saying "Get up, Gangan", and then to one of the Indian servants, "Man pull it", which makes us laugh very much.' Even so, both he and his brother, Albert, the future King George VI, were both frightened of their great grandmother when she was in a less playful mood and then they would often burst into tears and this would annoy her and she would ask petulantly what she had done wrong.[6]

Compared with what Henry Ponsonby called the peremptory manner in which she had treated her children, the indulgence generally shown to her grandchildren and great-grandchildren was extraordinary. One of her eldest daughter's sons once released a pet crocodile under her writing desk, an antic which his mother and her siblings would never have dared to perpetrate. Other children were permitted to build walls round her feet with empty dispatch boxes; and they remembered going for rides with her in her carriage and reducing her and themselves to helpless laughter. Her granddaughter, Margaret, the Duke of Connaught's child, was particularly naughty but she was usually forgiven because she was so 'funny'. The Queen was also amused rather than cross when Princess Beatrice's Alexander, known as 'Drino', wrote to her from Wellington College to beg her to send him some more pocket money. This she declined to do, telling the boy that he must learn to keep within his allowance. He replied to say she need not bother about the matter any more as he had sold her letter of refusal for thirty shillings.[7]

The children were not allowed to go too far, however; and, once they were old enough to sense her regal authority, they felt a certain awe in approaching her, just as she felt shy in their presence until she grew accustomed to their company, occasionally giggling apprehensively, giving diffident little shrugs of her shoulders when asking them questions. The Duke of Edinburgh's daughter, Princess Marie, known as 'Missy', and one day to be Queen of Rumania, recalled the walk to her room down hushed corridors in which grown-ups spoke in whispers.* And then the Queen's door opened 'and there sat Grandmama not idol-like at all, not a bit frightening, smiling a kind smile [the 'sweetest, most entrancing smile' which the composer and feminist, Ethel Smyth, had 'ever seen'] almost as shy as us children.'

Like the Queen's other grandchildren, however, Princess Marie knew that her grandmother could be strict as well as kind and shy. Princess Beatrice's daughter, Princess Victoria Eugénie, known as Ena, the future Queen of Spain, was told to be quiet in church at the Duke of York's wedding: nobody, she was told, talked in church. When the Archbishop began to read the service, however, Princess Ena called out 'But, Mummy, *that* man is talking.' On returning to Buckingham Palace the Queen severely told the child not to be pert. She had reason to be cross on other occasions with Princess Ena whose memories of her grandmother were accordingly less fond than those of her cousins, though she spoke of her 'lovely girlish voice and silver laugh'.

> She said [to Sir Harold Nicolson] that Queen Victoria never understood children and asked them so many questions that they became confused. She had a horrible bag of gold and coral out of which she would take sovereigns and give them to them. When it was too snowy at Balmoral to go out to Crathie Church, she would give them Bible talks in her room. That was a great ordeal, as she always lost her temper with their stupidity . . . No liberties were

---

* The silence of the Windsor corridors was often commented upon. 'It is quite remarkable, in fact almost uncanny, how quiet this enormous building is,' the Queen's German dresser, Frieda Arnold, wrote home in the 1850s, 'and sometimes one could imagine that the Castle was quite empty. For everyone goes about their business in the most calm and orderly fashion, and because of the carpets one hears nothing at all. People speak very quietly' (Benita Stoney and Heinrich C. Weltzien, *My Mistress the Queen*, 41).

permitted. The Battenberg children, being resident family, were always given dull nursery meals – beef, mutton and milk puddings – but visiting children were allowed éclairs and ices. Once Princess Ena, in indignation at this, said as her grace, 'Thank God for my dull dinner.' Queen Victoria was enraged at this and punished her.[8]

This, however, was a rare occurrence. She was seldom so cross with any of her grandchildren, most of whom she loved dearly. When Princess Ena was badly injured while riding her pony and Dr Reid felt obliged to tell her grandmother of the gravity of her case, the Queen said, 'I love these darling children so, almost as much as their parents.'

She took the greatest interest in their development and in that of all their many cousins; and it would have been too much to expect of her character that she should not require them to come to see her to subject them to cross-examination so as to elicit their qualities and attainments, as it would have been to expect that she should refrain from giving their parents advice about their upbringing and marriages. It was certainly predictable, for example, that she should tell the Princess of Wales that her sons should be kept 'apart from the society of fashionable and fast people', and advance the decided opinion that Princess Alice's daughter, Elizabeth, known as Ella, ought to be strongly discouraged from marrying the Grand Duke Serge, Tsar Alexander III's younger brother. She would *never* stand the climate for one thing; and, for another, Ella would be quite lost to her grandmother because, so the Queen said, 'Russia is *our real enemy* and totally antagonistic to *England*.'[9]

When her grandchildren were small the Queen delighted in arranging treats for them; and it became customary for her to give them all a gold watch on their tenth birthday.[10] She would have performing bears and Punch and Judy men brought to Windsor and Osborne for them; and once Buffalo Bill and his troupe came to put on their show below the East Terrace at Windsor; another day a man with a barrel organ and a monkey was summoned to the quadrangle for Princess Ena; and 'the Queen was much amused when the monkey climbed the portico and tried to find a way into the Castle through the dining room windows'.[11]

Once they had succeeded in overcoming the Queen's shyness as well as their own, her grandchildren clearly enjoyed their visits to Windsor and the company of their grandmother, her odd comments and forthright, unpredictable views. 'Grandmama so kind and dear as usual,' Princess

Victoria of Prussia told her mother, describing in her letters home the summer days, the green grass in the Park – 'no one knows what grass is until they come to England' – and the rhododendrons – 'like a dream' – the Queen making a speech, 'so well and without hesitation', as she presented new colours to a regiment in the courtyard, the drives to Frogmore and the picnic teas with the nurses in their long, rustling dresses running after children down the slopes, the Queen working so conscientiously at her papers in the shade of an immense cedar tree, the games of tennis on the courts below the East Terrace, the Eton boys rowing on the river in the evening and Uncle Bertie, charming and pleasingly raffish, coming to dinner and talking of a different world.[12]

55

✻✻✻✻✻✻✻✻✻✻

WOULD-BE ASSASSINS

'We shall have to hang some,
& it should have been done before.'

AS THE QUEEN'S CARRIAGE drove out of Windsor station yard on the late afternoon of 2 March 1882, she heard what she took to be an engine letting off steam. Then she saw people running about in all directions and a man being hustled away as two Eton boys hit him on the head and shoulders with their umbrellas. A superintendent of the Windsor police ran towards them and snatched a revolver from the man's hand. Brown was not as quick as usual in jumping down from his seat at the back of the carriage; and later the Queen described him as being 'greatly perturbed'.[1]

The would-be assassin, who was driven off in a cab to the police station by the superintendent, was, so the Queen was sorry to learn, a Scotsman. His name was Roderick Maclean and he fancied himself as a poet. When he was searched the police found an example of his work, dedicated to the Queen, together with a letter from Lady Biddulph, the Master of the Household's wife, informing him that Her Majesty did not accept manuscript poetry. It was also discovered that Maclean, after suffering a serious head injury, had spent fifteen years in a lunatic asylum from which he had not long since been discharged. At his trial on a charge of High Treason at Reading Assizes, his defence counsel maintained that no one could doubt that he was still insane. This contention was supported by several medical experts. The Queen, however, would have none of it; and when Maclean was found not guilty of attempting to murder Her Majesty 'on grounds of insanity', the verdict outraged her common sense.

How, she protested, could the man be found not guilty of attempted murder when numerous witnesses had actually seen him attempt it? If that was the law, she said, the law must be changed. And so it was: the following year an Act was passed providing for the new formula, 'guilty but insane'. Meanwhile, the two Etonians who had belaboured Maclean with their umbrellas were both promised a commission in the Guards.[2]

This was by no means the first attempt which had been made on the Queen's life. Four months after her marriage, when she had been three months pregnant with the Princess Royal, she had been driving up Constitution Hill from Buckingham Palace in an open carriage with Prince Albert one evening on their way to see her mother, who had not long since moved to Belgrave Square. The carriage was suddenly brought to a halt by a loud bang. 'My God! Don't be alarmed!' exclaimed the Prince, throwing his arms around his wife who was so little alarmed that she laughed at his agitation. She then noticed 'a little man on the footpath with his arms folded over his breast, a pistol in each hand', looking 'so affected and theatrical' that the Prince, by his own account, was 'quite amused'. The Queen saw the man take aim for a second time before the Prince pushed her head down as a bullet flew over it. The man was seized by John William Millais, a gentleman from Jersey, whose eleven-year-old son, John Everett Millais, a pupil at Henry Sass's school of drawing in Bloomsbury, had just raised his cap to Her Majesty.[3]

Mr Millais had no trouble in holding the assailant until the Queen's attendants rushed towards them as a gathering crowd began to shout 'Kill him! Kill him!' The Queen, still outwardly calm though now much alarmed, was driven up the Hill. 'We arrived safely at Aunt Kent's,' the Prince recorded. 'From thence we took a short drive through the Park, partly to give Victoria a little air, and partly to show the public we had not ... lost all confidence in them.'[4]

The assailant, 'an impudent, horrid little vermin of a man', as Lord Melbourne described him, was a frail, rather simple-minded youth named Edward Oxford who lived in decrepit lodgings which were found to contain not only numerous bulletins issued by some revolutionary society, but also – so unfounded and improbable rumours had it – letters from Hanover, the monogram of whose King, E. R. (Ernestus Rex, the former Duke of Cumberland) had been found on the pistols which Oxford had fired in the attack.

Oxford was arraigned on a charge of High Treason and was widely expected to be hanged; but, to the annoyance of both the Queen and of Lord Normanby, the Home Secretary, who could not believe that he was insane, as well as of Baroness Lehzen who observed that there was too much method in the man's madness, Oxford was sent to a lunatic asylum where he remained for twenty-seven years until given leave to emigrate after expressing his profound contrition. On being shown the pistols by Prince Albert the Queen reflected that they 'might have *finished me off*.'[5] This possibility made the poet, Elizabeth Barrett, 'very angry'. 'What,' she asked indignantly, 'is this strange popular mania for Queen shooting?'[6]

The Queen was again nearly 'finished off' two years later as her carriage was driven along the Mall where a man, described by Prince Albert as 'a little, swarthy, ill-looking rascal . . . of the age from twenty-six to thirty, with a shabby hat and of dirty appearance', pushed forward and, pointing a pistol at the Queen, pulled the trigger. The gun, however, was either not loaded or it misfired.

That evening the Prince talked to Sir Robert Peel; and, since the Queen felt sure that the man, who had managed to slink away in the crowd, would try again – and reluctant as she was to remain under threat in Buckingham Palace until he was apprehended – it was decided that she and the Prince should drive along the same route the next day. The coachman was told to drive rather faster than usual with 'two Equerries quite close to the carriage on either side'. An excuse was made to leave behind Lady Portman, the Queen's lady-in-waiting, who had been with her the previous day. 'I must expose the lives of my gentlemen,' the Queen said. 'But I will not those of my ladies.'[7]

As she and the Prince set off on the fine afternoon of 30 May 1842, their minds, as Prince Albert put it, were 'not very easy'. Numerous policemen in plain clothes were concealed around the Palace, behind the trees and in the Park. But as the carriage rolled along at a brisk pace in the sunlight, it seemed that their presence was unnecessary. On the return journey, however, the 'ill-looking rascal' was waiting, as the Queen expected. He pointed a pistol at her. She was close enough to him to hear the click of the hammer.

The man was seized, carried off, tried and condemned to death as a traitor, a sentence which so shocked and surprised the prisoner that he fainted in the dock. The Queen described it as being 'very painful' to her, but necessary as a deterrent. A plea of insanity had been advanced in court, but, as with Edward Oxford, she felt sure that this would-be assassin, John Francis, the son of a stage carpenter, was 'not the least mad' but 'very cunning'. She consequently heard with concern that his sentence was to be commuted to transportation for life on the grounds that there was some doubt as to whether or not the man's pistol had been loaded. She was, she said, 'glad, of course', that the man's life was to be spared; but she could not help feeling that hanging was a more effective deterrent than transportation, a view apparently shared by Edward Oxford himself who was said to have remarked to a warder that if he had been hanged 'there would have been no more shooting at the Queen'.[8]

As it was, only two days after Francis's reprieve the Queen was shot at yet again. This, however, appeared to be a not very serious attempt at assassination. The assailant was a miserable-looking midget, less than four feet tall, John William Bean, whose pistol contained far more tobacco and loose paper than gunpowder. He was sentenced to a mere eighteen months' imprisonment.

Nor was the next attack on the Queen a very serious matter. This took place on 19 May 1849 when an unemployed and unbalanced Irishman, William Hamilton, who had tried to manufacture a firearm with a few bits of wood and the spout of a tea kettle, eventually borrowed a pistol from his landlady with the intention of shooting at the Queen as she drove down Constitution Hill.[9] Since Hamilton omitted loading the gun before pointing it at the Queen and was, in any case, clearly insane, there was again no question of hanging the man who was sentenced to seven years' transportation. After this, the fourth occasion upon which the Queen's life had been threatened since she had come to the throne, Lord Shaftesbury wrote in his diary, 'The profligate George IV passed through a life of selfishness and sin without a single *proved* attempt to take it. This mild and virtuous young woman has, four times already, been exposed to imminent peril.'[10]

Alarmed as she had been by Hamilton, the Queen was far more upset as well as injured and affronted the following year by 'a very inconceivable attack' in July while she was on her way to visit her uncle Adolphus who was gravely ill at Cambridge House. In the carriage with her were Princess Alice, the Prince of Wales, Prince Alfred and one of the Queen's favourite ladies-in-waiting, Fanny Jocelyn. Her escort was a single equerry who became separated from the carriage as it squeezed through a narrow archway. On its emergence a pale, fair-haired young man whom the Queen had noticed before walking in the Park stepped forward from the crowd and hit the Queen a vicious blow over the head with the brass end of a stick which momentarily stunned her. The Prince of Wales, then nine years old, blushed a deep red; Fanny Jocelyn, having attended to the Queen, burst into tears; while the Queen herself struggled to her feet, calling out 'I am not hurt' to the people who were roughly manhandling her assailant, Robert Pate, a young, deranged, recently retired lieutenant in the 10th Hussars whose father had been High Sheriff of Cambridge. The Queen was deeply shocked.

> Certainly it is very hard & very horrid that I, a woman – a defence-less young [thirty-one-year-old] woman & surrounded by my children should be exposed to insults of this kind, and be unable to go out quietly for a drive [she wrote in her journal]. For a man to strike *any woman* is most brutal, & I, as well as everyone else, thinks this *far* worse than any attempt to shoot, which wicked as it is, is at least more comprehensible & more courageous . . . I own it makes me nervous out riding, and I stare at any person coming near the carriage.[11]

Lord Hardwicke, a lord-in-waiting, expressed the view, however, that the attack on the Queen was almost worthwhile because of the love it elicited afterwards. It was an opinion she herself had once expressed, claiming that it was worth going through the danger for the affection and sympathy which the people displayed towards her when she survived.

Certainly after Edward Oxford's attempt on her life she was greeted with the utmost enthusiasm, with people cheering and waving handker-chiefs when she appeared at the opera a few nights later; and, after Robert Pate's assault with his walking stick, she was loudly cheered in the streets on her way to the Royal Opera House, the 'lowest of the low being *most* indignant'. She was cheered also inside the theatre, although her late appearance with a black eye and a bruised face interrupted an exciting skating scene. The entire audience rose to their feet to applaud her and, when the hubbub had subsided, the cast gathered on the stage to sing 'God save the Queen'. Shaken as she was by Pate's attack, she had been advised not to go to the theatre that night. But if she did not go, she had protested, it would be thought she had been seriously hurt.

'But you *are* hurt, Ma'am.'

'Very well, then everyone shall see how little I mind it.'[12]

Gladstone expressed the dismissive opinion that all those who had shot at or threatened the Queen were crazy. But he could not suppose that all those Irish revolutionaries committed to the establishment of an independent republic in Ireland who were known as Fenians were lunatics; and these were considered to present a threat to her life as great as, if not greater than, that of the odd maniac. In the last months of 1867, for example, after receiving an alarming report from Manchester, where three Fenians had been condemned to death after the murder of a policeman, General Grey had thought it as well to surround Balmoral with soldiers. The Queen had thought Grey's proposal 'too foolish': the Fenians would never be 'so silly' as to take her hostage; and if they did they would find her a 'very inconvenient charge'. But she had consented reluctantly to some companies of the 93rd Highlanders being sent to protect her.[13]

After all it was not to be denied that the Irish had never 'become reconciled to English rule, which they hate! So different from the Scotch who are so loyal.' She told her eldest daughter that, although it was dreadful to have to press for such a thing, 'We shall have to hang some, & it ought to have been done before.' When the 'poor men' in Manchester were hanged, however, she prayed for them.

These hangings in Manchester led to threats of further violence:[14] there came a warning that eighty desperate Fenians were making for Osborne where they planned to kidnap or murder the Queen. General Grey had begged her to leave the island which was so dangerously exposed to an attack from the sea. Lord Derby also pressed her to do so. But she firmly stood her ground, suspecting that they were using the Fenians' threat to persuade her to return to Windsor or London from that restful retirement she needed. She was sorry to see General Grey 'so very much alarmed'; she would not, even so, leave Osborne. Although it made her feel 'like a state prisoner', she did agree, however, to have more soldiers and police to guard the house to which no one was to be admitted without a pass. She was pressed to have an armed bodyguard. This she refused to consider; but she was provided with one all the same.

When it transpired that reports of an attack on the island were entirely fanciful, the Queen berated her Ministers for giving credit to such 'an *absurd* and *mad* story', for allowing such 'extraordinary measures' to be taken against what now proved to be a 'disgraceful hoax'. The Fenians did pose a threat, though: one of their society shot and wounded Prince Alfred in March 1868 in Australia where he was then serving in the Royal Navy, a crime for which the assailant was executed soon afterwards. It was later suggested that when driving about London the Queen should be accompanied by the enormous, reassuring figure of the robust and aggressive Home Secretary, Sir William Harcourt. When he learned of this proposal Henry Ponsonby voiced the opinion that the sight of these two such contrasting figures riding along together would be 'most interesting'. The Queen's amused response to the suggestion was 'Good gracious, no!'

Towards the end of February 1872 she was threatened once again when a youth of seventeen, named Arthur O'Connor, a great nephew of the Chartist leader, Feargus O'Connor, waved a pistol at her, demanding the release of some Fenian prisoners, as her carriage was about to pass through the Golden Gate of Buckingham Palace. 'I was trembling v. much,' she confessed, 'and a sort of shiver ran through me.'[15] She grabbed hold of Lady Churchill's arm, crying, 'Save me!'

> I soon recovered myself sufficiently to stand up and turn round ... All turned and asked if I was hurt, and I said, Not at all. Then ... Arthur came up [and said] they thought the man had dropped something. We looked, but could find nothing when the postillion called out, 'There it is', and looking down I then did see shining on the ground a small pistol! This filled us with horror. All were as white as sheets, Jane C. almost crying, and Leopold looking as if he were going to faint. It is to good Brown and his wonderful presence of mind that I greatly owe my safety, for he alone saw the boy rush round and followed him![16]

Brown was rewarded by the Queen with a gold medal, an annuity of £25 and an expression of public thanks. At the same time Prince Arthur merely received a gold pin, much to the annoyance of the Prince of Wales who maintained that his brother had behaved just as bravely as the importunate ghillie.[17] Again it was proposed that the would-be assassin, who was sentenced by a lenient judge to a year's imprisonment, was insane; and again the Queen felt sure that her assailant knew perfectly well what he was doing. She asked Gladstone to have him transported at least, so that he should not return to assault her again. In the end O'Connor himself agreed to transportation, provided he could go to a country with a climate that suited him.

His threat to the Queen occurred just two days after the service which had been held in St Paul's to give thanks for the recovery of the Prince of Wales from typhoid fever; and the nation's sympathy for Her Majesty deepened the surge of loyalty to the Crown. Long queues of people formed outside Buckingham Palace to sign their names as a mark of sympathy for the Queen's ordeal; and when Charles Dilke attempted to make a speech in Bolton critical of the monarchy his words could not be heard above voices singing 'Rule Britannia' and 'God Save the Queen'. A proposal that a Select Committee should be appointed to examine the Civil List was lost in the House of Commons by 278 votes to 2. Anything like the enthusiasm, loyalty, sympathy and affection shown her after Roderick Maclean's attempt on her life was, the Queen said, 'not to be described'. In addition to numerous letters, she received within two days well over two hundred telegrams.[18]

It was worth being shot at, she observed, not for the first time, 'to see how much she was loved'. Certainly the threats and rumours of threats to her life, which continued well into the 1880s, helped for a time to quieten demands that she should show herself more in public.

✖✖✖✖✖✖✖✖✖✖

56

HOLIDAYS ABROAD

'La Regina d'Inghilterra!'

WHILE SHE CONSIDERED that the Prince of Wales spent too much time on his foreign trips, his visits to Paris and Biarritz, the French Riviera and German and Austrian Spas, the Queen herself travelled abroad frequently and in far grander style than her son, on occasions booking an entire hotel which she filled with as many as a hundred and rarely less than sixty of her entourage of servants, Indians, Highlanders, doctors, a dentist, a nurse, a French chef, M. Ferry, and his assistants, secretaries, detectives, equerries, grooms, ladies, dressers and a Director of Continental Journeys, J. J. Kanné, as well as innumerable trunks, cases and several evidently indispensable pieces of furniture, in addition to her bed and desk, various favourite pictures and photographs, and those mementoes and trinkets, bronzes, medals, miniatures, paperweights, inkstands and penknives which normally covered the walls and tables of her crowded rooms at Windsor, Balmoral and Osborne. Also taken abroad were her horses, her ponies, 'Sultan' and 'Flora', two or three of her carriages and, in later years, her donkey. When it was diffidently suggested to her that some of her suite might possibly be dispensed with, she replied certainly not, though some of them had little if anything to do.[1] Even when travelling in England she was accompanied by an enormous suite. In 1866, when, for once, she did not pay her usual May visit to Balmoral so as to be within easy reach of her Ministers during a political crisis and went instead to stay at Cliveden, she took with her three doctors, eighty-eight other persons, twelve ponies and eight carriages.

The entire assembly, together with supplies of English provisions, travelled on the Continent by her royal train at a speed of thirty-five miles an hour by day and twenty-five by night, stopping for an hour at eight o'clock in the morning so that the Queen could dress in comfort. Halts were also made at meal times and at times and places set out on a most detailed printed timetable. The timetables of Continental railways were in consequence frequently disrupted.

At the beginning of 1863, just over a year after the Prince Consort's death, the Queen had decided to visit Coburg, making as an excuse for her holiday there the state of her health. She had written to General Grey to say that she felt it '*almost a duty* to do something for her *wretched health* & nerves, to prevent further increase of depression & exhaustion'.

> God knows her *own* inclination would be to do *nothing* for her health [she had told him], as HER only wish is to see her *life end* SOON, but she feels that IF she is to go on, she *must* change the scene completely sometimes – (if it does not affect, & she hopes it does NOT, her duties) – consequently – going to Balmoral for a fortnight or 3 weeks in the *Spring* & to *Coburg* (Coburg only) in the Summer for 3 *weeks* – (beside visiting her dear Uncle at Brussels; which is a duty) & quite necessary.
>
> Her Beloved Angel wld *not* – if he were asked & saw *how* weak & bowed to earth with anguish & desolation she is – ever, ever increasing – object to her making these additional moves.[2]

The visit, however, had not altogether been a success: she had, on that occasion, and during a subsequent holiday at Coburg, been 'overwhelmed by the number of visitors and relations' who had called to see her; and in August 1865 she had proposed going to 'some *completely quiet* spot in Switzerland where she [could] refuse all visitors and have *complete* quiet.' She preferred Switzerland to Austria 'because the Prince knew it and she would rather see *nothing* he had not seen'.[3]

> 'Seriously, [she had written in a memorandum to General Grey] she thinks that if she is alive (and alas! she must live on) *next year* she must try and do something to get a little *complete* rest for she feels that *her nerves* and her *strength* are getting *more* and *more* *exhausted* and *worn*. . . She does not wish to travel *about* in *Switzerland* or to go and *see* anything very fatiguing for her strength and nerves would not stand that [but] to *live as simply* and in as retired a way as possible . . . The Queen has a real *longing* to try it.[4]

She had not been able to satisfy this longing in 1866 because of the war between Austria and Prussia; but in 1867 she wrote in her diary, 'Had a long talk with Maj. Elphinstone about a projected visit to Switzerland D. V. next year, which Dr Jenner is most anxious I should undertake for my health though it is terrible to do or see anything without my beloved Albert. Still I do long to see fine scenery, & Maj. Elphinstone is kindly going to try & find a nice place for me to go to.'[5]

She later told Elphinstone that unless she could 'find bracing air she wld *not* think of going to Switzerland at all'. 'Of course, *hot* sun and *hot* days she is prepared to put up with, but there must nevertheless *be fresh & cold air* besides.'[6]

The oppressive weather in London that summer and the next was intolerable and was made all the more so for her, since, as she explained to her eldest daughter, 'I don't perspire & am always in a dreadful, dry burning heat.' She could, she said, hardly hold her pen she was so stifled by the closeness of the atmosphere. She steeled herself to attend a garden party at Buckingham Palace where there were 'quantities of people on the lawn whom [she] had to recognize as [she] went along . . . It was vy *puzzling & bewildering*. . . Felt quite exhausted & faint & I had seemed to be in a dream, so totally unsuited to the scene'.[7]

Five weeks later she was preparing to set out for what she hoped would be the cooler climate of Switzerland where Major Elphinstone had found a large *pension* as well as a nearby chalet just outside Lucerne, both of which had been taken over in their entirety for the Queen's stay. As the day fixed for her departure approached, however, she began to worry that Lucerne might not be cooler than Osborne which was 'really like Africa, quite intolerable': it made her wish she could 'flee to some iceberg to breathe'. Indeed, she wished she was not going abroad after all, since it was 'misery to move':[8] she dreaded 'the whole thing a good deal'. Besides, she got 'tired very easily' and would be '*quite unequal*' to see any sights. 'All Picture Galleries & Exhibitions' she felt '*obliged* to give up'.[9] In her anxiety and apprehension about 'travelling *alone* without dearest Papa,' so she said, she became 'very unwell' with 'diarrhoea, most violent sick headaches and violent retching'. By 5 August, the day of departure, she had recovered, however. It was, as she recorded in her journal:

ABOVE The Prince and Princess of Wales with their first child, Prince Albert Victor, in May 1864.

RIGHT The Queen on her throne as Empress of India in 1876.

EMPRESS AND EARL;

OR, ONE GOOD TURN DESERVES ANOTHER.

Lord Beaconsfield. "THANKS, YOUR MAJESTY! I MIGHT HAVE HAD IT BEFORE! *NOW* I THINK I HAVE *EARNED* IT!"

Having been created Empress of India, the Queen bestowed an earldom on Disraeli who had declined a dukedom.

The invalid Prince Leopold, Queen Victoria's youngest son, with the physician, Sir William Jenner, and, in the check suit, the dandiacal courtier, the Hon. Alec Yorke.

ABOVE Princess Louise, the Queen's fourth daughter, the sculptress, who married the Duke of Argyll.

RIGHT Princess Beatrice, the Queen's youngest child, at the time of her marriage to Prince Henry of Battenberg in July 1885.

LEFT An attempt on the Queen's life at Windsor railway station by Roderick Maclean on 2 March 1882. The Eton boys attempting to restrain him in fact belaboured him with their umbrellas: they were both promised commissions in the Guards.

TOP The Queen caught smiling in a photograph by Charles Knight in c.1887.

ABOVE Sir James Reid, the Queen's personal physician, who offended her by marrying one of her ladies.

LEFT The Queen and her eldest daughter, the Empress Frederick, holding a portrait of the Emperor in 1889, the year after his death.

The Queen in the garden at Osborne in 1889 surrounded by members of her family, including three future kings: George V, in a white suit, with his hands on his second son, the future George VI, and, third from the left in a sailor suit, the future Edward VIII.

LEFT The Queen in her carriage at Grasse in 1891.

ABOVE The Queen and the Munshi, Abdul Karim, in 1894: the photograph which the Munshi contrived to have published in the press.

RIGHT The Queen at breakfast in the Oak Room at Windsor in 1895 with Prince and Princess Henry of Battenberg and their children, attended by her Indian servants.

The Queen struggling to read a letter towards
the end of her life.

LEFT The Queen's funeral procession leaving Windsor for the mausoleum at Frogmore.

BELOW The Royal Mausoleum at Frogmore with the recumbent marble effigies of Queen Victoria and Prince Albert by Carlo Marochetti which were still in the artist's studio when he died in 1867. The effigy of the Queen was made at the same time as that of her husband but was not brought here until after her funeral.

A very fine morning. – Breakfast out as usual & sitting a little while with Alice. Then took leave of her and Louis & [their] 4 dear little children with regret. – At ¼ p 12 left our dear peaceful Osborne with our 3 children [Princesses Louise and Beatrice and Prince Leopold] feeling sad at the parting with dear Alice . . . Janie E [the Marchioness of Ely, Lady of the Bedchamber], the Biddulphs [Sir Thomas Biddulph and the Hon Lady Biddulph, Honorary Bedchamber Woman], Colonel Ponsonby, Sir William Jenner, Fraulein Bauer [Ottilie Bauer, Princess Beatrice's Governess] & Mr Duckworth are with us. We rowed out to the *Victoria Albert* and were off by 1 . . .

As soon as we had passed the Needles, there was a groundswell & I had to go below, remaining there till we reached Cherbourg at ¼ p. 6. How it reminded me of the past, all seemed unaltered, & yet all is so changed for me'! What used formerly to be a delight makes me low & sad now.[10]

Travelling across France in the Imperial Train lent to her by Napoleon III, the Queen arrived in Paris feeling uncomfortable in the 'blazing heat' and very tired since she had been unable to sleep throughout the night because the railway carriage rocked 'so dreadfully' and was so hot, despite the footbath full of ice customarily placed in the Queen's carriage at such times. She was driven from the station to the British Embassy where the Empress Eugénie called to see her. She had some 'light dinner' at six o'clock, then went on a drive through Paris, regretting the destruction of the 'picturesque old streets' and the appearance in their place of the 'endless new formal building' planned by the Emperor's protégé, Baron Haussmann. She left Paris the next day without returning the Empress's call, a discourtesy which 'greatly vexed' the Imperial Court. 'It was no doubt a mere form,' commented Lord Stanley, the Foreign Secretary, after a conversation with the British Ambassador, 'and there was the excuse of want of time, but it is just on these points that the Imperial Court, as being *parvenu*, is touchy'.[11]

Upon her arrival in Lucerne the local newspaper described the distinguished visitor as 'a woman of about fifty [she had celebrated her forty-ninth birthday three months before], not tall, fairly corpulent [Lord Stanley had described her the previous month as 'growing enormously fat'], with a red face and clad in mourning for her departed husband'.

Flustered as she had been in the heat of the train, she was relieved to find her 'own dear Scotch sociable' waiting for her at the station, 'driven from the box with 4 horses by a local coachman. I entered into it with the Children. Kanné sat on the box & Brown behind.'[12]

She was equally pleased to discover the Pension Wallis 'very comfortable and very cool';* and for the next month she greatly enjoyed her holiday, sketching, going for rides and by steamer on the lake, nervously riding 'poor dear "Flora"' up mountain tracks and being carried down in chairs by porters, filling her journal with enthusiastic and rather trite descriptions of 'glorious scenery', 'feasts for the eyes', 'most splendid views', 'stupendous mountains . . . *beautiful* beyond belief', 'stupendous rocks, so grand and wild', 'pictures of indescribable beauty'.

So as not to be bothered by official recognition she was travelling under the pseudonym of the Countess of Kent, a title she later abandoned, since Prince Alfred was Earl of Kent as well as Duke of Edinburgh, choosing instead the Countess of Lancaster or the Countess of Balmoral (which sounded 'very pretty') though everyone knew quite well that she was Queen of England, a fact which was made quite clear not only by her generous largesse to the local children who ran after her open landau shouting '*Madame la Reine!*' but also by the sight of the royal standard flying over her hotel or villa and of John Brown sitting in the box-seat of her carriage, wearing his kilt and, on sunny days, incongruously, a topee, studiously ignoring the scenery which he affected to despise.[13]

'He is surly beyond measure,' Ponsonby recorded in April 1879 when the Queen went to Baveno on Lake Maggiore, 'and today we could see him all the way – a beautiful drive – with his eyes fixed on the horses' tails refusing to look up.' When they reached their destination, 'a lovely place', the Queen did not alight from the carriage. 'We believe it was because Brown would not allow her to get out.'[14] But Brown, who, as the Queen said, had an 'increasing *hatred* of being "abroad"', did have his uses on the Continent, as at home. 'J. B., of course, asks for everything for the Queen as if he were in Windsor Castle,' Ponsonby told his wife, 'and if anything cannot be got he says it must – and it is.'[15] He was, in fact, quite as domineering in Switzerland, Italy and Germany as he was

---

* The Pension Wallis, a handsome building on three floors, was specially equipped for the Queen's visit with numerous items bought locally and entered in the Lord Chamberlain's 'Statement of Her Majesty's Expenses on Tour in Switzerland' – 'furniture, carpets, baths and sundries, glass, china, looking-glasses, a telegraphic apparatus and, to put Jenner's mind at rest, a prodigious amount of cleanser for the patent WC' (Peter Arengo-Jones, *Queen Victoria in Switzerland*, 74).

in Scotland. In Coburg one day, for example, as he was about to take the Queen out for a drive, a German band appeared and started tootling and drumming in the street. 'Oh! I wish they would turn in,' she said. Immediately, Brown strode across to them and silenced them with four words directed at their conductor, 'Nix, nix boom boom!'[16]

The Director of Continental Journeys, J. J. Kanné, told Henry Ponsonby that Brown and Jenner between them would 'drive him mad ... Jenner, who has never seen foreign L [lavatories] before, runs about to each in a state of high disgust and says they must be entirely altered.'[17]

While Brown was permitted to do more or less as he liked on these foreign holidays, the Queen's gentlemen did not find her so undemanding. While she was staying at the Villa Clara, Baveno, Henry Ponsonby described how difficult she was to please on occasions:

> Our expedition to Milan was a failure. The Queen was annoyed because Paget [Sir Augustus Paget, the British Ambassador] wanted to telegraph about it. Her idea was that she should go quite incog ... driving about with the Highlander on the box ... Then it poured. I hinted at a postponement but she said no she would go. So we went. There was a crowd at the station but the people were kept back. At the Cenacola not many and a dozen police, but even here H. M. thought they were too close to the carriage.
>
> We saw the pictures in peace but in haste. At the Cathedral there was a crowd on the steps which increased inside ... This perturbed her and she complained to me that there were not more police. If she had gone as Queen we might have had fifty police there, but she had insisted over and over again that she would go quite privately ...
>
> As it rained the Queen drove in a shut carriage. She wouldn't go to the Brera – so we drove for an hour. And she wouldn't have Paget in her carriage – and she didn't ask Lady Paget to come. So ... she saw nothing. We men opened our carriage as it had ceased raining and saw a great deal. I stopped the carriage once and ran back to tell her these were San Lorenzo's columns. But this stopping of the carriage was coldly received and a crowd began to assemble to see the Highlander, so we went on – and I didn't trouble them again. In the evening the Queen began to reflect that she had seen very little. True. But whose fault?[18]

Insistent as she was about travelling incognito, she was perfectly content and was, indeed, pleased in her characteristically contradictory way, to be greeted with the by now familiar shouts of *'la Regina d'Inghilterra!'* from children by the roadside as her carriage passed by with its escort of *carabinieri* along the shores of Lake Maggiore.

As well as to Baveno and Lucerne the Queen went on holiday to Baden-Baden and Coburg, Darmstadt, Aix-les-Bains, and Mentone – where she stayed at the Châlet des Rosiers and the town was illuminated in her honour – to Charlottenburg, Biarritz, Hyères, Cannes, Florence and Grasse.*

At Florence, which she visited in 1888, 1893 and 1894, she stayed first at the Villa Palmieri – which was lent her by the Countess of Crawford and Balcarres and was specially painted and decorated for her stay – then at the Villa Fabbricotti from which she was escorted on protracted rounds of sightseeing by her Indian servants, much to the astonishment of the Florentines who took them for princes from her empire in the east. Having spent several hours in 1888 being wheeled round the Uffizi, she passed sadly by the Casa Gherini where Prince Albert had stayed in 1838. She remembered how he had marvelled at the sculptures of Donatello, which were 'far more beautiful' than he had imagined, and how he had developed his taste for Italian primitives.

The Queen also listened sadly to the music of the organ in the Badia which Prince Albert had played. He had played the piano, too; but this had not been a success, since the only instrument he had been able to hire in Florence was old and out of tune.

One day during this same visit, an English boy, the Hon. George Peel, saw 'policemen clearing the way for a little carriage in the Piazza del Duomo'. 'In it was an old lady with a companion,' Peel told Sir Harold Nicolson over sixty years later. 'It was Queen Victoria. She stopped the carriage, fumbled in her corsage, and drew out a locket which she held up to the [recently restored] façade [of the Duomo].' 'The Lady-in-Waiting afterwards told Peel that it was a miniature of the Prince Consort. She

---

* At Grasse she was a frequent guest at the estate of the immensely rich and awesomely imperious Alice Rothschild. One day while walking in the gardens she inadvertently strayed into a newly planted flower bed. ' "Come off at once!" Baroness Rothschild thundered at the Queen of England and Empress of India.

'The Queen came off. After that she referred to Alice, perhaps only half in jest, as "The All-Powerful One". Their friendship endured. So did the epithet. "The All-Powerful One" became Alice's nickname to her kin' (Frederic Morton, *The Rothschilds*, 189).

thought it would interest him to see how the Duomo looked after being repaired.'[19]

The Queen was tireless in her sightseeing in Florence which, so she said, 'I delight to do'. She went to the Palazzo Pitti and the Boboli Gardens, to Santa Croce and Santa Maria Novella, the Baptistery and the Bargello. The Crown Princess was 'quite wrong' to suppose she did not care for art and architecture, though she had in all honesty to concede she was no sightseer when it came to Greek and Roman remains. She spent hours in the Uffizi and was 'delighted with the treasures of art to be seen to such great advantage there'.[20]

Sir Augustus Paget's German wife, Walpurga Hohenthal, provided a description of her getting into her carriage in Florence in 1893 as she set out upon one of these excursions:

> The Queen generally keeps her own carriage waiting for an hour. At last she came out, after an infinity of rugs, shawls, parasols and drawing material had preceded her. Carpeted steps were pushed near the carriage and a grey-headed Highlander on one side and a lemon-turbaned Indian on the other, lifted the old lady into the large landau. The stalwart Highlander closed the door of the carriage after the other ladies had got in, while the Indian with his delicate brown hands, pulled the Queen's gauze veil over her face. In her young and bell-like voice she then called out: 'To the Ponte Vecchio.' She was in black with a round white felt hat.[21]

The Queen eagerly looked forward to these foreign holidays and she much enjoyed them, despite the amount of paperwork she had to attend to almost every day, John Brown's grumpiness, her constant regret that Albert was not there to share her pleasure with her and her admission that sightseeing tired her 'most dreadfully and finally bored [her] too'.[27] She filled letters and the pages of her journal with accounts of her diversions and enjoyments. She wrote of her ascent of Mount Pilate and the awesome sight of the St Gotthard Gorge, the even steeper ascent to La Grande Chartreuse where she asked for a glass of the monks' celebrated liqueur and where she was much taken with 'a very good-looking and tall young English monk with a beautiful, saintly, almost rapt expression' who knelt before her and kissed her hand, the peaceful woods outside Hyères where Henry Ponsonby saw her one morning, limping along with Lady Churchill, followed by her bath chair and her patient, white donkey,

'Jacquot', which she had bought from a peasant farmer whom she had come across on the shores of the Lac du Bourget. She wrote, too, of the delights of the Châlet des Rosiers which was surrounded by olive groves and had a beautiful view of the sea, the comfort of the Maison Mottet, later renamed the Villa Victoria, at Aix-les-Bains, where the scenery was 'quite splendid' and where, so Henry Ponsonby recorded, 'she heard noises below her room and, not being sure whether it was the regular rumblings of an earthquake or what, she sent for Hyam, the footman-in-waiting, who had the audacity to say "I think it must be Sir Henry."' 'It is true,' Ponsonby added, 'I do live just under the Queen and it is true I went to bed early, but I don't believe it was my snoring. However, the anecdote has caused great hilarity in our circles, in which I do not join.'[23]

The Queen also recalled with pleasure her excursion in 1889 from Biarritz into Spain, the first reigning English monarch to have been in that country, her drive through the streets of San Sebastian with the Queen Regent, Maria Christina, the cheering crowds, the black horses looking like animals in a painting by Velasquez, her reception by the officials of the municipality who did their best to make her feel at home by offering her a cup of tea which proved to be quite undrinkable. And she looked back with equal pleasure on her days staying at the Grand Hôtel at Grasse in 1891 when, although seventy-two, she behaved as though she were seventeen, so Marie Mallet thought, looking as 'fresh as a daisy' going out for a two-hour drive, though the mistral was at its height, and coming back covered in dust, as 'white as a miller'.[24]

In 1895 the Queen went to Cimiez and liked the place so much that she went back every year for the next four years, staying at first at the Grand, then at the Hôtel Excelsior, renamed in her honour the Excelsior Regina, where the President of France, Félix Faure, who was staying at the Riviera Palace, came to pay his respects. Since her interpretation of the protocol to be observed on such a reception of a president precluded her greeting him as she would have done a sovereign, she called the Prince of Wales over from Cannes and had him receive her visitor downstairs and bring him up. 'The three Princesses and the ladies were at the top of the stairs,' she recorded. 'I stood at the door of the drawing-room and asked him to sit down. He was very courteous and amiable, with a charming manner, so *grand seigneur* and not at all *parvenu* [his father had been a furniture maker in a small way of business in Paris]. He avoided all politics, but said kindly how I was *aimée par la population*, that he hoped I was comfortably lodged, etc.'*[25]

When staying at Cimiez the Queen frequently drove over to Nice, that 'Paradise of nature', where she regularly attended the Battle of Flowers, delighting in pelting the floats and keeping footmen busy in supplying her with plenty of blossoms. It was at Cimiez that she spent her last foreign holiday; and she left it with deep regret. 'I shall mind returning to the sunless north,' she wrote in her journal. 'But I am so grateful for all I have enjoyed here.'[26]

She had hoped to return to Cimiez the following year; but the increasingly outspoken attacks on her country in French newspapers had made another visit inadvisable while the Boer war was still being fought, so she decided to go to Ireland instead. It was 'entirely her own idea', she told the Empress Frederick, 'as was [her] giving up going abroad – and it will,' she added 'give gt pleasure & do good'.

Over fifty years earlier, in 1849, she had gone to Ireland with her husband and four eldest children and she had been much impressed by the good looks of the women, even though so many of them were in rags. They were 'really very handsome – quite in the lowest class . . . such beautiful black eyes and hair and such fine colour and teeth'. The crowds were 'noisy and excitable but very good-natured, running and pushing about, and laughing, talking, and shrieking' rather than cheering. She had landed at Cove which was renamed – but only temporarily renamed – Queenstown 'in honour of it being the first spot on which [she] set foot upon Irish ground'; and 'along the road to Dublin the masses of human beings', the bands, the 'waving of hats and handkerchiefs, the bursts of welcome which rent the air – all made it a never-to-be forgotten scene, when one reflected how lately the country had been in open revolt and under martial law' during the famine and the violence of the earlier 1840s which had led her to declare that, while their sufferings 'really were

---

* The Queen had been far less impressed by Francesco Crispi, who had called upon her with the King and Queen of Italy when she had been staying at the Villa Palmieri in Florence in 1888. 'The King [Umberto I] is aged and grown grey [he was only forty-four], the Queen is as charming as ever. To my astonishment Signor Crispi, the present very Radical Prime Minister, came into the room, and remained there, which was very embarrassing . . . They were most kind and amiable, making many excuses for Crispi's behaviour this morning – the King saying he was a very clever man, but had no manners' (Queen Victoria's Journal, 5 April 1888).

too terrible to think of', the Irish were 'a terrible people'.[27] The more one did for them, 'the more unruly and ungrateful they seemed to be'.[28] Prince George of Cambridge, who had been responsible for the military arrangements, confirmed that the Queen had been greeted with the utmost enthusiasm on this visit. It was, he had thought, 'impossible any longer to doubt that Irishmen are at heart thoroughly Royalistically inclined, if only the agitators would leave them in peace'.[29]

The Queen had returned to Ireland in 1861, when the Prince of Wales was attached to the Grenadier Guards in the Curragh Camp near Dublin. But she had not been in Ireland since; and she felt the bravery of the Irish soldiers in South Africa deserved recognition by her visit and by the establishment of a new regiment, the Irish Guards. As in 1849, she was much touched by the warmth of her reception by the loyalists, knowing nothing of the boos and catcalls of the Republicans and the tearing down of Union Jacks in the broken windows of shops in Dublin. Her equerry, Henry Ponsonby's son, Frederick, was with her and recalled:

> There were crowds of people practically all the way, but when we got into Dublin the mass of people wedged together in the street and in every window, even on the roofs, was quite remarkable. Although I had seen many visits of this kind, nothing had ever approached the enthusiasm and even frenzy displayed by the people of Dublin. There were, however, two places where I heard ugly sounds like booing, but they only seemed like a sort of bagpipe drone to the highly-pitched note of the cheering.[30]

'Felt quite sorry that all was over,' the Queen wrote on her return to England in April 1900. 'I can never forget the really wild enthusiasm and affectionate loyalty displayed by all in Ireland, and shall ever retain a most grateful remembrance of this warm-hearted, sympathetic people.'[31]

She had been in England for less than a month when news arrived from South Africa of the relief of Mafeking. The people went 'quite mad with delight', she recorded in her journal. She herself was visiting Wellington College where her grandson, Princess Beatrice's son, 'Drino', had started his first term; and she was greeted by a banner stretched across an arch to 'welcome the Queen of Mafeking'. When she returned to Windsor Castle she was welcomed by a crowd of Eton boys gathered in the Upper Quadrangle to sing patriotic songs to her. She leaned out of her window to say, 'Thank you, thank you', repeating the words many times; and, as she listened to the last song, the boys were intrigued to see an Indian servant appear by her side to hand her a scotch and soda.[32]

57

❊❊❊❊❊❊❊❊❊❊

DEATH OF BROWN

'I am in such terrible distress at the loss not only of my
best & most faithful attendant but at the loss of my
dearest and best friend.'

ONE MORNING IN MARCH 1883, a year after the attempt upon her life by the Scottish *soi-disant* poet, Roderick Maclean, John Brown had woken up at Windsor with a high fever and a return of the swellings on his face and head indicative of the erysipelas which had troubled him before. He was said to be 'quite helpless all day'. He had recently caught a severe cold while driving through an icy wind in an open dog cart to deliver a message from the Queen to Lady Florence Dixie, in Dr Reid's opinion 'rather a queer customer', who complained improbably that she had been assaulted by two men, possibly Fenians, dressed as women, and had been saved from serious injury only by the sudden appearance of her St Bernard dog.[1]

The days passed and Brown – who had spent hours searching for the Fenians or for clues that might lead to their apprehension – lay increasingly ill in the Clarence Tower. On 26 March Dr Reid noted that 'he was worse' and, additionally, suffering from delirium tremens.[2] The Queen was not, of course, told of this; indeed she was unaware of how ill he was. There was, in any case, no question of her going to see him, since she had fallen downstairs the week before and had subsequently suffered a succession of extremely painful rheumatic attacks and sleepless nights. 'She is confined to her couch,' Dr Reid wrote home to his mother, 'and has me in to see her very often.' She managed to walk round her sitting room, supported on his arm; but she could not climb the stairs.

On the 27th Reid reported to his mother that he thought that Brown would die; and by then the Queen had worked herself up 'into a great state of grief about him'.[3]

Brown did die that night; and, when told of his death by Prince Leopold, who had 'deep sympathy' for her 'without being sorry for the cause',[4] she was said to be inconsolable, in her own words 'very miserable and stunned'. Supported by Princess Beatrice, she managed to hobble up the stairs to Clarence Tower for the funeral service which was held in the room where her friend had died and where he lay as though in state for six days. A wreath of white flowers and myrtle placed on the coffin, which was to be taken for burial at Crathie, bore the legend: 'From his best and most faithful friend, Victoria R. I'.

'I have lost my *dearest best* friend who no-one in this World can *ever* replace,' she wrote to her grandson, Prince George of Wales. 'Never forget your poor sorrowing old Grandmama's *best & truest* friend.' 'He became my best & truest friend,' she repeated in a letter to the minister at Crathie. 'Weep with me,' she asked Brown's sister-in-law, 'for we all have lost the best, the truest heart that ever beat. My grief is unbounded, dreadful and I know not how to bear it, or how to believe it possible ... Dear, dear John – my dearest best friend to whom I could say everything & who always protected me so kindly. You have your husband – your support, but I have no strong arm now.'

To her daughter Vicky, the Queen wrote: 'I feel so stunned and bewildered. He protected me so – that I felt safe! And now all, all is gone in this world, and all seems unhinged again in thousands of ways ... The shock – the blow, the blank, the constant missing at every turn of the one strong, powerful arm and head ... This anguish that comes over me like a wave ... is terrible ... God's will be done but I shall never be the same again.'

She told Vicky's youngest daughter that Brown, 'for 18 years & ½ had never left [her] for a single day'.

'Friends have fallen on all sides,' she wrote to Tennyson who provided her with a tribute for the plinth of a life-size statue commissioned from Joseph Edgar Boehm:

> *Friend more than servant, Loyal, Truthful, Brave!*
> *Self less than Duty, even to the Grave*

'One by one I have lost those I cared for and leant on most,' the Queen lamented. 'And now again I have lost one who humble though he was – was the truest and most devoted of all! He had *no* thought but for me, my welfare, my comfort, my safety, my happiness . . . He was *part of my life.*' Even her letters to her young granddaughters were filled with such lamentations. 'I am in such terrible distress at the loss of my best & most faithful attendant . . . my *dearest* and *best* friend,' she wrote to one of them, Princess Victoria of Hesse. 'I am so *lonely* and since dear Grandpapa was taken have one by one lost *all* those who cld be a help & support to me – & this *one* of my *dear devoted, faithful* attendant and *trust* [*sic*] friend . . . whose help and support I miss hourly . . . The constant missing of that dearest Brown depresses me so terribly & makes everything so sad and joyless.'[5]

To others she wrote and spoke in similar terms, expressing a sorrow that she felt she would carry with her to her own grave.* She treasured the letters of condolence she received and she stuck the more feeling ones into a scrapbook. At the same time she decreed that Brown's room in the Clarence Tower should be preserved just as he had left it, and that a fresh flower should be placed every day upon his pillow. She set about raising memorials to him. As well as Boehm's statue at Balmoral, she ordered a granite seat inscribed with lines by Byron for Osborne and a life-size portrait from the German painter, Karl Sohn.† She had a eulogy printed in the *Court Circular* – which was five times as long as that accorded to her other 'most valued and devoted friend', Disraeli – a bronze tablet erected to his memory in the mausoleum at Frogmore – with the word 'insribed' mispelled thus and not corrected – the only

---

* Ten years before, she had written a letter of sympathy to the Duke of Cambridge on the death of his steward, which expressed her understanding of the grief that could be caused by the death of a trusted and devoted servant: 'Let me tell you how grieved I am at the great loss you have sustained in the loss of your faithful and excellent steward and I may add *friend*. No one perhaps can more truly appreciate your feelings than I do, who know what it is to have an attached, devoted and faithful confidential servant. Indeed such a loss is often more than those of one's nearest and dearest, for a faithful servant is so identified with all your feelings, wants, wishes and habits as really to be *part* of your existence and *cannot* be replaced' (FitzGeorge papers, 17 April 1873, quoted in Giles St Aubyn, *The Royal George: A Life of George, Duke of Cambridge*, 1963, 165).
† This portrait hung in Windsor Castle until, six days after his mother's death, King Edward VII had it removed and sent to Brown's surviving brother, William. It was kept at Crathie until 1944 when it was sold at auction for £4 12s. 6d. It was subsequently sold by Christie's in Edinburgh on 28 May 1998 to a private collector for £300,000 ('The Court Historian: Newsletter of the Society for Court Studies', vol. 111, 2 July 1998, 65).

memorial there not commemorating a member of her family; and, to members of the Household, she gave various mementoes, most unwanted, such as the blue and gold enamel locket containing Brown's portrait which was presented to James Reid. Every year thereafter she went to Crathie to lay a wreath of flowers on his grave. To the horror of the Household, she planned a biography of Brown to be written, she hoped, by Sir Theodore Martin, the fifth volume of whose life of Prince Albert had been published in 1880.

Sir Theodore declined the project on the rather suspect grounds of his wife's ill health; but, undeterred by this, the Queen decided to write a memoir herself with the help of a Miss Murray MacGregor. Her intention, she told Henry Ponsonby, to whom she sent the manuscript of the first part of the book for his comments, was to show that John Brown had meant far more to her than a faithful servant. Ponsonby, aghast at what he had read and disclaiming any right to be considered a literary critic, suggested that Her Majesty approach men who were experienced in the matter. The Queen responded by complaining that Ponsonby had not said whether or not he liked the extracts which she had sent him. Put on the spot in this way, Ponsonby replied at length, tactfully assuring her that the memoir would be of great interest to all who had known Brown but bringing himself to express the opinion that certain passages might lend themselves to misinterpretation and that there might be critics who would doubt the wisdom of her revealing to the public at large her 'innermost and most sacred feelings'.

To this the Queen retorted that the book was '*not* intended for publication but *for private* circulation'. She asked him to send the manuscript back to her as she wished to show it to Lord Rowton, Disraeli's former secretary, who did, at least, show 'gt interest in it'.[6]

Having read the manuscript, Rowton went to see Ponsonby. He fully agreed that it certainly should not be made public and suggested that some discreet printer should put it into type and by the time that this had been done, in about six months' time, Her Majesty 'would see how impossible it was to issue it'.[7]

Before this plan had been put into execution, however, Randall Davidson had become involved and had delicately suggested to the Queen that publication would be a mistake. She was as annoyed by Davidson's response as she had been by her Private Secretary's: she would certainly have the memoir printed. Davidson bravely repeated his advice in rather stronger terms. The Queen responded by demanding an apology and the withdrawal of his remarks. Davidson apologized but did not withdraw his advice and offered his resignation. For over a fortnight the Queen ignored his existence. Then she sent for him; she was perfectly agreeable; the memoir was not mentioned and, together with Brown's diary, was quietly destroyed. 'My belief,' Davidson commented, 'is that the Queen liked and trusted best those who incurred her wrath, provided that she had reason to think their motives good.'[8]

It did not, however, prove possible to prevent the publication, in February 1884, of a sequel to *Leaves from the Journal of Our Life in the Highlands*, covering the years from 1862 to 1882, which was dedicated to her 'Loyal Highlanders and especially to the memory of [her] devoted personal attendant and faithful friend JOHN BROWN' whose loss was 'irreparable', for he deservedly possessed her 'entire confidence'. 'And to say,' she added, 'that he is daily, nay, hourly missed by me, whose lifelong gratitude he won by his constant care, attention and devotion, is but a feeble expression of the truth.'

The book was to be a resounding success with the general reader, but the family deplored its publication. Her eldest daughter could not bring herself to say more than that it described Balmoral very well; the 87-year-old Duchess of Cambridge castigated its 'bad, vulgar English': the book, in her opinion, was 'so miserably futile & trivial! So dull and uninteresting'.[9] The Prince of Wales, holding 'very strong views on the subject', acknowledged the advance copy of the book which she sent him with a suggestion that it should be limited to private circulation. The Queen passed the letter to her secretary with a cross note to the effect that she thought it 'very strange that objections should come from that quarter where grt strictness of conduct [was] not generally much cared for [and where there was so] much talk and want of reticence'. To restrict the book to private circulation would be to limit the readership of the book to members of society, who were just the people least qualified to appreciate it. Changing tack, the Prince again wrote to his mother, this time to protest that, although he was well aware that the main purpose of the book was to describe her life in the Highlands, it might create surprise that the name of her eldest son never occurred in it.

To this the Queen riposted by asking if he had actually read the book himself or asked his 'so-called friends' to do so for him. Had he been kind enough to read it himself, he would have found that his name was mentioned on pages 1, 5, 8, 331 and 378. It would have been mentioned more often, the Queen did not forbear to add, if he had come to Balmoral more frequently.[10] But then, as she complained on other occasions, he was far too occupied with the pleasures of his social round to spare much time for that.

58

THE MUNSHI

'The Munshi occupies very much the same position
as John Brown used to do.'

IN THE SUMMER OF her Golden Jubilee Year of 1887, the Queen acquired the first of her Indian servants. She was delighted with them, and in particular with the stout and agreeable Mohammed Bukhsh and the taller, more handsome and ingratiating 24-year-old Abdul Karim, both of whom kissed her feet when they were presented to her at Windsor.[1] She had them stand behind her chair at breakfast as she ate a boiled egg in a gold eggcup with a gold spoon.[2] In accordance with her detailed instructions, they wore 'dark blue dress' when waiting at breakfast out of doors, with 'any "Pageri" (Turban) and sash they like, only not the *Gold Ones*'. At dinner they were to be dressed in scarlet and gold in winter, white in summer. Their hands clasped in front of their sashes, they stood motionless, Abdul Karim 'looking so distinguished' with his black beard and dark eyes in striking contrast with the white of his turban. In fact, she was quite sure, he was distinguished in his way, not really a servant at all: his father, she had been told, was a surgeon-general in the Indian Army. She raised him from the rank of *khitmagar* (waiter) to *munshi* (secretary), although he was barely literate; and, instead of cooking curries for her as he had done at first, he began to give her lessons in Hindustani. All photographs of him handing dishes to the Queen were destroyed.[3]

'I am learning a few words in Hindustani,' she wrote in her journal on 3 August. 'It is a great interest to me for both the language and the people, I have naturally never come into real contact with before.' The Munshi, as he came to be known, was a 'vy strict Master', though 'a perfect Gentleman'. 'He is zealous, attentive and quiet and gentle, has such intelligence and good sense,' the Queen told Dr Reid. 'He is useful for his great knowledge of his own language and . . . he will soon be able to *copy* a good deal for the Queen.'[4]

Her Household profoundly wished that she had never in any way come into contact with the Munshi. He was so tiresome, so infuriatingly pretentious, so very far from the docile, obedient, 'grave and dignified' man whom the Queen had described. Taking their dislike of him to be prompted by the racial prejudice she so much abhorred, she ignored such hints about Abdul Karim's unwarranted pretentions as they dared to insinuate. She gave him permission to enter the billiard room as though he were one of her official secretaries and even to have meals in the household dining room. She provided him with a fully furnished bungalow at Windsor, eventually allowing him the use of cottages at Balmoral and Osborne also. She commissioned a portrait of him from the Austrian artist, Rudolph Swoboda, and took great care in making a copy of it herself.[5]* She allowed him to bring over from India so many female dependants that every time Dr Reid was asked to attend Mrs Abdul Karim a different tongue, so he said, was put out for his inspection. The Queen firmly scolded another of her Indians for declining to carry a message for the Munshi; and she reprimanded her equerry, Sir Fleetwood Edwards, for attempting to place him with the dressers at a theatrical performance. The year after his arrival, so Dr Reid told Sir William Jenner, she took

---

* There are two portraits of Abdul Karim in the Durbar Corridor at Osborne which also contains a large collection of portraits of Indian dignitaries, soldiers, servants and of craftsmen who worked on the Durbar Room. All these were commissioned by the Queen who also commissioned the full-length portrait of the fifteen-year-old Maharajah Duleep Singh from F. X. Winterhalter. Impressed by the striking good looks of this boy who had been taken into British protection when his father was deposed, the Queen herself painted a portrait of him in watercolour, depicting him kneeling down to dress up Prince Arthur in Indian costume (Marina Warner, *Queen Victoria's Sketchbook*, 197–8). Thereafter Duleep Singh led a dissipated life for which he came to beg the Queen's forgiveness when she was staying at Grasse in 1891. 'The Queen said he was quite calm at first then wept bitterly imploring forgiveness and finally when she stroked his hand recovered his equanimity.' 'No wonder,' the Queen's maid-of-honour, Marie Adeane, commented, 'I believe he is a monster of the deepest dye and is treated far better than he deserves' (Victor Mallet, *Life with Queen Victoria: Marie Mallet's Letters from Court*, 48).

Duleep Singh's elder son, Prince Victor Albert, a godson of the Queen, married a daughter of the ninth Earl of Coventry. His father was told by the Governor-General of India at the time of his deposition in 1849 to present the famous Koh-i-Noor diamond to the Queen. When he died in 1893 the Queen sent a wreath with a message of sympathy from his 'affectionate friend & Godmother'.

him with her to Glassalt Shiel, her private retreat on Loch Muick.[6]

A few months later, when Abdul took to his bed with a painful carbuncle on his neck, the Queen visited him twice a day, 'examining his neck, soothing his pillows' and stroking his hand. When he began to get better the Hindustani lessons were resumed in his room.[7]

That year, at the Braemar games, he was allowed 'to make a very conspicuous figure among the gentry'.

> The Duke of Connaught was angry and spoke to me about it [wrote Henry Ponsonby upon whom the Queen had pressed an unwanted Hindu vocabulary to study]. I replied that Abdul stood where he was by the Queen's order and that if it was wrong, as I did not understand Indian Etiquette and H.R.H. did, would it not be better for him to mention it to the Queen. This entirely shut him up.[8]

What concerned the gentlemen of her Household more than all this was her appointment of Abdul Karim as her 'Indian Secretary'. She told Ponsonby that he was 'most handy' in this respect, 'helping when she *signs* by drying the signatures. He learns with extraordinary assiduity.'[9] There was no need to fear that she was indiscreet in employing him in this way. '*No* political papers of any kind are ever in the Munshi's hands, even in her presence,' she assured Lord Salisbury. 'He only helps her to read words which she cannot read or merely submissions or warrants for signature. He does not read English fluently enough to be able to read anything of importance.'[10] Yet her Ministers were inclined to believe that, while she did, indeed, keep confidential papers from him, she entrusted him with more responsibility than her account of his assistance implied, made recommendations at his request and was persuaded to see Indian affairs from an exclusively Muslim point of view. Certainly, when told of a proposal to found a Muslim college, she promised to subscribe to it, adding that she would do so, 'even if it should mean giving something to a Hindoo College – but they do not need help as they have plenty.'[11]

So much trust did the Queen appear to repose in Abdul Karim that it became a matter of serious concern that he was on very friendly terms with a young lawyer, Rafiuddin Ahmed, who was closely associated with the Muslim Patriotic League and was suspected of relaying to Afghanistan state secrets supplied to him by the Munshi.

The Secretary of State for India, Lord George Hamilton, expressed a doubt that it would be wise to send confidential papers to the Queen if she showed them to the Munshi and warned that Hindus in India would much resent a Muslim being trusted in the manner which Abdul Karim was. 'I do not think that the Munshi is as dangerous as some suppose,' Lord George told Lord Elgin, the Viceroy. 'Salisbury [the Prime Minister] concurs in that view.' But, he continued, the Munshi is 'a stupid man, & on that account he may become a tool in the hands of other abler men'.[12]

In 1894 a carefully worded protest to the Queen from four senior members of her Household about the indulgence shown to the Munshi, whose social origins were not as he pretended, drew forth a furious counterblast:

> To make out that the . . . poor good Munshi . . . is *low* is really *outrageous* & in a country like England quite out of place . . . She has known 2 Archbishops who were sons respectively of a Butcher & a Grocer, a Chancellor whose father was a poor sort of Scotch Minister, Sir D. Stewart and Ld Mt Stephen both who ran about barefoot as children . . . and the tradesmen Maple and J. Price were made Baronets . . . Abdul's father saw good & honourable service as a Dr & he [Abdul] feels cut to the heart at being thus spoken of. It probably comes from some low jealous Indians or Anglo-Indians . . . The Queen is so sorry for the poor Munshi's sensitive feelings.[13]

Determined to silence his critics, the Queen now sent a telegram to Sir Henry Ponsonby's son, who was then serving as an aide-de-camp on the Viceroy's staff in India and was about to become an equerry at Court, asking him to seek out the Munshi's father and to report upon his position.

> Of course I took steps to obey the Queen's commands [Frederick Ponsonby wrote in his memoirs] . . . And when I returned home and took up my appointment the Queen asked whether I had seen Abdul Karim's father and I replied that . . . the man was not a surgeon-general but only the apothecary at the jail . . . She stoutly denied this and thought I must have seen the wrong man . . . To mark her displeasure with me, the Queen did not ask me to dinner for a year.[14]

Frederick Ponsonby's revelation that the Munshi had lied about his parentage did nothing to lessen the Queen's regard for her 'Indian Secretary'. Randall Davidson and Prince Louis of Battenberg, who acted as go-betweens in the increasingly bitter dispute between the Queen and her Household, thought that the Queen was 'off her head' about her attitude to the exasperating man. She arranged for him to have a seat next to her lady-in-waiting at an evening entertainment; she persuaded the Prime Minister and the Secretary of State for India to have him created a Companion of the Order of the Indian Empire; she wrote to the Empress Frederick to ask her to show him her house at Kronberg when he was in Germany: he ate no meat, just fruit, and drank a little milk; the Queen hoped she was not being troublesome.[15] In 1894, when the Queen was staying at the Villa Fabbricotti in Florence, the Munshi sent an announcement to be inserted in the *Florence Gazette* together with a photograph of himself:

> The Munshi Mohammed Abdul Karim son of Haji Dr Mohammed Wazirudin . . . came to England in the service of the Queen Victoria Empress of India in the year 1887.
>
> He was appointed first for some time as Her Majestys Munshi and Indian clerk. From 1892 he was appointed as Her M's Indian Secretary. He is belonging to a good and highly respectable Family. All is Family has been in Govt. Service with high position . . . All the Indian attendants of the Queen are under him and he also wholes different duties to perform in Her Majesty's Service.[16]

While he was in Florence with the Queen, Dr Reid made a list of examples of the Munshi's dreadful behaviour, including his refusal to allow any Indians in the same railway carriage as himself, his appropriation of the bathroom and lavatory which had been allotted to Her Majesty's maids, and his complaint that Italian newspapers took too little notice of him. On learning of this complaint, the Queen told her wardrobe maid, Mrs Macdonald, to instruct her courier to see that more mention was made of him. 'The Italians,' Reid commented, 'say he is a "Principe Indiano" with whom the Queen is in love.'

Not long after the Queen's return from Florence, in January 1895, Frederick Ponsonby reported to the Viceroy, Lord Elgin:

> I find the Munshi is a more difficult question to grapple with than I had thought. I thought that no one here had any idea of what the Munshi really was, but I find that not only all the Household but also Princess Louise, P. Beatrice and Prince Henry . . . have spoken to the Queen about it and [the Prime Minister and Secretary of State for India] have done their best to explain to her the state

of affairs. But she won't listen to any of them and thinks they know nothing about it . . . It has been perfectly useless and the Munshi occupies very much the same position as John Brown used to do. I have been told that both your and Lady Elgin's letters are given him to read and that he retails all the news back to India.

There have been two rows lately, one when Edwards refused to go to tea with the Munshi and the other when Doctor Reid refused to take the Munshi's father round the hospitals in London, and in both cases the Queen refused to listen to what they had to say but was very angry, so as you see the Munshi is a sort of pet, like a dog or cat which the Queen will not willingly give up . . .

The Queen would listen to you if you could write and point out to her the importance of not elevating the Munshi to the position of a confidential adviser and explain to her what the feeling in India is with regard to the Munshi: that would be the only chance of getting her to listen.

At the tableaux the Munshi took a very prominent part, and a seat in the audience next to the Lady in Waiting (much to her disgust) was reserved for him by order from the Queen. The Khit-magar on duty helps the Queen to walk into dinner and even into the chapel here, so you will see how great is her opinion of all the natives here. I have now got to think it lucky that the Munshi's sweeper does not dine with us.[17]

When the Queen announced that she was going to take the Munshi in her entourage to Cimiez in 1897, the Household revolted since the presence of the man, now suffering from gonorrhoea, would entail their having to take their meals with him. They asked Harriet Phipps, the Queen's Personal Secretary, to tell Her Majesty that if the Munshi went to France they would regretfully have to resign. On being given this message the Queen lost her temper, which she had not done for years, and with a cataclysmic gesture she swept everything on her desk on to the floor.

For months the dispute continued, the Munshi causing further offence by arranging for the publication in the *Daily Graphic* of a photograph of himself with the Queen in which, document in hand, he appeared to be her mentor; Dr Reid becoming so worn out by the Queen's demands and intransigence, her complaints of being 'terribly annoyed and upset' by the 'stupid business', her being 'continually aggrieved' at her gentlemen wishing 'to spy upon and interfere with one of her people', that he fell ill and had to retire to bed with boils and carbuncles, while the gentlemen of the Household regaled each other with stories of the Munshi's outrageous presumption and of the Queen's peevishness and distress.

Lord Salisbury did what he could to help restore peace to the Household. Tactfully, he persuaded the Queen that when she went to Cimiez the French might not understand the position which 'Le Munchy' occupied in her Household and they might not be as polite as they should be. There was also the problem of arousing jealousy amongst her Hindu subjects should the Queen show particular favour to a Muslim. So the 'Indian Secretary' did not accompany the Household to Cimiez that year but to their consternation he turned up later, having invited his friend Ahmed to come as well. This was too much for them to stand.

Arthur Bigge, a 'clever, amiable and agreeable' – as well as that important consideration, 'good looking' – man who had, by then, succeeded Sir Henry Ponsonby as Private Secretary, insisted that Ahmed be sent away; while messages were sent to India requesting any information about the Munshi which might serve to persuade the Queen of his worthlessness. The Household themselves had done what they could to make her realize how impossible the man was. But it was 'no use', Frederick Ponsonby told the Viceroy's Private Secretary, 'for the Queen says it is "race prejudice" & that we are all jealous of the poor Munshi (!).'[18]

Lord George Hamilton thought that it would be as well not to make any more enquiries which might exacerbate this 'Court commotion'. He felt sure that the 'little storm' would soon subside, and that the Munshi would 'hereafter be on the decline'. Bigge assured him that the Household would ensure that the Munshi would now be put in his 'proper place'.

The Queen was determined, however, that the Munshi should not be humiliated. She had already 'got into a most violent passion' with Dr Reid who, with the support of the Prince of Wales, was brave enough to tell her that there were 'people in high places' who were saying to him that the 'only charitable explanation' of her support and defence of the Munshi was that she was not sane. She raged against Fleetwood Edwards for daring to oppose her giving way to the Munshi's demands that he should be appointed a Member of the Victorian Order. In enormously long letters to Dr Reid she complained of the distorted and exaggerated stories which were spread about her 'poor friend' who was so shamefully persecuted; and on Christmas Day 1897 during 'a most stormy talk for three quarters of an hour with the Queen about the Munshi', she grew, in Reid's words, 'quite mad with rage'.[19] She berated the India Office for suggesting that he was not a gentleman; when the Aga Khan came to Windsor she saw to it that he had a conversation with her 'Indian Secretary'; she told Lord Curzon, who succeeded Lord Elgin as Viceroy of India, not to believe the derogatory rumours circulating about the Munshi and his family; she asked the Lord Chamberlain, the Earl of Hopetoun, to set a good example at Windsor by being polite to him. She was equally attentive to the interests of Rafiuddin Ahmed to compensate for the 'disgraceful affair' of his being expelled from Cimiez, requiring that he be invited to a court ball, suggesting that he be employed in gathering information from Mohammedans that might be useful to the Government, and asking that he should be awarded a Jubilee medal which, after all, was given to 'clergymen, *actors*, artists', so why not to him?

Before her penultimate holiday at Cimiez, the Queen, who had long since taken to ending letters to the Munshi with the words, 'Your loving Mother', wrote to the Munshi to say: 'I have in my Testamentary arrangements secured your comfort and have constantly thought of you well. The long letter I enclose which was written nearly a month ago is *entirely* and solely *my own idea, not a human being will ever* know of it or what you answer me. If you can't read it I will help you then burn it at *once*. Your faithful true friend VRI.'[20]

She had already made her peace with Frederick Ponsonby whose revelation of the occupation of the Munshi's father had so offended her. Not once having invited him to dinner or even addressed a word to him during that year's visit to Cimiez – although one of the reasons for wanting him as an equerry was his good command of French, an ability of which she had taken note when seeing him perform in a French play at Osborne – she turned to him as she was leaving and said, 'What a pity it is to leave Nice in such beautiful weather!' For her, it was a kind of apology.[21]

After her return from Cimiez the gentlemen of the Household found the Munshi rather less obtrusive; but he retained his office and his cottages, and he retained the Queen's professed regard. And, although she confessed to Dr Reid that she sometimes quite dreaded seeing him because of the further 'trouble and mischief' he was liable to provoke, she resisted all hints that he should be sent back to India.[22] Indeed, Lord Salisbury was of the opinion that she quite enjoyed the squabbles he provoked since they were 'the only form of excitement she can have'.*[22]

---

* After the Queen's death her Indian servants were sent back to India with pensions; and, in the presence of the Munshi himself, most of his papers were burned on a bonfire at Frogmore Cottage where he had lived when the Court was at Windsor. In 1905 while he was on a tour of India, the Prince of Wales, the later King George V, went to see him at Karim Lodge, Agra. 'He has not grown more beautiful,' the Prince recorded, 'and is getting fat. I must say he was most civil and humble and really pleased to see us. He wore his C.V.O. which I had no idea he had got. I am told he lives quietly here and gives no trouble at all' (RA GV AA27/10, quoted in Sheila Anand, *Indian Sahib: Queen Victoria's Dear Abdul*, 103–4).

59

✳✳✳✳✳✳✳✳✳✳✳✳

DIAMOND JUBILEE

'No one ever, I believe, has met with such
an ovation as was given to me.'

'TODAY IS THE DAY,' the Queen wrote in her journal on 23 September
1896, 'on which I have reigned longer, by a day, than any English sovereign.'[1]

That autumn was a happy time for her. General Kitchener was doing
well in the Sudan; Lord Salisbury's third Cabinet, formed the year before,
was proving so much more amenable than any of Mr Gladstone's: 'Every
day,' she told Salisbury, 'I feel the blessing of a strong Government in
such safe and strong hands as yours.'[2] And, towards the end of September,
Princess Alice's beautiful daughter, Alexandra, known as Alicky, came
with her husband, Tsar Nicholas II, to stay at Balmoral.

The Queen had at first been much against Alicky's proposed marriage
to the Tsarevich. She had hoped that she would marry her grandson,
Prince Albert Victor, whom she had described, without too strict a regard
for the truth, as not only 'kind' and 'affectionate' but also steady;[3] and
she had viewed the prospect of the girl's marriage to the Tsarevich with
alarm 'on account of the country, the policy and differences with us and
the awful insecurity to which that sweet child will be exposed'. When his
father, Tsar Alexander III, died in November 1894 the Queen's fears for
the future were increased by the thought of the 'sweet innocent gentle' girl
being placed on 'that very unsafe Throne' and having her life 'constantly
threatened'.[4] It was a 'great additional anxiety' to her in her 'declining
years'.

Yet when she got to know Nicky she could well understand why

Alicky wanted to marry him: she had 'never met a more amiable, simple young man, affectionate, sensible and liberal-minded'. Besides, Anglo-Russian relations might well be improved by his marriage to Queen Victoria's granddaughter.

Nicky himself, who had stayed at Windsor in 1894, was made to feel quite at home. 'It feels funny to me,' he had told his brother Georgy, 'the extent to which I have become part of the English family. I have become almost as indispensable to [the Queen] as her Indians and her Scotsmen; I am, as it were, attached to her and the best thing is that she does not like me to leave her side . . . She exudes such enormous charm.'[5]

She much enjoyed the Tsar's company when he returned from Russia to stay at Balmoral in 1896; but he was not so taken with life in Scotland. He complained of having to go out shooting 'all day long'; and of the house being 'colder than Siberia'; and of suffering from toothache and a cheek 'much swollen from irritation at the stump of a decayed molar'.[6] On a particularly wet and stormy day he and the Tsarina were required to go to church where Lady Lytton thought it was 'very interesting seeing the two pews full of the Royalties and the Emperor and Empress standing by the Queen even in the Scotch Kirk [at Crathie] where all is simple and reverent'.[7] As though in relief that the visit was over, the Tsar gave the Master of the Household £1,000 to be distributed amongst the servants upon his departure, and to Sir James Reid who had cured his toothache he gave 'a gold cigarette case with his Imperial arms in gold and diamonds in the corner'.[8]

While he was still at Balmoral numerous telegrams 'kept coming in all day' to congratulate the Queen on her having reigned even longer than George III. 'People wished to make all sorts of demonstrations,' she wrote in her journal, 'which I asked them not to do until I had completed the sixty years next June.'[9]

Preparations for these celebrations in June had already begun; and the suggestion put forward by Joseph Chamberlain that, rather than European royalties as guests, prime ministers from the countries of the Empire should be invited to the Diamond Jubilee was gratefully accepted by the Queen who was profoundly thankful that she would not therefore have to fill Buckingham Palace and Windsor Castle with unwelcome relations and their suites and especially gratified that she would have a perfect excuse for not inviting the Kaiser. She did, however, invite her cousin, the King of the Belgians, and his younger daughter, Princess Clementina.

It was also proposed that, in view of the Queen's age, the programme of events should be less demanding than it had been ten years before. There was to be a family service in St George's Chapel on Sunday 20 June at eleven o'clock to coincide with services at other places of worship all over the country. At the Royal Family's service Prince Albert's *Te Deum* was to be sung as well as a Jubilee hymn set to music by Sir Arthur Sullivan.* Alfred Austin, by now Poet Laureate, had offered the words for this hymn; but Sullivan had rejected them as unsuitable and the hymn had been written instead shortly before his death by Walsham How, Bishop of Wakefield, at the request of the Prince of Wales.

On 22 June the early morning was overcast, but at a quarter past eleven, as cannon boomed in Hyde Park to announce the departure of the Queen from Buckingham Palace to St Paul's Cathedral, the sun came out as it had done for her Golden Jubilee in obedience to the tradition which had become known as 'Queen's Weather'. Wearing a black silk dress, which was rendered less lugubrious by panels of grey satin, and with white flowers and a white aigrette in her bonnet, the Queen drove to the Cathedral in an open landau with the Princess of Wales and Princess Helena who was taking the place of Her Majesty's eldest daughter since Vicky's rank as Empress prevented her sitting with her back to the horses.

The acclamations which greeted the Queen moved her to tears. 'How kind they are,' she said more than once, as the Princess of Wales leant forward to pat her hand in a gesture of both sympathy and congratulation. 'No one ever, I believe, has met with such an ovation as was given to me, passing through those six miles of streets,' she wrote in her journal.

---

* The Queen greatly admired Sullivan's music. She asked him for a complete set of his works, a request made to no other composer, not even Mendelssohn; and she sent Prince Albert's compositions for him to correct, as high a token of her regard as she could possibly have bestowed. Having heard his oratorio, *The Light of the World*, she declared it was 'destined to uplift British music'. Although she thought the plot of *The Mikado* 'rather silly', she found the well-known airs irresistible and she commanded a performance of *The Gondoliers* at Windsor Castle. She took pride in having urged Sullivan to try his hand at grand opera. 'You would do it so well,' she told him. Accordingly he dedicated *Ivanhoe* to her; and after the first night of that opera she told him that its success was 'a particular satisfaction to her' as she believed it was 'partly owing to her own instigation' that he had 'undertaken this great work' (Hesketh Pearson, *Gilbert and Sullivan* 161, 171, 183).

'The crowds were quite indescribable, and their enthusiasm really marvellous and deeply touching. The cheering was quite deafening, and every face seemed to be filled with real joy.'[10]

'We were seated under the right wing of the National Gallery & could see right down Pall Mall & right up Charing Cross,' wrote Lady Monkswell in her account of the procession. 'It was overwhelming looking round upon the sea of people.'

> We did not pay any attention to the first 7 carriages [she continued]. But we woke up very wide when those containing the little Battenberg, Connaught and Albany children came by, the children bowing their little best & beginning to look [very tired] . . . The papers say the little Duke of Albany fainted before he got home, & I can quite believe it . . . Then we beheld the dear old Queen, – & what a cheer they gave her, it made the tears come to my eyes. She was sitting quite upright & brisk in the carriage not looking flushed or overcome, but smiling & bowing. She was dressed in grey & black, & held in her hand the very long-handled black lace parasol lined with white, given her by Mr. Charles Villiers, the oldest M.P. [Lady Lytton's uncle, Member for Wolverhampton since 1835]. She held it high up so that we could see her face. Now I reflect upon it, her attitude expressing so much vigour, her bows which made so much impression upon me (I got one to myself at a Drawing-room & remember it *now*, & her keen blue eyes) what she had already done that week & what she had still to do. I cannot believe that she is in her 79th year.
>
> When she was passed & we felt that we had done our Jubilee I had an over-powering emotion of thankfulness & satisfaction that I, with husband & sons, had been present at this great, this tremendous occasion.[11]

The Queen rode along, the tears occasionally trickling down her cheeks, the Commander-in-Chief, Lord Wolseley, trotting in front of her, the Earl of Dundonald, colonel of the 2nd Life Guards, immediately behind, having some trouble with his mare and calling out 'Steady, old lady! Whao, old girl!' – injunctions which the Queen at first supposed to be addressed to her.[12]

After a short service conducted beside the Cathedral steps, the Queen drove on across London Bridge and through the gaily decorated streets of the East End which were filled with cheering people who seemed, she said, 'delighted to see their little old Queen'. She crossed Westminster

Bridge, drove through Parliament Square, past Horse Guards Parade and up The Mall back to the Palace. All had 'gone off splendidly' in the words of the Prince of Wales, the only mishap occurring when the 75-year-old Lord Howe, overcome by the heat, fainted and fell off his horse.

As in 1887, after the Golden Jubilee parade, the next few days were busy and tiring. Again there were receptions and garden parties, military reviews, banquets and parades of troops from all over the Empire, and a march past of some four thousand boys from several public schools, all cheering as they passed Her Majesty, the Eton and Harrow boys looking, she thought, rather smarter than the rest.

She was given a welcome quite as vociferous three years later when, after the relief of Ladysmith in February 1900, the second war against the Boers in South Africa seemed to be reaching a not too inglorious conclusion. Throughout both wars, the first to be fought against a white enemy since the Crimean War, she had maintained an indomitable confidence, condemning the Boers as a 'horrid people, cruel & over-bearing', bidding farewell to her soldiers with a lump in her throat, sending them parcels of knitted garments and 100,000 tins of chocolate, welcoming them home on their return, vainly endeavouring to ensure that coloured troops should serve alongside white in battle, visiting hospitals, and going to open one in Bristol, visiting Woolwich Arsenal where the cheers of the thousands of workers 'quite drowned out' the band playing 'God Save the Queen', confessing that reading telegrams always made her feel ill, often breaking down and crying, so Frederick Ponsonby said, over the long lists of casualties,[13] yet all the time insisting, even at the most worrying periods, that there was no one depressed in her own Household, that the war must be won even if the whole army had to go out. When A. J. Balfour, First Lord of the Treasury, came to Windsor with a gloomy report shortly after the British reverses in the 'Black Week' of December 1899, 'he was at once cut short with the characteristic, quick little bend of the head in which all regality seemed concentrated: "Please understand that there is no depression in *this* house; we are not interested in the possibilities of defeat; they do not exist." '[14]

As she had done during the Crimean War the Queen took great interest in the distribution of medals. 'There was a pathetic moment yesterday,'

Reginald Brett wrote in his diary after one investiture, 'when the Queen was wheeled up to Findlater and the other wounded V.C., both sitting in chairs. They were ordered to rise but the Queen said, "Most certainly not," and raised herself without help (a very unusual thing) and stood over them while she decorated them with the Cross.'[15]

60

LIFE AT COURT

'It was a great crime to meet her in the grounds . . . and
we all took good care that this should never happen.'

WHEN IN 1894 Frederick Ponsonby had arrived at Osborne aged
twenty-seven, he had found that all the senior gentlemen of the Household
had grown old in the Queen's service – two of them were eighty – and
that he himself as Junior Equerry had very little to do. After breakfast he
went to the equerries' room where he read the newspapers and wrote
private letters. At noon the Queen went out in her pony-chair, accompanied by a lady-in-waiting, a maid-of-honour or one of her daughters,
regardless of the weather: it was not considered in the least surprising
that Princess Beatrice suffered from rheumatism at an early age. As soon
as the Queen had driven away, the Household, who had to remain indoors
so long as the Queen was in the house, walked out too. 'But it was like
a lunatic asylum,' Ponsonby said, 'as everybody went alone in different
directions.'

Luncheon for the gentlemen was served at two o'clock, the Master
of the Household carving at one end of the table and the Junior Equerry
at the other. 'These luncheons were always very amusing,' Ponsonby
discovered, 'as there was much wit among the older men.'

At three o'clock the Queen went out driving again, this time in a
carriage and pair with an outrider in front and, if she were going to
Cowes or some other town on the island, an equerry riding alongside
the carriage, two equerries being required when Her Majesty had to attend
some sort of function. Again the gentlemen took the opportunity of the
Queen's departure to go out themselves, either for a walk or a ride, using

461

only those particular carriages, divided into five categories, which were allotted to their use, and making sure that they did not come across her, since, as Ponsonby said, 'it was a great crime to meet her in the grounds ... and we all took good care that this should never happen. If by any unlucky chance we did come across her, we hid behind bushes. Sir William Harcourt [the Chancellor of the Exchequer], walking one day with my father, looked up and saw the Queen coming down the path. There was only one small shrub near, and Harcourt asked whether he was expected to hide behind that, but as he was six feet four inches high, my father suggested that the wisest thing to do was to turn back.' Nor was it only Ministers and members of the Household who were required to avoid Her Majesty: new servants were not allowed to look her in the face, and when receiving orders had to gaze at the ground at her feet. If by chance they came across her in a corridor she would look straight ahead as though she had not noticed they were there.[1]

The Queen was in the habit of protesting strongly against the social prejudices of the upper classes. 'The division of classes is the *one thing* which is most dangerous & reprehensible,' she once wrote, 'never intended by the law of nature & wh the Queen is always labouring to alter.' Yet, the social hierarchy of her own Household was a rigid one: it was possible to cross the barriers, as John Brown had done, but the barriers were never lowered.

Having evaded the Queen, the members of the Household returned to the house when she did, the gentlemen being served tea in their own rooms, the ladies having 'a big tea' together. Then 'there was nothing for [Ponsonby] to do until dinner'.

The next year, however, Ponsonby was appointed Assistant Private Secretary and he then found his time fully occupied in cyphering and decyphering messages; dealing with a mass of correspondence which Arthur Bigge left for his attention; making notes of all the papers which were sent to the Queen in case an important document, which she might keep for as long as a week, did not return; copying out parts of despatches which the Queen wanted to keep for her files; learning shorthand; improving his German and studying the Almanac de Gotha so that he could make himself more familiar with the complicated ramifications of the royal family tree. He was also responsible for preparing the data on which the Queen based certain entries in her diary as she liked to be quite sure of the complete accuracy of her facts, though evidently she was not above allowing the occasional misstatement to appear when it cast her in a favourable or flattering light. Thus it was that in recounting the Queen's review of her colonial troops in 1897, Ponsonby – while knowing it to be false – included a statement, which had appeared in the newspapers, to the effect that Her Majesty had spoken to the Indian officers in Hindustani. When this was read out to her she objected, 'That's not true. I did not speak in Hindustani, but in English.' She was therefore asked if this part of the account should be omitted. 'No,' she decided. 'You can leave it, for I could have done so had I wished.'[2]

Another of Frederick Ponsonby's duties was to look after the Queen's birthday books by which she set great store, taking the latest volumes about with her wherever she went so that people on occasions mistook them for Bibles, and insisting that all the people who visited her should sign their names on the appropriate page. The German Secretary was nominally in charge of these books and was responsible for compiling their indexes. But he did not carry out his duties as well as he should have done, and the onus of keeping the books up to date fell upon Ponsonby. Once when the Queen was staying in Nice at the Hôtel Regina it was suggested to her that Sarah Bernhardt, who was acting at the theatre in the town, should be invited to give a recital in the hotel. The Queen was at first reluctant, knowing that Bernhardt's morals were far from being above reproach. Later, however, she changed her mind, attended the recital of Theuriet's *Jean Marie* which she thought 'quite marvellous, so pathetic and full of feeling', and, much impressed by the virtuosity of the great actress whose cheeks were wet with tears, she asked one of her ladies to present her to her so that she could compliment her. On Bernhardt's leaving the room the Queen sent to enquire if her autograph had been procured for the Birthday Book. Ponsonby was proud to have remembered to ensure that it was. He had watched with satisfaction mingled with astonishment as Bernhardt had taken the book from him, placed it on the floor, knelt in front of it, and scrawled across it, '*Le plus beau jour de ma vie*', followed by a flamboyant signature. Ponsonby proudly sent up the book for the Queen to see. But, having done his 'duty nobly', as he thought, he got 'no marks'. First of all it was the wrong book: he ought to have used the artists' book. Second, he should have prevented Miss Bernhardt from taking up the whole page.[2]

Towards the end of her life the Queen became an increasingly trying mistress because of her failing sight for which surgery was unsuccessfully proposed by 'one of the greatest oculists in Europe', Professor Hermann Pagenstecker, the Queen preferring to rely on belladonna to disperse the film. This proving less than satisfactory, her handwriting became increasingly difficult to read, while her secretaries were obliged to write in larger, more clearly formed characters and, therefore, more slowly.* Ponsonby, resourceful as ever, bought some copy-books printed for girls' schools with the help of which he perfected a completely new hand. He also bought 'some special ink like boot varnish'; and, having used this to write his document, he dried it over a copper tray heated by a spirit lamp, an invention of Sir Arthur Bigge's. But this method did not satisfy the Queen. Since the thick black ink showed through the paper, only one side could be used which rendered the documents she had to read too bulky for her taste. She, therefore, issued instructions for Ponsonby to revert to his former practice of writing on both sides of the paper. So Ponsonby applied to the Stationery Office for a supply of paper the same size as the sheets then in use but very much thicker. At first the new paper was acceptable; but, as the Queen liked to keep all messages in her room for some time, she soon found that the accumulation of paper was inconvenient: would Captain Ponsonby kindly revert to the ordinary paper.

'I grasped then that it was hopeless', Ponsonby recorded, 'and I consulted Sir James Reid as to whether it would not be possible to explain all the difficulties to her, but he said he feared her sight was going and that any explanation would therefore be useless. So I went back to the ordinary paper and ordinary ink, and of course received a message to

---

* The Queen's handwriting was as much a source of complaint in her family as it was among the members of her staff. For instance Tsar Nicholas II, husband of her granddaughter, Alexandra, complained to his wife, 'Her letters are so awfully difficult to read, and she has got a way of shortening her sentences and words in such a manner that I could not make out for a long time' (Andrei Maylunas and Sergei Mironenko, *A Lifelong Passion: Nicholas and Alexandra: Their Own Story*, 67).

say would I write blacker, but as it was hopeless I didn't attempt to alter anything.'*

In the end documents had to be read to her. Much of this reading was done by Princess Beatrice, her youngest child, which led to what Ponsonby called 'absurd mistakes'. Ponsonby wrote to his mother:

> The Queen is not even *au courant* with the ordinary topics of the present day. Imagine [Princess] B[eatrice] trying to explain ... our policy in the East. Bigge or I may write out long précis of [such] things but they are often not read to HM as [Princess] B[eatrice] is in a hurry to develop a photograph or wants to paint a flower for a Bazaar ... Apart from the hideous mistakes that occur ... there is the danger of the Q's letting go almost entirely the control of things which should be kept under the immediate supervision of the Sovereign ... The sad thing is that it is only her eyes, nothing else. Her memory is still wonderful, her shrewdness, her power of discrimination as strong as ever, her long experience of European politics alone makes her opinion valuable but when her sole means of reading despatches, précis, etc. lie in [Princess] B[eatrice], it is simply hopeless.[3]

Before going down to dinner all the men dressed up in knee-breeches and stockings even if they were going to the Household dining room rather than joining the Queen's dinner-party.† 'The silence in the house

* Shortly after the introduction of an improved version of the typewriter into England, a machine was purchased for use at Windsor. But the Queen evidently did not like it (Emden, *Behind the Throne*, 127). She was equally opposed at first to the introduction of the telephone. She commanded a private demonstration of this invention at Osborne House in 1878. Alexander Graham Bell's public relations officer, Kate Field, arrived on the island and from the nearby Osborne Cottage sang 'Kathleen Mavourneen' down the line to the Queen who was 'not much impressed' (Victoria Glendinning, *Trollope*, 1992, 448). In 1896, however, telephones were installed at Windsor Castle. The Queen was equally dismissive of that other invention, the motor car. 'I'm told,' she commented, 'that they smell exceedingly nasty and are very shaky and disagreeable conveyances altogether' (quoted in Nevill, 13). The Prince of Wales did not agree with her. Provided he was not accompanied by his wife, 'whose one idea was not to run over a dog', he delighted in being driven very fast in a large car equipped with a raucous horn in the shape of a four-key bugle (C. W. Stamper, *What I Know*, 191).

† The sculptor, Alfred Gilbert, who was summoned to Osborne in 1896 to execute a memorial to Prince Henry of Battenberg for Whippingham Church, arrived with evening clothes but without the regulation court dress. Fortunately his moulder, who had come to the Isle of Wight with him, had been a tailor in his youth and was able to convert Gilbert's evening trousers into knee-breeches for his appearance at dinner. A pair of lady's black silk stockings were borrowed and, after considerable difficulty, as it was a Sunday, shoes and buckles were procured from a local shoemaker. When Gilbert was thus equipped a message came from the Queen excusing him from wearing court dress; but by then he had no ordinary evening trousers to put on. When the Queen was

was almost oppressive at dinner-time,' Ponsonby said, 'and those who were asked to dine with the Queen solemnly walked down the corridor, with mosaic floors and statues, talking almost in a whisper . . . At Balmoral the Queen's dinners were necessarily not large as there were not many people to ask. The conversation was supposed to be general, but the custom was to talk to one's neighbour in very low tones, and those on the right and left of Her Majesty were the only ones who spoke up.' Occasionally, as the Queen's eyesight worsened, there were embarrassing moments when she failed to recognize her neighbour, as she did one evening in 1899 when the Master of the Household made a mistake in compiling the seating list which led her to turn to the French ambassador and, supposing him to be the Italian as the list had indicated, asked him, 'where is your King now?'[4]

At these dinners a great deal depended upon what kind of mood the Queen was in: when she was rather preoccupied and silent the meal was a dismal occasion. Ponsonby's father described a particularly depressing one. The Queen, who had a cold, sat between her son, Prince Leopold, who 'never uttered', and Lord Gainsborough, who was deaf. The prolonged silences were broken only by various types of cough, 'respectable', 'deep', or 'gouty', and by 'all the servants dropping plates and making a clatteration of noises'.[5] No doubt they were drunk, as they often were, the Queen, as Dr Reid said, being astonishingly lenient about drunkenness among her servants, and instructing him 'on no account to tell the Ladies and Gentlemen that Hugh Brown [John Brown's brother] had died of alcoholic poisoning!!'*[6]

Softly as those further away from Her Majesty spoke, she would often overhear a word and ask what they were talking about. Once, having heard Alick Yorke, the groom-in-waiting, mention something about a queen, she called across to him to ask which queen he was talking about. Told that it was Mary Tudor, she commented, 'Oh! My bloody ancestor.'

---

informed what had happened, she commented complacently, 'How clever!' (Isabel McAlister, *Alfred Gilbert*, London, 1929, 279).
* This was in 1872. The older the Queen grew, the more frequently drunk some of her servants became. Mary Adeane, who joined the Household as a maid-of-honour in 1887, said, 'the footmen smell of whisky and are never prompt to answer the bell [and] stare in such a supercilious way' (Victor Mallet, *Life with Queen Victoria*, 215).

It was Alick Yorke who, at another of the Queen's dinners, amused a German guest so much that a loud guffaw was heard at the other end of the table. The Queen asked Yorke to repeat the joke. Unwisely he did so; it was rather a risqué story; the Queen looked at him with her basilisk's stare and, mindful that there were young ladies present, delivered herself of her most celebrated reprimand: 'We are not amused.'*[7]

---

* The Hon. Alexander Yorke, fifth son of the fourth Earl of Hardwicke, who had joined the household in 1884, was, however, much indulged by the Queen who was fond of him as a kind of court jester. To others, Yorke's precious manner, his heavy scent and outlandish buttonholes were the cause of some disapproval and concern. On his appeareance one day with 'an enormous Malmaison Carnation' in his buttonhole, Lady Lytton asked her husband's Private Secretary, Austin Lee, rather apprehensively, 'Are button-holes worn now?' 'Well,' Lee answered, 'not the peony size of Alick's' (*Lady Lytton's Court Diary*, 97).

61

✳✳✳✳✳✳✳✳✳✳

DINNER PARTIES

'The tears ran down my cheeks which set off the Queen.
I never saw her laugh so much.'

THE COUNTESS OF LYTTON, who arrived at Court in 1895 to fill a vacancy which had occurred among the Queen's ladies-in-waiting, found most of Her Majesty's dinners rather irksome affairs. On her arrival one bitterly cold October afternoon she was greeted by Harriet Phipps, the Queen's Personal Secretary, who, like all the bedchamber women and maids-of-honour who did not have titles, was given the rank of a baron's daughter and was therefore known as the Honourable Harriet Phipps. Miss Phipps took Lady Lytton into a small room, formerly the Prince Consort's dressing room which was used for receiving visitors upstairs. She was presented with the Victoria and Albert Order which all the Queen's ladies wore, attached to a white ribbon, on their dresses. And, on returning to her room, she was told by a servant who knocked on the door: 'You are invited to dine with the Queen, miladi.'

She went down to the dining room where she waited with the other guests until the announcement, 'The Queen has arrived' drew them all to the door. The Queen came into the room, leaning on the arm of an Indian servant, went through to the dining room and took her place at the table. 'The beginning of the dinner was rather solemn,' Lady Lytton recorded in her diary. The Queen hardly spoke at all during the early courses; and it was not until she made some remark about the Spanish Ambassador having 'come in the afternoon and [expecting] to be received at once without making an appointment' that the atmosphere became more relaxed as the guests laughed 'for some little time' at this odd ignorance of protocol.[1]

At a subsequent dinner the atmosphere was 'very solemn and the room so cold'. On such occasions the Queen rejected dishes she did not like with 'a peevish *moue* with crumpled brow more eloquent than words', and she spoke little, and, when she did, her remarks were far from memorable. Indeed, Lord Ribblesdale said they were conventional in the extreme. 'One way or another,' he wrote in his memoirs, 'I must have dined many times at the Queen's dinner party, and I personally never heard her say anything at dinner which I remembered next morning.'[2]

At least the smaller and less formal dinners did not last very long since, throughout her life, the Queen continued to eat a great deal very rapidly, the courses of soup, fish, meat and pudding soon being despatched together with a large amount of fruit, preferably pears, oranges – which she ate with a spoon having scooped out a hole in the top – and apples grown in an orchard at Windsor extending to four acres.[3]

The food served was generally agreed to be excellent at all the four separate dinners which were served each evening, those for the lower servants, the upper servants, the Household and the Queen with her chosen guests. A kitchen staff, including a chef, four master-cooks, two assistant cooks, two roasting cooks, two yeomen of the kitchen, sixteen apprentices, as well as bakers, confectioners, pastrymen and some half a dozen kitchen maids, provided menus which the Aga Khan described as long and elaborate:[4]

> Course after course, three or four choices of meat, a hot pudding and an iced pudding, a savoury and all kinds of hot-house fruit ... The Queen, in spite of her age, ate and drank heartily – every kind of wine that was offered [she usually drank Scotch whisky, distilled especially for her by John Begg, with Apollinaris, soda or lithia water] and every course, including both hot and iced pudding.[5]

She preferred plain food, such as boiled chicken and roast beef, haggis and potatoes (twelve acres of these were devoted to their growth at Windsor), to anything exotic, but she liked a good helping and she liked her brown Windsor soup made no longer simply with ham and calves' feet as served to her children in the nursery, but including game, Madeira and shell-fish; and she loved her *crème de volaille*, her puddings, her cranberry tarts and cream, her chocolate cakes and chocolate biscuits, her 'stodgy trifle of jam and sponge cakes'.[6]

Marie Mallet complained that slow eaters like herself and Mr Gladstone 'never had time to finish even a moderate helping', because the servants, in Lord Ribblesdale's words, had 'a menial trick of depriving us of our plates as soon as the Queen had finished'. The lords-in-waiting, being 'mostly of the deferential breed', did not complain and were, therefore, all the more astounded when one evening a guest did complain. This was Lord Hartington who was in the middle of enjoying some mutton and green peas.

'The Queen could dispose of peas with marvellous skill and dexterity [Lord Ribblesdale said], and had got into conversation with Lord Hartington, thus delaying his own operations. They got on very well together. Though Lord Hartington, like Peel and the Duke of Wellington, had neither small talk nor manners, yet he seemed to me less shy with the Queen than with his neighbours. This may be accounted for, perhaps, by their both being absolutely natural and their both being in no sort of doubt about their positions.

'Well, anyhow, in the full current of their conversation the mutton was taken away from him. He stopped in the middle of a sentence in time to arrest the scarlet-clad marauder: "Here bring that back!"'

The members of the Household held their breath, but when Lord Ribblesdale looked up at the Queen he saw that she was amused. 'I knew this,' he said, 'by one of the rare smiles, as different as possible to the civil variety which, overtired, uninterested or thinking about something else, she contributed to the conventional observations of her visitors.'[7]

Mrs Mallet confirmed the observation of others that the atmosphere at the dinner table – as Sir Henry Campbell-Bannerman had found – was dependent upon the Queen's mood. Sometimes her conversation would take the form of a rigorous cross-examination; at others she was very gloomy and silent, especially when an uncongenial Minister was in attendance such as Charles Ritchie, at one time Home Secretary, a tall, dark Scotsman whom Marie Mallet described as being 'very vulgar and unrefined in all his ways, in short he has not the manners of a gentleman. He lifts up his loud voice at dinner and shouts under her very nose and last night I heard him deliver a lecture on Socialism to Her Majesty which I could perceive was not relished.'[8]

Dinners were equally uncomfortable occasions when members of the

Queen's Household or family died. On the occasion of the death of her lady-in-waiting, Lady Ely, she came into the dining room in deepest mourning and 'hardly uttered';*[9] and when, again at dinner, she heard of the death of Prince Henry of Battenberg, who had gone out to serve in South Africa, she 'hardly uttered' throughout the meal.

Yet normally in these last years she was more often cheerful and talkative than gloomy and silent. The Aga Khan found the 'facility and clarity' of her conversation 'astonishing'. 'She had an odd accent,' he added, making a comment not endorsed by others, 'a mixture of Scotch and German' with 'the German conversational trick of interjecting "so" pronounced "tzo" into her remarks'.†[10]

Often she would laugh until the tears rolled down her cheeks. The letters which Marie Mallet wrote to her mother and her husband contain many references to the Queen's spontaneous and sometimes uproarious laughter when at a 'hen dinner' with her ladies: 'the Queen laughed very much'; 'the Queen laughed more than ever'; 'she was immensely amused and roared with laughter, her whole face changing and lighting up in a wonderful way'; 'she was very funny at the evening concert . . . in excellent spirits and full of jokes'.[11]

Another of her maids-of-honour, Susan Baring, also wrote of the Queen's good humour during these ladies' dinners: 'It was rather amusing the Queen doing puppets of the German ladies, too killing!!'[12]

The celebrated comedian, J. L. Toole, who was well known for his imitation of the Queen, was once invited to Windsor and, after dinner, was summoned by Her Majesty who commanded him, 'Now, Mr Toole,

---

* A fortnight after Lady Ely's death the Queen drove in a closed carriage from Paddington to Kensal Green Cemetery to place a wreath on Lady Ely's grave. 'There were crowds out,' she recorded in her journal. 'We could not understand why, and thought something must be going [on], but it turned out it was only to see me . . . There were such crowds that the privacy of my visit was quite spoilt; still, I felt glad so many bore witness to this act of regard and love paid to my beloved friend' (Queen Victoria's Journal, 27 June 1890).

† The Queen still retained the clarity of her expressive speech. In October 1898 the recently appointed Clerk of the Council, Sir Almeric Fitzroy, having attended his first Council meeting at Balmoral, recorded in his memoirs: 'It was an impressive spectacle, on entering this small and rather meanly appointed room, to find the solitary occupant in this lonely woman . . . How little sensible was that shrivelled octogenarian figure to the emotions she excited, as, with the habitual dignity that belongs to her . . . she motioned with her left hand to the position I was to occupy . . . and with a clearness of articulation that is startling in its melodious resonance, she applied herself to the routine of a ceremonial at which she must have presided more than six hundred times' (Sir Almeric Fitzroy, *Memoirs*, i, 2).

imitate me.' Toole, aghast, demurred, but the Queen persisted. After the performance she was 'for a little while silent and serious, but then began to laugh, gently at first, and then more and more heartily. At last Her Majesty said, "Mr Toole that was very clever, and very, very funny, and you must promise me you will never, never do it again."'[13]

The Queen also still much enjoyed the theatricals and *tableaux vivants* performed by members of her family and Household, all the more so when Henry Ponsonby was no longer there to spoil them by having neither the time nor the inclination to learn his part.

The Queen did not take part herself. Yet, although Alick Yorke was nominally the director of most productions, she dominated the proceedings, not only choosing the play but attending the rehearsals, altering and censoring the dialogue, acting as costume adviser, supervising the making and painting of the scenery, and seeing to it that members of her immediate family were given all the leading parts.[14] On the evening of the performance she would enter after the rest of the audience and take up her position 'a little forward from them in a low armchair', so one of her servants recorded. 'A footstool is placed before her, and a small table holds her fan, opera-glasses, programme and book of the words. The applause is always led by the Queen, who taps either her hand or table with her fan.' She led the laughter as well as the applause; and frequently, to the great annoyance of the performers, she would explain the plot to her neighbours in an all too audible voice during the course of the production.[15]

When professional performances were staged she did not hesitate to censor the script if she considered it too *outré*. She made no objection to the Covent Garden production of *Carmen*; but when in 1893 the cast from the Lyceum of Henry Irving's production of Tennyson's tragedy *Becket* was summoned to Windsor she expressed misgivings to Ponsonby:

> The Queen is rather alarmed at hearing from the p^ce of Wales & p^ce George that there is some very strong language (disagreeable & coarse rather) in *Becket* w^h must be somewhat changed for performance *here* . . . Pr^ss Louise says that some *scenes* or perhaps *one* are very *awkward*. What can be done?
> The P^r of Wales thought Sir Henry sh^d see & speak to Irving. The Queen hates anything of that sort.[16]

In the event 'Irving acted well and with much dignity, but his enunciation is not very distinct, especially when he gets excited. Ellen Terry as "Rosamund" was perfect, so graceful and full of feeling and so young-looking in her lovely light dress, quite wonderfully so, for she is forty-six!'[17]

As well as performances of plays by professional companies and amateur theatricals, there were also concerts – once Ignacy Paderewski played for her at Windsor 'quite marvellously', proving himself 'quite equal to Rubinstein', and in 1898 she was 'simply enchanted' by a performance of Wagner's *Lohengrin*, 'so poetic, so dramatic ... full of sadness, pathos and tenderness, a most glorious composition';[18] and she was equally delighted by a performance of *Cavalleria rusticana* 'by a young Italian composer of the name of Mascagni'. It was 'a great success,' she said. 'I loved the music, which is so melodious, and characteristically Italian.'[19] She was later heard humming the 'wonderfully descriptive and plaintive airs' to herself.[20]

From time to time lectures were given in the evening. A 'very interesting lecture' was, for instance, given in September 1872 by the explorer and journalist, Henry Morton Stanley, 'a determined, ugly, little man – with a strong American twang', as the Queen described him.[21] Also, very occasionally, the furniture in the drawing room was pushed back and the Queen, despite her lameness, enjoyed a 'nice little impromptu dance, Curtis's band being so *entraînant*'. 'We had a quadrille, in which I danced with Eddy!!' she wrote of one such impromptu dance in October 1890. 'It did quite well, then followed some waltzes and polkas.'[22]

One evening at the Villa Clara in Baveno the Queen, having asked William Jenner how he had spent his day, was amused to be told that he and Fräulein Bauer, Princess Beatrice's ugly and formidably straitlaced German governess, had joined a party climbing the Rigi. They had been mistaken for man and wife and, on this erroneous understanding, had been required to make the descent squashed closely together in a chair. Imagining the doctor and the governess thus trapped, everyone tried not to laugh until Princess Louise, then nineteen, could not control herself any longer and everyone else then burst into laughter. 'The tears ran down my cheeks,' Henry Ponsonby commented, 'which set off the Queen. I never saw her laugh so much.' When Lady Churchill innocently enquired, 'Did you find it comfortable?' the laughter exploded once more.

'My laugh was at Jenner stuffing his napkin over his mouth to stop himself, at Mary Bids [Lady Biddulph] shaking and speechless at my side and at Bids's [Sir Thomas Biddulph's] solemn face.'[23]

There was also loud laughter when the Queen was told by Lord Dufferin of a naive American who asked his English hostess, 'How old are you? How long have you been married? I should like to see your nuptial bed.' Amused as she was, the Queen raised her napkin to protect Princess Beatrice and the maids-of-honour who were sitting on the other side of the table.[24]

Upon a later hilarious occasion, this time at luncheon, an old, deaf, garrulous Admiral was telling the Queen at inordinate length how a ship which had sunk off the south coast had been raised and towed into Portsmouth. Anxious to stop the Admiral's flow of boring detail about this salvage operation, the Queen tried to change the subject by asking him about his sister. Mishearing her, the ancient mariner replied, 'Well, Ma'am, I am going to have her turned over, take a good look at her bottom and have it scraped.' As the footmen in attendance withdrew behind a screen, the Queen 'put down her knife and fork, hid her face in her handkerchief and shook and heaved with laughter until the tears rolled down her face'.*

One evening in April 1888 she 'laughed incessantly and was full of all the interesting people she had seen [in Berlin]'. At subsequent Ladies' Dinners she was described as talking very freely, giving her opinions 'in a most decided and amusing manner', being altogether 'so amusing', reminiscing happily about the boredom she had experienced during a performance of Handel's 'Messiah' at York Minster when she was sixteen, roaring with laughter at Bernard Mallet's description of his wife's attempting to paint at Bruges where boys had spat at her canvas and thrown stones at her, laughing heartily at dinner again three days later, and then being 'most cheerful' and in 'excellent spirits' at a subsequent dinner, 'making jokes about her age [78] and saying she felt quite young and that had it not been for an unfortunate accident she would have been running about still'.[25]

---

* Except for the days of her inconsolable grief, she had always been prone to outbursts of uncontrollable laughter. When the sculptor, John Gibson, was working on his statue of her, he asked if he might measure her mouth. 'The proposal was so unexpected and droll that it was some time before the Queen could compose herself; directly she closed her mouth she burst out laughing again' (Sarah A. Tooley, *The Personal Life of Queen Victoria*, 142).

Nor were larger, more formal dinners always as strained as some guests found them when the Queen was in a disgruntled mood, unhappy or preoccupied. Reginald Brett, the Secretary of the Office of Works, son and heir of the first Lord Esher, told his son of a dinner in 1897:

> It was really quite an amusing and pleasant dinner for me. I was two off the Queen, between the Duchess of Connaught and the young Duchess of Hesse [the Duke of Edinburgh's daughter, Victoria Melita] who is called 'Duckie' . . . She was very shy at first, but we got on capitally later, and by the end of dinner there was quite a rag.
>
> The Queen was extraordinarily vivacious, full of smiles and chaff – a most wonderful thing.[26]

A few months later Brett, who had by then become Lord Esher on his father's death, was again a guest of the Queen at a dinner 'which went off well':

> The Queen was in good spirits and talked to me a good deal at dinner and afterwards. I was next but one to her, between Princess Beatrice and Lady Dudley. The latter looked very well, stately and young to be the mother of all those Wards! [seven of them]. A telegram [containing disturbing news about the Boer war] came at dinner and the Queen turned quite pale . . . She asked me if I had seen her new portrait by Angeli, and, when I said no, had it sent for into the corridor. It is wonderfully like.*[27]

After dinner in these later years the lady guests would play patience or whist while the men stood about 'at the end of the room in a very stiff way and very tiring to themselves', 'whispering discreetly'. Sometimes they would join the card games; but, according to Frederick Ponsonby, this activity was never very enjoyable, the packs 'usually being one card short', and 'no one having the least knowledge' of the rules of the game being played. Moreover, 'Lord Stafford, who was an equerry, had always been told that the danger of card-playing was that unscrupulous people

---

* The Queen was equally pleased with an earlier portrait by Heinrich von Angeli painted in 1875 which she thought 'absurdly like'. It was as though she 'looked at [herself] in the glass'. The artist had, in her opinion, painted her with 'honesty, total want of flattery, and appreciation of character'. In 1887 she was shown 'that grinning "Jubilee" photograph' of herself. 'Her daughters were indignant at its sale in the streets, and wished to have it stopped. All they could get her to say was "well really I think it is *very like*. I have *no* illusions about my personal appearance' (*Journal and Letters of Reginald, Viscount Esher*, 1934, i, 160). Indeed, she once told Vicky that she well knew that she had 'an ugly old face'.

looked over one's hand, and therefore held his hands so tightly under his chin that it took him nearly two whole minutes to find a card. Of course, no smoking was allowed.'[28]

The Queen, meanwhile, would sit in her chair, sipping coffee from a cup whose saucer was held by a page, occasionally asking someone to be brought up to speak to her and giving that 'curious, nervous laugh' of hers when a person whom she did not know very well was presented. 'About eleven the [card games] stop,' Lady Lytton recorded in 1896, 'and looks are sent across to the Queen ... When she takes her stick, as if by magic the servants outside know it and open the door and [an Indian servant] ... glides in, seizes the Queen's arm and she rises slowly, but still darts across the room when walking. At the door the Princes come and kiss her hand and then the Queen goes away and the Princesses follow. One feels very idiotic after this, and we either leave the drawing-room direct, or pass through the billiard-room where the Gentlemen of the Household remain.'[29]

62

✳✳✳✳✳✳✳✳✳✳✳

BOOKS

'I have nearly finished reading *Corleone* to the Queen
and she has been as much thrilled by the story
as if she were a girl of 18!'

ONE EVENING AT BALMORAL when the Empress Frederick was staying there the conversation at dinner turned to the novels of Marie Corelli which the Queen, like Mr Gladstone, much admired, maintaining that their author would rank as one of the greatest writers of her time. Her daughter, however, contended that they were utter tripe and, in a loud voice, sought support for this opinion from Frederick Ponsonby who was sitting at the far end of the table and had not heard the opinions expressed so far. Ponsonby contended that, while 'her books undoubtedly had a large sale, the secret of her popularity was that her writings appealed to the semi-educated. Whereupon the Empress clapped her hands and the subject dropped with startling suddenness.'[1]

Although she was by no means intellectual, the Queen was far from being as ill-read as was often supposed: Frederick Ponsonby averred that her taste in literature was 'said to be deplorable' and that 'she never liked the works of the great authors'. Yet her letters and journal entries contain numerous references to worthwhile books she had read, many of which she claimed to have admired or enjoyed.

She had been warned against reading novels as a girl; and in later life she confessed to feeling rather guilty when reading fiction. 'Read in [Bulwer Lytton's] *Eugene Aram* for some time while my hair was doing,' she had recorded in her diary in December 1838, 'and finished it; beautifully written and fearfully interesting as it is, I am glad I have finished it, for I never feel quite at ease or at home when I am reading a Novel, and therefore was really glad to go on to Guizot's *Révolution de l'Angleterre*.' She had already read Madame de Sévigné's letters, some of Racine's tragedies and Sully's memoirs. According to Lady Holland she told Guizot in March 1840 with what pleasure she had read his book. It was, so Lady Holland said, repeating a common fallacy, 'really one of the few books since her accession, & Hallam's [*Constitutional History of Englandl*] is the other, that she has read through'.[2]

Discouraged as she had been by her mother from reading novels, however, she confessed to having found James Fennimore Cooper's *The Last of the Mohicans* 'very interesting', though 'very horrible'; and had greatly enjoyed Sir Walter Scott's *The Bride of Lammermoor* which she had read aloud to Lehzen – there were later discovered to be no fewer than twelve copies of Scott's *Rob Roy* at Balmoral and thirty-two copies of his *Lady of the Lake*. As a child she had considered Scott her '*beau ideal* of a Poet'; and, in later life, she told Lady Lytton that of all the poets whose work she liked, Scott was still her favourite.

Before her marriage she had also been impressed by George Crabbe and by Washington Irving's *The Conquest of Granada*; and, unlike Lord Melbourne, she had found Dickens's *Oliver Twist* 'too interesting'. Later she noted having finished *Jane Eyre* (which was 'intensely interesting, really a wonderful book, so powerfully and admirably written'), Caroline Lamb's *Glenarvon* and Dumas's *Les Trois Mousquetaires* as well as *Northanger Abbey, Adam Bede* ('such knowledge of human nature, such truth in the characters', a book which she was 'delighted to read a second time' since she liked 'to trace a likeness to the dear Highlanders in Adam'), *The Mill on the Floss* ('wonderful and painful'), *Scenes of Clerical Life* ('admirable'), *Uncle Tom's Cabin*, Disraeli's *Coningsby* and his *Endymion*,* Charles Kingsley's *Hypathia*, Theodore Mügge's *Afrija* ('so intensely interesting, so poetical and romantic') and Charlotte M. Yonge's *Heartsease*. She began to read Trollope's *Barchester Towers* to her husband; but she did not like doing so: there was 'not enough romance in it' and 'the

---

* Evidently she did not read Disraeli's penultimate novel, *Lothair*, with great care. Having 'with happy promptitude', answered a question from the Duchess of Edinburgh as to whether or not she had read the book, by claiming that she had been the first person to do so, she was then asked if she did not think that Theodora, the enthusiastic supporter of Italian liberty, was 'a divine character'. 'The Queen looked a little perplexed and grave. It wd. have been embarrassing had the Dss. not gone on rattling away' (quoted in Stanley Weintraub, *Victoria*, 412).

people she could not interest herself in'. She preferred Fanny Burney's *Diary and Letters*, Mrs Gaskell's life of Charlotte Brontë, and Elizabeth Barrett Browning's verse – 'poetry,' she said, 'I like in all shapes', though Mrs Browning's *Aurora Leigh* was 'very strange', 'at times dreadfully coarse' and 'an incredible book for a lady to have written'; while Samuel Johnson's poetry she found 'very hard'. Lord Melbourne agreed with her. 'Hang it,' he said. 'It's as hard as Greek.' 'I am very fond of Burns's poems,' she declared unsurprisingly. 'They are so poetical – so simple in their dear Scotch tongue, which is so full of poetry.'

She was particularly taken with *Alice in Wonderland* by Prince Leopold's friend, the Revd Charles Dodgson, the eccentric young mathematical lecturer at Christ Church, Oxford who wrote under the name of Lewis Carroll. She told him so and said that she looked forward to reading others of his books. He sent her a volume which had been published five years earlier, *Syllabus of Plane Algebraical Geometry*.

Under Prince Albert's tutelage the Queen had begun to read fewer novels and more instructive works of non-fiction, such as Macaulay's *History of England from the Accession of James II* and Bishop Butler's *Analogy of Religion*. But after the Prince's death she was reluctant to find time to trouble herself with history and biography, though she did tackle *Charles Kingsley: His Letters and Memories of his Life by his Wife* which she found 'full of [her] sort of interest'.[3] And one day she spoke to Marie Mallet about A. J. Balfour's *The Foundations of Belief*. 'I must read some of it,' she said, 'but they tell me it is *very* difficult. I know it is beyond *me*. Have you read it?'

'Only partly Your Majesty.'

'Well, you must find some bit not too hard to read to me.'[4]

Nor did she much care for accounts of contemporary affairs. Kinglake's *Invasion of the Crimea* she thought 'very scurrilous';[5] and she described *With Kitchener to Khartoum* by the *Daily Mail* journalist, George Warrington Steevens, 'flippant', and she stopped Mrs Mallet's reading before she had finished it. She did, however, approve of the *Spectator*, 'a very sensible paper' and 'no longer as radical as it used to be'.[6]

But her greatest pleasure in her old age was in reading novels or rather in listening to novels being read to her. She expressed a particular enthusiasm for the works of Pauline Craven, a once highly popular novelist, the daughter of French émigrés, whom, so she told Mrs Mallet, she 'admired more than anyone', her novel *Récit d'une Soeur* 'above all'. She invited Mrs Craven to Osborne and asked her to send her all her works – there were a great number of them – after having written her name in all of them.[7]

She also much admired the now little-read American writer Francis Marion Crawford. She enjoyed his *Jaquissara* 'immensely' and, even more, his *Corleone*, a novel set in Rome which Marie Mallet read to her in 1898 not long after it had been published. 'I have nearly finished reading *Corleone* to the Queen,' Mrs Mallet told her husband, 'and she has been as much thrilled by the story as if she were a girl of 18! It is quite a treat to read to anyone so keen and I have enjoyed it immensely.'[8]

63

✖✖✖✖✖✖✖✖✖✖

BOOKMEN

'It is impossible to imagine a politer little woman.'

HAVING READ AND GREATLY ADMIRED Lord Tennyson's *In Memoriam* – although his *Holy Grail* had left her 'quite bewildered'[1] – the Queen asked to meet the poet who lived some fifteen miles from Osborne. Tennyson was reluctant to go: he was shy, he said, and would not know how to conduct himself. But on 14 April 1862, four months after the Prince Consort's death, he did go, taking his two sons and Benjamin Jowett, Fellow of Balliol, with him; and the visit was a success. The Queen described Tennyson as being 'very peculiar looking, tall, dark, with a fine head, long black flowing hair and a beard – oddly dressed but there is no affectation about him.' They talked about Prince Albert, of course; and Tennyson said he would have made a great king. Tears, gratifyingly, came into his eyes. The Queen asked him if there was anything she could do for him. He said there was nothing; but he would be grateful if she would shake his sons by the hand: the gesture might 'keep them loyal in the troublous times to come'.[2]

A meeting with the American poet, Henry Wadsworth Longfellow, was not so successful. The Queen made a few complimentary remarks to which Longfellow replied that he was surprised to find himself so well known in England. 'Oh, I assure you, Mr Longfellow,' the Queen said, according to the poet's own account, 'you are very well known. All my servants read you.' 'Sometimes,' said Longfellow, 'I will wake up in the night and wonder if it was a deliberate slight.' Oscar Wilde, to whom Longfellow related this story, observed afterwards that it was 'the rebuke of Majesty to the vanity of the poet'.[3]

The Queen also expressed a wish to meet Charles Dickens who, as a young man, had plagued his friends with wild protestations that he had fallen madly in love with the 21-year-old Queen, whose features bore more than a passing resemblance to those of his beloved sister-in-law, Mary Hogarth. He would die for Victoria, he wrote in a series of letters which gave rise to rumours that he had actually become demented. He said that he had wandered forlornly about the grounds of Windsor Castle and felt 'so heartbroken at the glowing windows of the royal bedchamber that he had cast himself down in the mud of the Long Walk'. He wished to be embalmed and 'kept on top of the triumphal arch of Buckingham Palace when she [was] in town, and on the north-east turret of the Round Tower when she [was] at Windsor'.[4]

Since then, at the time of the 1848 uprisings on the Continent, Dickens had declared himself a republican; but this had not lessened his pleasure at having the Queen in the audience at his production of a charity performance of *Every Man in his Humour* at the Theatre Royal, Haymarket and at a subsequent performance at Devonshire House where one of the actors, who was required by the script to smoke a pipe, was, at Dickens's insistence, merely to pretend to do so, since the Queen, as he said, 'couldn't bear tobacco'.

Having led the applause at this performance – in which, she noted in her journal, 'Dickens (the celebrated author) acted admirably' – she was anxious to see a subsequent production of Wilkie Collins's *The Frozen Deep* and offered Dickens a room at Buckingham Palace for this purpose. Dickens declined the offer, however, maintaining that, since his daughters had not been presented at Court, he did not want them to appear at Buckingham Palace for the first time as actresses. Dickens also refused to appear before the Queen as she asked him to do, after a performance of the play specially put on for her at the Gallery of Illustration in Regent Street.

'My gracious Sovereign,' Dickens wrote to his friend, John Forster, explaining his reasons for disobeying this royal command, 'was so pleased [with the performance] that she sent round begging me to go round and see her and accept her thanks. I replied that I was in my Farce dress, and must beg to be excused. Whereupon she sent again, saying that the dress "could not be so ridiculous as that", and repeating the request. I sent my duty in reply, but again hoped her Majesty would excuse me presenting myself in a costume and appearance that were not my own.'

It was, therefore, not until March 1870, shortly before his death, that Dickens appeared before the Queen at Buckingham Palace. Although he was unwell and had a swollen foot, the Queen did not break with convention by asking him to sit down. She herself remained standing, leaning over the back of a sofa for the hour and a half that the interview lasted.* She said that she had never been able to attend one of his readings from his works, hinting that he might give her a private performance. Some time before she had expressed a wish for a private reading from *A Christmas Carol*. He had regretted that he could not do so then; and now, giving the same excuse, he said that a mixed audience was essential for the reading's success. They spoke then of his American tour, and of such mundane matters as the servant problem and the high cost of food, education and Lincoln's dream before his assassination. As he prepared to leave she gave him a copy of her *Journal of Our Life in the Highlands*, inscribed 'from the humblest of writers to one of the greatest', and asked him for a set of his own works. She would like them, she said, that afternoon. At this he demurred: he would like to give her a special set, properly bound.

The Queen found him 'very agreeable, with a pleasant voice and manner'. He thought her 'strangely shy', so he told his sister-in-law, Georgina, 'and like a girl in manner'.[5]

---

* Dickens did not care to follow the example of Thomas Carlyle who, the year before, without being invited to do so, had taken a chair with the observation that he was a feeble old man. Carlyle described the Queen as a 'comely little lady, with a pair of kind, clear, and intelligent grey eyes ... still looks almost young ... still plump; has a fine, low voice, soft ... It is impossible to imagine a politer little woman; nothing the least imperious; all gentle, all sincere, looking unembarrassing – rather attractive even; makes you feel, too (if you have any sense in you) that she is Queen.' She 'sailed out towards [him] as if moving on skates and bending her head towards [him] with a smile'.

She described Carlyle as 'a strange looking, eccentric old Scotchman, who holds forth, in a drawling, melancholy voice, with a broad Scotch accent, upon Scotland and the utter degeneration of everything' (Queen Victoria's Journal, 4 March 1869).

64

❊❊❊❊❊❊❊❊❊❊

FAILING HEALTH

'After the Prince Consort's death I wished to die,
but *now* I wish to live and do what I can
for my country and those I love.'

TOWARDS THE END OF JULY 1900 the Queen received the news that
her second son, Alfred, Duke of Edinburgh, who had succeeded his uncle
as Duke of Coburg seven years before, had died at the Rosenau. An
alcoholic, he had been suffering from cancer of the tongue and for some
time had been estranged from his wife whom he blamed for the death of
their son, 'Young Affie', an unsatisfactory young man who had contracted
syphilis and, suffering from 'nervous depression', had shot himself after
a furious quarrel with his mother. The Queen felt 'terribly shaken and
broken' on hearing of her 'poor darling' second son's death, and at first
she 'could not realize the dreadful fact'. Following upon the deaths of
her youngest son, Prince Leopold, of Princess Alice's little daughter, May,
and of Princess Alice herself, who died of diphtheria at the age of thirty-
five on 14 December 1878, the seventeenth anniversary of her father's
death – a lamentable loss which occasioned a letter from her eldest sister
to their mother of thirty-nine pages* – the Duke of Edinburgh's death

* On the day of the death of Princess Alice – whose dying words were 'dear Papa' – the Queen
recorded in her journal: 'This terrible day come round again. Slept tolerably, but awoke very often,
constantly seeing darling Alice before me. When I woke in the morning, was not for a moment
aware of all our terrible anxiety. And then it all burst upon me. I asked for news, but nothing
had come. Then got up and went, as I always do on this day, to the Blue Room [where the Prince
Consort had died], and prayed there. When dressed, I went into my sitting room for breakfast.
Directly after, came another [telegram] with the dreadful tidings that darling Alice sank gradually
and passed away at half past 7 this morning! It was too awful! That this dear, talented, distinguished,
tender-hearted, noble-minded, sweet child, who behaved so admirably during her father's illness,
and afterwards, in supporting me in every possible way, should be called back to her father on

484

was the loss of a 'third grown-up child' which the Queen had had to bear. She had also lost 'three very dear sons-in-law' – Vicky's husband, Fritz, Beatrice's husband, Prince Henry of Battenberg ('beloved, noble "Liko"') who had died of malaria while serving in the Ashanti expedition in 1896 – 'causing such grief in the house', the Queen 'crying and sobbing much'* – and Princess Alice's widower, Louis IV, Grand Duke of Hesse, 'so dear and joyous – so loving and so young for his age', who had died after suffering a stroke in 1892. It was 'hard at eighty-one' to have to accept yet another death in the family.

It was all the harder to accept the death of the 'dear, lovable' Louis of Hesse, since it had come within a matter of weeks of that of the Prince of Wales's son and heir. Prince Albert Victor (Prince Eddy), Duke of Clarence, had died at Sandringham in January, six days after his twenty-eighth birthday, while his father was still recovering from his involvement in a scandalous court case in which it was revealed that he had been gambling at baccarat at Tranby Croft, a country house in Yorkshire, with a man accused of cheating. 'Poor poor parents,' lamented the Queen who had expressed the hope that the Tranby Croft case would prove a salutary 'shock to Society'. 'Poor, poor parents ... A tragedy *too dreadful* for words ... The Queen's impulse yesterday was to go to Sandringham but Dr Reid and all – said she must not run the risk of cold & fatigue etc. ... Poor May to have her whole bright future to be merely a dream.'[1]

In fact 'poor May', daughter of Francis, Duke of Teck, was not really to be pitied. Her marriage to Prince Eddy had been due to take place on 27 February that year and no one who knew the young man could suppose he would have made a good husband. He was pleasant enough, the Duke of Cambridge conceded, but 'an inveterate and incurable dawdler, never ready, never there'.[2] He was also weak-willed and impressionable, leading what the Queen had described in a letter to the young man's mother as a 'dissipated' life, a comment which prompted the Prince of Wales's Private Secretary, Sir Francis Knollys, to write to Sir Henry Ponsonby, 'I

---

this very anniversary, seems almost incredible, and most mysterious! To me there seems something touching in the union which this brings, their names being forever united on this day of their birth into another better world!' (Queen Victoria's Journal, 14 December 1878).

* 'We could have spared any of the Princes better than him,' Lady Monkswell commented, 'for he and Princess Beatrice and their four children always lived quietly with the Queen and made it pleasant and homely for her' (E. C. F. Collier, ed., *A Victorian Diarist: Later Extracts*, 6).

ask again *who* it is tells the Queen these things?' There was so little that escaped her notice. Prince Eddy had wanted to marry Princess Hélène d'Orléans, an attractive warm-hearted girl. Although she was a Roman Catholic whose father, the Comte de Paris, disapproved of the match, the Princess of Wales undertook to help her son overcome the difficulties which stood in the way of it. Rightly supposing that, as Princess Hélène was prepared to renounce her religion, Queen Victoria's affection for Prince Eddy, and the romantic appeal of young lovers in distress, would lead her to support a marriage which prudence frowned upon, the Princess of Wales urged her son to go to see his grandmother at Balmoral.[3] He quailed at the prospect of such an interview. 'You can imagine what a thing to go through,' he told his brother, George, 'and I did not at all relish the idea ... I naturally expected that grandmama would be furious at the idea, and say it was quite impossible etc. But instead of that she was very nice about it and promised to help us as much as possible, which she is now doing ... I believe what pleased her most was my taking Hélène into her, and saying we had arranged it entirely between ourselves without consulting our parents first. This as you know was not quite true but she believed it all and was quite pleased.'[4]

The Comte de Paris, however, proved resolute in opposition to his daughter marrying a Protestant young man of whom he had heard no good reports; and Prince Eddy was, therefore, compelled to look elsewhere for a bride. Having fallen in love with Lady Sybil St Clair Erskine and having failed to win her also, he had complaisantly agreed to marry the far more suitable Princess May of Teck, who was 'quiet and reserved' in the Queen's opinion, 'the reverse of *oberflächlich* [superficial]' and with 'such good manners wh. in the present day [were] not *too* frequent'.

Greatly distressed by Prince Eddy's death before this marriage could take place, his father made the highly extravagant claim that such a tragedy had 'never before occurred in the annals' of their family. Yet he knew in his heart that his lethargic and dandiacal elder son, whose mind, as his tutor had once put it, was 'at all times in an abnormally dormant condition', had been hopelessly ill-qualified for the position for which his birth had destined him and that his younger brother, Prince George, the future King George V, who obligingly agreed to marry Princess May in his brother's place, was far better suited to kingship. He was also, in his grandmother's opinion, 'so nice, sensible, & truly right-minded, & so anxious to improve himself.'*

In the years before and after Prince Eddy's death, the Queen had to mourn the loss of several other members of her family, as well as dear friends and ladies and gentlemen of her Household. General Grey and Sir James Clark had both died in 1870. Lady Augusta Stanley had died, five years before her husband, in 1876. Two years later, to what she said was her 'profoundest grief', Sir Thomas Biddulph contracted a fatal illness in Scotland. Gerald Wellesley, Dean of Windsor, followed Dean Stanley to the grave in 1882. 'Dear kind' Sir Henry Ponsonby never recovered from the paralytic stroke which incapacitated him in 1895. Sir William Jenner, whose ill health necessitated his retirement in 1890, died eight years later. Both Prince Alexander, 'Sandro', of Battenberg and the Prince Consort's brother, Ernest, Duke of Coburg, died in 1893; Augusta, the old Duchess of Cambridge in 1889, 'the last one gone,' as the Queen commented, 'who had a right to call me Victoria!' One of her favourite grandsons, Princess Helena's elder son, Christian Victor, Prince of Schleswig-Holstein, died in 1900 of enteric fever while serving with the 60th Rifles in South Africa.

'I could not believe it,' she wrote of this last death. 'It seemed too dreadful and heart-breaking, this dear, excellent, gallant boy, beloved by all, such a good as well as a brave and capable officer, gone.' She was 'dreadfully shaken and upset' as her ladies testified. Lady Lytton recalled the tears pouring down her cheeks as she squeezed her hand, silently acknowledging her sympathy; and Marie Mallet told her husband:

> Words fail me to describe the pall of sorrow that hangs over this house [Balmoral], the Queen is quite exhausted by her grief and that dear unselfish Princess Thora [Prince Christian Victor's sister] just heart-broken . . . When the Queen breaks down and draws me close to her and lets me stroke her dear hand I quite forget she is far above me and only realize she is a sorrowing woman who clings

* Prince George was created Duke of York in 1892. His father had wanted this title bestowed upon Prince Eddy. But the Queen had strongly objected since it was associated with her Hanoverian uncle who, however successful an administrator as Commander-in-Chief of the British Army, had led a far from blameless private life. She also objected to the title being conferred upon Prince Eddy's brother, Prince George, giving way with an ill grace. 'I am glad you like the title of Duke of York,' she told her grandson. 'I am afraid, I do not and wish you had remained as you are. A Prince *no one* else can be, whereas a Duke any nobleman can be, and many are! I am not very fond of that of York which has not very agreeable associations' (RA GV AA 10/39).

to human sympathy and hungers for all that can be given on such occasions. I feel thankful for my unreserved nature and power of showing what I feel, for I believe it is a comfort to her, just a little ... She is quite angelic, and does her best to keep up, but the effort is very great ... The curious thing is that she said to me, 'After the Prince Consort's death I wished to die, but *now* I wish to live and do what I can for my country and those I love.' Do not repeat this but it is a very remarkable utterance for a woman of eighty-two, and this is not the first time she has made the same remark.[5]

Mrs Mallet was worried by the deleterious effect the Queen's sorrow might have upon her health which was naturally not as robust as it had been, particularly in very hot weather. A stifling summer's day was 'quite dreadful for me, *who love cold*,' she had said years before, '& am always poorly & stupified in hot weather'. From the early 1880s she had been troubled with rheumatism in her legs, a complaint which Princess Louise, always ready with eccentric prescriptions, proposed should be treated by boiling the painful members in whisky every night. Temporarily the Queen had lost the use of her legs altogether in the emotional distress caused by the death of John Brown, as she had also done when the Prince Consort died. Then, as her eyesight began to fail, she also complained in frequent notes to Dr Reid of sciatica, neuralgic headaches, a husky voice, pain between her shoulders and in her hip, lumbago, gastric pain, nausea, trouble with her false teeth, occasional indigestion and what, in her hypochondriacal way, she supposed was heart disease.[6] Additionally, she suffered from bouts of insomnia for which she was prescribed doses of chloral, Dover's powder, ammonium bromide and tincture of henbane.*

> After grumbling about her very bad night [Reid recorded in one of many such comments] she said that perhaps after all she had more sleep than she thought, as, except once, she did not think she remained awake longer than five or six minutes at a time! Every time she wakes, even for a few minutes, she rings for her maids, who of course don't like it, and naturally call the night a 'bad' one. She has got into the habit of waking up at night, and I fear it may

---

* In earlier years, so she had told the Princess Royal, 'I always have standing on my night table near my bed wherever I go ... a bottle of camphor lozenges ... I am sure if I went anywhere without them I should fancy I could not get to sleep.' (Roger Fulford, ed., *Dearest Child*, 152).

not be easy to break this habit. Meantime I shall go on with Bromide
and Henbane, and give no opium.[7]

Fussy as she was about her health, and regularly as she called upon
her doctors for treatment, any reports that she was ill annoyed her
intensely; and she had been known in her old age to go out of her way
to fulfil some public duty, even coming down from Balmoral to do so,
rather than allow it to be supposed that she was really unwell. She could
not, however, disguise the fact that she was becoming increasingly lame:
she found it more and more difficult, and in the end impossible, to walk
without a stick or the help of someone's arm, and eventually she took
to being wheeled about in a chair.

Yet she did not allow her infirmities to interfere with her enjoyment
of life; nor did they prevent her from contriving to seem almost agile
when making an appearance in public. As late as the summer of 1900,
at a garden party at Buckingham Palace, the 'dear old lady' was described
by Lady Monkswell as being 'vivacious'. She 'wagged her head about and
looked this way and that through her spectacles'. Lady Monkswell was
'sure nothing escaped her'. 'When I thought of her immense age I felt I
ought to kneel as she passed ... Off she went back to Windsor – we
heard the crowd cheering her as she drove up Constitution Hill. I was
glad to notice that although she wanted a good deal of help she was able
to walk for herself and was not carried.'[8]

Marie Mallet's letters are full of references to the Queen's cheerfulness
and vivacity in these last years of her life. But by the end of the century
her general health had begun seriously to fail. On coming into waiting
at Osborne in February 1900, Marie Mallet's heart sank since Her Majesty
looked 'so much older and feebler'. She had a bad cough and could not
be kept awake when her ladies read to her in the evenings, rustle the
pages, wriggle in their chairs, and drop their fans as they would. Also
her digestion was becoming 'defective after so many years of hard labour'.
'If she would follow a diet and live on Benger's Food and chicken all
would be well,' Mrs Mallet thought. 'But she clings to roast beef and ices!
And what can you then expect? Sir James [Reid] has at last persuaded
her to try Bengers and she likes it and now to his horror, instead of
substituting it for other foods she adds it to her already copious meals
... And of course when she devours a huge chocolate ice followed by a

couple of apricots washed down with iced water as she did last night [25 July 1900] she ought to expect a dig from the indigestion fiend.'[9]

When she returned to Balmoral for a further spell of waiting, towards the end of October 1900, Mrs Mallet found the Queen looking 'very old and feeble'. 'She has grown very thin,' she wrote, 'and there is a distressing look of pain and weariness on her face ... She is far from well ... and yesterday we had thick fog worthy of London, which made her perfectly miserable.'[10]

On her return to Windsor from a 'wretchedly gloomy and dark Balmoral' in November, she was a little better but a large luncheon on the 14th and the need to shout to make herself heard by the deaf Princess of Wales exhausted her, and she was 'in pain and very feeble ... She resents being treated as an invalid and as soon as she feels a tiny bit better she overtires herself and collapses.' Marie Mallet's husband, Bernard, who was at Windsor that month, feared that 'it must be the beginning of the end'.

The Queen's brief entries in her journal this month and the next make pathetic reading:

> Felt very poorly and wretched, as I have done all the last days. My appetite is completely gone, and I have great difficulty in eating anything [5 November] ... I still have disgust for all food [9 November] ... Had a shocking night ... pain kept me awake. Felt very tired and unwell when I got up, and was not able to go to church, to my great disappointment [11 November] ... Had a very restless night, with a good deal of pain. Got up very late, and when I did felt so tired I could do nothing, and slept on the sofa [28 November] ... After a very wretched night, I passed a very miserable day, and could neither go out nor leave my room [2 December] ... Saw Sir Francis Laking [who] encouraged me by saying he thought I should in time get over this unpleasant dislike of food and squeamishness ... and recommended my taking a little milk and whisky several times a day [11 December] ... Had a very bad night and scarcely slept at all [18 December].[11]

That day the Queen left Windsor for the last time; but for once she was not looking forward to Christmas at Osborne. She was sleeping more fitfully than ever, despite the large doses of chloral she took with her Bengers; and she felt guilty that her unconscionable sleepiness in the daytime prevented her from attending properly to her work and correspondence. On Christmas Eve she went into the Durbar Room where the Christmas tree was traditionally kept according to the Prince Consort's wishes; but her eyes were so dim she could scarcely see the candles. 'I feel so very melancholy,' she wrote, 'as I see so very badly.' The next day, Christmas Day, she learned with great distress that her dear friend Lady Churchill, her companion in those happy, long-gone holidays in Scotland and for almost fifty years a most valued member of her Household, had died of heart failure in the night. 'The loss to me,' she said miserably, 'is not to be told . . . and that it should happen here is too sad.'[12]

65

✖✖✖✖✖✖✖✖✖✖

DEATH

'She kept looking at me and
frequently gasped, "I'm very ill." '

'ANOTHER YEAR BEGUN,' the Queen's first diary entry for 1901 recorded, '& I am feeling so weak and unwell that I enter upon it sadly.' A fortnight later her journal came to a close. The day after the last entry was written she saw Field-Marshal Lord Roberts, Wolseley's successor as Commander-in-Chief, and she talked to him about the war in South Africa which, like the strain of her visit to Ireland the previous year, had, so she believed, been largely responsible for her present ill health. She had conferred the Order of the Garter on Lord Roberts the week before and he had then observed how frail and ill she looked. On this later occasion she spoke to him for an hour; but she was far from as incisive as she usually was. The day before Reid had described her as being 'rather childish and apathetic'. On 16 January he reported:

> The Queen had rather a disturbed night, and was very drowsy all forenoon, and disinclined to get up, although she kept saying in a semi-confused way that she must get up. I saw her asleep in bed in the forenoon, as I was rather anxious about her, and the maids said she was too drowsy to notice me. This was the first time I had ever seen the Queen when she was in bed. She was lying on her right side huddled up and I was struck by how small she appeared . . . She did not get up till 6 p.m. when she had a dress loosely fastened round her and was wheeled into the sitting-room . . . At 7.30 I saw her and she was dazed, confused and her speech was affected.[1]

The next day Reid concluded that the Queen had had a slight stroke. On Saturday 19 January it was publicly announced that Her Majesty had not lately been in her usual health. Her children had been summoned. So had Randall Davidson who had recently been translated from Rochester to the bishopric of Winchester; and, in case his feelings were hurt, the Queen suggested that the Rector of Whippingham should also be sent for. Without any encouragement from his family in England, the Kaiser left for Osborne as soon as he heard how ill his grandmother was.

Early on Monday morning she asked the doctor, 'Am I better at all? I have been very ill.'

When he assured her she was, indeed, better, she said, 'Then may I have Turi?'

The small Pomeranian dog was placed on her bed; but he did not like it there and jumped to the ground. The Queen appeared not to notice his departure; and not long afterwards she lost consciousness. Intermittently she regained it later and when the Prince of Wales approached her bed and bent over her she recognized him and said, 'Bertie.' But when Sir James Reid returned to her bedside, she seemed to think it was her son and she kissed the doctor's hand repeatedly. Mrs Tuck, her chief dresser, realizing her confusion, asked her 'if she still wanted the Prince of Wales, and she said, "Yes". The Prince returned to her bedside and spoke to her and she said to him, "Kiss my face."'

When the doctor came back into the room, she smiled repeatedly when she heard his voice and assured him that she was ready to listen to his advice. 'I will do anything you like,' she said. 'She kept looking at me,' Reid wrote, 'and frequently gasped, "I'm very ill", and I each time replied "Your Majesty will soon be better."'

At some point Princess Louise heard her mother say, 'I don't want to die yet. There are several things I want to arrange.'

When the Kaiser arrived, to everyone's surprise, he behaved with unusual tact and delicacy. 'I had a good deal of talk with the Emperor who was full of touching loyalty to "Grandmama" as he always described her,' Randall Davidson wrote in a memorandum of the Queen's last days. '"She has been a very great woman [the Kaiser said]. Just think of it: she remembers George III, and now we are in the Twentieth Century. And all that time what a life she has led. I have never been with her without feeling that she was in every sense my Grandmama and made me love her as such. And yet the minute we began to talk about political things she made me feel we were equals and could speak as Sovereigns. Nobody had such power as she." [2]

He said that he would not go into his grandmother's room if her children thought it better that he should not. When he was taken in by the Prince of Wales, he went to the dying woman's bed and placed his good arm around her shoulders; and thus supported, with Reid on her other side, she died at half past six that evening, 22 January, holding a crucifix in her hand. [3]

'When all was over most of the family shook hands with me and thanked me by the bedside,' Reid recorded, 'and the Kaiser also squeezed my hand in silence. I told the Prince of Wales to close her eyes. Later the Prince said, "You are an honest straightforward Scotchman", and "I shall never forget all you did for the Queen." The Princess [of Wales] cried very much, shook hands and thanked me ... I left the dinner table to help the maids and nurse to arrange the Queen's body.'

In doing so he noticed that she had had a ventral hernia and a prolapse of the uterus, conditions he had not observed until then as, although he had been attending her for twenty years, he had never examined her body and had treated her 'purely through verbal communication'. [4]

The Queen, however, had reposed her implicit trust in him; and, well aware of this, Mrs Tuck had no hesitation in reading to him the paper which the Queen had given to her years before, detailing the actions which were to be taken immediately after her death and before the funeral.

66

✳✳✳✳✳✳✳✳✳✳✳

FUNERAL AND BURIAL

'Our whole talk had been of coffins
and winding sheets.'

THE QUEEN HAD ALWAYS HAD, as Henry Ponsonby had said and
the other members of her Household well knew, a consuming interest in
funerals. When the Duke of Clarence died, Dr Reid had advised her not
to go to the funeral on the grounds that her health might be affected by
such a depressing occasion. 'She replied that she was never depressed at
a funeral (!!) In fact she rather lost her temper.'[1]

'It is very curious to see how the Queen takes the keenest interest in
death and all its horrors,' Marie Mallet had written after a housemaid
had died at Grasse. 'Our whole talk had been of coffins and winding
sheets.' There was 'a sort of funeral service' for the housemaid in the
dining room of the Grand Hotel, the coffin in the middle of the room
'not even screwed down, everyone in evening dress, the servants sobbing;
it was too dreadful'. When the coffin was removed to the English church
the Queen had required her Household to visit it, then to attend a full
funeral service the next day.

Two days later the Queen had taken several members of her Household to Cannes cemetery to visit the tombs of various friends. 'We started
soon after 3.30,' Mrs Mallet had written, 'and were not home till ten to
seven! The gentlemen went in a separate carriage full to overflowing with
wreaths for the favoured tombs.'[2]

A week after this, various members of an unwilling Household had
been required to attend the funeral of an officer of the Chasseurs des
Alpes. 'As the Queen really enjoys these melancholy entertainments she

determined to see the procession and poor Major Bigge, much to his disgust, was ordered to put on full uniform and attend the ceremony which lasted nearly three hours.' 'It is certainly strange that the Queen should take such deep interest in the merest details of these functions,' Mrs Mallet had added after yet another funeral. 'A cheerful ceremony is always treated with the utmost indifference.' After Prince Henry of Battenberg's death, when there was 'a gloomy little service in honour of the burial day', Mrs Mallet had commented, 'these reiterated memorial services are very trying but I really think the Queen enjoys them.' She had been much concerned with what went into the coffin in addition to the corpse: Prince Henry, who had to be 'dressed in Ashanti uniform', had been required to have 'his rings left on, also a locket round his neck with Princess Beatrice's hair – the crucifix to be put in his hand with a piece of ivy, white heather, and myrtle from the Princess's wedding bouquet, and a small photo of the Princess attached to it'. There were to be 'three coffins, shell, lead, and oak'.[3]

Not only had the Queen taken great interest in the funerals of members of her family, of friends and acquaintances and even of strangers, she had also concerned herself with the details of the burials of her dogs. When her favourite Scottish sheepdog, Noble, which used to stand guard over her gloves, died at Balmoral, she 'was much upset', said Dr Reid, 'and cried a great deal. She said ... she believes dogs have souls and a future life: and she could not bear to see [Noble's] body, though she would have liked to kiss his head. Kingsley and many people, she says, believe dogs have souls. I had to increase the strength of her sleeping draught.' She sent Reid a note of instructions detailing the manner in which 'the Prince's beloved old dog' had been buried forty-three years before, and requiring that the body of Noble should be treated in a similar manner:

> I wish the grave to be bricked. The dear dog to be wrapped up in the box lined with lead and *charcoal*, placed in it ... I feel as if I could not bring myself to go and choose the spot. Dr Profeit [the factor at Balmoral] would perhaps suggest it. I will then tell Mr Profeit to write to Boehm to get a repetition of his statue of the dear Dog in bronze to be placed over the grave.[4]

Paying such attention to the burial of her beloved dogs, it was only to be expected that the Queen had carefully planned her own funeral as well as the actions to be taken immediately after her death, giving 'very minute directions' as to what she wanted done. These 'Instructions' had been entrusted to her dressers 'to be always taken about and kept by' whichever one of them might be travelling with her. They included details of what was to be put in her coffin 'some of which none of her family were to see'.

They included rings, chains, bracelets, lockets, shawls, the Prince Consort's dressing gown, a cloak of his which had been embroidered by Princess Alice and a plaster cast of his hand, numerous photographs, her lace wedding veil, and – to be placed in the Queen's left hand – a photograph of John Brown together with a lock of his hair.*[5]

The funeral, so the Queen instructed, was to be a 'Military Funeral' as befitted the 'Head of the Army', with her coffin on a gun carriage drawn by eight horses. Her detailed instructions also provided for places in the procession being found for the Munshi and her German secretaries. It was to be a white rather than a black funeral: the horses, she insisted, were not to be black.

This stated preference for a white funeral seems to have been either prompted or reinforced by a remark made by Lord Tennyson whom she had taken to see the Mausoleum at Frogmore. She had commented on the bright light which streamed into the interior from the windows. Tennyson replied that this was 'a great point & went on to say that he wished funerals cd be in white'. When he was buried twenty years after this conversation his coffin was covered with a white pall: the Queen wished to follow his example.[6]

Having satisfied himself that the Queen's 'Instructions' about the contents of her coffin had been carried out, and before letting the family know

---

* Like so many of her contemporaries, the Queen treasured a collection of strands of hair cut from the heads of 'the dear departed'. Some she was given: for example his executor gave her some of Dean Stanley's, part of which she sent on to her eldest daughter with the comment that 'it had to be disinfected' (*Dearest Mama: Private Correspondence of Queen Victoria and the German Crown Princess*, ed. Roger Fulford, 105). Some she asked for, as she did for a lock from the head of King Victor Emmanuel who, she discovered on its arrival, had dyed his once red hair black; and she sent for a tuft from the head of the Duke of Wellington whose manservant had to apologize for the small amount he was able to send, the demands from the family and friends being 'so great' (Spicer MSS, 4 October 1852 quoted in Elizabeth Longford, *Wellington: Pillar of State*, 400). The Duke's daughter-in-law, the former Lady Douro, acquired the Duke's walrus ivory false teeth.

that they could now return to the room, Reid – after helping to cut off the Queen's hair to be put into lockets – placed a bunch of flowers over Queen Victoria's hand to conceal John Brown's photograph.

The mourners then returned to the room; and the Prince of Wales, now King Edward VII, kindly sent for the Munshi so that he too could pay his last respects before the coffin lid was closed. The coffin, covered by a white satin pall, was then carried by a party of sailors down to the dining room, for the time being a mortuary chapel in which the air was heavy with the strong scent of tuberoses and gardenias. By the light of eight immense candles, four soldiers of the Queen's Company, Grenadier Guards, stood with reversed arms at the corners of the coffin which was covered with crimson velvet and ermine and the Queen's diamond-studded crown on a cushion. Above their heads hung a Union Jack which the Kaiser asked if he might keep, afterwards maintaining that it was his most valued possession.

On 1 February the Queen's coffin was taken down to Trinity Pier and across the Solent to Portsmouth in the royal yacht, the *Alberta*, while minute guns in the attendant warships boomed across the calm waters. The *Alberta* was followed by the King in the *Victoria and Albert*, and after that the Kaiser in his yacht. Next morning the coffin, in the care of Lady Lytton, was taken by train to Victoria Station past groups of people, dressed in black, kneeling by the lines as it steamed slowly by, the blinds of its windows drawn.[7]

In London the crowds, which had gathered in the streets to watch the gun carriage bearing the coffin roll by, were also clothed in black. Even the crossing-sweepers had tied bits of black cloth to their brooms. On the coffin stood the Imperial Crown, the orb and sceptre and the collar of the Order of the Garter.

Lady Monkswell was watching the procession from the upper window of a shop near Victoria Station:

> The streets were, indeed, a strange sight, thronged with chiefly decent, respectable & middle-aged people, every one in mourning [she wrote]. Even by 9 o'clock there did not seem room for another person on the pavement; they were all quiet & orderly . . . We saw all the Kings & Princes riding horses, & the 4 or 5 shut carriages for Queen Alexandra & the Princesses, pass up to the station. A little later came Lord Roberts riding; he was the only person the

people thought they might cheer . . . I did not concern myself much with whom the horsemen were, as my eyes were fixed so entirely upon the *one great object*, that, except for the Prince of Wales, now King, & the Kaiser, who rode a magnificent white horse, I saw nothing else & *that* I could hardly see because my eyes were filled with tears & I felt very shaky . . . Then I silently bid her farewell. The people stood uncovered & silent.[8]

Through streets lined with soldiers, to the sound of muffled drums, minute guns in Hyde Park and the clatter of the horses' hooves, the gun carriage passed slowly by to Paddington, the crowds watching in silence. Four monarchs followed the coffin on horseback, King Edward VII, Kaiser Wilhelm II, King George I of the Hellenes, and King Carlos of Portugal. A fifth King, Leopold II of the Belgians, drove in a carriage. Also in the procession were the German Crown Prince, and the Crown Princes of Rumania, Greece, Denmark, Norway and Sweden and Siam. The Emperor of Austria was represented by the Archduke Franz Ferdinand, the Tsar by the Grand Duke Michael Alexandrovitch and the King of Italy by the Duke of Aosta.

As in London, so also in Windsor, crowds of people stood quietly in the icy cold waiting to see the gun carriage drawn by men of the Royal Horse Artillery up the hill from the station to the Castle. They were kept waiting for longer than they had expected because of a mishap which the General Officer Commanding, Royal Artillery was afterwards required to explain to Lord Roberts:

> The RHA team had been so long standing at the station in the bitter cold that when the time came to move off, the horses got restless and out of hand and the splinter bar broke and there was almost a serious accident. The King was displeased and several of his suite got excited and did not improve matters.[9]

Prince Louis of Battenberg, a captain in the Navy and a Personal Aide to Queen Victoria, who was standing next to the coffin, went up to Frederick Ponsonby, who had been placed in charge of the arrangements at Windsor, and said to him, 'If it is impossible to mend the traces you can always get the naval guard of honour to drag the gun-carriage.'

Ponsonby proposed this to the King who agreed; but there were several Royal Artillery officers amongst the Queen's aides-de-camp who were furious that the men of the Royal Horse Artillery should be so ignominiously replaced. Sir Arthur Bigge, an Artillery officer himself, was 'particularly angry', so Ponsonby said; and he 'went off to expostulate with the King, who merely said, "Right or wrong, let [Ponsonby] manage everything; we shall never get on if there are two people giving contradictory orders." '[10]

So, using drag ropes, the sailors pulled the gun carriage through the Windsor streets, and up to the Castle's Long Walk towards St George's Chapel where the short funeral service was to take place while cannon fired a salute of eighty-one guns, one for each year of the Queen's life.

So well did the sailors carry out their task that King Edward suggested they should be given the duty of dragging the coffin to its final resting place in the Mausoleum at Frogmore. But Ponsonby demurred: 'the Artillery had been deeply mortified at their failures ... and would be much hurt if sailors took their place again ... The King quite realized they were not to blame ... but he really thought the sailors had been most effective ... I, however, pressed my point and finally he said, "Very well, the gun-carriage will be drawn by the Artillery, but if anything goes wrong I will never speak to you again." '[11]

Nothing did go wrong. On 4 February the Queen's coffin was carried out of the Albert Memorial Chapel in St George's and, accompanied by her family, it was taken to the Mausoleum, up the steps and through the door above which had been inscribed the words: 'His mourning widow, Victoria the Queen, directed that all that is mortal of Prince Albert be placed in this sepulchre. A.D. 1862. *Vale desideratissime!* [Farewell most beloved] *Hic demum Conquiescam tecum, tecum in Christo consurgeam* [Here at length I shall rest with thee, with thee in Christ I shall rise again].'

> Of all the ceremonials [Lord Esher thought], that in the Mausoleum was the simplest and most impressive. The procession from the sovereign's entrance, the Princess of Wales leading Prince Edward [the future Duke of Windsor] the other children walking, was very touching and beautiful. At the Mausoleum, the arrangements were left to me. Everyone got into the Chapel and the iron gates were closed ... the guardsmen brought in the coffin. The King and the Princes and Princesses standing on the right. The choir on the left ... Of all the mourners the Princess of Wales and the young [sixteen-year-old son of the Duke of Albany] Duke of Coburg displayed the most emotion.[12]

The service [Randall Davidson thought] was touching beyond words. After the Blessing it had been arranged that the Royal Family should all pass in single file across the platform looking upon the grave in which the two coffins then lay side by side. The King came first alone, but, instead of simply walking by, he knelt down by the grave. Then the Queen followed, leading the little Prince Edward by the hand. She knelt down, but the little boy was frightened, and the King took him gently and made him kneel beside him, and the three, in perfect silence, were there together – a sight not soon to be forgotten. Then they passed on, and the Emperor came and knelt likewise, and so in turn all the rest of the Royal Family in a continuous string. Then the Household or at least the few who had been invited to be present. As we left the building the rain or sleet began to fall.[13]

Lord Esher was left with the problem of the white stone figure of the Queen which had been made by Baron Marochetti at the same time as that of Prince Albert, the sculptor's last completed works. The Queen had told him about this figure the year before, but 'no one had heard of it ... After a minute enquiry, an old workman remembered that about 1865 the figure had been walled up in the stores at Windsor. The brickwork was taken down, and the figure found.'[14]

It was placed, as she had intended, on the tomb chest next to the effigy of the Prince. He is portrayed as facing upwards to the mosaics in the dome. Her young face inclines towards the husband whom she so deeply loved.

On the evening of the Queen's death, the novelist, Henry James, had come out of the Reform Club into Pall Mall. The streets around it seemed to him 'strange and indescribable'; passers-by spoke in hushed tones as though they were frightened. It was, for him, 'a very curious and unforgettable impression'. He had not expected to be so moved, since it was, after all, 'a simple running down of the old used up watch', the death of an old widow who had thrown 'her good fat weight into the scales of general decency'.[15]

Yet while writing letters later on the club's black-bordered stationery he 'continued to experience unexpected emotions'. He recognized that the death of the 'brave old woman' with her 'holding-together virtue' marked the end of an era. She had been a 'sustaining symbol'. He wrote to a friend: 'I mourn the safe and motherly old middle-class Queen, who held the nation warm under the fold of her big, hideous Scotch-plaid shawl and whose duration has been so extraordinarily convenient and beneficent'. It had 'prevented all sorts of accidents'.

As with the people walking the streets outside, James viewed the future with apprehension. He was assured that the new King was already making a good impression but the Victorian world with its faults and its virtues was already passing away; and, as for the future – in his own word, '*Speriamo*', one could only hope.

REFERENCES

The Queen's letters to her daughter, the Crown Princess of Prussia, later Empress, are kept, bound in some sixty blue volumes, at Friedrichshof, the house near Frankfurt which the Empress built and named in honour of her husband. They are the property of the Kurhessische Hausstiftung. The copyright, as all Queen Victoria's letters, belongs to Her Majesty Queen Elizabeth II. Selections from these letters, about a third of them, were skilfully edited by Sir Roger Fulford and published in five volumes by Evans Brothers (later Bell & Hyman) between 1964 and 1981. A sixth volume, edited by Agatha Ramm, was published in 1990 by Alan Sutton.

The Queen's letters to King Leopold are to be found in the earlier of the nine volumes of *The Letters of Queen Victoria: A Selection from Her Majesty's Correspondence*, published in three series of three volumes each by John Murray between 1907 and 1932. The first series of these letters was edited by Arthur Christopher Benson and Viscount Esher, and the second and third series by George Earle Buckle. They contain some two million words, both from the Queen's letters and her journals, extending over five thousand pages; and even so they represent but a small proportion of the papers which the Queen methodically collected and had bound for preservation in the Royal Archives at Windsor.

Regrettably, not all of the Queen's papers survived intact. For, in fulfilment of a charge imposed upon her by her mother, Princess Beatrice transcribed passages from the journals and burned the originals when she had finished with them. She often, in fact, went further than this, destroying whole entries which she thought unsuitable for transcription and substantially altering numerous passages which she did transcribe. But fortunately, unknown to her, Lord Esher made a copy of the earlier journals so that from the time they were begun in 1832 to the death of the Prince Consort in 1861 a complete typed version of them does exist.

Princess Beatrice was not alone responsible for the mutilation of Queen Victoria's papers. On the instructions of her brother, King Edward VII, letters from his mother to Lord Granville and papers concerning the Lady Flora Hastings affair were also destroyed, as were letters written by the Queen to Disraeli about various members of her family. The papers which survive, however, far outnumber those that were burned, and in addition to the material contained in the volumes mentioned above there are the letters from the Queen to the Empress Augusta in *Further Letters of Queen Victoria* from the archives of the House of Brandenburg-Prussia, edited by Hector Bolitho (Thornton Butterworth Ltd, 1938); the Queen's correspondence with Lady Canning in Virginia Surtees's *Charlotte Canning* (John Murray, 1972); extracts from her correspondence published in Monypenny and Buckle's six-volume *Life of Benjamin Disraeli* (John Murray, 1910–1920), in John Morley's *Life of William Ewart Gladstone* (three volumes, Macmillan, 1903), and in Arthur Ponsonby's *Henry Ponsonby, Queen Victoria's Private Secretary* (Macmillan, 1942). There are also entries from her journals published in the two volumes of Lord Esher's *The Girlhood of Queen Victoria* (John Murray, 1912) and in the five volumes of Theodore Martin's *Life of the Prince Consort* (1875–1880).

As well as at Windsor, there are large numbers of the Queen's papers at Broadlands. Brian Connell used a selection of these for his *Regina v. Palmerston: The Correspondence Between Queen Victoria and Her Foreign and Prime Minister, 1837–1865* (Evans Brothers Ltd, 1962); and Richard Hough made use of the Queen's letters to a much loved grandchild in *Advice to a Grand-daughter: Letters from Queen Victoria to Princess Victoria of Hesse* (William Heinemann Ltd, 1975). To these editors and their publishers I am most grateful for permission to reprint extracts in this book.

Several excellent biographies have been published since the appearance of Lytton Strachey's *Queen Victoria* in 1921. Among the most recent are Elizabeth Longford's splendid *Victoria RI* (1964), the first volume of Cecil Woodham-Smith's regrettably unfinished *Queen Victoria: Her Life and Times* (1972), Stanley Weintraub's *Victoria* (1987), Giles St Aubyn's *Queen Victoria: A Portrait* (1991), Monica Charlot's *Victoria: The Young Queen* (1991) and Juliet Gardiner's *Queen Victoria* (1997).

For full bibliographical details see Sources, pp. 523–33.

Abbreviations

RA Royal Archives
RAQVJ Royal Archives, Queen Victoria's Journal
CH Christopher Hibbert, *Queen Victoria in her Letters and Journals*

1 : THE FAMILY

1. *Creevey Papers*, 269.
2. Anderson passim; Duff, *Edward, Duke of Kent*, passim; Fulford, *Royal Dukes*, passim.
3. Greville, iv, 244–5.
4. Creevey, 284.
5. Ibid., 270.
6. RA 45340, Duke of Kent to Baron de Mallet, 26 January 1819.
7. Creevey, 271.
8. Hibbert, *George IV*, ii, 93.
9. Creevey, 425.
10. Quennell, *Private Letters of Princess Lieven*, 111.
11. Frampton, 267.
12. Aspinall, *Letters of Princess Charlotte*, 186.
13. Ibid., 262.
14. RA M2/68 quoted in Longford, *Victoria*, 20.

2 : THE PARENTS

1. Quoted in Woodham-Smith, 17.
2. Stockmar, i, 77.
3. RA Add. 7/1355, 1 February 1819.
4. Creevey, 276–7.
5. RA M3/1, 5 April 1819.
6. Stockmar, i, 78.
7. RA M3/3 24 May 1819, quoted in Woodham-Smith, 30.
8. RA M24/2 31 May 1819, quoted in Woodham-Smith, 30.
9. Quoted in Longford, *Victoria*, 24.
10. RA M4/26.
11. Ibid.
12. Hibbert, *George IV*, ii, 128–9; Charlot, 32–3; Longford, *Victoria*, 24.
13. RA Z/286, 19 January 1820.
14. Woodham-Smith, 44.
15. RA Y69/26 12 December 1842; RA Y82/101, 7 January 1859.

16. Quoted in Woodham-Smith, 46.

3 : THE CHILD

1. Quoted in Longford, *Victoria*, 28.
2. Lorne, 57–62.
3. John Lehmann, *Edward Lear and his World*, 1977, 68; Warner, 108.
4. RA MP 116/11, 23 March 1830.
5. Benson and Esher, i, 10.
6. Ibid., 10–11.
7. Hibbert, *George IV*, ii, 277–8.
8. Ibid.; Richard Edgcumbe, ed. *The Diary of Frances, Lady Shelley*, 1912–13, 146–7.
9. Edgcumbe, op. cit., 153.
10. Aspinall, *Letters of King George IV*, iii, 296.
11. RA Y36/132 15 April 1883.
12. Quoted in Hudson, 64.
13. RA Y 203/81.
14. Hudson, 73.
15. Benson and Esher, i, 18.
16. Low, *Queen Victoria's Dolls*; Tooley, 31.
17. Hudson, 16.
18. RA M3/36 1 April 1821.
19. Hudson, 55.
20. Quoted in Charlot, 43.

4 : CONROY

1. Greville, iv, 44.
2. Hudson, 14–15; Woodham-Smith, 258–9.
3. Hudson, 125.
4. Greville, ii, 294.
5. Hudson, 56.
6. RA M4/16, 12 January 1830; Hudson, 74.
7. Leigh Hunt, *The Old Court Suburb*, 1902, ii, 175, quoted in Woodham-Smith, 60; Tooley, 28.
8. Tooley, 32.
9. Charles Knight, ii, 170.

10. Greville, i, 214.
11. Wharncliffe, ii, 78–9.
12. Arbuthnot, ii, 186.
13. RA Y203/81, 2 December 1867.

5 : PROGRESSES

1. Quoted in Charlot, 40, 58.
2. RA M4/2, 30 June 1830.
3. RA M4/22, 1 July 1830; Greville, i, 196.
4. Charlot, 59.
5. RA M4/32, 26 June 1831.
6. Greville, ii, 150.
7. Quoted in St Aubyn, *Queen Victoria*, 27.
8. Lee, 31.
9. Quoted in St Aubyn, *Queen Victoria*, 28.
10. RA M5/78, 30 July 1835.
11. Hudson, 3.
12. Woodham-Smith, 89; Longford, *Victoria*, 42.
13. RAQVJ, 21 July 1832.
14. Ibid., 1 August–9 November 1832; Woodham-Smith, 88.
15. RAQVJ, 8 November 1832.
16. Greville, ii, 388, 4 July 1833.
17. RAQVJ, 2 August 1833.
18. Longford, *Victoria*, 43.
19. RA MP 115/73, 8 July 1836.
20. RA MP 115/75, 13 July 1836.
21. Quoted in Longford, *Victoria*, 43.
22. Woodham-Smith, 96; Esher, *Girlhood of Queen Victoria*, i, 104, 355.
23. RA MP 115/58, 22 August 1835.
24. Hudson, 26; RA M5/84, 2 September 1835.
25. Greville, iii, 258.
26. Hudson, 89.
27. Quoted in Woodham-Smith, 92.
28. RAQVJ, 25 September 1835.

6 : UNCLES

1. RAQVJ, 4, 6 October 1835; Longford, *Victoria*, 48–9.
2. Hudson, 104.
3. RAQVJ, 26 February 1838.
4. Hudson, 105.
5. RAQVJ, 14, 15 December 1835; 25 January 1836.
6. Woodham-Smith, 108.
7. RAQVJ, 18 April 1837.

8. RAQVJ, 4 June, 18 June 1836; RA 88/15 7 June 1836.
9. Warner, 4, 7, 51, 67.
10. RA Y88/14, 31 May 1836.
11. RA M4/64, 15 April 1837; Woodham-Smith, 125.
12. Hudson, 118.
13. Greville, iii, 308–11.
14. RA M7/14, 20; Woodham-Smith, 133.
15. RA M7/15.
16. Quoted in Woodham-Smith, 134.
17. RAQVJ, 24 May 1837.
18. RA Add. A 11/12, 8–13 June 1837.
19. Hudson, 129.
20. RA M7/67, Prince Charles Leiningen's Memorandum; Hudson, 121.
21. RAQVJ, 20 June 1837; Bell, 91.

7 : THE YOUNG QUEEN

1. Creevey, 664.
2. Ibid., 167.
3. Quoted in St Aubyn, *Queen Victoria*, 66.
4. RAQVJ, 20 June 1837.
5. Charlot, 83.
6. Greville, iii, 372–3.
7. Ibid.
8. *Croker Papers*, ii, 359.
9. RAQVJ, 20 June 1837.
10. Ibid.
11. Longford, *Victoria*, 66–73; Woodham-Smith, 140–48; Charlot, 87–91; St Aubyn, *Queen Victoria*, 65–70; Weintraub, *Victoria*, 99–101.
12. RA Z482/12, 17 August 1837.
13. RA M7/65.
14. Quoted in Woodham-Smith, 15.
15. Healey, *Coutts & Co.*, 295.
16. RAQVJ, 16 January 1838.
17. RAQVJ, 7 November 1837.

8 : MELBOURNE

1. RALP 13 November 1837.
2. Greville, iii, 373.
3. Boykin, 104.
4. Creevey, 668.
5. Quoted in Aronson, *Heart of a Queen*, 5.
6. Creevey, 666.
7. Lord Holland, *Holland House Diaries*, quoted in Healey, *The Queen's House*, 121; Granville, ii, 235.

8. Greville, iv, 40.
9. Ibid., iv, 41.
10. Mitchell, 41–2.
11. RAQVJ, 1 August 1838.
12. Mitchell, 3–5, 13.
13. Ibid., 31, 118; Longford, *Victoria*, 69–70; RAQVJ, 1 November 1837; Ziegler, *Melbourne*, 257–65.
14. Mitchell, 234; RAQVJ 2 July 1837.
15. Quoted in Mitchell, 235.
16. Greville, iv, 93.
17. Mitchell, 239.
18. Quoted in Ziegler, *Melbourne*, 124.
19. RAQVJ, 26 December 1838; 7 April 1839.
20. Mitchell, 24; RAQVJ, 6 April 1838.

9 : CORONATION

1. Frampton, 404–5.
2. Greville, iv, 19.
3. RAQVJ, 28 June 1838.
4. Raikes, ii, 107.
5. Oman, 287.
6. Martineau, 221.
7. Greville, iv, 72.
8. Lorne, 89.
9. Charlot, 123.
10. Greville, iv, 70–72.
11. RAQVJ, 28 June 1838.
12. Ibid.
13. Lorne, 90.
14. Ibid., 91.
15. RAQVJ, 6 July 1838.
16. Monypenny & Buckle, 1, 429–30; Jane Ridley, 217.
17. Longford, *Victoria*, 82–3.
18. RAQVJ, 28 June 1838.

10 : THE HASTINGS AFFAIR

1. RAQVJ, 13 December 1838.
2. Ibid., 28 June 1838.
3. Hudson, 151.
4. RAQVJ, 2 February 1839.
5. RAQVJ, 2 February 1829; Ziegler, *Melbourne*, 271; Charlot, 129; Longford, *Victoria*, 97.
6. Greville, iv, 134.
7. Lady Flora Hastings's statement, *Morning Post*, 14 September 1839, quoted in Charlot; Longford, *Victoria*, 95.
8. Sir James Clark's statement, *The Times* 6

October 1839, quoted in Charlot, 129, 131.
9. Quoted in Woodham-Smith, 166; Charlot, 130.
10. RA Z486/2, 17 February 1839.
11. Ibid.; Lady Flora Hastings's statement, *Morning Post*, 14 September 1839.
12. RA Z486/1, Certificate of Dr Clarke and Dr Clark.
13. RAQVJ, 19 September 1839.
14. RAQVJ, 7 June 1839.
15. RAQVJ, 23 February 1839.
16. Lady Flora Hastings's statement, *Morning Post*, 14 September 1839.
17. *Morning Post*, 14 September 1839: Lord Hastings to Lord Melbourne; Charlot, 133–4.
18. *Morning Post*, 14 September 1839, letter from Lady Flora Hastings to Hamilton Fitzgerald, 8 March 1839.
19. *Morning Post*, 14–18 September 1839.
20. RAQVJ, 16 April 1839.
21. Quoted in Longford, *Victoria*, 104.
22. RAQVJ, 27 June 1839.
23. Ibid., 1 July 1839.
24. RA MP/115/141, 29 April 1839.
25. RAQVJ, 10 July; 22 September 1839.

11 : 'A PLEASANT LIFE'

1. Quoted in St Aubyn, *Queen Victoria*, 63.
2. RA LP, 23 October 1837.
3. Creevey, 649.
4. St Aubyn, *Royal George*, 23.
5. RAQVJ, 10 May 1838.
6. Frampton, 403.
7. Greville, iv, 56.
8. RA LP, 7 October 1837.
9. Quoted in Longford, *Victoria*, 77.
10. RAQVJ, 22 August 1837.
11. RAQVJ, 29 August 1837; 3 October 1837.
12. Benson and Esher, i, 104, 27 June 1837.
13. RA LP, 29 June 1837.
14. Ilchester, 170.
15. Mitchell, 235.
16. Quoted in Hibbert, *Wellington*, 352.
17. Quoted in St Aubyn, *Queen Victoria*, 119.
18. Mitchell, 238.
19. Ibid.

12 : 'A HEADSTRONG GIRL'

1. Hudson, 81.
2. Ibid., 133.
3. RA M7/68.
4. RA Z483/3, 25 May 1839.
5. Greville, iv, 198–9; Hudson, 162.
6. Quoted in Longford, *Victoria*, 86.
7. RAQVJ, 22 March 1839.
8. RAQVJ, 7 May 1839.
9. Ibid.
10. RAQVJ, 7 May 1839.
11. RAQVJ, 8 May 1839.
12. Cecil, *Lord M.*, 328.
13. Charlot, 143.
14. Ibid.
15. RAQVJ, 9 May 1839.
16. Ibid.
17. Quoted in Longford, *Victoria*, 112.
18. Woodham-Smith, 174; Longford, *Victoria*, 112; Greville, iv, 200–203; Weintraub, *Victoria*, 121–3.
19. RAQVJ, 9 May 1839.
20. Ibid.
21. RAQVJ, 10 May 1839.
22. Greville, iv, 169–70.
23. Stockmar, i, 230.

13 : GERMAN COUSINS

1. *Watchman*, 4 May 1828, quoted by Charlot, 75.
2. Benson and Esher, i, 60–61.
3. RA Y88/11, 17 May 1836; Hudson, 116.
4. Rhodes James, *Albert, Prince Consort*, passim; Bennett, *King Without a Crown*; Weintraub, *Albert*, passim.
5. Grey, *Early Years*, 200.
6. Tooley, 205.
7. Stockmar, ii, 7.
8. RA LP, 24 May 1836.
9. Hough, *Victoria and Albert*, 123.
10. RA 88/15, 7 June 1836.
11. Jagow, 13.
12. RAQVJ, 25 May 1839.
13. Longford, *Victoria*, 75, 86; RAQVJ, 22 March, 12 April, 28 May 1839.
14. RAQVJ, 15–18 April; 24 June 1839.
15. Wyndham, 292.
16. Benson and Esher, i, 177, 15 July 1839.
17. Stockmar, ii, 2.
18. Benson and Esher, i, 186, 1 October 1839.
19. RAQVJ, 23 September 1839.
20. Cecil, 334.

14 : PRINCE ALBERT

1. RAQVJ, 11–14 October 1839.
2. Mitchell, 244.
3. RAQVJ, 14 October 1839.
4. RAQVJ, 15 October 1839.
5. Quoted in St Aubyn, *Queen Victoria*, 131–2.
6. Quoted in Longford, *Victoria*, 134.
7. Benson and Esher, i, 198.
8. RAQVJ, 14 November 1839.
9. Jagow, 26.
10. Ibid., 30.
11. Quoted in Weintraub, *Albert*, 85.

15 : THE BRIDEGROOM

1. Greville iv, 218; RAQVJ, 23 November 1839.
2. Croker, ii, 359.
3. Woodham-Smith, 201.
4. David, 116.
5. Woodham-Smith, 202.
6. *The Times*, 10 February 1840, quoted in Charlot, 171.
7. Quoted in Charlot, 171.
8. Longford, *Victoria*, 137–8; Charlot, 175.
9. Jagow, 58.
10. Martin, i, 58.
11. Greville, iv, 244.
12. Benson and Esher, i, 199.
13. Jagow, 37.
14. Greville, iv, 236.
15. Quoted in Woodham-Smith, 199.
16. Russell, 26.
17. Greville, iv, 244.
18. Jagow, 37.
19. Quoted in Woodham-Smith, 200.
20. Jagow, 41.
21. Benson and Esher, 199–200, 206; Longford, *Victoria*, 138–9.
22. RAQVJ, 7–8 February 1840.
23. Woodham-Smith, 202.
24. Longford, *Victoria*, 139–40; St Aubyn, *Queen Victoria*, 142–3.
25. RAQVJ, 9 February 1840.

16 : HONEYMOON

1. CH, 63, 10 February 1840, i, 217.
2. Tooley, 118.
3. Lorne, 120.
4. Ibid.
5. Hough, *Victoria and Albert*, 68–9.
6. Greville, iv, 239–40.
7. *Private Life*, 120.
8. RAQVJ, 10 February 1840.
9. Ibid.
10. Greville, iv, 240.
11. RAQVJ, 10–12 February 1840.
12. RAQVJ, 10 February 1840.
13. RAQVJ, 11 February 1840.
14. Ibid.
15. Benson and Esher, i, 217, 11 February 1840.
16. Greville, iv, 240–41.
17. Benson and Esher, i, 213.
18. Greville, iv, 241.
19. Woodham-Smith, 206–7.
20. *Private Life*, 83; Bloomfield, i, 130.
21. RAQVJ, 10 November 1839.
22. Benson and Esher, i, 199.
23. RA Y54/4, 28 May 1840.
24. RA Y54/8, 15 August 1840.
25. Charlot, 190.
26. Grey, *Early Years*, 319.
27. Bolitho, *Victoria*, 74.
28. Princess Lieven, *Une vie d'ambassadrice au siècle dernier*, 1903, 285, quoted in Charlot, 188.
29. Fulford, *Prince Consort*, 276.
30. Longford, *Victoria*, 145–6; Greville v, 49–50, 77–9, 124.
31. Charlot, 224.
32. RAQVJ, 28 February 1840.

17 : ROBERT PEEL

1. RA LP, 4 June 1840.
2. RA LP, 15 June 1840.
3. Longford, 'Queen Victoria's Doctors'.
4. Hibbert, *Wellington*, 355.
5. Bolitho, *Prince Consort and His Brother*, 21.
6. Woodham-Smith, 216.
7. Bolitho, *Prince Consort and His Brother*, 30.
8. RA George Anson's Memorandum, 28 May 1840.
9. Fulford, *Beloved Mama*, 172; Pakula, 27; Longford, *Victoria*, 153.

10. Fulford, *Beloved Mama*, 172; Pakula, 28.
11. RA Y90/11, 5 January 1841; Benson and Esher, i, 255.
12. Grey, *Early Years*, 246; Charlot, 196–7.
13. Bolitho, *Prince Consort and His Brother*, 34.
14. Theodore Martin, ii, 297.
15. Ibid., i, 113.
16. RA Y54/3.
17. Greville, iv, 413, 414.
18. RAQVJ, 28 August 1841.
19. Greville, iv, 409; Mitchell, 247.
20. Greville, iv, 407–8.
21. RA Y54/66–71.
22. Woodham-Smith, 223.
23. Greville, iv, 412–5.

18 : THE PRINCE AND THE HOUSEHOLD

1. RA Y54/100, 26 December 1841.
2. Ames, 15–17.
3. Watson, passim.
4. Stockmar, ii, 118–26.
5. Frederick Ponsonby, *Recollections*, 18.
6. Tooley, 137–8.
7. Records of the Lord Chamberlain's Department, quoted in Watson, 238.
8. Ibid., 49.
9. Jerrold, 185.
10. Jerrold, 219; David Duff, *Albert and Victoria*, 214.
11. Jerrold, 220.
12. Tooley, 146.
13. Watson, 234.
14. G. T. Curtis, *James Buchanan*, quoted in E. S. Turner, 326–7.
15. Jerrold, 253.
16. Ibid.
17. Erskine (Stanley correspondence), 176.
18. Greville, iv, 108.
19. Kennedy, 131.
20. Ibid., 32.
21. G. O. Trevelyan, *Life and Letters of Lord Macaulay*, 548–9.
22. Edwin Hodder, ed., *The Life and Work of the 7th Earl of Shaftesbury*, i, 236.
23. Greville, iv, 383.
24. Lyttelton, 389.
25. Frederick Ponsonby, 50.
26. Ibid., 51.
27. Greville, iv, 383.
28. Fulford, *Dearest Child*, 69.

29. RA Y203/78; RA Z491.
30. RAQVJ, 3 August 1843.
31. Fulford, *Prince Consort*, 242.
32. Lyttelton, 307.
33. Ibid., 357.
34. Ibid., 354.
35. RA Z491.

19 : ROYAL QUARRELS

1. Gerald Wellington, *Wellington and his Friends*, 139–40.
2. Ramsay, *Rough Recollections*, i, 66.
3. Lady Burghclere, *A Great Man's Friendship*: *Letters of the Duke of Wellington to Mary Marchioness of Salisbury*, 197; Muriel Wellesley, *Wellington in Civil Life*, 306.
4. Jagow, 72; Pakula, 29.
5. Fulford, *Dearest Child*, 78.
6. RAQVJ, 2 December 1841.
7. Quoted in Woodham-Smith, 226.
8. RAQVJ, 2 December 1841.
9. RA Add. U2/2, 16 January 1842.
10. Ibid.
11. RA Add. U2/4, 18 January 1842.
12. Ibid.
13. RA Add. U2/5, 19 January 1842.
14. Quoted in Woodham-Smith, 231.
15. RA Add. U2/7, 19 January 1842.
16. RA M12/1; RA Y54/100; RA M12/16, 17; RA M12/23.
17. Lyttelton, 319–22; Pakula, 34–6.
18. Pakula, 39.
19. Quoted in Woodham-Smith, 232.
20. RAQVJ, 24 September 1842.
21. Quoted in St Aubyn, *Queen Victoria*, 173.

20 : OSBORNE

1. RAQVJ, 1 October 1842.
2. Fulford, *Dearest Child*, 111–2.
3. Pakula, 41; Fulford, *Prince Consort*, 95.
4. Lyttelton, 338–9.
5. RA Y91/38, 6 February 1844.
6. Theodore Martin, i, 202.
7. Ibid., i, 208.
8. RAQVJ, 4 February 1844.
9. Fulford, *Dearest Child*, 140–41, 213, 215, 271.
10. RA Add. 40, 439; Woodham-Smith, 269–71.

11. Musgrave, 243.
12. RAQVJ, 8 February 1845.
13. RAQVJ, 19 October 1843.
14. RA 91/35, 16 January 1844.
15. RA Vic Y 92/16; Benson and Esher, ii, 35.
16. Theodore Martin, i, 322–3.
17. York and Stoney, 26.
18. Greville, v, 229.
19. RA Vic Y 92/16; Theodore Martin, i, 248.
20. Benson and Esher, ii, 36.
21. RAQVJ, 30 July 1847.
22. BM Add. 40, 440, 22 June 1845, quoted in Woodham-Smith, 275.
23. RAQVJ, 22 March 1845.
24. York and Stoney, 29–32; Mark Girouard, *The Victorian Country House*, 1971, 13.
25. Lyttelton, 364–5; York and Stoney, 39.
26. Ibid.
27. RAQVJ, 18 July 1854; York and Stoney, 132.
28. RAQVJ, 6 July 1849.

21 : TRAVELLING

1. RAQVJ, 2 September 1843.
2. Ibid.
3. Surtees, 95–8.
4. RAQVJ, 3–5 September 1843.
5. Theodore Martin, i, 181.
6. Jean Duhamel, *Louis-Philippe et la Première Entente Cordiale*, quoted in Woodham-Smith, 243.
7. Surtees, 109.
8. Ibid., 115.
9. E. C. Gaskell, *Life of Charlotte Brontë*, 1857, ii, 240.
10. Surtees, 110.
11. Monkswell, 33; quoted in St Aubyn, *Queen Victoria*, 335.
12. Gerald Wellington, *Wellington and His Friends*, 185.
13. Ibid., 197–8.
14. RAQVJ, 21 January 1845.
15. Ibid.
16. Hatfield House Papers, 8 October 1849, quoted in Hibbert, *Wellington*, 374.
17. Gerald Wellington, *Wellington and His Friends*, 198.
18. Greville, v, 146–8.
19. RAQVJ, 1 December 1843.
20. Greville, v, 148.

21. RAQVJ, 12 December 1843.
22. Greville, v, 198.
23. Ibid., iv, 192.
24. Ibid., v, 229–30.
25. RAQVJ, 20 August 1845.
26. Surtees, 163.
27. Greville, v, 229–30.

22 : BALMORAL

1. Quoted in St Aubyn, *Queen Victoria*, 191.
2. Jagow, 81.
3. Surtees, 115.
4. Benson and Esher, ii, 24.
5. RA Y206; Longford, *Victoria*, 212–6.
6. Greville, vi, 185–7.
7. Lyttelton, 393.
8. Quoted in St Aubyn, *Queen Victoria*, 201.
9. Fulford, *Dearest Child*, 139–40.
10. Victoria, *Leaves*, passim; Kerr, passim.
11. Quoted in Longford, *Victoria*, 237.
12. Rhodes James, *Rosebery*, 66.
13. Lytton, 37.
14. Princess Alice, 77.
15. *Private Life*, 117.
16. Rhodes James, 67.
17. Blake, 493.
18. Henry Ponsonby, 116.

23 : THE PRINCE OF WALES

1. Lyttelton, quoted in Hibbert, *Edward VII*, 5.
2. Ibid., 329; RA M13/46, 67, 68, 19–25 August, 29 September 1843.
3. RA 37/7, 10 December 1843; Longford, *Victoria*, 171–2.
4. RA M13/87, 18 August 1847.
5. Mitchell, 214.
6. RA M12/44.
7. RA M12/46.
8. Gibbs Papers, quoted in Magnus, *King Edward VII*, 7–8.
9. Lyttelton, 338.
10. George Combe's Reports, National Library of Scotland, MSS. 7437.
11. Magnus, *King Edward VII*, 6.
12. Surtees, 124.
13. Gibbs's Diary, quoted in Magnus, *King Edward VII*, 9.
14. Lincolnshire Papers, Bodleian MSS., quoted in Hibbert, *Edward VII*, 16.

15. Quoted in Hibbert, *Edward VII*, 16.
16. Ibid., 17.
17. York and Stoney, 108–10; Stoney and Weltzien, 33–4.
18. RA Add. A/25/168, 19 March 1866; Zeepvat, 45.

24 : PALMERSTON

1. Greville, iv, 207–8.
2. RAQVJ, 15 April 1845.
3. RAQVJ, 30 January 1845.
4. Quoted in Longford, *Victoria*, 181.
5. RAQVJ, 24 January 1846.
6. Mitchell, 249.
7. RAQVJ, 1 October 1842.
8. Quoted in Bolitho, *Albert the Good*, 234.
9. Quoted in Charlot, 262.
10. Benson and Esher, ii, 64.
11. Jasper Ridley, 275–6.
12. Jasper Ridley, Brian Connell, Bourne, passim.

25 : CHARTISTS

1. R. G. Gamage, *The History of the Chartist Movement* (1894), quoted in Best, 187.
2. Quoted in St Aubyn, *Queen Victoria*, 226.
3. CH 283, 30 October 1883.
4. Quoted in Longford, *Victoria*, 197–8.
5. Hibbert, *Wellington*, 380.
6. Benson and Esher, ii, 166–7, 4 April 1848.
7. Greville, vi, 51–2.
8. Theodore Martin, ii, 106.
9. Quoted in St Aubyn, *Queen Victoria*, 224–5.

26 : 'PAM IS OUT'

1. Quoted in St Aubyn, *Queen Victoria*, 217.
2. RAQVJ, 2 November 1848.
3. RAQVJ, 22 January 1849.
4. RAQVJ, 16 May 1850.
5. Ashley, 211–27; Jasper Ridley, 386–7.
6. RA C9/46, 12 August 1850.
7. Theodore Martin, ii, 307.
8. Charlot, 322.
9. RA A79/58, 8 October 1850.
10. Spencer Walpole, ii, 133.

11. Benson and Esher, ii, 392–400; Jasper Ridley, 396–7.
12. Theodore Martin, ii, 412.
13. Jasper Ridley, 398–400.
14. Greville, vi, 315–16.
15. RAQVJ, 20 December 1851.

27 : THE GREAT EXHIBITION

1. Benson and Esher, ii, 317–8.
2. Quoted in St Aubyn, *Queen Victoria*, 227.
3. *The Times*, 22 June 1851.
4. Hansard, vol. 112, 903, quoted in Woodham-Smith, 309.
5. Jagow, 176–7.
6. Quoted in St Aubyn, *Queen Victoria*, 230.
7. Wellington Papers, Hartley Institute, 2 April 1851, quoted in Hibbert, *Wellington*, 383.
8. Hansard, vol. 112, 905, quoted in Woodham-Smith, 309.
9. RAQVJ, 18 February 1851.
10. RAQVJ, 1 May 1851.
11. Ibid.
12. Asa Briggs, *Iron Bridge to Crystal Palace*, 172.
13. RAQVJ, 1 May 1851.
14. Theodore Martin, ii, 383.

28 : 'SCENES'

1. Benson and Esher, i, 480.
2. RA Z140/9–18.
3. RAQVJ, 31 December 1855.
4. RA Y206, Sir James Clark's Diary, 5, 15 February 1856.

29 : CRIMEAN WAR

1. RA Z171/13, 12 February 1845.
2. RAQVJ, 3 May 1855.
3. RAQVJ, 20, 22 February 1855.
4. RAQVJ, 18 April 1855.
5. RAQVJ, 22 November 1854.
6. Bolitho, *Further Letters*, 51.
7. Ibid.
8. RAQVJ, 8 December 1854.
9. Theodore Martin, iii, 503.
10. Panmure Papers, quoted in Hibbert, *Destruction of Lord Raglan*, 299.

11. Ibid., 300.
12. David, 326.
13. Raglan Private Papers D (1) 225, quoted in Hibbert, *Destruction of Lord Raglan*, 270.
14. RA G21/65/166.
15. Panmure Papers, 13 February 1855, quoted in Hibbert, *op.cit.* 256.
16. Ibid., 16 February 1855, quoted in Hibbert, *op.cit.*, 256.
17. Ibid., 24 June 1855, quoted in Hibbert, *op.cit.*, 256.
18. Quoted in Longford, *Victoria*, 241.
19. Hansard, 3rd series, 156.
20. Ibid.
21. Magnus, *Gladstone*, 119.
22. Weibe, vi, 405.
23. Pemberton, 30.
24. RAQVJ, 21 August 1856.
25. Jasper Ridley, 519–20; St Aubyn, *Queen Victoria*, 297.

30 : NAPOLEON III

1. RA J76/84, Prince Albert's memorandum, 12 September 1854.
2. RA Add. A19/37, 6 January 1853.
3. RA Add. A19/44, 20 January 1853.
4. RAQVJ, 16 April 1855.
5. Quoted in St Aubyn, *Queen Victoria*, 299.
6. Quoted in Aronson, *Heart of a Queen*, 102.
7. Greville, vii, 154.
8. Pakula, 59.
9. RA 76/92, 1 September 1855.
10. RA Z63, quoted in Woodham-Smith, 358.
11. Longford, *Victoria*, 251.
12. RAQVJ, 19 April 1855.
13. RAQVJ, 76/92, 1 September 1855.
14. RAQVJ, 18 August 1855.
15. Benson and Esher, iii, 135–6.
16. St Aubyn, *Queen Victoria*, 302.
17. Stoney and Weltzien, 17; Pakula, 57; Munich, 67; Weintraub, *Victoria*, 250–51.
18. CH, 133; Benson and Esher, iii, 136–8; Martin, iii, 321–38; RAQVJ, 18 August 1855; RAJ 76/92, 1 September 1855.
19. RAQVJ, 24 August 1855.
20. Greville, vii, 157.
21. Hibbert, *Edward VII*, 18.
22. Ibid.

23. Greville, vii, 158.
24. Aronson, *Heart of a Queen*, 108.
25. Pakula, 58.

31 : THE PRINCESS ROYAL

1. RA Add. A7/9; CH, 98, 29 September 1855.
2. Pakula, 65–6.
3. RAQVJ, 28 September 1855.
4. *The Times*, 3 October 1855; Charlot, 378–9; Pakula, 58.
5. *Punch*, September 1855 quoted in Charlot, 378.
6. RA Add. A7/9; CH, 98.
7. Ibid.
8. St Aubyn, *Queen Victoria*, 270.
9. *Leaves From the Journal of Our Life in the Highlands*, 10 September 1855.
10. Quoted in St Aubyn, *Queen Victoria*, 303.
11. RAQVJ, 15 January 1858; Kurtz, 105–6.
12. Malmesbury, i, 392–3.
13. Edmond Fitzmaurice, *Life of Lord Granville*, i, 288.
14. Jasper Ridley, 482.
15. RAQVJ, 25 January–2 February 1858.
16. Ibid.
17. RAQVJ, 25 January–2 February 1858.
18. Quoted in St Aubyn, *Queen Victoria*, 270.
19. Pakula, 78.
20. Charlot, 385.
21. Fulford, *Dearest Child*, 31–2, 5 February 1858.
22. Theodore Martin, iv, 169.
23. Fulford, *Dearest Child*, 45, 15 February 1858.
24. Pakula, 69–70.
25. RAQVJ, 7 January 1856; Pakula, 71.
26. Fulford, *Dearest Child*, 1–5; Thompson, 146.
27. Fulford, *Dearest Child*, 89.
28. Ibid., 56.
29. Ibid., 213.
30. Ibid., 195–6 and passim.

32 : INDIAN MUTINY

1. Hibbert, *Great Mutiny*, 59–90.
2. Quoted in St Aubyn, *Queen Victoria*, 306.
3. Quoted in Longford, *Victoria*, 280.
4. Hibbert, *op. cit.* 166.

5. Ibid., 165.
6. Ibid., 167.
7. Surtees, 232.
8. Theodore Martin, iv, 284.
9. Quoted in Woodham-Smith, 386.
10. Greville, vii, 175.
11. RAQVJ, 4 December 1855.
12. Greville, vii, 175.
13. Steuart Erskine, 303.
14. Theodore Martin, iv, 275.
15. St Aubyn, *Queen Victoria*, 304; Longford, *Victoria*, 279.
16. St Aubyn, *Queen Victoria*, 305.

33 : THE GERMAN GRANDSON

1. Bolitho, *Prince Consort and His Brother*, 177; Woodham-Smith, 375–7.
2. RA Z140, 1 October 1856.
3. Fulford, *Dearest Child*, 109, 29 May 1858.
4. Ibid., 115, 15 June 1858.
5. Ibid., 123, 21 July 1858.
6. Ibid., 24 July 1858.
7. Ibid., 131, 135, 21 September 1858, 5 October, 1858.
8. Ibid., 134, 27 September 1858; 139, 18 October 1858.
9. Quoted in Hough, *Advice to a Grand-daughter*, 126.
10. Pakula, 113–14.
11. Ibid., 114.
12. Ibid., 117.
13. Ibid., 124–6.
14. Fulford, *Dearest Child*, 159, 29 January 1859.
15. RA Z7/87, 28 February 1859; RA Z7/96, 12 March 1859.
16. Fulford, *Dearest Child*, 159.
17. Quoted in Woodham-Smith, 398.
18. Fulford, *Dearest Child*.
19. Quoted in Woodham-Smith.
20. RAQVJ, 25–7 September 1860.
21. Ibid., 1 October 1860.
22. *Memoirs of Ernest II, Duke of Saxe-Coburg and Gotha*, quoted in Woodham-Smith, 402; Weintraub, *Albert*, 393.
23. Ibid., Weintraub, *Albert*, 394.
24. Theodore Martin, iv, 225.
25. Ibid., iv, 259.
26. Ibid., iv, 274.
27. Fulford, *Dearest Child*, 310, 14 February 1861.

28. Theodore Martin, v, 274–5.
29. Fulford, *Dearest Child*, 308, 16 February 1861.
30. Ibid., 354, 1 October 1861.

34 : DEATH OF THE DUCHESS

1. Charlot, 87–92.
2. RA Z484/41, 2 March 1854.
3. RA Z484/32, 3 March 1854.
4. RAQVJ, 13 October 1850.
5. RAQVJ, 8 October 1849.
6. RA 95/20, 9 July 1850.
7. CH 90, 17 September 1852; Benson and Esher, ii, 394, 402; Charlot, 342.
8. RAQVJ, 15 March 1861.
9. Theodore Martin, v, 315.
10. RAQVJ, 9 April 1861.
11. Fulford, *Dearest Child*, 319, 300.
12. Kennedy, *My Dear Duchess*, 141.
13. RAQVJ, 24 March 1861; Benson and Esher, iii, 435–9.
14. Magnus, *King Edward VII*, 44.

35 : THE DISAPPOINTING HEIR

1. Fulford, *Dearest Child*, 174.
2. Ibid., 73.
3. Ibid., 147, 245; Hibbert, *Edward VII*, 25.
4. Fulford, *Dearest Child*, 109.
5. Corti, 54.
6. Ibid., 50.
7. Ibid., 51.
8. RA Add. U/32.
9. Corti, 59.
10. Theodore Martin, v, 87.
11. Corti, 63; Magnus, *King Edward VII*, 41.
12. Fulford, *Dearest Child*, 279.
13. RA Y107/12, 26 August 1861.
14. RA Z, 11/18, 6 April 1861.
15. Fulford, *Dearest Child*, 342.
16. Corti, 68, Magnus, *King Edward VII*, 46; Pakula, 143–5.
17. RA Add. MSS. A3/69.
18. RAQVJ, 30 September 1861.
19. Corti, 72.
20. Quoted in Hibbert, *Edward VII*, 45.
21. Magnus, *King Edward VII*, 50.
22. RA Z141/94.
23. RA Z141/95.
24. Corti, 72.

36 : DEATH OF THE PRINCE

1. Fulford, *Dearest Child*, 369–70, 27 November 1861.
2. RA Z140/62 undated.
3. RAQVJ, 3 December 1861.
4. Palmerston Papers, quoted in Woodham-Smith, 424.
5. RAQVJ, 6 December 1861.
6. Ibid., 7 December 1861.
7. Ibid., 8 December 1861.
8. Palmerston Papers, quoted in Woodham-Smith, 426–7.
9. RA Z142, 11 December 1861; Longford, *Victoria*, 298.
10. RAQVJ, 11 December 1861.
11. RA Add. U55, 19 December 1861.
12. Ibid.
13. RA Z142, 14 December 1861.
14. Ibid.
15. *Letters of Lady Augusta Stanley*, 291.
16. RA Z142, 14 December 1861.
17. McClintock, 46–7.

37 : THE GRIEVING WIDOW

1. RA Add. U 303/17, 16 January 1862.
2. RA Add. U 302/21, 11 March 1862.
3. Mallet, 4, 32.
4. Watson, 156.
5. Quoted in Weintraub, *Victoria*, 309.
6. *Private Life*, 66.
7. Quoted in Longford, *Victoria*, 308.
8. *Letters to the Duchess of Manchester*, quoted in Weintraub, *Victoria*, 316.
9. Gardiner, 108; *Letters to the Duchess of Manchester*, quoted in Weintraub, 314.
10. *Frogmore House and the Royal Mausoleum*, 40–42.
11. Palmerston Papers, 15 December 1861, quoted in Woodham-Smith, 430.
12. *Letters to the Duchess of Manchester*, 183.
13. Quoted in Longford, *Victoria*, 307.
14. *Letters to the Duchess of Manchester*, 186, 14 March 1862.
15. Pakula, 159.
16. Ibid., 160.
17. Corti, i, 82.
18. Fulford, *Dearest Mama*, 18 December 1862, 24.
19. Quoted in St Aubyn, *Queen Victoria*, 331.
20. Ibid., 332.
21. Quoted in Weintraub, *Victoria*, 334.

22. *Letters to the Duchess of Manchester*, 12 March 1862, 191.
23. Hughenden Papers, quoted in Longford, *Victoria*, 313.
24. Quoted in Weintraub, *Victoria*, 334.

38 : SÉANCES AND SERVICES

1. Fulford, *Dearest Child*, 7 October 1861, 356.
2. Princess Marie Louise, 57.
3. RA GV AA20/64, quoted in Wheeler-Bennett, 7.
4. Wheeler-Bennett, 8.
5. Martin, ii, 339–40.
6. Hough, *Advice to a Grand-daughter*, 76.
7. Lytton, 114.
8. Fulford, *Your Dear Letter*, 141.
9. Dorothy Thompson, 47, 124.
10. Portland, *Men, Women and Things*, 1937, 125.
11. RA Z264/2, 19 October 1873.
12. *Leaves from the Journal*, 29 October 1854.
13. Ibid., 14 October 1855.

39 : PRINCESS ALEXANDRA

1. RA Vic Add. MSS. A 22/71, quoted in Longford, *Victoria*, 308.
2. RA Vic Add. MSS. U 16.
3. CH, 161, 15 January 1862.
4. Corti, 81, 27 December 1861.
5. Quoted in Hibbert, *Edward VII*, 50.
6. Fulford, *Dearest Mama*, 105–6.
7. *Letters to the Duchess of Manchester*, 183.
8. Quoted in Longford, *Victoria*, 315.
9. RAQVJ, 18 September 1862.
10. CH, 162, 24 January 1862.
11. Quoted in Battiscombe, 36.
12. Ibid., 40–42.
13. CH, 172, 7 March 1863.
14. Ibid., 9 March 1863.
15. RAQVJ, 24 February, 9 March, 10 March, 1863.
16. Quoted in Hibbert, *Edward VII*, 62.
17. Battiscombe, 50; Longford, *Victoria*, 316; Magnus, *Edward VII*, 67–8; Monypenny and Buckle, ii, 119–21.
18. RAQVJ, 28 February 1863.
19. Ibid., 10 March 1863.
20. Quoted in Weintraub, *Victoria*, 320–21.
21. Quoted in Hibbert, *Edward VII*, 76.

22. Ibid.
23. Weintraub, *Victoria*, 327.

40 : THE RECLUSE

1. Munby, 90.
2. Grey Papers, Durham, 25 January 1863, quoted in Arengo-Jones, 16–17.
3. Ibid., 4 September 1863, 8, 26 May 1868, 32.
4. Arthur Ponsonby, 73–4.
5. Ponsonby Letters, quoted in Longford, *Victoria RI*, 386.
6. Ibid., 387.
7. Munby, 249.
8. Grey Papers, 17 December 1863, quoted in Arengo-Jones, 21.
9. Ibid., 4 September 1866, 22.
10. Ibid., 22 May 1868, 31
11. Disraeli, MSS, Bodleian, BXIX/A/52, 22 May 1868, quoted in Arengo-Jones, 32.
12. *Letters*, 2nd series, i, 218–19, 15 June 1864.
13. CH, 186–7, 8 December 1864; 192–3, 22 January 1866.
14. Quoted in Weintraub, 333.
15. Quoted in Longford, *Victoria RI*, 348.
16. CH, 192, 22 January 1866.
17. Munby, 218.
18. RAQVJ, 6 February 1866; *Letters*, 2nd series, i, 296.
19. Quoted in St Aubyn, *Queen Victoria*, 371.
20. CH, 197, 5 February 1867.

41 : DISRAELI

1. CH, 179, 12 November 1863.
2. Frederick Ponsonby, 58.
3. CH, 191, 25 October 1865.
4. Monypenny and Buckle, iv, 394; Blake, 431.
5. Blake, 487.
6. Ibid., 490.
7. CH, 90, 1 April 1852; Blake, 490–91.
8. *Letters*, 2nd series, i, 505, 26 February 1868; Blake, 491.
9. Monypenny and Buckle, vi, 453.
10. Sir H. Maxwell, *Life and Letters of . . . Fourth Earl of Clarendon*, ii, 346.
11. Blake, 491.
12. Quoted in Gardiner, 120.
13. Blake, 493.

14. Monypenny and Buckle, v, 339.
15. Quoted in St Aubyn, *Queen Victoria*, 383.
16. Quoted in Weintraub, 448.

42 : JOHN BROWN

1. Munby, 239.
2. Arthur Ponsonby, 127–9.
3. Bell, ii, 31.
4. Quoted in Longford, *Victoria*, 327.
5. Vincent, 47–8.
6. CH, 150, 21 October 1861.
7. McClintock, 33.
8. Quoted in Weintraub, 399.
9. CH, 188, 5 April 1865.
10. Ibid., 187, 24 February 1865.
11. RA Vic Add. MSS, A22/112, 26 December 1866.
12. Quoted in Longford, *Victoria*, 459.
13. Arthur Ponsonby, 126–7.
14. Quoted in Rose, *Kings, Queens and Courtiers*, 87.
15. Arthur Ponsonby, 127.
16. Ibid., 126.
17. Ibid.
18. Ribblesdale, 126.
19. Arthur Ponsonby, 124–6.
20. Ibid., 122
21. Ibid., 128.
22. Quoted in St Aubyn, *Queen Victoria*, 353.
23. RA C3/57–8.
24. McClintock, 182.
25. *Leaves from the Journal*, note to entry for 16 September 1850.
26. Elizabeth Longford, Introduction to *Leaves from the Journal of Our Life in the Highlands*, Folio Society, 1973, 19.
27. Baillie and Bolitho, *Letters of Lady Augusta Stanley*, 72.
28. CH, 192, 23 December 1865.
29. Magnus, *Edward VII*, 178.

43 : 'THE ROYALTY QUESTION'

1. Dilke Papers, quoted in Jenkins, *Sir Charles Dilke*, 145.
2. Hibbert, *Edward VII*, 108.
3. Arthur Ponsonby, 70.
4. Ibid., 211.
5. Reid, 162.
6. Arthur Ponsonby, 74.

7. CH, 193, 22 January 1866.
8. Arthur Ponsonby, 72.
9. Magnus, *Gladstone*, 212.
10. Quoted in Thompson, 204.
11. Ibid., 206.
12. Quoted in St Aubyn, *Queen Victoria*, 344.
13. CH, 315n.
14. Quoted in Longford, *Victoria*, 374.

44 : 'THE PRINCELY PAUPER'

1. RAQVJ, 29 March 1871.
2. RA Add. A1/16.
3. Quoted in St Aubyn, *Queen Victoria*, 342.
4. RAQVJ, 18 October 1871; CH, 226.
5. *Letters*, 2nd series, ii, 157, 160–61; RAQVJ, 18 September 1871.
6. *The Times*, quoted in Bolitho, *Victoria*, 241.

45 : TYPHOID FEVER

1. RAQVJ, 7 July 1867.
2. Macclesfield Papers, quoted in Battiscombe, 114–18.
3. Brett, i, 300.
4. Macclesfield Papers, quoted in Battiscombe, 116.
5. RA. Add A30/366, 10 January 1872.
6. RAQVJ, 29 November–31 December 1871; CH, 213–5, 29 November 1871–23 December 1871.
7. Arthur Ponsonby, 99–100; St Aubyn, *Royal George*, 162–3.
8. Arthur Ponsonby, 98.
9. RAQVJ, 14 December 1871.
10. CH, 215, 14 February 1872.
11. RAQVJ, 27 February 1872; Brett, i, 119–20; Longford, *Victoria*, 390; Jenkins, *Gladstone*, 348.
12. CH, 216; RAQVJ, 27 February 1872.
13. Longford, *Victoria*, 391.
14. *Letters*, 2nd series, 445–6.
15. Benson, *Victoria*, 232.
16. Quoted in Weintraub, 354.
17. Watson, 218.
18. Watson, 221–3; Rose, 52–3; Augustus Hare, *In My Solitary Life*, new edition, London, 1973, 229.
19. Hare, 52.
20. Arthur Ponsonby, *Sidelights*, 122, 128; Benson, *Victoria*, 226; Bolitho, *Victoria*,

245; Watson, 223; *Letters*, 2nd series, ii, 258–61.

46 : MAIDS-OF-HONOUR

1. Fulford, *Victoria*, 134.
2. Bell, 77.
3. Mallet, 4.
4. Reid, 176.
5. Ibid., 182–3.
6. 27 August 1899, quoted in Longford, *Victoria*, 572.
7. Reid, 188.
8. Ibid., 186.
9. Mallet, 44–5.
10. Guedalla, i, 227–9.
11. Martin, *Victoria*, 70.
12. Fulford, *Victoria*, 132.
13. Longford, *Victoria*, 567.

47 : SECRETARIES AND MINISTERS

1. Viscount Mersey, *A Picture of Life, 1872–1940*, 1941, 359.
2. Frederick Ponsonby, 16–17.
3. Arthur Ponsonby, 87.
4. Baron von Eckardstein, *Ten Years at the Court of St James's*, 1921, 43.
5. Ibid., 44.
6. Fulford, *Victoria*, 78.
7. Arthur Ponsonby, passim.
8. Quoted in Weintraub, 570.
9. Henry Ponsonby, 57–8.
10. Ibid., 60.
11. Reid, 44.
12. John Wilson, *C.B. A Life of Sir Henry Campbell-Bannerman*, 132–3.
13. Ibid., 133–5.
14. Quoted in Reid, 33.

48 : REGINA ET IMPERATRIX

1. Arthur Ponsonby, 244, 245.
2. Rhodes James, 64.
3. Ponsonby Letters, 27 January 1873 quoted in Longford, *Victoria*, 404.
4. Blake, 562–3.
5. Monypenny and Buckle, v, 827; Blake, 582–7.
6. *Letters*, 2nd series, ii, 28 September 1876.

7. Blake, 607.
8. Quoted in Longford, *Victoria*, 410, 19 June 1877.
9. Fulford, *Dearest Mama*, 28.
10. Quoted in Longford, *Victoria*, 411.
11. Ibid., 412.
12. Hibbert, *Disraeli and His World*, 106.
13. Blake, 613.
14. Ibid., 646.
15. Monypenny and Buckle, 632.
16. Quoted in Longford, *Victoria*, 415.
17. Blake, 649; Monypenny & Buckle, vi, 332; Longford, *Victoria*, 414.
18. *Letters*, 2nd series, iii, 37–8, 28 July 1879.
19. Ibid., 3rd series, i, 615, 12 June 1890.
20. Ibid., 2nd series, iii, 646, 17 May 1885.

49 : 'THE HALF-MAD FIREBRAND'

1. Fulford, *Dearest Mama*, 78.
2. Arthur Ponsonby, 184.
3. Monypenny and Buckle, vi, 538–9; Jenkins, *Gladstone*, 438–9; Longford, *Victoria*, 434; Morley, ii, 234–6; Fulford, *Dearest Mama*, 75; Henry Ponsonby, 187–9.
4. *Letters*, 2nd series, iii, 143, 20 September 1880; Blake, 716; Monypenny and Buckle, vi, 527.
5. Quoted in St Aubyn, *Queen Victoria*, 445.
6. *Letters*, 2nd series, iii, 181.
7. Blake, 747.
8. Ibid., 748.
9. Ibid., 750.
10. Longford, *Victoria*, 463.
11. Quoted in Weintraub, 458.
12. CH, 284, 9 February 1884.
13. CH, 289, 5 February 1885.
14. Quoted in St Aubyn, *Queen Victoria*, 456.
15. Ibid., 455.
16. *Letters*, 2nd series, iii, 594–5, 24 January 1885; St Aubyn, *Royal George*, 222–3.
17. *Letters*, 2nd series, iii, 619, 28 May 1885.
18. *Letters*, 2nd series, iii, 662, 11 June, 1885.
19. CH, 292–3.
20. Lady Geraldine Somerset, quoted in St Aubyn, *Royal George*, 228.
21. Arthur Ponsonby, 206.
22. *Letters*, 3rd series, i, 34, 1 February 1836.
23. Ramm, 28.
24. *Letters*, 3rd series, i, 119–24.
25. Viscount Milner, *My Picture Gallery*

1886–1901, quoted by Kenneth Rose in *The Later Cecils*, 13.

26. Quoted in Longford, *Victoria*, 492.
27. Ibid., 518.
28. *Letters*, 3rd series, ii, 145; CH, 323, 15 August 1892.
29. Brett, i, 161.
30. *Letters*, 3rd series, ii, 119 *et seq.*
31. Jenkins, *Gladstone*, 589.
32. Quoted in Longford, *Victoria*, 531.
33. Quoted in St Aubyn, *Royal George*, 301.
34. CH, 326–7, 28 February and 3 March 1894; Jenkins, *Gladstone*, 616–8.
35. *Letters*, 3rd series, ii, 370–71; RAQVJ, 3 May 1894.
36. *Letters*, 3rd series, ii, 404, 8 June 1894; St Aubyn, *Queen Victoria*, 515–18; Rhodes James, 336, 353; CH, 378, 11 March 1894.
37. Hibbert, *Edward VII*, 148.
38. Ramm, 215.
39. Ibid., 550.
40. CH, 337, 28 May 1898; Brett, i, 217.
41. Ponsonby Letters, 19 April 1875 quoted in Longford, *Victoria*.
42. Morley, ii, 764.
43. Magnus, *Gladstone*, 425.

50 : GOLDEN JUBILEE

1. CH, 309, 31 December 1887.
2. Salisbury Papers, quoted in Longford, *Victoria*, 499.
3. RAQVJ, 21, 22, 29 June 1887; CH, 305–7.
4. Lady Geraldine Somerset, quoted in St Aubyn, *Royal George*, 232.
5. Battiscombe, 174.
6. Quoted in St Aubyn, *Queen Victoria*, 489.
7. Longford, *Victoria*, 501.
8. St Aubyn, *Royal George*, 234.
9. Röhl, 676.
10. RA Z66/69 2 June 1887.
11. Röhl, 678.
12. Ibid., 679.
13. Ibid., 680.
14. Ibid., 681.

51 : DIE ENGLÄNDERIN

1. Pakula, 445; St Aubyn, *Queen Victoria*, 490.
2. Pakula, 436.

3. RA Z66/75.
4. RA Z66/76; Röhl, 659.
5. Röhl, 664.
6. Ibid.
7. Röhl, 690.
8. RA Z38/87, 15 November 1887; Röhl, 692–3.
9. Pakula, 458.
10. Ibid., 462; St Aubyn, *Queen Victoria*, 528.
11. Fulford, *Dearest Mama*, 60.
12. Quoted in Longford, *Victoria*, 505; Pakula, 463.
13. Ramm, 64.
14. Reid, 99.
15. Pakula, 482.
16. Ibid.
17. Fulford, *Dearest Mama*, 41.
18. Pakula, 483.
19. RAQVJ, 26 April 1888.
20. Corti, i, 302.
21. Quoted in St Aubyn, *Queen Victoria*, 533.
22. Ibid.
23. CH, 312.
24. Buckle, iii, 168–9.
25. RA Z41/49, 19 May 1888.
26. Pakula, 490.
27. Röhl, 679.
28. Ibid., 824.
29. RA Z44/33.
30. Quoted in Weintraub, 505.

52 : THE DAUGHTERS

1. Quoted in St Aubyn, *Queen Victoria*, 281.
2. RA Y104/13, 19 April 1859.
3. Fulford, *Dearest Child*, 287–8.
4. Hough, *Advice to a Grand-daughter*, 29.
5. RAQVJ, 1 July 1862; CH, 166, 2 July 1862.
6. Quoted in Rose, 147.
7. John van der Kiste, *Queen Victoria's Children*.
8. Quoted in St Aubyn, *Queen Victoria*, 412–13.
9. Ibid., 413.
10. *Letters*, 2nd series, i, 633, 29 November 1869.
11. Ponsonby Letters, 8 October 1870, quoted in Longford, *Victoria*, 368.
12. Ibid., 382.
13. Mallet, 40, 50, 216.
14. Reid, 102.

53 : THE SONS

1. Fulford, *Dearest Child*, 131, 236, 243.
2. RA C64/77, August 1874; RA Add. A 3/101, 22 November 1867.
3. RA Add. A 25/388, 22 November 1873; Stoney and Weltzien, 44.
4. CH, 205, 8 July, 5 August 1868.
5. RA 527/129–30.
6. McClintock, 25–6.
7. Fulford, *Dearest Child*, 146.
8. McClintock, 15, 25, 41, 52, 113, 220–21, passim.
9. RAQVJ, 3 February 1878.
10. *Augusta Stanley Letters*, 84–5.
11. Ponsonby Letters, quoted in Longford, *Victoria*, 569.
12. RA Y101/35, 26 August 1856.
13. Fulford, *Dearest Child*, 164, 2 March 1859.
14. Ibid., 208, 2 September 1859.
15. Quoted in Zeepvat, 8.
16. RA Y104/26, 26 August 1856.
17. RA Y199/334, 3 January 1860.
18. McClintock, 48.
19. RAQVJ, 15 April 1866.
20. RA Add. A/25/179, 8 July 1866.
21. Zeepvat, 51.
22. Ibid.
23. Fulford, *Your Dear Letter*, 184.
24. RA Add. A/30/336, 3 September 1868.
25. RA Add. A 30/15, 4 July 1870.
26. Zeepvat, 72.
27. Ibid., 81.
28. RA Z264/43, 4 June 1875.
29. Zeepvat, 114.
30. Ibid., 122.
31. Ibid, 150.
32. Ibid, 156–7.
33. CH 271, 18 November 1881; CH 273, 27 April 1882.
34. RAQVJ, 21 February 1882.
35. Fulford, *Beloved Mama*, 17.
36. CH, 285.
37. Zeepvat, 189.
38. *Lady Augusta Stanley Letters*, 146.
39. Ibid., 206.
40. RA Y206, Clark Diary, 5 February 1856.
41. RAQVJ, 29 April 1857.
42. Quoted in St Aubyn, *Queen Victoria*, 419.
43. CH, 234, 20 October 1873.
44. Pope-Hennessy, 218.
45. Henry Ponsonby, 119.
46. Fulford, *Dearest Mama*, 176, 177, 186.
47. Ibid., 144.
48. CH, 246, 25 July 1877.
49. RAQVJ, 23 July 1885.
50. Quoted in Weintraub, 475.
51. Quoted in Longford, *Victoria*, 518.

54 : THE GRANDCHILDREN

1. Mallet, 57, 100.
2. Bell, 90.
3. Mallet, 96.
4. Battiscombe, 122–3.
5. Windsor, *A King's Story*, 10.
6. Wheeler-Bennett, 19.
7. St Aubyn, 579.
8. Olsen, 359.
9. CH, 280; St Aubyn, 478.
10. Marie Louise, 19.
11. *Private Life*, 85–6.
12. *Queen Victoria at Windsor and Balmoral; Letters from her Grand-daughter*, James Pope-Hennessy, London, 1959, passim.

55 : WOULD-BE ASSASSINS

1. RAQVJ, 2 March 1882.
2. Ibid; CH, 272.
3. RA Prince Albert's Memorandum; RAQVJ, 2 March 1882.
4. RA Prince Albert's Memorandum.
5. Charlot, 221–3; Woodham-Smith, 212–3.
6. Forster, *Elizabeth Barrett Browning*, 109.
7. Baroness Bunsen, ed. *Memoirs of Baron Bunsen*, ii, 16, quoted in Longford, *Victoria*, 170.
8. CH, 69–70; Charlot, 222; Longford, *Victoria*, 169–70.
9. Benson and Esher, *Letters*, ii, 220.
10. Quoted in St Aubyn, *Queen Victoria*, 164.
11. RAQVJ, 2 September 1850.
12. Woodham-Smith, 310; Longford, *Victoria*, 193; St Aubyn, *Queen Victoria*, 164.
13. RAQVJ, 14 October 1867.
14. Ibid., 23 November 1867.
15. RAQVJ, 29 February 1872; Buckle, *Letters*, ii, iii, 198.
16. RAQVJ, 29 February 1872; CH, 227.
17. Longford, *Victoria*, 390.
18. Fulford, *Beloved Mama*, 116.

56 : HOLIDAYS ABROAD

1. Lytton, 75; Duff, *Victoria Travels*, passim.
2. Grey Papers, Durham, 5 February 1863, quoted in Arengo-Jones, 17–18.
3. Grey Papers, Durham, 29 August 1865, quoted in Arengo-Jones, 20.
4. Grey Papers, Durham, 28 August 1865, quoted in Arengo-Jones, 19.
5. RAQVJ, 4 August 1867.
6. RA Add. A25/204, 27–28 August 1867.
7. RAQVJ, 22 June 1868.
8. Quoted in Arengo-Jones, 48.
9. Ibid., 42.
10. RAQVJ, 5 August 1868.
11. Derby Papers, Liverpool, Diary 6 August 1868, quoted in Arengo-Jones, 54.
12. Ibid., 2 July 1868, quoted in Arengo-Jones, 44, 66.
13. Fulford, *Dearest Mama*, 35; Hough, *Advice to a Grand-daughter*, 35; Arengo-Jones, passim.
14. Arthur Ponsonby, 284.
15. RA Add. A 36/28 quoted in Arengo-Jones, 74.
16. Longford, *Victoria*, 459–60.
17. RA Add. A/36/28, quoted in Arengo-Jones, 74.
18. Arthur Ponsonby, 285–6.
19. Harold Nicolson, *Diaries and Letters*, entry for 2 February 1942.
20. Ramm, 65–7, 100.
21. Paget, *Embassies of Other Days*, 204.
22. Fulford, *Beloved Mama*, 56.
23. Arthur Ponsonby, 285.
24. Mallet, 41–54.
25. RAQVJ, 13 April 1898.
26. RAQVJ, 27 April 1899.
27. RAQVJ, 5 November 1847.
28. Buckle, *Letters*, 2nd series, iii, 162.
29. St Aubyn, *Royal George*, 45.
30. Frederick Ponsonby, *Recollections*, 63.
31. Quoted in St Aubyn, *Queen Victoria*, 556.
32. Bolitho, *Victoria*, 356.

57 : DEATH OF BROWN

1. Reid, 51–2.
2. Ibid., 52.
3. Ibid., 54.
4. Zeepvat, 177.
5. Hough, *Advice to a Grand-daughter*, 146; Fulford, *Beloved Mama*, 135–7; *CH*, 280–81; Hough, 45–6; Longford, *Victoria*, 452–3; St Aubyn, *Queen Victoria*, 420–24; Weintraub, 340–41; *The Court Historian*, vol. iii, 2 July 1998, 65.
6. Arthur Ponsonby, 146–7; RA Vic. Add. MSS. A12/903, A12/904.
7. Reid, 58–9; Bell, 207–8.
8. RA Z266/13, 2 January 1884.
9. Quoted in St Aubyn, *Royal George*, 265.
10. Magnus, *King Edward VII*, 178.

58 : THE MUNSHI

1. RAQVJ, 23 June 1887.
2. Reid, 128–9.
3. Arthur Ponsonby, 131.
4. Quoted in Anand, 18.
5. Warner, 198–9.
6. Anand, 21.
7. Ibid., 22.
8. Arthur Ponsonby, 131.
9. *CH*, Queen to Henry Ponsonby, 12 September 1887.
10. Salisbury Papers, quoted in Longford, *Victoria*, 540.
11. Quoted in E. F. Benson, *Victoria*, 345.
12. India Office Records, MSS, Eur. F84/126A, quoted in Longford, *Victoria*, 538.
13. Arthur Ponsonby, 131–2; Anand, 50; *CH*, 328.
14. Frederick Ponsonby, *Recollections*, 13–15.
15. Ramm, 176.
16. Reid, 139.
17. India Office Records Eur. F84/126B, quoted in Anand, 54.
18. Fulford, *Dearest Mama*, 56.
19. Quoted in Anand, 92.
20. RA U/104/20, quoted in Anand, 96.
21. Frederick Ponsonby, *Recollections*, 15.
22. Reid, 154.

59 : DIAMOND JUBILEE

1. RAQVJ, 23 September 1896.
2. *CH*, 333, 22 March 1896.
3. Quoted in St Aubyn, *Queen Victoria*, 575.
4. Ibid., 576.
5. Maylunas and Mironenko, *A Lifelong Passion: Nicholas and Alexandra*, 78, 204.
6. Reid, 124.
7. Lytton, 127.

8. Reid, 125.
9. RAQVJ, 23 September 1896.
10. Ibid., 20, 21, 22 June 1897.
11. Monkswell, 202.
12. Quoted in St Aubyn, *Queen Victoria*, 547.
13. Frederick Ponsonby, 75–6.
14. Cecil, *Life of Marquis of Salisbury*, iii, 191.
15. Brett, i, 214.

60 : LIFE AT COURT

1. Frederick Ponsonby, 11–25.
2. Ibid., 36–8.
3. Ibid.
4. Quoted in Weintraub, 602.
5. Henry Ponsonby, 119.
6. Reid, 158–9.
7. Mallet, xiii.

61 : DINNER PARTIES

1. Lytton, 22.
2. Ribblesdale, 118.
3. *Private Life*, 228–9.
4. Ibid., 139–40.
5. Aga Khan, 46–7.
6. *Private Life*, 140–42.
7. Ribblesdale, 119–20.
8. Mallet, 34.
9. Ibid., 37.
10. Aga Khan, 47.
11. Mallet, passim.
12. Reid, 177.
13. Musgrave, 213.
14. Reid, 116.
15. *Private Life*, 88–9.
16. Arthur Ponsonby, 82–3.
17. CH, 324, 18 March 1893.
18. RAQVJ, 24 May 1899.
19. Ibid., 26 November 1891.
20. Pope-Hennessy, 217.
21. RAQVJ, 9 September 1872.
22. Ibid., 11 October 1890.
23. Henry Ponsonby, 393.
24. Ponsonby Letters, quoted in Longford, *Victoria*, 420.
25. Mallet, 148.
26. Brett, i, 692.
27. Ibid., i, 672.
28. Frederick Ponsonby, 25.
29. Lytton, 22.

62 : BOOKS

1. Frederick Ponsonby, 51–2.
2. Holland, 183.
3. CH, 22, 36, 39–40, 116, 188, 265.
4. Mallet, 94–5.
5. Fulford, *Dearest Mama*, 177.
6. Ibid., 142, 173.
7. D.N.B. entry by Elizabeth Lee.
8. Mallet, 97, 142, 158, 173.

63 : BOOKMEN

1. CH, 218.
2. Ibid., 163, 218.
3. Richard Ellman, *Oscar Wilde*, 1987, 172.
4. Edgar Johnson, *Dickens*, 1953, i, 292–4.
5. Ibid., i, 624, 646, 733–5, 872–4, 1,000; ii, 1, 146–7; Peter Ackroyd, *Dickens*, 1,066.

64 : FAILING HEALTH

1. Quoted in Pope-Hennessy, 225.
2. St Aubyn, *Royal George*, 299.
3. Ibid., 208.
4. Pope-Hennessy, 198.
5. Mallet, 211, 212, 213.
6. Reid, 195, 196–8.
7. Ibid., 197–8.
8. Monkswell, 68–9.
9. Mallet, 197.
10. Ibid., 207.
11. CH, 347–8; RAQVJ, 17 September 1900, 1 January 1901.
12. Ramm, 258.

65 : DEATH

1. Reid, 201.
2. Bell, 353–4.
3. Reid, 209–12; Longford, *Victoria*, 559–62; St Aubyn, *Queen Victoria*, 593–7; Weintraub, 629–36.
4. Reid, 213.

66 : FUNERAL AND BURIAL

1. Reid, 119.
2. Mallet, 50.
3. Ibid., 52, 123.

4. Reid, 60–61.

5. Ibid.

6. RAQVJ, 6 March 1873.

7. Lytton, 203.

8. Monkswell, 80–81.

9. Dalton Papers, J. C. Dalton's Reminiscences, quoted in J. G. Fergusson, *Hounds are Home*, 162.

10. Frederick Ponsonby, 89.

11. Ibid., 91; Olivia Bland, *The Royal Way of Death*, 203.

12. Brett, i, 282.

13. Bell, 357.

14. Brett, i, 282.

15. Leon Edel, *The Life of Henry James*, 1972, iii, 425–7.

SOURCES

Ackroyd, Peter, *Dickens* (London, 1990).

Aga Khan, *The Memoirs of Aga Khan* (London, 1954).

Airlie, Mabell, Countess of, *Lady Palmerston and Her Times* (2 vols, London, 1922).

Albert, Harold A., *Queen Victoria's Sister* (London, 1967).

Alice, Grand Duchess of Hesse, *Letters to Her Majesty the Queen* (London, 1885).

Alice, Princess, Countess of Athlone, *For My Grandchildren: Some Reminiscences of Her Royal Highness Princess Alice* (London, 1966).

Ames, Winslow, *Prince Albert and Victorian Taste* (London, 1968).

Anand, Sushila, *Indian Sahib: Queen Victoria's Dear Abdul* (London, 1996).

Anderson, William James, *Life of . . . Edward, Duke of Kent* (Ottawa, 1870).

Arbuthnot *see* Bamford

Arengo-Jones, Peter, *Queen Victoria in Switzerland* (London, 1995).

Argyll, Duke of, *Autobiography* (2 vols, London, 1906).

Aronson, Theo, *Queen Victoria and the Bonapartes* (London, 1972).

   Victoria and Disraeli (London, 1977).

   Princess Alice, Countess of Athlone (London, 1981).

   Heart of a Queen: Queen Victoria's Romantic Attachments (London, 1991).

Ashdowne, D., *Queen Victoria's Mother* (London, 1974).

Ashley, The Hon. Evelyn, *The Life of Henry John Temple, Viscount Palmerston, 1846–1865* (2 vols, London, 1877).

Askwith, Betty, *The Lytteltons* (London, 1975).

Aspinall, A. (ed.), *Letters of George IV, 1812–30* (3 vols, Cambridge, 1938).

   (ed.), *Letters of the Princess Charlotte* (London, 1949).

   Politics and the Press, c.1780–1850 (London, 1949).

Asquith *see* Bonham Carter

Aston, G., *H.R.H. The Duke of Connaught* (London, 1929).

Bahlman, Dudley W. R. (ed.) *The Diary of Sir Edward Walter Hamilton, 1880–1885* (2 vols, Oxford, 1972).

Ball, T. Frederick, *Queen Victoria: Scenes and Incidents of Her Life and Reign*, (9th edition, 1886).

Balsan, Consuelo Vanderbilt, *The Glitter and the Gold* (London, 1953).

Bamford, Francis and the Duke of Wellington (eds), *The Journal of Mrs Arbuthnot, 1820–1832* (2 vols, London, 1950).

Barkeley, R., *The Empress Frederick* (London, 1956).

Barrett, Richard, *The Queen and Albert the Good* (privately printed, London, 1862).

Battiscombe, Georgina, *Mrs Gladstone: The Portrait of a Marriage* (1956).
Queen Alexandra (London, 1969).
Shaftesbury: A Biography of the Seventh Earl, 1801–1885 (London, 1974).

Beatrice, Princess (ed.), *In Napoleonic Days: The Private Diary of Augusta, Duchess of Saxe-Coburg* (London, 1941).

Bell, G. K. A., *Randall Davidson, Archbishop of Canterbury* (London, 1952).

Bell, H., *Lord Palmerston* (2 vols, London, 1936).

Bennett, Daphne, *King without a Crown: Albert, Prince Consort of England, 1819–1861* (London, 1977).
Queen Victoria's Children (London, 1980).
Vicky: Princess Royal of England and German Princess (London, 1983).

Benson, A. C. and Viscount Esher (eds), *The Letters of Queen Victoria: A Selection from Her Majesty's Correspondence between the Years 1837 and 1861* (3 vols, London, 1907).

Benson, E. F., *King Edward VII* (London, 1933).
Queen Victoria (London, 1935).
The Kaiser and His English Relations (London, 1936).
Daughters of Queen Victoria (London, 1939).

Best, Geoffrey, *Mid-Victorian Britain, 1851–1875* (London, 1971).

Blake, Robert, *Disraeli* (London, 1966).

Bloomfield, G., *Reminiscences of Court and Diplomatic Life* (2 vols, London, 1883).

Bolitho, Hector, (ed. with Albert Baillie, Dean of Windsor), *Letters of Lady Augusta Stanley* (London, 1927).
(ed.), *Later Letters of Lady Augusta Stanley* (London, 1929).
A Victorian Dean (London, 1930).
The Prince Consort and His Brother (London, 1933).
Victoria the Widow and her Son (London, 1934).
(ed.), *Further Letters of Queen Victoria* (London, 1938).
Victoria and Albert (London, 1938).
The Reign of Queen Victoria (London, 1948).

(ed.), *Later Letters of Albert, Prince Consort* (London, 1964).

Bonham Carter, Mark (ed.), *The Autobiography of Margot Asquith* (London, 1962).

Bourne, Kenneth, *Palmerston: The Early Years* (London, 1982).

Boykin, Edward (ed.), *Victoria, Albert and Mrs Stevenson* (New York, 1957).

Bradford, Sarah, *Disraeli* (London, 1982).

Bresler, Fenton, *Napoleon III: A Life* (London, 1999).

Brett, Maurice V. (ed.), *Journals and Letters of Reginald, Viscount Esher* (2 vols, London, 1934).

Briggs, Asa, *Victorian People* (London, 1954).

Iron Bridge to Crystal Palace: Images of the Industrial Revolution (London, 1979).

Brook-Shepherd, Gordon, *Uncle of Europe* (London, 1975).

Broughton, John, 1st Lord, *Recollections of a Long Life, 1786–1852* (6 vols, 1910–11).

Brown on the Throne (London, 1897).

Brown, Ivor, *Balmoral* (London, 1955).

Buchanan, Meriel, *Queen Victoria's Relations* (London, 1945).

Buckle, George Earle (ed.), *The Letters of Queen Victoria, 2nd series 1862–1885* (3 vols, London, 1926).

The Letters of Queen Victoria, 3rd series, 1886–1901 (3 vols, London, 1932).

Bulmer, Sir Henry Lytton [Lord Dalling], *The Life of Henry John Temple, Viscount Palmerston* (2 vols, London, 1870).

Cannadine, David, 'The Context, Performance and Meaning of Ritual: The British Monarchy and the "Invention of Tradition" c. 1820–1977' in Eric Hobsbawn and Terence Ranger (eds), *The Invention of Tradition* (Cambridge, 1982).

History in Our Time (New Haven, 1998).

Cecil, David, *The Young Melbourne* (London, 1939).

Lord M. (London, 1954).

Melbourne (Reprint Society, 1955).

Cecil, Lady Gwendolen, *Life of Robert, Marquis of Salisbury* (4 vols, London, 1921–32).

Chadwick, Owen, *The Victorian Church* (2 vols, London, 1966).

Chapman, Caroline, and Raban, Paul, *Debrett's Queen Victoria's Jubilee* (London, 1977).

Charlot, Monica, *Victoria: The Young Queen* (Oxford, 1991).

Clark, G. Kitson, *The Making of Victorian England* (London, 1962).

Colley, Linda, *Britons: Forging the Nation, 1707–1837* (New Haven, 1992).

Connell, Brian, *Regina v. Palmerston: The Correspondence Between Queen Victoria and her Foreign and Prime Minister, 1837–1865* (1962).

Corelli, Marie, *The Passing of the Great Queen: A Tribute to Queen Victoria* (London, 1901).

Corti, Egon Caesar, Conte, *The English Empress: A Study in the Relations Between Queen Victoria and her Eldest Daughter* (trans, Hodgson, E. M., London, 1957).

Court Historian: *Newsletters of the Society for Court Studies.*

Cowles, Virginia, *The Kaiser* (London, 1963).

Craik, D. M. M., *Fifty Golden Years: Incidents in the Queen's Reign* (London, 1887).

Creevey, Thomas, *The Creevey Papers: A Selection from the Correspondence and Diaries of Thomas Creevey* (ed. Sir Herbert Maxwell, 1903).
Creevey's Life and Times: A Further Selection from the Correspondence (ed. John Gore, London, 1934).

Creston, Dormer, *The Youthful Queen Victoria* (London, 1952).

Croker, John Wilson, *The Croker Papers: The Correspondence and Diaries of John Wilson Croker* (ed. Louis J. Jennings, 3 vols, London, 1884).

Cullen, Tom, *The Empress Brown* (London, 1969).

Cumming, Valerie, *Royal Dress: The Image and the Reality* (London, 1989).

D'Arblay, Madame [Fanny Burney], *Diary and Letters of Madame D'Arblay (1778–1840)* (ed. Charlotte Barrett, 6 vols, London, 1905).

Darby, Elisabeth and Smith, Nicola, *The Cult of the Prince Consort* (New Haven, 1982).

David, Saul, *The Homicidal Earl: The Life of Lord Cardigan* (London, 1997).

Dimond, Frances and Taylor, Roger, *Crown and Camera: The Royal Family and Photography, 1840–1920* (Harmondsworth, 1987).

Duff, David, *Edward of Kent* (London, 1938).
The Shy Princess (London, 1958).
Hessian Tapestry (London, 1967).
Victoria Travels: Journeys of Queen Victoria Between 1830 and 1900 (London, 1970).
(ed.) *Victoria in the Highlands: The Personal Journal of Her Majesty Queen Victoria* (London, 1971).
Albert and Victoria (London, 1972).

Duff, Ethel M., *The Story of H.R.H. The Duke of Cambridge* (London, 1938).

Edel, Leon, *The Life of Henry James* (2 vols, London, 1953–63).

Ellmann, Richard, *Oscar Wilde* (London, 1987).

Emden, Paul H., *Behind the Throne* (London, 1934).

Ensor, R.C.K., *England, 1870–1914* (Oxford, new edition, 1964).

Epton, Nina, *Victoria and Her Daughters* (London, 1971).

Ernest II, *Memoirs of Ernest II, Duke of Saxe-Coburg-Gotha* (London, 1888).

Esher, Viscount (ed.), *The Girlhood of Queen Victoria: A Selection from Her Majesty's Diaries, 1832–40* (2 vols, London, 1912).

Eyck, F., *The Prince Consort* (London, 1959).

Fitzroy, Sir Almeric, *Memoirs* (London, 1925).

Forster, Margaret, *Elizabeth Barrett Browning* (London, 1988).

Frampton *see* Mundy

Fulford, Roger, *The Royal Dukes* (London, 1933).

> *The Prince Consort* (London, 1949).
>
> *Queen Victoria* (London, 1951).
>
> *Hanover to Windsor* (London, 1960).
>
> (ed.), *Dearest Child: Letters Between Queen Victoria and the Princess Royal, 1858–61* (London, 1964).
>
> (ed.), *Dearest Mama: Letters Between Queen Victoria and the Crown Princess of Prussia, 1861–64* (London, 1968).
>
> (ed.), *Beloved Mama: Private Correspondence of Queen Victoria and the German Crown Princess, 1878–85* (London, 1971).
>
> (ed.), *Your Dear Letter: Private Correspondence of Queen Victoria and the Crown Princess of Prussia, 1863–71* (London, 1971).
>
> (ed.), *Darling Child: Private Correspondence of Queen Victoria and the German Crown Princess of Prussia, 1871–78* (London, 1976).
>
> See also Greville.

Gardiner, Juliet, *Queen Victoria* (London, 1997).

Gash, Norman, *Mr Secretary Peel* (London, 1961).

> *Sir Robert Peel* (London, 1972).

Gernsheim, Helmut, and Gernsheim, Alison, *Victoria R., A Biography with Four Hundred Illustrations Based on her Personal Photograph Album* (London, 1959).

Gilbert, Martin (ed.), *A Century of Conflict* (London, 1966).

Gillen, Mollie, *The Prince and His Lady: The Love Story of the Duke of Kent and Madame de St Laurent* (Toronto, 1970).

Girouard, Mark, *The Victorian Country House* (Oxford, 1971).

Gore, John, *King George V: A Personal Memoir* (London, 1941).

Gosse, Edmund, 'The Character of Queen Victoria' (*The Quarterly Review*, January–April, 1901, 301–37).

Gower, The Hon. F. Leveson (ed.), *Letters of Harriet, Countess Granville, 1810–1845*, (2 vols, London, 1894).

Gower, Lord Ronald Sutherland Leveson, *My Reminiscences* (2 vols, London, 1883).

> *Old Diaries 1881–1901* (London, 1902).

Granville *see* Gower

Greville *see* Strachey

Grey, Lieutenant-General, The Hon. Charles, *The Early Years of His Royal Highness the Prince Consort* (London, 1867).

Gronow, Rees Howell, *The Reminiscences and Recollections of Captain Gronow* (2 vols, 1889).

Guedalla, Philip, *The Queen and Mr Gladstone, 1845–1898* (2 vols, London, 1933).

Guest, John (ed.), *Essays by Divers Hands, XXXVIII* (Oxford, 1975).

Hamilton *see* Bahlman

Hardie, Frank, *The Political Influence of Queen Victoria, 1861–1901* (London, 1935).

    The Political Influence of the British Monarchy 1868–1962 (London, 1970).

Harrison, J. F. C., *The Early Victorians, 1832–51* (London, 1971).

Healy, Edna, *Lady Unknown: The Life of Angela Burdett-Coutts* (London, 1978).

    Coutts & Co, 1692–1992: The Portrait of a Private Bank (London, 1992).

    The Queen's House: A Social History of Buckingham Palace (London, 1997).

Heffer, Simon, *Power and Place: The Political Consequences of Edward VII* (London, 1998).

Heleniak, Kathryn Moore, *William Mulready* (New Haven, 1980).

Hibbert, Christopher (ed.), *Queen Victoria in Her Letters and Journals* (London, 1984).

Hobhouse, Hermione, *Prince Albert: His Life and Work* (London, 1983).

Holmes, Richard R., *Queen Victoria, 1819–1901* (1901)

Homans, Margaret, *Royal Representations: Queen Victoria and British Culture* (Chicago, 1999)

Hoppen, K. Theodore, *The Mid-Victorian Generation, 1846–1886* (Oxford, 1998).

Hough, Richard, *Edward and Alexandra: Their Private and Public Lives* (London, 1992).

    Victoria and Albert: Their Love and Their Tragedies (London, 1996).

    (ed.) *Advice to a Grand-daughter; Letters from Queen Victoria to Princess Victoria of Hesse* (London, 1975).

Howarth, T. E. B., *Citizen King: The Life of Louis-Philippe, King of the French* (London, 1962).

Hudson, Derek, *Munby: Man of Two Worlds* (London, 1972).

Hudson, Katherine, *A Royal Conflict: Sir John Conroy and the Young Victoria* (London, 1994).

Ilchester, The Earl of (ed.), *Elizabeth, Lady Holland to her Son, 1821–1845* (London, 1946).

Jagow, Kurt (ed.), *Letters of the Prince Consort 1831–61* (London, 1938).

Jenkins, Roy, *Sir Charles Dilke* (London, 1958).

    Gladstone (London, 1995).

Jerrold, Clare, *The Married Life of Queen Victoria* (London, 1913).

    The Widowhood of Queen Victoria (London, 1916).

Johnson, Edgar, *Charles Dickens: His Tragedy and Triumph* (2 vols, London, 1953).

Kennedy, A. L. (ed.), *My Dear Duchess: Social and Political Letters to the Duchess of Manchester 1858–1869* (London, 1956).

Kerr, John, *Queen Victoria's Scottish Diaries* (Moffat, 1992).

Kiste, John van der, *Queen Victoria's Children* (Gloucester, 1986).

with Jordan, Bee, *Dearest Affie . . . Alfred Duke of Edinburgh: Queen Victoria's Second Son* (Gloucester, 1984).

Knight, Charles, *Passages of a Working Life During Half a Century* (3 vols, London, 1864).

Knight, Cordelia, *Autobiography of Miss Cordelia Knight with Extracts from her Journals and Anecdote Books* (2 vols, London, 1861).

Kriegel, Abraham D., *The Holland House Diaries, 1831–1840* (London, 1977).

Kurtz, Harold, *The Empress Eugénie, 1826–1920* (London, 1964).

Lambert, Angela, *Unquiet Souls* (London, 1984).

Lee, Sidney, *Queen Victoria* (London, 1904).

King Edward VII (2 vols, London, 1925–7).

Lees-Milne, James, *The Enigmatic Edwardian* (London, 1986).

Lehmann, Joseph H., *All Sir Garnet: A Life of Field-Marshal Lord Wolseley* (London, 1964).

Lieven, Princess, *The Unpublished Diary and Political Sketches* (ed. Harold Temperley, London, 1925).

Lloyd, Christopher (ed.), *The Quest for Albion: Monarchy and the Patronage of British Painting* (London, 1998).

Longford, Elizabeth, 'Queen Victoria's Religious Life' (*Wiseman Review*, 236, summer, 1962).

Victoria R.I. (London, 1964).

'Queen Victoria's Doctors' (*A Century of Conflict*, ed. Martin Gilbert, 1966).

A Pilgrimage of Passion: The Life of Wilfrid Scawen Blunt (London, 1979).

(ed.) *The Oxford Book of Royal Anecdotes* (1989).

Darling Loosy: Letters to Princess Louise, 1856–1939 (London, 1991).

Lorne, Marquess of, *V.R.I. Her Life and Empire* (London).

Low, Frances H., *Queen Victoria's Dolls* (London, 1894).

Lyttelton, Lady Sarah Spencer, *Correspondence . . . 1787–1870* (ed. by her great-granddaughter, The Hon. Mrs Hugh Wyndham, London, 1912).

Lytton, Edith, Countess of, *Lady Lytton's Court Diary, 1895–99* (ed. Mary Lutyens, London, 1961).

Magnus, Philip, *Gladstone: A Biography* (London, 1954). *King Edward The Seventh* (London, 1964).

Mallet, Victor (ed.), *Life with Queen Victoria: Marie Mallet's Letters from Court 1887–1901* (London, 1968).

Malmesbury, Lord, *Memoirs of an ex-Minister* (2 vols, London, 1884).

Marie Louise, Princess, *My Memories of Six Reigns* (London, 1957).

Marie, Queen of Rumania, *The Story of my Life* (vol. 1, London, 1934).

Marshall, Dorothy, *The Life and Times of Victoria* (London, 1972).

Martin, Sir Theodore, *Life of H.R.H. the Prince Consort* (5 vols, London, 1875–1880).

Queen Victoria as I knew Her (London, 1908).

Martineau, Harriet, *Autobiography* (London, 1877).

Matthew, H. C. G., *Gladstone, 1809–1874* (London, 1982).

Gladstone, 1875–1898 (London, 1995).

May, John, *Victoria Remembered* (London, 1983).

Maylunas, Andrei and Sergei Mironenko, *A Lifelong Passion: Nicholas and Alexandra: Their own Story* (London, 1996).

McClintock, Mary Howard, *The Queen Thanks Sir Howard: The Life of Major General Sir Howard Elphinstone* (London, 1945).

Mitchell, L. G., *Lord Melbourne, 1779–1848* (Oxford, 1997).

Monypenny, William Flavelle and Buckle, George Earle, *The Life of Benjamin Disraeli, Earl of Beaconsfield* (2 vols, London, 1929).

Monkswell, Mary, Lady, *A Victorian Diarist: Extracts from the Journals of Mary, Lady Monkswell, 1875–1895* (ed. E. C. F. Collier, London, 1944).

A Victorian Diarist: Later Extracts from the Journals of Mary, Lady Monkswell (London, 1946).

Morley, John, *The Life of William Ewart Gladstone* (2 vols, London, 1905).

Morton, Frederic, *The Rothschilds: A Family Portrait* (London, 1961).

Mullen, Richard and Munson, James, *Victoria: Portrait of a Queen* (London, 1987).

Mundy, Harriet Georgiana (ed.), *The Journal of Mary Frampton* (London, 1885).

Munich, Adrienne, *Queen Victoria's Secrets* (New York, 1996).

Musgrave, Clifford, *Life in Brighton* (London, 1970).

Neale, Erskine, *The Life of Field-Marshal His Royal Highness, Edward, Duke of Kent* (1850).

Nevill, Barry St-John, *Life at the Court of Queen Victoria, 1861–1901* (Stroud, 1984).

Newsome, David, *The Victorian World Picture* (London, 1997).

Nicholls, David, *The Lost Prime Minister: A Life of Sir Charles Dilke* (London, 1995).

Nicolson, Harold, *Diaries and Letters, 1930–1964* (ed. Stanley Olson, London, 1950).

King George V: His Life and Reign (London, 1952).

Diaries and Letters (ed. Nigel Nicolson, 3 vols, London, 1966–68).

Noakes, Vivien, *Edward Lear* (London, 1969).

Noel, Gerard, *Princess Alice* (London, 1974).

Oliphant, Margaret, *Queen Victoria: A Personal Sketch* (London, 1900).

Oman, Carola, *The Gascoyne Heiress: The Life and Diaries of Frances Mary Gascoyne* (London, 1968).

Ormond, Richard, *Sir Edwin Landseer* (New York, 1982).

Paget, Lady, Walburga, *Embassies of Other Days* (London, 1923).

Pakula, Hannah, *An Uncommon Woman: The Empress Frederick* (London, 1996).

Parsons, Neil, *King Khama, Emperor Joe and the Great White Queen: Victorian Britain through African Eyes* (Chicago, 1998).

Pearson, Hesketh, *Gilbert and Sullivan: A Biography* (London, 1935).

Pemberton, W. Baring, *Lord Palmerston* (London, 1954).

Pocock, Tom, *Sailor King: The Life of King William IV* (London, 1991).

Ponsonby, Arthur, *Henry Ponsonby: Queen Victoria's Private Secretary: His Life and Letters* (London, 1942).

Ponsonby, Sir Frederick, (ed.) *Letters of the Empress Frederick* (London, 1928).
Sidelights on Queen Victoria (London, 1930).
Recollections of Three Reigns: Prepared for the Press with Notes and an Introduction by Colin Welch (London, 1951).

Ponsonby, Magdalen, *Mary Ponsonby: A Memoir, Some Letters and a Journal* (London, 1927).

Pope-Hennessy, James, *Queen Mary, 1867–1953* (London, 1959).
Queen Victoria at Windsor and Balmoral: Letters from her Grand-daughter, Princess Victoria of Prussia (London, 1959).

Potts, D. M. and Potts, W. T. W., *Queen Victoria's Gene: Haemophilia and the Royal Family* (Stroud, 1995).
The Private Life of Queen Victoria by One of Her Majesty's Servants (London, 1901).

Prochaska, Frank, *Royal Bounty: The Making of a Welfare Monarchy* (New Haven, 1995).

Quennell, Peter (ed.), *The Private Letters of Princess Lieven to Prince Metternich, 1820–1826* (London, 1937).

Raikes, Thomas, *A Portion of the Journal Kept by Thomas Raikes from 1831 to 1847* (4 vols, London, 1856–7).

Ramm, Agatha, *Beloved and Darling Child: Last letters between Queen Victoria and her Eldest Daughter, 1886–1901* (Stroud, 1990).

Redesdale, Lord, *Memories* (2 vols, London, 1915).

Reid, Michaela, *Ask Sir James: The Life of Sir James Reid, Personal Physician to Queen Victoria* (London, 1987).

Rhodes, James Robert, *Rosebery* (London, 1963).
Albert, Prince Consort (London, 1983).

Richardson, Joanna, *My Dearest Uncle* (London, 1961).
Victoria and Albert (London, 1977).

Ridley, Jane, *The Young Disraeli, 1804–1846* (London, 1995).

Ridley, Jasper, *Lord Palmerston* (London, 1970).

Napoleon III and Eugénie (London, 1979).

Roberts, Andrew, *Salisbury: Victorian Titan* (London, 1999).

Röhl, John C. G., *Young Wilhelm: The Kaiser's Early Life; 1859–1888*, (Cambridge, 1998).

Röhl, John C. G., Warren, Martin, and Hunt, David, *Purple Secret: Genes, 'Madness' and the Royal Houses of Europe* (London, 1998).

Rose, Kenneth, *The Later Cecils* (London, 1975).

King George V (London, 1983).

Kings, Queens and Courtiers (London, 1986).

Rowell, G., *Queen Victoria Goes to the Theatre* (London, 1978).

Russell, G. W. E., *Collections and Recollections* (London, 1898).

Schama, Simon, 'Balmorality: Queen Victoria's Very un-Victorian Ways' (*New Yorker*, 11 August 1997).

Somervell, D. C., *Disraeli and Gladstone: A Duo-Biographical Sketch* (London, 1932).

Stanley, Augusta, *The Letters of Lady Augusta Stanley: A Young Lady at Court, 1849–1863* (ed. the Dean of Windsor and Hector Bolitho, London, 1927).

Later Letters of Lady Augusta Stanley, 1864–76 (ed. the Dean of Windsor and Hector Bolitho, London, 1929).

Twenty Years at Court: From the Correspondence of Lady Augusta Stanley (ed. Mrs Steuart Erskine, London, 1916).

St Aubyn, Giles, *The Royal George, 1819–1904: The Life of H.R.H. Prince George, Duke of Cambridge* (London, 1963).

Edward VII, Prince and King (London, 1979).

Queen Victoria: A Portrait (London, 1991).

Stevenson, R. Scott, *Morell Mackenzie: The Story of a Victorian Tragedy* (London, 1946).

Stockmar, Ernst, Baron (ed.), *Memoirs of Baron Stockmar* (2 vols, London, 1872).

Stoney, Benita and Weltzien, Heinrich C., *My Mistress the Queen: The Letters of Frieda Arnold, Dresser to Queen Victoria* (London, 1994).

Strachey, Lytton, *Queen Victoria* (London, 1921).

Strachey, Lytton, and Fulford, Roger (eds), *The Greville Memoirs, 1814–1860* (8 vols, London, 1938).

Surtees, Virginia, *Charlotte Canning: Lady-in-Waiting to Queen Victoria and Wife of the First Viceroy of India, 1817–1861* (London, 1975).

Thompson, Dorothy, *Queen Victoria: The Woman, the Monarchy and the People* (New York, 1990).

Tingsten, Herbert, *Victoria and the Victorians* (translated from the Swedish and adapted by David Grey and Eva Leckstrom Grey, 1965).

Tooley, Sarah A., *The Personal Life of Queen Victoria* (London, 1897).

Trevor-Roper, Hugh, 'The Highland Tradition of Scotland: The Invention of Tradition' (eds Eric Hobsbawn and Terence Ranger, Cambridge, 1982).

Turner, E. S., *The Court of St James's* (London, 1959).

Turner, Michael, *Osborne House* (London, 1989).

Victoria, Queen (see also Benson, Brett, Esher, Bolitho, Hough, Hibbert, Duff, Fulford and Ramm), *Leaves from the Journal of Our Life in the Highlands from 1848 to 1861* (ed. Arthur Helps, London, 1868).

More Leaves from the Journal of a Life in the Highlands from 1862 to 1882 (London, 1884).

Letters of Queen Victoria from the Archives of the House of Brandenburg-Prussia (ed. Hector Bolitho, London, 1938).

Queen Victoria: Leaves from a Journal: A Record of the Visit of the Emperor and Empress of the French to the Queen, and of the Visit of the Queen and the Prince Consort to the Emperor of the French (ed. Raymond Mortimer, London, 1961).

Dear and Honoured Lady: The Correspondence between Queen Victoria and Alfred Tennyson (eds Hope Dyson and Charles Tennyson, Rutherford, New Jersey, 1971).

Vincent, John, *Disraeli* (Oxford, 1990).

(ed.) *Disraeli, Derby and the Conservative Party: The Political Journals of Edward, Lord Stanley, 1849–69* (Hassocks, 1978).

(ed.) *The Crawford Papers: The Journals of David Lindsay, 27th Earl of Crawford and 10th Earl of Balcarres.*

(ed.) *The Later Derby Diaries: Home Rule, Liberal Unionism and Aristocratic Life in Late Victorian England* (privately printed, 1981).

Walpole, Spencer, *The Life of Lord John Russell* (2 vols, London, 1889).

Warner, Marina, *Queen Victoria's Sketchbook* (London, 1979).

Watson, Vera, *A Queen at Home: An Intimate Account of the Social and Domestic Life of Queen Victoria's Court* (London, 1952).

Weibe, M. G. et al., eds., *Benjamin Disraeli Letters* (Toronto, six vols. to 1999).

Weintraub, Stanley, *Victoria* (London, 1987).

Disraeli: A Biography (London, 1993).

Albert: Uncrowned King (London, 1997).

Wellington, Gerald, 7th Duke of (ed.), *Wellington and his Friends* (London, 1965).

Wharncliffe, Lady, *The First Lady Wharncliffe and Her Family* (ed. Caroline Grosvenor and Charles Beilby, Lord Stewart of Wortley, 2 vols, London, 1927).

Wheeler-Bennett, John W., *King George VI: His Life and Reign* (London, 1958).

Whittle, Tyler, *Victoria and Albert at Home* (London, 1980).

Willis, G. M., *Ernest Augustus, Duke of Cumberland and King of Hanover* (London, 1954).

Wilson, John, C. B., *A Life of Sir Henry Campbell-Bannerman* (London, 1973).

Wilson, Robert, *The Life and Times of Queen Victoria* (2 vols, London, 1900).

Windsor, The Duke of, *A King's Story: The Memoirs of H.R.H. The Duke of Windsor* (London, 1951).

Woodham-Smith, Cecil, *Florence Nightingale, 1820–1910* (London, 1951). *Queen Victoria: Her Life and Times, vol. 1, 1819–1861* (London, 1972).

Woodward, Llewellyn, *The Age of Reform 1815–1870* (Oxford, 1964).

Wyndham, The Hon. Mrs Hugh (ed.), *The Correspondence of Sarah Spencer, Lady Lyttelton, 1787–1870* (London)

Wynn, Frances Williams, *Diaries of a Lady of Quality from 1797 to 1844* (ed. A. Hayward, London, 1864).

York, The Duchess of, and Stoney, Benita, *Victoria and Albert: Life at Osborne House* (London, 1991).

Young, G. M., *Early Victorian England, 1830–65* (2 vols, London, 1932).

Zeepvat, Charlotte, *Prince Leopold: The Untold Story of Queen Victoria's Youngest Son* (Stroud, 1998).

Ziegler, Philip, *Melbourne* (London, 1976).
   King Edward VIII: The Official Biography (London, 1990).

INDEX

Queen Victoria's name is abbreviated to QV, Prince Albert's to Pr. A., and the Prince of Wales's to Pr. of W.

Abercorn, 2nd Marquess and, *later*, 1st Duke of (1811–85), 176

Abercrombie, James, *later* 1st Baron Dunfermline (1776–1858), 51, 91

Aberdeen, George Hamilton Gordon, 4th Earl of (1784–1860), seasickness, 168; Balmoral, 177; and Gladstone, 193; Crimean War, 222; resigns, 227, 228; QV's appreciation, 318; QV sends for, 368

Adeane, Marie, *see* Mallet, Marie

Adelaide of Hohenlohe, Princess (1835–1900), 231

Adelaide, Queen (1792–1849)
    as Duchess of Clarence: marriage, 4; fecundity, 10; writes to Duchess of Kent, 27–8, 30; and Pss. V., 30, 33; personality, 30
    as Queen: Tory, 32; and King William's bastard children, 32; King William's birthday party, 46, 47; QV and, 54, 57; QV's wedding, 121; Christmas parties for children, 158n.

Afghan War, 365, 369

Aga Khan II (d. 1885), 453

Aga Khan III (1877–1957), 469, 471

Ahmed, Rafiuddin, 448, 452, 453

Aiton, William Townsend (1766–1849), 86

Albany, 1st Duke of, *see* Leopold, Prince, Duke of Albany

Albany, Charles Edward, 2nd Duke of (1884–1954), 410, 458

Albemarle, William Charles Keppel, 4th Earl of (1772–1849), 28, 56, 71, 116

Albert, Prince, *later* King George VI (1895–1952), 416

Albert, Prince, *later* Prince Consort (1819–61):
    and his children: games, 146; and Pss. Royal, 146, 183, 244–5, 256, 275; rehearses plays, 184; punishment, 185, 189; their education, 185; and Pr. Alfred, 258; Pss. Royal's engagement, 238, 239
    health: exhaustion, 124; illnesses, 262–3; insomnia, 275, 276, 277; little natural resistance, 102; melancholy, 262; needs sleep, 127; nervous system, 262; political problems and hard work take toll, 256; rheumatic pains, 275; seasickness, 119, 124, 165, 168
    interests and amusements: architecture, 163, 179–80, 201; art, 100n., 288, 434; chess, 125; deer-stalking, 179, 191; field-sports, 176; fishing, 177, 191; gardening, 191; hunting, 191; jokes, 232; music, 103, 125, 279, 304; nature, 103, 125, 176; organ playing, 158, 434; piano playing, 108, 123, 434; plays on words, 211; riding, 171; shooting, 177, 179, 191; swimming, 167
    personality: 100–1; behaviour with women, 128–9; clothes-conscious, 123; conscientiousness, 99, 100; fatalism 277; faults and foibles, 292; Greville on, 178; hardworking, 256; heavy humour, 100–1; hesitancy, 132; intelligence, 99, 178; nervousness, 121, 131; shyness, 128; QV on, 263; traits of character which annoy the aristocracy, 128
    and Pr. of W.: concerned over, 183, 269, 270; safeguards against corruption, 186;

Albert, Prince – *cont.*
  and Pr. of W. – *cont.*
    education, 187, 269; consults
    phrenologist, 187–8; recognizes his
    success, 271; and bride for Pr. of W.,
    273; Pr. of W.'s lack of enthusiasm for
    marriage, 274; shock over sexual
    misconduct, 274; forgiveness, 274
  private life: appearance, 99, 101, 216, 256;
    childhood, 99; education, 100; on
    Grand Tour, 100; in England aged
    sixteen, 101; King Leopold and, 105;
    and Stockmar, 110; old Royal Family's
    antagonism, 128; homesickness, 129;
    and Lehzen, 132, 151–2, 155; relaxed
    behaviour, 146; and Wellington, 148,
    170; death of his father, 159; Osborne,
    161, 163, 164; loves Scotland, 175–6;
    Balmoral, 177–80; designs his family's
    tartans, 181; Wynne-Carrington on,
    190; loves family celebrations, 191;
    cannot forgive Palmerston, 196; in
    Sant's portrait of Cardigan, 226; and
    Empress Eugénie, 233; celebratory
    bonfire, 240; carriage accident, 261;
    premonitions of death, 262; and Peel,
    265; death of Duchess of Kent, 267;
    angry with his brother, 273; last
    illness, 276, 277–81; opinion of
    Disraeli, 316; holds Gladstone in
    regard, 319; John Brown, 323; his
    greyhound, 414
  public figure: views future with some
    concern, 110; Order of the Garter, 111,
    121; 11th Prince Albert's Own Hussars,
    111–12; finance, 112–13; precedence,
    114–15, 116; his Household, 116–18;
    regency, 131; public engagements, 131;
    advance in status, 133–4; and Peel, 135,
    137; increasing responsibilities, 137–8;
    reform of Royal Household, 138,
    140–1; Buckingham Palace, 160; wins
    prestige, 171; honorary degree, 172;
    condemned over *battue*, 173; Bendinck
    attacks, 194; and sovereign's right to
    supervision of foreign policy, 196;
    memoranda on foreign relations, 198;
    and social reform, 200–1, 203; on
    Chartist marchers' leadership, 202;
    visits London slums, 203; and
    Palmerston, 206, 229; Great
    Exhibition, 210; popularity, 215;
    unpopularity exacerbated, 222;
    Crimean War, 223; and Napolean III,

230, 233, 253, 254; Indian Mutiny, 251;
    and Franco/Austrian War, 254–5; title
    of Prince Consort, 256; visits Royal
    Military Academy, 275; American Civil
    War, 276; commemorations, 286–7;
    monuments, 287–8, 327, 501; his
    understanding of constitutional
    monarchy, 367; and Aberdeen, 368
  and QV: her early opinion of, 102–3;
    she is entranced, 107–8; she proposes,
    109; in love, 109, 110; she wants him
    to have precedence, 115; his
    Household, 117–18; her bridesmaids,
    118–19; wedding eve, 119; wedding, 121;
    honeymoon, 123–4, 125; suggests short
    retirement from society, 124; his
    affection, 125; he writes about her, 126,
    131–2; he is denied her confidence,
    126; problems, 127–8; her pregnancy,
    131; birth of Pss. Vicky, 133; concern
    about her political sympathies, 134;
    contentment, 145, 147; he makes a
    pirouette, 146; quarrels, 149, 151–2, 216;
    he writes to her, 159, 217–18; birthday
    present 164; at Balmoral, 179; QV on,
    190; and her changing attitude to
    Melbourne, 194; and memorandum on
    Palmerston, 206; 'scenes', 218–20; on
    her relationship with their children,
    219; his unjust letter, 257; and her
    correspondence with Crown Pss.
    Frederick, 258; and death of her
    mother, 267; irritable with her, 278;
    dying, 279, 280; watches her mind,
    291; birth of Pss. Beatrice, 410;
    assassination attempts, 421, 422; and
    her reading matter, 479
  visits: Belgium, 168, 172; Chatsworth, 170;
    Coburg, 173; France, 167, 253; Ireland,
    187; Paris, 234; Prussia, 172, 261;
    Scotland, 175–6
Albert Edward, Prince of Wales, *see* Wales,
    Prince of
Albert Victor ('Eddy'), Prince, Duke of
    Clarence (1864–92), 455, 473, 485–6
Alexander, Grand Duke of Russia, *see*
    Alexander II, Tsar
Alexander I, Tsar (1777–1825), 7, 12
Alexander II, Tsar (1818–81), 96, 103, 361, 398
Alexander of Battenberg, Prince (1857–93),
    387, 438, 487
Alexandra of Denmark, Princess, *later*
    Princess of Wales (1844–1925): on
    QV's taste in wallpapers, 180n.;

Crown Pss. Frederick on, 272, 273; much sought-after as a bride, 272–3; QV and, 302–3; and Pr. of W., 302, 345, 465n.; personality, 303; QV on, 303, 305; anti-German, 305; and Schleswig-Holstein Duchies, 305, 306; premature birth of a baby, 306; popularity, 312; and Pss. Alice, 342; chronic unpunctuality, 343; Golden Jubilee celebrations, 380; Pss. Helena's marriage, 393; and Pss. Louise, 395n.; QV's advice on her sons, 418; Diamond Jubilee, 457; and Pr. Eddy, 486; deafness, 490; QV's death, 494; QV's funeral, 500, 501

Alexandra, Tsarina (1872–1918), 455

Alfred ('Affie'), Prince (1874–99), 484

Alfred, Prince, Duke of Edinburgh and Saxe-Coburg-Gotha (1844–1900): birth, 172; QV praises, 192; to go to sea, 258; QV compares Pr. of W. and, 268; appearance, 271; Pr. Wilhelm bites, 304–5; annuity, 311; and John Brown, 325; at Sandringham, 342; Ponsonby on, 353; QV's Golden Jubilee dress, 381; QV on, 396; personality, 397; marriage, 398; Pss. Beatrice's wedding, 412; with QV, 423; wounded, 426; Earl of Kent, 432; death, 484

Alice, Princess, later Grand Duchess of Hesse-Darmstadt (1843–78): birth, 165, 216; and Pr. of W., 184; her father's death, 279, 281; black trousseau, 286; and QV's health, 307; congratulates QV, 312; resentment against John Brown, 325; at Sandringham, 342; and QV, 391, 392, 423; wedding, 392; and Pr. Alfred's forthcoming marriage, 398; death, 484; embroidery of Pr. A's cloak, 497

Amberley, Katherine Russell, Viscountess (d.1874), 337, 352

Anderson, John Henry (1815–74), 191

Angeli, Heinrich von (1840–1925), 54n., 475n.

Anglesey, Henry Paget, 1st Marquess of (1768–1854), 35, 214

Anson, George (1812–49): appointed Pr. A's Private Secretary, 118; and Pr. A., 133–4; and Melbourne, 135; Gladstone and, 136; and Lehzen, 151; his house, 163; and Palmerston, 196; death, 265

Anson, Sir George, 118

Arabi Pasha (1839–1911), 371

Arbuthnot, Harriet (d.1834), 29, 228

Argyll, George Douglas Campbell, 8th Duke of (1823–1900), 394

Arnold, Frieda, 417n.

Arthur, Prince, Duke of Connaught (1850–1942): to church, 187; at Osborne, 191; annuity, 339; at Tel-el-Kebir, 371; QV on 398–9, 401; personality, 399; instructions and admonitions from QV, 400; army career, 400; marriage, 400, 401; Elphinstone and, 402; meagre reward, 426; and the Munshi, 448

Ashanti War, 365

Ashley, Anthony Ashley Cooper, Baron, later 7th Earl of Shaftesbury (1801–85): philanthropy, 68; and Melbourne, 89; at QV's wedding, 122; at Windsor Castle, 143–4; Factory Act, 199; Pr. A. and, 203
as Shaftesbury: on assassination attempts on QV, 423

Atholl, Duchess of (d.1897), 298

Augusta, Princess (1768–1840), 9, 12

Augusta ('Dona') of Schleswig-Holstein, Princess (1858–1921), 383, 388

Augustus, Prince of Coburg (1818–81), 105

Austin, Alfred (1835–1913), 343, 457

Bacon, Charles, 287

Baillie, A.V., 296

Balfour, Arthur James, later 1st Earl of Balfour (1848–1930), 139n., 459

Balmoral: QV buys lease, 177; QV on, 177; Grenville describes family life at, 178; QV and Pr. A., 179–81; Pr. A. designs new house, 179–80; food, 181; bagpipes, 181; cold, 181, 182; Lady Dalhousie on, 181–2; electric light, 181n., discomfort, 182, 357; domestic staff's accommodation, 182n.; P. of W., 187; workers' housing, 201; Florence Nightingale, 225; Pr. Frederick of Prussia, 239; commemorative stone to Pr. A. 287, 327; the widow, 290–1; Disraeli, 318; QV and John Brown, 322n.; John Brown, 323, 326; ghillies' balls, 326–8; Campbell-Bannerman, 357–8; QV exercises strict control, 358; Pr. Leopold, 404, 406, 408; protection of QV, 425; statue to John Brown, 442; the Munshi, 447; Tsar and Tsarina,

Balmoral – *cont.*
455, 456; copies of Scott's works, 478;
thick fog, 490

Baly, William (1814–61), 277

Baring, Mary, 408

Baring, Susan, *later* Lady Reid (1870–1961),
350, 351, 471

Baring, William Bingham, *later* 2nd Baron
Ashburton (1799–1864), 136

Barrett, Elizabeth (Elizabeth Barrett
Browning, 1906–61), 422

Barrington, George Barrington, 7th
Viscount (1824–86), 370

Bartley, George, 187

Bauer, Ottilie, 431, 473

Beaconsfield, Earl of, *see* Disraeli, Benjamin

Bean, John William, 423

Beatrice, Princess, *later* Princess Henry of
Battenberg (1857–1944): birth, 217, 259;
Pr. A. and, 278; encouraged to talk
about her father, 287; writes to Lady
Augusta, 315n.; QV dictates journal,
340; at Sandringham, 342; Campbell-
Bannerman and, 357; and Pss. Louise,
394n.; as a child, 410; indispensable to
QV, 411; marries, 412; honeymoon,
413; with QV to Switzerland, 431; and
the Munshi, 450; rheumatism, 461;
and QV's failing eyesight, 465

Beauvale, Lady, 183

Bell, Ingres, 380

Benson, Edward White (1829–96), 412

Bentinck, Lord George (1802–48), 194

Bentinck, Sir Henry (1796–1878), 225

Bernhardt, Sarah (1844–1923), 463–4

Bernstorff, Albrecht, Count von (1809–73),
306

Biddulph, Hon. Lady, 420, 431

Biddulph, Sir Thomas (1809–78), 314, 356,
431, 487

Bigge, Sir Arthur, *later* Baron Stamfordham
(1849–1931): QV's Private Secretary,
314; and John Brown, 325; Bismarck
and, 388; and Pss. Louise, 395n.; and
the Munshi, 452; and Frederick
Ponsonby, 462; attends a funeral, 496;
QV's gun-carriage, 500

Birch, Henry, 186–8 *passim*; 189

Bismarck, Otto, Fürst von (1815–98), 245,
364, 365, 387–8

Blatchford, Lady Isabella (d. 1866), 161

Blomfield, Charles James (1786–1857), 19

Blore, Edward (1787–1879), 160

Blunt, Wilfrid Scawen (1840–1922), 322n.

Boehm, Sir Joseph Edgar (1834–90), 322n.,
441, 442

Boer War, 437, 438; 2nd Boer War, 459

Bonaparte, Hortense de Beauharnais
(1783–1837), 232

Bradlaugh, Charles, 336

Breadalbane, (Lady Alma) Countess of
(d.1932), 408

Breadalbane, John Campbell, 2nd Marquess
of (1796–1862), 175

Brett, Reginald, *later* 2nd Viscount Esher
(1852–1930), 460, 475
as Lord Esher, 500, 501

Bright, John (1783–1870), 337

Brock, Mrs, Pss. V's nurse, 21, 22

Brodie, Sir Benjamin the elder (1783–1862),
83

Brontë, Charlotte (1816–55), 168

Brown, Archibald, 403, 405, 406, 410

Brown, John (1826–83): Ponsonby on, 321,
328, 432; rumour about QV and, 321;
caricatures and parodies on, 322;
appearance and background, 323;
relationship with QV, 322n., 323–9
passim; personality, 323–4, 326;
increasingly disliked, 324–6;
quarreling, 325; drunk, 325–6; extent
of his influence, 326; ghillies' balls,
326–7; QV on, 329; carries QV to bed,
340; public thanksgiving celebrations,
345; and QV, 360; Pss. Louise's
allusion, 395; treatment of, 399; Pr.
Leopold dislikes, 404; and attempt on
QV's life, 420; rewarded, 426; in
Switzerland, 432–3; grumpy, 435; ill,
440; death, 441; QV's grief, 441–2;
memorials, 442; mementos, 443;
biography, 443–4; and QV's coffin,
497; his photograph concealed, 498

Bruce, Lady Augusta (*later* Lady Augusta
Stanley, 1821–76): on Balmoral Castle,
180; Jenner and, 279–80; and QV, 280,
304; and Pr. A's death, 281; marries,
314; and *Our Life in the Highlands*,
329; on Pr. Leopold, 402; death, 487

Bruce, Robert (1813–62), 269–70, 273, 300, 301

Buccleuch and Queensberry, Walter
Montagu-Douglas-Scott, 5th Duke of
(1806–84), 175

Buchanan, James (1791–1868), 142

Buckingham Palace: Coronation Day, 70,
75; QV delighted with, 86; QV's
Declaration of Marriage, 111;
Conyngham's mistress, 117; wedding

breakfast, 122; QV and Pr. A. in the grounds, 125; Pr. A's writing desk, 131; birth of Pss. Royal, 132–3; domestic matters, 140; QV complains to Peel about, 159–60; gas and electric lighting, 181n.; Barnum's 'Greatest Show on Earth', 191; lamps smashed outside, 202; Great Exhibition conference, 210; QV and Pr. A. appear on balcony, 214; Pss. Royal's wedding breakfast, 243; Pr. A., 256; Golden Jubilee celebrations, 380, 381; Pr. and Pss. Arthur, 401; QV threatened, 426; signatures of sympathy, 427; garden parties, 430, 489; Diamond Jubilee, 457

Burdett-Coutts, Angela Burdett-Coutts, Baroness (1814–1906), 315n. 347

Buksh, Mohammed, 446

Bulteel, Elizabeth, 351

Cairns, Hugh McCalmont Cairns, 1st Earl (1819–85), 356–7

Cambridge, Adolphus, 1st Duke of (1774–1850): marriage and children, 4–5; solvency, 6; financial aid for Kent, 11; Viceroy of Hanover, 55; and Pr. A's precedence, 116; QV's wedding, 121; and Pr. A., 128; ill, 423

Cambridge, Duchess of, née Princess Augusta of Hesse-Cassel (1797–1889), 5, 128, 444, 487

Cambridge, Pr. George, 2nd Duke of (1819–1904): and QV, 86; Lady Augusta Somerset, 128; and Layard, 228; opposed to Ponsonby's appointment, 332–3; at Sandringham, 342, 344; on Gladstone, 376n.; on Irishmen, 438; QV's letter of sympathy, 442n.; on Pr. Eddy, 485

Campbell-Bannerman, Sir Henry (1836–1908), 357–8, 470

Canning, Charles John Canning, Earl (1812–62): Crimean War, 248–51 passim

Canning, Charlotte, Lady (d.1861): visit to Château d'Eu, 166–7; QV's dresses, 166, 168; in Belgium, 168; on Thüringen battue, 173; and Church of Scotland, 176; donations to Osborne museum, 192; QV and, 249, 250

Canrobert, François-Certain (1809–95), 225, 235

Canterbury, Archbishops of, see Edward White Benson, William Howley and Charles Thomas Longley

Cardigan, James Brudenell, 7th Earl of (1797–1868), 224–5

Cardwell, Edward, later Viscount Cardwell (1813–86), 346

Carisbrook, Alexander Mountbatten, Marquess of (1886–1960), 416–17

Carlos I, King of Portugal (1863–1908), 499

Carnarvon, Henry Howard Herbert, 4th Earl of (1831–90), 363–4

Caroline of Brunswick, Queen (1768–1821), 7

Caroline Matilda of Schleswig-Holstein, Pss., 408

Carpenter, William Boyd (1841–1918), 295

Carrington, Charles Wynn-Carrington, 3rd Baron (1843–1928), 345

Cavour, Camillo, Count (1810–61), 251, 252, 254

Cetewayo, Zulu King, 365

Chadwick, Sir Edwin (1800–1890), 201

Chamberlain, Joseph (1836–1914), 336, 456

Chambers, William Frederick (1786–1855), 83

Charlemont, Countess of (d.1876), 53

Charles Edward, Prince, Duke of Saxe-Coburg (1884–1954), 500

Charlotte of Mecklenburg-Strelitz, Queen (1744–1818), 4, 26, 158n.

Charlotte, Princess (1796–1817), 3, 6, 7, 8, 288

Charlotte of Prussia, Princess (1860–1919), 261

Charlotte, Queen of Württemberg (1766–1828), 12

Chartists, 199–203 passim

Chesterfield, George Philip Stanhope, 7th Earl of (1831–71), 341

Cholmondeley, George Cholmondely, 2nd Marquess of (1792–1870), 121

Christian of Denmark, Prince, later King Christian IX (1818–1906), 272, 380

Christian of Denmark, Princess, see Louise of Hesse-Cassel, Princess

Christian, Prince of Schleswig-Holstein-Sonderburg-Augustenburg (1831–1917), 311, 332–3, 393

Christian Victor, Prince of Schleswig-Holstein (1867–1900), 487

Churchill, Jane, Lady (1826–1900), 426, 435, 473, 491

Claremont Park: Pss. Charlotte's death, 8; Kents' honeymoon, 9; Leopold of Saxe-Coburg, 21, 23–4, 47; Pss. V. at, 21, 47; Louis-Philippe given shelter, 198; mausoleum, 288

Clarence, Duchess of, *see* Adelaide, Queen
Clarence, Dukes of, *see* Albert Victor, Prince *and* William IV, King
Clarendon, William Villiers, 4th Earl of (1800–1870): on QV in Scotland, 179; on thistle decorations at Balmoral, 180; Crimean War, 222; QV on, 229; on Napoleon III, 233; on QV, 235, 238, 309; and Pr. of W., 236; Pss. Royal's engagement, 239; on QV's behaviour after her mother's death, 267; distrusts Pr. A.'s doctors, 279; at Osborne, 287; and memorials to Pr. A., 288; on QV's artistic taste, 288; on QV's grief, 289; and balance of QV's mind, 291; on relations between QV and Pr. of W., 300–1; on QV's hatred of change, 314; on QV's predilection for Bright, 337n.; death, 339; on Pr. Louis of Hesse-Darmstadt, 391–2
Clark, Sir James (1788–1870): Pss. V.'s illness, 42–3; appointed QV's physician, 56; Lady Flora Hastings affair, 78–9, 81–2; press attack, 84; Pr. A. blames, 152; Scotsman, 177; 'uneasy', 219; and Crown Pss. Frederick's pregnancy, 259; Crown Pr. Frederick's confinement, 260; attends P.A., 277, 278; age, 314; QV and, 410n., death, 487
Clarke, Sir Charles (1782–1857), 79
Clementina, Princess, 457
Clifden, Nellie, 271
Coburg, Dowager Duchess of, 9, 12, 99
Cole, (Sir) Henry (1808–82), 210, 211
Collins, Robert Hawthorn, 406
Combe, George (1788–1858), 187–8
Connaught, Duke of, *see* Arthur, Prince
Conroy, Jane, 43
Conroy, Sir John (1786–1854): Kent's equerry, 14, 25; Duchess of Kent and, 24–7 *passim*, 31, 37, 48, 51, 265; history, 25; personality, 26; rank bestowed on, 26; and Pss. V., 26–7, 42, 44, 49, 51; dismissed from Chapel Royal, 34; 'Royal Progresses', 34; honorary degree, 35; and Dch. of Northumberland, 45; and King William's letter to Pss. V., 48; and Stockmar, 49; Stockmar's report on, 50; QV dismisses, 56; and Lady Flora Hastings, 78, 80; his demands, 90; ill reputation, 91; agrees to leave the country, 91; QV and death of, 265

Conroy, Lady, 25, 43
Conroy, Victoire, 27, 34, 43, 47
Conyngham, Elizabeth, Marchioness (d.1861), 20
Conyngham, Francis Nathaniel Conyngham, 2nd Marquess (1797–1876), 51, 52, 116–17
Corelli, Marie (*pseud.* of Mary Mackay, 1855–1924), 477
Corry, Montagu, *later cr.* Baron Rowton (d.1903), 369, 370, 443
Couper, Sir George (d.1861), 264
Court: etiquette, 141; dress, 142, 465; *Court Circular*, 142–3; dull evenings, 143; in mourning, 285–6; officials, 340; dullness of Court life, 357; daily routine at Osborne, 461–2; dinner parties, 468–71, 475–6
Coutts, Thomas (1735–1822), 23
Cowell, (Sir) John, 192
Cowley, Henry Wellesley, 1st Earl (1804–84), 252
Craven, Pauline, 479
Crawford and Balcarres, Margaret Lindsay, Countess of (d.1909), 434
Creevey, Thomas: and Kent, 3, 5, 6; on Sussex, 4; and Conroy, 27; on the young QV, 53, 61–2; and Lady Tavistock's dilemma, 62; on Buckingham Palace, 86
Crimean War, 221–7, 234, 240–1, 252
Crispi, Francesco (1819–1901), 437n.
Croker, John Wilson (1780–1857), 55–6, 111
Cubitt, Thomas (1788–1855), 163, 210
Cumberland, Duchess of (1778–1841), 4
Cumberland, Ernest, Duke of *and* (1837) King of Hanover (1771–1851): personality, 4, 23; appearance, 4; Conroy keeps Pss. V. from, 27; and Regency Bill, 31; QV's first Privy Council, 55; King of Hanover, 55n.; and Great Exhibition, 211
Cumberland, Prince George of, *later* George V, King of Hanover (1819–78), 23, 98
Curzon, George Nathaniel, Marquess (1859–1925), 453
Cust, Sir Edward (1794–1878), 142

Dalhousie, Marchioness of (1817–53), 181
Darnley, John Bligh, 4th Earl of (1767–1831), 11
Davidson, Randall (1848–1930): QV and, 293; QV on, 295; on QV's

relationship with John Brown, 321–2; on QV's charm, 349, 358–9; and QV's memoir of John Brown, 443–4; on QV's relationship with the Munshi, 449–50; summoned to Osborne, 493; and the Kaiser, 493–4; on QV's funeral, 501

Davys, George (1780–1864), 18, 48

Derby, Edward George Stanley, 14th Earl of (1799–1869):
  as Lord Stanley: moves vote of censure, 205–6
  as Lord Derby: declaration of trust in P.A., 223; QV sends for, 228; and French preparations for war, 254; resignations, 255; 316; not asked to sit down, 319; on QV, 431

Derby, Edward Henry Stanley, 15th Earl of (1826–93):
  as Lord Stanley: on QV's relationship with John Brown, 322; on QV's appearance, 340; French Imperial Court, 431
  as Lord Derby: attempting to prevent conflict, 363; resigns, 364; QV on, 369; presses QV to leave Isle of Wight, 425

Devonshire, Georgiana, Duchess of (1757–1806), 65n.

Devonshire, William George Spencer Cavendish, 6th Duke of (1790–1858), 35, 170–71, 213

Dickens, Charles (1812–70), 68, 199, 478, 482–3

Dilke, Sir Charles Wentworth, 1st Bart. (1810–69), 332, 340n.

Dilke, Sir Charles Wentworth, 2nd Bart. (1843–1911), 340 *and* n., 345, 427

Disraeli, Benjamin, *later* Earl of Beaconsfield (1804–81): on Coronation, 74–5; complains about Balmoral, 182; Corn Laws, 193–4; and P.A.'s visitors' book, 287; at P. of W.'s wedding, 304; P. of W.'s opinion of, 316; QV and, 316, 317, 360–61; on P.A., 316; background, 316–17; appearance, 317, 360; praises *Our Life in the Highlands*, 330; and Empress of India, 361; Suez Canal shares, 361; attitude to Turkish atrocities, 362; on Gladstone, 362; and Russo-Turkish conflict, 363, 364; Bismarck on, 364; Garter, 365; continuing correspondence with QV, 368; advice on Speech from the Throne, 369; death, 369; QV's grief, 369–70; and P. Leopold, 407; 'valued and devoted friend', 442; QV reads, 478

Dixie, Lady Florence, 440

Dodgson, Charles Ludwidge (1832–98), 406, 479

Dona, Princess, *see* Augusta of Schleswig-Holstein, Princess

Douro, Marchioness, *later* Duchess of Wellington (d.1904), 497n.

Duckworth, Robinson, 403–4, 431

Dufferin and Ava, Frederick Blackwood, 1st Marquess of (1826–1902), 474

Dundas, Sir David, 14

Dundonald, Douglas Cochrane, 12th Earl of (1852–1935), 458

Durham, Joseph (1814–77), 287

Dyce, William (1806–64), 163

Earle, Thomas, 287n.

Eastlake, Sir Charles (1793–1865), 100n.

'Eddy', Prince, *see* Albert Victor, Prince

Eden, Hon. Emily (1797–1869), 319

Edinburgh, Duke of, *see* Alfred, Prince

Edward, Prince, *later* King Edward VIII *and, after his abdication*, Duke of Windsor (1894–1972), 164n., 415–16, 500, 501

Edwards, Sir Fleetwood (1842–1910), 447, 451, 452

Elgin, Victor Alexander Bruce, 9th Earl of (1849–1917), 449, 450

Elizabeth ('Ella'), Princess (1864–1918), 418

Ellis, Sir Arthur, 141

Elphinstone, Sir Howard (1829–90), 281, 323, 399, 402, 430

Ely, Jane Loftus, Marchioness of (d.1890), 356, 431, 471

Ernest Christian Charles of Hohenlohe-Langenburg, Prince (1794–1860), 22

Ernest I, Duke of Saxe-Coburg (1784–1844), 99, 111

Ernest II, Duke of Saxe-Coburg (1818–93): Pr. A. and, 99; syphilis, 101; in England, 101, 108; bomb outrage in Paris, 242; Pr. A. angry with, 273; death, 487

Errol, Countess of, 139n.

Errol, William George Hay, 18th Earl of (1801–46), 133, 136

Erskine, Lady Sybil St Clair, 486

Esher, 2nd Viscount, *see* Brett, Reginald

Etonians, 381, 420, 421, 438–9

Eugénie, Empress of the French
    (1826–1920): bride of Napoleon III,
    231; Lord John Russell on, 231; QV
    and, 233–4, 431; appearance, 235–6; P.
    of W. and, 237; and Pss. Royal, 237;
    bomb outrage, 241, 242

Faure, Félix (1841–99), 436–7
Feodora of Leiningen, Princess (1807–72):
    journey to England, 11; in Devonshire,
    14; and Pss. V., 22 and n., 40, 42;
    marriage, 22; living in Germany, 33;
    QV writes to, 54, 60; QV's financial
    help, 58; attitude to prayer, 185
Ferdinand II, King of the Two Sicilies
    (1810–59), 204
Ferguson, Robert (1799–1865), 277
Field, Kate, 465n.
Fisher, John (1748–1825), 14, 19–20
FitzClarence, Lord Adolphus (1802–56), 45,
    46, 47, 165
FitzClarence, Lord Frederick (1799–1854), 7
Fitzgerald, Hamilton, 80, 81
Fitzherbert, Maria Anne (1756–1837), 6
Fitzwilliam, William Wentworth, 2nd Earl
    (1748–1833), 11
Frampton, Mary, 70, 86
Francis, John, 423
Francis Joseph, Emperor of Austria
    (1830–1916), 254, 255
Franco-Prussian War, 338
Frederick of Austria, Grand Duke, 172
Frederick William, Crown Prince, later
    Frederick III, King of Prussia and
    German Emperor (1831–88): and Pss.
    Royal, 238, 239, 240; personality and
    appearance, 238; wedding, 242–3;
    leaving England, 244; on Crown Pss.
    Frederick's confinement, 260; and
    QV, 299, 382, 384, 387; fighting in
    Prussian army, 306; Golden Jubilee
    celebrations, 380; illness, 384, 385;
    succeeds to throne, 386; death, 388,
    485; post-mortem, 389
Frith, William Powell (1819–1909), 411
Frogmore: Duchess of Kent, 264, 265; Royal
    Mausoleum, 288, 303, 305, 442–3, 497,
    500; Pr. and Pss. Christian, 393;
    Frogmore Cottage, 454n.

Garibaldi, Giueseppe (1807–82), 204
Garth, General Thomas (1744–1829), 26
George I, King of the Hellenes (1845–1913),
    380, 499

George III, King (1738–1820):
    grandchildren, 3; and Sussex, 4; dying,
    14; death, 16; passion for Handel, 39;
    appearance, 61; blindness, 77; mental
    imbalance, 97, 132, 172; Windsor
    uniform, 109; length of reign, 379
George IV, King (1762–1830):
    as Prince Regent: his establishments, 3;
    and Mrs Fitzherbert, 6; and Leopold
    of Saxe-Coburg, 7, 8; and Kent, 10–11;
    Pss. V.'s christening, 12–13; and Kent's
    widow and daughter, 15
    as King: succeeds to throne, 16; and Pss.
    V., 20, 21; and Duchess of Kent, 23;
    Hanoverian Order, 26; death, 29;
    coronation expenditure, 71; and Peel,
    94; mental instability, 132;
    Buckingham Palace, 159, 160;
    Shaftesbury on, 423
George, Prince, later King George V
    (1865–1936): talks to Esher, 344n.;
    wedding, 376; truth on, 413; on the
    Munshi, 454n.; and Pss. May of Teck,
    486; QV on, 487; title, 487n.
George Prince of Denmark (1653–1708), 112
Gibbs, Frederick Waymouth, 189
Gibson, John (1790–1866), 474n.
Gilbert, Sir Alfred (1854–1934), 465n.
Giles, James, 177
Gladstone, Catherine (1812–1900), 320, 358,
    374, 377
Gladstone, William Ewart (1809–98): on
    QV and new Government ministers,
    136; and Roman Catholicism, 193; on
    fall of Aberdeen's Government, 228;
    Chancellor of the Exchequer, 255; and
    QV, 295, 319–20, 378; Pr. A. holds
    him in regard, 319; QV on, 319, 320,
    360, 362, 367; Emily Eden on, 319;
    personality, 320; persuades QV to deal
    with matters of state, 331; and QV's
    reclusiveness, 336, 339; public
    thanksgiving, 345; visit of Shah of
    Persia, 347; enjoys Balmoral, 358n.;
    retires, 360; Bulgarian Horrors
    pamphlet, 362; championship of
    African races, 365; QV dislikes, 367,
    370, 373, 376n.; she treats him with
    'perfect courtesy', 368; QV's
    instructions, 368; on QV, 369;
    Ponsonby on QV's jealousy, 370–71;
    returns to office, 373, 374; Lady
    Augusta Stanley on, 373n.; Home Rule
    Bill defeated, 374; fourth term of

office, 375; final resignation, 376; death, 377; and attempts on QV's life, 425, 427; slow eater, 470; admires Corelli's works, 477

Glenlyon, George Stewart-Murray, 2nd Baron, *later* 6th Duke of Atholl (1814–64), 175

Gloucester, Princess Mary, Duchess of (1776–1857), 12, 15, 20

Gloucester, William Frederick, Duke of (1776–1834), 12

Gordon, Alexander Hamilton, 178

Gordon, Charles George (1833–85), 371

Gordon, Sir Robert (1791–1847), 177

Granville, Granville Leveson-Gower, 2nd Earl (1815–91), 101n., 242, 367, 368, 369

Great Exhibition: purpose, 210; difficulties foreseen, 211; Crystal Palace, 212, 213; public safety, 212; QV on, 213–14, 215; QV fascinated, 214; exhibits, 214

Gregory XVI, Pope (r.1831–46), 100

Greville, Charles Fulke (1794–1865): King William's disastrous birthday, 45–7; impressed by QV, 53–4; on her first appearance as Queen, 54–5; on a royal dinner party, 63–4; on Melbourne and QV, 67; on London on Coronation Day, 70; on Coronation clergy, 73; and Melbourne, 114, 135; and Wellington, 115; and P.A.'s precedence, 115; on invitations to QV's wedding, 122; on the going-away equipage, 122–3; and Peel, 134, 135; on Peel and QV, 136; boredom at Windsor, 144; and Lehzen, 150; on Osborne House, 162; on royal visit to Chatsworth, 170–1; on criticism of the Queen, 173–4; on Royal Family's life at Balmoral, 177–8; at Apsley House, 201; on Chartist march, 202; Granville and the Foreign Office, 208

observations on people: Pr. A., 171; Howley, 13; Kent, 5; Palmerston, 197, 265; Peel, 94; Pss. V., 28; QV, 54–5, 60, 62, 86, 96, 97, 121, 124, 125, 172, 174; Victor Emmanuel II, 252

Grey, Charles (1804–70): QV's Private Secretary, 298; and QV's reclusiveness, 307–8, 309, 331; death, 314, 487; Ponsonby and, 332; and QV, 334; and maids-of-honour, 350; protection of QV, 425

Grey, Charles Grey, 2nd Earl (1764–1845), 31, 32, 96

Grey, Sir George (1799–1882), 136

Grisi, Giulia (1811–69), 44

Gruner, Ludwig (d.1882), 100n., 163, 288

Guizot, François (1787–1874), 165, 478

Halford, Sir Henry (1766–1844), 50

Halifax, Sir Charles Wood, 1st Viscount (1800–85), 308, 336

Hamilton, Lord George (1845–1927), 448–9, 452

Hamilton, William, 423

Harcourt, Edward (1757–1847), 39 *and* n.

Harcourt, Sir William (1827–1904), 375, 426, 462

Hardwicke, Charles Yorke, 4th Earl of (1799–1873), 424

Harrowby, Dudley Ryder, 2nd Earl of (1798–1882), 315n.

Hartington, Spencer Cavendish, Marquess of, *later* 8th Duke of Devonshire (1833–1908), 367, 372, 470

Hastings, Dowager Marchioness of (1780–1840), 81

Hastings, Lady Flora (1806–39): appointed to Dch. of Kent's Household, 34; at Kensington Palace, 43; and Pss. V., 44, 45; QV and, 57, 77, 80, 83; suspected pregnancy, 78; Sir James Clark and, 78–9; blames Lehzen, 81; and Lady Tavistock, 82; death, 83; funeral, 84

Hastings, Francis Rawdon-Hastings, 2nd Marquess of (1808–44), 78, 80–1

Hatherton, Edward John Littleton, 1st Baron (1791–1863), 89

Hatzfeldt, Count (1831–1901), 353

Haussman, Georges-Eugène, Baron, 431

Hawaii, Emma, Queen of, 346, 383

Hawksmoor, Nicholas (1661–1736), 288

Haynau, Julius, Frieherr von (1786–1853), 206, 207

Heinrich, Prince of Prussia (1862–1929), 386

Helen of Waldeck, Princess (1861–1922), 408–10 *passim*

Helena, Princess, *later* Princess Christian of Schleswig-Holstein (1846–1923): birth, 176; and P.A.'s death, 281; her bridegroom, 311; QV and, 312, 393; appearance, 392–3; wedding, 393; and Pss. Louise's relationship with Bigge, 395n.; Diamond Jubilee, 457

Hélène d'Orléans, Princess, 486

Helps, (Sir) Arthur (1813–75), 298, 299, 329

Henry VIII, King (1491–1547), 165

Henry of Battenberg, Prince (1858–96): smoking, 353; and Pss. Louise, 395; QV and, 412, 413; and the Munshi, 450; death, 471, 485; QV's orders about his burial, 496
Herbert, Sydney, later 1st Baron Herbert (1810–61), 227–8
Hesse, Frederick, William Louis, Prince of, see Louis IV, Grand Duke of Hesse
Hobbs, Mrs, 258, 261
Holland, Elizabeth Vassall Fox, Lady (1770–1845), 81n., 89, 355, 478
Holland, Henry Vassall Fox, 3rd Baron (1773–1840), 62, 63, 264
Holland, Sir Henry (1788–1873), 279
Home, Daniel Dunglass (1833–86), 254
Hopetoun, John Adrian Hope, 7th Earl of (1860–1908), 453
Howe, Richard William Penn, 3rd Earl (1822–1900), 459
How, William Walsham (1823–97), 457
Howley, William (1766–1848), 13, 51, 56, 74, 153
Humbert, A.J. (1822–77), 288
Humbert of Italy, Prince, later King (1844–1900), 346
Hume, Joseph (1777–1855), 10, 11
Hyde Park: Coronation Day, 70; Coronation fireworks, 75; QV reviews troops, 109; Great Exhibition, 211, 213; military review in Shah's honour, 347; Golden Jubilee, 381–2; QV and Pr. A. drive through, 421; minute guns, 499

Ilchester, Henry Fox-Strangways, 3rd Earl of (1787–1858), 84
Ilchester, Maria, Dowager Countess of (d.1842), 7, 86
Indian Mutiny, 248–51
Innocent, Mrs, 259
Irene of Hesse, Princess (1866–1953), 388
Irving, (Sir) Henry (1838–1905), 472, 473
Ismail, Khedive of Egypt (1830–95), 346

James, Henry (1843–1916), 501–2
Jenkinson, Lady Catherine (1811–77), 35, 44–5, 51
Jenner, (Sir) William (1815–98): Physician Extraordinary to QV, 277; attends Pr. A., 278; 279–80; and QV's mental health, 308, 309; John Brown, 324; claims QV is ill, 331; Ponsonby and, 335, 356–7; with QV to Switzerland,

431; foreign lavatories, 433; and Fraülein Bauer, 473; death, 487
Jocelyn, Fanny, 424
Joinville, François Ferdinand, Prince de (1818–1900), 166
Joinville, Princesse de, 166
Jordan, Dora (1762–1816), 4
Jowett, Benjamin (1817–93), 481

Kanné, J.J., 428, 432, 433
Karim, Abdul, the Munshi (d.1909): appearance, 446; QV and, 446–54; personality, 447; female dependants, 447; ill, 448; in Florence, 450; Household aversion to, 451; causes further offence, 451; turns up at Cimiez, 452; becomes less obtrusive, 453; Pr. George on, 454n.; QV's funeral, 497, 498
Kaye, John (1783–1853), 19
Kean, Charles (1811?–68), 191
Kensington Palace: Pss. V's christening, 13; Sussex, 13; Dch. of Kent and Pss. V. return to, 15; Davys, 18; QV's childhood home, 19; Pss. Sophia, 26; Conroy, 27, 42, 43, 91; Dch. of Kent, 32, 46–7; Pss. V., 34, 42, 43; balls, 44; German cousins, 44; meeting of Privy Council, 53–4; Q.V.'s memories of, 85–6; Lornes' apartments, 395; Pss. Louise's statue of QV, 395
Kent, Edward, Duke of (1767–1820): death of Pss. Charlotte, 3; military career, 5; personality, 5–6, 7; Mme de St Laurent, 6; appearance, 7; Pss. Charlotte and Leopold of Saxe-Coburg, 7; and his wife, 9; seeks help from Regent, 10–11; journey to England, 11; birth of daughter, 12; Regent ignores, 13; in debt, 13; dwellings, 14; illness and death, 14–15; and Conroy, 25; possible infertility, 217n.
Kent, Princess Victoire of Saxe-Coburg, Duchess of (1786–1861): Kent and, 7, 8, 9; first marriage, 8; personality, 9; appearance, 9, 23; pregnancy, 10; journey to England, 11; birth of Pss. V., 12; Kent's illness and death, 14–15; Leopold of Saxe-Coburg and, 15, 23; and Pss. V., 17–18, 19, 48, 51; Lehzen and, 22, 34, 42; loneliness, 23; allowances, 23; Conroy, 24–7 passim; 31, 47, 48, 57–8, 90, 91; and

Wellington, 31; Regency Bill, 31–2; relationship with Court, 32; Pss. V.'s names, 32; attitude to King William's bastard children, 32–3, 57; and William IV, 33, 37, 45–7; 'Royal Progresses', 34, 37, 38; wants a country residence, 37–8; and Pss. V.'s indisposition, 42; arrival of Canterbury and Lord Chamberlain, 51–2; relations between QV and, 56, 92–3, 104, 264, 265; demand for rank, 56–7; Melbourne's opinion of, 57; debts, 58, 59; Coronation, 75; and Lady Flora Hastings affair, 79, 82; at Windsor Castle, 87; young Pr. A. on, 102; QV's wedding, 120, 121; birth of Pss. Royal, 133; Pr. A. and, 133, 254; Osborne, 162; and legitimacy of QV, 217n.; and QV's engagement, 264–5; death, 266; and chastisement of children, 401; Belgrave Square, 421

Kingsley, Charles (1819–75), 304, 478

Kitchener, Horatio Herbert Kitchener, 1st Earl (1850–1916), 455

Knight, Charles (1791–1873), 28

Knollys, Francis Knollys, 1st Viscount (1837–1924); 322n., 485

Kossuth, Lajos (1802–94), 207

Lablache, Luigi (1794–1858), 43, 44

Labouchere, Henry (1831–1912), 375, 412

Laird, John, 297

Lamb, Lady Caroline (1785–1828), 66, 185

Landseer, Sir Edwin (1802–73), 18, 54, 329, 414

Landsdowne, Henry Petty-Fitzmaurice, 3rd Marquess of (1780–1863), 228

Law, George Henry (1761–1845), 74

Layard, Sir Austen Henry (1817–94), 228

Lear, Edward (1812–88), 18

Lehzen, Louise, Baroness (d.1870): personality, 21; and Pss. V., 21–2, 34, 42, 43, 44, 50; created baroness, 26; 'Kensington System', 28; attempt to lessen her influence, 34; Pss. V.'s journal, 36; Dch. of Kent and, 42; Lady Catherine Jenkinson, 44; Dch, of Northumberland, 45; Conroy and, 45; news of QV's accession, 52; Attendant on the Queen, 56; at Coronation, 72; and Lady Flora Hastings, 77–8, 81; press attack, 84; QV and, 92, 132, 150–51, 155–6; Lord Alfred Paget and, 104; Pr. A. and, 132, 151, 152, 157; Mrs

Southey and, 153; to live in Hanover, 155; and assassination attempt on QV, 422

Leicester, Thomas Coke, 1st Earl of (1754–1842), 39

Leighton, Sir Frederic, later Baron Leighton (1830–96), 354

Leiningen, Charles Frederick, Prince of (1804–56), 45, 111

Leiningen, Emich Charles, Prince of (d.1814), 8

Leitch, William Leighton (1804–83), 18

Leopold I, King of the Belgians (1790–1865):
  as Prince Leopold of Saxe-Coburg: marriage, 7, 8; Prince Regent and, 7; and his sister, 8; assets, 9; Claremont, 9, 21, 23–4; Pss. V.'s christening, 12; takes care of Dch. of Kent and Pss. V., 15, 23; and Belgian throne, 24; Pss. V. and, 24, 39–40, 41, 43, 44, 49; personality, 24, 25; and Stockmar, 49
  as King Leopold I: second marriage, 24; and Conroy, 49; QV writes to, 54; advises QV, 54, 87; QV's diminutive size, 61; at Windsor Castle, 87; and QV, 88, 202; censures William IV, 98–9, and Pr. A., 99, 100, 105, 114, 118; marriage for Pss. V., 103; financial provision, 112; peerage, 114; Pr. A.'s Household, 117; birth of Pss. Royal, 133; QV and Pr. A. stay with, 168, 172; Palmerston and, 198; Pss. Royal's wedding, 243; funeral, 294; and QV and Pss. Alexandra, 302; urges·QV to show herself more, 310; death, 380

Leopold II, King of the Belgians (1835–1909), 380, 457, 499

Leopold, Prince of Coburg (1824–84), 105

Leopold, Prince, Duke of Albany (1853–84): birth, 216; haemophilia, 217, 402, 404, 409; QV writes to, 285; Pr. Wilhelm bites, 304–5; at Sandringham, 342, 343; in children's plays, 399; personality, 401, 408; QV on, 401, 402; and his mother, 401, 403, 405, 406–7; Lady Augusta Bruce on, 402; sent to France, 402; and Stirling, 403, 406; and Pss. Louise, 403; Duckworth, 403–4; loathes Balmoral, 404; Archie Brown, 405; at Oxford, 405–6; and Beaconsfield, 407, 408; marriage, 408–9; death, 409, 484; with QV to Switzerland, 431

Leopold of Saxe-Coburg, Prince, *see* Leopold I, King of the Belgians
Leveson-Gower, Frederick (1819–1907), 195
Liddell, Henry (1811–98), 406
Liddell, Hon. Georgiana, 146
Lieven, Dorothea von Benkendorff, Princess (1784–1857), 7, 60, 67
Lincoln, Bishop of, *see* Kaye, John
Lind, Jenny (1820–87), 304
Lister, Joseph, 1st Baron (1827–1912), 339–40
Liverpool, Charles Jenkinson, 3rd Earl of (1784–1851): Pss. V. and 50–51; Peel and, 95; at QV's wedding, 121; at Château d'Eu, 167; seasickness, 168; on relations between QV and her mother, 264
Locock, (Sir) Charles (1799–1875), 130, 131, 133
Londesborough, William Henry Denison, 1st Earl of (1834–1900), 341
London (*see also* Buckingham Palace, Hyde Park *and* Kensington Palace): Albert Memorial, 288; 316; Apsley House, 114, 201; Belgrave Square, 421; Carlton House, 3, 20; Chapel Royal, 34, 120, 243; Clarence House, 398; Constitution Hill, 71, 421, 423, 489; Covent Garden, 191; Cumberland Lodge, 20, 393; Guildhall, 41n., 60, 151, 215; Holborn Circus, 287n.; Horse Guards Parade, 459; Lambeth Palace, 295; Marble Arch, 160; Marlborough House, 367; National Gallery, 100n.; Paddington, 499; Palace of Westminster, 131; Pall Mall, 71, 501; Parliament Square, 459; Piccadilly, 71; Royal Albert Hall, 215, 288, 381; Royal Exchange, 215; Royal Horticultural Gardens, 301; Royal Opera House, 191, 424; St James's, 71; St James's Palace, 13, 43; St Paul's Cathedral, 345, 427, 457, 458; Temple Bar, 241; The Mall, 459; Trafalgar Square, 71; Victoria and Albert Museum, 215; Waterloo Station, 202; Westminster Abbey, 70, 71, 380, 381; Westminster Bridge, 458–9; Whitehall, 71
London, Bishop of, *see* Blomfield, Charles James
Longfellow, Henry Wadsworth (1807–82), 481
Longley, Charles Thomas (1794–1868), 304
Lorne, John Sutherland Campbell, Marquess of, *later* 9th Duke of Argyll (1845–1914), 394, 413
Louis of Battenberg, Prince, *later* 1st Marquess of Milford Haven (1854–1921), 449–50, 499
Louis IV, Grand Duke of Hesse-Darmstadt (1837–92), 286, 391–2, 412, 485
Louis XVIII, King of France (1755–1824), 6
Louis-Napoleon, Emperor of the French, *see* Napoleon III
Louis-Philippe, King of the French (1773–1850), 72, 165, 166, 167, 198
Louise of Hesse-Cassel, Princess, *later* Queen Louise of Denmark (1817–98), 301
Louise, Princess (1848–1939): birth, 201; QV and, 202; and Boehm, 322n.; dowry, 339; at Sandringham, 342; Campbell-Bannerman and, 357–8; personality, 394; her bridegroom, 394; wedding, 395; her statue of QV, 395; relationship with Bigge, 395n.; and Pr. Leopold, 403; truth on, 413; with QV to Switzerland, 431; and the Munshi, 450; bursts into laughter, 473; suggests a remedy for QV's rheumatism, 488
Louise of Prussia, Princess (1860–1917), 400, 415
Louise, Queen of the Belgians (1812–50): marriage, 24; and Pss. V., 41–2, 47; at Windsor Castle, 87; QV's visit to France, 166, 168; QV and Pr. A. go to see, 171; QV and death of, 265
Lyndhurst, John Singleton Copley, Baron (1772–1863), 74
Lyttleton, Lady (1787–1870): and Pr. A., 125; Wellington and, 144; on Pr. A., 146, 158, 163; and Lehzen, 150; Superintendent of royal nursery, 154; personality, 154; and Pr. of W., 155; on QV, 158, 179, 311; on Osborne, 163; on Pr. of W., 183, 186; and QV as mother, 184; and the royal children, 185
Lytton, Edith Bulwer-Lytton, Countess of (1841–1936): on servants' accommodation at Balmoral, 182n.; discusses bishops with QV, 295; QV shocks, 296n.; on Royalties at Scotch Kirk, 456; Yorke's buttonhole, 467n.; dinner with QV, 468, 476; QV's coffin, 498

Macaulay, Thomas Babington Macaulay, Baron (1800–59), 143

Macclesfield, Mary Frances Parker,
Countess of (1821–1912), 342–3
MacGregor, Miss Murray, 443
Mackenzie, Sir Morell (1837–92), 384, 385
Maclean, Roderick, 420, 427
McLeod, Norman (1812–72), 304
McNaghten, Daniel, 195
Mahon, Emily, Viscountess (d.1873), 130–31
Mallet, (Sir) Bernard (1859–1932), 351, 474,
490
Mallet, Marie (1862–1934):
as Marie Adeane: QV's maid-of-honour,
350, 351, 447n.; on QV's footmen, 466
as Mrs Mallet: on Pss. Louise, 395; her
son Victor and QV, 414; on QV at
Grasse, 436; on Duleep Singh, 447n.;
dinner with QV, 470; on Ritchie, 470;
QV's laughter, 471; QV's reading
matter, 479, 480; and QV's grief,
487–8; QV's indigestion, 489; QV's
interest in funerals, 495–6
Mallet, (Sir) Victor (1893–1969), 414
Malmesbury, James Harris, 3rd Earl of
(1807–89), 178, 242, 253
Maltby, Edward (1770–1859), 73
Manchester, Louise, Duchess of, later
Duchess of Devonshire (d.1911), 367
Manners-Sutton, Charles (1755–1828), 13
Manning, Henry Edward (1808–92), 211
Marcy, William (1786–1857), 142
Margaret of Hesse, Princess (1872–1954),
415
Margaret, Princess, later Pss. Gustav of
Sweden (1882–1920), 416
Maria Christina II, Queen Regent of Spain
(1858–1929), 436
Maria da Gloria, Queen of Portugal
(1819–53), 22, 77, 126
Marie, Princess, later Queen of Rumania
(1875–1938), 417
Marie Alexandrovna, Grand Duchess of
Russia (1853–1920), 398
Marie-Amélie, Queen of the French, 166
Marie Louise, Princess (1872–1957), 397n.
Marlborough, George Spencer Churchill,
5th Duke of (1766–1840), 34
Morochetti, Carlo (1805–67), 288, 501
Martin, Edward, 259
Martin, Sir Theodore (1816–1909), 308–9,
443
Mascagni, Pietro (1863–1945), 473
Maton, William George (1774–1835), 15
May of Teck, Princess, later Queen Mary
(1867–1953), 164n., 180n., 376

Mazzini, Giuseppe (1805–72), 242, 252
Melbourne, William Lamb, 2nd Viscount
(1779–1848): on QV, 18n.; succeeds as
Prime Minister, 38; personality, 64; at
Coronation, 71, 73, 74, 75; indisposed,
76; and Lady Flora Hastings affair,
78–84 passim; his laugh, 88; Ashley's
opinion of, 89; and Conroy, 90;
resignation, 92–3; and financial
provision for Pr. A., 112; tactlessness,
116; and Pr. A.'s Household, 117; and
Pr. A., 'stickler for morality', 118;
QV's wedding, 120; his dress coat, 122;
on QV's relationship with Pr. A.,
126–7; and Peel, 135, 194; admires Pr.
A., 135; and Pr. A.'s anger with
Lehzen, 151; and royal nursery, 154;
flagellation, 185; Leveson-Gower on,
195; death, 195; on QV's attitude to
Palmerston's marriage, 197; opposed
to reform, 200; on would-be assassin,
421; on Johnson's poetry, 498
and QV: she receives, 54; first Privy
Council, 55; advises her about Dch, of
Kent, 56, 57, 59; other advice, 62, 77,
94, 113, 114; their relationship, 64–9,
88–9, 92–3, 125; matter of the Queen's
Ladies, 94, 96; question of her
marriage, 104; she is snappy, 106; she
turns upon him, 115–16; after her
wedding, 122; agrees to write to her
regularly, 135; her 'unbounded
admiration and affection', 157; she
finds him tiresome, 194–5
Micklethwaite, Sir Peckham, 38n.
Millais, John William (d.1870), 421
Millais, (Sir) John Everett (1829–96), 421
Monkswell, Mary, Lady, 458, 485n., 498–9
Montefiore, Sir Moses, 41n.
Montpensier, Duke of (1824–90), 167
Montpensier, Mademoiselle de (Duchesse
de Montpensier, 1627–93), 167
Mordaunt, Sir Charles (1836–97), 332
Mordaunt, Harriet, 331, 332
Munby, A.J. (1828–1910), 307, 312, 321
Munshi, the, see Karim, Abdul
Murray, Lady Augusta, 4

Napier, Sir Charles (1782–1853), 84
Napoleon I, Emperor of the French
(1769–1821), 72, 236
Napoleon III, Emperor of the French
(1808–73): declares himself Emperor,
207; his intention of going to the

Napoleon III – *cont.*
　Crimea, 230, 232, 234; Pr. A. and, 230;
　personality, 230, 233; and Pss.
　Adelaide, 231; his Spanish bride, 231;
　State Visit to England, 232–4; QV
　and, 232–7 *passim*; 253, 254, 338;
　appearance, 233, 338; bomb outrage,
　241; assassination attempts, 242;
　Cavour and, 251; member of
　Carbonari, 252; changed relationship
　with England, 254; struck by
　coincidences, 294; in England after
　Franco-Prussian War, 338; Imperial
　Train, 431
Nash, John (1752–1835), 86, 160
Neild, John Camden (1780?–1852), 288n.
Nicholas I, Tsar (1796–1855), 140, 144, 221,
　286n.
Nicholas II, Tsar (1868–1918), 181, 455, 456,
　464n.
Nightingale, Florence (1820–1910), 225
Norfolk, Bernard Howard, 12th Duke of
　(1765–1842), 121
Normanby, Constantine Phipps, 1st
　Marquess of (1797–1863), 208
Northumberland, Duchess of (d.1866), 32,
　33, 45

O'Connor, Arthur, 426, 427
O'Connor, Feargus (1794–1855), 202
Order of the Garter: Pr. A., 111, 121, 145;
　Disraeli, 365; Napoleon III, 233;
　Palmerston, 229; Roberts, 492;
　Shaftesbury, 365; Shah of Persia, 348;
　Victor Emmanuel II, 253
Orléans, Duchess of (1814–58), 166
Orsini, Felice (1819–58), 242, 252
Osborne: Balfour's dilemma, 139n.; QV
　and Pr. A. buy, 161; QV entranced by,
　162; demolished and rebuilt, 162; Pr.
　A. designs, 163; QV loves, 163–4;
　Albert Smith lectures, 191; children's
　practical education, 191–2; Swiss
　cottage, 191–2; Peel tenders
　resignation, 195; workers' housing, 201;
　Pr. A. and Ashley, 203; French
　Emperor and Empress, 254; Pss. Royal,
　260–1; after death of Dch. of Kent,
　267; routine commemoration of Pr.
　A., 287; table-turning, 294; the widow
　at, 298; Pr. of W.'s honeymoon, 305;
　QV and Disraeli, 319; John Brown,
　324, 326; Pr. of W.'s convalescence,
　344–5; Gladstone's Cabinet at, 369;

Wolseley, 373; Pss. Alice's wedding,
　392; Marie Alexandrovna's opinion of,
　398; Pr. Leopold, 404; entertainments
　for grandchildren, 418; protection of
　QV, 425; heat 'quite intolerable', 430;
　granite seat commemorating Brown,
　442; the Munshi, 447; daily routine,
　461; telephone, 465n.; QV in failing
　health, 489; Christmas tree, 490; last
　Christmas, 490–91; QV's death, 494;
　QV's coffin, 498
Ossulston, Charles Bennet, Baron, *later* 6th
　Earl of Tankerville (1810–99), 63, 64
Owen, Robert (1771–1858), 11
Oxford, Bishop of, *see* Wilberforce, Samuel
Oxford, Edward, 421–2, 423, 424

Pacifico, David (1784–1854), 205
Paderewski, Ignacy (1860–1941), 473
Pagenstecker, Hermann, 464
Paget, Lord Alfred (1816–88), 104
Paget, Sir Augustus (1823–96), 433
Palmerston, Henry Temple, 3rd Viscount
　(1784–1865): Pss. V. on, 44; and
　William IV's illness, 50; on the young
　QV, 60–1; Foreign Secretary, 68, 196;
　history, 196; personality, 196, 197, 228;
　and European liberal movements, 198;
　provokes diplomatic crisis, 205; and
　Pr. A., 206, 229; and the Haynau
　affair, 206–7; and Kossuth, 207, 208;
　and politics of France, 207, 208;
　offered Lord Lieutenancy of Ireland,
　208; Crimean War, 221, 241;
　appearance, 228; gives way, 229; Order
　of the Garter, 229; Pss. Royal's
　engagement, 239; and relations with
　France, 242; Indian Mutiny, 249;
　support for Italian unity, 255; and Pr.
　A.'s illness, 277, 279; new method of
　conducting business, 298; Schleswig-
　Holstein Duchies, 305
　and QV: he instructs and charms her,
　196–7; her attitude changes, 197; she
　seeks his dismissal from office, 198;
　she has cause to complain, 204; her
　memorandum on, 206; she threatens
　to dismiss him, 207; she sends for,
　228; she appreciates him, 229; she
　recalls him, 255; QV and death of,
　265, 316
Palmerston, Viscountess, née the Hon.
　Emily Lamb (d.1869), 197
Panmure, Fox Maule, 2nd Baron, *later* 11th

Earl of Dalhousie (1801–74), 225, 226, 227, 234
Paris, Louis Philippe d'Orléans, Comte de (1838–94), 486
Parliament: Regency Bill of 1830, 31; Pr. A. in House of Commons, 194; Acts of social reform, 199; declaration of trust in Pr. A., 223; Conspiracy to Murder Bill, 242; QV and State Openings, 310–12, 331, 338, 362; Queen's Speech, 369
Pate, Robert, 424
Paxton, (Sir) Joseph (1801–65), 171, 212
Peacock, Thomas Love (1785–1866), 210
Pedro V, King of Portugal (1837–61), 279
Peel, Sir Robert (1788–1850): Melbourne on, 93; Wellington recommends, 93; seeks Wellington's support, 95; shy and awkward, 134, 146; Melbourne's advice, 135; and Pr. A., 137, 422; dances, 146; Osborne House, 161; Drayton Manor, 170; on QV, 193; resignations, 195, 196; no small talk, 470
and QV: Pss. V. meets, 44; matter of her Ladies, 94–6; her dislike, 113, 134; she becomes more accommodating, 135; increasing compatibility, 136; 193; her 'kind and true friend', 203
Persia, Nasru 'd-Din, Shah of, 347, 348
Phelps, Samuel (1804–78), 191
Phipps, Sir Charles (1801–66), 227–8, 279, 289, 324
Phipps, Harrier (b.1841), 317, 451, 468
Ponsonby, Frederick, later 1st Baron Sysonby (1867–1935): QV's opposition to his marriage, 315; on QV's relationship with John Brown, 323n.; on QV's visit to Dublin, 438; and the Munshi, 449, 450–1, 452; at Osborne, 461; Assistant Private Secretary, 462; duties, 463; problem posed by QV's failing eyesight, 464–5; conversation at dinner, 465–6; after-dinner card games, 475–6; Corelli's popularity, 477; and QV's taste in literature, 477; QV's funeral, 499, 500
Ponsonby, Sir Henry (1825–95): P.A.'s carriage accident, 262; advice on preaching, 296; stroke, 314; on Gladstone, 319; on John Brown, 321, 328, 432; at Balmoral, 327; personality, 332, 333; clothes, 333; and Jenner, 335, 356–7; at Sandringham, 344; on Duke

of Edinburgh, 353; on Wilde, 355n.; other duties, 356; and Reid, 357; and Campbell-Bannerman, 358; on Disraeli, 360; and Gladstone, 368; Pr. Leopold's letter to QV, 408; suspected of snoring, 436; and QV's biography of Brown, 443; and the Munshi, 448; theatricals, 472; bursts into laughter, 473; death, 487
and QV: his appointment as Equerry to, 332–3; understands her character, 333; his way of dealing with her, 334, 352; and forthcoming visit of Shah of Persia, 347; her replies to his submissions, 354; and her correspondence, 355; her unconstitutional behaviour, 363; his comments on her, 362, 370–1, 394, 416; she reprimands him, 411; to Switzerland, 431; he describes her visit to Milan, 433
Ponsonby, Mary, Lamb (1832–1916): on QV in Scotland, 179; Balmoral cold, 181; on Gladstone, 320; clever, 332; independence of mind, 333; and QV, 397n.
Portman, Viscountess (d.1865), 78, 79, 80, 81, 422
Portugal, Queen of, see Maria da Gloria, Queen of
Profeit, Alexander, 322n.
Profeit, George, 322n.
Prussia, Frederick William IV, King of (1795–1861), 140

Rachel, Mlle (d.1858), 144
Raglan, Lord Fitzroy Somerset, 1st Baron (1788–1855), 225, 226–7, 240
Raikes, Thomas (1777–1848), 72
Regent, Prince, see George IV, King
Reid, Sir James (1849–1923): QV's letters to Profeit, 322–3n.; and his engagement, 350–51; dinners, 357; Pss. Louise and, 395; and Pss. Ena's injury, 418; attends John Brown, 440, 441; attends QV, 440; she gives him a locket, 443; and the Munshi, 447, 451, 452; falls ill, 451–2; speaks out to QV, 452–3; present from Nicholas II, 456; QV's health, 488, 489, 492; her death, 494; Royal Family thanks him, 494; QV's interest in funerals, 495; her instructions on burial of her dog, 496; and contents of her coffin, 497–8

Ribblesdale, Thomas Lister, 3rd Baron (1828–76), 327

Richmond, George (1809–96), 54n.

Ritchie, Charles Thomson Ritchie, 1st Baron (1838–1906), 470

Roberts, Frederick Sleigh Roberts, 1st Earl (1832–1914), 492

Roebuck, John Arthur (1801–79), 227, 228

Rolle, John Rolle, 2nd Baron (1750–1842), 72

Rosebery, Archibald John Primrose, 4th Earl of (1783–1868), 63

Rosebery, Archibald Philip Primrose, 5th Earl of (1847–1929), 180, 182, 358, 373, 376–7

Rothschild, Alice, 434

Rothschild, Baron Lionel Nathan de (1808–79), 361

Rowton, Baron, see Corry, Montagu

Royal Household, 138–41

Rubini, Giovanni Battista (1794–1854), 44

Ruskin, John (1819–1900), 212

Russell, John Scott (1808–82), 210

Russell, Lord John, later 1st Earl Russell (1792–1878): at Balmoral, 178; and Palmerston, 196, 206, 207; QV seeks Palmerston's dismissal, 198, 205; appearance and personality, 204; Great Exhibition, 212; on forthcoming marriage of Napoleon III, 231; Foreign Secretary, 255; Schleswig-Holstein Duchies, 306

and QV: QV sees, 56; gives her unpalatable news, 92; finds her in tears, 93; gives her support, 96; she sends for him, 195, 228

Rutland, John Henry Manners, 5th Duke of (1778–1857), 171

Sahl, Hermann, 356

St George's Chapel: Garter banner, 128; Albert Memorial Chapel, 287, 500; Pr. A.'s coffin, 288; Pr. of W.'s wedding, 303, 304; Pss. Helena's wedding, 393; Pr. Leopold's tomb, 410, Royal Family's service for Diamond Jubilee, 457; QV's funeral service, 500

St Laurent, Julie de, 3, 6, 217n.

Sale, John (1758–1827), 18

Salisbury, Marchioness of (d.1839), 72

Salisbury, Robert Gascoyne-Cecil, 3rd Marquess of (1830–1903): hates Balmoral, 182; Mackenzie's knighthood, 385; and the Munshi, 452

and QV: necessity of understanding her character, 352; and his resignation, 373; their happy relationship, 374, 375; warns her against going to Germany, 387; and her 'only form of excitement', 454; she appreciates him, 455

Sandringham, 341–4

Sant, James (1820–1916), 226n.

Saxe-Coburg, Louise, Dowager Duchess of (d.1796), 99, 261

Saxony, Albert, King of (1828–1902), 354

Scott, (Sir), George Gilbert (1811–78), 288

Scott, Sir Walter (1771–1832), 68, 175, 478

Seymour, (Sir) Francis (1813–90), 299

Shaftesbury, 7th Earl of, see Ashley, Anthony Ashley Cooper, Baron

Shee, Sir Martin Archer (1769–1850), 354

Sibthorp, Charles (1783–1855), 212

Siebold, Madame, 11

Simpson, Sir James (1792–1868), 240

Singh, Sir Duleep (1837–98), 447n.

Smirke, Sir Robert (1781–1867), 170

Smith, Albert, 191

Smith, Revd Sydney (1771–1845), 62n., 68

Smith, William, 180

Smyth, Dame Ethel (1858–1944), 417

Snow, John (1813–58), 216, 217

Sohn, Karl (1805–67), 442

Somerset, Lady Augusta (1816–50), 128

Somerset, Lady Geraldine (1832–1915), 304, 380–81

Sophia, Princess (1777–1848), 26

Soult, Nicolas-Jean de Dieu, Duke of Dalmatia (1769–1851), 71–2

Southey, Mrs, 153, 154

Späth, Baroness, 11, 21, 33

Spencer, Hon. George (1799–1864), 154

Spring-Rice, Thomas, later 1st Baron Monteagle (1790–1866), 58

Stafford, Sir Henry Fitzherbert, 9th Baron (1802–84), 475–6

Stanhope, Lady Wilhelmina, 72

Stanley, Arthur Penrhyn (1815–81), 314, 324, 487, 497n.

Stanley, Lady Augusta, see Bruce, Lady Augusta

Stanley, Edward George Stanley, Baron, see Derby, 14th Earl of

Stanley, Edward Henry Stanley, Baron, see Derby, 15th Earl of

Stanley, (Sir) Henry Morton (1841–1904), 473

Stanley, Sir John Stanley, 1st Baron (1766–1850), 193–4
Stephen, Sir James (1789–1859), 189
Stevenson, Mrs Andrew, 61
Stewart, Dugald (1753–1828), 196
Stirling, Walter George, 403, 404
Stockmar, Christian Frederick, Baron (1787–1863): and Leopold of Saxe-Coburg, 49; personality, 49; and Conroy, 49, 90; reports to King Leopold, 50, 51, 77; QV and, 54, 56; concerned about QV, 97; and Melbourne, 135; administration of Royal Household, 138, 139, 140; and Lehzen, 150; memorandum on royal nursery, 154; royal children's education, 185–6; Gibbs's salary, 189; and Sovereign's right to supervision of foreign policy, 196, 197; in retirement at Coburg, 261; and Pr. of W., 269, 270; on a Prime Minister's position, 367
  and Pr. A.: on Grand Tour, 100; his concern over, 101, 262; tells him of QV, 110, 126; and Pr. A.'s unpopularity, 128; and Pr. A.'s hesitancy, 132; Pr. A.'s letters to, 151–2
Sullivan, Sir Arthur (1842–1900), 457
Sussex, Augustus, Duke of (1773–1843), 4, 13, 19, 55, 120–1
Sutherland, Duchess of (d.1868): QV reprimands, 62; Coronation, 71, 74; and Melbourne, 76; QV's wedding, 120; and Victor Emmanuel II, 253; her grandson, 394
Sweden, Charles V, King of (r.1859–72), 346
Swoboda, Rudolph, 447

Taglioni, Maria (1804–84), 44
Tamagno, Francesco, 144
Tamburini, Antonio (1800–76), 44
Tavistock, Marchioness of, 53, 62, 78, 82
Tennyson, Alfred Tennyson, 1st Baron (1809–92), 441, 472, 481, 497
Terry, (Dame) Ellen (1847–1928), 473
Thornycroft, Thomas (1815–85), 287–8
Thumb, General Tom, 191
Thynne, Lord John (1798–1881), 73
Titiens, Thérèse (1831–77), 141
Toole, John Lawrence (1830–1906), 471–2
Tories: William IV, 32; and Lady Flora Hastings affair, 80; attitude to QV's

match, 112; QV and, 112, 113, 115, 136; and Pr. A., 113, 115; at QV's wedding, 121; electoral victory, 134; and Lehzen, 151; QV on, 194
Torrington, George Byng, 7th Viscount (1812–84), 309
Trevelyan, (Sir) George Otto, 2nd Bart. (1838–1928), 340
Tuck, Mrs, 494
Turkey, Abdul-ul-Aziz, Sultan of (r.1861–76), 346

Umberto I, King of Italy (1844–1900), 437n.
Uxbridge, Henry Paget, Earl of, later 2nd Marquess of Anglesey (1797–1869), 117

Victoire, Princess of Coburg (1822–57), 105
Victor Albert, Prince (d.1893), 447n.
Victor Emmanuel II, King of Italy (1820–78), 252–3, 497n.
Victoria, Princess, the Princess Royal, later Crown Princess Frederick and then Empress of Prussia:
  as Princess Royal: birth, 132; Pr. A. and, 146, 183, 256–7; christening, 149; sickly, 149; tantrums, 154; and Lady Lyttelton, 154; and Pr. of W., 183–4, 189; QV on, 189; Great Exhibition, 213; presented to Napoleon III, 232; to Paris, 234; and Empress Eugénie, 237; Cr. Pr. Frederick and, 238, 239, 240; QV and, 238; wedding, 242–3
  as Crown Princess Frederick: her mother writes to, 243–7 passim; 257–61 passim; says farewell to her parents, 244; correspondence with Pr. A., 244–5, 275; first pregnancy, 257, 259; confinement, 260; at Osborne, 260–1; her parents' visit, 261, 262; on Pss. Alexandra, 272, 273; grief over Pr. A.'s death, 289–90; and her mother, 290, 387, 388; on QV, 290; and Pr. of W., 299; and Schleswig-Holstein Duchies, 306; disapproves of publication of QV's book, 330; Golden Jubilee celebrations, 380; on Pr. Wilhelm, 382, 386, 390; her husband's illness, 384; rumours and attacks, 385; and her husband, 386–7, 388; on Bismarck, 388; sends private documents to England, 389; and Pss. Louise's marriage, 394; and the Munshi, 450; opinion of works of Corelli, 477

Victoria Eugénie ('Ena'), Princess, *later*
Queen of Spain (1887–1969), 417, 418
Victoria of Hesse, Princess (1863–1950),
173n., 295, 392
Victoria of Prussia, Princess (1866–1929),
387, 418–19
Victoria, Queen of the United Kingdom of
Great Britain and Ireland and
Empress of India (1818–1901):
and Albert, Prince: birthday presents,
100n., 164; she is entranced by, 107–8;
she proposes, 109; his letter, 109; in
love, 110; public and Parliamentary
attitude to the match, 112–13; his
precedence, 114, 115, 172; question of
his Household, 117–18; her
bridesmaids, 118–19; wedding eve, 119;
wedding day, 122; honeymoon, 123–5;
excludes him from political business,
126; his nostalgia, 129; birth of Pss.
Royal, 133; contentment, 145, 147; he
makes a pirouette for her, 146;
quarrels, 149, 151–2, 216; her
adoration, 153, 157–8, 164, 216; on his
riding success, 171; at Balmoral, 179;
criticizes him to Pss. Royal, 190; holds
him up as example, 190; her faith in
his grasp of foreign politics, 197; and
social matters, 200–1; Great
Exhibition, 210, 213; scenes, 218–20;
his unpopularity painful to her, 223;
his carriage accident, 262; his illnesses,
262, 263; he breaks appalling news,
274; anxiety about his health, 275, 276,
277; her dying husband, 279–80; his
death, 281; perpetual commemoration,
286–7; Albert Memorial, 288;
Frogmore Mausoleum, 288–9; she
contemplates suicide, 289; mental
imbalance over his death, 291–2; she
remembers his faults and foibles, 292;
cause of his death, 299; State Opening
of Parliament, 310–11; anniversaries of
his death, 398n.
amusements and interests: art, 54n., 164
and n., 435; balls, 86, 96, 103;
battledore and shuttlecock, 87; clothes,
169n.; concerts, 473; dancing, 86, 103,
124, 125, 146, 236, 349, 473; distribution
of medals, 459–60; funerals, 495–6;
ghillies' balls, 327–8; Hindustani, 446,
448; lectures, 473; music, 88, 457n.;
poetry, 479; novels, 477–80; riding, 88;
sketching, 66n., 88, 179, 261;

sightseeing, 435; theatricals, 472–3;
trout fishing, 179
appearance: diminutive size, 61; eyes, 62,
458, 483n.; figure 61, 131, 204, 340, 431;
Greville on, 60; Lucerne newspapers
on, 431; plainness, 61; Mrs Stevenson
describes, 61
and her children (see also *and Prince of
Wales*): a strict mother, 184; they play
games, 184; their education, 185;
prayers, 185; Pr. Alfred, 191–2, 258,
396–8; takes them to Great Exhibition,
213; Pr. A. and her relationship with,
219; Pss. Royal, 238–40, 243, 244–7,
257; after death of Dch. of Kent, 267;
Pss. Beatrice, 278, 287, 410–13; younger
children's plays, 290; their fear of her,
344; with Empress Frederick, 387, 388;
her daughters, 391–5; Pss. Alice, 391–2;
Pss. Helena, 393; Pss. Louise, 394, 395;
Pr. Arthur, 398–400; Pr. Leopold,
401–10; deaths, 484–5
dress: Lady Canning deplores, 168–9;
coronation robes and crown, 71;
Declaration of Marriage, 111; Diamond
Jubilee, 457, 458; Privy Council, 54; in
Florence, 435; Golden Jubilee, 381;
jewels, 348; Pr. Leopold's wedding,
409; Pss. Louise's wedding, 395;
military attire, 241; mourning, 285,
303–4, 431; in Paris, 235; public
thanksgiving, 345; riding habit, 88;
robe of state, 75; State Opening of
Parliament, 312; visit to France, 166;
wedding dress, 120, 121; Windsor
describes, 415
grandchildren: preparations for birth of
first grandchild, 258–9; Pr. Wilhelm,
261, 304, 382, 383, 386, 387, 390, 457;
confides in a granddaughter, 293; birth
of George VI, 294; her presence at
births of, 414; 'Dear little things',
414–15; Pr. David and, 415–16;
indulgence to, 416; Drino, 416–17;
strictness, 417; Pss. Ena, 417, 418; she
arranges treats for, 418; Tsarina
Alexandra, 455; Pr. Eddy, 473, 486
health: after death of Pr. A., 291;
backache, 379; diarrhoea and
headaches, 430; excuse for holidays,
429; failing eyesight, 464, 465, 466,
488, 491; hypochondria, 488; ill at
Balmoral, 339–40; indigestion, 489;
insomnia, 440, 488; journal entries on,

490; lameness, 489; loss of use of legs, 488; mental imbalance, 172, 308, 314; poor health after Coronation, 76–7; post-natal depression, 202, 217; rheumatism, 379, 440, 488; sleepiness, 489, 490; stroke, 492

letter writing to: Q. Adelaide, 54; Pr. A., 117–18, 120, 125; Pss. Alice, 392, 398; Cambridge, 442n.; Pss. Feodora, 54, 231; Cr. Pss. Frederick, 257–398 *passim*; Pr. George of Wales, 441; granddaughters, 442; Grey, 429; King Leopold, 54, 99, 102–62 *passim*; 203, 215, 216, 249, 402; Pr. Leopold, 285; Melbourne, 124; the Munshi, 453; Peel, 162; Pss. Royal, 179, 243–4, 293; Stockmar, 159; Pr. of W., 394; Cr. Pr. Wilhelm, 389

Ministers:

Disraeli: her early view of, 316; he woos and flatters her, 317–18; at Osborne, 319; describes him to Rosebery, 360; gets her own way, 361; Suez Canal, 361; her admiration for, 361–2; lunch at Hughenden, 362–3; his return from Berlin, 364–5; Garter, 365; to continue correspondence with, 368; seeks is advice, 369; grief over his death, 369–70

Gladstone: she esteems, 319; finds him incompatible, 320; matter of Turkish atrocities, 362; his championship of African races, 365; her dislike, 367, 370, 373; tries to thwart his return to power, 367, 368; her instructions, 368; her jealousy, 370, 377; he angers her, 371; war in Sudan, 371; she declines to come down from Balmoral, 372; his fourth term, 375; Pr. George's wedding, 376; his final resignation, 376; his death, 377; her feelings towards, 377–8

Melbourne: she receives, 54; advice about her mother, 56, 57, 59; other advice, 62, 77; their relationship, 64–9, 88–9, 125; his indisposition, 76; his impending resignation, 92–3; her Ladies, 94, 96; question of her marriage, 104; she is snappy with him, 106; they discuss Pr. A., 108; she turns upon him, 115–16; at her wedding, 122; he agrees to write regularly, 135; consults him about nursery, 153–4; finds him tiresome, 194–5; his death,

195; and Palmerston's marriage, 197; his influence, 200

Palmerston: he instructs and charms her, 196–7; she praises him, 197; her attitude changes, 197; she seeks his dismissal from office, 198, 204–5; causes for complaint, 204; admires his speech, 205, 206; her memorandum on, 206; and the Haynau affair, 207; angry at his interference in French politics, 208; relief over his resignation, 209; she sends for, 228; Indian Mutiny, 249; she recalls, 255; his death, 316

Peel: she sends for, 93; subject of her Ladies, 94–5, 96; prepared to be more accommodating to him, 135; Greville on Peel and, 136; relationship between, 193; distressed at his resignation, 195; her praise, 196; her 'kind and true friend', 203

Wellington: she is angry with him, 113–14; invites him to her wedding, 116; at military review, 148; she has a cold, 148–9; he is host to, 169–70; advises her to leave London, 201

her mother: first day of reign, 56; antipathy between, 57; angry letters, 57, 58–9; Lady Flora Hastings affair, 82; unhappy relationship, 91–2, 104, 264; wedding day, 120, 121; improved relations, 265; death of the Dch., 266; mourning, 267; QV asks her advice, 401

opinions of other people: Pss. Alexandra, 303; Pr. Alfred, 396; Pss. Alice, 484n.; Pr. Arthur, 398–9, 401; Pss. Beatrice, 411; Bigge, 452; Brown, 329, 441, 442; Carlyle, 482n.; Pr. Christian Victor, 487; Davidson, 295; Derby, 369; Dickens, 483; Pr. Edward, 416; Empress Eugénie, 233–4; Faure, 436; Pr. George, 486–7; Gladstone, 319, 320, 360, 362, 367, 368, 373, 375, 377; Granville, 369; Pss. Helen of Waldeck-Pyrmont, 409; Pss. Helena, 393; Pr. Henry of Battenberg, 485; Henry Ponsonby, 334–5, 487; Pr. Leopold, 401; Lord John Russell, 204; Louis IV of Hesse, 392, 485; Pss. Louise of Prussia, 400; Pss. May of Teck, 486; the Munshi, 446–7; Nicholas II, 456; Palmerston, 229; Peel, 94, 113, 134; Salisbury, 374; Umberto I, 437n.; Cr. Pr. Wilhelm, 261, 390

Victoria, Queen of the United Kingdom of
Great Britain and Ireland and
Empress of India – *cont.*
opinions of others about her: Pr. A., 126;
Carlyle, 483n.; Clarendon, 235, 236;
Creevey, 53; Croker, 55–6, 111;
Dalmeny, 55; Davidson, 358–9;
Greville, 54–5, 62, 86, 96, 121, 124, 136,
174; Holland, 62; James, 501; Lieven,
60; Melbourne, 18n., 60; Palmerston,
60–61; Ponsonby, 323; Smyth, 417; Pss.
Victoria of Prussia, 418, 419;
Wellington, 55
personal matters: popularity, 60, 215; her
voice, 55, 61, 381, 417, 435, 471n., 483n,;
bathes Dash, 75; 'a pleasant life', 85–9;
suggestions of marriage, 98–9, 103;
attitude to marriage, 103, 104, 105,
314–15, 350–1, 392, 411; enjoys her
young relations' visit, 105; pregnancies,
130, 149, 216; birth of her babies,
132–3, 150, 172, 201, 216, 217; servants,
140, 397n., 442n., 462, 466; does not
care for babies, 149; journals, 150–51,
172n.; feelings about religion, 154, 185,
187, 188, 294–7; death of her father-in-
law, 158–9; Osborne, 161, 162, 163;
train journeys, 170, 202, 429, 431;
enchanted by Scotland, 176–7, 179; at
Balmoral, 178; 'Scottish' accent, 180–1;
impervious to cold, 181, 351; attitude
to Sundays, 187, 295; Great Exhibition,
210–15 *passim*; chloroform, 217; and
Sant's portrait of Cardigan, 226n.; on
bomb outrage in Paris, 241–2;
mourning, 286 *and* n.; accepts a
bequest, 288n.; feelings about afterlife,
293–4; superstitions, 294; the 'German
element', 305, 338; in seclusion,
307–10, 326; starts to make public
appearances again, 311; *Our Life in the
Highlands*, 329–30, 444; has outgrown
her grief, 349; and maids-of-honour,
350–51; prohibits smoking, 353;
difficult and demanding employer,
354, 464–5; devotion to animals, 355n.;
importance of anniversaries, 379,
397n.; and Gr. Dch. Marie
Alexandrovna, 398; enjoys company of
children, 414; entourage for holidays
abroad, 428; Indian servants, 434, 435,
446, 454n., 476; diary, 463; birthday
books, 463–4; handwriting, 464;
modern inventions, 465n.; dinner
parties, 468–71, 475–6; her preferred
food, 469; her smile, 470; Lady Ely's
death, 471; laughter, 471, 473, 474;
portraits, 475 *and* n.; reading matter,
477–80; deaths of friends, 471, 487;
deaths in the family, 484–5; dislikes
title Duke of York, 487n.; death,
492–4; burial of her dogs, 496; plans
for her own funeral, 496–7, 501
personality: abhors racial prejudice, 447;
attitude to servants, 396, 397n., 399,
466; cannot bear to be supposed
unwell, 489; charm, 85, 349, 358, 456;
cheerfulness, 489; compassion, 200;
composure, 289; conscientiousness, 85,
87, 298, 419; discrimination, 465;
frugality, 58; in general, 351–2;
generosity, 58, 140, 200n.; hard
worker, 308; hatred of change, 314;
hauteur, 62; hysterical outbursts, 217;
'little self-control', 218; memory, 465;
as mother, 184, 236; rages, 216;
reaction to deaths, 265–6; reluctance
to share authority, 127; self-centred,
62; self-control, 289; self-satisfaction,
271; self-willed, 85; shyness, 62, 328,
376, 417; stoicism, 216; stubbornness,
17, 96, 335, 372; shrewdness, 465;
temper, 17, 149, 153; thrift, 184;
tolerance, 140; truthfulness, 17;
vivacity, 489
as Pss. Victoria: birth, 12; christening,
12–13; and Pr. Leopold of Saxe-
Coburg, 15, 24, 41, 47; personality,
17–18, 26; education, 18–19; and her
uncles, 19–20; and George IV, 20, 21;
Claremont, 21, 47; and Lehzen, 21–2,
34, 44, 50; lonely childhood, 22; Pss.
Feodora, 22n.; Conroy, 26–7, 33, 47,
49, 50, 51; under 'Kensington System',
27–8; learns of future succession, 29;
Q. Adelaide and, 30, 33; on her
mother's quarrels with Royal Family,
32n.; William IV and, 33, 36, 46–7, 48;
'Royal Progresses', 34–5, 38–9; journal,
36, 44; her dog, Dash, 37, 38, 43;
music, 39, 43; eating habits, 39, 40, 43;
unwell, 39–40, 42; Q. Louise and,
41–2, 47; convalescent, 43; enjoyments,
43–4; German cousins, 44; Lady Flora
Hastings, 45; relations with her
mother, 48, 50, 51; seventeenth
birthday, 48–9, 102; Stockmar reports
on Conroy and, 50; and Liverpool,

50–1; receives news of her accession, 51–2; and Pr. A., 102; Christmas tree, 158n.

public figure: popularity, 60, 215, 424, 427; first Privy Council, 54–5; first day of her reign, 56; income, 58; Coronation, 70–75; Lady Flora Hastings affair, 77–84; unpopularity, 83–4, 321, 331, 340, 379, 380; change of Government, 92–7; matter of her Ladies, 94–6; Declaration of Marriage, 111, 113; her Household, 116; wedding day, 122; tour to meet Whig magnates, 134; and Court, 141–3; criticism of, 173–4, 176; Roman Catholicism, 193; Corn Laws reform, 193; sympathy with monarchies of Europe, 198; on poverty in Ireland, 198; and social reform, 200–1; denounces revolution, 201; Crimean War, 222, 223–7, 241, 459; and Raglan, 226–7; State Visit of Napoleon III, 231–4; State Visit to Paris, 234–7; review troops, 241; Indian Mutiny, 249–51; and Victor Emmanuel II, 252–3; and Napoleon III, 253; Franco-Austrian War, 254–5; Privy Council meetings, 298–9; Schleswig-Holstein Duchies, 305, 306; public appearances, 311; State Openings of Parliament, 310–13, 331, 336, 339; dreads changes of Government, 316; opening ceremonies, 331, 380; Ponsonby's appointment, 333; reclusiveness, 335–7, 339, 346–7; thanksgiving celebrations, 345; Shah of Persia, 347–8; replies to Ponsonby's submissions, 354–5; Empress of India, 361; and Turkish atrocities, 362; relations with Russians, 363–4; and Russo-Turkish conflict, 364; attitude to wars, 365–6; Speech from the Throne, 369; war in Sudan, 371–2; Golden Jubilee, 379–82; assassination attempts, 420–4, 426; efforts to protect, 425–6; pseudonyms, 432; congratulated on length of reign, 456; invitations to Diamond Jubilee celebrations, 456, 457; Diamond Jubilee, 457–9; second Boer War, 459–60; funeral procession, 498–9; funeral service in Royal Mausoleum, 500–1; Marochetti's sculpture, 501

relationships with others: Bernhardt, 463; Birch, 188; Bismarck, 387–8; Bright, 337 *and* n.; Brown, 321, 323–8 *passim*; 329, 441–4; Cowell, 192; Pr. Christian of Schleswig-Holstein, 393; Clark, 410; Dickens, 482–3; Elphinstone, 290n.; Empress Eugénie, 234, 341; Frederick William, Cr. Pr. of Prussia, 239; Lehzen, 153, 155–6; Longfellow, 481; Lady Lyttelton, 155; Gr. Dch. Marie Alexandrovna, 398; the Munshi, 446–54; Napoleon III, 232–7 *passim*; Singh, 447n.; Tennyson, 481; Toole, 471–2; Yorke, 467

visits: Blair Castle, 176; Cambridge, 172; Chatsworth, 170–71; Cimiez, 436–7, 452, 453; Coburg, 172–3, 301, 429; Florence, 434–5; France, 165–8, 253–4, 436; Ireland, 187, 437–8; King Leopold, 168, 172, 302; Milan, 433; Nice, 463; Paris, 234–7, 431; Prussia, 172, 261, 323, 387; Scotland, 175, 176; Spain, 436; Stratfield Saye, 169; Switzerland, 430, 431–4; Walmer Castle, 169 *and* n.

and Wales, Prince of: her feelings for, 183; relaxations, 184; she discusses him with Gibbs, 189; her letter about his father, 190; and death of Dch. of Kent, 267; concern and anxiety about him, 268–9; she gives him unreserved credit, 270–1; criticism, 271; and a bride for, 272–3; she considers him responsible for Pr. A.'s death, 299; relations between, 300–1; his wedding, 303–4, 305, 342; her disapproval, 332; he admonishes her, 332; at Sandringham during his illness, 342–4; his recovery, 344; she writes to Cr. Pss. Frederick about, 344–5; public thanksgiving for his recovery, 345; she sends for him to receive French President, 436; and sequel to *Our Life in the Highlands*, 444–5; as she is dying, 493

Villiers, Charles Pelham (1802–98), 458

Wales, Albert Edward, Prince of (1841–1910):
and Pss. Alexandra: first meeting, 273; anxious to propose, 301; engaged to be married, 302; wedding, 304; Sandringham clocks, 343; constantly together, 345

childhood: birth, 150; contented baby, 155; averse to learning, 183; his parents' attitude to, 183, 186; and Pss. Royal, 183–4, 189; his mother and, 184, 236;

Wales, Albert Edward – *cont.*
  childhood – *cont.*
    education, 186–7, 189–90; Holy
    Communion, 187; German accent, 187;
    phrenologist's report, 188; and Birch,
    188; and Gibbs, 189; and his father,
    190, 191; pleasures, 191; Great
    Exhibition, 213; and Napoleon III, 232,
    237; in Paris, 234, 236–7; and
    Clarendon, 236; and Empress Eugénie,
    237; Victor Emmanuel II and, 253
  opinions of others on: Bruce, 269; Lady
    Canning, 188; Dean of Christ Church,
    270; Cr. Pr. Frederick, 273–4
  personal matters: John Brown, 325n.;
    Mordaunt divorce case, 331–2; typhoid
    fever, 341, 343; recovery, 344; Pss.
    Helena's marriage, 393; Pss. Beatrice's
    wedding, 412; QV and his sons, 415;
    and attempt on life of QV, 423, 424;
    annoyed on his brother's behalf, 426;
    delight in motor cars, 465n.; Tranby
    Croft affair, 485; death of Pr. Eddy,
    486; and the Munshi, 498
  personality: charm, 269; in general, 186,
    269; QV on, 268, 269; rudeness, 190;
    temper, 189; violence, 190
  public figure: unveils statues of Pr. A.,
    287n.; opening ceremonies, 288;
    Schleswig-Holstein Duchies, 305–6;
    unpopularity, 332; popularity, 342;
    thanksgiving service for his recovery,
    345; Gladstone's pall-bearer, 377; to
    receive French President, 436;
    Diamond Jubilee, 459; QV's funeral,
    498, 499, 500, 501
  and Queen Victoria: her anxiety over
    him, 268–9; his grandson's date of
    birth, 294; her aversion to, 299, 300;
    improved relations, 301, 342; her
    disapproval, 332; he admonishes her,
    332; requests her to come down from
    Balmoral, 372; rare defiance, 377; and
    sequel to *Our Life in the Highlands*,
    444–5; as she is dying, 493, 494
  young man: death of Dch. of Kent, 267;
    appearance, 269; Italian tour, 269–70;
    favourable reports from Oxford, 270;
    popularity in America, 270–1; at
    Curragh military camp, 271; and Nellie
    Clifden, 271; urged to marry, 271–2,
    275; his father's shock and pain, 274;
    his father's forgiveness, 275; and Pr.
    A.'s death, 280, 281, 300

Waldersee, Count Alfred von, 390n.
Walewska, Madame, 254
Walewski, Alexander Florian, Count
  (1810–68), 231, 242
Walters, Catherine ('Skittles'), 322n.
Watson, (Sir) Thomas (1792–1882), 279
Watts, G.F. (1817–1904), 54n.
Webb, Sir Aston (1849–1930), 380
Wegner, Dr, 259
Wellesley, Gerald (1809–82), 320, 328, 487
Wellington, Arthur Wellesley, 1st Duke of
  (1769–1852): on Kent, 5; on royal
  dukes' allowances, 10; and Conroy, 27,
  91; and William IV, 30; and Dch. of
  Kent's claim to regency, 31; on
  contretemps between King and Dch.
  of Kent, 47; at Coronation, 71, 72;
  Lady Flora Hastings affair, 78, 91; his
  laugh, 88; and Peel, 93, 95; and Pr. A.,
  113, 134; ill, 114; and question of
  precedence, 115, 116; at QV's wedding,
  121; extreme deafness, 144; Windsor
  cold, 170, 181; Corn Laws, 193–4; and
  Chartists, 201, 202; Great Exhibition,
  212 *and* n., 214; Wellington College,
  311; and Pr. Arthur, 398; no small talk,
  470
  and QV: describes her first Privy
    Council, 55; affair of her Ladies, 95–6;
    her hostility, 113–14; her attitude
    softens, 116; her 'best friend', 148–9;
    her host at Walmer Castle, 169–70;
    her distress at his death, 265–6; she
    receives a lock of his hair, 497n.
Westall, Richard (1765–1836), 18
Westminster School, 72
Wharncliffe, Lady (d.1853), 28–9
Whigs: Dch. of Kent, 22; Reform Bill, 36;
  Melbourne on, 65; pronunciation, 65;
  Pr. A.'s Household, 118; at QV's
  wedding, 122; QV and, 134; Lehzen
  and, 151, Pr. A.'s opinion of, 194
Wilberforce, Samuel (1805–73), 186, 288
Wilde, Oscar (1856–1900), 353 *and* n., 481
Wilkie, Sir David (1785–1841), 54n.
Wilhelm I, King of Prussia and German
  Emperor (1797–1888), 385, 386
Wilhelm, Prince, *later* Wilhelm II, German
  Emperor (1859–1941): birth, 259–60;
  QV on, 261; at Pr. of W.'s wedding,
  304–5; his mother on, 382, 386; on
  QV, 382–3; cool reception in England,
  383; and his father's illness, 386; eager
  to succeed to throne, 387; at

Charlottenburg, 388; after his father's death, 389; and his mother, 389; his dislike of the English, 389n.; and his dying grandmother, 493; tactful behaviour, 493, 494; keeps Union Jack, 498; QV's funeral, 498, 499

William IV, King (1765–1837):
  as Duke of Clarence: his bride, 4; attitude to Dch. of Kent, 23
  as King: succeeds to throne, 29; personality, 30; Tory, 32; and Dch. of Kent, 32, 33, 34, 45–7; and Pss. V., 33, 44, 48; Pss. V.'s confirmation, 34; Dch. of Kent's 'Royal Progresses', 34–8 passim; naval salutes, 37; ill, 48, 50, 51; death, 52; expenditure on coronation, 71; King Leopold censures, 98–9; Buckingham Palace, 160

Willoughby de Eresby, Peter Drummond-Burrell, 22nd Baron (1782–1829), 121

Wilson, Dr, 11, 14, 15

Windsor Castle (see also St George's Chapel): Pss. Sophia, 26; death of George IV, 29; FitzClarences move into, 32; King William's contretemps with Dch. of Kent, 45–7; Prs. Albert and Ernest arrive, 107; Pr. A.'s writing desk, 131; guests get lost, 139; domestic extravagance, 140; guests' boredom, 143, 144; St George's Hall, 144, 232; concerts, plays and entertainments, 144, 191; military review in Park, 148; royal nursery, 153; Lehzen leaves, 155; Christmas, 158 and n,; Wellington on, 170; coldness, 181, 318; Palmerston's reprehensible behaviour, 196; Cardigan, 225–6; visit of Napoleon III, 232–3; Waterloo Chamber, 232; Pss. Royal's honeymoon, 243; Victor Emmanuel II, 252; Pr. A., 256; Dch. of

Kent's apartment, 264; Pr. of W. welcomed and congratulated, 271; Nellie Clifden, 271; Pr. A. perpetually commemorated, 286–7; Disraeli on, 318; Sultan of Turkey, 346; Shah of Persia, 348; Gladstones, 376, 378; Eton boys' celebrations, 381, 438–9; German royal private documents, 389; Marie Alexandrovna's opinion of, 398; silence, 417n.; entertainments for grandchildren, 418; Pss. Victoria of Prussia, 418–19; Clarence Tower, 441, 442; John Brown's portrait, 442n.; Nicholas II, 456; typewriter and telephones, 465n.; orchard and kitchen garden, 469
  QV and: Pss. V.'s rare visits, 33, 43; her attitude to, 87 and n., 159; her twentieth birthday ball, 103; her honeymoon, 123; a dance party, 124; she limits hospitality, 346–7

Windsor, Duke of, see Edward, Prince

Winterhalter, Franz Xaver (1806–73), 54n., 163–4, 398, 447n.

Wolseley, Sir Garnet, later 1st Viscount Wolseley (1833–1913), 371, 372, 373, 458

Wood, Sir Matthew (1768–1843), 11

Worth, Charles Frederick (1825–95), 237

Wynn-Carrington, Charles, later 1st Marquess of Lincolnshire (1843–1928), 190

York, Duchess of (1767–1820), 3–4, 12

York, Frederick, Duke of (1763–1827): childless, 3; and Kent, 5; marriage settlement, 7; Pss. V.'s christening, 12; and Pss. V. as a child, 20; death, 23

Yorke, Alick (1847–1911), 406, 466–7

Zulu War of 1879, 365